Paul Davies

Faith in the Millennium

Faith in the Millennium

Edited by Stanley E. Porter, Michael A. Hayes and David Tombs

Roehampton Papers, 7

Sheffield Academic Press

www.SheffieldAcademicPress.com

Published by Sheffield Academic Press Ltd
Mansion House
19 Kingfield Road
Sheffield S11 9AS
England

www.SheffieldAcademicPress.com

Typeset by Sheffield Academic Press
and
Printed on acid-free paper in Great Britain
by Antony Rowe Ltd,
Chippenham, Wiltshire

British Library Cataloguing in Publication Data

A catalogue record for this book is available
from the British Library

ISBN 1-84127-092-X

CONTENTS

ACKNOWLEDGMENTS

As ever, the editors wish to thank the sponsoring bodies at the University of Surrey Roehampton, formerly Roehampton Institute London, who made the conference on Faith in the Millennium in May 1999 so successful. These include the Faculty of Arts and Humanities, the Chaplaincy of Digby Stuart College, Southlands College and the Department of Theology and Religious Studies. We also owe a debt of gratitude to the efficiency of our speakers, who turned their spoken words into submitted manuscript in accordance with tight deadlines and admirable compliance with directives on style and format. Finally, Sheffield Academic Press deserve particular appreciation for the professional and scholarly way in which the volume is finally published.

ABBREVIATIONS

AB	Anchor Bible
AGJU	Arbeiten zur Geschichte des antiken Judentums und des Urchristentums
BBR	*Bulletin for Biblical Research*
BNTC	Black's New Testament Commentaries
EBib	Etudes bibliques
ENI	Ecumenical News International
FFNT	Foundations and Facets: New Testament
HNT	Handbuch zum Neuen Testament
HNTC	Harper's New Testament Commentaries
ICC	International Critical Commentary
JECS	*Journal of Early Christian Studies*
JETS	*Journal of the Evangelical Theological Society*
JSOT	*Journal for the Study of the Old Testament*
JSNT	*Journal for the Study of the New Testament*
JSNTSup	*Journal for the Study of the New Testament*, Supplement Series
JSOTSup	*Journal for the Study of the Old Testament*, Supplement Series
JSPSup	*Journal for the Study of the Pseudepigrapha*, Supplement Series
JSSR	*Journal for the Scientific Study of Religion*
KJV	King James Version
NAC	New American Commentary
NCB	New Century Bible
NICNT	New International Commentary on the New Testament
NIGTC	The New International Greek Testament Commentary
NIV	New International Version
NovT	*Novum Testamentum*
NovTSup	*Novum Testamentum*, Supplements
NTTS	New Testament Tools and Studies
PG	J.-P. Migne (ed.), *Patrologia cursus completa… Series graeca* (166 vols.; Paris: Petit-Montrouge, 1857–83)
RILP	Roehampton Institute London Papers
RP	Roehampton Papers
SBT	Studies in Biblical Theology
SNTSMS	Society for New Testament Studies Monograph Series

STS	Studies in Theology and Sexuality
TDNT	Gerhard Kittel and Gerhard Friedrich (eds.), *Theological Dictionary of the New Testament* (trans. Geoffrey W. Bromiley; 10 vols.; Grand Rapids: Eerdmans, 1964–1976)
THNT	Theologischer Handkommentar zum Neuen Testament
TLS	Theology and Liberation Series
TS	*Theological Studies*
TynBul	*Tyndale Bulletin*
WBC	Word Biblical Commentary
ZNW	*Zeitschrift für die neutestamentliche Wissenschaft*
ZPE	*Zeitschrift für Papyrologie und Epigraphik*

List of Contributors

John Anonby, Trinity Western University, Langley, BC, Canada

José Míguez Bonino, ISEDET, Buenos Aires, Argentina

Andrew Bradstock, King Alfred's College, Winchester

Anthony Cross, Paternoster Publishing, Carlisle

Rebecca Dudley, Christian Aid, London

Clive Erricker, Chichester Institute of Higher Education

Liam Gearon, University of Surrey Roehampton

Ron Geaves, University of Wolverhampton

Andrée Grau, University of Surrey Roehampton

Christopher Hamilton, Bedales School, Petersfield

Susan Hawley, Christian Aid, London

Michael A. Hayes, St Mary's College, Strawberry Hill, Twickenham

Stephen Hunt, University of Reading

Michael Kirwan, Heythrop College, University of London

Kevin McCarron, University of Surrey Roehampton

Ronald A. Nathan, London

Pat Pinsent, University of Surrey Roehampton

Stanley E. Porter, University of Surrey Roehampton

Wendy J. Porter, University of Surrey Roehampton

Michael Prior, St Mary's College, Strawberry Hill, Twickenham

Elizabeth Puttick, London

Anne Spalding, University of Manchester

Simon J. Taylor, Lincoln Theological Institute

David Tombs, University of Surrey Roehampton

Delia Whitbread, University of Surrey Roehampton

Introduction: Faith in the Millennium

Stanley E. Porter, Michael A. Hayes and David Tombs

'Faith in the Millennium' was the title of a conference held at Roehampton Institute London on 15 May 1999 and this collection of essays derives directly from it. The essays take various perspectives on the question, including theological, philosophical, historical, sociological, arts and literary. To reflect this diversity the volume is divided into three sections.

The first section on theological and philosophical perspectives opens with a chapter from José Míguez Bonino, who explores the Protestant Churches in Latin America and the challenges ahead for them. David Tombs's essay is also contextualized in Latin America as he explores the current crisis in liberation theology against its development over the past 40 years. He highlights that an option for the poor has been a long-standing component of Catholic social teaching and how this teaching still remains the focus and challenge of liberation theology. Michael Prior introduces the current situation in Israel–Palestine as a challenge to theology as well as to international affairs.

Clive Erricker's essay on 'Past Hopes, Past Fears, and Prospects for the Future?' investigates the possibility of a radical understanding of 'faith' for the twenty-first century based on a rereading of Kierkegaard and his relationship with twentieth-century writers who stand outside the ecclesial tradition. His argument centres on what he perceives as the rupture between metaphysics and faith, conceptual construction and spiritual aspiration, theory and action. Michael Hayes further explores the area of spirituality in his chapter. Contrasting its relationship with psychology, he explores the emergence of a 'fourth force' in psychology as a possible point of convergence and asks whether the language of transpersonal psychology mapping might indicate similar territory to Christian spiritual direction. Anne Spalding uses the work of Hannah Arendt to look back on the past and forward to the future in order to think about what we are doing to constitute a 'meaningful life'.

Rebecca Dudley and Simon Taylor offer perspectives on the Jubilee 2000 campaign, international debt and the theology of forgiveness in their respective chapters. The Jubilee 2000 campaign for debt relief has shown how ancient biblical categories like Jubilee debt relief still have power to motivate a successful political campaign for change. Looking at other challenges that Christian thinkers and activists will need to face in the new millennium, Susan Hawley explores the recent trends in theological reflection on, and religious responses to, globalization. Meanwhile, at a national level Ron Nathan calls for the Black Christian community to create a new or alternative hermeneutic and praxis in order to address the needs of Britain's black communities. This call is set against the background of the Black Christian community having survived colonialism and having become an integral part of the British Church scene.

Christopher Hamilton argues for a relationship between a mediaeval perspective on Christian faith and a modern one by drawing on Aquinas, Samuel Johnson, Kant, Bentham, Mill, Kierkegaard, Nietzsche and Kafka. Ron Geaves offers from an Islamic perspective an exploration of the rejuvenation that is taking place with the Naqshbandi tariqa, the largest Sufi order in the Muslim world.

The second section of this book examines faith in the millennium from an historical and sociological perspective. Exploring the major texts of the New Testament, Stanley Porter asks in his chapter, 'In what sense was earliest Christianity a millenarian movement?' Anthony Cross's chapter is an exploration of the life of Joachim of Fiore (c. 1135–1202) and the rise of various mediaeval reform and heretical movements. Andrew Bradstock discusses the contributions that millenarian and apocalyptic ideas can make to an understanding of the historical moments in which they emerge. He contrasts some contemporary movements with the rise of similar movements, notably during the European Reformation and the English Reformation.

Liz Puttick shows how New Religious Movements flourish during periods of rapid social change, arising as vehicles of protest and challenge. She further explores how they are responses to but also agents of transformation, offering a critique of society as well as established religions. Stephen Hunt charts the rise of post-millenarian ideas through the dynamics of the neo-Pentecostal movement in Britain and examines how it has been shaped by wider social considerations. These social considerations include the wider cultural milieu in which evangelical groups find themselves so that their millenarian thought reflects their relationship with society.

The third section of this book explores the topic of faith in the millennium from the perspectives of the arts and literature. In Michael Kirwan's ' "Such Beautiful Dignity in Self-Abuse": Millennial Refusals and the Appetites of Somatocracy', he draws on a dialogue between the contemporary writer Umberto Eco and the cardinal archbishop of Milan, Carlo Martini, on the theme of 'Apocalypse' to propose a unifying theological analysis of contemporary cultural preoccupations. He then examines some of the primary metaphors or expressions of 'somatocracy' including dysfunctional 'consumption', 'addiction' and 'asceticism'. Kevin McCarron assesses a range of novels within the genre of speculative fiction and considers various representations of futuristic religious faith within them. John Anonby develops the post-imperial and millennial implications of the African novelist Ngugi wa Thiong'o, while Liam Gearon explores 'A Theology of the Other', the latter drawing parallels between post-Vatican II theology, postcolonial theory and the writing of the novelist Brian Moore. Pat Pinsent discusses millenarianism in the seventeenth-century writing of Andrew Marvell and Anne Bradstreet, together with the visionary poetry and prose of Thomas Traherne.

Wendy Porter highlights the fact that music has had a place of importance in the Christian Church from its earliest foundations, and examines a musical text from the turn of each of three millennia. In each case, questions are raised regarding the nature of its relationship to the Christian Church, as well as possible insights into the faith of the Christian Church of the time. Delia Whitbread, using the medium of the stained glass rose window, shows the evolution of female iconography in comparative religious traditions and the subsequent dilution of the resonance and power once associated with the earliest images of the feminine. Andrée Grau, using dance as a medium of expression, explores the indigenous Tiwi people of the North Australian Island of Melville as a model to show how shifts in ideology found within many missionary movements of the nineteenth and early twentieth centuries established a syncretism that would respect both native and Christian ideologies in the later twentieth century.

The perspectives presented in these papers are various and diverse in their conception and articulation. Their unifying theme of Faith in the Millennium is one which the editors hope will prove to be both topical and of enduring academic importance.

Part I
THEOLOGICAL AND PHILOSOPHICAL PERSPECTIVES

THE PROTESTANT CHURCHES IN LATIN AMERICA IN THE NEW MILLENNIUM

José Míguez Bonino

I must avow, from the start, that my approach to this question will not be unprejudiced. I cannot ignore the fact that there are in the Anglo-Saxon mind deeply introjected 'visions' of Latin America—its idiosyncrasies, character, culture. Besides—not unrelated but in a different direction—some recent literature has, rather lightly, given the impression of a massive turn to Protestantism that promises to transform the culture and move Latin America to a 'modern' and 'progressive' society.[1] I know that many Anglo-Saxon people have not bought these stereotypes (and this probably applies to most people reading this essay) but reading some of the things that have been published, particularly in Britain and the USA, suggests that these views are quite widespread. Against this background, my essay is an attempt to present a much less 'triumphalist' and more nuanced and differentiated picture. In such an essay, however, all I can do is simply to take a 'glance' at four areas that seem to me a necessary 'prologue' for a more detailed study of the subject. Probably this will be well-known territory for many, but at least I wanted to make explicit how I look at the 'challenge' to Protestant Churches in Latin America in the next decades (as for the entire 'century' or the 'new millennium', I prefer to leave it in God's hands). The four areas will be, first, the direction of the social, political and economic life for the next decades; secondly, the 'religious

1. This interpretation was first suggested in 1954 by Emilio Willems in an article entitled 'Protestantism as a Factor of Cultural Change in Brazil' (*Economic Development and Cultural Change* [1954], pp. 321-33) and developed in 1967 in his book *Followers of the New Faith* (Nashville: Vanderbilt University, 1967). Recently, David Martin has generalized this interpretation in his widely read book *Tongues of Fire: The Explosion of Protestantism in Latin America* (Oxford: Basil Blackwell, 1990).

field' in general; thirdly, the Protestant Churches; and, fourthly, theologico-pastoral challenges that seem (to me, at least!) to be prioritary.

Conditions and Forecasts

I hear frequently—both in Latin America and outside—the Latin American scene painted in terms of 'the recovery of democracies', 'emerging economies' and 'entrance into globalization' as characterizing the present and future of the continent. While this is partly true, it has to be seen in the light of other facts as well.

We all celebrate, to be sure, the demise of the military regimes and the return to democracy—fragile, imperfect and largely formal as it is—in Chile, Brazil, Argentina, Bolivia, Paraguay, Uruguay, and the end of internal military confrontation in El Salvador and Guatemala. But, at the same time, we cannot ignore other decisive trends, also partly initiated by the military regimes. Thus, the Economic Commission for Latin America (ECLA), an instrument of the United Nations hardly suspect of revolutionary leanings, speaks of the 1980s as 'the lost decade'. It is characterized, ECLA says, by a 'marked process of globalization...of national economies', accompanied by 'fall in production, international indebtedness, regressive redistribution, fall in salaries and in the social expense (education, health, security) per inhabitant'. In the later part of the 1980s and the first years of the 1990s all countries went through processes of 'adjustment', anti-inflationary programmes, efforts to stabilize the balance of payments and obtain deferments in meeting the service of the debts, the shrinking of the state, privatization. The results to date have been the growth of the debt, the loss in the purchasing power of the 'frozen' salaries (no less than 30 per cent in five years), increasing unemployment, which has now become structural, more regressive taxes, concentration of wealth in the highest two-tenths of the population, increasing marginality and criminality. Lest we think all of this is due to the proverbial inefficiency of the Latin American—'siesta people'—we can see some of these signs, perhaps in a less dramatic way, in European societies and in the celebrated 'tigers' of South East Asia.[2] In Latin America, ECLA suggested

2. Curiously enough, the concentration of wealth at the top 15 per cent of the population, the loss in the salaries in the lower levels and the percentage of people below the poverty line seems to be noted also in the United States of America in the midst of a flowering economy. See, for instance, H. Daly and J. Cobb, *For the*

a way of measuring success: the relation between growth and equity. In its report ECLA places seven countries in the square of growth without equity, ten in that of 'neither growth nor equity' and two in that of 'equity without growth'. Summing up, Latin America has no country that combines growth and equity. Nobody dares today—and this view is accepted by some of the more conspicuous economists of the developed world—to insist in the classic answer: 'Let us grow, the market knows how to distribute and we'll see that the "trickle down" effect will soon begin to function.' In fact, almost all Latin American countries are going into recession (from annual growth of 4–7 per cent in the 1990s we are now moving down to negative figures of minus 2 to minus 5 per cent). The well-known ghosts of illiteracy, infantile disease, drug traffic, delinquency are not simply a passing 'moment'—they are projecting themselves at least into the next decades. The 'priorities' indicated by ECLA in 1994—education, a greater investment in social expense and conditions of competitiveness at the international level, while included in all political programmes and speeches, are further and further away.

It is not my intention to paint an apocalyptic picture. Some of the international 'gurus' are doing it much more effectively (cf., for instance, recent analyses by Bill Gates,[3] amazingly, as if they had no part in or responsibility for what is happening and without suggesting any ways of turning the tide that they promoted!). There is no need to exaggerate. Reality is exaggerated enough, as anybody with eyes open can see. It is in this society that Protestant—and other Churches and religious expressions—will have to operate in the next decades.

The Religious Field

If we broadly define 'religious field' as the dynamics of the relations between the different religious expressions within a particular area or region at a specific historical period,[4] we must admit that the last 20 or 30 years have witnessed very significant changes, probably world-wide but at least in the area with which I am concerned. Whether as

Common Good (Boston: Beacon Press, 1996); Wallace Peterson, *The Silent Depression* (New York: W.W. Norton, 1996).

3. Bill Gates, *The Road Ahead* (Harmondsworth: Penguin Books, 1996).

4. See P. Bourdieu, 'Genèse et structure du champ religieux', *Revue Française de Sociologie* 13.3 (1971), pp. 295-334.

'accompanying music', as a quest for meaning, as 're-enchantment of the world', as the last hope of the marginal or as subjective compensation for an objectified, depersonalized and mechanical world, religion seems to recover a relevance that looked to be definitively lost. In the first place, we see a *heating* of the religious field. Harvey Cox has recognized it in his recent book on Pentecostalism: 'Since then [1965, when he wrote *The Secular City*] religion—or at least some religions—seems to have gained a new lease on life. Today it is secularity, not spirituality which may be headed for extinction.'[5] Secondly, religious life becomes more and more *pluralized and globalized*: as we shall see, we cannot any more designate a country, an area or an ethnic or linguistic group as Catholic, Protestant, or even as Christian, without immediately qualifying it by indicating the new religious expressions that have either come from outside or grown or been revived from inside the area. Finally, it becomes a *conflictive field*, in so far as these different religious groups vie for the support of the people. Whether this is a passing phenomenon or inevitable aspect of the economic, cultural and communications globalization, the fact is that it has already changed the religious landscape of the world, and certainly has become very visible in Latin America.

This basic trends—'heating', 'pluralization' and 'conflictivity'—are present in Latin America against a particular background. Latin America has usually been seen as a homogeneous cultural and religious world shaped and controlled by the Roman Catholic Church. That has never been totally true. Latin American Catholicism is itself—behind and below the unified hierarchical structure—a plural phenomenon in which the Hispanic Catholicism transplanted by the conquerors and colonizers, the Popular Catholicism that represents a syncretistic amalgamation with different indigenous cultures and religions, the Afro-American Catholicism of Brazil and the Caribbean, the Vatican Catholicism of Pius IX and the baroque piety from Italy and Spain live together, sometimes in conflict, sometimes in peaceful coexistence, sometimes parallel to each other. But the last 30 years have significantly changed the picture. At least four aspects of the change deserve to be mentioned:

First, the self-assertion of indigenous and Afro-American cultures and communities, which have begun, particularly around the debates at

5. Harvey Cox, *Fire from Heaven* (Reading: Addison-Wesley, 1995), p. xv.

the fifth centenary of the European conquest, to reclaim their ethnic, cultural and religious identity.

Secondly, the new religious movements, whether imported from outside like Buddhism, diverse versions of Hinduism (mostly syncretistic movements with different origins), Islam and gnostic groups or semi-religious phenomena like the 'New Age', which are now represented in different proportions in all Latin American countries.

With regard to the first group—indigenous and Afro-American religiosity, we should realize that we are not dealing with 'a new reality' in terms of numbers or intensity but with forms of syncretism in popular indigenous religion that are now claiming the indigenous root they have had to hide or disguise since the time of the conquest and colonization, but which had been present all the time. The second group—new religious movements—does represent, in some more secularized countries or social sectors (new middle classes), a 'return' to religion. In this sense, it is interesting to note that the study of religion, totally banned in our national universities born on the crest of positivism, is now gaining ground. In both cases we cannot speak of a 'massive' return to religion but of a significant increase in its 'visibility'.

Thirdly, the movements of renewal within Catholicism, and fourthly the much-advertised growth of evangelical Protestantism. I shall presently return to these two.

Although I would prefer to defer to a Catholic scholar the evaluation of movements and conditions in Latin American Roman Catholicism, I must, since Catholicism is the earliest and most extended Christian presence in Latin America, venture a few comments in order to have a more adequate vision of the whole religious field.[6]

Since the early 1940s insightful lay and religious leaders and theologians of the Latin American Catholic Church have been calling attention to the fact that the commitment to the faith could not any more be taken for granted. They have called for what has been variously called 're-evangelization', 'mission' and lately 'a new evangelization'.

6. Among the countless publications and studies devoted to the analysis of the present situation of Roman Catholicism in Latin America, I recommend a recent book of José Comblin, a Belgian Catholic priest who has lived in Latin America throughout all this process: J. Comblin, *Called for Freedom: The Changing Context of Liberation Theology* (Maryknoll, NY: Orbis Books, 1998). At several points I have made use of his analysis.

John XXIII, after receiving the reports and proposals of Latin American bishops, theologians and lay leaders for Vatican II, declared Latin America 'a missionary field' for the Catholic Church. In a brief summary, we can speak of at least four ways in which this effort has found expression, particularly since the late sixties.

Since Leo XIII's *Rerum Novarum* (1891) 'the social question' has been one of the ways in which the Catholic Church has asserted its presence and message in the world. In Latin America, Catholic Action in its different forms has been one way of conveying this message. But particularly after Vatican II, the Bishops Conference of Medellín in 1968 and those that came after that, papal visits and letters and episcopal statements have presented the 'social doctrine of the Church' as the instrument through which Latin America could face in a Christian way its crucial problems—this has a significant role in Catholic thinking about mission.

How this is done raises some critical issues. The traditional relation of Latin American Catholicism to economic and political power suggests one way: through education and associations of national and Latin American intellectual, political and economic leadership, the Church can influence society in the direction of her social doctrine and thus contribute to social change. Some lay movements like Opus Dei, Communione e Liberazione (usually called 'integrist') have adopted this line. At the other end are those who think that changes ought to emerge from the base of the Church: the BEC/CEB (Base Ecclesial Community) has been the way in which a significant number of priests and lay people have tried to put together evangelization—Bible study, prayer, celebration—and social action. The Theology of Liberation has been both a product and an instrument of the BEC movement. A certain clash between the 'ecclesiology' of the 'integrists' and the BEC is unavoidable. While the BECs continue, perhaps in a less visible way than ten years ago, their theological and pastoral leadership has met in many places the opposition of Catholic authorities.

We should not forget, however, that while all these efforts are very significant, the great majority of Catholics in Latin America—particularly in the countryside and the poor 'barrios', but also in the lower middle class, adhere to the traditional popular piety and also increasingly to the charismatic Catholic movements. In the conditions of poverty, marginalization and deprivation of great masses, the pilgrimages to sanctuaries, the veneration of Mary and the saints seem to be increasing even in the more 'secularized' Latin American countries like Uruguay and in the somewhat 'de-religionized' middle sectors.

Protestantism in Latin America

When one speaks today of Protestantism in Latin America, people from the Anglo-Saxon world will immediately want to know about 'Pentecostal growth'. This is reasonable, because it is the most significant 'new' development in Protestantism and, possibly, in the whole Latin American religious picture. It has been the object of an endless number of sociological and ethnological studies. But we are still far from adequately understanding or estimating the scope and meaning of this growth. Outside Latin America, it has been exaggerated in both numbers and influence. The growth has had peaks at several points in time, in Chile, Brazil or Argentina, Central America and Mexico. Some of the numbers quoted are totally unreliable. In many cases—Chile, for instance—after a peak moment, growth diminishes and seems to reach a certain ceiling. Signs of a slowing down are present in most of South America. To call attention to this fact is not to underestimate the significance of this movement. It has changed the face of Protestantism and, to some extent, of the whole religious field. But it is totally misleading and out of proportion to hail it as *the* crucial event in Latin American society.[7]

It is important to point out that Pentecostalism and charismatic movements in Latin American Protestantism take different forms in Latin American society. There are different types of Pentecostalism and their growth may have different consequences. There is a 'creole' or 'native' Pentecostalism which grows basically through social networks—in the neighbourhood, in house Churches, through work relations—and is centred in the congregations that spring and extend 'in chain'. There is the mass movement, the spectacular multitudinarian meeting of the star evangelists. And there are the new 'neo-pentecostal' movements, centred in the miracles of healing, the promise of prosperity and the

7. We do not have many reliable statistics, partly because national censuses do not always include religious affiliation, or they present the alternatives in ways that distort the picture, partly because the numbers given in many books are confused or inflated. Besides, we would need a more detailed comparative analysis that would take into account different geographical, social, economic, ethnic and cultural areas of growth.

extraordinary experiences—casting out demons, people who fall down, the Toronto Blessing, the Spiritual War, etc. These are not neatly separated phenomena. But there is, it seems to me, a significant religious and theological difference in several ways. Some are centred on participation: the convert becomes an agent of the Spirit, a missionary, a 'producer'; others are centred on 'receiving', when a person has a 'consumer' relation to his/her faith. In the former the experience is basically a 'community' experience—a finding of the Spirit, personally but with the other; in the latter it is a 'mass' experience, just beside the other. With all necessary caveats, one could say that social growth, when it happens, may be seen, in one case, as a result of the dignity and the power of a new identity; in the other, offered and interpreted as a sort of barter or exchange deal: you 'invest' your faith and 'receive' your reward as prosperity.

Naturally, Pentecostalism is not the whole of Protestantism. Protestant/evangelical Churches have been in Latin America since the 1840s. They came in three streams: as missions from so-called 'mainline' Churches—Methodists, Baptists, Christian Church, Presbyterians, Lutheran in the 1840s and 1850s; as immigrants or business and trading groups and persons about the same years, from Germany, France, Holland, Scandinavia, North Italy (Lutheran, Reformed, Anglican, Waldensians, Mennonites); and from the Anglo-Saxon Holiness Movement at the end of the century—Salvation Army, Nazarenes, Pilgrims, Evangelical Missionary Alliance. In the last 50 years, the membership of the mainline and immigrant Churches (probably with the exception of Southern Baptists, who have significantly grown) have just maintained the rate of growth of the total population while the third group has grown, though not at the rate of Pentecostalism.

If we look at the presence of these Churches in terms of their public role, the mainline Churches have been more concerned with social issues: at an earlier point, the defence of religious freedom and the concern for education and social service, and lately, gathered around issues like human rights and social justice. The 'evangelical wing' and Pentecostalism, on the other hand, while practising different forms of charitable activities, have on the whole refused participation in anything that looks political or para-political. It is all the more interesting that now, as these Pentecostal and Holiness Churches become more significant numerically, they begin to develop an active interest in political participation, creating evangelical political parties or participating in other political groups. In Brazil, Venezuela, Colombia, Peru and Central America, evangelicals of different Churches have been voted into government positions—not always with the best results, one must confess.

This change is particularly important for my concern with the future role of Protestantism. The influence of right-wing North American missionaries and groups has been quite visible in Central American countries and created conflicts between so-called fundamentalist and liberal evangelical Churches. However, in the last ten or twelve years, the growth of the Latin American Theological Fraternity (FTL), bringing together the evangelical tradition and social concerns, the significant movement in younger Pentecostal leadership, developing the theological and social implications of their experience and the increasing exchange of people from different streams of Protestant traditional, immigration and evangelical Churches are opening a hopeful prospect of ecumenical theological and practical cooperation, as witnessed five years ago by the Third Latin American Evangelization Congress (CLADE III)[8] and in the increasing exchange between the Latin American Council of Churches (CLAI) and the Latin American Theological Fraternity (FTL).[9]

Challenges in the New Millennium?

So far these comments have been basically descriptive—though I have not tried to hide my own opinion. In the kind of religious field fore-

8. The report of CLADE III is an excellent source for an understanding of the theological, missionary and social concerns of the largest number of Protestant/evangelical Churches in Latin America: *CLADE III: Tercer Congreso Latinoamericano de Evangelización* (Buenos Aires: Fraternidad Teológica Evangélica, 1993). A new congress, CLADE IV, has just taken place 2–10 September 2000 in Quito, Ecuador, with an even larger and more representative participation of most Latin American Evangelical Churches. The report will be available soon.

9. In 1994, in Argentina, for instance, the Argentine Federation of Protestant Churches (FAIE), the Christian Alliance of Evangelical Churches in Argentina (ACIERA) and the Confederation of Pentecostal Churches (CEP) drew together their requests for changes in the national constitution, including issues related not only to religious liberty and equality but also to human rights, the condition of the indigenous population and other social concerns. In 1999, the three ecumenical institutions, while retaining their own identity, organized the National Christian Evangelical Council (Consejo Nacional Cristiano Evangélico (NCE) as an organ of consultation and representation.

seeable in the short and medium term, we can risk taking for granted that Protestantism will include a wide variety of types that will make it very difficult to define, on clearly historical or sociological criteria, what should be included in the term 'Protestantism'. In other words, the attempt to make a 'map of Protestantism' will be an almost impossible task. This anticipates a certain confusion and conflictivity but also forms of association across traditional confessional borders. The themes of identity and associative affinity will probably acquire greater importance. In a time of uncertainty, new conditions, problems and needs, we can easily rush for order. It seems to me that we should not try to introduce order 'too soon'. We already see this tendency in confessional organizations, ecumenical bodies and national Churches. Besides, facing the multiplicity of religious associations, not a few Latin American states seek to sanction laws—sometimes called 'of religious liberty'—that intend to 'regulate' religious activity. On the contrary, I think it is a time for taking up (but seriously) the famous (and never practised) slogan of Maozedong: 'Let a hundred flowers bloom'. Let us give to the Spirit time and space to dig her own channels. Let us not try to design the plan of the house before we know the family that will live in it.

The danger is greater than we may think. History shows that ecclesiastical structures have been modelled after the structures of power and participation of the existing social and political systems—tribe, empire, feudalism, monarchy, republic. Today we can already see religious movements assuming the style of corporations. Probably to some extent this is unavoidable and no doubt, as in many other times, God can use it. But if we really want to serve a process of 'ecumenization' rather than simply integrate ourselves as the religious component of a globalization ruled by sheer domination and the 'laws of the economy', we cannot rush to 'freeze' the dynamic reality of the present religious field with a simple and hurried formal manipulation of the structures that we now have. We should rather begin 'building from below', trying to discern the direction of the Spirit, permanently opening the road to participation, working with replaceable 'moving walls', letting the tasks that we discover define the structures and functions that we need. Perhaps in that way we can contribute to design the plans of the 'ecumenical house' that humankind needs for the next century.

The question of identity is not solved by trying to trace very carefully the borders but rather by sticking to the centre. In this sense, there are some crucial questions that Protestant Churches have to answer.

First, will the Protestant Churches accompany in solidarity and in a pastoral spirit the growing oppressed and marginalized majorities in their religious and social quest or will they simply satisfy themselves with a 'stable clientele' in the middle and middle-high class?

Secondly, will they enter the 'religious market' with the offer of 'salvation products'—health, inner peace, earthly prosperity and a future in heaven—or will they invite the people to the discipleship of a Lord who offers forgiveness, peace and eternal life but who also demands prophetic courage, active solidarity and the effort to build a different world?

Thirdly, will they be a group of closed communities of refuge or will they recruit members for open communities of evangelizing witness, solidarity and service?

Fourthly, how will the Protestant Churches define the centre of their message: through a reductionist partiality—soteriological, ethical, pietistic, apocalyptic or social—or will they embrace the wholeness of the biblical message?

Fifthly, will they privilege the 'success' of an aggressive, introverted and combative confessional or denominational militancy or the witness to a gospel that inspires a spirit of cooperation and unity?

We know now that an 'identity' is not something static and supra-historical but a self-perception that is generated in the consciousness of a people or a group in the interaction of objective and subjective conditions, an inter-subjective creation, in relation to an 'other'—that is, within plurality and difference. The identity of Protestantism, thus understood, is created from the identities of its different Churches, in dialogue with our people and culture and in the open dialogue with the world Church. There is not one only way of being Protestant. It is the interaction of these different ways of being Protestant that makes possible the creation of symbols that are wide enough to include the diversity. On the contrary, exclusive symbols are what threatens to destroy the identity of the people of God.

Will the different streams of Protestantism be able to articulate, starting from their biblical and evangelical vocation, an understanding of the faith which is at the same time true to its history and capable of assuming the questions, give an answer to the fears and offer a historical concreteness to the hopes of our people? Will the evangelical Churches, now grown in numbers, visibility and interest in participation in the wider society, find effective and genuinely evangelical ways of relating with civil society? Will they be ready to give up the 'social strike' for which they have been rightly criticized while at the same time rejecting the temptation to use their new power to exercise control or obtain privileges?

These questions are meant as a challenge. The future of Protestantism in Latin America will not be defined simply by the conditions of the religious field but also, and perhaps primarily, by the behaviour of the Churches themselves. Our question is not what will happen to Protestantism, but what will the Protestant Churches do?

LATIN AMERICAN LIBERATION THEOLOGY FACES THE FUTURE

David Tombs

Introduction

During the 1970s Latin American liberation theology seemed to offer a blueprint for Church renewal that ensured it would be at the forefront of theological thought well into the future. Yet at the turn of the millennia a growing consensus has arisen that the future of liberation theology is uncertain and that it may have entered a decline in the 1990s from which it might not recover. Both conservative opponents of the movement and sympathetic observers agree that liberation theology faces a crisis. When liberation theologians discuss what might lie ahead, the future is uncertain. Hostile critics are more likely to speak of the movement's 'failure' while proponents and sympathizers speak in terms of 'change'. This paper adopts the latter perspective and examines the background to the current crisis in terms of complex 'change' rather than simple 'failure'.[1] It suggests that the future of liberation theology as a movement may be uncertain—and the terminology of 'liberation' now problematic—but liberation theology's achievements since the 1960s (its pastoral commitment, political engagement, methodology and epistemology) will be valuable guides for any Christian theology

1. For more detailed accounts of the crisis itself, see, for example, J. Comblin, *Called for Freedom: The Changing Context of Liberation Theology* (trans. P. Berryman; Maryknoll, NY: Orbis Books, 1998); P. Berryman, *Religion in the Megacity: Catholic and Protestant Portraits from Latin America* (Maryknoll, NY: Orbis Books, 1996); I. Linden, *Liberation Theology: Coming of Age?* (London: Catholic Institute for International Relations, 1997); J.M. Vigil, 'Is There a Change of Paradigm in Liberation Theology?', *SEDOS* 29.12 (1997), pp. 315-21 (315); F. Betto, 'Did Liberation Theology Collapse with the Berlin Wall?', *Religion, State and Society* 21.1 (1993), pp. 33-38; M. Löwy, *The War of the Gods: Religion and Politics in Latin America* (London: Verso, 1996); G. De Schrijver (ed.), *Liberation Theologies on Shifting Grounds* (Leuven: Leuven University Press, 1998).

that is to offer a prophetic social witness in the new millennium. To support this claim it is helpful to give an overview of different phases in the development of liberation theology since the 1960s.[2]

The Emergence of Liberation Theology in the 1960s

The Second Vatican Council meetings in Rome (1962–65)—usually referred to as Vatican II—introduced sweeping reforms into the Roman Catholic Church and reorientated its relationship to the world. The social teaching in the Council documents known as *Lumen Gentium* (Dogmatic Constitution of the Church, 21 November 1964) and *Gaudium et Spes* (Pastoral Constitution on the Church in the Modern World, 7 December 1965) were particularly important for the emergence of Latin American liberation theology in the late 1960s. *Lumen Gentium* spoke of the Church as 'the People of God' in a way that helped to identify the Church much more positively with the temporal realm (see especially §§9–17). *Gaudium et Spes* challenged the Church to read the 'signs of the times' and respond to them.[3] The document's opening sentence indicated the Church's commitment to the poor: 'The joy and hope, the grief and anguish of the men of our time, especially of

2. The development of liberation theology as a social movement in the 1960s and 1970s has been superbly documented by C. Smith, *The Emergence of Liberation Theology: Radical Religion and Social Movement Theory* (Chicago: University of Chicago Press, 1991). My purpose is to complement this through an examination of liberation theology as a *theological* movement from the 1960s to the present. Two 'First World' critics who have already completed suggestive work along these lines are Paul Sigmund (Princeton) and Georges De Schrijver (Louvain). Sigmund's *Liberation Theology at the Crossroads* (Oxford: Oxford University Press, 1990) argues that there was more popular participation and less Marxist emphasis in liberation theology after the mid-1970s. De Schrijver examines the 1980s and 1990s in terms of a shift from economc class analysis to a broader cultural analysis in 'Paradigm Shift in Third-World Theologies of Liberation: From Socio-Economic Analysis to Cultural Analysis?', in *idem* (ed.), *Liberation Theologies on Shifting Grounds* (Leuven: Leuven University Press, 1998), pp. 3-83. De Schrijver's book offers useful responses (and his own reply) to his thesis. I would generally agree with the basic arguments in these two works but I believe that they need to be located in a broader framework of changes and will attempt to sketch such a framework in this essay.

3. The influential phrase 'signs of the times' is especially associated with *Gaudium et Spes*, §4.

those who are poor or afflicted in any way, are the joy and hope, the grief and anguish of the followers of Christ as well' (§1).

This new social emphasis encouraged the Church in Latin America to embrace the poor as its special concern in the years immediately after Vatican II. In so doing it drew upon and developed the idea of the poor's special rights that dates back as least as far as the very first Catholic social encyclical (Leo XIII's *Rerum Novarum* in 1891).[4] *Rerum Novarum* (The Condition of Labour) recognized that 'the poor and helpless have a claim to special consideration' by civil authorities.[5] John XXIII had recently restated the same principle of special consideration in 1963 in *Pacem in Terris*.[6] Prior to the 1960s the Church had seen the defence of these rights as the responsibility of the civil authorities. The Church's own role had been restricted to charity rather than justice. After Vatican II, social justice for the poor was also to be an issue for the Church and integral to its mission. Where civil

4. *Rerum Novarum* is usually seen as the formal beginning of what is widely referred to as 'the Catholic social tradition'. The tradition does not have precise boundaries but is made up of Papal encyclicals, Conciliar documents and other authoritative documents of the magisterium. The major documents are gathered together in D.J. O'Brien and T.A. Shannon (eds.), *Catholic Social Thought: The Documentary Heritage* (Maryknoll, NY: Orbis Books, 1998), and all quotations here are taken from this version. In practice, the influence of Catholic social teaching may be much less than the Catholic ideal (and its impact varies from Catholic to Catholic and from issue to issue). Nonetheless, it remains a potentially very powerful influence. In comparison with the Protestant Churches, the Catholic social tradition is highly centralized and carries great status within the Church. At least in theory, the social tradition is backed by the Church's full authority.

5. The full passage reads: '...it is the duty of the public authority to prevent and punish injury, and to protect each one in the possession of his own. Still when there is a question of protecting the rights of individuals, the poor and helpless have a claim to special consideration. The richer population have many ways of protecting themselves, and stand less in need of help from the State; those who are badly off have no resources of their own to fall back upon, and must chiefly rely upon the assistance of the State' (*Rerum Novarum*, §29).

6. In 1931 Pius XI used the fortieth anniversary of *Rerum Novarum* to issue his own social encyclical *Quadragesimo Anno* (After Forty Years). In §25, he quoted Leo's principle and made it his own. In 1963 John made the same point in his social encyclical *Pacem in Terris*: 'Considerations of justice and equity, however, can at times demand that those involved in civil government give more attention to the less fortunate members of the community, since they are less able to defend their rights and to assert their legitimate claims' (*Pacem in Terris*, §56).

authorities failed to heed their responsibility to the poor, the Church would need to take up their cause. This development in the tradition provided the basis for the Church in Latin America to make their commitment to the poor.

At the end of Vatican II the Council of Latin American Bishops (CELAM) decided to hold a major meeting in 1968 at Medellín (Colombia) to discuss the implications of Vatican II for their continent.[7] In 1967 Paul VI's social encyclical *Populorum Progressio* (1967) provided further material for the Medellín agenda. In preparation for the main council the following year, 38 priests from throughout the continent met to discuss *Populorum Progressio* at the invitation of CELAM in November 1967. The priests signed a communiqué that called for a whole-hearted commitment to the Church's social tasks, called for more priests to devote themselves to ministry to the poor, and stressed the need for changes to redress injustices against the poor and win their true freedom.[8] Each of these points had important political implications that marked a new course for the Church in its relation with society and the civil authorities: a radically new direction for the traditionally conservative Church.[9] Nonetheless, when the bishops themselves finally met at Medellín they confirmed these brave new directions for the Church in even more forceful ways.

The Medellín Conference was the single most important Church event for the foundation of liberation theology. The documents from Medellín are uneven but its social teaching comes out most strongly in the documents on justice, peace and poverty of the Church. In these

7. CELAM is commonly used to designate both the Council of Latin American bishops as an organizational body and their major conferences. CELAM (the organization) was set up at a meeting in 1955 in Rio de Janeiro at a conference now referred to as CELAM I. The conference at Medellín is widely known as CELAM II. The other two general conferences are CELAM III (Puebla, Mexico, 1979) and CELAM IV (Santo Domingo, Dominican Republic, 1992). In addition to the general conferences (sometimes called 'extraordinary' meetings) CELAM also meets annually for 'ordinary' meetings. It was the annual meeting in 1965 (held in Rome during Vatican II) that led to the second general conference at Medellín.

8. See 'Between Honesty and Hope', in A.T. Hennelly (ed.), *Liberation Theology: A Documentary History* (Maryknoll, NY: Orbis Books, 1990), pp. 58-61.

9. Despite a number of radical social reformers throughout its five hundred-year history (most famously the sixteenth-century Dominican friar, Bartolomé de las Casas) the Latin American Church had traditionally been a conservative social bastion.

documents, the Church made a commitment to the poor that had three key features. First, they denounced injustice and defended the poor as an integral part of Christian mission. Recognizing and naming the suffering of the poor as injustice rather than misfortune (or providential ordering) reflected a new political awareness in CELAM's social teaching. For example, the *Document on Justice* echoed *Populorum Progressio* that 'misery, as a collective fact, expresses itself as injustice which cries to the heavens' (§1).[10] The bishops went on to commit the Church to assist the poor and serve as their advocates: 'The Church—the people of God—will lend its support to the downtrodden of every social class so that they might come to know their rights and how to make use of them' (§20).

Secondly, Medellín called for a clearer witness to the Church's teaching in its own institutional life. The *Message to the Peoples of Latin America* called on the Church to live a 'true scriptural poverty expressed in authentic manifestations that may be clear signs for our people. Only poverty of this quality will show forth Christ, Savior of humankind, and disclose Christ, the Lord of history'.[11] The *Document on the Poverty of the Church* developed this and summarized the tasks that confront the Church:

> In this context a poor Church: denounces the unjust lack of this world's goods and the sin that begets it; preaches and lives in spiritual poverty, as an attitude of spiritual childhood and openness to the Lord; is itself bound to material poverty (§5).[12]

10. CELAM, 'Document on Justice', in Hennelly (ed.), *Liberation Theology*, pp. 97-105 (97); cf. *Populorum Progressio* (§30). The denunciation of poverty in §§1-2 of the *Document on the Poverty of the Church* is equally emphatic: 'The Latin American bishops cannot remain indifferent in the face of the tremendous social injustices existent in Latin America, which keep the majority of our peoples in dismal poverty, which in many cases becomes inhuman wretchedness. A deafening cry pours from the throats of millions of men and women asking their pastors for a liberation that reaches them from nowhere else' (Hennelly [ed.], *Liberation Theology*, pp. 114-18 [114]). Likewise the 'Message to the Peoples of Latin America' reports: 'Its human potential, more valuable than the riches hidden in its soil, makes of Latin America a promising reality brimming with hope. Its agonizing problems mark it with signs of injustice that wound the Christian conscience' (Hennelly [ed.], *Liberation Theology*, pp. 90-94 [90]).

11. Hennelly (ed.), *Liberation Theology*, p. 93.

12. It sets out the consequence of this in §9: 'The Lord's distinct commandment to "evangelize the poor" ought to bring us to a distribution of resources and apos-

In §10 the bishops spoke of their 'duty of solidarity with the poor'. Poverty in the Church's institutional life is closely connected to its social commitment to the poor in wider society. The Church committed itself to material poverty so that it could strengthen its solidarity with the poor and live more easily in spiritual poverty.[13]

The third feature of the Church's commitment to the poor was the recognition of poverty as a structural issue in terms of class oppression and the theological judgment that this was a sinful situation. This was clearest in the *Document on Peace*:

> If development is the new name for peace [*Populorum Progressio,* §87], Latin American underdevelopment, with its own characteristics in the different countries, is an unjust situation which promotes tensions that conspire against peace... When speaking of injustice, we refer to those realities which constitute a sinful situation (§1).[14]

The Document addressed both class tensions in terms of internal colonialism and international tensions in terms of neo-colonialism. In Latin America it picked out 'extreme inequalities between social classes' (§3) and deplored the way that 'some members of the dominant sectors occasionally resort to the use of force to repress drastically any attempt at opposition' (§6). At an international level it repeated *Populorum Progressio*'s condemnation of the 'international imperialism of money' (§9)—a social teaching that stretched back to the social encyclical *Quadragesimo Anno* (1931). It noted that the countries that produced raw material remained poor while the manufacturing countries enrich themselves (§9) and criticized the progressive debt that absorbed the greater part of Latin American gains (§9).[15]

tolic personnel that effectively give preference to the poorest and most needy sectors and to those segregated for any cause whatsoever, animating and accelerating the initiatives and studies that are already being made with that goal in mind. We, the bishops wish to come closer to the poor in sincerity and fellowship, making ourselves accessible to them.'

13. 'This solidarity means that we make ours their problems and their struggles, that we know how to speak with them. This has to be concretized in criticism of injustice and oppression, in the struggle against the intolerable situation that a poor person often has to tolerate, in the willingness to dialogue with the groups responsible for that situation in order to make them understand their obligations' (§10).

14. See 'Document on Peace', in Hennelly (ed.), *Liberation Theology*, pp. 106-13.

15. See also 'Document on Justice', §11 (p. 101). 'Many of our workers... experience a situation of dependence on inhuman economic systems and institutions: a situation which for them borders on slavery'.

The arguments and movements represented at Medellín came together under a name provided by Gustavo Gutiérrez, a Peruvian priest. Gutiérrez developed the term 'liberation' in a way that would be crucially important in focusing the new outlook into a pastoral and theological movement for freedom.[16] Discussions of 'dependency' in other disciplines—most especially economics—emphasized the need for 'liberation' as an alternative to development. This inspired Gutiérrez to make the same shift in theology. In July 1968—the month before Medellín—he presented a paper at a meeting of priests and laity in Chimbote, Peru. It was entitled 'Towards a Theology of Liberation'.[17] The political, existential and theological applications of the term liberation reflected the holistic understanding of salvation to which Medellín had pointed. Liberation proved a rich and inspirational term, and was ideally suited to the revolutionary context of the late 1960s. It was not surprising that this new movement quickly came to be known by the name 'liberation theology'.

Gutiérrez had an influential role at Medellín and the bishops' pastoral commitment to the poor reflected many of his contributions. After Medellín he continued to work on the Chimbote paper and presented a revised version of it in 1969 at a SODEPAX conference in Cartigny, Switzerland.[18] In these early works, Gutiérrez developed the political implications that accompanied an authentic pastoral commitment to the poor in history and argued for a new methodology in Latin American

16. The term liberation can be found in many places at Medellín and Gutiérrez noted at Chimbote that there was already talk of the theology of liberation, but it was his own use of the term that made it such a central term for the new movement.

17. Independently of Gutiérrez, the Brazilian Protestant theologian Rubem Alves submitted his doctoral dissertation at Princeton in 1968 under the title 'Towards a Theology of Liberation'. This was published the following year, but changed at the publishers request to *A Theology of Human Hope* (Washington, DC: Corpus Books, 1969). In Spanish translation it changed again to *Opio o instrumento de liberación* (Montevideo: Tierra Nueva, 1970). Alves and Gutiérrez first realized the similarities of their perspective when they met at the conference in Cartigny, 1969.

18. G. Gutiérrez, 'Notes on a Theology of Liberation', in SODEPAX, *In Search of a Theology of Development: Papers from a Consultation on Theology and Development Held by SODEPAX in Cartigny, Switzerland, November 1969* (Geneva: WCC, 1970), pp. 116-79. SODEPAX (Committee on Society, Development and Peace) was jointly set up by the WCC and the Pontifical Commission for Justice and Peace early in 1968 and ran for three years.

theological work. Gutiérrez stressed that theology had to be responsive to new times and circumstances; theology cannot just repeat abstract and timeless truths. For Gutiérrez, theology had to interpret people's historical commitment to God (and to their human neighbours) in the light of revelation. In a now famous passage he said

> theology is a reflection—that is, it is a second act, a turning back, a reflecting, that comes after action. Theology is not first; the commitment is first. Theology is the understanding of the commitment, and the commitment is action.[19]

Viewed from this perspective, the liberation theology that emerged in the 1960s had at least three distinctive features. First, it advocated a pastoral commitment to the poor that had political implications for both Church and society. Secondly, it endorsed a methodological approach that put commitment to social action first and made participation in struggles for justice a precondition for theology. Thirdly, it used a terminology of liberation that expressed the movement's distinctive features in a way that was both relevant and profound. Hopes for liberation and freedom went to the heart of the movement's political ideals, theological thought and methodological process.

In 1971, Gutiérrez published his highly influential work, *A Theology of Liberation*.[20] This developed his work from Chimbote, Cartigny and elsewhere and systematized these three principles from the 1960s for the new movement to build upon in the 1970s. 'Liberation theology' was a perfect name to represent the new course that the Church in Latin America set for itself in the late 1960s and early 1970s. However, since it was this terminology of liberation that became problematic in the 1990s it is important to be clear that from the very beginning liberation theologians stressed that their work was not just about a new theme or terminology for theology. It was also a new commitment to the poor and a new methodological approach to the practice of theology. It was because these three innovations came together in such a mutually empowering way that liberation theology would be so influential in the 1970s.

19. G. Gutiérrez, 'Toward a Theology of Liberation', in Hennelly (ed.), *Liberation Theology*, pp. 62-76 (63).

20. G. Gutiérrez, *A Theology of Liberation: History, Politics and Salvation* (trans. C. Inda and J. Eagleson; Maryknoll, NY: Orbis Books, 1973 [Spanish orig. 1971]).

The Development of Liberation Theology in the 1970s

In the 1970s progressive priests and nuns responded to Medellín's commitment to the poor. The 1970s were difficult years in Latin America. Military coups took place in Bolivia, Chile and Uruguay (1973), and Argentina (1976). Repression also increased in countries already under military regimes (especially noticeable in Brazil after 1968, El Salvador after 1969 and Peru after 1975). By 1978 only Colombia, Venezuela and Guyana in South America were free from military dictatoship.[21] In Central America, the Somoza dictatorship held sway in Nicaragua and the military controlled Honduras, El Salvador and Guatemala.

In the face of widespread repression and harassment liberation theology and the popular Church made impressive headway and seemed to offer signs of a major Church renewal. Three particularly important new emphases that received much greater attention in the 1970s can be seen in the Documents of the third General Meeting of the Council of Latin American Bishops at Puebla, Mexico in 1979 (known as CELAM III): first, the terminology of the 'option for the poor'; secondly, a new form of popular participation that incarnated the ideals of liberation theology in the base communities; and thirdly, the 'conversion' of the Church and the transformation of theology through its contact with the poor, especially in the base communities.

If the terminology of 'liberation' played a crucial role in initiating the movement in the late 1960s and early 1970s, the idea of an 'option for the poor' was equally important in setting the agenda from the 1970s onwards. The phrase both reflected and reinforced the transformation of the Church by the poor. Critics of liberation theology objected to the idea of an 'option' that was not supported by Church tradition and claimed that it made the Church and theology partial and exclusive. However, although the terminology might have been new, the basic idea of an 'option' had clear precedents in Catholic social tradition and the Gospels. Special concern for the rights of the poor (as a responsibility for civil authorities) had been part of the social tradition since *Rerum Novarum*. The Church's recognition of its own social responsibilities to the poor (beginning in the early 1960s and reinforced by Vatican II) suggested that the principle should be extended from civil

21. See P. Lernoux, *Cry of the People: The Struggle for Human Rights in Latin America—The Catholic Church in Conflict with U.S. Policy* (New York: Penguin Books, rev. edn, 1982 [1980]), esp. p. 10.

authorities to the Church itself. Liberation theologians also pointed out the Bible—and especially the Gospels—showed the same preferential interest in the poor.[22] The poor were most in need and the Church had a special responsibility to stand alongside them.

In the 1970s, Latin American liberation theology developed these principles and precedents into a concerted programme of pastoral action and referred to this as an 'option' for the poor. At the end of the decade, Puebla's classic phrase 'preferential option for the poor' (§1134) clarified that this option was—and always had been—a 'preferential' concern and never an exclusive one.[23] What made the option so controversial was that the Church did not shy away from the political conflicts that solidarity with the poor inevitably involved in situations of structural injustice.

Alongside this development, Medellín had already encouraged the growth of the nascent base community movements.[24] During the 1970s the CEBs (Base Ecclesial Communities) spread rapidly in many Latin American countries.[25] Their strength varied from place to place but they

22. See D. Tombs, 'The Hermeneutics of Liberation', in S.E. Porter and D. Tombs (eds.), *Approaches to New Testament Study* (JSNTSup, 120; Sheffield: Sheffield Academic Press, 1995), pp. 310-55.

23. 'We affirm the need for conversion on the part of the whole Church to a preferential option for the poor, an option aimed at their integral liberation' (CELAM, *Puebla: Evangelization at Present and in the Future of Latin America: Conclusions* (Official English edition of the Third General Conference of Latin American Bishops, Puebla, Mexico, 1979; Slough: St Paul Publications; London: Catholic Institute for International Relations, 1980), §1134. It would be mistaken to see the term 'preferential' as a later toning down of an exclusive idea. The option for the poor had never been intended in an exclusive sense. In November 1971 the Peruvian bishops presented their forceful contribution to the Bishops Synod on Justice in Rome. In this they pledged themselves to 'opting for the oppressed and marginal peoples as personal and communal commitment'. The preferential—as opposed to exclusive—sense of the option was clarified in the next sentence: 'This option does not exclude any individual from our charity; rather opting for those who today experience the most violent forms of oppression is for us an efficacious way of also loving those who, possibly unconsciously, are oppressed themselves by their very different situation of being oppressors.' See Bishops of Peru, 'Justice in the World', *IDOC* (December 1971), pp. 2-18 (§8); reprinted in Hennelly (ed.), *Liberation Theology*, pp. 125-36 (128).

24. See 'Document on Justice', p. 104.

25. In English the CEBs are sometimes referred to as CCBs (Base Christian Communities).

were especially influential in Brazil and Central America.[26] The communities played an important role in the dissemination of liberation theology among ordinary people. Many base community members were transformed into social activists through contact with liberation theology. However, this transformative dynamic went both ways. A less expected feature of this process was that priests, women religious, pastoral workers and theologians were themselves transformed by their contact with the poor. Closer contact with the communities generated a second phase in liberation theology's commitment to the poor. In the 1960s the Church had started to commit itself socially to the poor. In the 1970s, the poor started to 'convert' the Church and the progressive Church started to commit itself to the theological authority of work with the poor as a fourth distinctive feature of the movement.

A number of factors contributed to this transformation.[27] One of the most important was the new political context of the 1970s. The first phase of liberation theology had been set in the 'atmosphere of liberation' of the late 1960s. The second phase was marked by repression and persecution in the 1970s. The rise of authoritarian regimes throughout the region and escalating conflict between Church and state provided a context of persecution and martyrdom. The Church committed itself to the poor at a time when their suffering was most acute and it was particularly dangerous to challenge the powers of the militarized state. Thus in 1980 Gutiérrez looked back on the changes liberation theology had undergone in the 1970s and noted the transformative influence of the poor on the Church:

26. A classic example is the record of the Solentiname community presented in the work of E. Cardenal, *The Gospel in Solentiname* (trans. D.D. Walsh; 4 vols.; Maryknoll, NY: Orbis Books, 1976–82).

27. The methodological principles of the first phase of liberation theology developed in the late 1960s (especially authentic solidarity and the theology as a second step) were important factors in facilitating this transformation. Without these assumptions the priests and theologians might have been less willing—or perhaps less able—to make such an important shift. Since the priests and theologians were already committed to these principles the shift could be made as an extension to what was already believed. This may explain why so many liberation theologians could make the shift from first phase to second phase successfully in the 1970s, whereas shifts to the third or fourth phases in the 1980s and 1990s have proved far harder.

> After Vatican II and the stimulus of the Medellín Conference, we creatively reappropriated the gospel expression about evangelizing or 'preaching the good news to the poor'. Reinforced by an option for the oppressed and commitment of solidarity with them, a series of rich and promising initiatives took place all over Latin America... Then came the irruption of the poor. At a terrible price the common people began to become the active protagonists of history. This fact gave us deeper insight into the whole matter of evangelization. Working in the midst of the poor, exploited people, whom we were supposedly going to evangelize, we came to realize that we were being evangelized by them. Here the CCBs played a major role. The Puebla Conference commented on this when it noted that the Church discovered the 'evangelizing potential of the poor' through its involvement with the poor and such communities.[28]

The poor were not just passive objects of an option made by the Church. The poor were the active subjects who made the option real and thereby transformed the Church. Many communities showed that they were able to take over and live out the Church's option for them with enthusiasm and dignity. Part of the background to this was Paulo Freire's work on a 'pedagogy of the oppressed' and his rejection of 'banking education'. Freire had emphasized that liberating education had to make the people subjects and not just objects. This required a faith in the people as partners in a dialogue and not just recipients of information.[29] In the base communities, this was developed in Bible reading circles that valued the contribution of all participants in a mutual search for new understanding. The Bible readings in base

28. G. Gutiérrez, 'The Irruption of the Poor in Latin America and the Christian Communities of the Common People', in S. Torres and J. Eagleson (eds.), *The Challenge of Basic Christian Communities* (EATWOT International Ecumenical Congress of Theology, São Paulo, Brazil, 20 February–2 March 1980; Maryknoll, NY: Orbis Books, 1981), pp. 107-23 (120). Likewise, at the same conference, Sobrino writes: 'Neither *Evangelii Nuntiandi* nor Medellín placed any stress on persecution or martyrdom either. They both re-emphasize the need for subjective witness in the evangelization process. Both, Medellín in particular, stress the need for poverty and the necessity of becoming poor in order to be in solidarity with the poor. But the essential nature of witness is not viewed in terms of persecution and martyrdom' (J. Sobrino, 'The Witness of the Church in Latin America', in Torres and Eagleson [eds.], *The Challenge of Basic Christian Communities*, pp. 161-88 [171]).

29. See D. Collins, *Paulo Freire: His Life, Works and Thought* (New York: Paulist Press, 1978).

communities showed how the poor could bring their personal experiences to the Bible and offer theological insights that professional exegetes might miss.[30]

As a result, liberation theology in the 1970s started to make explicit how a theological commitment to the perspective of the poor should accompany the political commitment of the 1960s. Jon Sobrino describes how the new contact and appreciation of the poor contributed to this theological shift in the 1970s:

> The important thing about the decade of the 1970s, then, was our rediscovery of the real life of the impoverished majorities, together with our evangelical rediscovery that it is to them that the good news of the gospel is addressed. In this perspective, the poor become the locus, the place, of the Christian life.[31]

The lives of the poor became not just an ethical priority for social work but also a historical *locus* where God was revealed in a special way. This introduced what might be called a new 'epistemological option' into liberation theology—a new way of knowing God in and through the lives of the poor. Sobrino expresses this clearly when he says, 'This means that the poor are the authentic *theological source* for understanding Christian truth and practice.'[32] God had made both a social option and a theological option for the poor in the life of Christ. The theological commitment to the poor meant that Latin American liberation theologians judged their priorities and procedures in terms of their relevance to the poor and took the experiences of the poor as the starting point for their theological work.

Liberation theology's epistemological option for the poor of the 1970s did not materialize *ex nihilo*. Just as the Church's social option had developed out of existing strands in the traditions, so the epistemo-

30. See esp. C. Mesters, *Defenseless Flower: A New Reading of the Bible* (Maryknoll, NY: Orbis Books, 1989 [Portuguese orig. 1983]); C. Rowland and M. Corner, *Liberating Exegesis: The Challenge of Liberation Theology to Biblical Studies* (London: SPCK, 1990).

31. J. Sobrino, *Spirituality of Liberation: Towards a Political Holiness* (trans. R.R. Barr; Maryknoll, NY: Orbis Books, 1988 [Spanish orig. 1985]), p. 3.

32. J. Sobrino, *The True Church and the Poor* (trans. M. O'Connell; Maryknoll, NY: Orbis Books; London: SCM, 1984), p. 93. See also: 'The poor are not simply beneficiaries of liberation. By the mere fact that they exist, for believers they are the historical locus of God, the "place" where God is found in history' (Sobrino, *Spirituality of Liberation*, p. 24).

logical option came out of what had already gone before. The emphasis was discernibly new, but it could not have arisen without the earlier methodological breakthrough of the 1960s.[33] There were hints in this theological direction at Vatican II and Medellín but it was the progressives in the Latin American Church that developed these tentative suggestions and made them central to their practice in the 1970s. On the strength of this approach, Latin American liberation theology in the 1970s rose to international prominence as a creative new force that appeared to offer renewal for the life of the Church and the practice of theology.

The terminology of an 'option for the poor', the spread of the CEBs and the distinctive epistemological orientation developed in partnership with the CEBs were the most important developments of the decade. These developments built on and deepened the work of the 1960s to initiate a new phase in liberation theology. They did not replace the earlier breakthroughs (which remained essential to the movement) but took them to new levels.

The Maturation of Liberation Theology in the 1980s

The 1970s extended the option for the poor from the political to the epistemological realm. However, the Puebla Documents from the end of the decade are also noteworthy for the more inclusive definition of poverty and the poor than had previously been common in some class-based accounts. In their 'Conclusions' the bishops noted that 'the poor do not lack simply material goods. They also miss, on the level of human dignity, full participation in socio-political life' (§1135). They explained: 'Those found in this category are principally our indigenous peoples, peasants, manual laborers, marginalized urban dwellers and, in particular the women of these social groups. The women are doubly oppressed and marginalized' (§1135).[34] This definition of oppression

33. It came out of the experiences of theologians, priests, religious and pastoral workers who committed themselves to the poor and sought to reflect theologically on the implications of this commitment.

34. It is curious that both these passages from §1135 are given in a footnote, and it is the only footnote in the published record, as there are no other footnotes for any of the documents! Gutiérrez states that the original intention had been for these to be part of the text but that they were relegated to a footnote after the meeting.

wider than just social class at Puebla in 1979 pointed to debates that would find even greater prominence in the 1980s.

A key feature in the 1980s was the need to extend the analysis of oppression from a class-based to a more inclusive social framework. This was one of both the great strengths and the great weaknesses of the decade. It was a strength in as much as a more comprehensive analysis was urgently required. Theologians in other contexts (especially feminist and black theologians in North America, and other Third World theologians in Africa and Asia) increasingly criticized the limitations of Latin American liberation theology on these grounds.[35] Gutiérrez (who was more sensitive to these wider concerns than many other liberation theologians) sketched the new agenda at the start of the decade at the meeting of the Ecumenical Association of Third World Theologians in São Paulo:

> The Church of the Third World must commit itself to those struggles for liberation that take up specific concerns of ethnic, racial and sex groups, within the overall framework of the struggle of the poor. Indigenous peoples, blacks, and women of the popular classes will always deserve special attention from our Church and a growing concern on the part of our theology.[36]

In response to these needs, a new wave of liberation theologians emerged who were more sensitive to the new challenges and better able to deal with them. This was especially true for women theologians who became much more prominent during the 1980s.[37] Many of their works addressed gender issues from personal experiences that their male colleagues either lacked or were reluctant to engage. However, Latin American women theologians with academic training are few in number and there were limits on what they could do. Unfortunately, most male theologians failed to respond to their leadership.

35. Engagement with ecological theology and issues of sexuality were equally absent from the work of Latin Americans in the 1960s and 1970s but would have to wait even longer for any attention.

36. 'EATWOT International Ecumenical Congress of Theology, São Paulo, Brazil, 20 February–2 March 1980: Final Document', in Torres and Eagleson (eds.), *The Challenge of Basic Christian Communities*, pp. 231-46 (245).

37. See the various contributors to E. Tamez (ed.), *Through Her Eyes: Women's Theology from Latin America* (Maryknoll, NY: Orbis Books, 1989 [Spanish orig. 1986]).

The challenge to broaden the analysis to engage with race, indigenous culture and gender in the 1980s did not generate the creative and empowering response that was required, and this contributed to the 1990s crisis in the movement. In the 1970s, the addition of an epistemological option had deepened the political concerns of the 1960s in a way that gave new momentum to the movement while preserving its basic focus. Liberation theologians had found the transition from the first phase (late 1960s) to the second phase (1970s) an empowering experience which strengthened their commitment to the poor. It proved harder to adjust to the challenges of the third phase in the 1980s. The failure of many male liberation theologians to address adequately the new agenda had many causes, including their areas of academic expertise, their personal backgrounds and their institutional traditions. Few liberation theologians who had been prominent in the 1970s were suitably trained or experienced to take this work forward with the same force and energy that they had shown in earlier work. Apart from a small number of theologically articulate women, the majority of Latin American liberation theologians found gender and race to be alien issues.

Many liberation theologians had experience in poor neighbourhoods, had undertaken personal vows of poverty as part of their vocation and had found ready support for their stance in the bible.[38] By contrast, their personal experiences usually did not prepare them to recognize or address race, cultural or gender differences as pressing concerns. They also lacked a strong heritage within their institutional identity that would support them with such challenges. The patriarchal culture that the Church shared with almost every single other social institution in Latin America was an enormous barrier to their engagement with sexism. The privileges of the European heritage that many of them shared may also have impeded their recognition of racial issues. The Catholic social traditions that had offered such firm support when dealing with economic poverty and political freedoms offered virtually nothing of value on gender issues, indeed it was usually part of the problem rather than part of a possible solution. The attempt to explore new dimensions of oppression and deepen the appreciation of poverty

38. Because the Bible is permeated with patriarchal values, feminist theology requires a more complex hermeneutics than generally adopted in Latin American liberation theology.

therefore met with limited success. Male liberation theologians had been emotionally and intellectually open to political and economic transformation but were much less familiar with or open to challenges of race and gender.

There is justification in talk of the 'failure' of Latin American liberation theology on these grounds. It is a failure that had always existed but the 1980s showed its real extent and it persisted into the 1990s.[39] Despite the explicit challenges of the 1980s many liberation theologians made only token attempts to widen their perspective and some dismissed the new agenda as merely secondary issues, which could be addressed after the real priorities (politics and economics), had been resolved. Others made more genuine efforts but provided few new insights.[40] Their failure to respond adequately dissipated the energy of their efforts in other areas, reduced the originality and creativity of their work, and slowed the momentum of the movement.

It would, however, be very misleading to see these difficulties as the only—or even the primary—causes of the crisis in the 1990s. Other factors in the 1980s also need to be recognized as being responsible for precipitating the crisis in liberation theology.

Perhaps most important, the political and economic map of Latin America had started to change. In political terms the 1970s had been the decade of dictatorship but the 1980s saw a shift to formal democracy in many countries (for example, Argentina in 1983, Brazil in 1985 and Chile in 1989). These were welcome changes and in most countries the worst of the political repression abated. However, the majority of poor Latin Americans remained excluded from meaningful participation in the political process. At the economic level, during the 1980s 'Silent Revolutions' swept the continent and ushered in new neo-

39. This failure is seen most clearly in the nearly complete absence of works on sexuality by male liberation theologians despite its importance for understanding the real lives of the poor and the various oppressions that women face. I examine this failure in more detail in D. Tombs, 'Machismo and Marianismo: Sexuality and Liberation Theology', in M.A. Hayes, W.J. Porter and D. Tombs (eds.), *Religion and Sexuality* (STS, 2; RILP, 4; Sheffield: Sheffield Academic Press, 1998), pp. 248-71.

40. See Elsa Tamez's interviews of leading male liberation theologians in *Against Machismo: Rubem Alves, Leonardo Boff, Gustavo Gutiérrez, José Míguez Bonino, Juan Luis Segundo and Others Talk about the Struggle of Women* (Oak Park, IL: Meyer–Stone Books, 1987).

liberal economic policies that widened the gap between rich and poor.[41] In response to the debt crisis many countries looked to boost growth by giving the free market and free trade a free reign. At the same time, governments imposed harsh 'structural adjustment' plans to slash spending on social services (including food subsidies, welfare benefits, education and health). Working conditions and union rights suffered as private enterprise capitalized on its new freedoms. The result was a partial gain in economic productivity in some sectors and prosperity for a few but the destruction of whole industries elsewhere and unemployment or underemployment for many.

Liberation theology in the 1960s and 1970s called for liberation from dependency. As the 1980s progressed it seemed that liberation theologians had misread the economic and political signs of the times and misled the hopes of their followers. Limited political freedoms had been won but did not resolve the economic injustices. Within the new democracies the option for the poor remained a pressing priority, but liberation was as distant as ever and dependency was deepening. Furthermore, the class-based analysis and politics of the previous phases of liberation theology were less suited to the new situation. The new poverty did not fit the straightforward class terms that had been used previously but there were no ready alternatives to replace them.

The search for alternatives in the 1980s was also severely hampered by the need for liberation theology to defend itself. Vatican criticisms made many liberation theologians more cautious in what they said.[42] Theologians who were under special scrutiny, including such leading exponents as Gustavo Gutiérrez and Leonardo Boff, had to spend more time responding to criticisms (often very unfair ones) and less time on their own creative theological work. At the same time, indirect attacks were made against liberation theology by appointing more conservative bishops to dioceses that had previously been supportive of the movement. Finally, the Vatican moved to absorb liberation theology into its own vocabulary and muted the distinctiveness of the Latin American approach. Thus in *Sollicitudo Rei Socialis* ('On Human Concern', 1987) John Paul II endorsed the 'option or love of preference for the poor' (§42). Essentially, the Vatican's restoration policy combined firm

41. See D. Green, *Silent Revolution: The Rise of Market Economics in Latin America* (London: Cassell, 1995).

42. See P. Lernoux, *People of God: The Struggle for World Catholicism* (New York: Viking, 1989).

discipline for 'errant' liberation theologians alongside a hostile takeover and asset-stripping of the original liberation theology enterprise. After asserting its managerial control over the trademark, the Vatican then relaunched a much 'safer' product, which had some similarities in appeareance but had far softer political edges.

Linked to the success of this counter-offensive, the base community movement that had been integral to liberation theology's success in the 1970s started to weaken during the 1980s. Opposition to the popular Church within national hierarchies (strongly supported by Rome) reduced institutional support for the communities in many areas. Training courses, national meetings and other resources that had supported the base communities were withdrawn. The process of political democratization in many countries opened up alternative forums for political discussion and social action and some members of the communities left as a result. Other community members were attracted to Protestant Churches—most usually fundamentalist or Pentecostal—which spread dramatically during the decade, especially in Central America and Brazil.[43]

Both the progressives and traditionalists in the Catholic Church saw the spread of these Protestant Churches as detrimental to society but for rather different reasons. The progressives focused their criticism on the depoliticized gospel of heavenly salvation while the traditionalists saw it as a challenge to the institutional role of the Church in Catholic societies. The tendency was to stereotype and dismiss the entire movement rather than to recognize its diversity and seriously engage with what made the Protestant Churches so organizationally effective or so attractive to converts in Latin America's new political and economic context. The religious situation became far more pluralist than ever before and liberation theology could no longer expect to be the only active and energetic movement among the poor. Since the 1980s Pentecostal

43. On Central America, see esp. D. Stoll, *Is Latin America Turning Protestant? The Politics of Evangelical Growth* (Berkeley: University of California Press, 1990); D. Stoll and V. Garrard-Burnett, *Rethinking Protestantism in Latin America* (Philadelphia: Temple University, 1993). On Brazil, see especially Berryman, *Religion in the Megacity*, pp. 9-101; M.A. Vásquez, *The Brazilian Popular Church and the Crisis of Modernity* (Cambridge Studies in Ideology and Religion; Cambridge: Cambridge University Press, 1998), pp. 74-98; J. Burdick, *Looking for God in Brazil: The Progressive Catholic Church in Urban Brazil's Religious Arena* (Berkeley: University of California Press, 1993), pp. 182-220.

Churches have continued to grow while membership of base communities has shown a marked decline. Some critics have suggested that, although liberation theology opted for the poor in the 1970s, since the 1980s many of the poor have opted for Pentecostalism.

On a more positive front the 1980s witnessed a new attention to spirituality and contemplation in the work of some liberation theologians. Gutiérrez had already indicated in *A Theology of Liberation* that there was a 'great need for a spirituality of liberation'.[44] In the 1980s he developed this in a number of his writings.[45] The rise of Sendero Luminoso or 'Shining Path'—an armed revolutionary movement based loosely on Maoist strategies and committed to the violent overthrow of society—and the response of government security forces unleashed new terror on the Peruvian people.[46] Gutiérrez's heart-felt meditations on the 'God of Life' in a culture of death are very different in tone from his work of the early 1970s but conveyed in an equally impressive way his solidarity with the poor and outrage at the injustices that they suffered.[47]

Likewise, Jon Sobrino's focus on spirituality was influenced by the 'suffering in hope' of the Salvadoran people as the country degenerated into civil war during the 1980s.[48] His work during the period continued to focus on Christology and one of the most challenging themes that he worked with was the idea of a Crucified people. In close collaboration with Ignacio Ellacuría—and inspired by the legacy of Archbishop Oscar Romero—Sobrino read the idea of the Suffering Servant and Crucified Christ into the suffering and deaths of the Salvadoran people

44. Gutiérrez, *A Theology of Liberation*, p. 136.

45. See esp. G. Gutiérrez, *The God of Life* (trans. M. O'Connell; Maryknoll, NY: Orbis Books; London: SCM Press, 1991 [Spanish orig. 1982, 1989]); *idem*, *We Drink from our Own Wells: The Spiritual Journey of a People* (trans. M.J. O'Connell; Maryknoll, NY: Orbis Books; London: SCM Press, 1984 [Spanish orig. 1983]); *idem*, *On Job: God-Talk and the Suffering of the Innocent* (trans. M.J. O'Connell; Maryknoll, NY: Orbis Books; London: SCM Press, 1987 [Spanish orig. 1985]).

46. On Sendero Luminoso, see D. Scott Palmer (ed.), *Shining Path of Peru* (London: Hurst, 1992) and D. Poole and G. Rénique, *Peru: Time of Fear* (London: Latin America Bureau, 1992).

47. Particularly noteworthy is Gutiérrez's reformulation of his methodological principle to emphasize contemplation as well as action as the first step on which critical reflection builds as the second step. See esp. Gutiérrez, *On Job*, pp. xi-xiv.

48. Sobrino, *Spirituality of Liberation*.

in ways that brought both ancient history and current reality to life.[49] Works like these in the 1980s are some of the most thought-provoking writings by liberation theologians. They deepen the spiritual commitment to the liberation process and generate provocative insights into God's concern for the poor. However, they were not enough to overcome the growing problems that the movement faced as the 1980s progressed. While the new insights were very valuable, less attention was given to analysis and reflection on the new economic and political context. There was increasing recognition that straightforward talk of liberation was problematic and earlier assumptions about economic dependency over-simplistic but little was offered as an alternative.

By the end of the 1980s liberation theology was already suffering serious weaknesses. Its social analysis was more open to question, its theology was under attack, its supporters in Latin America were being replaced and its roots in the popular Church were weaker. It was still a powerful influence within the Church and theology but it was much less well equipped to cope with the dramatic changes that lay ahead. Both the strengths and weaknesses of the movement at this time were illustrated in an ambitious project to systematize liberation theology's contribution that began in the mid-1980s. The collaborative project involved a number of well-known liberation theologians and was called the *Theology and Liberation* project. It was intended to provide a comprehensive statement on doctrinal areas in a 50-volume work. The *Theology and Liberation* project shows that liberation theology was very far from being a spent force during the 1980s. However, it also illustrated many of the mounting problems. It started with an outstanding contribution from Leonardo and Clodovis Boff that synthesized the key themes and methodology of the movement in their short overview *Introducing Liberation Theology*.[50] After this a further 11 books were

49. J. Sobrino, *Jesus in Latin America* (trans. various; Maryknoll, NY: Orbis Books, 1987 [Spanish orig. 1982]). After Ellacuría's assassination along with five other Jesuits, their housekeeper and her daughter by the Salvadoran military on 16 November 1989, Sobrino continued to develop this theme into the 1990s. See especially J. Sobrino, *Jesus the Liberator: A Historical-Theological View* (trans. P. Burns and F. McDonagh; Maryknoll, NY: Orbis Books; Tunbridge Wells, Kent: Burns & Oates, 1994 [Spanish orig. 1991]); *idem*, *The Principle of Mercy: Taking the Crucified People from the Cross* (trans. various; Maryknoll, NY: Orbis Books, 1994 [Spanish orig. 1992]).

50. C. and L. Boff, *Introducing Liberation Theology* (trans. P. Burns; TLS, 1;

published by eminent liberation theologians.[51] These reflected the wider theological range of the movement in the 1980s but sales were poor and it seemed that interest in liberation theology was in decline. The project never realized its ambitious hopes and it was eventually suspended in 1993. The difficulties with the *Theology and Liberation* Series were a clear indication that despite the maturity of its theological writing the liberation theology movement at the turn of the decade was now facing a serious crisis in much of its work.

The weaknesses in the liberation theology movement of the 1980s—an economic context of dependency but little hope of liberation, institutional pressures within the Church and greater competition from outside it and the problems of engaging with new challenges in a creative and energizing way—became further entrenched in the 1990s and their effects became much more apparent.

The Crisis in Liberation Theology in the 1990s

The 1990s brought many of the weaknesses in liberation theology to a head in a serious crisis for the movment. First, in terms of global social context, the fall of the Berlin Wall in 1989 showed the power of the neo-liberal economic forces at work across the world. During the 1990s the globalization of the free market posed further major questions to the economic analysis at liberation theology's core. Secondly, at an institutional level the rising tide of Pentecostalism and sustained pressure from the Vatican continued to have their effect. Thirdly, at a theological level, liberation theologians continued to engage with more diverse perspectives in their writing but struggled to preserve a clear political and economic analysis. There was no ready-made terminology to replace the dependency-liberation axis of the 1960s and 1970s and the new challenges they faced fragmented their previously clear focus. Each of these factors are important to an understanding of the problems that liberation theology faced in the 1990s.

The fall of the Berlin Wall and the break-up of the former Soviet Union and Eastern Europe brought to a head the economic shifts of the

Maryknoll, NY: Orbis Books; Tunbridge Wells: Burns and Oates; 1987 [Portuguese orig. 1986]).

51. The books were published simultaneously in Spanish and Portuguese in Latin America and then translated into English for publication in the USA by Orbis Books and in the UK by Burns & Oates.

1980s and anticipated a new stage in global economic relations. It would be wrong to see the fall of the Berlin wall as proof of the 'triumph' of capitalism and the 'failure' of liberation theology in the 1990s.[52] The primary influence on liberation theology has always been the experiences of the poor and not Marxist theory or hopes for a socialist state. While discussion of the importance of Marxism and socialism had featured in some of the movement's earliest works, since the mid-1970s they had given very little attention to these issues. At a practical level, hardly any liberation theologians had endorsed the versions of socialism institutionalized in the Soviet Union or Eastern Europe. The simplistic argument that liberation theology fell along with socialism and the Berlin Wall is therefore to be rejected. However, the economic and political realignments represented by the fall of the Wall are related to the crisis in liberation theology and cannot be entirely ignored.

Despite the many flaws of the socialist regimes in the Soviet Union and Eastern Europe, at least in the 1960s and 1970s these had been an alternative to free-market capitalism that showed that life could be different. The possibility of an alternative informed the basic formulation of liberation and dependency. Liberation theologies have had to rethink many of these assumptions and hopes. There are few grounds for optimism that capitalism will bring relief to the poor. The financial shocks that have hit Mexico and Brazil in the 1990s suggest that neo-liberalism will not bring economic salvation (and will certainly not aid social equality) in the twenty-first century any more than it did in the twentieth. However, there is no longer confidence in viable alternatives. The economic problems are obvious but solutions remain elusive. The suffering of the poor remains the same but the faith and hopes of the 1960s and 1970s have been replaced with uncertainty and doubt.

Secondly, the Vatican has continued its policy of consolidating its control over national bishop conferences (mainly through conservative episcopal appointments) and harshly disciplining individual theologians. Pressure on Leonardo Boff led him to resign from the Franciscan

52. An over-simplistic argument represents the collapse of socialist regimes in the former Soviet Union and Eastern Europe as historical proof that liberation theology is discredited at a historical level. Liberation theology is seen to have failed because the Marxist philosophical foundations—on which it is presumed to rest—cannot support it.

order in 1992. In 1995, Ivone Gebara (a Brazilian nun who had been at the forefront of women's contributions to liberation theology) was criticized for remarks she had made to the magazine *Veja* in 1993 about abortion, which the magazine misleadingly published under the title 'Nun Says Abortion Not a Sin'.[53] In 1995 her religious order—the Canonesses of St Augustine—were pressured into sending her to study in Europe for two years.[54]

At the same time the Vatican also continued to make the language of liberation its own, but repeatedly emphasized the distinction between the 'reductionist' political version and the 'authentic' gospel version of liberation. The overall effect of this has been that overt conflict with liberation theologians has receded. In a way liberation theologians can legitimately claim official support and Vatican sanction for their work. However, it has become even harder for liberation theologians to preserve the political edge in their message and distinguish themselves from the depoliticized way that others use their language.

At the same time the Pentecostal Churches have made headway at astonishing rates and in some places appear to be a serious challenge to Catholicism's claim to represent the majority.[55] Elsewhere in this volume, José Míguez Bonino assesses the positive and negative consequences such growth might have. The attraction of such Churches among all sectors of Latin American society shows that liberation theology cannot just ignore or dismiss them as a foreign imperialism.

As in the 1980s there have also been factors internal to the movement that have influenced the development of the crisis. There has also been further movement, as in the 1980s, towards new issues for reflection in liberation theology's expanding analysis of oppression and injustice. Indigenous and ecological issues were added alongside the 1980s' interest in race, culture and gender to extend and expand its class analysis.[56] As in the previous decade, in principle this wider perspective is

53. See *The Tablet* 249 (1 July 1995), p. 851; I. Gebara, 'The Abortion Debate in Brazil: A Report from an Eco-Feminist Philosopher and Theologian under Siege', *Journal of Feminist Studies in Religion* 11.2 (1995), pp. 129-36.

54. She was originally meant to go to France but instead ended up in Belgium (where she had previously been a student at Louvain).

55. See the different contributions in E.L Cleary and H.W. Stewart-Gambino (eds.), *Power, Politics and Pentecostals in Latin America* (Boulder, CO: Westview Press 1997).

56. On ecology and the environment, see L. Boff, *Ecology and Liberation: A*

an appropriate and necessary development for their message to preserve its integrity. However, in practice the diffusion and complexity made communication of a central message even more difficult and contributed to the feeling that the movement had in some sense lost its way.

Each one of the challenges noted above is serious and taken together they pose an important question of whether liberation theology will survive as a movement beyond the twentieth century. As the impact of the first generation fades there are few signs of a strong second generation to take their place and revitalize their movement. Many critics of the movement have been eager to pronounce it dead. However, even if liberation theology does not continue in the new millennium, its so-called 'failure' needs to be kept in perspective and its extraordinary achievements should never be forgotten. While liberation theology always had important limitations—and these certainly became more apparent in the 1990s—the same is true for any theological movement that engages with social issues on the historical plane. Liberation theology's terminology may now seem dated in the neo-liberal world economy, its social analysis often too limited and its theological foundations increasingly questionable, but the same criticism could be made of any other theology. None of liberation theology's difficulties in reading the signs of the times and presenting a prophetic response belong to liberation theology alone.

Looking to the future, the terminology of 'liberation' (which was once a key strength) now makes the movement vulnerable to dismissive superficial judgments. In the new millennium the movement may be forced to leave this terminology behind. However, in an unjust world that remains far from the promise of the kingdom of God, the methodological, epistemological and ethical principles on which liberation theology rested will continue to be relevant. If liberation is no longer the helpful term it once was—and others have co-opted it anyway—the 'theology of liberation' might come to an end. Even so, those who follow God's option for the oppressed in the twenty-first century will no doubt find other theological terms to express their hopes in ways that move the movement's agenda forward and build on its insights. As

New Paradigm (trans. J. Cumming; Maryknoll, NY: Orbis Books, 1995 [Portuguese orig. 1993]); *idem*, *Cry of the Earth, Cry of the Poor* (trans. P. Berryman; Maryknoll, NY: Orbis Books, 1997 [Portuguese orig. 1995]). On inculturation and indigenization, see M.M. Marzal *et al.*, *The Indian Face of God in Latin America* (trans. P.R. Hall; Maryknoll, NY: Orbis Books, 1996).

Gustavo Gutiérrez has said, 'I was a Christian long before liberation theology and I will be a Christian long after liberation theology.'[57]

Conclusion

This brief overview of different phases in liberation theology has explored the 1990s crisis against the earlier development of the movement in the 1960s, 1970s and 1980s. Looking back on these earlier decades it is possible to identify the different key advances that were made in the 1960s and 1970s. First, a pastoral concern for the poor (originating in the 1960s) that involved political commitment and solidarity with their struggles. Secondly, a methodology that linked theology to social analysis and rooted reflection in action (originating in the 1960s) and actively incorporated the poor in a process of liberative action and reflection through the CEBs (originating in the 1970s). Thirdly, a terminology of 'liberation' (originating in the late 1960s) and 'option for the poor' (originating in the 1970s) that provided a clear focus for the movement. Fourthly, an epistemology that recognizes the struggles of the poor as a special locus of God's revelation (originating in the 1970s).

The achievements of liberation theology and the growth of the Church of the poor in the 1970s were based on these principles. The social context permitted a clear vision of the economic and political challenges, a firm basis for solidarity and a unified programme for change. By contrast, the 1980s were a decade of tension and change for liberation theology. The restoration of limited democracies in the political sphere and the rise of neo-liberalism and globalization in the economic arena put question marks against the categories that liberation theology had previously depended upon to articulate its option for the poor. In the 1960s and 1970s liberation theology's class-based analysis of political and economic issues had been its greatest strength. The new situation was harder to interpret. Unfamiliar with the new economic issues and uncertain over new political forces, liberation theology's social critiques started to lose their previous edge. In addition the Vatican's sustained attack on liberation theology diverted its energies and made the movement more cautious in its political and economic stances. Finally, these difficulties coincided with liberation theology's

57. R.M. Brown, *Gustavo Gutiérrez: An Introduction to Liberation Theology* (Maryknoll, NY: Orbis Books, 1990), p. 22.

own attempts to diversify the analysis of oppression beyond class-based political and economic categories. This was an important and necessary development but not all liberation theologians were fully committed to it or well placed to undertake it.

When neo-liberal capitalism 'triumphed' with the fall of the Berlin Wall, it seemed to many observers that liberation theology no longer had a valuable contribution to make on economic justice. The argument in this essay has been that the crisis in liberation theology in the 1990s has more complex origins, which are rooted in developments in the 1980s and earlier. Furthermore, although the problems in the 1990s are real ones—especially in regard to the terminology of liberation—they do not invalidate the importance of the principles on which liberation was built or prove that liberation theology has no relevance for theology in this new millennium. Liberation theology first arose in response to the cries of the poor. The global situation today is worse rather than better than in the 1960s. There are more poor people in Latin America and those who are poor are poorer than ever before. Despite ambitious programmes to cut poverty in the next century the urgent need for social justice is unlikely to disappear. Whether a recognizable movement called liberation theology persists or not, the issues that it dealt with will continue to remain just as pressing as before. The terminology may vary but Christian theology will need to keep faith with and build upon the ethical, methodological and epistemological principles of liberation theology if it is adequately to engage with these issues in the new millennium.

Israel–Palestine: A Challenge to Theology

Michael Prior

The Palestinian–Israeli conflict is one of the most explosive issues in international affairs. Its beginnings can be traced to the First Zionist Congress in Basle on 29–31 August 1897. In the vision of Theodor Herzl (1860–1904), the founder of the Zionist movement, the purpose of the Congress was to lay the foundation stone for a legally secured home in Palestine for the Jewish people. Herzl had already set out his plans in his pamphlet *Der Judenstaat.*[1] In addition to providing 'a house to shelter the Jewish nation', the project would 'advance the interests of civilisation, by establishing a cultural station, on the shortest road to Asia, a task Jews were ready to undertake as the bearers of culture'.[2]

Reflecting typical nineteenth-century European colonialist attitudes, Herzl presented the proposed state for Jews as 'a portion of the rampart of Europe against Asia, an outpost of civilisation [Herzl's term was *Kultur*] opposed to barbarism'.[3] He reflected elsewhere also the typical world-view of European racist superiority. He assured the Grand Duke

1. Herzl composed the first draft of *Der Judenstaat* between June and July 1895. He summarized his scheme in the London *Jewish Chronicle* (17 January 1896), 'A "Solution of the Jewish Question"'. The editorial was sceptical of 'a scheme which is the outcome of despair'. For several more years the editor continued to view Zionism as 'ill-considered, retrogressive, impracticable, even dangerous'.

2. *Protokoll des I. Zionistenkongresses in Basel vom 29. bis 31. August 1897* (Prague: Selbstverlag–Druck von Richard Brandeis, 1911), p. 15.

3. *The Jewish State* (New York: Dover, 1988), p. 96. The original German, *Der Judenstaat: Versuch einer Modernen Lösung der Judenfrage* (Leipzig and Vienna: M. Breitenstein's Verlags-Buchhandlung, 1896), was translated into English by Sylvie d'Avigdor as *A Jewish State*, and in 1946 as *The Jewish State*, and published by the American Zionist Emergency Council. *Der Judenstaat* might be translated more appropriately by 'The State for Jews', to distinguish it from the implications of a Jewish state (*Jüdischer Staat*).

of Baden that Jews returning to their 'historic fatherland' would do so as representatives of Western civilization, bringing 'cleanliness, order and the well-established customs of the Occident to this plague-ridden, blighted corner of the Orient'.[4] As Joseph Conrad might have put it, Herzl's state for Jews would be an 'outpost of progress' in 'the heart of darkness'.

It was inevitable from the beginning that the relationship between the immigrant Zionist Jews and the indigenous Palestinian Arabs would result in conflict, since the Zionist movement was determined to establish a state for Jews in a territory that was already inhabited,[5] and in which Jews constituted less than 5 per cent of the total population.[6] We shall see that 'ethnic cleansing' was foreseen as necessary, was planned for, and was put into operation at the first opportunity (1948–49), and again in 1967.

But why should the State of Israel, founded in 1948, any more than the existence of any other state, be a challenge to theology? There are

4. *The Complete Diaries*, vol. I, p. 343. Herzl began his diaries in 1895, and continued until shortly before his death. Seven volumes of the letters and diaries have been published: vol. I, 1983, *Briefe und Autobiographische Notizen. 1886–1895*; vol. II, 1983, *Zionistiches Tagebuch 1895–1899*; vol. III, 1985, *Zionistiches Tagebuch 1899–1904* (vols. I–III ed. Johannes Wachten *et al.*); vol. IV, 1990, *Briefe 1895–1898*; vol. V, 1993, *Briefe 1898–1900*; vol. VI, 1993, *Briefe Ende August 1900–Ende Dezember 1902*; vol. VII, 1996, *Briefe 1903–1904* (vols. IV–VII ed. Barbara Schäfer *et al.*) (Berlin: Propylaen Verlag). Raphael Patai edited an English translation of the diaries in five volumes: *The Complete Diaries of Theodore Herzl* (trans. Harry Zohn; New York: Herzl Press, 1960). In general, I quote from Patai's edition (rendered Herzl 1960), which I have checked against the original in Wachten and Schäfer. Where I judge it to be important, I give the original German (or other language) from the latter (rendered Herzl 1983–96). I indicate the volume number of the English translation by 1, 2, etc., and the German ones by I, II, etc.

5. Herzl visited Rome on 23 January 1904, and met King Victor Emmanuel III and Pope Pius X. To Herzl's request for a Jewish state in Tripoli, the king replied, 'Ma è ancora casa di altri' (But it is already the home of other people) (Herzl 1983–96: III, 653).

6. There are no exact figures for the number of Jews in Palestine before World War I. Justin McCarthy estimates that in 1880 there were some 15,000 Jews in a total population of approximately 450,000. By 1914 the population of Palestine was c. 710,000, of which some 38,000 (still 5 per cent) were Jews. See further Michael Prior, *Zionism and the State of Israel: A Moral Inquiry* (London: Routledge, 1999), p. 12 n. 10.

two categories of reasons, I suggest. The first derives from the general moral question attendant upon the forcible displacement of an indigenous people from its homeland. The second springs from the unique place which the land (Canaan, *Eretz Yisrael*, or, later, Palestine) has in the sacred scriptures of both Jews and Christians, and the significance attached to the land as the location of the state for Jews. In addition, there is the positive assessment of the State of Israel on the part of the majority of religious Jews of various categories, and in certain Christian ecclesial and theological circles. This is particularly pronounced in those engaged in Jewish–Christian dialogue. Moreover, somewhat on the periphery of scholarship and ecclesial affiliation, many in the broadly fundamentalist evangelical wing of Christianity ascribe unique theological significance to the State of Israel. Manifestly the necessary displacement of the indigenous Arab population of Palestine in order to establish a state for Jews is a challenge to morality. Let us examine the matter further.

The Bible and the Land

The theological element in the problematic is seen at its starkest in the claim that, by the decree of the one Lord of the Universe, the land belongs exclusively to the Israelites and their descendants in perpetuity. According to the determination of the State of Israel the sole descendants who have a legitimate claim to 'return' are 'Jews'—the precise definition of which is an ongoing source of controversy within modern Israel—hailing from any part of the globe, who themselves were never displaced from Palestine. The recently uprooted and expelled Palestinian Arabs, by way of contrast, have no right of return.

Not infrequently, the claim is made that the Bible legitimates the implementation of the Zionist political programme. For people who ascribe divine provenance to the biblical text, there could not possibly be a higher legitimating authority. In the propagandistic claim of David Ben-Gurion, Israel's first Prime Minister, the Bible is the 'Jews' sacrosanct title-deed to Palestine...with a genealogy of 3,500 years'.[7] The claim also pervades the mainstream theology of the Jewish religious establishment, and can be found in much Christian ecclesial and theological opinion. Indeed, the assertion that the Bible provides the ulti-

7. *The Rebirth and Destiny of Israel* (New York: Philosophical Library, 1954), p. 100.

mate divine approval for the establishment of the State of Israel is so pervasive, not only in Christian Zionist and Jewish Zionist circles but even within mainstream Christian Theology and university biblical studies, that the very attempt to raise the issue is sure to elicit opposition. The opposition normally takes the form of personal abuse, and, on occasion, the intimidation of publishers.

There is, of course, a profound problematic surrounding the moral character of the relevant traditions of the biblical narratives themselves, since the gift of the Land of Canaan to the Israelites is inextricably related to the divine mandate to subject the indigenous population not simply to expulsion but to genocidal extermination. By modern standards of international law and human rights, then, the land narratives of Exodus–Joshua mandate 'war crimes' and 'crimes against humanity'. Readers might seek refuge in the claim that the problem lies with the predispositions of the modern reader, rather than with the text itself. One cannot escape so easily. One must acknowledge that much of the Torah, and the book of Deuteronomy in particular, contains menacing ideologies and racist, xenophobic and militaristic tendencies. Nevertheless, biblical scholars appear to be oblivious to this embarrassing fact and retain a high esteem for the book, assessing it to be a theological treatise *par excellence*, and the focal point of the religious history of the Old Testament.[8]

Read with a literalist naiveté these traditions predicate a god who is a xenophobic nationalist and a militaristic ethnic cleanser. Reliance on the authority of a gift of land from such a god, then, is problematic for

8. Indeed, in the 1995 Lattey Lecture in Cambridge University, Professor Norbert Lohfink argued that Deuteronomy provides a model for an utopian society in which there would be no poor (*The Laws of Deuteronomy: A Utopian Project for a World without any Poor?* [Cambridge: Von Hügel Institute, 1996], and in 'The Laws of Deuteronomy. A Utopian Project for a World without any Poor' [without the question mark], *Scripture Bulletin* 26 [1996], pp. 2-19). In my role as the formal proposer of a vote of thanks, I invited him to consider whether, in the light of that book's insistence on a mandate to commit genocide, the utopian society would be possible only after the invading Israelites had wiped out the indigenous inhabitants. The protocol of the Lattey Lecture left the last word with me, and subsequently I was given a second word, being invited to deliver the 1997 Lattey Lecture, for which I chose the title, *A Land Flowing with Milk, Honey, and People* (Cambridge: Von Hügel Institute, 1997, and in *Scripture Bulletin* 28 [1998], pp. 2-17). However highly one esteems the theological thrust of Deuteronomy, one must acknowledge that the narrative does require the genocide of the indigenous population.

any reader who might presume that the divinity would be sufficiently moral to entertain the values of the Fourth Geneva Convention and the Universal Declaration of Human Rights, at least. Moreover, at the level of reception, these biblical traditions have fuelled virtually every form of militant colonialism emanating from Europe, resulting in the sufferings of millions of people and loss of respect for the Bible.[9] Were it not for their religious provenance, such biblical sentiments would be regarded as incitements to racial hatred. On moral grounds, therefore, one is forced to question whether the Torah in fact provides divine legitimacy for the occupation of other people's land and the virtual annihilation of the indigenes.[10]

Yet not all religious people are satisfied with the claim that the Bible legitimizes 'ethnic cleansing'. Moreover, recent biblical scholarship, aided by increasing archaeological evidence, makes it impossible to

9. In my *The Bible and Colonialism: A Moral Critique* (Sheffield: Sheffield Academic Press, 1997), I focus on three different regions and periods in which each colonialist enterprise gained the support of a distinctive religious ideology: the invasion of Latin America in the fifteenth century, the Dutch incursion into the Cape Colony of southern Africa in 1652 and its sequel in the nineteenth and twentieth centuries, and Zionist settler-colonialism of Palestine in this century. Earlier, while the Crusader Templars ate their meals in silence they enjoyed public readings from the Bible, with special emphasis on the books of Joshua and Maccabees. All found inspiration in the ferocious exploits of Judas, his brothers and their war-bands in reconquering the Holy Land from cruel infidels (see Desmond Seward, *The Monks of War: The Military Religious Orders* [London: Penguin Books, 1995], p. 32).

10. G.E.M. de Ste Croix, the greatest authority on the history of class politics in the ancient world, notes the unprecedented character of the biblical traditions of divinely mandated ferocity: 'I can say that I know of only one people which felt able to assert that it actually had a divine command to exterminate whole populations among those it conquered; namely, Israel. Nowadays Christians, as well as Jews, seldom care to dwell on the merciless ferocity of Yahweh, as revealed not by hostile sources but by the very literature they themselves regard as sacred. Indeed, they continue as a rule to forget the very existence of this incriminating material... There is little in pagan literature quite as morally revolting as the stories of the massacres allegedly carried out at Jericho, Ai, and Hazor, and of the Amorites and Amalekites, all not merely countenanced by Yahweh but strictly ordained by him... The Greek and Roman gods could be cruel enough, in the traditions preserved by their worshippers, but at least their devotees did not seek to represent them as prescribing genocide' (G.E.M. de Ste Croix, *The Class Struggle in the Ancient Greek World from the Archaic Age to the Arab Conquest* [London: Gerald Duckworth, 1981], pp. 331-32).

evaluate the biblical narratives of land as pointers to what actually happened in the period portrayed in the text. In the wake of the seminal works of Thomas L. Thompson and John Van Seters,[11] it is now part of the scholarly consensus that the patriarchal narratives of Genesis do not record events of an alleged patriarchal period, but are retrojections into a past about which the writers knew little, reflecting the author's intentions at the later period of composition, perhaps that of the attempt to reconstitute national and religious identity in the wake of the Babylonian exile.[12] Therefore, it is naïve to cleave to the view that God made the promise of progeny and land to Abraham after the fashion indicated in Genesis 15.

Neither do the Exodus–Settlement accounts present empirical facts of history. The archaeology of Palestine shows a picture quite different from that of the religiously motivated writings of the Bible. The evidence from archaeology and extra-biblical literature, supplemented by insights from the independent methodologies of geography, sociology, anthropology, historical linguistics, Egyptology, Assyriology, etc. points in an altogether different direction from that implied by Joshua 1–12. It suggests a sequence of periods marked by a gradual and peaceful coalescence of disparate peoples into a group of highland dwellers whose achievement of a new sense of unity culminated only with the entry of the Assyrian administration. The Iron I Age settlements on the central hills of Palestine, from which the later kingdom of Israel developed, reflect continuity with Canaanite culture and repudiate any ethnic distinction between 'Canaanites' and 'Israelites'.[13] The biblical narrative, then, unless read in a naïve, literalist fashion, offers little succour to ethnic cleansers.

The Religious Significance of the State of Israel

The State of Israel is problematic for theology also in virtue of the fact that its existence attracts a unique vocabulary of approval. The existence of the state, although thoroughly despised as an aspiration by

11. Thomas L. Thompson, *The Historicity of the Pentateuchal Narratives: The Quest for the Historical Abraham* (Berlin: W. de Gruyter, 1974), and John Van Seters, *Abraham in History and Tradition* (New Haven: Yale University Press, 1975).

12. See further Prior, *The Bible and Colonialism*, pp. 216-23.

13. See further Prior, *The Bible and Colonialism*, pp. 228-47, and *Zionism and the State of Israel*, pp. 159-83.

mainstream Orthodox and Reform Judaism until the 1930s and 40s, has in more recent times been elevated into a core element of Jewish self-identification. As such it has implications for Christians also, since the legitimacy and appropriateness of the state for Jews is an integral component of both parties in mainstream Jewish–Christian dialogue. The general flavour of that discourse is detected in the volume reflecting upon 20 years of the dialogue since the Second Vatican Council's Declaration on the Relationship of the Church to Non-Christian Religions (*Nostra Aetate*, 28 October 1965).[14] The dialogue is posited on the premise that both parties, Christians as well as Jews, must accept the self-definition and self-designation of the other. One encounters in the volume claims such as,

> A free Jewish State with Jerusalem as its capital represents the core of Jewish existence and aspirations (Rabbi A. James Rudin).
>
> The living reality of the State of Israel should evoke the respect and admiration of the Christian theologian. How could the renewal of the land be anything to the theologian but a wonder of love and vitality, and the reborn state be anything but a sign of God's concern for his people? (Monsignor John Oesterreicher).
>
> Christians should 'rejoice in the return of the Jewish people to a small sliver of their ancient homeland—if not from compassion and a sense of justice at least from a sense of guilt and repentance' (Father Edward Flannery).[15]

The adulation of Zionism is no less striking in Father Robert F. Drinan, Dean of Boston College Law School. With language that would have surprised Herzl, Drinan describes the Zionist visionary as having pursued his 'messianic pilgrimage' with a zeal 'infused with a compelling humanitarianism combined with traces of Jewish mysticism'. And now Herzl has died, the 'mystery' and 'majesty' of Zionism appears in its glory from his tomb.[16]

14. Eugene J. Fisher, A. James Rudin and Marc H. Tanenbaum, *Twenty Years of Jewish–Catholic Relations* (Maywah, NJ: Paulist Press, 1986).

15. In *Twenty Years of Jewish–Catholic Relation*: Rudin, p. 17; Oesterreicher, p. 35; Flannery, p. 76, who also claims that Zionism is 'a sacred word' with an 'honourable history', and hence support for the state is a *sine qua non* of the dialogue ('the Jewish–Christian embrace', p. 79). For a fuller discussion of the proclivities of the Jewish–Christian dialogue see Prior, *Zionism and the State of Israel*, pp. 123-31.

16. Robert F. Drinan, *Honor the Promise: America's Commitment to Israel*

Biblical Prophecy and the Eschatological Significance of the State of Israel

If such an affirmative stance towards the State of Israel is not uncommon in mainstream Christian reflection it assumes millennial and eschatological proportions in the estimation of a significant body of Christians. The evangelical fundamentalist wing, of which Christian Zionism is an integral element, adds its own distinctive theological perspective. While it is only on the fringes of Church life in Europe, the evangelical fundamentalist wing is particularly influential in the USA.[17]

While allowing for variations in location and among groups, characteristically Christian Zionism takes its cue from a particular reading of certain passages of the Bible, leading to a peculiar theological interpretation of the State of Israel. It proclaims that the ingathering of the Jewish people and the rebirth of the nation of Israel are in fulfilment of biblical prophecies. Since God gave the land to the Jewish people as an everlasting possession, they have absolute rights over all of it, including Judaea, Samaria, Gaza and the Golan Heights. God will bless or curse nations in accordance with their treatment of the Chosen People of Israel.

The Reformation was the vehicle through which a matrix of belief patterns and values favourable to subsequent Zionism infused Western Protestant thought in the sixteenth century, found multiple expression in several parts of Europe in the seventeenth century and continued to find expression in Protestant millenarian circles ever since. The theological claims of John Nelson Darby (1800–82) laid the foundations for the development of fundamentalist evangelical Christian Zionism. He devised a distinctive theology for the final days of history, dividing history into seven periods (dispensations), beginning with Creation, and ending with the millennial kingdom of Jesus, following the Battle of Armageddon. Rather than subscribing to the view that the Church had replaced Israel, Darby claimed that Israel would replace the Church, which was a mere parenthesis to God's continuing covenantal relationship with Israel. Those portions of biblical prophecy and apocalyptic

(Cape Town, NY: Doubleday, 1977), pp. 32, 39.

17. The following discussion is summarized from my *Zionism and the State of Israel*, pp. 134-47.

which had not been fulfilled already would be completed in the future.[18] With his authority waning in Britain, Darby concentrated on North America, where he influenced such evangelical leaders as William E. Blackstone, C.I. Schofield and Dwight L. Moody.[19]

Blackstone (1841–1935) saw Zionism in terms of the fulfilment of biblical prophecy. In 1878 he published his *Jesus Is Coming*,[20] supporting his dispensationalist theology with abundant use of the Bible, especially the prophetic texts that speak of restoration. Despite Jesus' own reticence about details of the end time,[21] Blackstone interpreted contemporary catastrophes as 'signs of the times'.[22] Having visited Palestine in 1889 he judged the agricultural settlements of the first *aliyah*, as well as the antisemitic pogroms in Russia and Roumania, the weakening of the Ottoman hold on the land and the talk a Jewish state also to be 'signs of the times', indicating that the end time would come very soon.[23]

18. Darby invoked the apocalyptic language of Col. 3.4 and 1 Thess. 4.15 to postulate a two-stage Second Coming of Christ. The first 'invisible appearing' would involve the 'rapture of the saints': the faithful remnant of the Church, especially his own followers, would go up to meet Christ in the air, before his appearing on earth. The raptured saints, having joined the Lord in the air, would return to earth with him after seven years, as indicated in 1 Thessalonians. The seven-year long rapture in the air would be marked on earth by the 'Great Tribulation' of natural disasters, wars and civil unrest. After the rapture, a faithful Jewish remnant would observe the Law and rule on earth for a millennium. Darby's views were countered by B.W. Newton, his chief assistant in Plymouth, who proposed that the Jews would be restored only after the return of Christ, who would bring them to faith in the messiah, making them into a kingdom of priests and a holy nation (*The Christian Witness*, V [Plymouth: The Christian Witness & Tract Depot, 1838], p. 306).

19. D. Wagner, *Anxious for Armageddon: A Call to Partnership for Middle Eastern and Western Christians* (Scottdale, PA and Waterloo, ON: Herald Press, 1995), p. 89.

20. The original 96-page tract was expanded, the third edition (1908) to a book of 250 pages, which sold over a million copies.

21. E.g., concerning the coming of the Son of Man: 'But about that day and hour no one knows, neither the angels of heaven, nor the Son, but only the Father' (Mt. 24.36; also 25.13).

22. E.g., the unclean spirits of the lawless trio of communism, nihilism and anarchy were preparing the way for the Antichrist (*Jesus Is Coming* [Chicago: Revell, 1908], pp. 234-35).

23. Biblical prophecy was on the way to fulfilment: 'On that day the Lord will

In 1891, Blackstone organized a national campaign to urge President Benjamin Harrison to support the establishment of a Jewish state in Palestine, with the morally superior USA acting like a modern Cyrus speeding the return of the Jews. The petition, the so-called Blackstone Memorial, urged the President and Secretary of State, James G. Blaine, to

> use their good offices and influence with the governments of the European world...to secure the holding at an early date of an international conference to consider the condition of the Israelites and their claims to Palestine as their ancient home, and to promote, in all other just and proper ways, the alleviation of their suffering.

It called upon the powers to give Palestine back to the Jews as in 1878 they had given Bulgaria to the Bulgarians, Serbia to the Serbians and Cyprus to Great Britain.[24]

With no convening of an international conference in sight, Blackstone continued to lobby politicians. He assured them that the 'signs of the times' were as predicted by the Hebrew prophets, and that 'the title deed to Palestine is recorded...in hundreds of millions of Bibles now extant in more than three hundred languages of the earth'.[25] He

extend his hand yet a second time to recover the remnant that is left of his people, from Assyria, from Egypt, from Pathros, from Ethiopia, from Elam, from Shinar, from Hamath, and from the coastlands of the sea' (Isa. 11.11). Blackstone saw in even the date of the First Zionist Congress (1897), just 1,260 years after the Muslim capture of Jerusalem in AD 637, resonances with biblical prophecy. He alluded to Dan. 12.7: 'The man clothed in linen, who was upstream, raised his right hand and his left hand toward heaven. And I heard him swear by the one who lives forever that it would be for a time, two times, and half a time, and that when the shattering of the power of the holy people comes to an end, all these things would be accomplished' (*Jesus Is Coming*, p. 241).

24. While appeal is made to sympathy, justice and humanity—rather than to theological principles—the Memorial does say, 'Why not give Palestine back to them? According to God's distribution of nations it is their home—an inalienable possession from which they were expelled by force.' The Memorial carried the signatures of 413 prominent Americans, including the Chief Justice, the Speaker of the House of Representatives and the Chairman of the Foreign Relations Committee. In a letter accompanying the Memorial, and signed only by himself, Blackstone invoked his eschatological framework and his sense of the fulfilment of Isa. 49.22, Ezek. 34 to support the motion.

25. *Jesus Is Coming*, p. 235. Moreover, hearing that Herzl was considering Uganda or Argentina as a location for his *Judenstaat*, Blackstone sent him a Bible, marking every passage that referred to Palestine, with instructions that it alone was

resubmitted the memorial to President Theodore Roosevelt in 1903, and by 1916 had prepared a second memorial that was presented to President Woodrow Wilson on 30 June 1917, stressing the urgency of obtaining benign action in favour of the Jews and public USA support for the Zionist project before Christ's imminent return.[26] Lobbying the USA President, members of Congress *et al.*, has been developed into a fine art since by the evangelical wing of USA Christians.[27]

Typically, the modern dispensationalism found within fundamentalist evangelical Christian circles predicates that the present age is the penultimate one. The birth of the State of Israel on 14 May 1948 was the first clear sign of the fulfilment of biblical prophecy. Christ will return in glory soon and bring matters to a cataclysmic triumph over the forces of evil at Armageddon. The Jews, having returned to their ancient homeland, allowed themselves to be ruled by a Jewish impostor of the Messiah. The return of Jesus, the true Messiah, will end the anti-Christ's rule and establish the millennial kingdom. Those Jews who survive will welcome Jesus as their Saviour. During the thousand-year reign, Jesus will establish his capital in Jerusalem, the centre of world government, and the Jewish people now living within the boundaries of the ancient kingdom of David will assist him in its administration. Furthermore, Israel's amazing (or even 'miraculous') victory over Arab armies in June 1967 confirms the prophetic scenario.[28]

to be the site of the Jewish state. In 1916 he presented a second petition to the President of the USA, this time coordinating with American Zionist leaders, Louis Brandeis, Steven Wise and Jacob de Haas. The Zionist leaders passed over Blackstone's real hopes for the Jews and his disparagement of the Jewish Law as an agent of salvation as the price for his support for the Zionist venture.

26. See further P.C. Merkley, *The Politics of Christian Zionism 1891–1948* (London: Frank Cass, 1998), pp. 59-92.

27. However, American Christian support for Zionism was not the preserve of the evangelical wing of Christianity, but included within its number some of its great theological thinkers of the century, e.g., Reinhold Niebuhr, Paul Tillich and the archaeologist, William Foxwell Albright. See further Merkley, *Politics of Christian Zionism*, pp. 134-45, and Prior, *Zionism and the State of Israel*, pp. 162-70.

28. The war of 5–11 June 1967 marked the beginning of my interest in the Arab–Israeli conflict. Although not matching the Nintendo-like portrayal of the new war journalism pioneered in the Gulf War, the television pictures, reports and comment portrayed a classic David-versus-Goliath conflict, with diminutive, innocent Israel repulsing its rapacious Arab predators. Later that summer, billboards in London's Golders Green, quoting the Hebrew prophets, assured readers that those who trusted in biblical prophecy would not be surprised by Israel's victory. I was to

The evangelicals have had significant influence over American policy since the 1970s. When it came to power in 1977, the Likud Party in Israel, under the leadership of Prime Minister Menachem Begin, began to use religious language to advance its agenda, and efforts were made to forge bonds between evangelical Christians and pro-Israel lobbies. The stage was set for promoting a cynical alliance between the ultimately conversionist goals of evangelical Christianity and the political aspirations of expansionist Zionism. The evangelical Christian constituency was a major factor in the election of Jimmy Carter to the Presidency in 1976, and the swing of the evangelical 'right' from Carter to Ronald Reagan in the 1980 presidential election was a major factor in the former's defeat. Reagan himself was open to a fundamentalist evangelical reading of the Old Testament, regarding Armageddon as the goal of history (Rev. 16.16) and contemporary events as signs leading up to it.[29]

The 'clammy embrace' of fundamentalist evangelical Christianity and expansionist Zionism has been carefully orchestrated and heavily financed. To this day, the influence of the North American evangelical right wing, together with the power of the Jewish lobby, is a major factor preventing the USA from exercising even-handedness in the Middle East. Successive Israeli governments have entered into a marriage of convenience with the International Christian Embassy in Jerusalem, happy to use it as a means of gaining support for Israel from some groups of Christians, while ignoring that body's eschatological expectations.

That the State of Israel is esteemed in (some) religious circles as a polity of distinctive value and of unique religious significance is not

learn much later that the 1967 war inaugurated a new phase in the Zionist conquest of Mandated Palestine, one that brought theological assertions and biblical interpretations to the very heart of the ideology that propelled the Israeli conquest and set the pattern of Jewish settlement. See further Prior, *Zionism and the State of Israel*, pp. 84-99.

29. In an intimate phone conversation with Tom Dine, the Executive Director of the American Israel Political Affairs Committee (AIPAC), Israel's powerful US lobby, President Reagan said, 'You know, I turn back to your ancient prophets in the Old Testament and signs foretelling Armageddon, and I find myself wondering if—if we're the generation that's going to come about. I don't know if you've noted any of those prophecies lately, but believe me, they certainly describe the times we're going through' (see Don Wagner, 'Beyond Armageddon', *The Link* 25 [1992]: 1-13 [1]).

sufficient to posit the state as a challenge to theology. That challenge arises mainly because of the underside of the creation of the state. Let us review the situation from the perspective of the victims.

The Nakba

The extent of the *Nakba* (the Palestinian term for the catastrophe of 1948) that the wars of 1947–49 and 1967 caused for the Palestinian Arabs can be assessed in several ways. The planned and comprehensively executed expulsion of the majority of the indigenous Arab population of Palestine in 1948 constitutes the original sin. The estimates of the number of Palestinian Arabs expelled in 1948 fall between 700,000 and 800,000.[30] This constituted 54 per cent of the total Palestinian population of Mandatory Palestine, and has grown to create a diaspora in excess of five million.[31] Moreover, about six million dunums (1.25 million acres) of land were summarily divided among the old and new Jewish colonies.[32]

30. Elia Zureik surveys the estimates, showing that they fall within the range 700,000–800,000 ('Palestinian Refugees and Peace', *Journal of Palestine Studies* 93 [1994], pp. 5-17 [p. 11, table 3], but more recently Salman H. Abu-Sitta argues for a total figure of 935,000 (*The Palestinian Nakba 1948: The Register of Depopulated Localities in Palestine* [with accompanying map, 'Palestine 1948 50 Years after Al Nakba. The Towns and Villages Depopulated by the Zionist Invasion of 1948'] [London: Palestine Return Centre, 1998], p. 14). Janet Abu Lughod puts the number at around 770,000–780,000 ('The Demographic Transformation of Palestine', in Ibrahim Abu Lughod (ed.), *The Transformation of Palestine: Essays on the Origin and Development of the Arab–Israeli Conflict* [Evanston: Northwestern University Press, 2nd edn, 1987], pp. 139-63 [161]).

31. According to the 1994 report of the United Nations Relief and Welfare Agency's Commissioner General, there were 504,070 'refugees' in the West Bank, 42 per cent of the population, and 643,000 in the Gaza Strip, 75.7 per cent of the population (Bernard Sabella, 'Demographic Trends in Jerusalem and the West Bank', in *Arab Regional Population Conference, 8–12 December 1996, Cairo* [Liège: International Union for the Study of Population, 1996], pp. 177-96 [193]). The UNRWA 1995 Report estimated that there are now some 4,645,248 Palestinian displaced persons in camps throughout Syria, Lebanon, Jordan and beyond. Abu-Sitta calculates that the maximum estimate of Palestinians in 1998 is 8,415,930, of which 5,477,745 are refugees (*The Palestinian Nakba 1948*, p. 15).

32. W. Khalidi (ed.), *All that Remains: The Palestinian Villages Occupied and Depopulated by Israel in 1948* (Washington, DC: Institute for Palestine Studies, 1992), p. xxxiii.

The period 1947–49 falls into two distinct phases of belligerence. Although Western historiography concentrates on the regular war phase—from 14 May 1948 to the various Arab–Israeli armistices concluded in 1948–49—and portrays Israel as a tiny, poorly armed and pacific newborn nation being attacked in its cradle and without provocation by the overwhelming force of the regular armies of the surrounding Arab countries, the first civil war phase (29 November 1947–14 May 1948) was the more decisive.

The available evidence confirms that the Jewish community in Palestine was militarily and administratively vastly superior to the Palestinian Arabs, being far better armed, organized and led. The critical part of the first phase began in the first week of April 1948, with the execution of the two new operational plans, Plan Gimmel and Plan Dalet. Plan Gimmel aimed at buying time for the mobilization of forces to carry out Plan Dalet, the master plan for establishing by force of arms Jewish control of the areas assigned to it by the UN Partition plan, for expelling as many Palestinian Arabs as possible, and for conquering as much additional Arab territory as was feasible and, in addition, Jerusalem. The 'ethnic cleansing' of Arab villages followed quickly, and lines of Arabs were expelled in a manner that recent events in Kosovo help one to imagine.

The stereotypical methods of ethnic cleansing were employed: surprise attack against civilian populations assisted by continuous mortar and rocket bombardment; Zionist radio stations broadcasting threats of dire punishment and advising on modes of escape; the massacre of some 254 inhabitants of Deir Yassin, including women and children, some of whose bodies were thrown into a well, doused with kerosene and set alight.[33] That massacre promoted dread in the surrounding Arab villages, whose inhabitants abandoned their homes immediately.[34] The execution of Plan Dalet is the principal explanation for the departure of most of the Arabs of Palestine.[35] Hundreds of thousands were driven

33. A former Stern Gang intelligence officer, a participant in the massacre, wrote of some of the brutality involved (*Ha'aretz*, 25 April 1993). His testimony and that of a Mossad intelligence officer on the scene are summarized by N.G. Finkelstein (*Image and Reality of the Israel–Palestine Conflict* [London: Verso, 1995], p. 189 n. 16).

34. See Prior, *Zionism and the State of Israel*, pp. 24-26.

35. I. Pappé, *The Making of the Arab–Israeli Conflict, 1947–51* (New York: Macmillan/St Anthony's Press, 1992), p. 93.

over the borders by the victorious Jewish brigades. By 23 April Plan Dalet had achieved its purpose.

That the international community has paid little attention to the wilful destruction of some 418 Palestinian villages[36] is a tribute to the determination of the State of Israel to preserve one of its best-guarded secrets. Until recently no publication gave either the number or location of these villages, and the fact that they were completely destroyed helps perpetuate the claim that Palestine was virtually an empty country before the Jews entered. However, rather late in the day, a number of substantial publications,[37] together with the testimonies of individuals,[38]

36. There is an inconsistency in the determination of the number of Palestinian localities destroyed. Benny Morris lists 369 villages and towns and gives the date and circumstances of their depopulation, relying mostly on recently released Israeli files (*The Birth of the Palestinian Refugee Problem, 1947–1949* [Cambridge: Cambridge University Press, 1987], pp. viii-xviii). Khalidi's figure of 418 is based on the villages or hamlets (only) that are listed in the Palestine Index Gazetteer of 1945 falling inside the 1949 Armistice Line (*All that Remains*). Abu-Sitta's register of 531 includes the localities listed by Morris and Khalidi, and adds those of the tribes in the Beer Sheba District (*The Palestinian Nakba 1948*).

37. E.g., Khalidi, *All that Remains*; N. Masalha's *Expulsion of the Palestinians: The Concept of 'Transfer' in Zionist Political Thought, 1882–1948* (Washington, DC: Institute for Palestine Studies, 1992), and *A Land without a People: Israel, Transfer and the Palestinians, 1949–96* (London: Faber & Faber, 1997); and Abu-Sitta's *The Palestinian Nakba 1948*.

38. For example, J.I. Toubbeh, *Day of the Long Night: A Palestinian Refugee Remembers the* Nakba (Jefferson, NC, and London: McFarland, 1998), and the earlier ones of E. Chacour, *Blood Brothers: A Palestinian's Struggle for Reconciliation in the Middle East* (Eastbourne: Kingsway Publications, 1985), and *We Belong to the Land* (San Francisco: Harper, 1992); A. Rantisi, *Blessed are the Peacemakers: The Story of a Palestinian Christian* (Guildford: Eagle, 1990); M. Raheb, *I Am a Palestinian Christian* (Minneapolis: Fortress Press, 1995); and the most recent, R. Abu El-Assal's *Caught in Between* (London: SPCK, 1999). Note especially the theological analysis of N.S. Ateek, *Justice and Only Justice: A Palestinian Theology of Liberation* (Maryknoll, NY: Orbis Books, 1989), and the ongoing field work of individual scholars, such as May Seikaly, who are recording the memories of the distress of the Palestinians in 1948 (see her 'Justice and Reconciliation—Living with the Memory. Legitimacy, Justice and Nationhood', in N.S. Ateek and M. Prior (eds.), *Holy Land—Hollow Jubilee: God, Justice and the Palestinians* (London: Melisende, 1999), pp. 105-10. Moreover, the Washington-based Institute of Palestine Studies and Oxford University's St Anthony's College are sponsoring programmes on Palestinian historiography.

provide an abundant Palestinian narrative of 1948 and after to challenge the dominant Israeli one.

The War of 1967

The June 1967 war resulted in the capture of the West Bank (including East Jerusalem) from Jordan, the Golan Heights from Syria and Gaza and the Sinai from Egypt. Eventually, in 1972, Israel conceded that its pre-emptive strike against Egypt initiated the war. In the light of subsequent events, Israel's intent to reap the fruits of victory, which the war certainly would bring, must be considered a likely explanation for her military aggression. Top of the list of such inevitable fruits was the neutralization of the Arab states and, most particularly, the undermining of Egyptian President Nasser's capacity to unify and modernize the Arab nation. But there were other motives also.

With victory in the war, Zionism finally had achieved its goal of controlling the whole of Palestine west of the Jordan. The speed with which Israel proceeded to benefit from its victory suggests that 'the territorial fulfilment of the Land of Israel', only partly achieved in 1948-49, was one of the central aims of its aggression. But Israel's new 'demographic problem' became clear with the realization that the total Arab population of Israel (some 400,000) and the Occupied Territories came to over 1.3 million, which, mindful of the relatively higher Arab birth rate, could lead to the Zionist nightmare of Palestinians equalling the number of Jews in the land. Immediately after the war, talk of '(compulsory) population transfer' and 'organized emigration' came to the fore for a second time. In the immediate aftermath of the war, the Israeli government discussed plans for solving the 'demographic problem', albeit in secret, information that has come to the surface only gradually, largely due to the tenacity of some Israeli journalists. They reveal that Premier Levi Eshkol convened secret meetings of the cabinet between 15 and 19 June to discuss the demographic problem arising from the fact that, unlike the situation in 1948, the majority of the Palestinians remained *in situ*, even though some 320,000 fled or were expelled.[39]

39. For a discussion of the background to, and the actual evictions carried out by the Israeli army during and after the 1967 war, see Nur Masalha, 'The 1967 Palestinian Exodus', in G. Karmi and E. Cotran (eds.), *The Palestinian Exodus, 1948–1998* (Reading: Ithaca, 1999), pp. 63-109.

William Wilson Harris's investigation of the 1967 exodus[40] estimates that about 430,000 of a pre-war population of some 1.4 million left the territories occupied by Israel, including the Golan Heights and Sinai between June and December 1967, mostly in June. Israel ethnically cleansed the Golan Heights of the 100,000 Syrians who had lived in 143 communities before 1967, leaving only four villages inhabited to this day by some 16,000 Druze. The Israeli expulsions in 1967 and various deportations since, carried out with that unique form of 'legality' practised in Israel, but altogether in contravention of a range of human rights' conventions, emphasized the essential link between the fulfilment of the Zionist dream and the concomitant requirement to deport the Arab population. Yet Israel has remained largely impervious to international criticism.

The Palestinian *Nakba* of 1948 and 1967, when measured in terms of the victims of the most perduring refugee problem of the twentieth century, together with the quotidian oppression that the Arabs of Palestine experience, whether as fourth- or fifth-class citizens of the State of Israel or as victims of the longest belligerent occupation by a foreign power in recent times, should be sufficient to challenge the theological achievement and significance of the State of Israel. Moreover, there is compelling evidence that those catastrophes were not accidents of war, but were intended, planned for and systematically executed.

Moreover, Israel's war crimes did not end with the war of 1948–49, but were followed by state terrorism against its neighbours, including civilian targets, during the 1950s.[41] At least two members of the Netanyahu cabinet were key players in crimes against humanity during that period.[42] Indeed several of the leaders of the state, including at least six Prime Ministers (Ben-Gurion, Eshkol, Begin, Shamir, Rabin and

40. *Taking Root: Israeli Settlement in the West Bank, the Golan and Gaza-Sinai, 1967–1980* (Chichester: Research Studies Press, 1980).

41. See Prior, *Zionism and the State of Israel*, pp. 209-10 for more details concerning the massacre in the Bureij refugee camp in Gaza, in the West Bank village of Qibua, and the some 3,000–5,000 unarmed civilians killed by the IDF without compunction between 1949 and 1956. The IDF atrocities were in Kafr Qasim (October 1956); in Khan Yunis and Rafah some days later; in Samu (West Bank) in 1966; air attacks on Irbid (Jordan, 1968), on the Abu Za'abel factory (Egypt, 1970), Bahr al Baqr (Egypt) and Beirut (1981), etc., all killing civilians.

42. Ariel Sharon was Foreign Minister, while Rafael Eitan served as Minister of Agriculture and Environment.

Peres), three of them honoured by the award of the Nobel Peace Prize in an Orwellian farce, also were perpetrators of crimes against humanity. To the individual acts against Arab villages one must note too Israel's merciless assaults on Lebanon (1968, 1978, 1981, 1982, 1993 and 1996).

Ethnic Cleansing as the Goal of Zionism

The expulsion of the (majority of the) indigenous Arab population of Palestine was a *sine qua non* for the establishment of a viable Jewish state in a land already inhabited by a people that had no intention of 'folding their tents' and moving on. Herzl and his supporters were in no doubt that the enterprise would require the expulsion of the indigenous people. But that was a small price to pay, especially when someone else was paying.

The fate of indigenous people was a matter of little importance to those sharing typical nineteenth-century European colonialist attitudes and supporting the grand European enterprise of civilizing the natives. Although 99 per cent of the land of Palestine was Arab-owned, *Der Judenstaat* ignored the Arabs who constituted 95 per cent of the indigenous population. The aspirations of the colonizers overrode every other consideration. Privately, Herzl and the majority of Zionists after him were in no doubt that the realization of the Jewish dream would require a nightmare for the indigenous population. Despite public protestations to the contrary, Zionist leaders from the beginning were aware of the demographic reality in Palestine.

An item in his diary entry for 12 June 1895 signals Herzl's plans. Having occupied the land and expropriated the private property of its inhabitants, 'We shall endeavour to expel the poor population across the border unnoticed, procuring employment for it in the transit countries, but denying it any employment in our own country.' He added that both 'the process of expropriation and the removal of the poor must be carried out discreetly and circumspectly'.[43] In public, however, he

43. I offer this translation of 'Die arme Bevölkerung trachten wir unbemerkt über die Grenze zu schaffen, indem wir in den Durchzugsländern Arbeit verschaffen aber in unserem eigenen Lande jederlei Arbeit verweigern' (Herzl 1983–96: II, 117-18), in preference to Zohn's translation, 'We shall try to spirit the penniless population...' (Herzl 1960: 1, 87-88).

showed a different face. This kind of duplicity was a characteristic of Zionist discourse, producing 'a not-undeserved reputation in the world for chronic mendacity'.[44] Moreover, after his death in 1904, Herzl's diaries were held by the Zionist movement, and until 1960 only edited versions were released, carefully omitting his 'population transfer' plans.

Israel Zangwill, although he had seen the situation in Palestine for himself in 1897, spoke of 'a land without a people for a people without a land', a phrase widely invoked in the West to win support for the Zionist venture. Realizing that Palestine was twice as thickly populated as the United States, he added in April 1905, that

> [We] must be prepared either to drive out by the sword the tribes in possession as our forefathers did or to grapple with the problem of a large alien population, mostly Mohammedan and accustomed for centuries to despise us.

He left Vladimir Jabotinsky (who later founded Revisionist Zionism) in no doubt that the Zionist enterprise required a new world order, with no place for sentimental argument that the indigenous Arab population would not leave voluntarily:

> If we wish to give a country to a people without a country, it is utter foolishness to allow it to be the country of two peoples.[45]

Chaim Weizmann, later to become the first President of Israel, spoke of the necessity of fitting the gem (the Jewish people without a country) into the ring (the country without a people). He described the native population as the rocks of Judea, obstacles that had to be cleared on a difficult path.[46] After the Balfour Declaration, Zangwill campaigned for transfer, declaring that an 'Arab exodus' was 'literally the only "way out" of the difficulty of creating a Jewish state in Palestine':

> We cannot allow the Arabs to block so valuable a piece of historic reconstruction... And therefore we must gently persuade them to 'trek'...

44. C. Sykes, *Crossroads to Israel: Palestine from Balfour to Bevin* (London: Collins, 1965), p. 26.

45. I. Zangwill, *Speeches, Articles and Letters of Israel Zangwill, Selected and Edited by Maurice Simon* (London: Soncino, 1937), p. 210.

46. See S. Flapan, *Zionism and the Palestinians, 1917–1947* (London: Croom Helm, 1979), p. 56, and D. Ingrams, *Palestine Papers, 1917–1922: Seeds of Conflict* (London: John Murray, 1972), pp. 31-32.

> There is no particular reason for the Arabs to cling to these few kilometres. 'To fold their tents' and 'silently steal away' is their proverbial habit: let them exemplify it now.[47]

The Zionist enterprise meant an *Arab rein* Palestine,[48] and throughout the 1930s its leaders held secret meetings with the British government and with Arab leaders with a view to ensuring it.[49] At the 5 May 1936 meeting of the National Council of the Yishuv (the Jewish community in Palestine), Ben-Gurion was explicit:

> If we want Hebrew redemption 100 per cent, then we must have a 100 per cent Hebrew settlement, a 100 per cent Hebrew farm, and a 100 per cent Hebrew port.[50]

The Jewish Agency Executive in October 1936 overwhelmingly approved detailed plans for the expulsion of the Arab population.[51] Accepting the Peel recommendations of the partition of Palestine (1937) as a temporary expedient, Ben-Gurion wrote in his diary,

> The compulsory transfer of the Arabs from the valleys of the proposed Jewish state could give us something which we never had, even when we stood on our own feet during the days of the First and Second Temple (12 July 1937).

And he emphasized his determination to have it carried out. On 27 July he wrote somewhat disingenuously to his 16-year-old son Amos,

> We have never wanted to dispossess the Arabs [but] because Britain is giving them part of the country which had been promised to us, it is only fair that the Arabs in our state be transferred to the Arab portion.

By 5 October he reverted to adult-speak:

47. I. Zangwill, *The Voice of Jerusalem* (London: Heinemann, 1920), pp. 103, 93.

48. According to Moshe Menuhin, future Zionist leaders schooled in the Hebrew Gymnasia Herzlia in Palestine had it drummed into their young hearts that 'the fatherland must become ours, "*goyim rein*" (clear of Gentiles–Arabs)', *The Decadence of Judaism in our Time* (Beirut: Institute for Palestinian Studies, 1969), p. 52.

49. See Masalha, *Expulsion*, p. 22.

50. D. Ben-Gurion, *Zichronot* (Memoirs) (4 vols.; Tel Aviv: 'Am 'Oved, 1971–72), p. 163.

51. For details, see Masalha, *Expulsion*, pp. 53-57.

> We must expel Arabs and take their places...and if we have to use force...then we have force at our disposal.[52]

While the Twentieth Zionist Congress (3–21 August 1937) was divided on details of the Peel partition plan, most of the speakers were of one mind with regard to transfer. Its morality was accepted, only its feasibility was in doubt,[53] and the Zionist Executive lost no time in forming the (first) Population Transfer Committee in November 1937.

On 7 June 1938, Ben-Gurion replied to the Jewish Agency Executive Committee:

> The State...must enforce order and security and it will do this not by moralising and preaching 'sermons on the mount' but by machine-guns, which we will need.

While Ben-Gurion, Yosef Weitz (the moving spirit of the Population Transfer Committee, and Director of the Land Department of the Jewish National Fund) and other Zionist leaders advocated compulsory 'transfer', they did so only in closed Zionist circles.[54] Moreover, Ben-Gurion deleted references to 'transfer' in published protocols and instead wrote of Zionist intentions to create 'one law for the foreigner and the citizen in a just regime based on brotherly love and true equality...that will be a shining example for the world in treating minorities'.[55] Shabtai Teveth, his biographer, acknowledges the disjuncture between Ben-Gurion's public protestations and his private aspirations.[56] The debates of the Jewish Agency Executive in June 1938 marked the culmination of discussions on Zionism's core requirement of Arab transfer. There was consensus on its moral acceptability, which is scarcely surprising in the light of the goal of the Zionist enterprise.

While the Zionist leadership realized that transfer would have to await the end of the World War, Weitz's unedited diary indicates his overall assessment of the situation.[57]

52. Ben-Gurion, *Zichronot*, pp. 297-99, 330-33, and Shabtai Teveth, *Ben-Gurion and the Palestinian Arabs* (Oxford: Oxford University Press, 1985), p. 189.

53. See Masalha, *Expulsion*, pp. 69-73.

54. See Masalha, *Expulsion*, pp. 108-17.

55. See B. Morris, 'Falsifying the Record. A Fresh Look at Zionist Documentation of 1948', *Journal of Palestine Studies* 24 (1995), pp. 44-62.

56. Teveth, *Ben-Gurion and the Palestinian Arabs*, pp. 198-99.

57. Weitz's unedited diary, from 1932 until his death in 1970, is in the Central Zionist Archives in Jerusalem (see Masalha, *Expulsion*, pp. 130-41). He edited five volumes, which were published in 1965 as *Yomani Veigrotai Lebanim* (My diary

> Amongst ourselves it must be clear that there is no room for both peoples in this country... After the Arabs are transferred, the country will be wide open for us... When the war is over...the only solution is the Land of Israel, or at least the Western Land of Israel, without Arabs. There is no room for compromise on this point... The only way is to transfer the Arabs from here to neighbouring countries, all of them, except perhaps Bethlehem, Nazareth, and Old Jerusalem. Not a single village or a single tribe must be left... There is no other solution.[58]

Weitz's visits up and down Palestine convinced him more and more that the complete transfer of the Arab population was the only solution (see his entries for 18 and 20 March, 4 May, 26 June and 17 July 1941)—the purchase of land would never achieve the necessary result.[59] Because the Arabs were too many and too well rooted in the country, the only way was to cut and eradicate them from the roots, and replace them with Jewish redeemers planted on the land (26 June 1941). If the Arabs could be removed to northern Syria and Iraq, and the frontiers of the Jewish state were to stretch north to the Litani River, and to the east to include the Golan Heights, Palestine would not be small at all. From then on, all Yishuv activities should be directed towards working out a secret plan based on the removal of the Arabs, a plan that the Yishuv should inculcate into American political circles, and he added, 'We will not live here with the Arabs' (22 June 1941).

On 10 July 1941, Weitz proposed that the Jewish Agency should appoint a three- to five-member committee to investigate ways of implementing the evacuation of the Palestinian Arabs to Syria, Iraq and Transjordan. They agreed, and Weitz proposed himself, Zalman Lifschitz and Yosef Nahmani for membership of the second Transfer Committee. With the leadership of the Yishuv (Ben-Gurion, Weizmann, Moshe Shertok, Eliezer Kaplan, Golda Meir, Weitz, *et al.*) intent on population transfer, it was only a matter of time before the plans would be enacted. The first opportunity came in 1948.

While the Yishuv contained a number of factions that advocated binational options (e.g. *Brit Shalom*, whose members included Judah

and letters to the children) (Tel Aviv: Massada). For a discussion of disjunctures between the original hand-written diary and the sanitized public version, see Morris, 'Falsifying the Record'.

58. Weitz (20 December 1940), in Masalha, *Expulsion*, pp. 131-32.

59. Indeed, as late as 1937, despite its relentless efforts, the Jewish National Fund, which owned more than one-half of the land of the Yishuv, had managed to purchase only 3.5 per cent of Palestine.

Magnes, Martin Buber and Hans Kohn), they had little impact on policy. The main division was between the Revisionists—founded by Jabotinsky in 1925, advocating a 'revision' of the Mandate to include Transjordan—who were maximalist and uncompromising, and the more pragmatic, gradualist Labour Zionists. Jabotinsky put his trust firmly in armed force:

> The Arabs must make room for the Jews in Eretz Yisrael... We Jews, thank God, have nothing to do with the East... The Islamic soul must be broomed out of Eretz-Yisrael.[60]

Denial of History

Characteristically, the adulation of the State of Israel that one detects in some Christian circles is contingent upon a distinctive reading of all Jewish history, and an interpretation of the intentions and achievement of Zionism that conflicts with historical truth as well as with good sense. It broadly accepts the propaganda of the State of Israel, which has proved to be one of the most successful disinformation campaigns in modern times. The fabricated Zionist history claims that the Zionists intended no ill to the Arabs of Palestine, and that their intentions did not necessitate a clash or displacement; that, nevertheless, Israel was born into an uncharitable, predatory environment; that Zionist efforts at compromise and conciliation were rejected by the Arabs; that, in the course of the 1947–49 war, the Palestinian leadership ordered their people to quit their homes.

The fabricated history also claims that 'the land was empty' and neglected; that it was redeemed by Jewish labour, which made the desert bloom; that Zionism never damaged, and indeed benefited the natives, who nevertheless remain ungrateful; that the Zionists acted without the assistance of interested imperial powers; that the few unsavoury actions in 1947–49 were the result of the stresses of war; and that all its wars and invasions, and its actions against the Palestinians were purely defensive, and so forth. That fabricated history has

60. See Masalha, *Expulsion*, p. 29. The Irgun (founded in 1935, and commanded in the 1940s by Menachem Begin, future Prime Minister and Nobel Peace Prize winner) and LEHI (the 'Stern Gang', which broke from the Irgun in 1940, and was later co-commanded by Yitzhak Shamir, also a future Prime Minister) were the ideological descendants of Jabotinsky's Revisionism, as is Benjamin Netanyahu's Likud Party.

moulded the perceptions of much of the international community. Even in the face of overwhelming evidence to the contrary, the cant is repeated, not least in religious and theological circles.

Conclusion

The background to the Palestinian *Nakba* is well known. The establishment of the State of Israel in 1948 devastated the indigenous Palestinian culture. Some 780,000 Arabs were driven from their homes in the first wave of Zionist 'ethnic cleansing', and, to ensure that they would not return, some 418 of their villages were razed to the ground. The almost total annihilation of Palestinian society in 1948 is matched by the denial of its history. The conquest of Palestinian society was extended in 1967, this time bringing theological assertions and biblical interpretations to the very heart of the renewed ideology of Zionism. In the process of securing their own homeland, Zionists uprooted another people. Abu-Sitta's description of the Palestinian tragedy holds the moral and theological problematic in sharp relief:

> The Palestinian Nakba is unsurpassed in history. For a country to be occupied by a foreign minority, emptied almost entirely of its people, its physical and cultural landmarks obliterated, its destruction hailed as a miraculous act of God and a victory for freedom and civilised values, all done according to a premeditated plan, meticulously executed, financially and politically supported from abroad, and still maintained today, is no doubt unique.[61]

The determination to create a state for Jews abrogated any possibility of its being guided by universalist values, guaranteeing equality to all its people. Despite the rhetoric of the Preamble to its Declaration of Independence (14 May 1948), the State of Israel does not foster the development of the country for the benefit of all its inhabitants, nor is it based on freedom, justice and peace. There is not equality of social and political rights for all its inhabitants irrespective of religion, etc. Israel is essentially a state for the Jews, dramatically demonstrated by the Zionist expulsion of the majority of the indigenous Arab population and the levelling of their villages to ensure they could not return.

In their determination to present an unblemished record of the Zionist achievement, the fabricators of propagandistic Zionist history rewrote

61. Abu-Sitta, *The Palestinian Nakba 1948*, p. 5.

not only their history, but the documents upon which such a history was based. The aim was to hide things said and done, and to bequeath to posterity only a sanitized version of the past. The argument from the compelling need of Jews to settle in a Jewish state does not constitute a right to displace an indigenous population. It is a dubious moral principle to regard the barbaric treatment of Jews by the Third Reich as constituting a right to establish a Jewish state at the expense of an innocent third party. Surely the victims of Auschwitz would not have approved.

As we have seen, the 'transfer' of the Arab population was promoted by virtually the whole pantheon of Zionist ideologues, albeit mostly in secrecy, thereby comprehensively unmasking the myth of the benevolent and peaceful intentions of Zionism. Furthermore, Israeli appeal to an exclusively 'defensive ethos' is merely a public relations device, as well as an exercise in conscious self-deception, assuaging both world opinion and the consciences of Zionists. Moreover, the consistency with which the State of Israel is excused from having to conform to international law and decent behaviour is one of the great eccentricities of twentieth-century political ethics.

The widespread Western support for the Zionist enterprise is particularly striking from a moral perspective. Whereas elsewhere the perpetrators of colonial plunder are objects of opprobrium, the Zionist conquest is widely judged to be a just and appropriate accomplishment, with even unique religious significance. Much of the rationale for this derives from literalist interpretations of particular traditions of the Bible: the Zionist prize is no more than what the Jewish people deserves in virtue of God's promises. However, there must be a place for examining the modern conflict from the perspective of the victims, the equivalent of reading the biblical text 'with the eyes of the Canaanites', that is, with a sensitivity to the moral question of the impact that the Zionist conquest and settlement have had on the indigenous population of Palestine.

Mainstream Christian theological commentary on Israel–Palestine is driven by guilt feelings concerning the treatment of Jews in the past, and is characterized by a detachment from the international political context of Zionism, by naiveté or misinformation concerning the realities of its conquest of and rule over Palestine, and by a certain paralysis of conscience regarding the unjust treatment of the indigenous population. Christian Zionism is insensitive to the human rights of the

Palestinians and tends to support Israeli governments indiscriminately, while having little respect for Judaism as such. In such circles, biblical attitudes of justice, mercy, love of one's enemies, etc. are either ignored or reinterpreted when applied to Israel.

Zionism, however one estimates its value to international Jewry, is responsible for the dispossession, dispersion and humiliation of the indigenous Arab population of Mandated Palestine over the last 50 years. While such devastation is not unique in the history of human civilization, it does have distinctive features. Most alarmingly from a moral perspective, the injustice to the indigenous population is passed over in most Western discourse, including biblical and theological scholarship, and in some religious circles is even clothed in the garment of piety.

SURVIVING THE GUILLOTINE: PAST HOPES, PAST FEARS, PROSPECTS FOR THE FUTURE; THE APORIA OF FAITH

Clive Erricker

> Knowledge is a 'leprosy of the mind'...every recipe for salvation erects a guillotine.[1]

Introduction: Religion and Faith

The terms religion and faith are usually understood as relational, that is, the latter derives from the former or is, at least, in need of it as a vehicle toward truth. We can understand this relationship as presuming a systemic and structural necessity in the way in which faith is made possible. By this I mean that there is a certain prescription placed upon faith according to the demands exacted by religion. These demands are legitimated by the invocation of tradition and doctrine. Tradition legitimates itself by virtue of the notion of historical continuity, pronounced as 'orthodoxy', orthodoxy is certified by doctrine. Therefore doctrine is the 'litmus test' of 'true faith' as opposed to heresy. If we seek to understand what the political and epistemological presumptions of this process entail we arrive at some interesting conclusions. For example, the claim has to be that an ahistorical truth is maintained within the political processes to which religion conforms itself. It also has to be the case that this truth is capable of expression linguistically, that is, in particular conceptual formulations that are not open to reformulation or translation. By translation here I mean reconceptualization.

My contention is that the above relationship between religion and faith is both false and ultimately untenable. I shall seek to show this both through analysing particular historical examples pertaining to this contention and by showing that the relationship between language, and thus

1. E.M. Cioran, *A Short History of Decay* (Oxford: Basil Blackwell, 1975 [1949]), pp. 88-89.

conceptualizations of reality, and any possibility of a 'knowledge' of 'reality' thus conceived, and the possibility of a 'reality' understood on this basis, is both flawed and irreconcilable with a notion of faith. In doing so I intend to create a rupture between religion and faith and suggest that the future possibilities for faith lie outside and beyond theology, in so far as it is wedded to an ecclesia. This places faith within the context of paradox or aporia, that which is not deducible but yet remains within the play of possibilities (between the possible and impossible).[2]

Kierkegaard and Faith

A useful starting point for examining this rupture is Kierkegaard. In *Philosophical Fragments* he lays out the paradox that Reason always encounters. In the analysis of this I am particularly concerned with Kierkegaard's method:

> What then is the Unknown? It is the limit to which the Reason repeatedly comes, and in so far, substituting a static form for the dynamic, it is the different, the absolutely different. But because it is absolutely different, there is no mark by which it could be distinguished. When qualified as absolutely different it seems on the verge of disclosure, but this is not the case; for the Reason cannot even conceive an absolute unlikeness.[3]

As a consequence:

> It is impossible to hold fast to a difference of this nature. Every time this is done it is essentially an arbitrary act, and deepest down in the heart of piety lurks the mad caprice which knows that it has itself produced the God (the Unknown).[4]
>
> Thus the God becomes the most terrible of all deceivers, because the Reason has deceived itself.[5]

As a result, Kierkegaard posits an inversion of the respective merits of folly and wisdom, as usually conceived and sited by theological orthodoxy:

2. For Derrida's understanding of aporia, see M. Hobson, *Jacques Derrida: Opening Lines* (London: Routledge, 1998), p. 52.
3. Søren Kierkegaard, *Philosophical Fragments* (trans. David Swenson; Princeton, NJ: Princeton University Press, 1962), p. 55.
4. Kierkegaard, *Philosophical Fragments*, p. 56.
5. Kierkegaard, *Philosophical Fragments*, p. 57.

> For the fool says in his heart that there is no God, but whoever says in his heart or to men: Wait just a little and I will prove it—what a rare man of wisdom is he![6]

In his footnote to this Kierkegaard comments: 'What an excellent subject for a comedy of the higher lunacy!'

We should note that neither the 'fool' nor the 'man of wisdom' comes out of this well, both being consigned to 'lunacy' as Kierkegaard's paradoxical reasoning subverts the project of knowledge per se. We may finish with his terse reminder that 'the God is not a name but a concept'.[7] In other words there is neither God nor no God, there is only the Unknown, which is unknowable by reason and therefore beyond comprehension.

This leads Kierkegaard to the *leap*—the act of passion that cannot be based on the Reason.[8] Within Kierkegaard's method we can uncover two issues of paramount importance. The first is that any resort to naming the unknowable, or presuming that a conceptualization of the unknowable constitutes knowledge of it, is a deceit, which confounds the possibility of faith. The second is that any possibility of faith is performative—it depends on acting without knowing.

Kierkegaard has brought us to the impasse of undecidability as experienced by the individual who desires faith. Derrida introduces us to the politics of undecidability.

Derrida and Undecidability

Where Kierkegaard uses paradox and irony to argue against a systematic metaphysics we find that Derrida uses deconstructive analysis in developing his hermeneutic of Undecidability. As with Kierkegaard, Derrida's intention is to destabilize knowledge, to show it cannot achieve what it claims, and, as a result, brings about closure rather than opening up possibilities. If we consider his argument in Plato's Pharmacy we gain a sense of what this means.

In Plato's Pharmacy,[9] Derrida revisits the final section of Plato's Phaedrus in which the inventor-god Theuth exhibits his inventions to the Great God-King Thamus (Ammon). Thamus considers the merits of

6. Kierkegaard, *Philosophical Fragments*, p. 54.
7. Kierkegaard, *Philosophical Fragments*, p. 51.
8. Kierkegaard, *Philosophical Fragments*, p. 59.
9. Jacques Derrida, 'Plato's Pharmacy', in *Dissemination* (trans. A. Bass; London: Athlone Press, 1981 [1972]).

each one. When it comes to writing, Theuth proclaims it as 'a pharmikon for memory and wisdom'.

Pharmikon could be translated as 'magic potion' or as recipe, cure or remedy. Derrida notes the ambiguity of the word's meaning. In Greek it can mean either cure or poison. Like 'drug' it can have good and bad aspects. The pharmakon is an undecidable, but some translations resolve the word by cutting out one of its poles.

Theuth offers it as a remedy or recipe, Thamus perceives it as a poison: 'Those who write will stop exercising their memory and become forgetful...as for wisdom, you offer your students a mere appearance of it, not the reality...'[10]

Writing is an undecidable that has been returned decided. But the pharmakon, Derrida argues, cannot be fixed down within Plato's oppositions. The pharmakon has no proper or determinate character. It is the play of possibilities.

Derrida attributes the need to decide on undecidables to the way in which knowledge is formed: according to binary opposition, which is the basis of conceptualization and the structure of language. Let us consider 'faith' in this context of undecidability.

Kierkegaard's notion of faith can be said to fit with Derrida's description of an undecidable because of its pharmakonic quality. That is, the leap of faith cannot be presumed to have a decidable outcome prior to the act. In other words we cannot know, in advance of the act, whether it will result in a 'cure' or a 'poison' in terms of resolving our existential situation.

If Kierkegaardian faith is placed before the judge Reason, it will be returned decided as not leading to wisdom. But, if we translate faith into a decidable, that is, change its character so that it can be accommodated by Reason, the judgment returned can go the other way—it can be understood as leading to wisdom. My contention is that this is precisely what religion does when it speaks of faith. By turning faith into a decidable religion becomes the judge of faith and, at the same time, defines its character. Thus we can speak of 'true faith' and 'false faith', truth and heresy. Binary oppositions can now be applied. However, this can only be done by turning faith into a decidable, that is, by denying its inherent character, at least in the Kierkegaardian sense. What faith loses in this translation is the existential possibility it pos-

10. Plato, *Phaedrus and the Seventh and Eighth Letters* (Harmondsworth: Penguin Books, 1973), pp. 274b-75b.

sessed for Kierkegaard in relation to the Unknown. In submitting to the judgment of religion faith gains definition, but at the cost of the play of possibilities that faith opens up. In other words what we might call doctrinally regulated faith is a betrayal of faith itself and its performative possibilities. Faith suffers the same fate as the Unknown, being conceptually imprisoned in the concept 'God'. It is situated within the language games and power moves of 'knowledge'. It becomes resited within the province of epistemology. Thus religion renders faith impotent, emasculated, by virtue of its imprisonment within the systematic constructions of metaphysics, with the intent that faith can then be presented as a known means of achieving a known end, this being expressed in doctrine. The importance of this move is revealed in the political authority that proceeds from it.

Religion as Reiterated Authority

By such a conceptual framing of both faith and (what now becomes) its object (God), religion creates a fixed ordering of decided values that is 'true' and then judges on this basis by invoking the authority of a presumed known transcendental authority that is itself legitimated on the basis of religion's ownership of a creedally formulated declaration of what constitutes faith. In this way religion manages to claim knowledge that transcends the self-referential system of signs of which it is a part. The contradictory nature of such a situation should now be clear.

Despite it being the case that religion itself is a conceptual construct, and as such open to the judgment made according to decidability (is it good or bad?), it seeks to occupy a political position in which it presents itself as the judge of decidability, the arbiter of what is cure and poison, good and bad. It does this by virtue of the invocation of 'faith' as a basis for such authority (faith has now become a foundational epistemological principle). Thus it uses an undecidable (faith), or in Kierkegaard's terms a paradox, to legitimate its conceptual framework and thus its claim to knowledge. Such legitimation is untenable, but nevertheless it is politically beneficial, which allows us to understand the specific aim of such a legitimation: power.

As an example of the manner in which this power move is executed consider the following quotations from Andrew Wright's *Spiritual Pedagogy*:[11]

11. A. Wright, *Spiritual Pedagogy: A Survey, Critique and Reconstruction of*

> True rationality lies...in understanding that accommodates itself to the objective claims of the actuality of divine revelation. Authentic faith is rooted in...a relationship with the Trinitarian God dependent on the mediation of revelation through scripture and ecclesiastical tradition.[12]

> If Christian spirituality, in its historical continuity, is incompatible with romantic and post-modern formulations, then the latter can claim universality only by deconstructing orthodox Christian discourse and colonising it within its own frame of reference.[13]

In the first statement Wright presumes that 'divine revelation' can be understood as 'objective', that 'authentic' faith is determined by its assent to Trinitarian doctrine and that this will be recognized by scripture's and tradition's pronouncements being ratified. In other words faith is determined as authentic according to its assent to foundational claims and these can be confirmed as authentic by virtue of appeal to 'objectivity', which is a scientific criterion. This satisfies most of the criteria claimed for knowledge in the modern period and previous to it.

In the second quotation two further criteria are introduced: universality (which is the corollary of objectivity) and historical continuity (which is the criterion for affirming the authenticity of orthodoxy). In this series of assertions Wright seeks to ensure that 'faith' is bound within the criteria of knowledge that operate within religion and science in the modern era. Only in conforming to these does it gain any credence. This is a significant example of how religion seeks to ensure its own political purposes without sufficient justification or apologia. This is wholly Platonic in its form of decidability.

On a point of greater detail we may observe that historical continuity presumes that statements made in one context are transferable, without change in meaning and interpretation, to another. Derrida challenges this notion of context on the basis of his term 'iterability'.[14]

Language, Derrida says, is a 'non-masterable dissemination'. Communication is always subject to iterability, repeatable, but repeatable with difference. That is, repeatability implies repetition *elsewhere* and

Contemporary Spiritual Education in England and Wales (Abingdon: Culham College Institute, 1998).

12. Wright, *Spiritual Pedagogy*, p. 72.

13. Wright, *Spiritual Pedagogy*, p. 69.

14. See J. Derrida, *Of Grammatology* (trans. G.C. Spivack; Baltimore, MD: Johns Hopkins University Press, 1974 [1967]), and *idem*, *Margins of Philosophy* (Brighton: Harvester Press, 1982 [1972]).

so undermines the stability of 'context', which presumes the repetition of statements at different times and places being able to preserve the same meanings. (Derrida identifies citation and grafting as two ways in which repetition occurs in new contexts.) On this basis reiteration cannot be said to amount to a guaranteed, masterable passage of meanings.

When the above analysis is applied to what we call religion it acts as a deconstructive identification of the way in which an apparent continuity can be established in the context of historical, cultural and political change. In the process of change an apparent historical continuity is established that depends upon signification. For Derrida the 'sign' has two aspects, as with Saussure[15] and Barthes:[16] the signifier and the signified. The first is a sensory perception (spoken or written word), the second is a concept or meaning associated with that sensory perception. Thus 'cat' and the associated concept of 'cat'. A sign, to be a sign, necessarily is the relationship between these two things.

It is impossible to think outside these cultural constructs unless other significatory relationships are introduced to us. So, in religious terms, the word 'Christ' and the concept of 'Christ' are bound in this relationship. This may seem to create a stable historico-conceptual continuity if it weren't for the characteristics pertaining to iterability. Iterability can be understood as using signification for different purposes and ends according to the specific political desires of different groups in different contexts.

Thus iterating the words of Jesus at the last supper in the context of the mass confers upon the sacrament a particular signification relating to its indispensability for salvation, yet it is problematic trying to read such formal sacramental significance back into the last supper event, it has to be grafted on. This manoeuvring is at the centre of all language games as an attempt to ensure that binary oppositions are kept in place and that the signified has some transcendental significance, in order to serve the ends of the group in question. It prevents recognition of undecidability. The role of the signified in this complex process is to provide recourse to authority beyond that of the group itself, an authority that is absolute or objective, transcends discourse and 'is the determination of Being as *presence* in all senses of this word'[17]. Thus the

15. F. de Saussure, *Course in General Linguistics* (New York: Philosophical Library, 1959).

16. R. Barthes, *Mythologies* (Paris: Seuil, 1970).

17. J. Derrida, 'Structure, Sign and Play in the Discourse of the Human Sciences',

signification given to 'Christ' that contradicts the possibilities of signification. However, no signified of itself has this possibility because it is inherently part of the self-referential system of language. So how is this done? The means of ensuring the efficacy of the repetition of the signified is through context, that is, by creating a sense of the signification applying in every new context as it applied previously. In this way historical continuity is established and the apparent changelessness of the signified assured, giving the impression that what is being addressed is a timeless truth. Historical continuity, however, is simply the tool of tradition and its invention. It refers to nothing more than a group claiming to be the legitimate heirs to tradition (orthodoxy) to the exclusion of others (heterodoxy). This claim is made despite iterability undermining 'context' as a final governor of meanings, and the signified always deriving from a signifier embedded in language.

We now find ourselves approaching religion on the basis of *its* undecidability—we can now 'play' with its value rather than being subjected to the 'knowledge' it is intended we imbue by knowing-through-it. This paves the way for a positive reconsideration of the possibilities of faith without recourse to doctrine as the 'fixation' of knowledge within the trammels of tradition.

Beyond Decidability

If we presume the possibility of faith leading to wisdom the question then becomes how, instrumentally speaking, can religion act in the service of faith? To interrogate this we need to recognize the difficulty with and limitations of definition. As Bauman observes,

> 'Religion' belongs to the curious, and often embarrassing concepts, which one perfectly understands until one wants to define them. Postmodern mind...resigns itself to the tendency of definitions to conceal as much as they reveal and to maim and obfuscate while pretending to clarify and straighten up. It also accepts the fact that all too often experience spills out of the verbal cages in which one would wish to hold it, that there are things of which one should keep silent since one cannot speak of them, and that the ineffable is as much a part of the human mode of being-in-

in *Writing and Difference* (trans. A. Bass; London: Routledge & Kegan Paul, 1978 [1968]), p. 279. This essay is an excellent introduction to this theme in Derrida's earlier writings.

> the-world as is the linguistic net in which one tries (in vain as it happens…) to catch it.[18]

Thus we may say that the word religion, as a signifier, cannot be tied to a signified that matches with our experiencing of the world. This happens in two ways. First, the attempt to create a discrete thing, 'religion', which can be identified, always suffers from slippage into the cultural and the political insofar as we seek to locate it in human affairs. Secondly, as we attempt to locate it in the experience of individuals as a matter of faith or the spiritual, it slides out of our capacity to conceptualize and so classify and name. It disappears into the ineffable. So, we may ask, what would religion be but the name attached to that which seeks to control the worlds of the cultural, political and spiritual?

In this particular essay Bauman suggests that we should not look too naively on the way in which the Churches have prospered, particularly during their period of dominance. He muses on why

> we have come to believe the Churches far and wide which, whenever pressed, insist that they provide the service necessitated by the overwhelming human urge to get answers to 'fundamental questions' of the purpose of life and to placate the fears that arise from the absence of a good answer. One wonders, though; there is little in the daily routine which prompts such eschatological enquiry.[19]

He suggests that the answer rather lies in the way in which the Churches, 'like other producers of goods and services, had to occupy themselves first with the production of their own consumers: they had…to make their work indispensable'.[20] And he calls upon Foucault's assessment of how this was done:

> [a]ll those techniques of examination, confession, guidance, obedience, have an aim: to get individuals to work at their own 'mortification' in this world. Mortification is not death, of course, but it is a renunciation of this world and of oneself: a kind of everyday death. A death which is supposed to provide life in another world.[21]

18. Z. Bauman, 'Postmodern Religion?', in Paul Heelas (ed.), *Religion, Modernity and Postmodernity* (Oxford: Basil Blackwell, 1998), pp. 55-78 (55).

19. Bauman, 'Postmodern Religion?', pp. 56-57.

20. Bauman, 'Postmodern Religion?', p. 59.

21. M. Foucault, in L.D. Kritzman (ed.), *Politics, Philosophy, Culture: Interviews and Other Writings, 1977–1984* (London: Routledge, 1988), p. 59.

The point made here is that the concern for personal salvation depends upon the insertion of that into the concerns of the individual, it does not naturally arise out of the *Lebenswelt* of the individual; it is formulated by, in Derridean terms, an undecidable (death) being turned into a decidable, the afterlife with its binary polls of heaven and hell, out of which emerges the concern for personal salvation, dependent on mortificatory practices.

It follows that if 'faith' is to have any meaning in a world that no longer buys the afterlife package or the religious construction generally, it must concern itself with the everyday precisely for the everyday's sake. In other words any sense of the 'spiritual' has to be sited in the concerns of everyday narratives rather than impressed by religious meta-narratives. The *concept* of faith, religiously defined, will be lost but the possibility of performative acts, in everyday life, being imbued with something of the character of faith may remain. What would Kierkegaard's leap of faith amount to in this context? I suggest that moving beyond the theorizing about knowledge, by giving up the idea that such theories are necessary for action, is an equivalent of Kierkegaard's recognition that reason did not lead to faith, but confounded it. The Unknown, when translated into the immanent context of the everyday becomes that which can exist in the space between conceptualization at the abstract level and between entities, person and person, people and things, at the concrete level (deprived of its capital letter and of its transcendental inferences). In effect, without the possibility of naming, it is what it is possible to create, in a temporal and fleeting sense, in the spaces in which, in Walter Benjamin's phrase, the exchange of experiences and the creation of community occur.[22] In this context faith, rather than being what we might call a linguistic reduction of a performed act, which serves ideological pretensions rather than any spiritual purpose, can be understood as a struggle against both social entropy and meta-narrological imperialism.

This seems to me to be a constructive way of moving on from the insights of both Kierkegaard and Derrida. Whist theologians following Kierkegaard, notably Karl Barth, seized upon Kierkegaard's understanding of God as Wholly Other to legitimate a transcendentalist orientation in twentieth-century Christianity, this only served to justify a salvific form of thinking. If we concentrate on Kierkegaard's idea and

22. W. Benjamin, 'The Storyteller', in H. Arendt (ed.), *Illuminations* (London: Jonathan Cape, 1970 [1955]), pp. 83-109 (91).

method of paradox as the fulcrum of his thinking, for example, as expressed in the parable of the humble maiden and the king, we may interpret his aim as seeking to ensure that paradox and its lack of resolution was the only way to maintain the possibility of faith within an *immanence* that had no contrary.[23] In other words the charge is to prevent the resolution of paradox both by reason and transcendentalism. In Derrida's terms this is to prevent those who would wish to be the judges of decidability being able to make their judgments. Living as the 'humble maidens' becomes encountering whom we encounter as what they appear to be for us, and acting within that relational understanding. This is a political situation in which we wrestle with the idea of faith. Faith, as a result, can only be understood within the matter of relationships, wholly immanent, not as the pursuit of some salvific goal.

Given the above reconstruction of the idea of faith we might describe it as an antidote to despair, which brings it closer to our sense of hope, and which has a poignant connection to Walter Benjamin's own suicide when prevented from crossing the border into Spain, when, as a Jew, he fled from the Nazi invasion of France.

Walter Benjamin and the Significance of Story

In *The Storyteller: Reflections on the Works of Nikolai Leskov*,[24] Benjamin asserts that storytelling is coming to an end: 'Less and less frequently do we encounter people with the ability to tell a tale properly... It is as if...the securest among our possessions, were taken from us: the ability to exchange experiences.'[25] Benjamin further identifies that the epic of the story, mediating universal experience, is replaced by the fortuitous character of events in the novel. The novel is the contemporary genre that gives form to subjective experience.[26] Behind Benjamin's observations lies the notion that the epic, or past forms of storytelling, no longer speak to our experience in a world 'where language is reduced to the prolific exchange of *information*',[27] and that the result is the loss of the precondition for wisdom.

23. Kierkegaard, *Philosophical Fragments*, commentator's introduction, Nils Thulstrup, p. xxiii.

24. Benjamin, 'The Storyteller'.

25. Benjamin, 'The Storyteller', p. 83.

26. Benjamin, 'The Storyteller', pp. 87-89.

27. Benjamin, 'The Storyteller', p. 89.

In an analogy offered in the 'Theses on the Philosophy of History',[28] he speaks of a puppet constructed to play a winning game of chess whatever the opponents move. To do this he has to be guided and his hands moved by a hunchback who sits beneath the chess table and is an expert chess player. The puppet he names as 'historical materialism' and suggests it can win so long as it engages the services of theology (the hunchback) 'which today, as we know, is wizened and has to keep out of sight'.[29]

Benjamin's point is that in every era, and significantly our own, a new attempt must be made to wrest tradition (and by implication theology) away from a conformism that is about to overpower it.

If we attempt to piece together the implications of Benjamin's theses we may suggest that the conformism he refers to as historical materialism can be identified in the present modernist policies of government. These policies and their mythological structure require a spiritual and moral underpinning to persuade us of their veracity, which is provided by theology/tradition in its wizened form. The result is that we no longer find the stories of the epic, which we can identify with scripture, speaking to our experience. However, the novel form retains this capacity owing to its relatively autonomous nature—it still speaks of the exchange of experiences and relates the subjectivity of experience, inviting resonance and response. Thus it evokes the spiritual vitality of the reader. Scripture used in the service of doctrine, by contrast, is incarcerated within a theological tradition that has lost the capacity to see its own stories as of relevance to the 'outsider' (and possibly to its own believers).

If we take Benjamin's observations on board, with some modification, we might say that our experience of the character of modern life is reflected in the novel form, which creates a narrative that leaves open the possibilities of experience and the storying of experience in a way the epic fails to do because of its intention to reveal a continuity of understanding, not only within its own narration but by expressing an understanding of beginnings, ends and values that extends beyond that which is congruent with the temporal and the mortal. The metanarrative that underpins and acts as a commentary on the Christian scriptures offers a case in point. Lyotard's incredulity toward such

28. W. Benjamin, 'Theses', in Arendt (ed.), *Illuminations*, pp. 255-66 [255].

29. Benjamin, 'Theses', p. 255.

meta-narratives[30] is well founded by both examining their inner consistency and their relationship with our experience. The canonization of stories and texts as 'scriptures' produces an alienating effect.

In so far as we can speak of such a thing as theology, as Benjamin does, it must disassociate itself from the wizening effect of serving both particular political ideologies and religious ones if it is to retain any sense of relevance or connection with the notion of faith. In relating Benjamin's observations, we might speculate that loss of faith is not due to a lack of force in doctrinal governance but to a loss of the thread of narrative, which in turn results in a lack of trust and belonging in community. Perhaps, more in accordance with the instructions of the revered, for example, Christ and the Buddha as they are entitled, we ought to pursue the means or the method and leave the ends to look after themselves.

The Moral Economy of Religious Ideology

The moral economy of religious doctrine can never deal with the complexity of faith, which is always situated in unresolved human situations that are akin to the novel form rather than the formulated abstractions that underpin the epic forms of narrative expression that religion employs. The human condition (in so far as we can speak of such a thing) lacks both a beginning and an end and has no discernible plot or complete characters, and yet it is in this context that faith has to register its substantive influence. When the situation is overlaid with a meta-narrological prescription, ostensibly seamless, complete, authorized and legitimated, the business of faith gives way to buying into a package deal that satisfies the egocentric desire for personal salvation (if you are among the under 30s you buy into the desires of youth; if you are over 50 you contact Saga; if you are close to demise the Church has something to offer). The relational environment of need in community is replaced by a free-market economy of religious and nationalist dispute and power not dissimilar to the armaments industry and, in a sense, part of it.

The unintentionally ironic character of the following utterance by General Lemay, recruiting for the CIA at a university in the United

30. J.-F. Lyotard, *The Postmodern Condition: A Report on Knowledge* (Manchester: Manchester University Press, 1984 [1979]), p. xxiv.

States, speaks for itself as an example of the way in which religious rhetoric becomes bound up in nationalist ideology and economic gain:

> Our patriotism has to be intelligent patriotism. It has to go deeper than blind nationalism or shallow emotional patriotic fervour. We must continually study and understand the shifting tides of our world environment. Out of this understanding we must arrive at sound moral conclusions. And we must see to it that these conclusions are reflected in our public policies... If we maintain our faith in God, our love of freedom and superior global airpower, I think we can look to the future with confidence.[31]

With regard to an earlier age, John Morrill comments on the reputation and motivations of Oliver Cromwell on his 400th birthday as follows:

> His face, with its famous warts, is one of the best known of all faces, and so is the essence of his life: his nerveless self-belief during more than 30 military engagements; his muscular Christianity based on an utter assurance of being not only one of those called to salvation but also called to be the instrument of God's will; and that darkest of stains—the massacres of Drogheda and Wexford, the Hiroshima and Nagasaki of his times, the *in terrorem* sacking of two Irish towns that induced the bloodless surrender of many more.
>
> What smarts is not that moral economy but his letters glorifying in the bloodshed, his failure to rise above the bigotry of the age that had seen Catholics and Protestants massacre one another for the best part of a century to avenge the last atrocity by the other.[32]

We might remark, however, that the recurrence of atrocity was legitimated by that moral economy; operating as the arbiter of justice, the salve to conscience and in defence of power.

Michael Oakeshott makes clear the basis of the distinction between Benjamin's position and that of religious ideology in speaking of the contrasting ethical motivations that have influenced Christian tradition, which he refers to as 'idealised ethics' and 'habits of morality and community':

> In the earliest days, to be a Christian was to be a member of a community animated by a faith and sustained by a hope—faith in a person and

31. P. Agee, *Inside the Company: CIA Diary* (Harmondsworth: Penguin Books, 1975), p. 14.

32. J. Morrill, 'Oliver Cromwell: Much More than a Rough-Humoured Ayatollah', *The Observer*, 25 April 1999, p. 29.

> hope for a coming event. The morality of these communities was a custom of behaviour appropriate to the character of the faith and to the nature of the expectation... The nearest thing to a moral ideal known to these communities was the ideal of charity; the nearest thing to a moral rule was the precept to love God and one's neighbour.
>
> ...But over these earliest Christian communities, in the course of two centuries, there came a great change. The habit of moral behaviour was converted into the self-conscious pursuit of formulated moral ideals—a conversion parallel to the change from faith in a person to belief in a collection of abstract propositions, a creed.
>
> This change sprang from...the necessity of translating a Christian way of life into a form in which it could be appreciated by those who had never shared the original inspiration and who, having to learn their Christianity as a foreign language, needed a grammar.
>
> From this time in the history of Christendom a Christian habit of moral behaviour (which had sprung from the circumstances of Christian life) was swamped by a Christian moral ideology, and the perception of the poetic character of human conduct was lost.[33]

The linguistic turn (the understanding that language can never escape its own self-referentiality) no longer permits us to name the object of faith in an ideological sense. This does not prevent the presence of narrative in which, for some, it might appear in a relational manner, common to both what Oakeshott refers to as 'the poetic character of human conduct' and Benjamin's 'storytelling' as an attempt to articulate experience. The difference is that the former seeks to assert the cognate reality of the object in some known, objective or absolute sense (a known truth), the latter has the status of seeking to attend to a process of narration and action that coheres the fissures and randomness of everyday life without attempting to impose any formally conceptualized structure upon it.

Beyond Liberalism

It is usually assumed that liberalism in religious and political affairs can act as an antidote to the ideological tendencies I have referred to thus far. Here I should like to insert an argument to the contrary. We might say that liberalism can be identified as occupying that space in which the narratives of others are treated empathetically but one's own epis-

33. M. Oakshott, *Rationalism in Politics and Other Essays* (London: Methuen, 1977), pp. 77-78.

temological identity is still defended. In religious terms Peter Berger offers a suitable example of this with his 'signals of transcendence'.

In *Redeeming Laughter*,[34] Berger seeks to argue that the comic can act as a signal of transcendence that points beyond itself once 'perceived in the light of faith'.[35] But it is precisely this manoeuvre of shifting from narrative to ideology that Berger is caught within, and utilizes:

> Every instance of the comic is an escape from reality—healthy physically, psychologically, and sociologically, but an escape all the same. The real world of empirical existence must in the end reassert itself; the counter-empirical world of the comic must be seen as an illusion. Comedy is fundamentally counter-factual; tragedy reveals the hard facticity of the human condition. *But as soon as all this is perceived in the light of faith* [my italics]—*etsi Deus daretur*—the assertions of reality and illusion are reversed. It is the hard facts of the empirical world that are now seen as, if not illusion, a temporary reality that will eventually be superseded. Conversely, the painless world of the comic can now be seen as an adumbration of a world beyond this world.[36]

Berger's use of 'faith' relating to a world beyond makes cognate that which is beyond cognition in order to establish what he calls the 'meta-empirical' as the ultimately real. In doing so he is seeking to provide an argument for an ideological position he seeks to defend, a sort of apologetics. While not hard nosed, like dogmatics, it is the usual, often sophisticated, form of defence in retreat that can be found in Schleiermacher,[37] Otto[38] and other Christian and religious apologists. In each case they are attempting to ensure that 'faith' through certain experiencings is defended in relation to religious (doctrinal and ideological) claims.

But in the context of the experience of the comic (or any other of the phenomena that Berger points to) there is no decidability possible as to what overall construction of reality can be entertained or affirmed. Rather we are left with the paradoxes that the phenomena present us with. The riddle remains and Berger is as guilty as those who refuse to

34. P.L. Berger, *Redeeming Laughter: The Comic Dimension of Human Experience* (Berlin: W. de Gruyter, 1997).

35. Berger, *Redeeming Laughter*, p. 210.

36. Berger, *Redeeming Laughter*, p. 210.

37. See F. Schleiermacher, *On Religion: Speeches to its Cultured Despisers* (New York: Harper & Row, 1958).

38. See R. Otto, *The Idea of the Holy* (Oxford: Oxford University Press, 1958).

take any notice of the presence and influence of the comic (presumably hard-nosed empiricists and rationalists) in trying to use it to argue for a revised conceptual reformulation of reality, with its own binary oppositions (this world/the next world, etc.). What Berger *uses* faith for is this religious construct. Rather, we might understand faith as residing within the process of the comic (as a process) that contributes to enduring the everydayness of things. It cannot be extrapolated from that—and that is all faith is. It does not point to anything. Faith cannot point to or act in the service of knowledge, and in so far as religious pronouncements seek to advertise themselves as knowledge or 'knowledge possibilities' rather than *perform* as narrative 'faith' is corrupted.

The position I have argued, in summary, is that there is an illegitimate use of the term faith, in relation to 'religion', what we might call a linguistic deceit, the purpose of which is to relate faith to knowledge. However, if we create a rupture between faith and religion (operating as a knowledge system), we can seek to understand 'faith' as a *performed* act toward some 'spiritual' purpose freed from the construals that religion places upon it.

It follows that understood as a 'performed act' within the process of narration, what Lyotard refers to as 'the pragmatics of narrative knowledge',[39] and I prefer to refer to as 'narrative pragmatics', faith is located within community rather than a process isolated within the individual. We might say that we have pursued Kierkegaard's radical critique to the point where we have collapsed his residual tension between the immanent and the transcendent, the individual and the other (with both big and little 'o'). I am now seeking to find out what useful purpose these terms 'faith' and 'spiritual' might serve in this context. What I am not doing is bringing some prior definition of these terms *to* this context. Equally, I am not presuming these terms represent any 'thing' in 'the world of appearances',[40] that is, have to be measured against some reality. The possibilities of performing such an epistemological feat have collapsed once we understand language to be a part of the experienced world, not an interpreter or arbiter of it. In short, through language we construct an environment (in the many faceted meanings of that term, which includes the idea of community) that can have no pretensions to represent any reality by means of correspondence. It just is

39. Lyotard, *The Postmodern Condition*, pp.18-23.

40. M. Foucault, *The Order of Things: Introduction to the Archaeology of the Human Sciences* (New York: Vintage Books, 1973).

what it is for us. I am trying to place faith and the spiritual in this context. If you like it is liberation theology without the theology, but allowing for the sort of theology that liberation theology espouses—grass roots theological activity as praxis—as a legitimate communal activity conducted by a particular 'faith' group. In this respect I find myself in a similar position to that which Anthony Swift finds himself in, as he reports in Children for Social Change:[41]

> As an agnostic, I anticipated another realm of terminological difficulty arising from the fact that the work of street educators was conceived within a religious framework, albeit that of liberation theology where socialism and Christianity most readily converge (I, of course, would wish to put the latter in small case). Some educators who are militants of liberation theology regard what they are doing as working to 'realise the Kingdom of God on Earth' or to 'rescue the Christ who is in all of us'. However, they do not use such terms dogmatically and are talking about consciously rescuing or resurrecting our essential humanity amid the forces that would deny it. For them the work is a celebration of faith. For me and doubtless the many non-Christian educators it is just one of the best ideas around.[42]

In citing the above I have to qualify some of the language that Swift uses in order to situate myself alongside both him and the liberation theologians engaged in such work. I have to release the word faith from its solely Christian positioning and understand it as part of the process of what is happening that can be interpreted within different narrative frameworks by different groups involved. The important issue is that the praxis is rooted in the solidarity of affirming the need for the action itself, not in a theological interpretation that contextualizes the action. The latter for me is a secondary use of the term faith, which is prefaced by faith as a need to perform/act. In other words the absence of the latter, particular narrative use of the term, would not lead to a cessation of the praxis being performed, it would simply be narrated differently, for example in the way that Swift does.

Swift also uses the phrase 'essential humanity'. For me such a phrase takes us back into a quasi-doctrinal state of affairs. In terms of Foucault's prison-house of concepts and Derrida's warnings on iterability, this becomes a dangerous term. That, however, does not prevent me

41. A. Swift, *Children for Social Change: Education for Citizenship of Street and Working Children in Brazil* (Nottingham: Educational Heretics Press, 1997).

42. Swift, *Children for Social Change*, p. 3.

from situating myself alongside Swift for the purposes of praxis—given that the praxis is the primary concern. Thus I can interpret 'faith' in this context as the process of the acts being performed.

There is a sense in this process of a number of narratives coming together to address a particular issue that is common to all of their concerns and values, identified in each as a kind of moral imperative. This, Swift identifies as the following: 'What Brazil's street educators do...is assume a personal responsibility for reversing the social exclusion of the children they work with.'[43] Taking this to be the case, it would seem that faith in the first instance is the commitment to a certain sort of transformation in social and moral affairs, prior to and with precedence over any particular ideological commitment into which that praxis becomes translated, which performs as a theoretical or doctrinal explanation, that is, a rationalization and contextualization of the praxis. If that were not the case it would be expected that the relationship between doctrine as a motivating force and praxis as its practical outcome would mean the praxis being irrelevant if the doctrine were abandoned. In other words a loss of 'faith' in relation to the doctrine would mean that the street educators would have no further reason or motivation for their efforts. In the specifics of the situation as reported by Swift this would appear to be incomprehensible.

What would have to be the case for this to happen would be a sudden loss of commitment to the rights and needs of the children in question, what Swift refers to as 'rescuing our essential humanity amid the forces that would deny it'.[44] Swift advertises his own narrative reasons for involvement as 'trying to recover some sense of community and individual purpose following the social vandalism of the Thatcher–Reagan era'.[45] And, we might add, following the moral and spiritual vandalism of religion in the name of faith. The above situation could serve as an example of what Newman and Holzman refer to as a 'moving beyond the rational towards the "performative" which is a political activity of bringing about change that is dependent on method rather than the theorizing character of "knowing" '.[46]

43. Swift, *Children for Social Change*, p. 2.
44. Swift, *Children for Social Change*, p. 3.
45. Swift, *Children for Social Change*, p. 3.
46. F. Newman and L. Holzman, *The End of Knowing: A New Developmental Way of Learning* (London: Routledge, 1997), p. 63.

Earlier Benjamin had commented as follows:

> The tradition of the oppressed teaches us that the 'state of emergency' in which we live is not the exception but the rule. We must attain to a conception of history that is in keeping with this insight. Then we shall clearly realise that it is our task to bring about a real state of emergency.[47]

Benjamin was writing as a Marxist opposing the rise of Fascism, and it would be difficult now to know exactly how such a conception of history could be arrived at, considering my objections to knowledge. However, it acts as a warning against the (meta) historical constructs of others, which I am opposing.

Conclusion

It may seem that we have arrived at a point where 'faith' admits of no definition, and it seems to me that this is an appropriate conclusion to make. This does not mean that the political and existential possibility of faith is denied. Its enemies at least can be identified. The first would be those who seek to establish moral autocracies legitimated by religious ideology. These rely upon the construction of tradition to enforce a distinction between truth and falsehood, using salvation as the weapon of arbitration.

The alternative to such a schema is to recognize not ideology, a divisive principle, but narrative, a potentially cohering process, as the way of distinguishing between two different moral 'species', the second of which would be those who understand faith primarily as pointing to a relationship with a transcendental entity, thus playing down if not entirely nullifying the significance of what we might call the importance of moral habit or relational responsibility and communal need. While not entirely distinct from our first group, it is more a matter of being able to recognize your target by virtue of identifying the power moves of their rhetoric and responding accordingly to avoid its seductive influence.

One way of describing the sort of differentiation I wish to make is by analogy with prostitution as the illicit selling of goods and services in order to satisfy personal desires. I have no particular problem with this in relation to the usual commodity of sex. In fact its legalization would

47. Benjamin, 'Theses', p. 259.

at least provide regulation. However, the purveyors of faith, as a commodity, to satisfy desires for personal salvation, have more to answer for. The prostitution of faith, in this respect, has never been made illegal but contrarily has often underpinned the regulatory systems operating in societies as party to religious, political and moral ideologies. It is this state of affairs that demands scrutiny in order, in Lyotard's words, to provide an 'outline of a politics that would respect both the desire for justice and the desire for the unknown'.[48]

The aporetic is only a confusion for those who wish to impose their own doctrinal classification in relation to such matters, whether scientific or religious.

48. Lyotard, *The Postmodern Condition*, p. 67.

THE EMERGENCE OF A FOURTH FORCE IN PSYCHOLOGY: A CONVERGENCE BETWEEN PSYCHOLOGY AND SPIRITUALITY?

Michael A. Hayes

This essay presents a literature review of various authors who have explored a developing convergence of psychology and spirituality at the dawn of a new millennium. In terms of psychology there is a spectrum of schools, thought and practice, which include psychology, counselling, counselling psychology, psychotherapy and psychiatry. Within each of these divisions there are further distinctions and differentiation. Duffy notes that the point of convergence and differentiation on this spectrum is 'intentionality'.[1] Because of their focus on intentionality, this essay initially does not distinguish between the terms psychology and psychotherapy. The essay will interpret spirituality in a Christian context and highlight the need to make a clear differentiation between what is understood as religion and what is understood as spirituality. It also presents the findings of some recent research that supports this perception of a developing convergence between psychotherapy and spiritual direction, while recognizing that there is a distinct sphere of operation for each of the two disciplines.

Vaughan[2] writes about the traditionally perceived antagonism between psychological growth and the spiritual quest. Noting that the former often dismisses the latter as escapist, delusion or a crutch, while the latter considers the former as an irrelevant distraction, Pargament takes a similar position when he writes that 'psychology has accused religion of everything from dogmatism and intolerance to social repression and mental illness. Psychology has, in turn, been accused of

1. M. Duffy, 'Counselling Psychology USA: Patterns of Continuity and Change', *Counselling Psychology Review* 5.3 (1990), pp. 9-18, quoted in P. Clarkson and M. Pokorny, *The Handbook of Psychotherapy* (London: Routledge, 1994), p. 7.

2. F. Vaughan, *The Inward Arc* (Nevada City, CA: Blue Dolphin Publishing, 1995 [1985]).

arrogance, elitism, amorality, and selfishness.'[3] Grame *et al.*[4] suggest three reasons that help to create a barrier between spirituality/religion and psychotherapy: (1) that the religious experience of an individual is often not accepted by the medical profession and scientists; (2) that there are varying meanings of the term 'religion' together with a bias against religion by researchers; (3) that there is a lack of meaningful dialogue that includes different languages used, the tendency to undervalue each other, the lack of interest in integration and lack of knowledge to facilitate integration.

Despite these mutual negative claims both Vaughan and Pargament urge a drawing together of the vision and way of working of both disciplines. Healey notes that 'in some respects, issues regarding the integration of psychotherapy and religious experience or spirituality have come full circle'.[5] Clay, and Shafranske and Maloney,[6] also see a movement toward integration. Indeed Moore calls for a renaissance that will be a bridge between the religious and scientific worlds and hold them together.[7] While it is not the case that psychology and religion are similar, with psychology enabling the individual to have a sense of control over their lives and religion enabling the individual to accept their limitations and engage in a reality beyond themselves, rather it is the case that these approaches to human capacity and human limitation complement each other.

3. K. Pargament, *The Psychology of Religion and Coping: Theory, Research, Practice* (New York: Guildford Press, 1997), p. 7; A. Ellis, *The Case against Religion: A Psychotherapist's View and the Case against Religiosity* (Austin: American Atheist Press, 1986); P. Vitz, *Psychology as Religion: The Cult of Self-Worship* (Grand Rapids, MI: Eerdmans, 1977).

4. G. Grame, J. Tortorici, B. Healey, J. Dillingham and P. Winklebaur, 'Addressing Spiritual and Religious Issues of Clients with a History of Psychological Trauma', *Bulletin of the Menninger Clinic* 63.2 (1999), pp. 223-39.

5. B. Healey, 'Religion and Spiritual Issues in Psychotherapy—General Issues' (Paper presented at the Menninger Conference on Dissociative States: Multiple Personality and Other Trauma-Related Disorders, Topeka, KS, p. 2). Quoted in Grame *et al.*, 'Addressing Spiritual and Religious Issues'.

6. See Grame *et al.*, 'Addressing Spiritual and Religious Issues', p. 227; R. Clay, 'Psychologists' Faith in Religion Begins to Grow', *APA Monitor* 27(8).1 (1996), pp. 35-50 (48); E. Shafranske and H. Maloney, 'Clinical Psychologists' Religious and Spiritual Orientations and their Practice of Psychotherapy', *Psychotherapy* 23.1 (1990), pp. 72-78.

7. T. Moore, *Care of the Soul: How to Add Depth and Meaning to your Life* (London: Piatkus, 1992), p. xiv.

In the introduction to *Towards a Psychology of Being*, Maslow suggested a 'higher' rung to his ladder of human evolution in the process of 'self-actualisation'—the other rungs in the hierarchy of needs were psychological safety, love, belonging and esteem. He said:

> I should say also that I consider Humanistic, Third Force Psychology to be transitional, a preparation for a still 'higher' Fourth Psychology, transpersonal, transhuman, centred in the cosmos rather than in human needs and interest, going beyond humanness, identity, self-actualisation and the like.[8]

Transpersonal psychotherapy has come to be known as a 'fourth force' in psychotherapy. The term 'fourth force' is used to make a distinction among the major traditions of psychotherapy, the 'first force' being considered as *behavioural*, with its origin in the work of Pavlov (1902); the 'second force' being *psychoanalysis* with Freud (1893) as its founder; the 'third force' being *humanistic/existential*, with Moreno (1908) as its founder.[9] Keutzer reflecting on the genre of transpersonal psychotherapy offers the following distinction:

> The goal of behaviourism is the good adjustment of the patient, the goal of psychoanalysis is the rendering conscious the unconscious, that of humanistic therapy is the achieving of self-actualisation; existentialism, however, strives for 'authenticity'. In contradistinction to these schools, then, the goal for transpersonal therapy could be said to be transcendence—the recognition, acceptance, and realisation of ultimate states, or 'enlightenment'.[10]

Rowan[11] gives the following map of therapies by column: the first column lists those that do not touch on the transpersonal; the second column lists therapies that touch on the transpersonal, but not in any

8. A. Maslow, *Towards a Psychology of Being* (New York: Van Nostrand, 2nd edn, 1968), pp. iii-iv, cited in C. Keutzer, 'Transpersonal Psychotherapy: Reflection on the Genre', *Professional Psychology: Research and Practice* 15.6 (1984), pp. 868-83.

9. P. Clarkson in Clarkson and Pokorny, *The Handbook of Psychotherapy*, pp. 20-21, offers a very useful chart mapping the major traditions of psychotherapy in terms of founder; date when active; comments about philosophy, orientation and practice; application; aetiology; techniques; goals; other workers; focus.

10. C. Keutzer, 'Transpersonal Psychotherapy: Reflections on the Genre', *Professional Psychology: Research and Practice* 15.6 (1984), pp. 868-83 (870).

11. J. Rowan, *The Transpersonal: Psychotherapy and Counselling* (London: Routledge, 1998 [1993]), pp. 128-29.

systematic or worked-out way; the third column lists therapies that explicitly acknowledge the importance of the transpersonal and have established strategies for working with the transpersonal:

Behaviour Modification	Adlerian Therapy	Biosynthesis
Behaviour Therapy	Bioenergetics	Jungian Analysis (Zurich School; Archetypal School)
Cognitive Therapy	Co-Counselling	Primal Integration
Jungian School (London School)	Existential Psychotherapy	Psychosynthesis
Kleinian Analysis	Feminist Therapy	Transpersonal Psychotherapy
Personal Construct Therapy	Gestalt Therapy	
Psychoanalysis (Classical School)	Open Encounter	
	Person-Centred Therapy	
	Psychoanalysis (Object Relations School)	
	Psychodrama	
	Transactional Analysis	

How might transpersonal psychology be defined?[12] The United Kingdom Council for Psychotherapy National Register of Psychotherapists[13] defines transpersonal psychotherapy as an 'orientation which includes

12. J. Fadiman, 'The Transpersonal Stance', in R. Walsh and F. Vaughan (eds.), *Beyond Ego* (Los Angeles: Tarcher, 1980), pp. 175-81, explains: 'A basic assumption of transpersonal psychology is that there is more to you than your personality... The very word "transpersonal" means through or beyond the personality... One therapeutic goal is to align the personality within the total self so that it functions appropriately... A goal, within the context of transpersonal therapy, is to encourage and develop those tendencies which allow an individual to disidentify from the restrictions of the personality and to apprehend their identity with the total self' (p. 177; cited in Keutzer, 'Transpersonal Psychotherapy', p. 870). Walsh and Vaughan in *Beyond Ego* state: 'The term transpersonal was adopted after considerable deliberation to reflect the reports of people practicing various consciousness disciplines who spoke of experiences of an extension of identity beyond both individuality and personality. Thus transpersonal psychology cannot strictly be called a model of personality because personality is considered only one aspect of our psychological nature; rather it is an inquiry into the essential nature of being (p. 16; cited in Keutzer, 'Transpersonal Psychotherapy', pp. 870-71). C. Keutzer, 'Physics and Consciousness', *Journal of Humanistic Psychology* 22 (1982), pp. 74-90 (76), describing transcendent experiences, observes that there is general agreement that they include '(1) the highest state of consciousness; (2) a self-transforming perception of one's total union with the infinite; and (3) an experience beyond time and space—an experience of the timelessness which is eternity, or unlimited unity, with all creation' (cited in Keutzer, 'Transpersonal Psychotherapy', p. 871).

13. Published by Routledge.

the spiritual dimension rather than the content of therapy. It views the human psyche as having a central core Self or Soul as the centre of identity as well as a personal ego.'[14] According to Frances Vaughan[15] transpersonal psychology is concerned with experiences and aspirations that lead people to seek transcendence. Keutzer,[16] however, makes a distinction between 'transcendent experience' and 'transcendence' itself. She notes that when Walsh, Elgin, Vaughan and Wilber introduced a definition of 'transcendent experience' they confined their definition to an experience of an altered state of consciousness that included ineffability—an indescribable experience; noetic—heightened clarity and understanding; altered perception of space and time; an appreciation of the wholistic, unitive nature of the universe, including a sense of unity with the self—a state of oneness. Transcendence, however, is considered as the goal of the transpersonal therapy, which Fadiman described as 'the daily experience of a state known in different traditions as certainty, liberation, or gnosis'.[17]

Because of the difficulty of describing precisely states of heightened awareness in this sense, writers tend to use metaphors to describe that

14. S. Grof defines transpersonal as 'experiences involving an expansion or extension of consciousness beyond the usual ego boundaries and beyond the limitations of time and/or space'. F. Vaughan says 'the transpersonal holds that a large spectrum of altered states of consciousness exist, that some are potentially useful and functionally specific (i.e. possessing some functions not available in the usual state but lacking others) and that some of these are true "higher" states. Higher is used in Tart's (1973, 1875a) sense of possessing all the properties and potentials of lower states, plus some additional ones. Furthermore, a wide range of literature from a variety of cultures and growth disciplines attests to the attainability of these higher states.' (Both quoted in Rowan, *The Transpersonal*, pp. 6-7.) R. Assagioli, in *A Manual of Principles and Techniques* (Wellingborough, Northants: Crucible, 1970 [1965]), as the founder of Psychosynthesis, sees spiritual development in this context as 'a long and arduous journey, an adventure through strange lands full of surprises, difficulties and even dangers. It involves a drastic transmutation of the "normal" elements of the personality, an awakening of potentialities hitherto dormant, a rising of consciousness of new realms, and a functioning along a new inner dimension' (p. 39).

15. Vaughan, *The Inward Arc.*

16. Keutzer, 'Transpersonal Psychotherapy', p. 871; R. Walsh, D. Elgin, F. Vaughan and K. Wilber, 'Paradigms in Collision', in Walsh and Vaughan (eds.), *Beyond Ego*, pp. 36-53.

17. Fadiman, 'The Transpersonal Stance', p. 180, cited in Keutzer, 'Transpersonal Psychotherapy', p. 871.

which can be termed the numinous. For example, this is what Wilber calls a 'spectrum of consciousness'[18] or the idea of journey or a ladder (Maslow), or pilgrimage (many Christian writers). The exploration continues with artists,[19] theologians, psychologists, counsellors and psychotherapists and others each adding their own perspective. Postmodernity's critique of modernity opens up questions of premodernity that can facilitate bridging the earlier separation of spirituality and psychology. In other words there is a timely opportunity presented with the advent of postmodernity. We are moving from a world-view where rational thought alone was given worth to a world-view where the religious, the numinous, as well as the rational are included in the exploration. The role of religion and religious experience has become a legitimate area of debate and discussion. According to Worthington, Kurusu and McCullough,[20]

> religious experience is not only part of multiculturalism but also consistent with the overall direction of post-modern culture. The acceptance of some role of religion in counselling[21] has thus exploded into the mainstream of counselling and clinical psychology over the last decade.

While there has been a growth and development of counselling and psychotherapy schools there has not been a proportional decline of interest in things religious. Indeed Gallup and Castelli 1989 figures show that 90 per cent of Americans said that they never doubted God's existence; with 82 per cent believing in miracles; 79 per cent reporting

18. K. Wilber, *The Spectrum of Consciousness* (Wheaton, IL: Theosophical Publishing House, 1989 [1977]).

19. For example, R. Hughes, *The Shock of the New: Art and the Century of Change* (London: Thames & Hudson, 1996 [1980]), describes the American artist Jackson Pollock as attempting to deal with the 'spiritual' when he says 'Pollock, not a widely read man but by no means the cowboy aesthete myth, owned and often pursued a copy of Kandinsky's essay *Concerning the Spiritual in Art*. Nor was he, in any orthodox sense of the word, religious, yet he was preoccupied with such metaphysical questions as he thought art could pose; and the role of art Kandinsky insisted on, an evocation of the "basic rhythms" of the universe and their vague but imaginable relationship to inner states of mind, was of the most passionate to Pollock' (p. 313).

20. E. Worthington, T. Kurusu and M. McCullough, 'Empirical Research on Religion and Psychotherapeutic Processes and Outcomes: A 10-Year Review and Research Prospectus', *Psychological Bulletin* 119.3 (1996), pp. 448-87 (448).

21. In their study the term 'counselling' is used generically to refer to counselling and psychotherapy.

that they are sometimes very conscious of God's presence.[22] Downey refers to another Gallup study that predicts that the largest sales increase in non-fiction books in the twenty-first century will be in religion/ spirituality, with an 82 per cent projection growth in sales between 1987 and 2010.[23] Worthington *et al.*, in their ten-year review of empirical research on religion and psychotherapeutic processes and outcomes (1984–94), show that between 1993 and 1995 the American Association of Christian Counsellors had grown from 2,000 members to 16,000.

Acknowledging William James's[24] warning of not foreclosing a description of religion, Pargament understands religion as 'a process, a search for significance in ways related to the sacred'.[25] He locates religion at the intersection of the sacred and the significant. The term 'religion'[26] is sometimes used generically to refer to spirituality and religion. However, the use of the term 'religion' can have negative overtones, and I would therefore suggest that, similar to the differentiation between transcendent experience and transcendence, a further differentiation between religion and spirituality needs to be made. Smith (1996) makes a useful distinction:

> *Spirituality*: That dimension of our being—related to the physical and psychological dimensions—which gives our lives meaning and calls us towards our higher self, usually expressed as some form of relationship with a Divine being (sometimes called God). *Religion*: A particular framework (which includes a belief structure, a moral code, an authority structure and a form of worship) within which people find nourishment for the spiritual dimension of their lives and explore their spiritual journey in the company of others.[27]

In surveying the current thinking on the complex relationship between spirituality and religion, Grame *et al.*,[28] highlighting the works

22. Pargament, *The Psychology of Religion*, p. 2.

23. M. Downey, *Understanding Christian Spirituality* (New York: Paulist Press, 1997), p. 6.

24. W. James, *The Variety of Religious Experience* (London: Fontana, 1960).

25. Pargament, *The Psychology of Religion*, p. 22.

26. For Ninan Smart a definition of religion will include six dimensions: ritual, mythological, doctrinal, ethical, social and experiential (*The Religious Experience of Mankind* [Glasgow: Collins, 1969], pp. 15-25).

27. A. Smith, *The Tablet*, 9 March 1996, p. 332.

28. Grame *et al.*, 'Addressing Spiritual and Religious Issues', pp. 223-39; R. Ingersoll, 'Spirituality, Religion, and Counselling: Dimensions and Relationships', *Counselling and Values* 38 (1994), pp. 98-111; J. Sachs, 'Religious Issues in

of Ingersoll, Sacks, Sermabeikian, Siporin and Tortorici, explore the distinctiveness of each. Spirituality tends towards a transcendence beyond the cultural concreteness of human expression and action. It seeks to find expression by relating to the universal, the supernatural, the moral, and does that in a manner that goes beyond that which can be defined and described. It can be expressed as a sense of right relationship with the self, the world and the sacred.

Religion, on the other hand, is precisely described in terms of human observation and practice. It is the way in which the individual (in relationship with other) expresses their relationship to the 'Other' through worship, ritual, beliefs. It is the concrete expression, the framework through which the individual (in community) seeks to express their spiritual awareness. Religion is the response of the person in relation with others to the transcendent and tends to be expressed in cultural, communal, institutional, behavioural, moral and intellectual ways. Spirituality and the spiritual speak from the inner being of the person directly to the transcendent and can only be described in terms of mystery and openness to being and creation. The language of soul, of energy and essence are common ways of seeking to talk to the focus of the spiritual in an individual.

Downey offers this distinction: 'Spirituality broadly understood refers to the human quest for personal integration in the light of levels of reality not immediately apparent...when the quest involves an explicit reference to God or the divine, then the spirituality is religious.'[29] Worthington, Kurusu and McCullough[30] point out that a person may be spiritual but not religious or religious but not spiritual, while Schneiders observes that every person 'has a capacity for spirituality or is a spiritual person'.[31]

Psychotherapy', *Journal of Religion and Health* 24.1 (1985), pp. 26-30; P. Sermabeikian, 'Our Clients, Ourselves: The Spiritual Perspectives and Social Work Practice', *Social Work* 39.2 (1994), pp. 178-83; M. Siporin, 'Current Social Work Perspectives on Clinical Practice', *Clinical Social Work Journal* 13.3 (1985), pp. 198-217; J. Tortorici, 'Abuse of the Sacred and the Need for Spiritual Healing in the Treatment of MPD' (paper presented at a Menninger Conference on Dissociation States: Multiple Personality and Other Trauma-Related Disorders, Topeka, KS, February 1993).

29. Downey, *Understanding Christian Spirituality*, p. 32.

30. Worthington, Kurusu and McCullough, 'Empirical Research', p. 449.

31. Quoted in U. King, 'Spirituality in a Postmodern Age', in U. King (ed.), *Faith and Praxis in a Postmodern Age* (London: Cassell, 1998), pp. 94-112 (100).

Establishing this distinction between religion and spirituality enables us to return to consider the complementarity of psychology and spirituality. The review of the literature outlined here highlights a growing awareness, particularly from a psychological perspective, of the need to include a 'spiritual' reality in the psychological debate. As theology and, by implication, spirituality for the Christian includes human experience as a source for reflection, the insights of psychology and the tools of psychotherapy become more available to those who work with the 'spiritual' dimension of their lives.[32] Furthermore, I would suggest that by focusing the discussion on transpersonal psychotherapies (see Rowan's chart above) and on spiritual direction[33] a convergence between psychology and spirituality begins to emerge.

In the Christian context spiritual direction has a long and rich tradition. The desert tradition of the fourth century in the Christian era celebrated the significance of the Abba–monk relationship as an important resource for growth, which for the monk was an attempt at the alignment of his will with the will of God. This relationship between the Abba/Amma and the monk/nun was key in the process of discernment for the monk/nun in their relationship with God. The presence of a spiritual guide or spiritual director or *geron* in the Greek tradition or *starets* in the Russian tradition, is constant in Christian spiritual movements. This relationship underscores the significance of the community

King in the same chapter also quotes from Elena Lugo, describing spirituality as 'a fundamental vital source and point of reference for our mind, will and heart, a basis of orientation or conscious direction of human activity and inquiry. Spirituality is the pursuit of meaning, of an intimation of purpose and sense of vital connection to one's ultimate environment—the dimension of depth in all of life's endeavours and institutions. In short, a spirituality functions as a principle of enlightenment, integration and finality without which our self-reflection, self-realization and self-surrender would become superficial, chaotic and aimless' (p. 98).

32. See R. Barnes, 'Psychology and Spirituality: Meeting at the Boundaries', *The Way Supplement* 69 (1990), pp. 29-42; P. Sheldrake, *Spirituality and History* (London: SPCK, 1991).

33. W. Barry and W. Connolly, *The Practice of Spiritual Direction* (New York: HarperCollins, 1991), describe spiritual direction as 'directly concerned with a person's actual experiences of his [her] relationship with God... [It is] help given by one Christian to another which enables that person to pay attention to God's personal communication to him or her, to respond to this personally communicating God, to grow in intimacy with this God, and to live out the consequences of the relationship' (p. 8).

context in which spiritual direction takes place. Lonsdale notes the importance of the 'community of faith' as the context for the formation of a mature Christian.[34] Indeed, from a Christian incarnational viewpoint genuine integral spirituality will include a community dimension.

A convergence, however, between psychotherapy and spiritual direction does not mean a merger, as Houdek observes when he makes a useful distinction between these two disciplines:

> These two disciplines ordinarily concentrate on problem areas of life and generally seek resolution through an emotional understanding of personal history or by modifying personal decision making and behaviour from a psychodynamic perspective. This interpersonal relationship may lack any conscious awareness or reference to God, mystery, or faith. In contrast, spiritual direction deals explicitly with spiritual themes in life, embracing the totality of one's life and experience.[35]

The development of qualitative research in psychology, such as discourse analysis, has given tools for the systematic investigation of spiritual experiences.

The Adult Attachment Interview[36] (AAI) is one example of discourse analysis used in current psychological research. The AAI is rooted in attachment theory as developed by John Bowlby, which specifically highlights relationship as key in the understanding of human develop-

34. See, for example, D. Lonsdale, 'Towards a Theology of Spiritual Direction', *The Way* 32.4 (1992), pp. 310-20; K. Leech, 'Viewpoint', *The Tablet*, 22 May 1993, p. 634; Sheldrake, *Spirituality and History*.

35. F. Houdek, *Guided by the Spirit: A Jesuit Perspective on Spiritual Direction* (Chicago: Loyola Press, 1996), p. 7.

36. The Adult Attachment Interview (AAI) was developed by George, Kaplan and Main in 1985 as a semi-structured interview in which a specially trained interviewer asks the participant to reflect on early attachment relationships and experiences in the light of current experience. The interviewer, by giving the participant the opportunity to describe the quality of early significant relationships and to confirm this description with actual episodic memories, provides a sensitive test of the person's model of relationships and their overall coherence in describing and justifying it. The transcript is coded into one of four major categories through a discourse analysis: Secure Autonomous; Dismissing of Attachment; Preoccupied/ Entangled; Unresolved/Disorganized. More specific scales measure such aspects as lack of memory to justify statements; underlying anger towards caregivers; passivity of discourse; idealization of one or more parents; derogation of one or more parents; fear of loss or separation from caregivers; the development of a metacognitive stance on the memories of childhood; and the overall coherence of the argument in the transcript.

ment. It underscores the importance of early relationships and the development of an internal working model of self as significant in psychological development. As *relationship* in its many facets is key to both psychotherapy and spiritual direction, it is an important convergent, and the AAI is a useful tool for investigating the interface of psychotherapy and spiritual direction

The purpose of this essay is not an in-depth analysis of the AAI Attachment Interview. However, in research I carried out recently with ten psychotherapists and ten spiritual directors using the AAI but also exploring further questions regarding religion and religious experience, some useful insights emerged. In this study the psychotherapists were all trained in a transpersonal school of psychotherapy and the spiritual directors trained in an Ignatian school of spiritual direction.[37] In this research both groups were asked in addition to the AAI:

(a) To what extent does religion give you an interpretation of your day-to-day reality?
(b) To what extent do you feel the presence of God or a higher being?

The analysis of the responses of both groups to these two question in research is outlined in Figures 1–4.

Figure 1 shows that all the spiritual directors practise their religion while only 1 out of 10 psychotherapists are committed and 3 out of 10 sometimes practise; the remainder have no religious practice. In contrast, Figure 2 shows that in both groups all claim to have 'spiritual experiences'. Figure 3, on the other hand, shows that only 8 out of 10 spiritual directors make use directly of the 'spiritual' in their life, and 2 out of 10 only indirectly. In contrast, 5 out of 10 of the psychotherapists use the 'spiritual' directly in their life, with 3 out of 10 making an indirect use and 2 out of 10 making no use. Figure 4 shows that all the spiritual directors strongly 'feel' the presence of God/higher being, while only 8 out of 10 psychotherapists feel it strongly and the remaining 2 feel it sometimes.

37. Ignatian spiritual direction owes its origin to the Spanish-born St Ignatius of Loyola (1491–1556), founder of the Society of Jesus—the Jesuits. It uses as a basic text the *Spiritual Exercises* of Ignatius. W. Meissner, *Ignatius of Loyola: The Psychology of a Saint* (New Haven: Yale University Press, 1992), p. 87, describes the *Spiritual Exercises* as 'one of the most influential works in western civilization. It became a guide for spiritual renewal in the Roman church during the entire Counter-Reformation and has been a primary influence in the spiritual life of the church ever since'.

Figure 1. The Participants' Practice of Religion

Figure 2. Spiritual Experience of Participants

Figure 3. Participants' Use of the Spiritual in Life

Figure 4. Participants' Experience of the Presence of God/Higher Being

Spiritual directors often use language from the Christian tradition in answering these questions, such as

> I think of the whole paschal mystery and the nonsense of the cross but the reality of the resurrection and a risen Christ...whose wounds are still there...are the kinds of images that come(s) from faith and ...the reality of the relationship with God.

The psychotherapists equally use language descriptive of their experience, although not often rooted in a particular religious tradition. For example,

> Yes... I mean it's an intrapersonal, it's an interpersonal and there is a transpersonal thing.

Congruent with the differentiation between religion and spirituality identified by Grame *et al.* and Downey and Smith in the literature review above, a similar differentiation emerged in both groups. Responses from psychotherapists included:

> Well none really...in terms of religion...but certainly...you know... I have a spiritual feeling...

Supporting Lonsdale's observation of the community dimension in spiritual direction, spiritual directors responded, for example, with

> I understand religion to be the public or communal articulation of...personal spirituality.

Further, for psychotherapists a 'spiritual experience' is often understood in terms of a peak experience. For example,

> I think...I've come to experience it more...it but it's in like little bursts and not...often.

While for spiritual directors a 'spiritual experience' engages every dimension of life, which include the highs and lows, peaks and troughs, or joys and sufferings, as when, for example, a participant says

> ...the sense that God is in all the mess.

This matches with Houdek's[38] understanding that spiritual direction is concerned about a person's life in all its dimensions.

In conclusion, the literature review outlined above indicates a desire on behalf of some researchers and commentators in psychology to

38. Houdek, *Guided by the Spirit*, p. 7.

engage in a new dialogue with the numinous, the spiritual dimension of the individual. Conversely as those engaged in spiritual direction begin to include human growth as part of their endeavour then the insights of psychotherapy become for them a valuable tool. While spiritual direction tends to take place in an overtly religious context, its thrust is the spiritual quest of the person. In this sense, a fourth force in psychotherapy working also with the spiritual dimension of the individual can be seen to deal with similar issues. This I would suggest is the convergence that both the literature review and my own research has begun to discern. The research presented here supports the convergence and highlights the fact that when a distinction is made between religion and spirituality a common ground in terms of language emerges. A willingness to explore this common ground between transpersonal psychotherapy and spiritual direction challenges the perceived antagonism between psychological growth and the spiritual quest.

FAITH FROM PAST TO FUTURE: THINKING ABOUT HUMAN MEANING-MAKING IN RELATION TO THE WORK OF HANNAH ARENDT

Anne Spalding

There has been considerable discussion about significant people and events of the past millennium and speculation about the new one. This gives us the opportunity to evaluate our past together, rather than solely as individuals, and perhaps to reach common decisions about some of our priorities for the future. To contribute to this discussion, in this essay I am concerned with illuminating our past and present priorities. These priorities are not abstract ideals but reflect our motivation in life, so they are, in James Fowler's description, part of our faith. Here faith is about the meaning we make of life. What is essential for a meaningful human life was a concern of Hannah Arendt's, so I discuss some of what Arendt considered vital for humans in order to reflect on our own way of faith or making meaning.

Faith and Making Meaning

In the prologue to her book *The Human Condition*, Hannah Arendt expressed concern that in 'the modern age' society only addresses people's need to earn a living and no longer knows of 'higher and more meaningful activities'.[1] In the rest of the book she elaborated on the values and activities she saw as lacking in Western society and yet necessary for a meaningful human life. She addressed this primarily to secular society, and this is a surprise if making meaning in life is thought of as the prerogative of religions and those involved in religious practices. Arendt, however, drew from philosophical and political sources, as well as from her doctoral studies on the concepts of love in

1. H. Arendt, *The Human Condition* (Chicago: University of Chicago Press, 1958), p. 5. She considered the (Western) 'modern age' to be from the seventeenth century up to her own time.

the writings of Saint Augustine, and arguably from her own experience as a liberal Jew (in Germany and as a refugee from the Nazis).[2] Arendt's assumption, then, was that making meaning is a human rather than a specifically religious concern. This fits with James Fowler's description of faith as 'our way of finding coherence in and giving meaning to the multiple forces and relations that make up our lives'.[3] Indeed, Fowler maintains that '[f]aith, classically understood...is an orientation of the total person, giving purpose and goal to one's hopes and strivings, thoughts and actions'.[4] In these terms, it can be said that 'everyone has a religion'.[5]

This meaning-making faith may or may not use conventional religious concepts and practice. Also, wherever the concepts stem from, the background they form for our life is not necessarily coherent and structured.[6] In fact, this 'ultimate environment' is often unconscious or tacitly held, and its nature therefore unnoticed, although it is our reality, shaping our initiatives and responses in life. Indeed, it forms our comprehensive perception of what constitutes true power, true value and the meaning of life. Its significance, however, does not imply a static image. Changes, in fact, occur when key elements in this environment are seen in a new light and are found wanting. Consequently, changes usually occur with human development (Fowler's main interest) but less predictable changes may also occur, for example, if an individual's principal concern in life is work and he or she is made redundant, or if family was the primary concern and this is removed through death or members leaving. Unsurprisingly, then, it has been argued from a psychological point of view that simply accepting other people's values is not sufficient for adults, rather that the 'path to holiness lies through questioning *everything*'.[7] Such an emphasis on questioning is echoed in

2. See, for example, H.F. Pitkin, 'Conformism, Housekeeping, and the Attack of the Blob: The Origins of Hannah Arendt's Concept of the Social', in B. Honig (ed.), *Feminist Interpretations of Hannah Arendt* (University Park, PA: Pennsylvania State University Press, 1995), pp. 51-81.

3. J.W. Fowler, *Stages of Faith: The Psychology of Human Development and the Quest for Meaning* (London: HarperCollins, 1995 [1981]), p. 4.

4. Fowler, *Stages of Faith*, p. 14.

5. M.S. Peck, *The Road Less Travelled: A New Psychology of Love, Traditional Values and Spiritual Growth* (London: Arrow, 1990 [1978]), p. 199.

6. Fowler, *Stages of Faith*, pp. 28-31.

7. Peck, *The Road*, pp. 207-208 (italics original).

Hannah Arendt's motivation for writing *The Human Condition*—'to think what we are doing'.[8]

Arendt herself was not much concerned with either holiness or psychological health but with the world of human affairs and actions within it. Nevertheless, both action and relationship are intrinsic to meaning-making faith: Fowler writes that faith 'is an active mode of being and committing...[and that] faith is always *relational*; there is always another in faith. "I trust *in* and am loyal *to*..." '[9] Faith in this sense, then, is not simply an internal subjective experience but is developed and practised in the context of other people. Story is important here, forming and supporting the images that give the context for our perception of valuable and meaningful action.[10] Faith, however, remains something we *do* (a verb, not a noun), even if we can partially express it in story or in more formal beliefs.[11] Arendt also valued story in making human reality, and she was aware of the inadequacy of the 'dead letter' of recorded words wholly to capture the 'living spirit' of thought, speech and action.[12] As we consider some aspects of Arendt's work in the remainder of this essay, we should be aware of the living nature of meaningful human existence.

Also, this study cannot be an exhaustive one, either in terms of elements making up faith, or in terms of Arendt's work. It is, rather, an opportunity to follow Arendt in thinking about what we are doing. We may or may not come to agree with the values and activities she saw as supremely important but we can consider them seriously, and use them to reflect on our own way of faith in the past and on how we may faith in the future.

Where Is Meaning?

The most meaningful activities, according to Arendt, take place among other humans. From Arendt's work, then, we can consider the nature of the world of other humans and the significance of this world—in comparison to the significance of either our own minds or bodies, or an 'other world'—in the way we make meaning. Arendt herself felt that

8. Arendt, *Human Condition*, p. 5.
9. Fowler, *Stages of Faith*, p. 16.
10. Fowler, *Stages of Faith*, p. 17.
11. Fowler, *Stages of Faith*, pp. 25-27.
12. Arendt, *Human Condition*, pp. 95, 169.

the world of other humans is of central importance, since, for example, she found that we humans need the presence of other humans who see and hear what we do to assure us of the reality of ourselves and of the world.[13] This centrality is also seen in Arendt's description of the world as a distinctively human place: she saw the world as the communal context within which human nature can express 'its special singularity' rather than its common ground with the rest of nature.[14] Moreover, this communal context is a public place, accessible to citizens, rather than being the private context of the family or household. Indeed, Arendt felt that the public aspect is so important to humans that 'even the greatest forces of intimate life—the passions of the heart, the thoughts of the mind, the delights of the senses—lead an uncertain, shadowy kind of existence unless and until they are transformed, deprivatized and deindividualized, as it were, into a shape to fit them for public appearance'.[15] In Arendt's understanding, therefore, human identity essentially requires openness and orientation to the world of other humans.[16] We may question here whether the world of human affairs, particularly that beyond the family, is essential or peripheral in the way we faith.

Arendt's description of the world is based on the understanding that it is precisely *this* world that is the place for meaningful life. She was critical of Christianity, therefore, for its alienation from the communal world of human affairs through its otherworldly concerns. She understood, for example, that Jesus taught 'the activity of goodness', but that 'goodness obviously harbors a tendency to hide from being seen or heard', and so 'goodness that comes out of hiding and assumes a public role is no longer good, but corrupt in its own terms'.[17] This does not mean Arendt was advocating badness, rather she found that ambition for goodness led at least early Christians to live as far removed as possible from the public realm of human affairs. For this to be so, the martyrdom of Christians must be seen as always arising from gladness to leave this world rather than sometimes being brought about through rejection of the martyrs' understanding of, and efforts for, life in it. We may question, therefore, whether Arendt's interpretation of Jesus'

13. Arendt, *Human Condition*, p. 50.

14. Cf. P. Bowen-Moore, *Hannah Arendt's Philosophy of Natality* (London: Macmillan, 1989), p. 108.

15. Arendt, *Human Condition*, p. 50.

16. Cf. Bowen-Moore, *Natality*, p. 110.

17. Arendt, *Human Condition*, pp. 74-77. Presumably from Mt. 6.

teaching is the necessary one. Nevertheless, in reflecting on Arendt's view, we may ask whether those of us who are Christian continue to take from human society without returning anything to it. Also, whether or not we faith within a particular tradition, we may ask what place the world of human affairs has in our faith or whether faith for us is an entirely private affair.

Historically, Arendt saw disengagement from the world—she called it 'world alienation'—being strengthened through 'Luther and Calvin's attempts to restore the uncompromising otherworldliness of the Christian faith', but here the emphasis on individual salvation contributed to what Max Weber called 'innerworldly asceticism'.[18] In fact, any discipline or practice that concentrated on the self and lost sight of the world of others was subject to Arendt's criticism. She found world alienation, for example, in modern science and modern philosophy because of their shared 'assumption that what was true and therefore indisputable owed its discovery solely to the mind'.[19] In these views, therefore, the reality of the world outside ourselves, including the world of other humans, is doubted. For the same loss of the reality of the world of humans, Arendt was critical of personal introspection, which she saw as 'the sheer cognitive concern of consciousness with its own content'.[20] This dismissal of interior life was not, however, absolute. We have seen, for example, that she advocated thinking about what we are doing. Also, the work of others suggests that many people need a period of becoming aware of, and trusting, their own perspectives rather than accepting other people's,[21] and it seems possible that Arendt's own period of introspection as a young adult helped form her conviction that human meaning is not found in interior absorption. Perhaps, then, we should question not only whether our way of faith includes mental searching

18. Arendt, *Human Condition*, p. 251.

19. Bowen-Moore, *Natality*, p. 117.

20. Arendt, *Human Condition*, p. 280.

21. Cf. Fowler, *Stages of Faith*, pp. 174-83. Women, in particular, may go through a marked period of trusting only themselves when others have let them down (M.F. Belenky, B.M. Clinchy, N.R. Goldberger and J.M. Tarule, *Women's Ways of Knowing: The Development of Self, Voice and Mind* [New York: Basic Books, 1986], pp. 52-86). Also, Carol Gilligan found that women have to learn 'selfishness' as well as 'responsibility' as they develop in moral decision-making (C. Gilligan, 'In a Different Voice: Women's Conceptions of Self and of Morality', in M.R. Walsh [ed.], *The Psychology of Women: Ongoing Debates* [New Haven: Yale University Press, 1987], pp. 278-320).

but whether in pursuing these questions we have become alienated from the communal world of humans.

Arendt felt that the mental patterning in the scientific world-view dominant in the modern West has not only led to alienation from the world of human affairs but also to the loss of the world of the senses.[22] In other words, she saw that the priority of the mind in science has diminished the reality of the physical world separate from ourselves, and Arendt found that with this the transcendent world also disappears. That Arendt was concerned with the transcendent at all may be a surprise, since we often frame our faith questions in terms of either the transcendent or the material, whereas Arendt argued that there is a need to transcend the material world in concept and thought as a part of meaningful involvement in this world. She also argued that transcendence beyond an individual and beyond an individual's life-span is linked to an 'authentic concern with immortality'.[23] She understood immortality as 'the potential immortality of the people', which she found in both the Hebrew creed and in the ancient Greek *polis*, and was clear in contrasting this with 'the pagan immortality of the world', with 'the Christian immortality of individual life' and with the modern perception of mortal/physical life as the ultimate good.[24] This suggests that an understanding of immortality and transcendence is part of faith and that where we locate these makes a significant difference to our motivation and actions in this world.

In and around Christianity, there have always been tensions between immortal and mortal, and between transcendent and immanent.[25] Arendt is not alone, therefore, in her perception of Christians alienated from this world, at first through expectations of the end of the world, then through the evident mortality of human achievements combined with the 'gospel of an everlasting individual life'.[26] Modern reactions to this alienation include those of feminists who in various ways have made initiatives towards greater integration of the world and human relation-

22. Arendt, *Human Condition*, p. 288.

23. Arendt, *Human Condition*, p. 55.

24. Arendt, *Human Condition*, pp. 315-16.

25. See, for example, 1 Cor. 15.50-57; 2 Cor. 5.1-10; and discussion leading to the agreement at the Council of Chalcedon (451 CE) that Jesus Christ was one being yet with two natures, fully divine and fully human.

26. Arendt, *Human Condition*, pp. 74, 21.

ships in theological thinking and practice.[27] Arendt herself, as we have seen, advocated emphasis on the world of humans, but, unlike some modern initiatives, this did not lead to a central focus on the human body and human physical and emotional needs.[28] As ever, Arendt's concern was that lifestyles that centre on the body and human needs can lose the world in which humans can share and communicate.[29] She was not, however, in favour of lifestyles that remove all the pain and effort of human needs since she found that this led to substituting vicarious life for real life; rather, Arendt felt 'the necessities of life, of individual survival as well as of continuity of the species, were taken care of and guaranteed' in the private realm of the household so that a citizen could take part in the meaningful activities in the public realm.[30] Modern feminists are suspicious of this division between the public and private realms since it appears to exclude many women from meaningful activities.[31] Debate on interpretation continues then, but Arendt's work suggests that, at the least, our physical circumstances have relevance for meaningful life. Also, Arendt's work altogether raises pertinent questions over where we primarily find meaning—in our bodies, our minds or among others, in this world or another.

What Does Meaning Need?

According to Hannah Arendt, then, meaningful activity takes place among humans, but it is not sufficient simply to be among other humans. For her, meaningful activity is 'action', and this needs both initiative from individuals and an environment among humans that

27. See, for example, the work of Rosemary Radford Ruether, Carter Heyward and Mary Grey.

28. For example, in the variety of perspectives and practice of 'spiritual feminists' who are trying to develop a religion consistent with the natural world and with qualities traditionally or biologically associated with being female; M. Raphael, *Thealogy and Embodiment: The Post-Patriarchal Reconstruction of Female Sacrality* (Sheffield: Sheffield Academic Press, 1996).

29. So, for example, she wrote, 'The *animal laborans* does not flee the world but is ejected from it in so far as he is imprisoned in the privacy of his own body, caught in the fulfilment of needs in which nobody can share and which nobody can fully communicate' (Arendt, *Human Condition*, pp. 118-19).

30. Arendt, *Human Condition*, pp. 119-20, 45, 30-31.

31. For a summary of feminist critiques, see M.G. Dietz, 'Feminist Reception of Hannah Arendt', in Honig (ed.), *Feminist Interpretations*, pp. 17-50.

accepts and welcomes initiative. Arendt saw initiative or 'the capacity of beginning something anew' as an expression of human natality in that we first contribute something new to the human world through being born—also bringing the potential of further new beginnings—and thus she saw initiative as essential to humans.[32] Indeed, she said that 'action' rests on 'an initiative from which no human being can refrain and still be human'.[33] From a slightly different perspective, Fowler confirms that human action always involves initiatives as well as responses, and says that we seek to fit our actions into, or oppose them to, the larger patterns of action and meaning that we perceive.[34] Our understanding of the arena in which humans can act, therefore, is part of the way we faith. From Arendt's work we can consider both the nature of this arena—here considering issues of dominance and of conformity—and the attitudes—to human uniqueness, to thought, and to the world of humans—which Arendt found significant for meaningful action.

We have seen that Arendt thought meaningful activity takes place in a public place rather than within the privacy of family or household. Indeed, she particularly valued the opportunity to speak and act among one's peers and she claimed, contrary to her own experience, that the necessary mutual respect was not possible in families.[35] Certainly, in households with an authoritarian head there are few opportunities for others to show initiative[36]—an experience with which women in patriarchy are familiar! Arendt herself was concerned that too often in the public realm initiative is similarly discouraged. She found that both spontaneous action and outstanding achievement are often excluded in public society by the 'innumerable and various rules' that are imposed, rules that 'normalize' the members and produce conformity of behaviour.[37] These rules are not necessarily imposed by an identifiable ruler, but Arendt found that 'the rule by nobody is not necessarily no-rule',

32. Arendt, *Human Condition*, p. 9.

33. Arendt, *Human Condition*, p. 176.

34. Fowler, *Stages of Faith*, p. 24.

35. Cf. Arendt, *Human Condition*, pp. 49, 242-43. A friend described Arendt and Blücher's marriage as 'a Dual Monarchy'; E. Young-Bruehl, *Hannah Arendt: For Love of the World* (New Haven: Yale University Press, 1982), p. 267.

36. Cf. Arendt, *Human Condition*, pp. 27-28.

37. Arendt, *Human Condition*, p. 40.

indeed, it may be a cruel and tyrannical rule.[38] Arendt also found that 'the more people there are, the more likely they are to behave and the less likely to tolerate non-behavior'.[39] Whether or not we immediately recognize this description, we need to ask to what extent we make meaning through conforming to the expectations of specified or generalized others. In fact, Fowler's research showed that many adults remain in a way of faith based on conformity with what 'they' expect.[40] Caricatures of religious faith are usually based on this (with some justification) but religious faith is not necessarily conforming faith and conforming faith is not necessarily religious.[41] Since making meaning through conformity is an unexamined way of meaning-making, the conformity is unrecognized until the way of faith is beginning to change. Interpersonal relationships are important for those with conforming faith, and this gives support to Arendt's view that here difference and distinction between people, as well as speech and action involving initiative, have become intimate, individual and private matters.[42] Arendt argued in favour of privacy for some aspects of life but she felt that action that is only private diminishes human meaningfulness.[43]

In contrast to conformity, then, meaningful activity for Arendt assumes the recognition that human beings are not 'endlessly reproducible repetitions of the same model'.[44] We can see, for example, that each birth is new and unique although it is one of many births. Similarly, Arendt felt that for action to be meaningful each human must act from his or her unique perspective, and the action reveals this individuality, making each person's action different from that of any other.[45] This is not, however, uniqueness for its own sake, since there must also be awareness of an equality between humans that provides the ground for understanding one another: Arendt called this combination 'the

38. Arendt, *Human Condition*, p. 40.

39. Arendt, *Human Condition*, p. 43.

40. Fowler, *Stages of Faith*, pp. 151-73.

41. 'Conforming faith' is the National Society (Church of England) for Promoting Religious Education's name, rather than Fowler's, for this way of making meaning (*How Faith Grows: Faith Development and Christian Education* [London: National Society; Church House Publishing, 1991], pp. 24-27).

42. Cf. Arendt, *Human Condition*, p. 41.

43. Cf. Arendt, *Human Condition*, p. 49.

44. Arendt, *Human Condition*, p. 8.

45. Arendt, *Human Condition*, pp. 179-82.

paradoxical plurality of unique beings'.[46] In practice, Arendt found that action is frequently related to specific, physical, objective realities that are of common interest. These are literally *inter-est* in the sense of lying between people, able to relate and bind them together in the real but intangible world that is the 'web' of human relationships.[47] Anything that destroys this web of relationships and 'the in-between which relates us to and separates us from others' reduces the opportunity for meaningful action.[48] Arendt found that this in-between is removed in (romantic) lovers' absorption with each other, as well as through conformity, authoritarianism and totalitarianism, all of which remove, in varying ways, the opportunity to act from different perspectives. In addition, Arendt maintained that 'aspiration toward omnipotence always implies...the destruction of plurality',[49] and this needs further discussion in the light of the monotheistic religions and their religious practice. In the context of this essay, however, we can consider whether the way we make meaning includes the opportunity to be unique and, if so, whether this uniqueness isolates us or relates us to others.

It is, of course, impossible to speak and act from one's uniqueness if one's thoughts and meanings are taken directly from others, however significant those others seem. Rather, it has been rightly said that 'thought—not only its content but its process—forms us, [and] develops our uniqueness', although we should be clear that thought here is not 'climbing up into the head', nor 'developing cleverness or even acquiring a great deal of information which could be recalled on demand',[50] but it is a quest for meaning. Fowler describes this sort of thought beginning when making meaning through conformity is found unsatisfactory.[51] Some people advocate moving from conformity to thought—it has been said, for example, 'There is no such thing as a good hand-me-down religion'[52]—but Arendt felt more urgency than

46. Arendt, *Human Condition*, pp. 175-76.

47. Arendt, *Human Condition*, pp. 182-84.

48. Cf. Arendt, *Human Condition*, p. 242.

49. Arendt, *Human Condition*, p. 202.

50. G.M. Jantzen, 'Necrophilia and Natality', *Scottish Journal of Religious Studies* 19.1 (1998), pp. 101-21 (117).

51. Fowler, *Stages of Faith*, pp. 174-98. Scott Peck describes a similar process in M.S. Peck, *The Different Drum: Community-Making and Peace* (London: Arrow, 1990 [1987]), pp. 187-93.

52. Peck, *The Road*, p. 208.

this. She found that the by-product of thinking is conscience and so saw thinking as essential to minimize evil actions.[53] She reached this conclusion after witnessing a Nazi war trial, where she found the striking characteristic of the defendant 'was not stupidity but a curious, quite authentic *inability to think*'.[54] So thought is necessary to act both against evil and for a truly human life, and, despite the need to stand back from the active busyness of everyday life for thought, Arendt felt thinking might surpass all other activities.[55] We may ask ourselves the extent to which we value thought in our own way of making meaning.

Thinkers are sometimes accused of sitting in ivory towers but this was not Arendt's ambition, since both thought and action in her description are motivated by love for the world, *amor mundi*. Arendt said that *amor mundi* means 'to care more for the world...than for ourselves, for our immediate interests and for life...',[56] a view we usually associate with giving up our unique perspective and thoughts in favour of other peoples'. Clearly this was not Arendt's understanding, and her work shows a paradox between awareness of self and of others, between the plurality of unique beings and love for the world. This is consistent with Fowler's description of 'balanced faith'.[57] Fowler found that this way of making meaning is unusual before mid-life and knows 'the reality of irrevocable commitments and acts', so it is perhaps unsurprising that Arendt's biographer says that '[w]hen her marriage gained a new stability and her childhood oppression—her lack of trust—lifted, when she finally felt at home, Hannah Arendt wanted to write of her *amor mundi,* her love of the world'.[58] We also need to recognize that this love is not sentimental but stems from the will; it is not manipulative, quite different from 'I want to have you' or 'I want to rule you', and Arendt summed up the approach as ' "*Amo: Volo ut sis*",

53. Cf. Bowen-Moore, *Natality*, p. 73.

54. From H. Arendt, 'Thinking and Moral Consideration: A Lecture', *Social Research* 38.3 (Autumn 1971), p. 439 (Arendt's italics), also cited in Bowen-Moore, *Natality*, pp. 72-73. The defendant was Adolf Eichmann, and Arendt's reports on this trial are in H. Arendt, *Eichmann in Jerusalem* (London: Faber & Faber, 1963).

55. Cf. Arendt, *Human Condition*, p. 325.

56. From Arendt's unpublished university course lecture, 'Introduction to Politics', cited in Bowen-Moore, *Natality*, p. 55.

57. Fowler, *Stages of Faith*, pp. 184-98. 'Balanced faith' is the National Society's name, not Fowler's (National Society, *How Faith Grows*, pp. 30-33).

58. Fowler, *Stages of Faith*, p. 198; Young-Bruehl, *Hannah Arendt*, p. 262.

"I love you; I want you to be" '.[59] All of this raises challenging questions for us on whether our way of faith does or could include this sort of love for others, or whether we find our own individuality or conforming identity of greater importance. Thinking these issues through for ourselves and in relation to the human contexts in which we share will inevitably mean assessing the past and looking toward the future.

Looking Back and Looking Forward

As we look back at the beginning of a new millennium, we can see such features as national, cultural and religious new beginnings and what has provided continuity from then until now. In this our own birth provides a specific beginning and our subsequent lives give us a specific perspective and human context. From evaluation of the past, we can make decisions about the direction and extent of our priorities for meaningful life in the future. Arendt's work challenges us particularly to consider the beginnings of birth in a communal context, life continuing in a physical context and the urgency and limitations in working for meaningful life in future generations.

We have already seen that for Arendt meaningful activity in each generation is action in the world of human affairs, and that action is an expression of human natality. In this understanding, physical birth is a beginning for the individual. The birth of a child also provides a new beginning for lovers absorbed in one another, who, Arendt felt, are returned to the wider context of human relationships through the child, 'love's own product'.[60] In addition, Fowler confirms that '[o]ur first experiences of faith and faithfulness begin with birth', through the degree of fidelity in the reception we are given in this world by those who care for us, so that, long before a child can sort out language or conscious meaning-making, the 'love, attachment, and dependence bind the new one into the family, [and] he or she begins to form a disposition of shared trust and loyalty to (or through) the family's faith ethos'.[61]

59. Arendt developed this understanding of love from Duns Scotus's thinking in mediaeval theology, seeing it as 'the same love with which supposedly God loves men, whom He created only because He willed them to exist and whom He *loves without desiring them*' (H. Arendt, *The Life of the Mind/Willing* [London: Secker & Warburg, 1978], p. 136).

60. Arendt, *Human Condition*, p. 242; cf. Bowen-Moore, *Natality*, pp. 16-18.

61. Fowler, *Stages of Faith*, pp. 16-17.

Arendt emphasized, however, that the new beginnings of birth are not simply personal, since she observed that we are born into a communal context: 'Every man [*sic*] is born a member of a particular community and can survive only if he is welcomed and made at home within it'.[62] In her own life a significant part of her identity and meaning was rooted in being Jewish, and she early learnt to defend her cultural and racial heritage.[63] This was not an uncritical identification with the Jewish people as a whole, since Arendt also found that the community of other humans asks of the one born among them, 'Who are you?', and the response to this displays both individual uniqueness and identification with the communal context.[64] Responding in this way may not be an easy task—for Arendt her Jewishness was a fact of her birth but also needed embracing 'with hard-won gratitude'.[65] The speech and action required for this process are also on-going, so that physical birth brings the potential of new beginnings to the wider world of human affairs. Altogether, then, our own beginnings in family and community make a difference to the way we, as adults, make meaning and act meaningfully, whether we act from or against our past. The challenge is in identifying the inheritance of the past in our present way of faith.

Both physical birth and human initiative in action take place in an existing web of relationships and they affect the future of that relational web. This change has an identifiable beginning at birth but the contribution of the life that follows it is full of uncertainties, and action often has a similar identifiable beginning with uncertain consequences, so natality has been said to bring with it 'the force of unpredictability'.[66] Arendt recognized that uncertainties can generate unease but she herself welcomed the opportunities inherent here because she felt that 'everything human [is inevitably carried] to ruin and destruction if it were not for the faculty of interrupting it and beginning something new'.[67] In this

62. H. Arendt, *Crises of the Republic* (New York: Harcourt Brace Jovanovich, 1972), pp. 87-88. I have kept Arendt's masculinist language despite my own discomfort with it: in much of her work I am convinced she was considering all humans and not distinguishing men.

63. Bowen-Moore, *Natality*, p. 14; Young-Bruehl, *Hannah Arendt*, pp. 11-12.

64. Bowen-Moore, *Natality*, p. 18.

65. Bowen-Moore, *Natality*, p. 13.

66. Bowen-Moore, *Natality*, p. 22; cf. Arendt, *Human Condition*, pp. 144, 184.

67. Arendt, *Human Condition*, pp. 166, 246.

perspective, the risks of new beginnings are less than the consequences of not taking initiative. New beginnings, however, are not in themselves necessarily moral, hence Arendt's concern that action is taken in the attitude of *amor mundi*, love for the world.[68] *Amor mundi* gives an urgency to act both to preserve the world with its opportunities for meaningful human action and to make human beginnings 'ever possible' in the future.[69] In other words, the hope and expectation of *amor mundi* is that the world, as a place for action, will endure, and that newcomers will be anticipated and welcomed into its communal experiences. In the light of this, we might consider whether the way we faith takes any account of the future, particularly the future of the human world beyond our private lives.

If all this seems impossibly intangible, it is worth observing that, for Arendt, the world of human relationships has a physical context. She understood that manmade artefacts, such as buildings and objects for use, provide the stability and solidity necessary 'to house the unstable and mortal creature which is man'.[70] The stable context comes from these artefacts having a durability beyond the activity of producing them and potentially beyond the lives of those who made them, so that the 'artificial' world of things 'is meant to outlast and transcend them all'.[71] In fact, Arendt expected objects to become used up but she made a distinction between objects made simply to be consumed and those that are sufficiently enduring to form the necessary reliable physical world for humans. Unsurprisingly, she regretted that in the modern 'waste economy', things never last long enough 'to surround the life process in their midst'.[72] This does not imply that Arendt wanted human artefacts to be too precious to use. Indeed, usefulness is one of their purposes. Nevertheless, she found that there is a distinction between usefulness and meaningfulness, to the extent that 'utility established as meaning generates meaninglessness'.[73] Meaning, then, is beyond the objects themselves and their usefulness: Arendt said that meaning 'must be permanent and lose nothing of its character, whether

68. Cf. Bowen-Moore, *Natality*, p. 44.
69. Bowen-Moore, *Natality*, pp. 103, 19.
70. Arendt, *Human Condition*, p. 136.
71. Arendt, *Human Condition*, pp. 7, 96.
72. Arendt, *Human Condition*, p. 134.
73. Arendt, *Human Condition*, p. 154.

it is achieved or, rather, found by man or fails man and is missed by him'.[74] From this, we can ask ourselves what is the place of physical objects and location(s) in the way we find meaning, and whether such objects aid both the continuity from the past and the looking toward the future that Arendt found essential for a truly human life.

Finally, one commentator felt that Arendt described men who 'strive endlessly to be superhuman'.[75] Arendt certainly argued with urgency for human initiative in action to provide a future for the world of human affairs but there does also seem to be recognition of individual finiteness in Arendt's work. For example, *amor mundi* 'acknowledges the fact that while human beings do indeed belong to the world for a short time, the world does not belong to them exclusively', because the world also belongs to past and future generations.[76] Similarly, Arendt said that *amor mundi* or love dedicated to the world 'is possible because *we* shall not live forever. To be dedicated to the world means among other things: not to act as though we were immortal.'[77] The emphasis I see in Arendt's work, then, is to do what we can when we can, always acting in acceptance of the contribution of past and future generations. This is quite different from ways of making meaning that look for absolute, unchanging patterns. We may consider, then, whether in our ways of faith we hold a balance between what we contribute and the contributions of other generations. Also, if Fowler is right that humans change their way of making meaning through the course of their lives, and Arendt is right that thinking takes place in that moment between past and future, then for faith to be living and life to have meaning there is a continuing need to 'think thought anew'.[78] There may be personal occasions on which this is particularly relevant, but as we begin the new millennium, we have an unparalleled opportunity to look back together over the past century and millennium and then to look forward to meaningful life in the new one.

74. Arendt, *Human Condition*, p. 155.

75. Pitkin, cited in Dietz, 'Feminist Reception', p. 26.

76. Bowen-Moore, *Natality*, pp. 49-50.

77. From Arendt's unpublished 'Introduction to Politics', cited in Bowen-Moore, *Natality*, p. 56.

78. Cf. Bowen-Moore, *Natality*, pp. 98-99, 158.

Conclusion

Arendt's work directs our attention to the significance of the wider web of human relationships in making meaning. In her understanding, this is the location of meaningful life, rather than solely in our minds or our bodies, or related to an 'other world'. Meaningful life is also something we do, not something we have, and an environment of respect for the uniqueness of others as well as love for our shared world of human relationships beyond our private relationships is essential for meaningful action as Arendt described it. Her work, therefore, gives a specific expression to Fowler's understanding that faith is always active and relational, whether we are conscious of this or not, and Arendt advocates a way of making meaning usually only found by more mature people. Both Fowler and Arendt are clear that thinking is essential for this meaning-making. Arendt's own thought about the world of human affairs brought her to appreciate and appropriate, although not uncritically, the individual and communal past, and so to promote the centrality of this shared human world for future meaningful action. At our present turn of the millennia, we too can think about significance in past achievements and actions and look towards meaningful life in the future, not only for our individual lives but in the communal human context we share.

A Matter of Interest: International Debt as a Challenge to Faith

Rebecca Dudley

Introduction

> There is a Christianity which takes off fetters instead of binding them on—that breaks every yoke—that lifts up the bowed down. It passes, link by link, until it finds the lowest link in humanity's chain—humanity's most degraded condition. [This Christianity]...reaches down its arm and tells them to stand up.[1]

The above lines are from one of the speeches of Frederick Douglas, who escaped slavery in the southern United States, and survived to become one of the most eloquent abolitionists in the nineteenth century. Opening with the words of Frederick Douglas is apt, and not only for their theological message about the nature of God. People who know what it is like for their countries to be burdened with unpayable debts compare the economic stranglehold of creditors over the poor countries to slavery. By this analogy, modern Christians and others of good will are invited to become the new abolitionists. This essay has three parts. First, to briefly introduce the debt crisis and explain why it matters: if you like, debt as a matter of interest. The second and third parts give two different kinds of answers to the question, Why is debt a matter of Christian faith? In the second part I will give my own answer. In the third part I will expose a process by which readers might determine their own answers. If you like, debt as a matter of faith, parts one and two.

Debt, I will argue, is a crucial issue for people of faith around the world.[2] From a Christian standpoint, this is not only because people are

1. F. Douglas, *Life and Writings*, cited in J.P. Wogaman and D.M. Strong (eds.), *Readings in Christian Ethics* (Louisville, KY: Westminster/John Knox Press, 1996), p. 210.

2. Delegates from all major world faiths are engaged in a formal dialogue with the World Bank to challenge and enrich the latter's criteria for development.

suffering because of unpayable debts. It is also because exploring issues of debt and redemption can enrich Christian faith and make it deeper and profoundly more meaningful.

Debt as a Matter of Interest

So where do we start in considering international debt? I would like to suggest that we start by recognizing that, in one sense at least, the people of Britain stand with the rest of the world, in the red. As the personal finance magazine *Your Money* states: 'Many of us do not clear our credit card balances every month. According to Alliance and Leicester, there is typically £13 billion outstanding on credit cards nationally.'[3] That is £13 *billion*. Another article says, 'Datamonitor reports that only 30 per cent of us pay off our balances in full every month, which leaves a lucrative 70 per cent of us paying what many might regard as extortionate rates of interest.'[4] If we want to consider debt from a standpoint of faith, we have to begin with the fact that we are in the red.

But our starting point is also to look around us at a world in which unpayable debt has been identified as one of the pressing moral issues of our time. In 1996 Desmund Tutu said, 'Now that we have accomplished this extraordinary business of ridding the world of apartheid, the next moral campaign, the most urgent issue ought surely to be international debt.'

The Jubilee 2000 campaign is designed to address this pressing moral issue. The aim of the campaign is cancellation of debt on a case-by-case basis for the poorest countries of the world. It is pushing a political process that has won support in both Conservative and Labour governments.

Because the World Bank is a major creditor institution, this dialogue necessarily encompasses debt payment issues. For the papers, contact Wendy Tyndale, Coordinator of the Faiths, World Faiths Development Dialogue, 33-37 Stockmore Street, Oxford, OX1 1JT, United Kingdom. E.g. Occasional Paper No. 2, *Papers Presented by the Faiths' Delegates at the Consultation on the World Bank's World Development Report 2000/1 on the Themes of Values, Norms and Poverty, Johannesburg 12–14 January 1999.*

3. Update from editor, *Your Money* (Matching Hat Ltd, Penthouse Suite, 143 Charing Cross Road, London, WC2H OEE), February/March 1998, p. 4.

4. *Your Money*, pp. 14-15.

It is first important to know, however, how the debt crisis came about.[5] There was a glut of credit available at low interest rates in the 1970s, credit that was sold to poor countries. The developing countries of the 1970s snapped up these loans for all sorts of reasons, from very noble to scandalous. A few years later interest rates increased hugely, so that governments found they could not service the loans without making massive cuts in other expenses. Over time many countries found they had repaid the amount of the capital several times in loan payments. Most of the worst-hit countries are in Africa. 'In 1994, for every £10 it received in aid, Sub-Saharan Africa owed £11.50 in debt payments, of which it actually managed to pay off £6. Any delay in repaying added to the interest, which simply had to be repaid later.'[6]

Starting in the late 1970s, new loans came from international institutions like the International Monetary Fund (IMF) and the World Bank, which had been set up to stabilize economies. These loans had conditions: countries had to earn more and spend less. The recipe for this was changes that weakened national currencies and export markets. But the poor suffered the worst direct effects of the conditions: cuts on subsidies for basic foods, health care, education, credits for poor farmers to tide them over to harvest, and so forth.

The programmes and conditions on economy are called structural adjustment programmes in English, and have and other local names around the world. In Zimbabwe, visitors report that even ordinary people in remote rural villages call them ESAPs from the local acronym—and they know that they are deadly. For example, a newsletter for farmers' groups says, 'ESAP is the worst kind of animal: killing poor people.'[7]

From Nigeria, Dr Adabayo Adedeji, of the African Centre for Development Strategy says, 'Debt is tearing down schools, clinics, and hospitals, and the effects are no less devastating than war.'[8] From El Salvador

5. For more extended discussion, see Christian Aid, *The New Abolitionists: Slavery in History and the Modern Slavery of Poor Country Debt* (London: Christian Aid, 1997); *idem*, *One Every Second* (London: Christian Aid, 1997); *idem*, *Forever in Your Debt* (London: Christian Aid, 1998).

6. P. Spray, *Change the Debt Rules* (Internal Christian Aid document, September 1997).

7. J. Woodruffe, interview, Christian Aid, May 1995.

8. I. Hanson and A. Travis (eds.), *Breaking the Chains: The New Jubilee 2000 Debt Cutter's Handbook* (London: Jubilee 2000, 1999), p. 44.

it feels like war too. A community worker from San Salvador says, after the peace treaty in El Salvador,

> We say that the war of the poor against the rich has finished. But the war of the rich against the poor has not finished. And that is precisely what foreign debt is. It is the war of the rich, the powerful, the owners of this world, against the poor.[9]

In their traditional role of childbearing and rearing and caring for family members, women take the pressure of the debt crisis: caring for relatives in the hospital when there is no staff, making ends meet for the children to eat, walking long distances for antenatal and postnatal care that is increasingly scarce in some countries. Women take the brunt because they fill the factories in the so-called free enterprise zones of the Caribbean and Asia where work is low-skilled, pay is low and unions are not welcome.

And most of all, perhaps, children are affected. Children die of preventable illnesses because clinics have shut and preventive health care is not available, and they die of hunger-related causes because subsidies on basic foods like milk and bread have been lifted and prices have skyrocketed. They die because work is scarce, jobs are precarious and wages are low for their parents. They die because government credits and other assistance for poor farmers are withdrawn. From a parish in Peru, an American priest says that the debt crisis is a massacre of the innocents. And he says, 'Children have a way of dying quietly.' For example, Thekla Msigwa lives in the village of Milo in Tanzania. Last August, a colleague went with visiting health workers, funded by the local Church and Christian Aid, to meet her. She had a daughter, Winnie, who was two years and eight months old. Winnie was seriously malnourished. The health workers gave her advice on what to feed her daughter, but she was not sure that she could. She said, 'I will try to follow the programme but I am worried because I don't have the income. Milk is very expensive.'

This, then, is why debt is a matter of interest: because milk is very expensive. UN figures, again from 1997, estimate that there are now 1.3 billion people who live on the income equivalent of 60 pence a day.[10] Debt is a matter of interest because unpayable debt is one of the chief

9. N. Davies, interview, Christian Aid, El Salvador, July 1998.

10. United Nations Development Programme, *Human Development Report, 1997* (Oxford: Oxford University Press, 1997), p. 10.

barriers to one billion people escaping poverty. But proposals for one-off cancellation of unpayable debts in the poorest countries of the world are possible. They are already on the table. Some are already fact.

The British government has taken the lead, and recently the German government has reversed its policy on debt relief. The campaign has notched up some notable successes: the IMF has just agreed in principle that 50 billion dollars' worth of gold reserves can be used for debt relief. Chancellor Gordon Brown is reviewing the current process for debt relief to see whether it can be speeded up and extended to more countries. And hundreds of fine economists and social policy analysts across a political spectrum and around the world are working on how to reform the system that creates unpayable debts and makes the poor pay them. Reforming the system is not simple. The undoing of evil never is. To undo evil in this case depends on political systems being open and accountable, democracies that are strongly based on healthy local institutions and political controls in creditor countries that check irresponsible lending.

Debt as a Matter of Faith: Part 1

The Jubilee 2000 campaign has been launched in over 60 countries around the world, from the US to Zambia, Sweden to the Philippines. Churches have comprised a principal base of support for this campaign. *But, why? Why is debt a subject of Christian faith?* In other words, why should we be concerned with it, pray about it, study or preach about it in our Churches? I would like to suggest three reasons why debt is a subject of Christian faith. I will write now as if all are committed to Christian faith. I realize that this may not be the case, but I believe that engagement of personal values, visions and commitments cannot be separated from this study. In the next two sections of this essay, I would like to answer the question in two ways. First, the easy way, which is to give you my answer. Then the harder way, which is to try to expose a process by which others might reflect on what their answer might be.

First, I would like to suggest that the language we use about faith—debt, bondage, slavery, redemption, freedom—has an *economic reality* behind it. I will come back to that below by looking at particular Bible texts, but the reason that debt is a subject of faith is that by trying to understand debt we can bring the Bible off the page and our faith to life.

Debt slavery and freedom from it are core stories and images in the Bible—in fact, they are what we might call one of the 'main roads' through the story of salvation. One example is the way we use the word *redeemer*. We don't usually think about the original meaning of this word. The word *redeemer* comes from the word used for someone who pays off a debt and thus frees us. As Peter Selby writes,

> We have lost touch with the roots of one of the most important metaphors that have been used about the person and work of Christ. For by seeing our debt to God and Christ's repayment of that debt as a spiritual truth (for which we easily mean…a truth that is not based in the material world) we are allowed to let the financial world look after itself and go its own way.[11]

So debt is a subject of faith because exploring debt can bring Christian faith alive.

The second reason that debt is a matter of Christian faith is that debt is about money and money is a big part of our lives. Getting and spending it, acquiring enough savings for the future and paying off debts now are some of the chief concerns of adult life. As Dietrich Bonhoeffer preached in the early 1920s, 'If we wish to have Jesus, then he demands the right to say something decisive about our entire life.'[12]

However, all the energy and anxiety around money, which we know from experience and read about in the Bible, are not often matched by the attention given to the issue in Church. It is a hard subject. But the difficulty and importance of money in our lives makes it an even more appropriate subject for prayer and study.

The third reason debt is a matter of Christian faith is related to the nature of God. The God we are striving to follow is defined in the Old Testament as a God who hears the cry of people who are suffering and promises to deliver them (for example, see Exod. 6). A God who hears the cry of the people is a foundation for the Hebrew understanding of who God is: according to some scholars the basis of the theology of the Psalms, for example. This nature of God is the foundation for the Jubilee legislation too (see Lev. 25.38). A fifth of the world's people are suffering because of unpayable debt. They are not slaves but they are not free either. All through their lives debt will affect their health care

11. P. Selby, *Grace and Mortgage: The Language of Faith and the Debt of the World* (London: Darton, Longman & Todd, 1997), p. 6.

12. Selby, *Grace and Mortgage*, p. 20.

and education. And debt will be a barrier to them escaping from poverty. The God we know from the Bible is also one who inspires people to dream about how things could be different and better (see Isa. 65) even in the worst of times. God does not expect his people to be resigned to slavery.

So I have three personal answers to why we should pray and think and work on debt as a matter of interest for our Christian faith—because it helps us understand our faith better, because it touches an area that is central to our lives and because the nature of God is to hear a suffering world and inspire people to dream and work for a better one.

But for thoughtful readers, I don't think it is good enough just to give you my answers as if they are the only ones. I would like, therefore, to move to the harder part of this paper. The second part of what I would like to do is to expose an approach to thinking theologically about debt. If we don't explore the issue of money enough in Church, how do we begin? What are the resources we bring to the task? The next part of this essay attempts to expose a process for further reflection.

Debt as a Matter of Faith: Part 2, Exposing a Process

We do not start this process from a neutral standpoint. Professionally, my educational work includes studying writings on Leviticus and the Lord's prayer and interpreting them in liturgy and preaching for Churches. I work during the day on publications for Christian Aid Week with reflections on faith and poverty that reach over half a million Churchgoers. But in the evenings, I take care of my children and confront my credit card bills and slight nagging worries about my pension and whether it will provide sufficiently. My pension is of course tied into the stock market and therefore into the global financial system that causes such hardship to the poor. My own ties to the global financial system are typical of most Churchgoers of relative affluence in the north.

So I would like to suggest an old approach to sorting out this tangle in our heads about how debt, and the wider money issues it points to, relate to our faith. I would like to propose that we work with the classic sources that have always informed the theology of individual Christians and the Church. There are at least five sources. There is not enough space in this to explore them, but I would like at least to note them. They are: (1) the Bible, (2) Church tradition, (3) the Church universal, (4) our own experience and (5) prayer.

They all work together, and each can help to interpret the others. Let us begin with the Bible. Debt stories and images are at the core of our Christian faith, grace, freedom and redemption. They spoke to people's real lives; what people knew about money and its power to enslave. To try to rediscover an economic dimension of these scriptures is to try to face these real truths for our own lives.

The central paradigm of the Old Testament, which defines the identity of the people of Israel, is that they became slaves, but God heard and delivered them. It is instructive to consider how they became slaves: in Genesis 47 we read that after a famine they had nothing to exchange for food but their bodies and their land. They forfeited these last possessions and went into slavery.

Later in Exodus 5 we find a succinct study of what slavery means. Pharaoh commanded, 'You shall no longer give the people straw to make bricks; let them gather straw for themselves.' But they still had to make the same number of bricks. Why? Because Pharaoh said 'they were idle liars'. Forced to make bricks without straw, forced to produce for others, punished for not having the means, they suffered the arbitrary and brutal power that is used against the weak. This is one reason why many people who know what it is like to try to pay off their countries' debt compare it to slavery—forced to produce bricks without straw they are punished further for not having the means. In Exodus God heard the cry of the people and freed them. This story is the basis for the laws enacted to keep people from falling below a certain line when they got into debt, including the famous jubilee legislation in Leviticus 25 that has inspired the Jubilee 2000 campaign. These laws were designed to keep people from falling back into slavery from which they had been freed.[13]

Finally, and perhaps most powerfully, there are the stories of people who are very close to becoming slaves. As Neh. 5.1-5 says,

> There was a great outcry of the people against their Jewish kin...for there were those who said, 'We are many, we must get grain, so that we can eat and stay alive.' And others said, 'We are having to pledge our houses, our fields and our vineyards, in order to get grain during the famine.' And others said, 'We are having to borrow money on our fields and vineyards to pay the king's tax.' Now our flesh is the same as that of our kindred; our children are the same as their children, and yet we are forcing our sons and daughters to be slaves, and some of our daughters

13. See Lev. 25.39-42; Deut. 15.

have been ravished; we are powerless, and our fields and our vineyards now belong to others.

This text includes what I believe must be one of the most searching in the Old Testament: '*Our children are the same as their children, and yet we are forcing our sons and daughters to be slaves.*' Nehemiah is angry, and persuades the nobles to stop taking interest on their debts, restore everything they have taken and take nothing more from the people. This is a window on to the ancient world and the terror of debt slavery and how it related to what we sometimes call 'biblical' poverty. It is worth noting that by biblical poverty we mean appalling destitution. Debts and slavery related to debt were one of the chief causes of biblical poverty.

If we turn to the New Testament, debt slavery was still a fearful possibility for some and a reality for many others in the time of Jesus. We often say that the teaching of Jesus is memorable because he talks about everyday things, and one of the everyday realities he talks about is debt slavery and the fear of it. For example, in both Matthew 18 and Luke 7 he makes a point about grace and forgiveness. The kingdom of heaven, he says, is like a king who wished to settle accounts with his slaves (Mt. 18.23). The gist of the story is that the servants who owe their king should be as gracious as the king is to those who owe him. This is the condition on the forgiveness of debts that is given in the Lord's prayer, Matthew 6. Forgive us our debts as we forgive our debtors.

But is debt not a metaphor for sin in both the parables and the prayer? Are we really supposed to be taking them literally, talking about money debts? Well, the language has many layers, and money debts are not the only meaning.[14] But they are one meaning, I would argue, and for two reasons.

14. R. Rustin, 'Forgive Us our Debts', address, 23 January 1998, Oxford. Rustin provides a helpful footnote, echoed by other scholars: 'Commentators usually tell us that "debt" is a metaphor for sin (Schweitzer, Fenton, Green, who says it was used thus by the rabbis). It would clearly be wrong to be narrowly literal about it. The parable of the unforgiving servant shows that something wider than material debt is at stake in the "releasing" that is expected of Jesus' disciples. However in view of Matthew's persistent use of the language of debt, where he might have used the normal Greek word for sin (*hamartia*) as in Luke 11.4, it does not seem wrong to suggest that remission of debts should be part of the work of forgiveness among the disciples. Anyone alive to the basic meaning of the words would have made the connection, unless hardened by generations of "religious" usage or by self-interest.'

First, the level of indebtedness in society at the time of Jesus had led to growing social and economic inequality.[15] In fact, debt was literally a burning issue! Roger Rustin notes that in the year 66 CE, only 30 years after the death of Jesus, Jewish revolutionaries set fire to the house of the high priest Ananias and then 'took their fire to the record office, eager to destroy the money lenders' bonds, and to make impossible the recovery of debts, in order to secure the support of an army of debtors' (Josephus, *War* 2.425). The source for the report, Josephus, a contemporary historian, has nothing but contempt for the poor. About three years later, Josephus reports, 'a young hot head called Simon bar Gioras took advantage of the breakdown in the political order, set up camp in the Judea hill country and proclaimed liberty for slaves and rewards for the free, so collecting the scum of the whole district' (*War* 4.508). In this context of social anxiety about debt, New Testament scholar John Kloppenborg writes, 'Bread and debt were quite simply the most immediate problems facing the Galilean peasant, day labourer, and non-elite town dweller. Alleviation of these two anxieties would be the most obvious benefits of God's reign.'[16] It is unlikely that any ordinary hearers of Jesus would have understood *debt* simply as *sins*. The presence of bread and the absence of debt would have been two signs that the first petition of the prayer had come to pass: Thy kingdom come.

The second reason why we have to include an economic dimension to our understanding of debt is that this is the way that Jesus announced his ministry. In Lk. 4.16 Jesus quotes Isaiah 61 to announce good news to the poor, release to the captives, recovery of sight to the blind and freedom for the oppressed.

These are jubilee terms—terms of release and freedom—that would have been familiar to all of the Jewish hearers of Jesus' message. Of course, there are many meanings to this announcement, and it is sometimes easy for us to forget an obvious one. As Steven Mohammed of the New Testament Church of God in Trinidad says, 'Good news for the poor is that they are poor no more.'[17]

15. See Selby, *Grace and Mortgage*; L. Green, *Jubilee: The Kingdom of God and our New Millennium* (Sheffield: Urban Theology Unit).

16. Cited in Selby, *Grace and Mortgage*, p. 132.

17. Quoted by Joel Edwards, Director, Evangelical Alliance, in an address to Churches Together in England Assembly, Swanwick, England, July 1997.

I mentioned above that there were other sources that we can find helpful as we try to understand our faith in relation to debt issues. After the Bible, the second classic source for Christian theology, and for our own exploration of what debt means for our faith, is Church tradition. For 1,600 years the weight of Church tradition was unanimous that it was not acceptable to charge interest on loans. Charging interest, as Peter Selby points out,

> was expressly forbidden to clergy by the third century Councils of Arles (314) and Niceae (325), the ban extended to laity in the fourth century council. It continues to be condemned in the Middle Ages in a tradition that Martin Luther maintained.[18]

We know that there were hypocrisies in the practice of this policy and that it led to persecution of Jews by Christians, as they were legally allowed to hold the purse strings. But it is challenging that in all the history of the Church John Calvin was the first major Church thinker to consider a change in this policy. As a result, we can contrast the whole weight of the tradition of the Church with the widely held attitudes in our Churches today. There is a critical edge of Church tradition waiting to be recovered for our own times.

Besides the Bible and Church tradition, we can learn about what debt means for our faith by trying to listen to as many voices as possible within the world Church. This helps to keep us honest too. Consider the words of Rachel Gomez, in El Salvador:

> The effects of debt on our communities are critical. People do not have enough food or jobs. Things are very expensive and every day interest and inflation gets higher. Children are abandoned to work on the streets. Young people have no direction and a sense of meaninglessness.

Her colleague, Luis Alberto Garcia, puts this in terms of a challenge for our faith. He says:

> The war of the rich against the poor has not finished. And that is precisely what foreign debt is. So it is in this moment that the year of the Lord's grace should be announced and proclaimed. It is necessary to remind the powerful of this world that they can't become owners nor take power over human life, nor of the planet itself. All we have, all that is here, is God's. It belongs to God and to no one else.

So far, I have tried to answer the question about what debt has to do with faith. I gave you my three answers. I have also discussed three

18. Selby, *Grace and Mortgage*, p. 124.

sources that can inform our own theology about debt and how it matters for faith: the Bible, Church tradition and the universal Church. There are two more sources that are also very important. They are our personal experience and prayer.

Our own difficulties and experience are a source for theology that matters. In fact, as the credit card bills land on our doorsteps, we know, as profoundly as the people who wrote the Bible, what it is like to live in a world that is in the grip of money as a God. John Hull, Professor of Education at Birmingham University, has spent much of his career researching barriers to adult Christian learning.[19] In recent years he has been probing the effects of the money culture on spirituality. He believes now that worship of what he calls the 'Money God' is the most formidable obstacle to learning in faith.

He says that we invest in money all the qualities we invest in God, but less explicitly. 'There is a structural and psychological analogy between Money and God', he says.[20] For example, as money is the ground and value of all commodities, so too we say that God is not an entity among entities, but the ground and source of value of all else. Our spiritual language about God expresses a belief that God is the means through which our desires will be fulfilled. But our everyday actions reveal that we actually believe this about money; it is the means through which we will achieve all our other desires. We read that our hearts long for God as the hart longs for the flowing stream. In fact, the words of Psalm 42 could have been written to describe how I feel about money as I contemplate my personal finances. Let me be clear. We know the grip of the Money God as profoundly as the people who were inspired to write the Bible. One strand of the tangled web we weave about debt and the money issues it raises for our faith is idolatry. M.P. Joseph, a theologian writing from India, roots the entire debt crisis in this idolatry. International debt, he says, is 'the crisis of faith today. The God of death is worshipped as the real God when the God of life is ignored or condemned as heresy.'[21]

19. J. Hull, *What Prevents Christian Adults from Learning?* (London: SCM Press, 1985).

20. J. Hull, 'God and the Global Economy', address, Cardiff, November 1998.

21. M.P. Joseph, 'Worship of Moloch: A Theological Critique of National Debt', in J. Widyatmadja and J. Damanik (eds.), *'No More Yoke on our Neck': 50 Years of Independence of Indonesia* (Surakarta: Action Group on Social and Development Policy, Social Welfare Guidance Foundation, 1995).

The good news is we can get free of the grip of the Money God. The bad news is that we have to confront our own tendencies to idolatry. That is why, as Luis Garcia can see from El Salvador, the Jubilee 2000 campaign 'also has to be a search for the conversion of all humanity, a sign of hope for everyone in which the rich will also benefit'.

One difference between God and money is how we talk about the subjects in Church. We try to be specific about God in Church. But when we talk about money we become curiously vague. It is a weakness of our Church life that John Hull points out when he says that although in many respects we are living in the grip of the power of global capital that reaches into the lives and hearts of each of us, we have not developed the resources or the courage in Churches to try to confront this in prayer and study. 'We are in danger of worshipping the Money God in all aspects of our lives', he says, 'and all we have in the Churches is a theology of stewardship.'

If this is true, we will need all our wits and resources to try to unseat the idol who threatens to take the place of God in our lives—the Bible, Church tradition, the experience of the world Church and trying to discern our own experiences and feelings about money.

All this about worshipping money is very tough, very personal, very painful and very complex. And the only way out of these dilemmas is straight though the middle. So, the relationship of debt and the money issues it points to and our Christian faith is the perfect subject for prayer. That is the last of the resources we bring to an exploration of debt and faith. This is the kind of prayer that might be the first thing we do. If we do it honestly, it won't be the last.

Conclusion

The poor of the world are in the grip of unpayable debts that they are nonetheless expected to pay. In the second and third part of the essay, there were two answers to the question, What does debt have to do with faith? First, my own answers: debt slavery and freedom from it are at the core of our Christian faith. Throughout the Old Testament and in the New Testament God hears the cry of the people and promises to set us free. That is who God is.

In the third part of the essay I tried to expose an approach to considering the issues using the classic tools of theology: resources from the Bible, the universal Church, our own experiences and difficulties. As a matter of *interest*, all of these sources suggest to us that it is in each of our interests to explore debt as a matter of *faith*. Study of *debt* leads us into a *Bible* where people testify to the power of the Money God and the possibility that we can be free from it. And the *Bible* leads us into the *world* where we know all too well this power and we need to hear that we can be free. The health of our faith and the health of the world are profoundly linked. Isaiah saw the link so clearly:

> If you remove the yoke from among you...if you pour yourselves out for the hungry... The Lord will guide you continually, and satisfy your needs in parched places, and make your bones strong... And you shall raise up the foundations of many generations; and you shall be called the repairer of the breach, the restorer of streets to live in (Isa. 58.9-12).

FORGIVENESS, THE JUBILEE AND WORLD DEBT

Simon J. Taylor

Introduction: Forgiveness as a Theological and an Economic Theme

Peter Selby's work on debt focuses specifically on the language that both faith and economics have in common. He writes that

> the language of gift and debt...of mercy and demand, of forgiveness and judgment, of calling to account and remission of dues, all turns out to be deeply embedded not simply in deviates about 'social ethics'—what the gospel *im*plies, or how it can be *ap*plied—but in the way in which the gospel has been understood and the Christ at the centre of it has been understood.[1]

Thus for Selby, the (economic) language of debt is at the heart of Christian theology. How we understand debt will affect how we understand the gospel and vice versa. This is not simply an 'ethical' question, independent of the content of our faith, but is entwined with the very substance and expression of that faith. As H.R. Mackintosh said,

> Forgiveness clearly is one of the *foci*—although not necessarily the only one—from which it is at once possible and natural to survey the whole circumference of Christian truth, and to determine the relationship which obtains between one conviction and another. It implies a distinctive view of God, of man, of sin, of the universe as supernaturally constituted, of Jesus.[2]

This close connection between forgiveness, as an economic term to do with debts, and the heart of Christian theology forms the starting point for this essay. It cannot be seen any more clearly than in the Lord's

1. P. Selby, *Grace and Mortgage: The Language of Faith and the Debt of the World* (London: Darton, Longman & Todd, 1997), pp. 8-9.
2. H.R. Mackintosh, *The Christian Experience of Forgiveness* (London: Nisbet, 1927), p. 1.

Prayer. 'Forgive us our debts, as we forgive our debtors' is the language both of theology and of economics.[3]

I hope to explore the use of language of forgiveness in the current debate about debt relief. This language provides a point of contact between the theological and economic spheres in a way that resists a simple reduction of one to the other. Language of forgiveness is neither simply economic nor simply theological, in whatever sense of those words you want to use. I shall outline an understanding of forgiveness from a theological perspective, which should provide some categories for an understanding of proposals of debt relief. Using these categories, I shall examine two proposals for debt relief, those enshrined in the Heavily Indebted Poor Countries Initiative, which is the scheme advocated by the World Bank and the International Monetary Fund (IMF), and the proposals of the Jubilee 2000 campaign. I offer these reflections as a Christian theologian, rather than as an economist, but I do offer them as an understanding of forgiveness, which I hope will be of relevance to the issue at hand.

Cheap, Costly and Too-Costly Forgiveness

The reason for the intimate connection between forgiveness and the central tenets of Christian faith is that forgiveness is bound up with the saving work of Christ. Forgiveness, for Christian theology, is not arbitrary, nor a minor religious nicety. Rather it is a constituent part of Christian faith, centred on and shaped by the cross and resurrection of Christ. Forgiveness is therefore inescapably concerned with, and rooted in, the nature of God as revealed in Christ. The Christian understanding of forgiveness thus has a twofold nature: God's forgiveness of us being taken as a model for our forgiveness of each other. 'Forgive us our debts, as we forgive our debtors.'

We must begin by saying that God's forgiveness is also God's judgment. In forgiving us, God also judges us. This is fundamental for a

3. There is some variation between the versions of the Lord's prayer found in Matthew, Luke and the *Didache*. Matthew uses the word ὀφειλήματα (Mt. 6.12), Luke uses ἁμαρτίας (sins) in the first clause, but ὀφείλοντι in the second (Lk. 11.4). The *Didache*, another important source for the prayer, uses ὀφειλεῖν (*Did.* 8.2). In all three, therefore, the root ὀφειλ- is used. This word has as its primary meaning a debt, although it had also become an established way to speak of sin by the first century (see *TDNT*, V, pp. 559-66).

correct understanding of forgiveness. It is as we are forgiven that we come to see fully that for which we are forgiven. We *are* forgiven, but we cannot ignore the fact that for there to be sin to be forgiven, it must be acknowledged as *sin*, it must be judged sinful. Judgment and forgiveness are correlates, they cannot be considered in isolation. It would be wrong to speak of judgment without speaking of God's forgiveness; equally it is wrong to speak of forgiveness without mentioning God's judgment. It is for this reason that the Church has decisively linked forgiveness and repentance in its liturgy. From the earliest call of Jesus to 'repent and believe in the gospel' (Mk 1.14), through the Apostles' call to 'repent and be baptised' (Acts 2.38), to the liturgical practices of confession and absolution, there is no forgiveness that is not bound up with repentance.

Much of my argument so far draws on the work of Dietrich Bonhoeffer, and in particular his rejection of 'cheap grace'. For Bonhoeffer,

> Cheap grace is the preaching of forgiveness without requiring repentance, baptism without church discipline, Communion without confession, absolution without personal confession. Cheap grace is grace without discipleship, grace without the cross, grace without Jesus Christ, living and incarnate.[4]

Coming out of the context of nineteenth-century German liberal Protestantism, Bonhoeffer was to find the individualist and privatized understanding of forgiveness it taught utterly bankrupt in the face of the Third Reich.[5] Bonhoeffer, like Barth before him, had become convinced that the liberal Protestantism of his teachers was a cheapened version of the Christian gospel, so cheapened that it may have ceased actually to be the Christian gospel. In this 'cheap forgiveness', sin is no longer confronted and so it is no longer dealt with.

Essentially, I think, there are two elements to Bonhoeffer's criticisms of cheap grace. First, he rejects it because it is not *grace*, that is, it is not the grace offered by God but an alternative grace. Instead it is a falsely reassuring grace. 'Cheap grace is the grace we bestow on ourselves.'[6] The second criticism Bonhoeffer has of this grace is that it is ineffec-

4. D. Bonhoeffer, *The Cost of Discipleship* (trans. R.H. Fuller and I. Booth; London: SCM Press, 1959), p. 36.

5. Cf. Bonhoeffer, *Discipleship*, p. 46: 'Deceived and weakened, men felt that they were strong now that they were in possession of this cheap grace—whereas they had in fact lost the power to live the life of discipleship and obedience.'

6. Bonhoeffer, *Discipleship*, p. 36.

tual. This is primarily a result of it being a grace other than God's grace. Since cheap grace is not really grace at all, the forgiveness it pretends to bestow is not really forgiveness. On the basis of this, we can distinguish an understanding of forgiveness that is to be avoided, which we may call, following Bonhoeffer, 'cheap forgiveness'.[7] Cheap forgiveness is forgiveness that seeks to avoid the requirement of judgment and repentance. In its avoidance of these it ceases to be efficacious forgiveness, it ceases to be grace, because it fails to address the sin for which forgiveness is required. Instead we should look for a 'costly forgiveness', derived from Bonhoeffer's account of 'costly grace', which faces the issue of judgment as a necessary part of forgiveness:

> Such grace is *costly* because it calls us to follow, and it is *grace* because it calls us to follow *Jesus Christ*. It is costly because it costs a man his life, and it is grace because it gives a man the only true life. It is costly because it condemns sin, and grace because it justifies the sinner. Above all, it is *costly* because it cost God the life of his Son...and what has cost God much cannot be cheap for us. Above all, it is *grace* because God did not reckon his Son too dear a price to pay for our life, but delivered him up for us. Costly grace is the Incarnation of God.[8]

'Costly forgiveness' will require an embodiment of that forgiveness in repentance and discipleship. For Bonhoeffer, forgiveness issues in the life of discipleship, and he speaks of the 'mutual relationship between grace and discipleship'.[9] Gregory Jones writes that 'forgiveness is a craft that must be learned...and embodied over time as people seek to become holy in communion with God and one another'.[10] Both Bonhoeffer and Jones offer profound and insightful visions of Christian forgiveness. What is unusual about each of their accounts is that both Bonhoeffer (a Lutheran) and Jones (a Methodist) advocate the recovery of the discipline of confession. For Bonhoeffer, confession is 'liberation through truth'.[11] It is God working through the Church to counteract the isolating effects of sin and to enable the 'break-through to com-

7. On this see also L. Gregory Jones, *Embodying Forgiveness: A Theological Analysis* (Grand Rapids: Eerdmans, 1995), ch. 1.

8. Bonhoeffer, *Discipleship*, p. 37.

9. Bonhoeffer, *Discipleship*, p. 47.

10. Jones, *Embodying*, p. 13.

11. D. Bonhoeffer, *Life Together* (trans. J.W. Doberstein; London: SCM Press, 1954), p. 86.

munity'.[12] This communal aspect is very significant. Bonhoeffer writes that

> [s]ince the confession of sin is made in the presence of a Christian brother, the last stronghold of self-justification is abandoned. The sinner surrenders; he gives up all his evil. He gives his heart to God, and he finds the forgiveness of all his sin in the fellowship of Jesus Christ and his brother. The expressed, acknowledged sin has lost all its power. It has been revealed and judged as sin. It can no longer tear the fellowship asunder. Now the fellowship bears the sin of the brother. He is no longer alone with his evil for he has cast off his sin in confession and handed it over to God. It has been taken away from him. Now he stands in the fellowship of sinners who live by the grace of God in the Cross of Jesus Christ. Now he can be a sinner and still enjoy the grace of God. He can confess his sins and in this very act find fellowship for the first time. The sin concealed separated him from the fellowship, made all his apparent fellowship a sham; the sin confessed has helped him to find true fellowship with the brethren in Jesus Christ.[13]

Out of this we can begin to see that forgiveness is an activity that involves us in community, and indeed enables the foundation of community. This community is based on a twofold mutuality. The first mutuality is the mutual acknowledgment and naming of sin in confession. This is the communal resistance to cheap grace. The second mutuality is the confession to another who recognizes themselves as a sinner; as Bonhoeffer puts it, '[o]nly the brother under the Cross can hear a confession'.[14] It is a sinner that pronounces pardon. The forgiven life is a life in the community of sinners. This involves mutual forgiveness based on God's forgiveness. This is the communal expression of grace. As an earlier writer on forgiveness has put it, '[t]he pardoned life, when equal to its idea, is a life in which each is debtor to all the rest'.[15]

It is in this way that we are to understand the two petitions of the Lord's Prayer, 'forgive us our debts, as we forgive our debtors'. Forgiveness is based on God's judgment and condemnation of sin. Forgiveness that does not acknowledge and condemn sin is cheap forgiveness and is neither Christian nor effective. For there to be real forgiveness of sin, there must be true confession and acknowledgment of that sin. This

12. Bonhoeffer, *Life Together*, p. 87.
13. Bonhoeffer, *Life Together*, p. 88.
14. Bonhoeffer, *Life Together*, p. 93.
15. Mackintosh, *Christian Experience*, p. 268.

enables the creation of a community of the forgiven sinners based on a mutuality of forgiveness. This costly forgiveness is both Christian and effective in all its costliness.

There is also a third position that we should consider alongside cheap and costly forgiveness. If cheap forgiveness denies our status as sinners, then we might speak of a 'too-costly forgiveness', which emphasizes it too much. Here I have moved beyond Bonhoeffer's two categories to add a third. Too-costly forgiveness is, I think, a necessary addition, as it helps us to see the theological problems caused by an overemphasis on the cost of costly forgiveness at the expense of forgiveness. If forgiveness is too costly, then sin still dominates, there is no forgiveness, no freedom from sin, no foundation for community, no grace. Too-costly forgiveness allows judgment to have the final word, rather than grace. It is, to rework Bonhoeffer, repentance without forgiveness, discipline without baptism, confession without communion, personal confession without absolution, discipleship without grace. It is to concentrate on the sin that is forgiven rather than the forgiveness that releases us from sin. This goes against the insight that Gregory Jones brings to the subject, writing that '[w]e have been judged, and thus we acknowledge our sinfulness; but that judgment is wholly in the service of grace, healing, and holiness'.[16] Too-costly forgiveness is not efficacious, because in its refusal to let go of the sin forgiven it refuses the possibility of forgiveness.

In advocating an understanding of forgiveness that avoids the pitfalls of cheap and too-costly forgiveness, we have paid special attention to the role of judgment. Here we are faced with a final problem. Gregory Jones rightly reminds us that 'forgiveness invariably involves power and the dynamics of power-relations'.[17] The danger of the approach I have suggested, at least when understood in the context of my forgiving another, is that it allows me to use the need for judgment to achieve a position of power over my neighbour. Here the issue is not about the cost of forgiveness, but who is to bear the cost of forgiveness. In addressing this, we must pay attention to the mutuality that we identified earlier as being involved in forgiveness. Among human beings, we are all sinners, we all stand in need of forgiveness both from God and from one another. The cost of forgiveness, if it really is forgiveness, will be

16. Jones, *Embodying*, p. 147.
17. Jones, *Embodying*, p. 148.

shared. It will be costly to both forgiver and forgiven. The cost of forgiveness cannot be borne entirely by the one forgiven. If it costs the forgiver nothing, then it is not true forgiveness, since the forgiver has not given up the claim on the forgiven implied by the need for forgiveness. If the granting of forgiveness fails to acknowledge the mutuality involved in forgiveness, then the forgiveness offered is not true forgiveness, but serves only to bolster an ideological claim to power on the part of those claiming to forgive.

Forgiving Debts

We are now in a position to begin to assess what our account of forgiveness can say to the current debate on world debt. We should begin by noting that the language of forgiveness is used by a variety of different agencies in connection with debt. To illustrate this, a quick internet search of the IMF and World Bank websites produces a number of references to the HIPC Initiative and specific instances of debt relief. The World Bank and IMF speak of a United States proposal to the review of the Heavily Indebted Poor Countries (HIPC) Initiative of 'complete forgiveness' of certain claims,[18] an earlier World Bank report speaks of 'Grants and Debt Forgiveness in Africa',[19] and an IMF press release quotes a Mozambican minister as saying that 'it would have been our desire to receive total debt forgiveness' from the HIPC Initiative.[20] My straw poll foundered somewhat when the Jubilee 2000 website refused all attempts to be searched. Elsewhere, however, I did find Martin Dent, one of the founders of Jubilee 2000, speaking of Lloyd's Bank's 'fear as to how to set limits to this principle of forgiveness'.[21] It is clear that the language of debt forgiveness does permeate the debate

18. World Bank and IMF, 'Heavily Indebted Poor Countries (HIPC) Initiative—Perspectives on the Current Framework and Options for Change', 2 April, 1999, Table 1 [http.//www.imf.org/external/np/hipc/options/index.htm].

19. L. Hernández and S.N. Katada, 'Grants and Debt Forgiveness in Africa' (Washington, DC International Finance Division, International Economics Department, World Bank, September 1996).

20. Tomáz Salomão cited in 'Debt Relief Package of Nearly US$3 Billion Approved for Mozambique', IMF press release, 7 April 1998 [http.//www.imf.org/external/np/sec/pr/1998/PR9812.htm].

21. M. Dent, 'Theological Help in an Urgent Economic Crisis: Jubilee 2000', *Crucible* 33 (1994), pp. 24-35 (28).

on debt relief, along with other terminology, such as that of cancellation of debt or debt relief. These three terms appear, at least to me, to be used almost interchangeably.

Having established, all too briefly, the linguistic basis for my remarks, I now want to ask what the discussion of forgiveness with which I began has to contribute to the ongoing debate about debt forgiveness. There are two key concepts that emerge out of the above discussion. The first is that of judgment. Without this, we saw, any understanding of forgiveness is cheapened. Yet without the emphasis on the grace of forgiveness, this leads all too easily to what I have called 'too-costly forgiveness'. The other concept that comes out of the preceding discussion is that of mutuality. At its most basic, this is the recognition that forgiveness is something that occurs in the context of a community. The crucial issue that the concept of mutuality in forgiveness raises is where the cost of forgiveness is borne. The question that must concern us here is whether we can see these as relevant to the debate about world debt, and if so how. It will hardly be surprising to learn that I think that these concepts are very relevant to the debate. The concept of judgment provides an important contribution to the debate over the conditionality of debt. This is an important aspect of the current debate and the campaigns associated with it. More controversially, I think that the concept of mutuality provides an important impetus towards rethinking the context in which debt forgiveness has been discussed. I shall look at each in turn.

Conditionality is relatively uncontroversial in principle. The HIPC Initiative has a number of conditions attached to it concerning level of indebtedness, a track record of good economic performance, and a maximum level of reduction. The Jubilee 2000 campaign is calling for the cancellation of all unpayable debts, which accordingly requires that the minimum condition of unpayability be attached to the debt. The specific conditions that each require will be considered in greater detail later. In general, we can say, therefore, that conditionality attached to debt relief serves at least two functions. It serves to ensure that the money released by the forgiveness of debt is used in appropriate ways and that the country which has received debt relief does not immediately fall back into the position of having an unsustainable debt. The IMF paints the broad picture well when it states that

> unconditional debt cancellation risks debt relief being squandered on corruption, military expenditure, or grandiose projects with little if any

> benefit in terms of sustainable growth or poverty reduction. In addition, this could further erode support for aid flows in developed countries.[22]

The twin requirements of sustainability and poverty reduction are broadly (and perhaps only broadly) agreed by most participants in the debate. This is, I think, appropriately understood as an attempt to avoid 'cheap forgiveness'. It takes seriously the reasons for indebtedness and the reasons for the forgiveness of debt.

What remains is a concern to avoid too-costly forgiveness, and this is where most of the debate over the relief of the current debt problem has occurred. Too-costly forgiveness is characterized by a domination by the concept of judgment, and a failure to allow real forgiveness to occur. In terms of conditionality, this would mean that the conditions imposed are too onerous, and the failure to allow the amount of debt forgiven to reach a level at which a significant difference to the debtor economy would be made. It is clear that in looking at the prospects for debt relief under the HIPC Initiative and the proposals of Jubilee 2000, we must be concerned with whether they will allow this, or whether they fail to bring real debt forgiveness. The issue here is again one of the need to make a judgment.

As we saw earlier, the mutuality of community functions as a continuing context for forgiveness. This context cannot prevent bad judgments about forgiveness and its cost, but it does provide a means by which the relationship of creditor and debtor may be examined. We noted earlier that forgiveness involves a relationship of power, and that there is a constant danger of the power to forgive being abused so that the cost of forgiveness falls only on the forgiven. The two forms of mutuality that we identified are important here. The mutual recognition of sinfulness is significant because it implies that both debtors and creditors have a responsibility in the problems that have arisen over debt in the current context. Loans must not only be asked for, they must be granted. Responsible borrowing finds its counterpart in responsible lending. There is an element of risk in the creation of debt and this must be shared between creditor and borrower. It is not responsible to lend when it is clear that the debtor will not be able to repay and that a situation of deepening indebtedness will result. Nor, however, is it responsible to simply allow debtors who have squandered their loans to be

22. IMF, 'HIPC Initiative: The IMF's Response to Critics', September 1998 [http.//imfnt1x.imf.org.80/external/np/hipc/res.htm].

given more money to squander. The issues of moral hazard here must be addressed by any proposed debt forgiveness.

Beyond this, however, there is the mutual recognition of forgiveness. What is needed from debt forgiveness in regard to this is the willingness to admit errors and to change policies, and above all to surrender the power over the debtor that is conferred on the creditor by the debt. In short, a commitment not to take any one economic model as ideologically given, but rather to recognize the need for continual reassessment of such models, and to allow former debtors to become fully equal members of the international community. Without this, conditionality in relation to debt forgiveness can be at best ineffective, and at worst, a naked manipulation of the debtor countries.

I shall now turn to look at the concrete proposals for debt forgiveness proposed by the HIPC Initiative and Jubilee 2000. In both cases, I shall use the issues of conditionality and the sharing of risk as the basis of my analysis. The categories of cheap and too-costly forgiveness will also prove helpful as we approach the strategies that are currently at the fore of the debate.

The Heavily Indebted Poor Countries Initiative

The HIPC Initiative is a joint initiative launched in September 1996 by the World Bank and the IMF. It recognizes that 'many heavily indebted poor countries (HIPCs) continue to have difficulty in paying their external debt-service obligations, largely because of exogenous factors, imprudent debt-management policies, and the lack of sustained adjustment or implementation of structural reforms' and aims 'to reduce the debt burden of all eligible HIPCs to sustainable levels'.[23] It takes a case-by-case approach and aims to reach a sustainable level of debt for the countries it considers. It builds on both existing debt relief measures (the Brady Plan and the Paris Club flow reschedulings) and also on the structural adjustment policies that the IMF and World Bank have been advocating for a number of years now. Its greatest significance lies in the fact that it represents a coordinated approach to debt forgiveness among all the creditors, including the multilateral financial institutions. One commentator from outside the institutions responsible for the Initiative has suggested that

23. A.R. Boote and K. Thugge, *Debt Relief for Low Income Countries: The HIPC Initiative* (IMF Pamphlet Series, 51; Washington, DC: IMF, 1997), p. v.

> HIPC may be the single most important step toward resolving the debt crisis of the 1980s and 1990s. Its fundamental contribution is the recognition, for the first time, that any long term resolution of the problem requires debt CANCELLATION and that all lenders, including the multilaterals, must participate.[24]

The Initiative's achievement in bringing together all creditors in a unified strategy to obtain a once and for all exit from the problems of the indebtedness of the HIPCs is hugely significant.

At present HIPC is undergoing a thorough review process, and between that and the G-7 summit in Cologne in June 1999 it seems likely that its terms will be expanded. However, here I am considering the Initiative as it was set up in 1996, which is the form of the Initiative until such time as the review or the G-7 changes it. The Initiative is open to all countries who are eligible for the IMF's Enhanced Structural Adjustment Facility (ESAF)[25] and who are only eligible for funds from the International Development Association (IDA).[26] There are currently 41 countries classified by the World Bank as HIPCs. Of these, 31 meet these entry requirements.[27]

The first stage of the Initiative requires countries to follow a programme of adjustment and reform supported by the IMF and World Bank for three years. During this period the country will get conventional assistance from the relevant donors and creditors. The aim of this

24. J. Hanlon, 'HIPC Heresies and the Flat Earth Response' (London: Jubilee 2000 Coalition, April 1998), p. 2.

25. ESAF is the concessional support given by the IMF to poor countries undertaking structural adjustment to bring their macro-economic policies into line with IMF preferences.

26. The IDA is that branch of the World Bank that lends at concessional rates of interest. It is only available to poor countries. IDA-only countries are those who are ineligible for the Bank's normal loans.

27. See Development Committee of the World Bank and the IMF, 'The Initiative for Heavily Indebted Poor Countries: Review and Outlook', 22 September 1998, p. 7. Of the ten countries that do not meet the entry requirements for the Initiative, one (Nigeria) is not IDA-only. Most of the remaining nine (Angola, Burundi, Democratic Republic of Congo, Equatorial Guinea, Liberia, Myanmar, São Tomé and Príncipe, Somalia and Sudan) have recently suffered conflicts and thus require different treatment. At present there are no arrangements for post-conflict countries, but this seems likely to be changed following the review of the Initiative. Of these nine, the Development Committee report suggests that only Angola and Equatorial Guinea are likely to have potentially sustainable debt.

first phase is to establish a track record of good performance on a macroeconomic level. This track record is

> necessary to ensure a lasting solution not only to the country's debt problems but to its underlying economic difficulties; it will also be necessary in order to give confidence to creditors and donors that the exceptional assistance will be put to good use.[28]

After three years the 'decision point' is reached. At this point a calculation is made of the sustainability of the debt of the country undergoing the Initiative. If the country's projected debt is decided to be sustainable, then the country is taken out of the Initiative and given continuing support by conventional means. If the projected debt is deemed to be unsustainable, then the country enters the second stage of the HIPC Initiative. Here a second period of three years' good performance is established, and debts are continued to be rescheduled, but at a more concessional rate. This culminates in the completion point, when the debt stock of the country is reduced by up to 80 per cent of its Net Present Value (NPV),[29] and adjustments made to the debts owed to the multilateral institutions in order to make the country's debt sustainable. The World Bank and IMF believe that the Initiative

> should enable HIPCs to exit from the debt-rescheduling process...implementation of the initiative should remove debt as a barrier to economic development and growth and enable HIPC governments to focus on the difficult policies and reforms required to remove the remaining impediments to achieving sustainable development.[30]

They estimate that by 2000, at least six countries should have passed the completion point.[31] Of these Uganda and Bolivia have already reached that point.

It would be very hard to describe the HIPC Initiative as cheap forgiveness. The exclusion of ten HIPCs from entry into the initiative and the six-year time frame for its implementation in any individual country force us to resist this conclusion. The IMF, in particular, has empha-

28. Boote and Thugge, *HIPC Initiative*, p. 20.

29. NPV is the 'sum of all future debt-service obligations (interest and principal) on existing debt, discounted at the market interest rate' (Boote and Thugge, *HIPC Initiative*, p. 39). It is equivalent to the amount that would have to be invested now in order to meet projected debt service payments.

30. Boote and Thugge, *HIPC Initiative*, p. v.

31. Development Committee, 'Review and Outlook', p. 10.

sized the centrality of the use of ESAF programmes to the effectiveness of the Initiative. The IMF brief guide to the Initiative states that

> [c]entral to the Initiative is the country's [being considered for debt forgiveness under the HIPC Initiative] continued effort toward macroeconomic adjustment and structural and social policy reforms.[32]

Rightly cautious toward seeing debt relief as a *panacea* for poverty relief, Michel Camdessus (the Managing Director of the IMF) has suggested that it be seen as

> just one—at times essential—component of a package of policy change and financial support available to any eligible country determined to enter into a partnership with the international community to pull itself out of poverty.[33]

He goes on to suggest a fivefold strategy for helping the poorest countries, of which policy adjustment and structural reform is the first. With the weight that is given to such issues, the HIPC Initiative cannot be seen as cheap forgiveness.

Most of the criticisms of the HIPC Initiative have been concerned with the cost of its forgiveness. The Initiative, while widely welcomed as an important development in the way the international community considers the issue of indebtedness, has been criticized at virtually every stage. Two fairly obvious criticisms are the eligibility of countries and the timescale involved in obtaining forgiveness under the HIPC Initiative. The HIPC Initiative recognizes 41 HIPCs, while the Jubilee 2000 campaign believes there to be 52.[34] The requirement that three years' track record of adherence to ESAF is required is a further limiting requirement, with Oxfam noting that this effectively limited the number of countries eligible at the time of the Initiative's launch to two,

32. IMF, 'Debt Initiative for the Heavily Indebted Poor Countries (HIPCs)', September 1998 [http.//imfnt1x.imf.org/external/np/hipc/hipc.htm].

33. M. Camdessus, 'Addressing Concerns for the Poor and Social Justice in Debt Relief and Adjustment Programmes', speech to a Conference on the Ethical Dimensions of International Debt, Seton Hall University, New Jersey, 22 October 1998 [http.//imfnt1x.imf.org.80/external/np/speeches/1998/102298.htm].

34. Jubilee 2000 believes Gambia, Guyana, Haiti, Jamaica, Malawi, Morocco, Peru and Zimbabwe should be added to the list of HIPCs recognized by the international financial institutions. See I. Hanson and A. Travis (eds.), *Breaking the Chains: The New Jubilee 2000 Debt Cutter's Handbook* (London: Jubilee 2000, 1999), pp. 42-43. I am grateful to Jenny Humphreys for this reference.

Uganda and Bolivia.[35] This brings up the issue of the timescale involved in the Initiative. Whereas previous Paris Club programmes had required only three years before rescheduling took place, the HIPC Initiative doubles this, requiring three years before the decision point and a further three years before completion and additional debt relief.[36] Countries emerging from situations of conflict, and thus in most need of aid, must start from the beginning of the six-year timetable in order to qualify for forgiveness under the Initiative. Oxfam's assessment of this is clear. 'Stated bluntly, six years is too long for countries emerging from conflict or facing chronic social and economic problems related to debt to wait for debt relief.'[37]

Serious as they are, these criticisms do not affect significantly the structure of the Initiative. It would be relatively easy to broaden the entry requirements and speed up the process. Indeed, there is some evidence that this is likely to happen.[38] However, there are some problems that are markedly more significant. Not the least of these is the definition of sustainable debt that the HIPC Initiative uses. According to the Initiative,[39] the debt stock of a country is considered to be sustainable if they fall within the range of '200 percent to 250 percent for the debt-to-exports ratio expressed in NPV terms[40] and 20 percent to 25 percent for the ratio for debt service to exports[41]'. These target ranges are country specific, but the ranges themselves are fixed. To give some context to these figures, the debt-service-to-export ratio agreed for the UK after the Second World War was 4 per cent and that for Germany agreed in 1953 was 3.5 per cent. The high levels of Germany's debt repayments after the First World War were between 13 per cent and 15 per cent.[42] That the UK and Germany should now be taking a lead in reducing the debts of the HIPCs is only right, given that the HIPC Initiative, as it

35. Oxfam International, 'Assessment of IMF–World Bank Debt Reduction Initiative', March 1996 [http.//www.oneworld.org/oxfam.policy/papers/debt.htm].

36. Hanlon, 'HIPC Heresies', p. 6.

37. Oxfam, 'Assessment'.

38. See A. Brummer, 'Britain Is Debt Relief's Talmudic Prophet', *The Guardian*, 24 April 1999, p. 23.

39. Boote and Thugge, *HIPC Initiative*, p. 10.

40. This is the ratio of the NPV (see above, n. 30) to the total annual export of a country.

41. This is the ratio of annual payments of the interest and principal of a loan to total annual exports.

42. See Hanlon, 'HIPC Heresies', pp. 14-15.

now stands, demands of HIPCs five times the levels of repayment that both countries agreed after the last war.[43]

If there must be a suspicion that the cost of forgiveness under the HIPC Initiative is too high, then we must also ask where that cost is to fall. Here particular attention must be paid to the Initiative's insistence on good performance under ESAF before any forgiveness is offered. Structural adjustment programmes have been a feature of the work of the World Bank and the IMF since the 1980s. They consist of macro-economic policies that a country has to put in place before debt relief or future loans will be provided by the multilateral financial institutions. These reforms are intended to promote economic growth in the countries that adopt them. Typically they involve a country expanding its export capacity so as to obtain foreign capital (usually dollars) through cash cropping, government spending cuts, privatization, wage freezes and price increases. A full assessment of the impact and the problems associated with structural adjustment would require far more space than is available to this essay. What is clear is that these problems are major problems. The drive to exports has left countries dependent upon imported food, which in turn leaves them vulnerable to currency fluctuations. Oxfam describes such programmes as 'ineffective, even on its own terms',[44] and one commentator has even called these programmes a form of 'economic genocide'.[45] For our purposes, what must suffice is the recognition that in all of this no power is allowed to remain with the debtor country government. The structural reforms are an effective means of removing the debtor government's control over their own

43. Oxfam have also expressed reservations about the choice of indicators for debt sustainability. They argue that the concentration on debt to export ratios does not capture the scale of HIPCs' vulnerability to debt. Oxfam suggests three further indicators: export concentration (reflecting the dependence on just one product for a large proportion of export income); debt to public revenue ratio (reflecting the proportion of government expenditure that is taken up by debt service); and balance-of-payments weakness (reflecting the amount by which aid is paid by donor countries back to themselves in debt relief). The HIPC Initiative considers each of these factors to be relevant as indicators of vulnerability, but Oxfam argues that in practice only the debt/export ratios are used to decide qualification for HIPC Initiative debt relief (see Oxfam, 'Poor Country Debt Relief: False Dawn or New Hope for Poverty Reduction?', 1998 [http.//www.oneworld.org/oxfam/policy/papers/ debtdawn.htm]).

44. Oxfam, 'Poor Country Debt Relief'.

45. M. Chossudovsky, *The Globalisation of Poverty: Impacts of IMF and World Bank Reforms* (London: Zed, 1997), p. 37.

economic policies. Structural adjustment programmes have the ultimate effect of undermining democracy and promoting the interests of the rich creditor nations. They have resulted in an effective guarantee of an abundant supply of cheap commodities for consumers in the richer countries, while promoting the dependence of poorer economies on these exports. Moreover, the very adjustments made to debtor economies are not required of the rich countries. As Paul Spray of Christian Aid has suggested, we need 'structural adjustment in northern industrial nations to remove economic obstacles'.[46] In all of this there is no acknowledgment of the risks involved in lending, but the risks in borrowing are plain to see. The one-sided nature of the risk involved here is reflected in the absolute lack of criticism that has come from the World Bank and the IMF regarding the role of creditors, while they are happy to warn that a lack of conditions attaching to forgiveness 'risks debt relief being squandered on corruption, military expenditure, or grandiose projects with little if any benefit in terms of sustainable growth or poverty reduction'.[47] The costs of debt forgiveness under the HIPC Initiative fall largely on the shoulders of the HIPCs.

The proof of any debt relief package is in the question, Has it worked? In March 1998, Uganda reached its completion point and was given a package of debt relief that the IMF calculations state are worth US $650 million, or US $350 NPV.[48] The Debt Sustainability Analysis released by the IMF and the IDA states that 'with assistance under the HIPC Initiative, Uganda's debt situation would become sustainable and Uganda would exit from the debt-rescheduling process'.[49] Michel Camdessus greeted the news warmly, saying that he was 'certain that this will be an extremely positive signal to the rest of the world'.[50] However, by February 1999 Clare Short, the Secretary of State for International Development, was to conclude that 'the review [of the HIPC Initiative] concerning Uganda, which has just received debt relief, was

46. Cited in C. Caufield, *Masters of Illusion: The World Bank and the Poverty of Nations* (London: Macmillan, 1997), p. 159.

47. IMF, 'Response to Critics'.

48. IMF, 'Uganda to Receive US$ 650 million in Debt Relief', press release, 8 April 1998 [http.//imfnt1x.imf.org/external/np/sec/pr/1998/PR9813.htm].

49. IMF and IDA, 'Uganda: Initiative for Heavily Indebted Poor Countries Completion Point Document' (Washington: IMF and IDA, 20 March 1998), p. 11.

50. IMF, 'Camdessus Applauds Debt Relief for Uganda under HIPC', press release, 24 April 1998 [http.//imfnt1x.imf.org/external/np/sec/nb/1997/NB9707.htm].

very disappointing. As a result of the fall in coffee prices,[51] it is as badly off as it was in the first place'.[52] In fact Uganda faced an increase in debt service of about $12 million p.a. after HIPC, and it was only after some of the debt relief was brought forward that any resources were released for social expenditure.[53] When this is added to a recently leaked IMF document that states that '[i]n absolute terms the [HIPC] initiative may not be significantly reducing debt service from the current levels paid' and that '[t]he US dollar amounts of debt service owed by Burkina Faso and Mali are expected to increase',[54] the result is damning. The HIPC Initiative on its present terms is a manifest failure.

The HIPC Initiative is certainly not a variety of cheap forgiveness, but the restrictions it imposes are so steep that forgiveness is not a result of its lengthy and arduous proceedings. The definition of sustainable debt that it uses, together with its entry requirements and timeframe would be enough to brand it as a harsh variety of too-costly forgiveness. Where particular attention is required beyond this analysis is over the programmes of structural adjustment that form a central plank of the Initiative. Not only are these too-costly, but they reject any mutual responsibility for the creation of debt that is now causing such sustained damage to the lives of people in HIPCs. The costs involved in debt cancellation under the HIPC Initiative fall on the HIPCs themselves. It is the HIPCs that must change their behaviour, not the creditors. In fact, the ESAF programme may be seen as such a naked use of power that it must be wholeheartedly rejected as a strategy for debt forgiveness and poverty relief.

The Jubilee 2000 Coalition

The Jubilee 2000 Coalition is a broad organization bringing together NGOs, trade unions, religious groups and individuals. It has groups active in all the G-7 countries, in Africa and in Latin America. Given

51. The IMF/IDA Debt sustainability analysis assumes that coffee exports from Uganda will grow in volume by 2 per cent p.a. from 1999 and remain priced in real terms at US $1.4 per kg from 1999 (IMF and IDA, 'Uganda', p. 12).

52. Answer to question in the House of Commons from Mrs Maria Fyfe MP. Cited in Jubilee 2000 Coalition, 'Uganda Debt Unsustainable Again', press release, 19 February 1999 [http.//www.jubilee2000uk.org/news/uganda1902.html].

53. Jubilee 2000, 'Uganda'.

54. L. Elliott and C. Denny, 'Fund Admits Debt Plans Will Fail Poor', *The Guardian*, 19 April 1999, p. 21.

the diverse nature of its make-up, the position of the Coalition is not always clear. Different members of the coalition are free to disagree on the specifics of how debt forgiveness is to work. Thus a recent document concerning proposed changes to the HIPC Initiative produced by the World Bank and the IMF devotes space to Jubilee 2000, as well as to the different proposals made by Oxfam, CAFOD and Eurodad, all of whom are members of the Coalition.[55] In practice, however, this is one of Jubilee 2000's greatest strengths, enabling it to bring a great deal of analysis and campaigning pressure to bear on creditor governments and the multilateral financial institutions, notably the World Bank and the IMF. As my chief documentary sources for Jubilee 2000's position I have taken the three declarations cited by the World Bank/IMF review,[56] some policy papers originating both from the London office and from before the first Jubilee 2000 international conference in Rome 1998, and some papers written by Martin Dent, one of the founders of Jubilee 2000.

The first question to be asked of Jubilee 2000 is, therefore, whether the forgiveness it offers is too cheap. The Accra Declaration's first demand is for '[t]he immediate and unconditional cancellation of Afrikas's [*sic*] external debts'[57] and discussions at their international conference in Rome certainly covered the possibility that debt relief should be unconditional. The working group at this conference noted five arguments for complete cancellation: the one-time nature of the call; the need to reject the system that has caused the debt crisis; it is a politically feasible goal in some countries; it could be a bench mark rather than a strategy; and it would lead to a call for the writing off or down of middle-income country debt as a second phase of the campaign.[58] It need not be the case that a complete cancellation of debt is cheap forgiveness, but it is important to note that all of Jubilee 2000's statements refer to conditions that should be attached. The Accra Decla-

55. World Bank and IMF, 'Heavily Indebted Poor Countries'.

56. These are the Accra Declaration of 19 April 1998, 'A Jubilee Call for Debt Cancellation and Economic Justice', adopted by the first international Jubilee 2000 conference in Rome on 17 November 1998; and the Tegucigalpa Declaration of 27 January 1999.

57. Jubilee 2000 Coalition, 'ACCRA Declaration', 19 April 1998 [http.//www.oneworld.org/jubilee2000/accra.html].

58. Jubilee 2000 Coalition, 'Rome Jubilee 2000 Policy Discussion', 17 November 1998 [http.//www.jubilee2000uk.org/policy_papers/discussion.html].

ration moves on to talk of how money freed by such forgiveness should be spent, as well as other recommendations for reform of the international financial system. The Rome conference in its statement calls for 'debt cancellation by the year 2000, including: 1. Unpayable debt... 2. Debt that in real terms has already been paid. 3. Debt for improperly designed policies and projects. 4. Odious debt.'[59]

The petition that it has circulated calls for 'the cancellation of the unpayable debts of the most impoverished nations by the year 2000'. The most obvious conditionality of the Jubilee 2000 campaign takes two forms, its call for a one-off cancellation of debts to mark the millennium, and the notion of unpayable debts. Martin Dent describes the one-off nature of the call as an attempt to meet

> two apparently contradictory requirements... On the one hand we have to uphold the general principle that debts must be honoured on which the vast structure of commerce, of banking and of loans for enterprise depend, and on the other we have to correct the huge and intolerable imbalance that now leaves the poorer part of the human family in unpayable debt to the richer part, inhibiting recovery and exacerbating the contrasts in living standards.[60]

While there is clearly some unease about conditional debt relief, to which we must return, Jubilee 2000 calls for debt forgiveness to be accompanied by a number of other features. This means that there is an element of conditionality, at least to the extent that they acknowledge that a simple writing off of debt is not enough. We cannot accuse the Coalition of advocating a blanket cheap forgiveness.

An assessment of whether Jubilee 2000 is actually calling for too-costly forgiveness is best achieved through an account of the worries that the Coalition has about conditional debt relief. This will also enable us to see where the costs of the debt forgiveness that Jubilee 2000 advocates will fall. The main concern expressed by Jubilee 2000 about conditionality is over its imposition by creditors. Thus the Rome declaration states that 'creditor governments, international financial institutions and commercial banks, which are chiefly responsible for the debt crisis, should not set the conditions for debt cancellation'.[61] The working group at the Rome conference discussing this point came to a decisive agreement that

59. Jubilee 2000, 'Rome Policy Discussion'.
60. Dent, 'Theological Help', p. 30.
61. Jubilee 2000, 'Jubilee Call'.

> creditors cannot set the conditions for debt cancellations. There is a need for a framework for debt cancellation, to ensure that the funds released are used beneficially. But this framework must be set by the people of the South for the benefit of the people of the South. People and people's organisations in the North should campaign for this.[62]

This is a rejection of the IMF/World Bank approach of tying debt forgiveness to ESAF programmes. However Jubilee 2000 are rather less precise about the structures that should be put in place to set up the framework that it sees as necessary. There is a clear emphasis on the role of civil society, rather than just debtor governments. The working group report that 'there was agreement that even democratic governments could not be allowed to resolve debt issues without the integral involvement of civil society'.[63] The Coalition is moving towards the idea of arbitration as the best mechanism for determining levels of debt forgiveness. The Rome declaration states that '[t]ransparent and independent arbitration should be available to cancel debt',[64] and the Tegucigalpa Declaration envisages arbitration taking a form such that '[d]ebtors and creditors will appoint an equal number of judges for a Tribunal or Arbitrage Jury. In the case of debtors, this would include participants from a broad cross section of society'.[65] The key themes that come from the various statements of the Coalition are transparency and accountability, an analogy to domestic insolvency proceedings and a debtor voice. Perhaps the clearest attempt to give an account of such arbitration is the proposal for a Debt Review Body (DRB) made by Ann Pettifor.[66] Pettifor suggests that a DRB be set up for each debtor country at its request either to the United Nations or to the International Court of Justice. It would commission a full audit of outstanding debt and ask for government plans for economic recovery, reconstruction and support for the poor. Its hearings would be open, public and well publicized and would determine the amount of debt to be cancelled

62. Jubilee 2000, 'Rome Policy Discussion'.

63. Jubilee 2000, 'Rome Policy Discussion'.

64. Jubilee 2000, 'Jubilee Call'.

65. Jubilee 2000 Coalition, 'Tegucigalpa Declaration. Jubilee 2000 Latin American and Caribbean Platform: *Yes to Life, No to Debt*' [http.//www.jubilee2000uk.org/latin_america/declaration.html].

66. A. Pettifor, 'Concordats for Debt Cancellation: A Contribution to the Debate' (London: Jubilee 2000 Coalition, 30 March 1999) [http.//www.jubilee2000uk.org/features/concordats.html].

based on human development criteria and on the costs of reconstruction and economic recovery. Its conclusions would be binding, with penalties for violation. Pettifor's paper remains a contribution to an ongoing debate, rather than a policy statement on behalf of Jubilee 2000. Thus we must be careful not to place too much weight on her proposals. Nevertheless it remains the fullest suggestion of what a procedure that is transparent and accountable and gives a voice to civil society from debtor countries might look like.

Jubilee 2000, therefore, cannot be accused of suggesting cheap forgiveness. The Coalition has paid a great deal of attention to the costs of forgiving debt. Its most significant difference from the HIPC Initiative lies in the way in which it seeks to spread and enforce the costs of the conditions placed upon that forgiveness. Thus it also escapes the charge of offering a form of too-costly forgiveness in the way that the HIPC Initiative does. Although its proposals remain tentative, Jubilee 2000 offers the best account of what true debt forgiveness might involve.

Conclusion

This essay does not intend to be the last word on the complex problem of debt forgiveness. It does attempt to peer behind the statistics and to examine the understanding of forgiveness with which two of the leading positions in the debate operate. The HIPC Initiative has been found to operate with an understanding of forgiveness that is very costly and allows the cost to fall entirely on the debtor. This is a form of what I have called too-costly forgiveness, and the extent of its cost barely enables it to be described as forgiveness. To the extent that the Jubilee 2000 campaign recognizes that the costs of forgiveness must be shared between creditor and debtor, it reflects a recognition that both are responsible for the relationship of indebtedness. Its understanding of forgiveness is costly, but reflects better the understanding of forgiveness with which I began. Bonhoeffer wrote that 'the call to follow Christ always means a call to share the work of forgiving men their sins',[67] and in the context of the world today, this also means sharing the work, and the cost, of forgiving debts.[68]

67. Bonhoeffer, *Discipleship*, p. 80.

68. I am grateful to Jacky Humphreys for her comments on an earlier draft of this essay.

Finding God in Consumption: An Intimate Theology of Globalization

Susan Hawley

Introduction

The term globalization is the most often used description of the shape and direction of the world today. Anthony Giddens stated in his 1999 Reith Lectures, 'Globalisation is not incidental to our lives today. It is a shift in our very life circumstances. It is the way we now live.'[1] Any theology that seeks to be contextual has in one way or another to be a theology of globalization.

But what do we mean by globalization? What is this context we cannot escape? What are its challenges to faith and how do we talk about God in an age of globalization? Globalization is increasingly characterized by growing inequality, economic instability and social exclusion. All of these represent fundamental challenges to Christians today. But there is another aspect of globalization that I want to focus on here, and that is the way in which it has become, as Giddens puts it, 'an "in here" phenomenon...influencing intimate and personal aspects of our lives'.[2]

What I will argue here is that in order to respond to this particular side of globalization Christianity needs a theology of consumption. That is, Christians need to find ways of talking about God in a context where Christians as humans are increasingly defined by our consumption patterns, and where the quest for more and more consumption threatens substantially to redefine any space for God.

Focusing on consumption in theological terms is crucial because it is through consumption that people personally experience globalization as an everyday phenomenon. Through their consumption patterns, whether

1. *The Observer*, 11 April 1999, p. 31.
2. *The Observer*, 11 April 1999, p. 31.

it be eating fruit flown in from other countries or taking a holiday, people are increasingly linked to the other side of the world by what they buy. Consumption is therefore the medium through which people are most able and likely to attempt to shape globalization: it is the new sphere of political and social action. A theology of consumption, if it is to be politically as well as personally meaningful, has also, as I will argue, to be a theology of consumer action. Theology has to go where it has previously feared to tread: into the aisles of Tesco's and the inner pockets of wallets.

In this paper I will look at the nature of global consumption, the spiritual challenges that it poses, what the Bible says about consumption, and finally discuss some signs of hope, where new theologies of consumption and thence of globalization are being constructed from below.

Consumption

Consumption today is one of the main engines of global economic growth. As a recent United Nations Development Programme (UNDP) report has described:

> World consumption has expanded at an unprecedented pace over the 20th century, with private and public consumption expenditures reaching $24 trillion in 1998, twice the level of 1975 and six times that of 1950. In 1900 real consumption expenditure was barely $1.5 trillion.[3]

Indeed, so important has consumption become in the global economy, that when 'the unknown American consumer' went on '*the biggest shopping spree in history, accounting for half of all world economic growth*' in 1998, the world was brought back from the brink of a disastrous global recession.[4]

Of course, consumption in and of itself is neutral, but its present patterns are anything but. Today's consumption patterns are becoming the major cause of indebtedness, inequality, social exclusion and environmental destruction. Household indebtedness as a proportion of national income, for instance, has risen dramatically: in Britain between 1980 and 1990 it rose from 38 per cent to 80 per cent.[5] In Brazil, meanwhile,

3. United Nations Development Programme (UNDP), *1998 Report* (New York: United Nations, 1998), p. 1.

4. *The Observer*, 9 May 1999, p. 4.

5. H. Schutt, *The Trouble with Capitalism: An Enquiry into the Causes of*

consumer debt is over $6 billion, and is particularly concentrated among lower-income households. In good times, of course, there is nothing wrong with this. In bad times, it is disastrous.

But we also see a massive inequality in consumption. Globally, 20 per cent of the world's population account for 86 per cent of private consumption. The richest 20 per cent consume 45 per cent of all meat and fish, 58 per cent of total energy, 84 per cent of all paper and own 87 per cent of the world's vehicle fleet. Consumption is increasingly a luxury of the rich. Most worryingly, in 70 countries with nearly a billion people, consumption is declining and is actually lower than 25 years ago. The average African household consumes 20 per cent less than 25 years ago.

These trends in consumption are creating on a global scale a situation of social, economic and cultural exclusion. Those who are not part of the consumption boom are being pushed to the margins. As the UNDP report notes: 'When there is heavy social pressure to maintain high consumption standards and society encourages competitive spending for conspicuous displays of wealth, inequalities in consumption deepen poverty and social exclusion.'[6]

At the same time, marketing and advertising are changing the definition of what constitutes a necessity. Spending on advertising is increasing world-wide faster than population or incomes, and at a conservative estimate is around $435 billion annually.[7] To put this into perspective, the United Nations estimates that with $40 billion a year the international community could help provide basic social services to everyone in the world. And on a more human level, it would take a worker in a Chinese toy factory 523 years to earn the sum Mattel spends advertising the Barbie doll in one day.[8]

One consequence of the growth and pervasiveness of advertising is that the amount of income needed to reach consumption aspirations has been rising. In the US it actually doubled between the mid-1980s and the mid-1990s at a time, it is important to note, that employment was becoming less secure, more flexible and for some increasingly elusive.[9]

Global Economic Failure (London: Zed Books, 1998), p. 186.

6. UNDP, *1998 Report*, p. 6.
7. UNDP, *1998 Report*, p. 7.
8. 'Globalisation and Employment', *Panos Briefing* 33 (May 1999), p. 18.
9. UNDP, *1998 Report*, p. 6.

The Spiritual Challenges of Consumerism

According to the Korean Brazilian theologian, Jung Mo Sung,

> from the religious point of view, the current situation is a spiritual crisis. Shopping has become a substitute for church, and solidarity with other people is being replaced by competition and scorn for the poor, who do not consume and therefore do not exist.[10]

The message of faith is indeed increasingly having to compete with the message of consumerism. Advertising is a prime example. Advertising knows no limits to what and how it will try to sell something. The recent advert for the fizzy orange drink Tango, for instance, had a picture of a boy kneeling and praying: 'Please, God, let it be Tango.' In Brazil, things are even cruder. A maker of sweets tried recently to tempt the evangelical community with an advert in which a sweet wrapped in biblical text was promoted as 'the word of God in every mouth'. Religion and spirituality have become cultural symbols with which to sell goods, and in the process are turned into commodities.

This commodification of spirituality is clear in another recent advert for the internet on the London Underground, which had as its caption

> Thanks to excite.co.uk this woman found her astrologically ideal partner on-line. Amazingly, she also searched for her entire family tree, played backgammon with Christoph in Munich, found a local restaurant with an exclusively vegan menu, bid for an original Art Deco lamp and discussed spirituality with a Tibetan monk. All before her morning coffee. If she can, why can't you?

As this advert suggests, spirituality can be reduced in advertising speak to a momentary activity that gratifies some immediate need. It becomes something that is easy, comfortable, compartmentalized and unchallenging.

The message of consumerism given through advertising also offers an idealized version of the world—a kind of cheap global community with easy solutions. The accountancy firm Price Waterhouse, for instance, boldly proclaims in its adverts that 'together we can change the world', Gillette pronounces its own 'Good News' and a construction company calls itself 'GlobalVision'. In creating a particular interpretation of the world and constructing a vision of the future—in images that are relentlessly upbeat, positive and fun—advertising and corporate

10. Quoted in *ENI*, 21 September 1998, p. 22.

spin become in themselves 'a spiritual formation'.[11] They sell to us a virtual or illusory community that is far removed from the hard work needed to construct real communities based on solidarity and love.[12]

Of course, this version of the world pushed by business and increasingly our own political leaders carefully hides and distorts reality—a reality that the gospel does not allow us to ignore. The image of a positive global world in which all can participate as shoppers hides the fact that, as John Hull puts it,

> [w]e do not live in a global village but in a rich village, outside of which five sevenths of the world's people live in various degrees of poverty... The iron curtain has passed away...but the place has been taken by the money curtain... It is invisible to those of us on the inside because we can see right through it, but to the poor majority outside the money curtain, it stands as a glittering barrier through which they cannot pass.[13]

But there is a further danger. Consumer culture is becoming a kind of 'hyper-culture', which has become, as Ritzer puts it, 'McDonaldized'. In the spiritual realm, McDonaldization is, according to Dennis Hiebert, 'the banishment of meaningful, living spirituality that leaves persons less than fully human'.[14] He argues that there is a real danger of Christians McDonaldizing their own worship and message in an uncritical form of inculturation. Argentinian Pentecostals, for instance, argue that if Jesus were here today he would use a mobile phone and fly around in a helicopter. And it is not just Christians that are adapting themselves. In Thailand, for example, the Dhamakaya Buddhist temple has created a storm with its successful use of aggressive marketing techniques, which, according to the Buddhist scholar Dr Suwana, 'answers the spiritual void with something that's simple, concrete, modern and does not force them to give up their consumerist lifestyles'.[15]

How should Christians engage with this hyper-culture, then, and how should they respond to the spiritual challenges that consumerism throws up?

11. Simon Barrow, quoted in *ENI*, 18 November 1998, p. 23.

12. I. Burkett, 'Coca-Community: Corporately Imagined Communities and the Global Colonization of Place', *Development* 41.2 (1998), pp. 59-64.

13. 'Education and Mission', sermon preached by John Hull in Bishop's Cleve, 31 January 1999.

14. D. Hiebert, 'The McDonaldization of Protestant Organisations', paper given at ACTS/Ilkley Conference, Newbury, UK, June 1998.

15. *Guardian*, 26 March 1999, p. 18.

Towards a Theology of Consumption

The writer of Ecclesiastes might not have had a mega shopping centre around the corner from him, but he certainly understood the human impulse that attracted people there:

> I have learnt why people work so hard to succeed: it is because they envy their neighbours. But it is useless. It is like chasing the wind...it is better to have only a little, with peace of mind, than to be busy all the time with both hands, trying to catch the wind (Eccl. 4.4-6).

Consumerism, then, from the wisdom perspective in the Bible is grasping after illusion. It is chasing the wind. It can never make one truly happy, and it distorts human relationships. This idea is picked up in the New Testament in James, who asks 'Where do all the fights and quarrels among you come from?... You want things, but you cannot have them, so you are ready to kill; you strongly desire things, but you cannot get them, so you quarrel and fight?' (Jas 4.1-2). The desire for goods destroys community and creates jealousy and misunderstanding.

It is because of this that there is such a strong injunction against the hoarding of goods and against greed in the Bible. The command not to covet is central to the code of ethics created at Sinai. Jesus, meanwhile, warned his listeners to 'watch out and guard yourselves from every kind of greed; because a person's true life is not made up of the things he owns, no matter how rich he may be' (Lk. 12.15). Indeed throughout the New Testament, Erich Fromm says,

> we find the central postulate that people must free themselves from all greed and cravings for possession and must totally liberate themselves from the structure of having, and conversely, that all positive ethical norms are rooted in an ethics of being, sharing and solidarity.[16]

It would be wrong, however, to see consumerism today as just about greed or the desire for belongings. It is a message pushed by a powerful system with strong corporate interests behind it. Which is why some identify the current situation as one of idolatry, where false gods, or the money god, are worshipped instead of the true God. In Revelation, Babylon is condemned because 'your businessmen were the most powerful in all the world, and with your false magic you deceived all the peoples of the world' (Rev. 18.23). Today the 'false magic' of

16. E. Fromm, *To Have or to Be* (London: Abacus, 1978), p. 61.

advertising does indeed seek to seduce the world to a way of life that creates exclusion and is blind to the reality of injustice and poverty.

But a theology of consumption cannot just be a 'no' to the current situation. As Villa-Vicencio writes, 'The prophetic task of the Church must include a thoughtful and creative "Yes" to options for political and social renewal.'[17] A theology of consumption must provide the ground work for creative alternatives. Ched Myers has laid much of this groundwork with what he calls a 'theology of enough'.[18]

A theology of enough states that there is enough for everyone, that everyone's basic needs can and should be met and that we should accept limits for ourselves so that there is enough to go around. The miracle of the manna falling from the sky, as the Israelites suffer hunger in the desert on their way to the promised land, is central to such a theology. Each family was only to gather enough for its needs, and no one was to 'store up' any extra (Exod. 16.16-20). As a result 'The one who gathered much did not have too much, and the one who gathered little did not have too little' (Exod. 16.18). But when people did try to store it up, the manna rotted.

The Sabbath is also central to such a theology. The Sabbath as a day of rest is, according to Fromm, a day when 'one lives as if one *has* nothing, pursuing no aim except *being*, that is, expressing one's essential powers: praying, studying, eating, drinking, singing, making love'.[19] Or as Brueggeman puts it, 'Sabbath means that there's enough bread, that we don't have to hustle every day of our lives.' The Sabbath represents an alternative to the current system, it prefigures the Kingdom of God as a time when there will be a different way of living, rooted in respect for the gift of life given by a generous God, and in an ethic of 'enough for all'. And that is why Jesus wanted to reclaim the Sabbath from stultifying and hypocritical religious laws.

The theology of enough is a countercultural theology—it calls for 'cultural disobedience', [20] or living in exile within the dominant culture. It is about creating a different kind of culture that is full of hope, is

17. Quoted in R.J Schreiter, *The New Catholicity: Theology between the Global and the Local* (Maryknoll, NY: Orbis Books, 1997).

18. C. Myers, 'God Speed the Year of Jubilee', *Sojourners Magazine*, May-June 1998.

19. Fromm, *To Have or to Be*, p. 57.

20. R. Van Drimmelen, *Faith in a Global Economy: A Primer for Christians* (Geneva: WCC Publications, 1998), p. 135.

rooted in sharing, resists the desire to acquire more and more and seeks to transform the world. As Brueggeman puts it,

> The ideology devoted to encouraging consumption wants to shrivel our imaginations so that we cannot conceive of living in any way that would be less profitable for the dominant corporate structures. But Jesus tells us that we can change the world... He demonstrated that the world is filled with abundance and freighted with generosity. If bread is broken and shared, there is enough for all.[21]

This cultural disobedience is also expressed through reorienting our consumption towards greater self-sufficiency. The prophetic vision of Isaiah fits well with this. He envisions a future in which 'people will build houses and live in them themselves—they will not be used by someone else. They will plant vineyards and enjoy the wine... They will fully enjoy the things they have worked for' (Isa. 65.21-22).

But a word of warning. The theology of enough is a prophetic theology. But is there a danger that it sets up ideals that are impossible for ordinary people to follow and are therefore disempowering? Is a theological critique of consumerism in danger of becoming a misplaced moralism which does not actually fit with why people consume or try to understand the deeper human reasons behind certain types and styles of consumption?

The anthropologist Daniel Miller argues that consumerism is often based on the values of thrift and good value, rather than extravagance and greed.[22] Consumption, he argues, is in itself a highly moral activity, based very much on ethical principles of home and family. At the same time, styles of consumption can also be about expressing belonging to a group that fulfil deep social needs. They can also be a means of claiming self-worth in a society that undermines it, or a channel for youth revolt and creativity. People can find in consumerism an empowerment, a way of being that is youthful and fun in an age of uncertainty and anxiety. Condemning consumerism, then, can risk misunderstanding the cultural context of our time.

A theology of consumption needs to take this on board. That is, while maintaining the ideals of a theology of enough, it has to look at what

21. W. Brueggeman, 'The Liturgy of Abundance, the Myth of Scarcity', *Christian Century*, 24–31 March 1999, pp. 342-47.

22. D. Miller, 'Consumption as the Vanguard of History', in *idem* (ed.), *Acknowledging Consumption: A Review of New Studies* (London: Routledge, 1995), p. 19.

are empowering models of consumption. It needs to outline a way of consuming that liberates. It needs to empower people to reintroduce values into daily economic activity which for too long has been portrayed as valueless—such values as responsibility, stewardship for creation and accepting limits in order that others might meet their basic needs. But it also needs to create an awareness of the economic power behind consumption. And that is where a theology of consumer action comes in.

Signs of Hope

Will Hutton said several years ago, ‘As consumers we are kings, as producers we are serfs.’ Daniel Miller, who has recently written an anthropology of capitalism today, takes it one step further. He claims that as consumers we are in fact ‘global dictators’, and that as dictators we have an enormous power to influence the shape of the global economy. He writes,

> It is not the proletariat today whose transformation of consciousness would liberate the world, but the consumer… Today it is the process of consumption itself that must be engaged, through an act of self revelation, into taking responsibility for the power that it wields without consciousness, and therefore largely without responsibility.[23]

He goes on to say,

> In the global economy, we cannot escape the foundational ethical principles by which taking responsibility for others is the same process by which we take responsibility for ourselves… If we can rise to consciousness in our consumption activities as the vanguard of history, then there is at least the glimmer of hope that responsibility could confront irresponsibility in citizenship, and morality could confront the amorality of the market.[24]

Miller’s claims are backed up by the recent admission of a senior Shell executive that Shell’s greatest fears are not government regulation or a fall in oil prices, but a Western consumer revolt.[25]

Consumer consciousness is indeed on the rise, mainly in the form of increased customer complaints and the rise of ‘ethical’ name brands.

23. Miller, ‘Consumption’, p. 19.
24. Miller, ‘Consumption’, pp. 49-50.
25. *Guardian*, 7 June 1999, p. 2.

The huge success of a campaign by the Church development agency, Christian Aid, in the UK on how supermarkets treat the workers in developing countries behind their products is a good example. Churchgoers gathered together their till receipts to show supermarkets how much custom they were worth. As a result many supermarkets were brought into a process called the Ethical Trading Initiative. Such actions are the beginning of a praxis of a theology of consumption.

But there are also signs of hope in local grassroots organizing towards alternative consumption styles. In New York, for instance, a coalition of youth organizations and neighbourhood centres is inspiring kids to stop buying or take back to the store Nike trainers. But it is also

> asking young people to face not only what Nike has done to its workers abroad but what Nike is doing to them, through advertising that mercilessly pushes $50 shoes without which some refuse to go to school (and for which others steal). This advertising is, in [a youth worker, Leo] Johnson's words, 'sucking the brains out of their heads'.[26]

In the Philippines and the Pacific Islands, women are forming themselves into Citizens' Alliances for Consumer Protection to confront what Mary John Mananzan calls 'the single most dramatic consumer problem' facing them—that of imported food. In the Solomon Islands, these consumer activists have created the concept of the 'supsup' garden, which uses mixed cropping, recycling of waste, composting, organic growing techniques to produce the basic food basket of the islanders. As Mananzan says, 'The supsup garden is an important means of ensuring that nobody starves in Paradise.'[27]

These are just a few examples of the mustard seeds of consumer action that threaten to change the system from below. If they were increasingly brought together with some of the more mainstream efforts at consumer consciousness-raising and action, then these small beginnings could indeed begin to make a difference and change the nature of globalization from the inside out. As Mananzan puts it:

> There is no blueprint for an alternative to globalization. The different efforts, different forms of resistance, and initiatives at alternative systems...must be encouraged and shared and somehow coordinated. Out of these radical energies, a tangential energy could somehow bring a

26. W. Tabb, 'Progressive Globalism: Challenging the Audacity of Capital', *Monthly Review* 50 (1999), p. 9.

27. M.J. Mananzan, 'Emerging Alternatives to Globalization and Transformative Action', *Voices from the Third World* 21.2 (December 1998), pp. 119-33.

> quantum leap to something qualitatively new and bring about a fundamental societal transformation.[28]

Brave words at the turn of the millennium. But the gospel demands that we always live in hope.

28. Mananzan, 'Energy Alternatives'.

The Black Church in the New Millennium

Ronald A. Nathan

Introduction

In order for the black Christian community to face the challenges of the third millennium it is important for us to be cognizant of where we have come from. For example, we (the Black Church) must ask ourselves what were the forces that shaped our thinking, behaviour, institutions, philosophies and theologies?

We do recognize that there are those, black and white, who are impatient with this need to look back before moving into the future, their perceptions being that such matters as African heritage, slavery, colonialism and suchlike are irrelevant in paving a new way ahead. To forget the past is a request that is impossible for us to entertain, as we are a sum total of all that we have experienced as a people.

The main focus of this essay will be to look at the past influences, present priorities and future prospects and challenges of the Black Church in the UK. I prefer to use the term 'Black Church' as a generic term for the myriad of politically correct terms and names associated with the Christian denominations prevalent among 'people of colour'. This term will be used to describe primarily 'West Indian' congregations.

The Black Church Looking Back

The advent of the Black Church in the UK was synonymous with the demise of the British Empire. British colonial citizens made their way to the mother country with hopes of finding a better way of life, rebuilding its cities and developing its infrastructure. The onslaught of racism, class, cultural and theological differences experienced by many black Christians convinced them to join together for worship and a common spirituality. Therein lie the humble beginnings of the Black Church phenomena.

There were other black Christians who stayed within the historic denominations of which they were members in the Caribbean and African countries. These include Anglicans, Roman Catholics, Baptists and Methodists. The struggles of both Christian groups contributed to the collective experience of racism and social injustices that impinged upon the lives of the British black communities.

It should be noted that the Black Church in the UK has been influenced by black religious traditions of the USA, African religious retention and its intercourse with European Christian denominations. These influences came through a variety of denominational, cultural and fraternal ties. They are recognizable in the Church's worship, polity and practices.

Those who migrated from the Caribbean territories in the late 1940s and 1950s were shaped by a colonial mentality and viewed the mother country as their own. They did not wish to cause trouble and therefore were considered to be conservative in nature. The Churches they started in the front rooms of their homes reflected this conservatism. Those Churches whose primary religious experience was rooted in the Holiness tradition had not experienced models of Christianity that encouraged involvement at a political or policy level.

Many had heeded the concept of 'keep politics and religion separate' and that 'they were now saved from that' worldly endeavour.

It seems to be a common experience of first-generation migrants that they shun confrontation in the domestic politics of their adopted country. Their main concerns are for their families' survival, be that physical or economic. What is also true of these groups is that they find it a necessity to maintain and replicate the same or similar institutions (including religious ones) as may have existed at home. This is especially so in an environment considered to be at best indifferent, and at worst hostile to the newcomers.

This historical glance back should make us ask where were the models for political engagement, civic responsibility and prophetic churchship in 1950s Jamaica, Barbados, Trinidad, Kenya and Ghana? We know that with few exceptions the British colonial civil service and much of the then clergy did not foster any independent political or theological tradition.

Those models that existed did so on the periphery of society and were marginalized by the establishment. Examples of these include the Spiritual Baptists and Shango religions in Trinidad, Tobago, Barbados and

Grenada, the Cumina, Pocomina and Rastafarian religions in Jamaica, the Harris Church in Ghana and the Ivory Coast, and Gikuyu congregations associated with the Mau Mau rebellions in Kenya.

The years 1930–50 were tumultuous ones in the British West Indies, with political and industrial unrest seething. The talk of federation and independence, union strikes and political agitation was rife in the aftermath of the heyday of Garveyism.

Migration offered an escape from the social and economic hardships of the islands. They looked to the north, but the Monroe directive limited West Indians' access into the USA. The next best place to go to was the heart of the empire, where there was the promise of political stability and the possibility of employment.

The Black Church and Christian Service

At the end of the twentieth century there are approximately 150,000 black Christians located in the Black Church with another 100,000 others to be found in the historic denominations. There have been growing awareness, respect and relationships among these two groups. This has resulted in a coming together in such organizations as the African and Caribbean Evangelical Alliance, the Senior Black Clergy conferences, the Black Christian Civic Forum, the Churches Commission for Racial Justice, the Association of Black Clergy and the International Ministerial Fellowship of Great Britain, to name a few.

Sociologists and politicians, black and white, not familiar with this angle to the Black Church's history had concluded that the Black Church's other worldly rhetoric also meant that it was without social relevance. They had heard the dynamic preaching, seen the pulsating performances of our lively choirs and noted the phenomenal Church growth and heightened profile of the Black Church. Upon these they based their conclusions, they pointed to the absence of any reciprocal growth in proactive and advocacy work by these congregations on the behalf of the wider black community.

A closer look at what the Black Church was and is still doing show that several of the relevant issues facing the black community were being addressed. At a grass roots level, several Churches were tackling the social issues through project-based activities. These activities have had an impact on the development of the black community that is seldom calculated and therefore not acknowledged. This is evident in the Black Church's provision of services, for example:

Elderly drop-in centres
Advisory centres for immigration matters
Drug awareness programmes
Saturday schools
Representation on race relations institutions (e.g. Commission for Racial Equality and the Churches Commission on Racial Justice).
Job clubs etc.
Participation on Police Consultative Groups and other philanthropic organizations.

This approach has left the Black Church open to accusations from black unionists, pressure groups and social workers of letting the government off the hook by such provision, rather than investing in and carrying out advocacy work that would lobby and agitate for change.

Another resource that has been consistently overlooked by social commentators is the human resources that are developed within the context of the Black Churches. The Revd David Greaves, the National Bishop of the New Testament Assembly, states

> that what often goes unnoticed by the public is the church's provision of a 'safe space' for many young people, to develop leadership skills and build confidence. It is also in the church's environs that they are able to dream dreams and to see visions which have resulted in many going on to further education.

He further believes that sufficient credit is not given 'to the policy changes which have taken place within the Church's project areas as a consequence of their involvement at the local level'.

Having accepted that the Church's contribution as outlined above is significant it still leaves the Black Church in a dilemma. This dilemma is in respect to the scope of the Church's ministry as it pertains to the leadership of the black community and, by inference, its responsibility to the wider British society. This is reflected in the tensions that exist, first, in the priority the Black Church gives to its central programme, that is, redemption and salvation, and whether this includes a commitment to justice and equality. Secondly, what are its methods and strategies for social change? This is still unclear amidst its denominationalism and parochialism. Thirdly, there is its conservatism that flies in the face of the biblical tradition of a radical and prophetic Church. These all contribute to restrict the Black Church's capacity for united action.

What is evident to all and sundry but missed by many black Christian leaders is that the Black Church represents the most organized and best resource of organizations in the black community. The social expectations and vision of the black community as pertaining to the Black Church has always seemed to be wider than that which the Black Church has for itself.

It is this widening 'credibility' gap that embroils the Church and the black community in controversy. The black community reminds the Black Church of the biblical quotation 'to whom much is given much is required'.

The Black Church in the Twenty-First Century

There is a significant legacy of black British Christian involvement in social and political activism spearheaded by the likes of Rev. Robert Wedderburn (1763), Olaudah Equiano (1745), Phillis Wheatley (1761) and Pastor Daniel Ekarte (1904).

There are also theological and philosophical traditions at the roots of black Christianity. One of these is particularly related to the current discussions of the millennium, that is, the teachings on millennialism. This can provide another resource for the Black Church to draw from in its relation to the social, political, cultural and spiritual contexts in a multicultural society like the UK.

Millennialism is the belief rooted in Christian tradition and thought that history will be fulfilled in a golden age based on Rev. 20.1-7. It has been observed that millenarian sects or movements always picture salvation as collective, terrestrial, imminent, total and miraculous.[1]

Black millennialism of the nineteenth and early twentieth century identified this golden age with ancient Israel and the hope of entering the Promised Land of Canaan. Black millennial thought can be categorized into three types: cultural millennialism, millennial Ethiopianism and progressive millennialism.

Cultural millennialism denotes the ideology of Blacks working out the millennium through the forces of Western civilization, that is, education, Anglo-Saxon culture, American democracy and republicanism.

1. N. Cohn, *The Pursuit of the Millennium: Revolutionizing Millenarians and Mystical Anarchists of the Middle Ages* (London: Paladin).

Millennial Ethiopianism denotes a radical break with the Old World and posits a pan-African millennium, a future golden age continuous with a glorious African past accompanied by God's judgment of white society and Western civilization.

Progressive millennialism is a more traditional type of millennial thought that emphasized the role of the Church, evangelism, missions and reform in giving birth to the millennium on earth. Although it also had notes of pan-Africanism and strong social criticism concerning race relations, it was unlike millennial Ethiopianism, and it reveals an optimism that the millennium will be marked by racial equality and harmony.

Millennialism combined with pan-Africanism and Ethiopianism supplied a holistic black religious quest for a golden age that was firmly rooted in the earthly realities. This tradition has manifested itself in a number of different ways in black communities in the USA and the Caribbean. It has, however, been allowed to languish in a dusty corner of premillennial eschatological dogma in the Black Church in the UK.

I now wish to focus on a number of trends that point to the development of the Black Church in the new millennium. These trends will have a major impact upon the nature of interchurch relations, missions and evangelism and theological development.

Future Trends and Challenges

The Black Presence in British Christianity

The visible presence of black Christians across the ecclesiastical spectrum will be much more noticeable in years to come. They will represent the difference between the generation that migrated to the UK and the ones that were born and or educated here. They will also be a reflection of the social mobility facilitated through higher and further education which has been endorsed and preached from the Black Church pulpits. One major difference in their attitude would be their desire to be in leadership roles and their intolerance with paternalism and racism.

This black presence will be mainly female, which follows on from the fact that black women are moving ahead faster, educationally and economically, than their male counterparts. This will challenge the popular idea in the media and in the perception of some policy makers that blacks are prone to underachieving and dropping out. This trend would therefore support my assertion that the Black Church is one of the fastest socially mobile constituencies in the black community.

The Growth and Prominence of the African Charismatic and Pentecostal Churches

In the last 20 years, the growth of the Black Churches in the UK has been mainly amongst the African-led congregations. These congregations are primarily West African, evangelical/Pentecostal and charismatic in orientation. Not located in any one denominational group, they are very dynamic and mostly led by African Church leaders who have moved out of other professional fields into Christian ministry.

These Churches' leadership is characterized by a flamboyant and entrepreneurial style which in itself is a challenge to the traditional black 'West Indian' Churches. There is a strong emphasis on faith and prosperity, which gives these Churches an image of success and upward mobility. Their Church government is somewhat autocratic and patriarchal, which supports the notion of strong leadership. They will be at the forefront of television evangelism, mass evangelistic campaigns and foreign missions. These are patterned on the example of American evangelical fundamentalism.

Black British Theology

During the past 20 years there has been a sprinkling of black Christians who have been influenced by the development of Black theology in the USA and the Republic of South Africa. This influence has come through theological education overseas, be that in the USA or the Caribbean. There has been the creation of a number of networks across the UK, which has become a focal point for encouraging and developing black British theologians.

Apart from organizing conferences covering a wide spectrum of issues, these groups have shown a willingness to stand up and be counted as a legitimate expression of black theological development in the UK. They have established a number of courses on black theology within British theological institutions. At a local congregational level a number of seminars are held catering for different levels of experience and exposure.

In 1998 these networks launched their own journal, *Black Theology in Britain: A Journal of Contextual Praxis*. This demonstrates the determination of black liberation theologians to engage British life and to articulate this engagement in the literary and oral traditions.

This coming of age of the black British theologian will also challenge the stereotype of the Black Church and encounter a much more positive response from the black community. There are many hurdles for these groups to manoeuvre over or around, none as important as the need constantly to gain a hearing in the Black Churches and other black Christian forums. Related to this would be the establishment of models that would challenge young black people with their action-orientated programmes that deal with the oppression of black people, socially, culturally, economically and politically. An example of these models would include the following:

(a) The development of our own theological institutions that would produce Christian leaders who understand their mission to include community leadership, political and economic theory and community organizing.
(b) The development of local Churches with a holistic gospel programme that is prepared to address the total needs of the black person, black community and the wider society. This would include a hermeneutic model that is proactive towards political engagement, that is, utilizing socioeconomic analysis in its formation and interpretation of its theology and practice.
(c) The development of a leadership style and organizational structure that encourages its membership to use its gifting to act as a leverage for the betterment and strengthening of the black community and wider community relations.
(d) The developments of structures that further empower black women for all forms of leadership, including the emerging womanist theology.

One such model for transformation is the recently created Black Christian Civic Forum, which has as one of its aims to bring political and informed information to the black Christian community. It has been able to establish itself among the Black Church denominations and a wide cross-section of black Christians in the historic denominations.

Faith communities in the new millennium will have to grapple with black British liberation theologians speaking with a Cockney or Liverpudlian accent and whose perception will be informed by a hermeneutic of suspicion on behalf of the poor and the disadvantaged.

I now wish to look at the changing British scene and its implications for the Black Churches.

All Change

Whatever the theology, structure or programme of the black Christian community we will have to 'engage the powers', to use Walter Wink's term. We will have to recognize the changing face of our world. From the rapid rise in information technology to the widespread apathy towards party politics in the UK, on one hand, to the long arm of injustice manifesting itself in ethnic conflicts or globalism on the other. We as black Christians and our leaders have the awesome responsibility to equip our children for the future and to leave them a legacy of institutions and traditions that faces up to the reality of our world in the twenty-first century.

The subject set before us today is a highly complex and integrated one. It covers a wide range of disciplines, including theology, philosophy, cultural studies, economics, politics, education and the social sciences. These are worked out in the tensions of our social relationships and the physical environments we share as a human family. This very complexity has made some Christians, black and white, throw up their hands in despair and surrender responsible civic education and action to others.

A recognition and awareness of these changes has to be accompanied by an understanding of the structure's ability to exercise authority, power and control over the individual, local communities and society. In other words, that they have the capacity to add to or take away from the quality of life of the people. Jesus' words 'I am come that you might have life and have it to the full' are indicative of the need for a change from oppressive systems and wicked regimes of power.

We in the Black Churches realize that the new century brings with it an era of change that has resulted in humanistic and secularist social philosophies and cultural pluralism that are all underpinned by postmodernism. There are further challenges presented by urbanization, mobility and the growing underclass in the midst of affluence. The dominant role of the entertainment industry in shaping the behaviour patterns and values of our youth cultures and countercultures has not gone unnoticed by us. A further realization is that these cannot be overlooked or ignored by the Christian community, and certainly not by the Black Churches—nor can they be tackled by Christian service that is reactive.

As a black liberation theologian I am amazed that some black evangelicals would, on one hand, accept the doctrine of original sin and the need for personal repentance, but are, on the other hand, unable to grasp that it stands to reason that the institutions and structures developed by these 'sinful' persons also fall short of the glory of God and therefore are also in need of conversion and transformation.

For in my use of the term 'structures' I am speaking of systems that evolve over time, that orchestrate and regulate our lives. These structures cover much of our lives, for example, education, criminal justice, constitutional reform and civil rights. Then there are the military, monetary and taxation systems, domestic and international trade, to mention just a few. These structures give meaning, significance and value to our human activities either individually or collectively.

Conclusion

The heart of the matter for the Christian Church, therefore, is how do we apply biblical truth to the public square so that it contributes to the philosophical assumptions, content and extent of the structures, their operations and their policies, thus redeeming the times and the cultures?

The critical question for the Black Church in Britain as we enter the twenty-first century is, Have we done enough to ensure the quality of life of the community of which we are a part? Our laid-back behind-the-scenes approach may be safe but does it answer the needs of the black community and even more so does it obey the teachings of the Church to be salt in the earth and light to the world?

Further Reading

Beckford, R., *Jesus Is Dread* (London: Darton, Longman & Todd, 1998).

Fryer, P., *Staying Power: The History of Black People in Britain* (London: Pluto Press, 1984).

Fulop, T.E., 'The Future Golden Day of the Race: Millennialism and Black Americans in the Nadir, 1877–1901', in T.E. Fulop and A.J. Raboteau (eds.), *African-American Religion* (New York: Routledge, 1997), pp. 227-54.

Haynes, A., *The State of Black Britain*, I (St John's, Antigua: Hansib Caribbean, 1996).

—*The State of Black Britain*, II (St John's, Antigua: Hansib Caribbean, 1997).

Kenyatta, J., *Facing Mount Kenya* (Nairobi: Heinemann Educational Books, 1984).

Mohabir, P., *Pioneers or Settlers?* (London: Scripture Union, 1991).
Pemberton, E., 'African Slave Religions in the Caribbean', *Black Theology in Britain* 2 (1999), pp. 90-116.
Walker, S.S., *The Religious Revolution in the Ivory Coast* (Chapel Hill, NC: University of North Carolina Press, 1983).
Williams, E., *From Columbus to Castro: The History of the Caribbean* (London: Andre Deutsch, 1975).
—*The Negro in the Caribbean* (Brooklyn: A. & B. Publishers, 1994).
Wood, W., *Keep The Faith Baby* (Oxford: Bible Reading Fellowship, 1994).

Reflections on the Relation of Self and Other in Mediaeval and Modern Christianity

Christopher Hamilton

Introduction

The aim of this essay is to explore a fundamental difference in the relation between self and other in mediaeval and modern Christian thought. Most importantly, I wish to discuss a profound difference in the nature of that relation on account of the increasing value that is placed in modern Christian thought on the notion of inwardness. I shall argue that this emphasis raises problems to which faith in the new millennium must respond if it is to remain the vital force in western culture that it has been in the last two millennia.

It goes without saying that in so rich a system of thought and experience as Christianity is, and in an essay with the broad sweep of the present type, there is no possibility here of doing justice to all that might be said on the chosen topic. The most that one can hope for is to alight upon a perspective that is helpful in what it reveals, is not gratuitously distorting in what it leaves out and which captures at least part of the truth. Further, there are no doubt other perspectives on the present topic that may provide further material for reflection, but there is no reason to suppose that they must be incompatible with what is said here: the issues discussed here are complicated and the more help we get from different perspectives in the attempt to understand them the better.

Thomas on the Four Kinds of Law

The richest and most well worked-out theology that mediaeval Christianity provided was that of St Thomas Aquinas, and it is on his thinking that I propose to concentrate at the outset. Thomas's religious outlook involves a very subtle account of the relation between self and other. In order to trace out this relation we may begin with a consideration of Thomas's account of the law.

Thomas thinks of the law in four ways.[1] First, God himself is an Eternal Law: Law is a name of God, like wisdom or goodness. Secondly, there is a law that is in us by nature (natural law) and dictates: pursue good and shun evil. Thirdly, there is enacted law, which we can derive from the natural law. Injunctions of enacted law would include, for example, prohibitions on killing. Fourthly, there is God's law, which Thomas divides into the Old Law and the New Law. I shall concentrate here on Thomas's thinking on natural law and on the Old and New Laws.

The Natural Law

For Thomas, all created things are good. Or, more exactly, all things that have being are good. And being is something that each created thing can have to a different degree. For the more a thing's potentialities are actualized the more being it has and, accordingly, the better it is. On this account, God, who is pure actuality, is perfect while everything else has only limited goodness since it has some potentialities that are unrealized.[2]

Human beings, for Thomas, share many of their features with the rest of creation. In particular, we are not alone in possessing the capacities of nutrition, growth and reproduction and in having the faculties of sensation, memory and imagination. What we have, however, which we do not share with the rest of the created world, is reason, and Thomas follows Aristotle in claiming that it is a life in accord with reason that fulfils our nature and is morally good. For he claims that, God having made us in his image, it is in our nature to do as God wishes us to do. Our natural inclination, properly understood, is thus to act in accordance with our reason, and this Thomas identifies with morally good behaviour.[3] Hence, Thomas thinks of natural law as the rational creature's participation in the eternal law: God imprints in our minds his eternal law, which we thus have in us by nature.[4]

Since Thomas thinks that God has imprinted his law on the mind of each of us, it follows that, for Thomas, even aside from our duties

1. St Thomas Aquinas, *Summa Theologiae* 1a2ae qu.91-108 (hereafter cited as ST).
2. ST 1a2ae qu.18, art.1, response (hereafter cited as resp.).
3. ST 1a2ae qu.18, art.5, resp.
4. ST 1a2ae qu.90, art.4, resp.

towards others, we have certain moral duties towards ourselves. For if I do not live the life of reason then at a fundamental level I am in conflict with myself, for I am in conflict with what I most fundamentally am. We can express this by saying that, according to Thomas, I have a duty of *care of self*. But, of course, I also have a duty of *care of others*, and this will support my duty of care of self, for the other shares the same fundamental nature with me. That is, the fact that the other's mind shares the same nature as my own and that our ultimate *telos* lies in the same place means for Thomas that a central way in which I pursue my own good is through pursuing the good of others. Hence it is that Thomas follows Aristotle in emphasizing the value of friendship based on concern for the other's virtue. Unlike Aristotle, however, he does not restrict this to all free-born males: he extends it to all human beings, and in doing so enriches—and to some extent leaves behind—Aristotle's notion of friendship by thinking of this friendship as a friendship in love or charity.[5]

Thomas thinks not only that we all share the same fundamental nature. He also thinks that the natural law can never be completely erased from our hearts, that we can never completely lose all our natural goodness, however evil we might be.[6] This is connected with the fact that evil remains a negative in Thomas's system, a privation of existence, and is thus not merely dependent upon goodness for its concrete existence in the world but is also dependent upon goodness in conceptual terms. Evil is conceptually recessive to goodness: without the concept of the latter we could never form the concept of the former. Thus, each individual human being has worth, however corrupt or evil he or she may seem. No one is beyond redemption and we must be ready to give unconditional forgiveness for acts committed against us. For there is always something in the evildoer that can respond to this forgiveness and to the call to a better life, which, in part, works through this forgiveness. In short, the natural law in all human beings creates a fellowship among us all.[7]

We can deepen these comments on the relation between my good and the good of others—between care of self and care of other—in Thomas's system by turning to look at his comments on the New Law and the Old Law.

5. ST 2a2ae qu.23ff, esp. at qu.25, art.4, resp.
6. ST 1a2ae qu.94, art.6, resp.
7. ST 2a2ae qu.25, art.6, resp.

The New Law, the Old Law, Grace and Guilt

For Thomas, the Old Law is the law that Christianity recovers from Judaism. Thomas does not reject the Old Law. On the contrary, he says that 'the precepts of the decalogue are immutable in so far as they embody justice in its essence'[8] and that there can be 'no doubt that the Old Law was good'.[9] The crucial distinction between the Old Law and the New Law is that the former governed only the external acts of men and women while the latter governs the soul. Hence it is that Thomas speaks of the connexion of grace with the New Law. '[T]here are five effects of grace in us: firstly, the healing of the soul; secondly, willing the good; thirdly, the efficacious performance of the good willed; fourthly, perseverance in the good; fifthly, the attainment of glory.'[10] The fact that the New Law is a law that governs the soul and not merely external action is expressed in this striking thought of Thomas's:

> [S]piritual men are not subject to the law for, through charity shed into their hearts by the Holy Ghost, they fulfil the law of their own will... [W]hat a man does by the Holy Spirit are the deeds of the Spirit rather than of the man himself.[11]

Thus the grace of the Holy Spirit, poured into the heart and hence constituting the New Law, means that God is immanently present in living in accordance with the New Law. That is, living in accordance with the New Law means being in the closest touch with God that it is possible to be in this life, since the soul is then filled with the spirit of God: God is within.

Why do human beings stand in need of the New Law of grace? The answer is that they are fallen, for sin entered the world through the turning of the human will away from God. By this sinning human beings lost their freedom from 'guilt and unhappiness'.[12] And, for Thomas, being guilty is now, after the fall of man, something that reveals the most fundamental condition of human beings. The guilt in question is not itself an emotion or feeling of guilt. It records the fact that the will

8. ST 1a2ae qu.100, art.8, resp.
9. ST 1a2ae qu.98, art.1, resp.
10. ST 1a2ae qu.111, art.3, resp.
11. ST 1a2ae qu.93, art.6, resp.
12. ST 1a qu.83, art.2, resp.

is corrupt and leads human beings away from their true good, God. It is therefore explanatory in reflections on how it is that human beings are capable of evil. Thus it is that man's guilt, on this picture, explains his other moral failings: guilt is the condition that explains any particular instance of wrongdoing.

As I have noted, this guilt is not an emotion of guilt. But there is, I think, an important point to be made here. For the guilt that characterizes man's state or condition—what one might call *primordial* guilt—is plausibly thought of as having a non-contingent connexion with the *predominance* of guilt as an emotion in response to wrong-doing. I shall refer to this *emotion* of guilt as 'experienced guilt' in order to distinguish it from primordial guilt in the sense just explained. What is meant by the predominance of guilt?

Consider the following point. It seems plausible to suppose that any normal human being, from any culture and at any stage (beyond, perhaps, the most rudimentary) in that culture's development will have a tendency to suffer psychological pain of some form or another for what is conceived of, by that human being, as, in the broadest sense, some wrongdoing. This pain could be experienced by a subject in various ways: guilt, shame, dishonour, self-disgust, self-contempt, self-despite and so on, although these ways are clearly not exclusive of one another. Guilt predominates for a subject when this psychological pain is mainly experienced by that subject as guilt, that is, when the subject more often experiences the psychological pain caused by his sense of his wrongdoing as guilt than any other moral emotion. Within the Christian tradition of which Thomas provides us with the best mediaeval account there is a deep connexion between the predominance of experienced guilt and primordial guilt. Where man's most fundamental nature is conceived in terms of primordial guilt, this will have a tendency to give rise to the predominance of experienced guilt among the moral emotions. Moreover, the influence will also work in the reverse direction: the predominance of experienced guilt will tend to justify further the sense that human beings are primordially guilty. Hence it is that the emphasis in the Christian tradition on guilt, even if couched mainly in terms of primordial guilt, will tend to support experienced guilt.

Thus, within the Christian tradition guilt is conceived of as something that is a *source* for wrongdoing and a *reaction* to wrongdoing. These two aspects of the operation of guilt support and strengthen one another: they do this, at least in part, by making each other, and their role with respect to one another and the moral-emotional life of human beings, intelligible, that is, by being explanatory of one another and of other aspects of man's behaviour.

Guilt and Inwardness

Within Thomas's system there is a deep and important link between primordial guilt and the concept of inwardness. How is this link forged? We may begin from the idea that the self is not something that we can characterize in non-moral, or at any rate non-evaluative, terms. But which terms are used alters the sense of how deep the self is. The self is not like a container that holds, or could hold, now this, now that content. Rather, the shape of the self depends upon how it is conceived. To think of the self as primordially guilty is to think of it as being such that, at any depth at which it could be investigated, there is a still further depth at which it could be explored and this is so because it is conceived on this model as something that has dark depths that can never be brought to light. On this picture, there is always more 'down there', which is working in ever more subtle ways against virtue and purity of motive—a thought that obviously goes beyond the idea that the drives of the self (sometimes) need to be controlled by virtue. Another way to put this point is to say that for Thomas, as for the central tradition of Christian thinking, the ideal of human conduct that affects others is that such conduct be entirely free of self-interest. Yet, as Samuel Johnson remarked: 'To act from pure benevolence is not possible for finite beings. Human benevolence is mingled with vanity, interest, or some other motive.' And this means that the Christian *cannot but fail* in his or her attempts to act as required by his or her system of belief. The self will always throw up something which is not purely benevolent or free of self-interest, and even if the subject cannot be sure what that is in any given case, and even if he or she suspects that, in a given case, the act was free of self-interest, he or she must assume that this was not the case and that self-interest was at work there after all. Thomas himself puts this point in terms of the idea that the theological virtue of charity is the 'mother and root of all virtue'[13] but that it is impossible to have this virtue in its perfect form, from which it follows that we can only fail to be the kind of virtuous creatures which God wants of us. Grace is

13. ST 1a2ae qu.62, art.4, resp.

what is required to complete our virtue and that is something which exceeds the human, all too human and, indeed, shows up its very limitations.

If the notion of primordial guilt is quite absent from one's conceptualizations of the self, then the self will not be thought to have the kinds of inner depths in question. And although many different conceptualizations are available which would construe the self as having depths, it does seem that thinking of the self as primordially guilty is a conceptualization that represents the self as deeper than other conceptualizations allow, and that is so for the reasons given, namely, that here the self is thought of as working against virtue. There is thus no contingent connexion between the emphasis that Christianity places upon (primordial and experienced) guilt and inwardness. Thomas, in fact, provides us with a conception of the *maximally deep self*.

This connexion between primordial guilt and depth helps to explain why it is that (experienced) guilt has such a power to poison a life—even in an age, such as ours, which places little overt emphasis upon primordial guilt but which is very strongly attached to the idea of the self as having inner depths. For even as we may wish to be free of guilt, the experience of this moral emotion can be a synecdoche for, or emblematic of, the depth of the inner life which we have reason to want. Thus we can remain attached to the experience of guilt for what we think it shows about our inner life. And hence it is that there is a contrast between guilt and shame. As Bernard Williams has pointed out, when one experiences shame one wishes to hide in order to relieve one's discomfort. But, as he correctly says, '[w]ith guilt, it is not like this; I am more dominated by the thought that even if I disappeared, it would come with me'.[14] Another way of putting the point is to say that the experience of guilt is the experience of the inner voice,[15] whereas shame is the experience of being looked at. Thus guilt seems more intimately deep in what one is than shame.

14. B. Williams, *Shame and Necessity* (Berkeley: University of California Press, 1993), p. 87.

15. Cf. H. Morris, 'Guilt and Shame', in *On Guilt and Innocence: Essays in Legal Philosophy and Moral Psychology* (Berkeley: University of California Press, 1976), pp. 59-63.

The Relation of Self and Other

Guilt, then, is intimately connected with the notion of inwardness. And within Thomas's thinking it is this which means that care of self and care of other are profoundly dependent upon one another. For in spiritual and psychological terms love of one's neighbour is centrally, if not exclusively, construed by him as the effort to remove the dark depths of the self by achieving a direct openness to others (and thus to oneself) through removing anything in the soul which could work against others. Removal of—or work against—guilt, on the one hand, and love of the other, on the other hand, are two sides of the same process within Christian morality. We can, perhaps, see this most clearly in those fourth- and fifth-century Desert Fathers whom Peter Brown has discussed. St Anthony, for example, was loved as 'someone whose heart had achieved total transparency to others'.[16] The monk of the desert was the man 'who had gained a heart that was all of one piece, a heart as unriven by the knotted grain of private, unshared meanings and of private, covert intentions as was the solid, milk-white heart of the date-palm'.[17] Moreover, the monk's heart was like a book. 'What required infinitely skilled exegesis and long spiritual experience were the "movements of the heart", and the strategies and snares that the Devil laid within it.'[18]

For Christian thinkers, then, there can be no clear distinction between care of self and care of other. And it is primordial guilt with its connected notion of inwardness—together with the natural law imprinted on our hearts—that forges this intertwining of the two forms of concern.

The Impact of the Reformation

Mediaeval Christian thinking, as provided by Thomas, thus links together care of self and care of other in a profoundly intimate relation. According to this system, I seek my own good as I seek that of the other and vice versa.

The modern period, starting from around the time of the Reforma-

16. P. Brown, *The Body and Society* (New York: Columbia University Press, 1988), p. 226.

17. Brown, *The Body and Society*, p. 227.

18. Brown, *The Body and Society*, p. 229.

tion—especially with the work of Luther and Calvin—represents in many ways the gradual crumbling of this conception of a deep intimacy between the concerns of the individual and his or her fellow human beings. We must try to trace out why this is so.

There are two important shifts that we see in the thinking on the relation between self and other in Reformation thinking. The first is that the thinkers of the Reformation placed even greater emphasis upon inwardness. It was inwardness that, to these thinkers, came to be absolutely central to the constitution of Christian faith. Whence this idea? One reason is simply that they were reacting against the legalistic conception of morality that the nominalism of the fourteenth and fifteenth centuries unwittingly brought with it. But there was also a deeper reason. This is to be found in the fact that the thinkers of the Reformation insisted with renewed emphasis that man's nature was utterly corrupt and had no resources within itself to enable human beings to move through their own effort towards the *telos* of their life, namely, the vision of God in a life after this. But as I have already argued, there was always within Christianity a deep conceptual and psychological relation between guilt and inwardness for Christian thinking and thus the increased emphasis on guilt by Reformation thinkers naturally brought in train an increased emphasis upon inwardness.

This emphasis upon inwardness had, as Max Weber famously argued,[19] a peculiar result. For much of life, but most especially the life of production—economic activity—broke free from the strictures of Christian morality under which it had formerly stood, since it had nothing to do with the inwardness of human beings. Nevertheless, and somewhat paradoxically, such activity came also to be considered to be an outward sign of inner salvation. But precisely because this idea was of a paradoxical nature, the uneasy alliance between the emphasis upon inwardness and the outer indication of just what the true nature of one's inner state was began to break down rather rapidly. The economic sphere developed away from being any kind of indication of the inner until it developed its own norms and became an end in itself. And as social life became more and more orientated by capitalistic modes of economic activity, which this development in religious thinking had helped to set in train, other aspects of life that had formerly fallen under the strictures of Christian morality came to be understood and assessed

19. M. Weber, *Die protestantische Ethik und der 'Geist' des Kapitalismus* (Bodenheim: Athenäum Hain Hanstein, 1993 [1904–1905]), *passim*.

in terms of the same kind of bureaucratic rationality that characterized, and continues to characterize, capitalistic acquisition itself.

What we have here, then, is a development of Christian morality that issues in a deep cleft between the inner and the outer and no clear way in which these two are held together. And this cleft had a profound effect on the relation between care of self and care of other within Christianity. For it meant that there was no longer felt to be a deep intimacy of concern across them. On the contrary, the rise of Reformation thinking tended to conceptualize the individual as isolated, left more or less to his or her own devices to work out his or her salvation in the privacy of the inner self with God. Morality came to be conceived of less and less as an enterprise in which we together work out our destiny and more and more as a mere system of rules of non-interference that leaves space for the individual to retreat into the inner life and meet God there. Hence the rise of theories that tend to assimilate morality to the law and think of it largely in terms of rules on a legal model. And hence also the rise of state of nature theories that view morality largely in terms of contract. Strangely enough, Luther's hostility to an empty formalism in moral and spiritual matters and an emphasis on the individual in his or her relationship to God led to an ever greater legalism. Moreover, this legalistic view of morality was further encouraged by the Counter-Reformation, which saw itself in the business of laying out the rules and laws that had to be followed for true membership of the Roman Church and which all but lost the inner life from sight.

Atheistic Responses to the Reformation

One response to the development of the inner away from the outer is to abandon religious faith. If this happens, then two polarized positions tend to emerge from the wreckage. For since care of self and care of other are no longer seen as intimately bound up with one another, it is possible that either the one or the other comes to be emphasized at the expense of what was previously its counterpart. That is, under these conditions either care of self is no longer seen as a moral issue or care of the other ceases to be of great significance in the moral life. The first of these developments I should like to illustrate through the work of Jeremy Bentham; the second through that of Nietzsche.

Bentham was, of course, a utilitarian. He believed that the criterion of the moral goodness of an action lay only in its tendency to promote happiness or reduce unhappiness, and he understood happiness to consist in pleasure and unhappiness to consist in pain. He allowed into his thinking no distinction between the quality of different pleasures and thus famously asserted that push-pin was of no greater value than poetry, provided only that it give pleasure. This view has been amply criticized by moral philosophers, but what has been less often criticized in his philosophy is the fact that there is, as Mill put it,[20] a complete blank in Bentham's system on the question of self-education or self-development. For Bentham, it makes no sense to think of morality as involving anything that we could recognize as a self-concern. The inner life is of no interest to him and the moral agent is to be concerned only with the other.

Why has this aspect of Bentham's philosophy been so little criticized? The central reason is that moral philosophers of the modern era, particularly in the English-speaking world, have been almost as indifferent to the inner life as Bentham was. For example, it is only very recently —in the last 20 years or so—that philosophers in the analytic tradition have shown any interest in the virtues as dispositions of character, and they are still indifferent to many other features of the inner moral and spiritual life. There is thus in the mainstream of moral philosophy almost no discussion of the nature of a person's spirit;[21] of what it is to learn and grow morally and spiritually by being moved; of moods and temperament; of what sense, if any, can be made of purity and of the ways in which certain experiences can have a cathartic effect on the self; of the way in which the inner life can be haunted by images or ideas; and so on. Without knowing it, and even as they take themselves to be opposed to him, modern moral philosophers very largely follow in Bentham's footsteps in their indifference to the inner life. But the point has wider application than merely to philosophy. For, as Edward Craig[22] and Iris Murdoch[23] have in their different ways pointed out, we live in an age where the dominant picture of the moral subject is that of an agent acting in the world, and this emphasis leaves out

20. J.S. Mill, 'Bentham', in *Mill on Bentham and Coleridge: With an Introduction by F.R. Leavis* (London: Chatto & Windus, 1950), pp. 39-98, esp. p. 71.

21. I have said something about this notion in C. Hamilton, 'Ethics and the Spirit', *Philosophical Investigations* 21.4 (1998), pp. 313-37.

22. E. Craig, *The Mind of God and the Works of Man* (Oxford: Clarendon Press, 1987), esp. ch. 5.

23. I. Murdoch, *The Sovereignty of Good* (London: Ark, 1970), *passim.*

inner life. The cleft between inner and the outer that was wrought by the Reformation has, for many in the modern world, meant the end of the notion of care of self as a moral concern. Indeed, there are very few of our contemporaries for whom the idea that morality centrally or importantly is concerned with one's relation to oneself makes any sense.

If Bentham represents the apotheosis of indifference to the inner life as a moral notion, then Nietzsche represents the reverse. For him, care of the other is in many ways no longer truly a moral matter. That is, for Nietzsche, the rules that we need to get on with one another are not fundamentally of moral significance: they are primarily matters of prudence. For this reason, he thinks that the great man can act with a completely clear conscience on those who are below him in the hierarchy of noble life. As he puts it, the mass of people exist merely for the great man and may be used by him as he sees fit. On the other hand, Nietzsche makes a great deal of the inner life. A vast amount of his work is concerned with developing strategies whereby we may purify our inner life of what, in the *Genealogy of Morals* and elsewhere, he calls its slavish elements—*ressentiment*, guilt, envy and the like—and this culminates in his notion of an affirmation of life, the ability to want to live one's life over again just as it has been. This will include the affirmation of even those parts of one's life which were painful or contained suffering, and it is in this, perhaps, that we see most strongly his emphasis on the development of the inner life, for an affirmation of one's pain and suffering involves the ability to be sufficient unto oneself, that is independent of the way the world goes.[24]

What is thus of great interest in both Bentham and Nietzsche is that, despite their disagreement on almost every point of principle and detail, they share something in common, namely, that they are neither of them able to make sense of a care of self which is also a care of others. Of course, they represent, as I have said, the extremes of the split between the inner and outer which Reformed Christianity bequeathed to the modern world. They do so because they rejected Christian belief, a central reason for which was precisely that split between the inner and the outer to which Christianity had been subject.

But how do things stand for those in the modern world who retain allegiance to the Christian faith?

24. I have explored Nietzsche's notion of the affirmation of life at greater length in C. Hamilton, 'Nietzsche on Nobility and the Affirmation of Life', *Ethical Theory and Moral Practice* 3.2 (2000), pp. 169-93.

A Revitalized Faith?

The split between the inner and the outer has been for some Christian thinkers not a reason to doubt the validity of Christian faith but has been welcomed as involving the possibility of a revitalized relationship to God. Central here is Kierkegaard, who pressed extremely hard on the concepts of both inwardness and guilt in his thinking. Kierkegaard saw the outer as providing no grounding for faith at all and thus turned his energies towards trying to reconstitute Christianity from the resources of inwardness. I have elsewhere argued that there is a great deal to be said for this move.[25] Roughly, what can be said in favour of it is that it makes clear, and focuses our minds on the idea, that faith is fundamentally a spiritual matter which has to do with how and in what way it deepens an individual's inner life. But there are doubts about this way of proceeding and since I have, as noted, concentrated elsewhere on its advantages, I wish here to air some of the difficulties it raises.

There are, I think, two central problems attendant upon the conception of faith we are now considering. These are, first, that it may mean we overlook the idea that Christian faith has usually seen itself in the business of making truth claims about the world and its relation to God, and, secondly, that it leaves the relation between the moral structure of the inner life and the nature of one's moral relations with others extremely unstable. The two are connected, as we shall see—indeed, the second problem cannot be properly understood without understanding the first—but I shall concentrate on them in turn.

In postwar English-speaking philosophy it has largely been through thinking inspired by the work of Wittgenstein that the denial that someone who has a religious belief makes or needs to make metaphysical claims about the world has been articulated. Let us, therefore, turn briefly to Wittgenstein and then see how his thinking has been used by those influenced by him who are also sympathetic to religious faith.

The central Wittgensteinian point concerning religious beliefs is that we should not think that those who deny religious beliefs are *contradicting* those who hold or assert such beliefs. For example, it is argued that the person who says that he does not believe God exists does not contradict someone who says she does believe God exists as he would

25. C. Hamilton, 'Kierkegaard on Truth as Subjectivity: Christianity, Ethics and Asceticism', *Religious Studies* 34.1 (1998), pp. 61-79.

if he said that he does not believe that there is a chair in the next room to someone who said she did believe there was a chair so situated. For, so the argument goes, in questions of religious belief matters of evidence are entirely inappropriate, and so in assertions of belief or disbelief the conceptual background—precisely *evidence*—that would support the possibility of contradiction is missing. Wittgenstein seems to have thought this because he thought it plain that the evidence for Christian belief was so slim that no rational person could possibly rest his or her belief on it. Anyone who looked for evidence of that belief would be, according to Wittgenstein, superstitious and unreasonable.[26] But since it is manifestly the case that many have believed and that their belief has been important to them in some way, indeed in the very deepest way, Wittgenstein supposed that there must be some other way of understanding their belief, that is, a way that pays no attention to evidence at all. Hence Wittgenstein is reported as saying, 'The point is that if there were evidence, this would in fact destroy the whole business.'[27]

Wittgenstein himself did not do much to make this account of religious belief any clearer: his comments remain embryonic. But others have sought to build on his account. One of these is Raimond Gaita, and I should like briefly to consider some of his comments, since this will, I think, allow us to get clearer about the problems to which the kind of account of religious belief we are considering is exposed.

Gaita denies that religious belief needs support from anything metaphysical. In support of this he considers what someone might mean if he says that he 'believes *literally* that there is a God, that He receives our prayers, that everything that happens is an expression of His will and that He created heaven and earth and all things in them'.[28] If, for example, such a person says that God knows everything, does this mean that God knows his telephone number? Gaita says that that seems to him to be nonsense and that 'this kind of literal-mindedness misconstrues the grammar of serious religious belief'.[29] Gaita goes on to say that the important point about religious speech is that, when it is thus serious, it is connected with what deepens our lives in certain ways.

26. L. Wittgenstein, *Lectures and Conversations on Aesthetics, Psychology and Religious Belief* (ed. C. Barrett; Oxford: Basil Blackwell, 1978), p. 59.

27. Wittgenstein, *Lectures and Conversations*, p. 56.

28. R. Gaita, *Good and Evil: An Absolute Conception* (London: Macmillan, 1991), p. 220.

29. Gaita, *Good and Evil*, p. 220.

Thus he says:

> The difficulty I have with what some people call a literal belief in religious propositions is in connecting them with anything spiritual. If someone says that to believe in God is to believe that there is some X with attributes a-n and that it knows my telephone number, then that is to speak of God in a way that is not yet spiritual.[30]

As an example of the deepening he has in mind Gaita gives the following example from Pablo Casals:

> For the past eighty years I have started each day in the same manner. It is not a mechanical routine but something essential to my daily life. I go to the piano and I play two preludes and fugues of Bach. I cannot think of doing otherwise. It is a sort of benediction on the house. But that is not the only meaning it has for me. It is a rediscovery of the world of which I have the joy of being a part. It fills me with awareness of the wonder of life, with a feeling of the incredible marvel of being a human being… I do not think that a day has passed in my life when I have failed to look with fresh amazement at the miracle of nature.[31]

Gaita says that this draws our attention to connexions between goodness, attention, love and purity. He denies that this is a conception of religious goodness, yet he calls it a 'kind of ethical other-worldliness'. He says he calls it that in order 'to emphasise that the sense of other-worldliness is ethically conditioned rather than the other way about, as most who say they are humanists because they are not religious, would think it to be'.[32] He says that we could say that Casals spoke of life as a gift and that he speaks in the accent of gratitude. But Gaita says that someone who so speaks does not need to think that there is someone to whom he or she is grateful such that that idea would require metaphysical support or justification. Further, he clearly thinks that if someone says that life is a gift from God this no more needs metaphysical support than does the claim that life is a gift, for he goes on:

> The person who speaks of life as a gift but who cannot speak of it as God's gift might say that to be religious in the 'strict sense' is to be able to speak of God and to speak His name in prayer. That does not mean

30. Gaita, *Good and Evil*, p. 221.

31. Gaita, *Good and Evil*, p. 215; the original is in *Joys and Sorrows: Reflections by Pablo Casals, as told to Albert E. Kahn* (New York: Simon & Schuster, 1970), p. 17.

32. Gaita, *Good and Evil*, p. 217.

> that if someone is not religious in the strict sense, then they are not religious at all, or that they are religious in a waffly sense. If such a person may be said to speak out of an implicit recognition, or even love of, God then they speak religiously even if they would only shrug their shoulders at such a claim. There are first- and third-person asymmetries here.[33]

I have a great deal of sympathy with Gaita's approach here, but it is not free from problems. The central of these can be seen if we ask the key question, Why should examples such as that of Casals be appropriated by religious thinking—by 'God-talk'? Consider another example. Erich Heller says of Nietzsche and Rilke that they sought to

> re-assess and re-define all experience in thought and feeling; to show that the traditional modes of thought and feeling, in so far as they were determined, or decisively modified, by Christian transcendental beliefs—and to which of them does this not apply?—had been rendered invalid by the end of religion; to replace them; to overcome the great spiritual depression, caused by the death of God, through new and ever greater powers of glory and praise; to adjust, indeed to revolutionize, thought and feeling in accord with the reality of a world of absolute immanence; and to achieve this without any loss of spiritual grandeur.[34]

When Rilke and Nietzsche praised existence and expressed a gratitude for life, we cannot say that they were really Christians in disguise or that they spoke out of an implicit recognition, or love of, God, nor even that they were on their way to such a recognition. There is no way that we can coopt their view to a Christian outlook. Yet this, it seems, is what Gaita must be committed to doing. And the reason for this is that, as Heller points out, so much of what we are and what we want to say has been formed by Christianity that those who want to say anything new are always faced by the following problem: either they try to create a new vocabulary, in which case it is highly likely that they will simply be misunderstood by their contemporaries; or they try to breathe a new and different set of ideas into vocabulary of Christian provenance or colouring, in which case their modes of thinking and feeling will probably not be appreciated for what they are and will be assimilated to that which they are trying to overcome. This, I cannot help feeling, is what is happening in the case of Gaita's thinking about what it is to speak in religious language.

33. Gaita, *Good and Evil*, p. 225.

34. E. Heller, *The Disinherited Mind* (Cambridge: Bowes & Bowes, 1952), p. 140.

'Whom Does Christianity Deny?'

Certainly one can see that a view such as Casals' is admirable and enviable, and one would like to make it part of one's own life. My worry, it will be clear, is simply about assimilating it to a Christian point of view. And central to that worry is the fact that, in denying that Christian belief need make any metaphysical claims, the Wittgensteinian view draws upon and deepens the split between the inner and outer that is characteristic of modern Christian belief. And this leaves the relation between self and other unclear. We can see this perhaps most clearly if we turn for a moment to some comments by Paul Tillich:

> I have written of the God above the God of theism. This idea has been misunderstood as a dogmatic statement of a pantheistic or mystical character. First of all, it is not dogmatic, but an apologetic, statement. It takes seriously the radical doubt experienced by many people. It gives one the courage of self-affirmation even in the extreme state of radical doubt. In such a state the God of both religious and theological language disappears. But something remains, namely, the seriousness of that doubt in which meaning within meaninglessness is affirmed. The source of this affirmation of meaning within meaninglessness, of certitude within doubt, is not the God of traditional theism but the 'God above God', the power of being, which works through those who have no name for it, not even the name of God.[35]

This description could in many ways fit Casals who himself found no solace in traditional religion and who was plagued by doubts about the meaninglessness of pain and suffering in this world. And what this shows, I think, is that the inner life of the believer—or doubter?—as Tillich conceives of him has become so free of any specific content that it can issue in nothing very specific by way of care of self. The structure of faith as a state of inwardness which makes no claims about the outer world—except how frighteningly meaningless it is—and which itself is beset by vagueness means that the moral life of the believer—if that is what he or she is—begins to lose the possibility of offering anything distinctive by way of care of self. And, *a fortiori*, this vagueness must issue in a vagueness about how care of self is supposed to connect with care of other and what the latter can consist in. The *distinctively Christian* notions of care of self and care of other and, correlatively, the way

35. P. Tillich, *Systematic Theology*. II, Pt. III. *Existence and the Christ* (London: SCM Press, 1990), p. 12.

they are bound together, wither. And it is, I believe, on account of this very vagueness of the Christian notions of care of self and care of other that there is an increasing tendency for those who consider themselves believers to acquiesce in adopting the prevailing moral values. This has resulted in a kind of vacuity at the heart of many professions of faith. Nietzsche was amazed and angered at this:

> Where has the last feeling of decency gone, of respect for oneself, when even our statesmen—otherwise thoroughly impartial and anti-Christians in their actions—still call themselves Christians and go to communion?... A young prince at the head of his regiments, resplendent in expressing the egoism and superiority of his people—but *without* any shame declaring his allegiance to Christianity! *Whom* does Christianity deny? *what* does it call 'world'? That one is a soldier, a judge, a patriot; that one defends oneself; that one values one's honour; that one wants one's advantage; that one is *proud*... Every action of every moment, every instinct, every value-judgement which issues in *action* today is anti-Christian: what sort of a *monster of falsity* must modern man nonetheless be to have *no shame* in being called a Christian![36]

Or, as Mr Vincy says in more restrained terms to Mr Bulstrode (*Middlemarch*, ch.13): 'I don't see anybody...who is not worldly... The only difference I see is that one worldliness is a little bit honester than the other.'

A Way Forward?

I have suggested that contemporary Christian morality is suffering from a looming vacuity in its centre and that this means that Christians more and more tend towards identifying passing moral concerns in the culture at large as their own, leaving little room for a distinctively Christian moral message. This is why it is now possible to ask, 'What's "Special" about Christian Morality?'[37] It is not that this is an unworthy question to ask or to seek to answer. But the very fact that it *is* raised and that one tries to answer it betrays a deep uneasiness about whether there is, after all, anything special about Christian morality and what

36. F. Nietzsche, *Der Antichrist* §38 (ed. G. Colli and M. Montinari; Kritische Studienausgabe, 6; Munich: Deutscher Taschenbuch Verlag, 1988), my translation.
37. Denis F. O'Callaghan, 'What's "Special" about Christian Morality?', in M.A. Hayes and L. Gearon (eds.), *Contemporary Catholic Theology: A Reader* (Leominster: Gracewing, 1998), pp. 369-74.

that might be. I should like to end by suggesting, not an answer to the question, but a direction in which one might look.

I noted earlier that both the Reformation and the Counter-Reformation had a tendency to assimilate morality to the following of rules or laws, leaving the inner life of the believer adrift. And this understanding of morality is the dominant one in modernity. Both Christians and atheists are living in the modern world in an age of moral minimalism in which it is taken to be sufficient for moral probity to follow the laws of the land and avoid overt hostility to others. It seems to me that if Christianity is to remain a powerful and nurturing moral and spiritual force in this new millennium then what it needs to do is to move away from a conception of morality—of moral minimalism—that is overly preoccupied with rules and duties, and to concentrate again on those richer aspects of morality that are so often overlooked by the contemporary world. And this, it seems to me, is exactly what the documents of Vatican II attempt to do. That is, I believe that Vatican II took up just that challenge which is presented by the split of the inner and the outer—the split of care of self and care of other—that I have discussed here. For Vatican II sought to forge a new—or, at any rate, reinvigorated—vocabulary in which to understand our moral and spiritual relation to ourselves and to one another. Such a vocabulary would do away with moral codes that seek to simplify the difficult and serious task of living a life while providing some of the materials needed to give a distinctively Christian content to both care of self and care of other and their relation to one another. How successful Vatican II has been in that attempt is as yet unclear: we are only just beginning to absorb its lessons.

THE HAQQANI NAQSHBANDIS: A STUDY OF APOCALYPTIC MILLENNIALISM WITHIN ISLAM

Ron Geaves

Introduction

It is not surprising that the much-heralded arrival of the year 2000 has aroused considerable interest within Christianity, there being a strong tradition of millennialism with long-held apocalyptic beliefs concerning the triumphant return of Jesus Christ. The advent of both the first and second millennia have seen a growth of sects expecting the imminent arrival of the Messiah and the final assault on and defeat of the forces of Satan at Armageddon. It is less well known that Islam also maintains strong eschatological traditions that can be compared to Christian beliefs concerning the end time even though the Islamic calendar has only recently reached 1420 and cannot therefore be described as millennial. However, as will be seen, the year 1400 holds a significance for Islam which, when coinciding with the millennium, adds weight to beliefs concerning the immediacy of the end time.

Whereas much Christian thought concerning the new millennium is centred on the future of the faith in the twenty-first century rather than faith in the apocalyptic tradition and its imminent fulfilment, traditional Muslims tend to hold more literal eschatological beliefs. Within most forms of orthodox Christianity the possibility of the millennium heralding the fulfilment of apocalyptic visions of the end time has receded to the extent that the belief has been pushed to the fringes of the religion or even out into new alternative spiritualities. In both these locations these beliefs can function to express alienation with certain aspects of contemporary western society. Muslim expectations of the end time, devoid of the major debates that transformed western Christianity over the last three hundred years, such as the Enlightenment and more recently, postmodernism, remain far more apocalyptic and literal in their interpretation of events. In addition to the above reasons for the differences between the two faith traditions, there is the fact that Islam remains a religion practised predominantly by rural populations in spite of increasing urbanization in the Muslim world. Such rural believers are far more likely to retain their literal interpretation of traditional beliefs. Even in the urban areas Islam has proved to be far more resistant to secularization than western Christianity and this too may have an influence on the differing attitudes to apocalyptic end time traditions.

This article will explore the teachings of a contemporary Muslim leader, Shaykh Nazim al-Haqqani of the Naqshbandi Sufi *tariqa* (order),[1] who has developed traditional Muslim doctrines concerning the end time into a full-blown prophetic millennial message that dovetails with some Christians' expectations of the return of Jesus. In order to understand the Shaykh's (spiritual master) teachings on this subject it will be necessary to locate them in the context of both traditional Muslim beliefs concerning the Last Day (*Yaum al-Din*) and the unique contemporary factors that may have predisposed the Shaykh to millennialism.

The Haqqani Naqshbandis

Although Shaykh Muhammad Nazim Adil al-Haqqani an-Naqshbandi can trace his Sufi lineage through his mother's ancestry to Jalalu'd-Din Rumi and on his father's side to Shaykh Abdul Qadir Jilani,[2] it is in the

1. The Naqshbandi *tariqa* is the largest and most widespread of the Sufi orders. As with most Sufi *tariqas* it is organized as local autonomous groups that wax and wane in importance and size according to the reputation and leadership of the particular charismatic spiritual guide. Before Turkish secularization, the Naqshbandi *tariqa* was strong in both Turkey and Syria. The *silsilah* (spiritual lineage) of Shaykh ad-Daghestani can be traced back through the great Indian master, Shaykh Ahmad Sirhindi (d. 1625), rather than through the Central Asian or Turkish branches. The Indian branch of the *tariqa* returned to the Middle East through the initiation of Murad ibn Ali al-Bukhari by the son of Shaykh Ahmad Sirhindi. Al-Bukhari made Damascus his centre from where he travelled thoughout the Middle East before dying in Istanbul in 1720. The Turkish branch of the *tariqa* was strong in the towns and there were over 50 centres in Istanbul in the 1880s (J. Spencer Trimingham, *The Sufi Orders in Islam* [Oxford: Oxford University Press, 1998], p. 95).

2. Jalalu'd-Din Rumi was the founder of the influential Ottoman *tariqa* known as the Mevlani. They are well-known for their whirling movement, known as turning, in order to achieve ecstasy. Rumi's poetry has been translated into many

Naqshbandi *tariqa* that he has developed his own considerable spiritual achievements. Shaykh Nazim was born in Cyprus in 1922 and after completing his high school education went on to study for a degree in chemical engineering at the University of Istanbul. While in Istanbul he began to study Arabic and the *shari'a* (religious law) but he also received permission from Shaykh Jamal al-Lassuni (d. 1955) to study the spiritual path of Islam. Shaykh Nazim pursued the study of seven Sufi *tariqas* (Naqshbandi, Chishti, Qadiri, Mawlawi, Rifa'i, Shadhili and Badawi) but it was the Naqshbandi *tariqa* that attracted him and in which he discovered his spiritual home. He continued his studies of the Naqshbandi *tariqa* under the guidance of Shaykh Sulayman Arzurumi, who advised him to continue his journey by seeking instruction from Shaykh Abdullah ad-Daghestani, who was residing in Damascus.[3] The meeting with Shaykh Abdullah ad-Daghestani was to transform Shaykh Nazim's spiritual life.

Throughout Cyprus the Shaykh continued to teach the *tariqat* (inner path) according to the Naqshbandi way, later expanding his activities to Lebanon, Egypt and even Saudi Arabia. In 1952 he moved back to Damascus and married one of the daughters of his Shaykh. From that time he lived in Damascus, studying under the guidance of the *Grand-shaykh* (the master of a master or founder of an order) until Abdullah ad-Daghastani's death in 1973. Shaykh Nazim underwent rigorous spiritual training in close proximity to his Shaykh, including a number of lengthy retreats in famous locations, such as the mosque of Abdul Qadir Jilani and the Prophet's mosque in Medina. These periods of isolation were interrupted only when he performed the five prayers with other Muslims. During this period he continued to spend three months of every year in Cyprus where he organized parties of Muslims to accompany him on the *Hajj* (the annual Muslim pilgrimage to Mecca).[4]

After the death of the *Grandshaykh*, Shaykh Nazim extended his missionary activities to include Europe. From 1973, he began to visit

languages and is popular in the West. Shaykh Abdul Qadir Gilani is the founder of the world-wide Qadiri *tariqa* but is also believed by many to be the ultimate Sufi saint.

3. The biographical details concerning Shaykh Nazim can be found in the movement's literature or on their websites. A good source is http.//www.naqshbandi.net/haqqani/sufi/Sh.Nazim.html.

4. www.naqshbandi.net/haqqani, p. 3

London regularly, and then in 1991 he made his first journey to the USA. Shaykh Nazim has been particularly successful in promoting the spiritual teachings of Sufism to large numbers of non-Muslims. In the USA there are now over 20 centres dedicated to establishing the Haqqani Naqshbandis under the guidance of Shaykh Nazim's *khalifa* (a disciple appointed to teach), Shaykh Muhammad Hisham Kabbani. Many of the western followers have gone on to become Muslims under Shaykh Nazim's charismatic influence.

When Shaykh Nazim first visited the UK, he had a ready audience in the Turkish-Cypriot Muslim community, which had mainly settled in London escaping the civil war that had afflicted Cyprus. During his first visit he attracted a young Muslim of Pakistani background named Shahid, whose parents had lived in south Turkey. Through Shahid's involvement, the Shaykh's message was able to move into the subcontinent migrant communities and today there are small groups of *murids* (disciples) in most of the major centres where the subcontinent Muslims have settled. However, it was the Turkish-Cypriot community which provided Shaykh Nazim with a base in Britain.

As the Grand Mufti (Muslim religious leader) of Cyprus he is able to attract large audiences of Turkish-Cypriot migrants, and many of them have become *murids*. Other members of the community simply regard him as one of the prominent religious leaders from their place of origin. It was the Turkish-Cypriot community who purchased the first mosque in Shacklewell Lane in north-east London and later the second mosque in Peckham, south-east London. Both districts of London are strong centres of migration from Cyprus, but they also include other populations of Muslims from West Africa and the subcontinent. The two mosques are managed by the Cypriot community and function as social and worship centres for them throughout most of the year. The surge of international activity when the Shaykh is present attracts attention from the other Muslim communities in the area and has added to the Shaykh's facility to cross ethnic borders when attracting followers.

The current headquarters of the Haqqani Trust is the former convent, St Anne's Priory, in north London, now renamed the Haqqani Islamic Priory. The Shaykh traditionally spends the month of Ramadan in the UK. At this time the Haqqani Priory is full to capacity with followers from most parts of western Europe and North America. The Shaykh travels between the three London centres, teaching, preaching, holding audiences with both *murids* and interested people, attending prayers and *dhikr* gatherings.[5] It is in the month of Ramadan that the Shaykh's talent for transcending the barriers of ethnicity is most evident. At this time a truly international community of *murids*, representing both converts and Muslim-born followers, gathers around him in great numbers. Ramadan also provides an opportunity to observe the relationship between *murids* and a charismatic shaykh renewing the Naqshbandi *tariqa* by extending its activities into the non-Muslim world. Individuals from both the converts and the born Muslims describe their meeting with the Shaykh as transformative. Muslim followers are likely to recount visionary dreams that preceded their meeting with the Shaykh and to describe their previous experience of Islam as incomplete or nominal. On the other hand, western converts relay stories of how one glimpse of the Shaykh enabled them to recognize that he was their master. They sometimes described experiences of 'coming home' or perceiving the Shaykh as the most beautiful human being they had ever seen. For many of the western converts it was the experience of contact with the Shaykh's presence that convinced them to become followers, and only later did they consider becoming Muslims.

The Shaykh's Eschatology

The Shaykh's teachings concerning the Muslim end time contain the essentials of Muslim doctrine with regard to Isa (Jesus), *Al-Dajjal* (Antichrist) and *Yaum al-Din* (the Last Day). However, it is his confident and detailed specifics that provide the unique vision uniting Muslim doctrine and millennial expectations. As early as 1985 (1406) the Shaykh was developing his warning of the imminence of the end time:

> We know that this world is being prepared for huge appearances. In a short while there will be a common change, physically and then spiritually. Time is over now. All nations and all mankind are being prepared for something that is approaching soon. These are huge events, unexpected huge events.[6]

5. *Dhikr* or remembrance of the Names of Allah is central to Sufi spiritual discipline. The difference between the *tariqas* is usually associated with the variety of forms of remembrance associated with the founder-saint. However, there is considerable similarity between the practices of the *tariqas*.

6. Shaykh Nazim al-Haqqani, *The Secret behind the Secrets behind the Secrets* (Berlin: Duru, 1985), back cover.

In recent publications of extracts of his speeches around the world, the Shaykh is specific concerning the year 2000 and the events that he predicts will take place in the twenty-first century:

> The biggest trouble is in front of us, which will wipe away six out of seven people. People cannot imagine the tragedy that will happen in the war to come. It can come in 1996, or in 1997, or in 1998, or in 1999. It will not wait for the year 2000 to come.[7]

However, in spite of these dire warnings concerning the years prior to the millennial year, the twenty-first century will herald a golden age founded on truth and justice:

> The twenty first century will oppose everything which belongs to the satanic kingdom. It will all be destroyed and the Heavenly Kingdom will be founded and established.[8]

The Shaykh bases his vision on Islam's prophetic traditions, found in the Hadith,[9] rather than any deep knowledge of the book of Revelation in the New Testament. For example, he explains that time will soon be over because, according to an Hadith, the Prophet stated that Allah bequeathed the Muslims one day if they obeyed the *shari'a* and an extra half day if they began to depart from its instructions. Muhammad went on to explain that one day of Allah was a thousand years for human beings. Consequently, the people of Islam would not be on the earth for more than 1500 years. According to the above calculation the last days have already begun.[10] In the final paragraph of *Defending Truth* published in 1997 the Shaykh expresses his own hope to remain alive for the momentous events which will take place in the first half of the twenty-first century:

> The next century will only be for True Ones. It will start with the coming of Jesus. No one can change that. He will follow the *Shari'ah* of Muhammad and for forty years this world will be like Paradise; with justice, respect, worshipping, love, mercy, blessings, lights... All nations

7. Shaykh Nazim al-Haqqani, *Secret Desires* (London: Zero Productions, 1996), p. 116.

8. Nazim, *Secret Desires*, p. 116.

9. The Hadith are the second source of scriptural authority within Islam. They consist of six major collections of sayings and actions of Muhammad. For a Muslim they provide a way to imitate the Prophet's *sunna* or exemplary role in manifesting the ideal of submission to Allah's revelation contained in the Qur'an.

10. Nazim, *Secret Desires*, p. 83.

> begged to reach that period and so do we. I don't know. Since I was young I have been asking Allah the Almighty to give me a chance to be with those True Ones.[11]

However, it is in a series of speeches given in 1985 to western followers of the Hindu teacher, Sai Baba, at their community in Schweibenalp near Basle in Switzerland, that the Shaykh gave his most developed exposition of the events which he believes will take place at the end time. The full picture becomes evident only by trawling through the speeches given by the Shaykh over a three-day period in July. What emerges is a remarkably detailed vision of the millennium.

According to the Shaykh, both the salvific figure of the *Mahdi* and *Al-Dajjal* are already here. The *Mahdi* is in direct lineage from the Prophet and his parents remain alive in Jeddah, Saudi Arabia. He was recognized by those with the necessary spiritual capacity in his childhood. However, his spiritual power is so great that ordinary human beings cannot look upon his visage and remain alive. Therefore, he has gone into seclusion accompanied by 99 spiritually elite companions in the inhospitable region of the desert between Saudi Arabia and Yemen known as the Empty Quarter. He is now between 40 and 50 years old but will remain in seclusion until after the final battle of Armageddon, a war that will be fought between the East and the West. The West will be victorious but six out of seven people will die in the conflict.

After this final war the *Mahdi* will appear in Damascus and rally the Muslims to him with the cry of '*Allah hu Akbar*!' (God is Great). On this cry all modern technology throughout the world will fail. He will then move on to Istanbul carrying the flag of the Prophet. At this point the Antichrist will arrive in Jerusalem from Horacan in Iran and then circumambulate the world for 40 days. At the present time, the Antichrist is chained on an unknown island by Allah's command. However, he is already at work in the world through the agency of 30 deputies. When the Antichrist encircles the globe, the second saviour figure, Jesus Christ, will descend from heaven to meet the *Mahdi* in Damascus at the tomb of John the Baptist. Jesus will ascend the minaret of the tomb at the time of *fajr* (morning prayer). He will then make the prayer call from the minaret and will be transported down from the minaret by two angels. He will then lead the Muslims in *fajr* prayer. In his hands

11. Shaykh Nazim al-Haqqani, *Defending Truth* (London: Zero Productions, 1997), p. 91.

he will hold a sword that will slay the Antichrist. The Shaykh is certain that this second coming will take place before the year 2000 is completed.

Once the Antichrist is killed, people will live on earth for 40 years in peace and tranquillity comparable to Paradise. In the decade following the fortieth year the seeds of sin will begin to reappear. On the fiftieth year Jesus will die and be buried next to Muhammad in Medina. Immediately on the death of Jesus, Allah will send a sweet-smelling wind that will bring painless death to all the believers. The unbelievers will remain to die shortly after, painfully. When no living human beings remain, the final judgment will begin for all humankind born since the creation of Adam and Eve.

Muslim Eschatological Traditions

Islam shares with Christianity the belief in final judgment, the centrality of Jesus' role in that inevitable event and the idea of a final victorious struggle over the forces of the Antichrist (*al-Dajjal*). The Qur'an shares with the New Testament the belief that God will judge all human beings on the Last Day, which will involve the physical resurrection of all the dead from the grave. According to the Qur'an, judgment will be based on the moral qualities of human actions but, in particular, the prerogative that a person believes in God and has not fallen into idolatry or *shirk* (polytheism) and not associated any other being with God. Watt points out that Muslims often tend to think of salvation as bestowed upon a righteous believing *ummah* (community) rather than an individual. However, the Qur'an itself provides examples of Allah on the Last Day judging both individuals and communities.[12]

As this essay is concerned with the end time, it will concentrate on the judgment to be given to Muslims as the ultimate community of God, who are believed to have accepted the final revelation and the last Prophet, rather than individuals who practise the faith. The principal difference between the two aspects of judgment in Islam is that individuals are measured throughout their lifetime and receive the rewards of their respective actions while living and in the grave. The final judgment will come on the Last Day when all communities will be assembled behind their respective prophet for Allah's judgment. It is in this

12. M. Watt, *The Formative Period of Islamic Thought* (Oxford: Oneworld Publications, 1998), p. 31.

respect that Islam shares with Christianity not only the belief in final judgment at the Last Day but also the central role of Jesus (Isa) in that ultimate event.

Muslims, particularly the millions of traditional believers who have been in contact with the beliefs of the influential Sufi tradition, believe that Jesus taught the inner or esoteric dimension of the primordial religion passed on through the prophets from Adam to Muhammad. Unlike Moses or Muhammad he did not herald a new revealed law (*shari'a*) but taught a spiritual way (*tariqa*) based on the love of God. Islam therefore acknowledges this special function of Jesus independent of the other prophets in that he did not bring with him a law, neither did he renew the previous Jewish revelation. This special role is acknowledged in the Qur'an, which calls Jesus the 'spirit of God' (*ruh Allah*) and confirms his supernatural birth from an immaculate and virgin mother.[13] For this reason, Jesus is given high status among the prophets of God, but Islam does not recognize the filial relationship to God or the Trinitarian definition of Christ's divinity.[14]

However, it is not only Jesus' birth that is special but also his death. It is the unique nature of Jesus' death that provides Muslims with his key role in Islam's eschatology. It is difficult to assess the contribution of Christian teachings concerning the end time and, in particular, Jesus' final victory over the forces of evil in a triumphant return. Cragg argues that the rapid expansion of Islam into Christian territories from the eighth century onwards would have provided easy access to millennial traditions concerning Jesus.[15] However, the importance of the contribution of Islamic doctrine to the acceptance of such influences from Christianity should not be overlooked.

The Qur'an itself promotes the doctrine of 'Manifest Success' that is so influential in determining the dynamics of the Muslim faith in his-

13. Mary (Miriam) is the first woman of Islam in that she is without sin. The Qur'an states: 'Behold! The angels said: "O Mary, Allah has chosen you and purified you. Truly he has chosen you above the women of all nations"' (Surah 3.42). Jesus is born from the spirit of God entering Miriam but this should not be confused with the Christian trinitarian view of the Holy Spirit. In Islamic doctrine the Spirit of God approximates the idea of emanation but is distinct from Allah even though it issues forth from him; it is therefore regarded as an aspect of his creation.

14. S. Hussein Nasr, *The Ideals and Realities of Islam* (London: Mandala Press, 1991), pp. 33-34.

15. K. Cragg, *Jesus and the Muslim* (Oxford: Oneworld, 1999), p. 57.

tory. In particular, the first Muslims' success at the Battle of Badr (623 CE) confirmed the theological position that associated worldly success with proof of Allah's special favour. The later battle of Uhud (625 CE), although not a total defeat, severely challenged the doctrine of 'Manifest Success'. The theology that links worldly success with divine approval has to resolve the challenge of failure. The setback at Uhud was explained by Muslims as a just consequence of their own lack of commitment to Allah's revelation. The solution to worldly failure was therefore deemed to be renewed commitment to the faith. This cycle of political failure, military defeat or economic and social decline being accompanied by religious revival has continued in the Muslim world to the present day.

The early rapid expansion of the Arab empire under the Umayyad and Abbasid dynasties in the first centuries of Islam did not challenge the doctrine of 'Manifest Success': on the contrary, it provided confirmation to the faithful of Allah's promise and his pleasure in his final community of believers. However, there were those who felt that the worldliness of the rulers and their courts were a departure from the piety and simplicity of the Prophet and his companions. In addition, the consequent fragmentation of Muslim territory into competing sultanates, the invasion of the Mongols in the thirteenth century and the halting of Muslim expansion into Europe, with the consequent expulsion from Spain in the fifteenth century, all led to an increasing sense of unease in the Muslim psyche with regard to 'Manifest Success'. Although a succession of religious revivals took place throughout this period, they were not able to prevent the social and political decline of the *ummah*. This sense of unease increased in the eighteenth and nineteenth centuries as a result of colonial domination by various European powers.

Yet it was inevitable to the believer that 'Manifest Success' promised to the final recipients of Allah's revelation must occur some day. Cragg comments that the decline of the Muslim community was reinforced by well-known Hadiths attributed to the Prophet, explicitly stating that there would be a decline from the glorious days of the Prophet and the three generations that followed him.[16] The Muslim world had an example of a golden age at the time of the Prophet but its subsequent decline meant that it would need to be seen again before the Last Day if

16. Cragg, *Jesus and the Muslim*, p. 58.

Allah's promise of 'Manifest Success' was to be fulfilled.

The doctrine of 'Manifest Success' also applies to the mission given by Allah to his chosen human messengers, the prophets. In the absence of Christian teachings concerning the death and resurrection of Jesus Christ and his salvific role, it was inevitable that Islamic doctrine would be uneasy with the crucifixion. In addition to the Qur'an's adamant denial of the crucifixion, such a terrible end was inconceivable to the Muslim religious psyche, as it appeared to preclude the possibility of 'Manifest Success'. Jesus is regarded as the messenger to the Jews, but they had not accepted him. Allah could not permit such an ignoble death to his chosen messenger. Even though the crucifixion is denied, Jesus requires final success to his mission just as the Muslim community needs the fulfilment of Allah's promise regarding their ultimate victory. It is not surprising therefore that Islam looks to Jesus rather than the final prophet, Muhammad, as the key player in the end time. In Muslim eschatology, both the penultimate prophet of God and the final community of revelation will achieve ultimate and manifest success.

Although Muslims do not accept the crucifixion and resurrection of Jesus that is so central to Christian faith, they do believe in his literal physical ascension to Paradise.[17] Cragg argues that Jesus is available for the eschatological role as it 'follows from his being raptured to heaven, in contrast to the demise and burial of Muhammad in Medina'.[18] In this respect Jesus is unique in that he is the only prophet to continue in his physical body beyond the bounds of death. All the other prophets' bodies are in the grave and await the final Day of Judgment. It is this physical existence of Jesus' body that is important in understanding his eschatological role. In Islam the grave is the destination of all human beings, including the prophets of God. Jesus therefore has to return to the world where he will play a crucial role in the final period before the Last Day. He will confront and defeat *al-Dajjal*, who is regarded as the

17. The foundation upon which Muslims build the idea of the physical ascension of Jesus is in the Qur'an: 'As for their claim that they killed the Messiah Jesus, Mary's son, the messenger of God, the truth is that they did not kill him, nor did they crucify him. They were under the illusion that they had. There is a lot of doubt about this matter among those who are at odds over it. They have no real knowledge but follow only surmise. Assuredly they did not kill him. On the contrary God raised him up to Himself' (Surah 4.157-159). Later tradition develops the idea of the substitution of Judas Iscariot as a semblance of Jesus.

18. Cragg, *Jesus and the Muslim*, p. 57.

cause for both Muslim lack of compliance and non-Muslim lack of acceptance of the final revelation and its requirement for obedience and submission. A great battle will take place after Jesus has acknowledged Islam as the final manifestation of the religion of God, destroyed all crosses[19] and brought the people that he was chosen to guide, namely the Jews and the Christians, to the revelation contained in the Qur'an. As Cragg states, 'The Antichrist is defeated eschatologically by Jesus as the agent, but by Islam in the event.'[20]

After fulfilling his mission of bringing humanity back to Islam Jesus will live for 40 years in a world guided by true Islam and will then die. As expressed by Shaykh Nazim, it is believed that Jesus will be buried in an empty tomb that has been kept for him next to Muhammad and two of the first Caliphs in the mosque at Medina. At the death of Jesus, an archangel will sound a trumpet and all humans will die. There will then follow the resurrection and the Final Judgment. At this ultimate event, all the prophets, including Jesus, will act as intercessors and helpers for their respective people.[21] Cragg analyses the role of Jesus in the last days and summarizes that

> it stems from Islam's own need of millennial 'finality'. Precisely because Islam had a totally successful inauguration, and because of that inauguration, by the same token, could not be made perpetual but, on the contrary, fell into rapid compromise as history sees it, a final future would be needed to make good in the end what had been 'the seal of the prophets' at the start.[22]

As with Shaykh Nazim, in some variations of Muslim eschatology, Jesus' role in the end time comes to be linked to that of the *Mahdi*. There can be little doubt that the Sunni tradition has been influenced in this respect by beliefs of the minority Shi'a traditions whose ideas may first have been adopted by some Sufi *tariqas*. Watt points out that messianic beliefs may have first occurred after the death of Ibn al-Hanifiyya in 700 CE, but the full-blown Shi'a doctrine of the *Mahdi* does not

19. The crosses will be destroyed not because they are a symbol of Christianity but because they represent the mistaken doctrine that Jesus was crucified. However, it cannot be denied that it represents to the Muslim psyche the final vicory of the Crescent over the Cross.

20. Cragg, *Jesus and the Muslim,* p. 59.

21. N. Daniel, *Islam and the West* (Oxford: Oneworld, 1993), p. 347.

22. Cragg, *Jesus and the Muslim*, p. 57.

traditionally occur until the death of the twelfth Imam, Mohammed al-Mahdi.[23] Nasr explains the Shi'a belief that the twelfth Imam went into minor occultation after the death of his father.[24] By this he means he disappeared from public view and ruled the Shi'a community by appearing on occasions to four chosen representatives. Shi'a doctrine affirms that the last Imam went into major occultation rather than suffer physical death at the hands of enemies. The Imam is believed to have been raised to a protective invisible sphere by Allah where he remains alive as the ruler of the universe or *Mahdi*. At the end of time he will return to bring truth and justice to a war-torn world that will be filled with the peace of Islam. The perfect government of human society cannot occur until the return of the *Mahdi*.

The belief in a messianic *Mahdi* who would come to restore Islam has crossed into Sunni traditions, especially amongst the Sufi *tariqas*, whose own leaders were often heralded as the *Mahdi*, particularly when engaged in successful *Jihad* (religious war) in later centuries against the invading European colonial powers. This transmigration from Shi'a sects into traditional Sunni beliefs via the Sufi *tariqas* may have occurred as a result of the Safavid movement itself. Nasr explains that the Safavids began as a Sufi order that became powerful as a result of their excellent organization, and developed to exercise authority over all of Persia, thus creating the Safavid dynasty, which ruled over the country[25] and only finally disappeared with the overthrow of the Shah by Ayatollah Khomeini. The potential contradiction that both Jesus and the *Mahdi* are involved in the Last Days has been resolved in some traditional Sufi lore by providing Jesus with the role of herald, who will prepare the world for the arrival of the *Mahdi*. However, none of the eschatological roles given to Jesus in traditional Sunni belief have been lost except that the *Mahdi* is believed to rule over the governance of human society in the final years before the Last Day.

23. Watt, *The Formative Period*, p. 47. Ibn al-Haniyya was a son of Ali, the son-in law of the Prophet and first Imam of the Shi'as. He was a child of Ali from another wife and not from the Prophet's daughter, Fatima.

24. Nasr, *The Ideal and Realities*, p. 166. Occultation (*al-ghaibat*) refers to the doctrine prevalent in Shi'a that their Imams were allowed to remain hidden from public view for their own protection. The final Imam is provided with *al-ghaibat al-kubra* (the major occultation) whereby he is concealed by Allah until the last days.

25. Nasr, *The Ideal and Realities*, p. 167.

The role of Jesus in the end time within traditional Muslim belief and in particular among Sufis has been reinforced by the unique character given to the penultimate prophet. I well remember the excitement of discovering the carved quotation in Fatehpur Sikri,[26] the city of the Mughal emperor Akbar (1553–1603 CE), attributed to Jesus. It reads as follows: 'Jesus (peace be upon him) said: "This world is a bridge. Pass over it, but build not your dwelling here."' Cragg states with considerable justification that 'nowhere is Islamic awareness of Jesus more lively or more perceptive than in the Arabic, Persian, Turkish, and Urdu poems of the mystics of Islam'.[27] Jesus' withdrawal from the world, his deep compassion, his 40 days of retreat in the desert, his celibacy, and above all his intimacy with God, mark him out as the perfect example of a contemplative saint or *awliya* (a friend of God), as the Sufis refer to their own masters. The mood of transience, abstention and withdrawal in the above quotation is supported by many more derived from the Gospels.[28] They are closely suited to the Sufi mystical temperament, but, in addition, Jesus' renunciation and unworldliness, although sometimes compared unfavourably with Muhammad's leadership qualities, fitted him perfectly for the end time role.

Throughout the nineteenth century, several prominent Sufis were heralded as the *Mahdi* by their followers. Usually they were among those successful in maintaining *jihad* against European incursion into Muslim territory.[29] Muslim eschatology linked famines and natural disasters to both the imminent arrival of the end time and to the decline of belief. Sirriyeh notes that it was inevitable that the success of the increasing European domination and the acquisition of so many Muslim

26. The city of Fatehpur Sikri, near to Agra, was constructed by Akbar after his decision to move the Mughal court away from Delhi. Fatehpur Sikri is now disused due to problems with the water supply. It is speculated that one of the reasons for Akbar moving his court was the presence of his Sufi master in Fatehpur Sikri.

27. Cragg, *Jesus and the Muslim*, p. 60.

28. A comprehensive list of sayings attributed to Jesus can be found in Al-Ghazali's famous work *Ihya Ulum al-Din* (Religion: its meaning and practice revitalised). Cragg provides an excellent selection of these quotations and readers may see for themselves their parallels to Gospel themes (*Jesus and the Muslim*, pp. 47-49).

29. Sayyid Ahmad Barelwi (d. 1831) of India and Sayyid al-Mahdi (d. 1902), the son of the founder of the Sanusiyya *tariqa* in Libya were both involved in armed struggle against the British.

lands by unbelievers would lead to many being convinced that the end time was near.[30] She describes how many believed that with the approach of the Islamic year 1300 (1882–83) the *Mahdi*'s return was imminent.[31] The beginning of the century is always likely to have special significance, since many traditional Muslims believe that every hundred years heralds the coming of *mujaddid*, or a specially devout Muslim whose role is to renew the faith.

However, it is with the arrival of the Islamic year 1400 that Muslim expectations of the end time dovetail with the Christian millennium, and it is this that is most fully expressed in the prophetic preaching of Shaykh Nazim al-Haqqani of the Naqshbandi *tariqa*.

5. *Conclusion*

It is not in any way exceptional for a traditional Muslim, particularly when rooted in the Sufi tradition, to hold eschatological beliefs involving the *Mahdi*, Jesus and *al-Dajjal* in conflict before the Last Day. This essay has explored Muslim doctrine and beliefs concerning the end time and demonstrated their significance, in particular to Sufis and the millions of Muslims influenced by their teachings. However, in my experience it is not usual for Sufi *shaykhs* or other Muslim leaders to be as specific as Shaykh Nazim al-Haqqani. In addition to the Shaykh's prophetic certainty, his linking of Muslim apocalyptic traditions to the millennial equivalent in Christianity is unique.

The Shaykh's visionary experience of the end time is firmly rooted in Muslim tradition and borrows heavily from Hadith accounts. His Sufi identity provides the traditional affinity with the penultimate prophet of Islam, but there are more compelling reasons unique to the Shaykh's perceived mission to carry Islam to the West that may provide the solution to his visionary conviction that Muslim and Christian traditions of the end time coalesce in the year 2000. The Shaykh's background is Turkish and his home is on the divided island of Cyprus. His sympathies and outlook are essentially Ottoman and he longs for the return of the Ottoman caliph as the political leader of Muslims around the world. This background has given him closer contact with Christians and their traditions than is usual for Muslims in the Arab heartlands or further

30. E. Sirriyeh, *Sufis and Anti-Sufis* (London: Curzon, 1999), p. 34.
31. Sirriyeh, *Sufis and Anti-Sufis*, p. 34.

east. He is well aware of the dual status of Istanbul as a Muslim city and as the ancient capital of Byzantine Christianity, and his continued residence in divided Cyprus must be a constant reminder of the abiding conflict between the two religious traditions.

It is, however, in the Shaykh's exceptional ability to gain converts from the West that it is possible to achieve further insight into his millennial convictions. Since his arrival in western Europe and subsequent visits to the USA, the Shaykh has reached out to western spiritual seekers as well as to Muslim migrant communities. He preaches that mysticism lies at the heart of all religions and is prepared to be invited to Hindu and Buddhist centres that attract western seekers. He has been a guest at several new religious movements of eastern origin and the majority of his western followers have come from alternative lifestyle backgrounds that have often involved intense alienation from contemporary western culture and personal histories of conscious attempts to find a spiritual solution in their lives.

Berger asserts that modern societies are marked by an expansion of the variety of alternatives available in all areas of life, including religion and world-views. However, the shift in consciousness, although liberating, is also accompanied by an increasing sense of alienation. This alienation may result in a search for religious certainty usually associated with premodern society.[32] One of the common themes of this renewed search for religious meaning has been the emphasis on the experiential dimension of religion. Berger states that one of the distinctive features of eastern traditions is the idea that the divine is found within oneself as the ground of one's own being.[33] The focus of spiritual disciplines thus becomes the method to initiate the experience of the divine within, usually in the form of some kind of unitive apprehension of communion or union involving cessation of ego-consciousness. Such ideas are not the property of Indian yogis or Buddhist monks but are familiar to mystics of all the major world faiths. There is a strong current of opinion amongst western truth seekers that the mystical experience is universal and unites all religions at their core. Sufism is an established mystical tradition that also offers the religious certainties of Islamic doctrine. Köse notes that evidence was found to indicate

32. P. Berger, *The Heretical Imperative: Contemporary Possibilities of Religious Affirmation* (London: Collins, 1980), pp. 22-23.

33. Berger, *The Heretical Imperative*, p. 159.

similarities between conversion to Islam through Sufism and conversion to new religious movements.[34] His study also found that converts to Islam through Sufism were likely to have tried other forms of eastern religion prior to their contact with Sufism.

The Shaykh is not only a contemporary living master of an eminent mystical tradition that offers a means of direct access to the divine, he is also a prophetic visionary who exemplifies his own teaching. For western seekers brought up on the values of empiricism but dissatisfied with the products that resulted from the empirical world view, the Shaykh's visionary mysticism offers a charismatic alternative that remains experiential. Although not developed into a coherent doctrine, there is a general sense among many of these seekers of truth that the state of the world is indicative of the last days. The Shaykh's firm belief in the Muslim end time's imminence awakens his audiences' own general sense of unease with the era in which they are living. His certainty and detail are unusual but are surely rooted in his own experience as a visionary mystic as well as Muslim tradition. However, his precise prophecies run the risk of all predictions concerning events that are so near in the future. The danger of them remaining unfulfilled may create a conflict between the requirement amidst his western followers for visionary or mystical experience and their potential to dismiss incredulous belief.

34. A. Köse, *Conversion to Islam* (London: Kegan Paul International, 1996), p. 145.

Part II
Historical and Sociological Perspectives

Was Early Christianity a Millenarian Movement?*

Stanley E. Porter

Introduction

It is a commonplace among biblical scholars and theologians to speak of early Christianity as a millenarian movement. Originally, this millenarianism meant the literal thousand-year reign of Christ on earth, with his followers, to occur between his parousia or return (the second coming) and the last judgment of believers and non-believers.[1] The use of the term has been greatly expanded, so that it has become one form of Christian eschatology that is characterized by 'the intrusion of god's kingdom of Justice, in relentless combat with the oppressive structures of this world'.[2] In this form, the concept has been applied to a wide range of theological issues, both ancient and contemporary, including those of so-called liberation theology. The concept of millenarianism has spread as well to the social sciences, and is apparently a common description to apply to certain 'religious movements that expect imminent, total, ultimate, this-worldly, collective salvation'.[3] The result of such a widespread conception is to be found in the contents of this volume itself, where the concept of a millennium is seen to provide the controlling metaphor for analysis of the past, present and future. How-

* A revised and shorter version of this essay is to appear in S. Hunt (ed.), *Christian Millenarianism* (London: Hurst; New York: New York University Press, in press [2001]).

1. The nature of the second coming or parousia of Christ has been a controversial one. For discussion of some of the major proponents and issues, see S.H. Travis, *Christian Hope and the Future* (Downers Grove, IL: InterVarsity Press, 1980), esp. pp. 63-92.

2. See C.E. Hill, *Regnum Caelorum: Patterns of Future Hope in Early Christianity* (Oxford Early Christian Studies; Oxford: Clarendon Press, 1992), p. 1.

3. Hill, *Regnum Caelorum*, p. 1 n. 1, quoting Y. Talmon, 'Millenarism', in D.E. Sills (ed.), *International Encyclopedia of the Social Sciences* (17 vols.; New York: Free Press, 1968), X, pp. 349-62, here p. 349.

ever, the term is obviously being used in a number of different ways: most of them are metaphorical, but a few of them are literal; some are precise in their formulation, concentrating on such things as economics, while others are far looser in conception, invoking a much more vague notion that has almost no formal or conceptual links with historical Christianity. Such a broad definition may make for a successful volume of essays, with a range of interests expressed, but it makes for havoc in terms of defining the concept in a meaningful and useful way across a range of problems. This is especially true when one is attempting to define the specific origins of the movement, and test this reconstruction against a number of early documents.

The same complaint can be made of discussion of millennialism in terms of the New Testament. The concept of early Christianity being a millenarian movement is widespread and pervasive in discussion of the movement, so much so that in many ways it serves as a governing paradigm for discussion and analysis of the movement. For example, Robert Jewett sub-titled his detailed study of the Thessalonian letters as 'Pauline Rhetoric and Millenarian Piety'.[4] However, when one examines what millenarianism means in New Testament studies, one finds a wealth of different conceptions. For example, Jewett clearly invokes a model drawn from social-scientific analysis, using the framework of a people expecting imminent salvation.

Once one opens up the definition of the topic, one realizes that there is an abundance of secondary literature to consider, focused around the various major ways of viewing this topic, and the subject is much more often discussed in terms of several broader topics of discussion in New Testament studies. For example, Ernst Käsemann, in a now-famous essay, once pronounced that 'Apocalyptic was the mother of all Christian theology'.[5] By this he meant that the apocalyptic mindset was the basis of the development of Christian thought. Apocalyptic thought is

4. R. Jewett, *The Thessalonian Correspondence: Pauline Rhetoric and Millenarian Piety* (FFNT; Philadelphia: Fortress Press, 1986); cf. H.C. Kee, *Christian Origins in Sociological Perspective* (London: SCM Press, 1980).

5. E. Käsemann, 'The Beginnings of Christian Theology', in his *New Testament Questions of Today* (trans. W.J. Montague; SBT, 41; London: SCM Press, 1969), pp. 82-107 (102); cf. also his 'On the Subject of Primitive Christian Apocalyptic', in *New Testament Questions*, pp. 108-37. The perspective of Käsemann has been soundly criticized, but the influence of apocalyptic on understanding the New Testament remains.

governed by increasing frustration by an oppressed group that in despair looks to the direct intervention of God to rescue them from their oppression. Apocalyptic thought is typically seen as a Jewish perspective,[6] to be found in some of the later prophets and especially developing during the intertestamental period, including such works as Daniel, *1 Enoch* in its several parts, the *Testaments of the Twelve Patriarchs*, *Sibylline Oracles* 2, *2 Baruch* and *4 Ezra*, possibly some of the Qumran documents,[7] among others. Christianity is, according to this perspective, simply the culmination of a major thread of Jewish thought. Since this Judaism expected a resurrection,[8] and spoke of a 'millennial' kingdom,[9] Christianity must also have expected these things. Another way in which millenarian thought is introduced into discussion of early Christianity is in terms of the distinction between early Christianity as a charismatic movement, in which the Spirit was seen to be active, as the followers of Christ expected his imminent return, and the rise of early Catholicism, in which the disappointed expectation was replaced by formal structures to guide the Church in its day-to-day life. Again, Käsemann was very important in making this distinction, and it figures largely in discussion of matters of authenticity for various New Testament books.[10] Those that evidence the life of the Spirit, such as many of the letters of Paul (e.g. 1 Corinthians), are clearly genuine, but books that reflect the growth of institutionalization, such as the Pastoral Epistles, are clearly not authentic to Paul but were written later in the light of later developments in the Church, when a word from the apostle was thought relevant to the changing ecclesial situation. A third way that millenarian thought is often discussed in New Testament studies is in

6. However, many of the chief elements of apocalyptic thought, including its imagery, symbolism and visionary elements, may be found in other Hellenistic literature of the times. For discussion, see T.F. Glasson, *Greek Influence in Jewish Eschatology: With Special Reference to the Apocalypses and Pseudepigraphs* (London: SPCK, 1961), including discussion of resurrection (pp. 26-32) and the intermediate state (pp. 33-47).

7. See Hill, *Regnum Caelorum*, pp. 5 n. 14, 41-52.

8. Resurrections are found in 2 Macc. 7.9, 23; 14.46; *Pss. Sol.* 14.3-7; *4 Ezra* 7.32; *2 Bar.* 50–51; *1 En.* 51.1; *T. Benj.* 10.

9. Millennial kingdoms are spoken of in *1 En.* 6–36, 91–104; *2 En.* 33.1 (1000 years); *Pss. Sol.* 11.1-8; *Jub.* 23.27 (1000 years); *4 Ezra* 7.28-29 (400 years); *T. Isaac* 6-8 (millennial banquet).

10. E. Käsemann, 'Paul and Early Catholicism', in *New Testament Questions*, pp. 236-51.

terms of the expectation of the kingdom of God, spoken of by Jesus in the Gospels.[11] There is serious debate among New Testament scholars over whether Jesus had any messianic self-consciousness, that is, whether he saw himself as God's anointed person for redemptive purposes of Israel, and whether he had any foreknowledge of his own death and possible resurrection.[12] The risen Christ was soon believed to have departed from this earth with the expectation of his imminent return.

I am not sure that any of these perspectives, however, indicates that Christianity was a millenarian movement in a specific and meaningful sense. It indeed was a movement that had apocalyptic elements to it, and had an eschatological thinking that expected the return of Christ, his so-called parousia; there was certainly growth and development in its institutional structures; and there was early and pervasive belief in the kingdom of God. Nevertheless, none of these models necessarily focuses upon the specific issues involved in millenarianism. One of the major problems is that I am not convinced that we have arrived at a firm enough definition of what millenarianism means. It seems to be interpreted in most discussions as a fairly loose concept, which does not seem to have definable temporal, conceptual or institutional boundaries. Before we can expand the definition to be more inclusive, we need first to see in what sense Christianity thought of a future literal period of time, that is, a thousand years (or some other lengthy period of time), at the beginning of which Christ as messiah would return to establish his actual rule on earth as a prelude to the end of the age.[13] With this definition in mind, I would like to look at the major passages in the New Testament related to this concept, to see if early Christianity can be defined as a millenarian movement in this specific and precise sense.

11. This is a huge topic of discussion, and cannot be surveyed here. For a history of discussion through primary texts, see B. Chilton (ed.), *The Kingdom of God* (Issues in Religion and Theology, 5; Philadelphia: Fortress Press; London: SPCK, 1984); and through description, see B. Chilton, 'The Kingdom of God in Recent Discussion', in B. Chilton and C.A. Evans (eds.), *Studying the Historical Jesus: Evaluations of the State of Current Research* (NTTS, 19; Leiden: E.J. Brill, 1994), pp. 255-80. For recent helpful works, see G.R. Beasley-Murray, *Jesus and the Kingdom of God* (Grand Rapids: Eerdmans, 1986); B. Chilton, *Pure Kingdom: Jesus' Vision of God* (Grand Rapids: Eerdmans; London: SPCK, 1996).

12. All of these topics, and more, are discussed in C.A. Evans, *Jesus and his Contemporaries: Comparative Studies* (AGJU, 25; Leiden: E.J. Brill, 1995).

13. See Hill, *Regnum Caelorum*, p. 5.

References to a Millennium in the New Testament

It may come as a surprise to find that there is only one passage in the New Testament that refers to a thousand-year reign, and that is in the book of Revelation. Of course, in apocalyptic literature, there are a number of different time periods referred to for the reign of God, including 400 years and 1000 years, and even an indefinite period. Even if we extend the boundaries of the time period in either direction, this passage remains as the only one to consider in terms of a specific reference to a period of such length. If this were the only passage considered, this would potentially make for a very short essay. However, there are a number of other biblical authors who make suggestive comments who are also worth considering. These include passages in Hebrews, 2 Peter, the Gospels and Paul.[14] These too will be considered, before drawing some conclusions regarding whether early Christianity was a millenarian movement.

Revelation 20.2-7

Revelation 20 contains the only passage in the New Testament that refers directly to a thousand-year reign of Christ. The passage comes near the end of the book, after a number of events have taken place, and before the ultimate events regarding the new heaven and the new earth are related. The passage reads:

> And I saw an angel coming down out of heaven, having the key to the Abyss and holding in his hand a great chain. He seized the dragon, that ancient serpent, who is the devil, or Satan, and bound him for a thousand years. He threw him into the Abyss, and locked and sealed it over him, to keep him from deceiving the nations any more until the thousand years were ended. After that he must be set free for a short time. I saw thrones on which were seated those who had been given authority to judge. And I saw the souls of those who had been beheaded because of their testimony for Jesus and because of the word of God. They had not worshiped the beast or his image and had not received his mark on their foreheads or their hands. They came to life and reigned with Christ a thousand years. (The rest of the dead did not come to life until the thousand years were ended.) This is the first resurrection. Blessed and holy are those who have part in the first resurrection. The second death has no power

14. Several of these passages have been suggested, and are briefly treated by Hill, *Regnum Caelorum*, pp. 155-63, from whose study I have greatly benefited.

> over them, but they will be priests of God and of Christ and will reign with him for a thousand years. When the thousand years are over, Satan will be released from his prison and will go out to deceive the nations in the four corners of the earth...to gather them for battle (NIV).

Let me make some observations that are pertinent to the topic of this essay. Of course, this is the passage from which various Christian theologies have developed doctrines concerning the millennium. There is no denying that a 'millennium' is mentioned here, and it has been understood in terms of Christ's return as being pre-millennial, that is, before the millennium, and in some way inaugurating it; post-millennial, that is, at the end of the millennium, as its fitting climax; or a-millennial, which does not mean that there is no millennium, but that essentially the millennium is understood as being co-terminous with the existence of the Christian Church, with Christ's return occurring at the end.[15] According to the definition I am using for millennialism, only the first of these positions, the pre-millennial, really has pertinence to the discussion. On that basis, and since that view, although occasionally ably defended, commands far from consensus, the millennialism of even Revelation 20 should be called into question. In order to approach our question of whether early Christianity was millenarian, rather than whether later or modern biblical theologians are millenarians, however, let me examine this text more thoroughly. The first set of observations concerns the passage itself, and the second set concerns the book of Revelation.

This passage is very intriguing, not least because of its intense imagery. Much of the book of Revelation is filled with a variety of suggestive, yet allusive imagery.[16] It is fair to say that there have been numerous attempts to understand the imagery of the book, none of which has commanded anything remotely close to universal assent. Some of the more intriguing imagery concerns visions of a heavenly

15. For discussion of various millenial views, see J.W. Mealy, *After the Thousand Years: Resurrection and Judgment in Revelation 20* (JSNTSup, 70; Sheffield: JSOT Press, 1992), pp. 15-28; and G.K. Beale, *John's Use of the Old Testament in Revelation* (JSNTSup, 166; Sheffield: Sheffield Academic Press, 1998), pp. 356-93, who concludes for the thousand years as reference to a lengthy period of time.

16. For a description of this passage in context, see R. Bauckham, *The Theology of the Book of Revelation* (New Testament Theology; Cambridge: Cambridge University Press, 1993), pp. 106-108.

throne (ch. 4), a personified revivified lamb that is worshiped (ch. 5), various seals (ch. 6), plagues (ch. 15), bowls (ch. 16), and a variety of other persons and beings, such as the two witnesses (ch. 11), the woman and the dragon (ch. 12), the beast from the sea (ch. 13), the beast from the earth (ch. 13), and the whore of Babylon (ch. 17). No one has yet provided a convincing explanation of all of these images. Perhaps the most sensible means of analysis is to realize that there is a kind of symbolic imagery at play here, which progresses from persecution through God's judgment to a time of triumph in the New Jerusalem (ch. 21). Quite probably these images had correlates in the world in which they were written,[17] although here too scholars disagree. The passage itself that was cited above is part of this conglomeration of imagistic and highly symbolic writing. There is the angel coming from heaven, a place called the abyss, a dragon who is said to be the devil or Satan, who is bound and thrown into the abyss. There are also thrones on which judges sit, the souls of apparently Christian martyrs, and a resurrection, though this is said to be only the first resurrection, which has produced those who reign with Christ.

The major scholarly opinion is that the book of Revelation was probably written at the earliest during the time of the Roman emperor Domitian, who ruled from 81 to 96 CE. Even this is not certain, with scholars arguing from a time around the death of Nero (54–68 CE) to much later.[18] Once written, however, few biblical books were suddenly accepted as Scripture. One of the last to establish itself within what became the Christian canon was the book of Revelation. The general history of its reception is that the book was known fairly early but met with a mixed response, with the earliest references to it probably dating to about the mid-second century, and serious reaction to it coming late in that century.[19] There was also a surprisingly wide variety of interpre-

17. See W.M. Ramsay, *The Letters to the Seven Churches of Asia and their Place in the Plan of the Apocalypse* (London: Hodder & Stoughton, 1904), esp. pp. 93-127.

18. See L.M. McDonald and S.E. Porter, *Early Christianity and its Sacred Literature* (Peabody, MA: Hendrickson, 2000), pp. 554-57.

19. See D. Guthrie, *New Testament Introduction* (Downers Grove, IL: InterVarsity Press, 3rd edn, 1970), pp. 931-34. It probably stretches things to say that it was widely read because of the seven letters at the beginning (R.H. Mounce, *The Book of Revelation* [NICNT; Grand Rapids: Eerdmans, rev. edn, 1998], p. 21), although this probably does circumscribe its earliest area of reception.

tation, with varying types of literalistic and figurative interpretation applied.[20]

From both internal and external factors, we can conclude several things regarding the millennial influence of the book of Revelation. First, as in many other Jewish millenarian texts, the imagery, vivid and provocative though it is, is not entirely clear in Revelation, and even appears to introduce elements that are beyond the confines of a simple and straightforward millennial position. We have those who are human co-rulers with Christ, the term of the binding of the dragon or Satan is for a fixed time, before his release, and he is said to be confined to a place called the abyss. Charles argued that the millennium begins 'when the martyrs, and the martyrs only, are raised in the first resurrection and become priests of God...and of Christ, and reign with Christ personally on earth for a thousand years (xx. 4-6), with Jerusalem as the centre of the kingdom'.[21] But as Swete points out, Charles must introduce into his description of this passage ideas that are not found in it, but are gleaned from Rev. 5.10, 20.9 and 21.10, which are not necessarily part of the same chronology or scene at all.[22] The most that can probably be said of this passage is that it endorses the ultimate triumph of Christ and his followers against the oppressive enemies. This time of triumph on earth is seen as a prelude to the lasting and enduring one of God's eternal rule in the new heaven and the new earth, which includes the new Jerusalem that comes down from heaven (ch. 21). It is in chs. 21 and 22, not ch. 20, that much of the imagery of traditional millennial thought is to be found. Explanations of this strange ordering of the imagery have included the thought that the author died in the midst of his writing, and various theories of multiple or compound authorship.[23] All of these attempts indicate that, at least in so far as traditional millennial imagery is concerned, the ordering runs contrary to what might have been expected. Secondly, the possible impact of this work on earliest Christianity is probably quite minimal, due to its date of composition and its pattern of limited use in the early Church. The book was probably written at the end of the period of earliest Christian for-

20. On the history of interpretation, see J.M. Court, *Myth and History in the Book of Revelation* (Atlanta: John Knox Press, 1979), pp. 1-19.

21. R.H. Charles, *A Critical History of the Doctrine of a Future Life in Israel, in Judaism, and in Christianity* (London: A. & C. Black, 2nd edn, 1913), p. 407.

22. H.B. Swete, *The Apocalypse of St John* (London: Macmillan, 1906), p. 261.

23. See Hill, *Regnum Caelorum*, pp. 173-74.

mation, and has since been embroiled in controversy that has rarely subsided.

In other words, if one wishes to establish earliest Christianity as a millennial movement in strict terms, one needs to look elsewhere than in the book of Revelation, and perhaps not even there.

Hebrews 12.22-24

The book of Hebrews speaks of followers of Christ coming to Mount Zion, the heavenly Jerusalem, the city of the living God. In Heb. 12.22-24, they are an assembly with thousands upon thousands of angels gathered with God, the judge of all people, Jesus, who is the mediator of a new covenant, and the spirits of the perfected righteous. One of the major areas of dispute regarding these verses is who the spirits of the perfected righteous are. Some have taken them as elect angels,[24] but most scholars take them as humans, either pre-Christian believers, believers whose names are inscribed even if they have not yet entered heaven,[25] or, most likely, any departed Christian.[26] The background to the book of Hebrews is too obscure to use as a definitive means of interpretation.[27] The book is written in some of the most refined Greek in the New Testament, and is filled with much Old Testament and Jewish imagery. It is quite possible that the book was written by a Gentile or Diaspora Jew to a group threatened by returning to Judaism (ch. 6) and hence to a Jewish audience who might be tempted by some of the structures of their previous religious life. The author of Hebrews wishes to assure his readers that, in a real sense, these followers of Christ are already gathered with God and Jesus in a heavenly place with other fellow believers. This is used to give assurance that there is nothing more to be gained by indulgence in Jewish practices, and in fact much to lose by refusing the sacrifice of Christ as sufficient.

24. C. Spicq, *L'épitre aux Hébreux* (EB; 2 vols.; Paris: Gabalda, 1953), II, 407-408; H. Montefiore, *The Epistle to the Hebrews* (HNTC; San Francisco: Harper & Row, 1964), p. 231.

25. J. Moffatt, *A Critical and Exegetical Commentary on the Epistle to the Hebrews* (ICC; Edinburgh: T. & T. Clark, 1924), p. 217.

26. B.F. Westcott, *The Epistle to the Hebrews* (London: Macmillan, 1889), pp. 413-16, who notes that here angels and humans are together; F.F. Bruce, *The Epistle to the Hebrews* (NICNT; Grand Rapids: Eerdmans, rev. edn, 1990), pp. 358-60; W.L. Lane, *Hebrews* (WBC, 47A, B; 2 vols.; Dallas: Word Books, 1991), II, p. 469.

27. See P. Ellingworth, *The Epistle to the Hebrews* (NIGTC; Grand Rapids: Eerdmans; Carlisle: Paternoster, 1993), pp. 3-36, esp. 34-36 on canonization.

There are several elements of this passage that have millenarian characteristics. There appears to be a reign of Christ, except that here it seems to be a reign of God *and* Christ, and it is not on earth but in the heavenly Jerusalem, and is a heavenly realm concurrent with the earthly one. Even if the elect are still on earth, they are not depicted as being in a millennial kingdom, since the heavenly Jerusalem seems to be emphasized. There is no indication in Hebrews of how long this heavenly Jerusalem is to last. In fact, it would seem to be that the period should last for eternity, since the argument is that followers of Christ already have a secure inheritance on the basis of his sacrifice, not needing to do anything further to merit their salvation. In other words, this passage does not provide a model of millenarian belief. The passage also does not mention a future resurrection of the dead, so it is difficult to determine his chronology here (cf. 11.35, where it may indicate that he believes in one).[28] It appears that judgment occurs at the time of death.

Even if there were to be millenarian elements in Hebrews, there are problems with its defining force on early Christianity. Although probably written before the fall of Jerusalem, the book of Hebrews was the subject of dispute for some time, with the Eastern Church being more willing to accept it early on as Pauline but the Western Church resisting this. Several later canonical lists do not include Hebrews. By the time that it was realized that Paul was not the author, and it was accepted as authoritative, we are no longer in the period of earliest Christianity.

2 Peter 1.11

2 Peter speaks in 1.11 of how those brethren who make their calling and election secure will receive a rich welcome into the eternal kingdom of our Lord and saviour Jesus Christ.[29] This passage clearly refers to a kingdom of Christ, who is seen here as the saviour-messiah, although it is also possible that the compound appellative is simply seen as his name. Bauckham notes that this is one of only a few references in the New Testament to Christ's kingdom, as opposed to God's.[30] However,

28. Bruce, *Hebrews*, p. 360.

29. The phrase 'our Lord and saviour Jesus Christ' only appears in 2 Pet. 1.11; 2.20; 3.2, 18 in the New Testament.

30. R.J. Bauckham, *Jude, 2 Peter* (WBC, 50; Waco, TX: Word Books, 1983), p. 191, citing Mt. 13.41; 16.28; Lk. 1.33; 22.29-30; 23.42; Jn 18.36-37; 1 Cor. 15.24-25 (discussed below); Col. 1.13; 2 Tim. 4.1, 18; Heb. 1.8, plus references in the Apostolic Fathers.

some interpreters attempt to correlate this Petrine reference to the kingdom with what they see as Paul's description of the kingdom as intervening between Christ's resurrection and his return (see below, on Paul).[31] Nevertheless, this kingdom is said to be eternal, not one of a thousand years and not one that will be terminated in anticipation of other events to follow.

The book of 2 Peter was one of the formally disputed letters of the early Church, according to Eusebius (*Hist. Eccl.* 3.3.4; 6.25.8). He said that some disputed whether this book was written by Peter. It is not clear at what date the book was written (dates from 60 to 160 CE have been suggested), but it perhaps began exerting influence in the second century, since there is quite a bit of apparent attestation for it.[32] For those who entertain apostolic authorship, the date of composition would have had to be no later than 64 or 65 CE. However, if what Eusebius says is true, that the book was disputed, even if written by Peter it appears not to have had the kind of lasting influence that one might have expected. If the book was written later, then it could not have had an influence upon earliest Christianity, that is, the Christianity of the first century. For these several reasons, one cannot argue that early Christianity was a millenarian religion on the basis of 2 Peter.

The Gospels

The Gospels have often been thought to provide evidence for the millenarianism of early Christianity.[33] There is no doubt that Jesus speaks

31. See J.N.D. Kelly, *A Commentary on the Epistles of Peter and Jude* (BNTC; London: A. & C. Black, 1969; repr. Grand Rapids: Baker Book House, 1981), p. 310; and Bauckham, *Jude, 2 Peter*, p. 191, but both of whom argue for the similar perspective noted below.

32. On authorship, see Bauckham, *Jude, 2 Peter*, pp. 158-63, who has an excellent summary of the evidence.

33. I do not include reference to Mk 13 = Mt. 24 = Lk. 21, since the references to the kingdom in these passages (Mt. 24.14; Lk. 21.31) are too obscure, and do not seem to indicate the framework being discussed here. For recent discussion of these passages, and how they might be interpreted, see T.R. Hatina, 'The Focus of Mark 13.24-27: The Parousia, or the Destruction of the Temple?', *BBR* 6 (1996), pp. 43-66; N.H. Taylor, 'Palestinian Christianity and the Caligula Crisis. Part II. The Markan Eschatological Discourse', *JSNT* 62 (1996), pp. 13-41; and E. Adams, 'Historical Crisis and Cosmic Crisis in Mark 13 and Lucan's *Civil War*', *TynBul* 48.2 (1997), pp. 329-44. Nor do I discuss Mt. 27.51-53, with its highly apocalyptic imagery, but not readily apparent millennial language.

of his kingdom in numerous places, and Jesus' teaching of the kingdom is undoubtedly authentic material, according to the standard of recent historical-Jesus research.[34] However, the nature of that kingdom has been an item of serious debate. Some have argued for a thoroughly proleptic approach to the kingdom, a view that has been prominent since around the turn of the century in much German scholarship.[35] Others, in reaction, have argued for a present kingdom, brought with Jesus' coming. This was the view of Dodd, who unfortunately based his view on a grammatical mistake.[36] The mistake has been corrected, but the perspective remains. Others have argued for the imminent kingdom.[37] With this much diversity, it is difficult to utilize such a framework to define the millenarian nature of the movement. However, even if one could define the imminence of the kingdom, one would still need to define its length and boundaries. Here one begins to run into difficulties, since there is no indication that the kingdom is earthly or has any terminal point. In fact, some of the evidence says otherwise. In Lk. 23.42-43, Jesus is recorded as speaking with one of the others being crucified. The man says, 'Jesus, remember me when you come into your kingdom' (NIV), to which Jesus replies, 'I tell you the truth, today [σήμερον] you will be with me in paradise' (NIV). There is a textual variant in this verse that has 'in' (ἐν), rather than 'into' (εἰς).[38] This would perhaps indicate belief at least on the man's part of Jesus returning to inaugurate a kingdom. It is also possible that the man thought that Jesus would raise him from the dead.[39] In any case, in Jesus' answer it appears that here Jesus' kingdom is equated with a heavenly kingdom, not one on this earth. Regarding the two temporal dimensions, the time of entering and the time of ending, 'today' would seem to indicate that

34. See Chilton, *Pure Kingdom*, *passim*.

35. See A. Schweitzer, *The Mystery of the Kingdom of God: The Secret of Jesus' Messiahship and Passion* (trans. W. Lowrie; London: A. & C. Black, 1925).

36. C.H. Dodd, *The Parables of Jesus* (New York: Charles Scribner's Sons, rev. edn, 1961), pp. 21-59. On pp. 29-30, he makes his classic mistake regarding the verb φθάνω. See S. McKnight, *A New Vision for Israel: The Teaching of Jesus in National Context* (Grand Rapids: Eerdmans, 1999), p. 73.

37. W.G. Kümmel, *Promise and Fulfilment: The Eschatological Message of Jesus* (trans. D.M. Barton; London: SCM Press, 1957).

38. The evidence is debatable, but probably εἰς is the better reading.

39. A. Plummer, *A Critical and Exegetical Commentary on the Gospel According to St Luke* (ICC; Edinburgh: T. & T. Clark, 1896), p. 535.

very day on which the man will die, but there is no indication given that this would only be for a period of one thousand years. Some have tried to explain 'today' as simply a reference to Jesus inaugurating redemption or the kingdom through his death and resurrection.[40] While this may be acceptable theology, it goes against the sense of the verse, which gives no indication of any future inauguration apart from the events in question at the time.[41]

The parable of Lazarus in Lk. 16.19-31 is often said to indicate that there is some form of intermediate state or kingdom before the final judgment.[42] In the parable, Lazarus dies and goes to Abraham's side, while the rich man dies and goes to hell. While the two men are in these two places, there is a conversation involving them and Abraham, regarding whether there is any relief for the rich man or warning that can be given to his family. There are a number of problems with using this parable to indicate the millenarian beliefs of early Christianity. The first is the fact that this is probably a parable. Parables are stories told by Jesus that often make a number of telling points. If the point of the story here is one regarding the millennial kingdom, it is an obscure and poorly made one, since there are a number of confusing or contradictory features. One is that Jesus is telling the story, but is not present in the kingdom, if it is to be equated with the bosom of Abraham. Instead, Abraham is the major figure in this place. There is no temporal indication given, and it certainly is not a literal place on earth. Most of the early interpreters, as well as modern interpreters, would take the bosom of Abraham as a place to be equated with heaven. Where there is mention of 'resurrection' (vv. 27-31) , if this is not simply a reference to a visit from the dead, the concept is dismissed, since it is said that

40. J.A. Fitzmyer, *The Gospel According to Luke* (AB, 28, 28A; 2 vols.; Garden City, NY: Doubleday, 1985), II, p. 1510; R.H. Stein, *Luke* (NAC, 24; Nashville: Broadman & Holman, 1992), p. 593.

41. See W. Grundmann, *Das Evangelium nach Lukas* (THNT, 3; Berlin: Evangelische Verlagsanstalt, 1971), p. 434; I.H. Marshall, *The Gospel of Luke* (NIGTC; Grand Rapids: Eerdmans, 1978), p. 873; J. Nolland, *Luke* (WBC, 35A, B, C; Dallas: Word Books, 1993), III, p. 1152; D.L. Bock, *Luke* (Baker Exegetical Commentary on the New Testament; 2 vols.; Grand Rapids: Baker Book House, 1996), II, p. 1857; J.B. Green, *The Gospel of Luke* (NICNT; Grand Rapids: Eerdmans, 1997), p. 823.

42. See Fitzmyer, *Luke*, II, pp. 1125-29.

Lazarus cannot return, and that those on earth would not believe if someone were to arise from the dead anyway.[43]

There are also a number of places in John's Gospel that have been interpreted as giving indications of the millennial nature of early Christianity. In Jn 14.2-4, Jesus is recorded as telling his disciples that in his father's house are many rooms, and that he is going there to prepare a place for them, and that he will return and take them to be with him. As Hill records,[44] there has been a variety of interpretation of this passage. Some have thought that this indicates an event occurring at the time of the death of the disciples,[45] at the time of the return of Christ, the so-called parousia,[46] the spiritual union that his disciples will have with him at his resurrection and the coming of the Paraclete,[47] or a combination of these explanations, including present spiritual position in Christ and future heavenly abiding with the Father.[48] In order to understand how this imagery is to be understood, one needs to appreciate the overall conceptual thought of the Gospels. This is perhaps best represented by Jesus' comment to Pilate in Jn 18.35-36, when Pilate asks Jesus regarding his kingdom. Jesus says: 'My kingdom is not of this world. If it were, my servants would fight to prevent my arrest by the Jews. But now my kingdom is from another place' (NIV). The perspective of the Gospel seems to be that Jesus is the initiator of an other-worldly kingdom, not an earthly millennial kingdom.

The Pauline Letters

The last place to look for support for Christianity as a millennial movement as defined here is in Paul. Apart possibly from the book of James, and there is much dispute over this, Paul was probably the earliest writer of the New Testament documents. He wrote the bulk of his letters

43. Bock, *Luke*, II, pp. 1361-62.

44. Hill, *Regnum Caelorum*, p. 157, who provides the following explanations and representation of scholarly opinion.

45. R. Bultmann, *The Gospel of John: A Commentary* (trans. G.R. Beasley-Murray; Oxford: Basil Blackwell, 1971), pp. 601-602.

46. L. Morris, *The Gospel According to John* (NICNT; Grand Rapids: Eerdmans, 1971), p. 639.

47. C.H. Dodd, *The Interpretation of the Fourth Gospel* (Cambridge: Cambridge University Press, 1953), pp. 395, 403-405.

48. R.H. Gundry, ' "In my Father's House are Many Μοναί" (John 14.2)', *ZNW* 58 (1967), pp. 68-72.

between c. 50 and 65 CE, and this corpus comprises the earliest body of Christian writings. Even the 7 letters usually recognized today as authentically Pauline comprise about one-fifth of the New Testament (with the corpus of 13 letters being over one-quarter). There is a long tradition of interpreting Paul as a millenarian thinker. In modern times, one of the major advocates has been Albert Schweitzer, who proposed that, consonant with other Jewish apocalyptic eschatology, Paul believed in a millennial kingdom. A Pauline distinctive, according to Schweitzer, was belief in two resurrections, one for those believers who have died (allowing them to participate fully in the millennial kingdom) and one for those alive at the return of Christ at the end of the millennium.[49] Since the time of Schweitzer, there has been widespread acceptance of the idea of Paul as an apocalyptic eschatologist.[50] This is not the place to evaluate this entire construct, but instead I will focus upon those passages that might give indication of Paul's belief in a millennial kingdom. Within this body of material, there are four major passages within the Pauline letters that merit attention. These passages vary in length and significance, with the first two being most important for this discussion.

1 Thessalonians 4.13-18. The first passage is 1 Thess. 4.13-18, where Paul tells his readers that he does not want them to be ignorant about those who have died, or fallen asleep (that is Paul's language), before the return of Christ. He then develops a chronology for this return, with those who are alive at Christ's return not preceding those who have died. Starting with v. 15, Paul says,

> we who are still alive, who are left till the coming of the Lord, will certainly not precede those who have fallen asleep. For the Lord himself will come down from heaven, with a loud command, with the voice of the archangel and with the trumpet call of God, and the dead in Christ will rise first. After that, we who are still alive and are left will be caught up with them in the clouds to meet the Lord in the air. And so we will be with the Lord forever (NIV).

49. A. Schweitzer, *The Mysticism of Paul the Apostle* (trans. W. Montgomery; London: A. & C. Black, 1931), pp. 65-68, 74-100, esp. p. 94, where he says, 'The doctrine of the two Resurrections was not found by Paul already in existence.'

50. See J.C. Beker, *Paul the Apostle: The Triumph of God in Life and Thought* (Philadelphia: Fortress Press, 1980); *idem*, *Paul's Apocalyptic Gospel: The Coming Triumph of God* (Philadelphia: Fortress Press, 1982).

The major question here, in so far as this essay is concerned, is whether Paul is here positing two resurrections, one for those who are asleep in Christ, which occurs during the millennial kingdom and allows their participation in it, and one at the end for those who are alive, as Schweitzer posited.[51]

Several observations are to be made on this passage. One of the major issues among scholars is whether Paul is now writing about a subject he has mentioned before to the Thessalonians but never expounded, that is, an eschatological resurrection, or whether he is clarifying an issue already discussed, in particular, the fate of those who have died before the resurrection and who might have been suspected to miss out on or enjoy a lesser resurrection.[52] Scholarship is divided on this issue, and with arguments on both sides, this is not the place to adjudicate such a dispute. The more important issue is whether Paul is speaking of a millennial kingdom, and whether there is a time lag between the resurrection of the dead in v. 16 and the living in v. 17. Whether Paul is introducing new concepts about the eschatological resurrection or not, it is certainly far from clear that he is talking about some form of intermediate earthly reign of Christ, regardless of length. At best he is speaking of a heavenly reign, since that is where Christ is situated (v. 16). The word translated 'after that' (ἔπειτα) is used as a word of sequence in Paul, but usually indicates a sequential or following on, not an extended period of time.[53] If this is the case here, Paul is depicting not two resurrections, but a single resurrection at the 'return' (παρουσία) of Christ, which results in a progression of those dead in Christ preceding those alive, but both groups ending up meeting the Lord in the air and being with him. As Davies states, 'There is no need to postulate that Paul here introduces the belief in a twofold resurrection under pressure from the logic of Jewish apocalyptic.'[54] Best introduces

51. Schweitzer, *Mysticism in Paul*, p. 92.

52. See J. Holleman, *Resurrection and Parousia: A Traditio-Historical Study of Paul's Eschatology in 1 Corinthians 15* (NovTSup, 84; Leiden: E.J. Brill, 1996), pp. 23-26, 69-72.

53. See J.E. Frame, *A Critical and Exegetical Commentary on the Epistles of St Paul to the Thessalonians* (ICC; Edinburgh: T. & T. Clark, 1912), p. 175. See 1 Cor. 12.28; 15.6, 7, 23, 46; Gal. 1.18, 21; 2.1.

54. W.D. Davies, *Paul and Rabbinic Judaism: Some Rabbinic Elements in Pauline Theology* (Philadelphia: Fortress Press, 4th edn, 1980), p. 291.

the idea that Paul speaks of the dead being raised to the earth and then they and the living are taken up.[55] This seems to be beyond the concerns of what is being said in the text. Neither does Paul entertain here the state of those who are dead.[56] More importantly, Marshall, following the meaning of 'meet' to indicate the process by which a dignitary was met outside and brought back to a city,[57] has posited that those resurrected and Christ meet and then return to the earth, and that this is where all are with the Lord.[58] However, this is not what the text says. It does not say where this being with the Lord takes place, only that it is forever (v. 17).[59] Further, these ideas do not appear to grow out of an apocalyptic context, but out of Paul's concern for those who have died in the faith, even if apocalyptic language is used.[60] It appears that one must import an apocalyptic framework, such as Schweitzer's, if one wishes to see his scheme here. Lastly, the return seems very much to be placed within a context of Paul expecting the imminent return of Christ, probably during his lifetime. Paul perhaps develops in his thought at this point, indicating in a later work such as Philippians that he is content with his own death before the return of Christ (see below). The point here is that the timing of his own death in regard to the return of Christ does not seem to have any bearing upon his belief in or theology of this return.

55. E. Best, *A Commentary on the First and Second Epistles to the Thessalonians* (BNTC; London: A. & C. Black, rev. edn, 1977), p. 198.

56. The intermediate state is an issue of scholarly concern in 2 Cor. 5.1-10, and is treated below.

57. On controversy over the meaning of ἀπάντησις (meeting), see M.R. Cosby, 'Hellenistic Formal Receptions and Paul's Use of ΑΠΑΝΤΗΣΙΣ in 1 Thessalonians 4.17', *BBR* 4 (1994), pp. 15-33; refuted by R.H. Gundry, 'A Brief Note on "Hellenistic Formal Receptions and Paul's Use of ΑΠΑΝΤΗΣΙΣ in 1 Thessalonians 4.17"', *BBR* 6 (1996), pp. 39-41.

58. I.H. Marshall, *1 and 2 Thessalonians* (NCB; Grand Rapids: Eerdmans, 1983), p. 131.

59. A. Plummer, *A Commentary on St Paul's First Epistle to the Thessalonians* (London: Robert Scott, 1918), p. 77; cf. L. Morris, *The First and Second Epistles to the Thessalonians* (NICNT; Grand Rapids: Eerdmans, rev. edn, 1991), p. 146.

60. See A.F.J. Klijn, 'I Thessalonians 4.13-18 and its Background in Apocalyptic Literature', in M.D. Hooker and S.G. Wilson (eds.), *Paul and Paulinism: Essays in Honour of C.K. Barrett* (London: SPCK, 1982), pp. 67-73.

1 Corinthians 15.20-28. The second passage is 1 Cor. 15.20-28.[61] In many ways this passage, written possibly five years later than 1 Thessalonians, reflects a similar orientation to the return of Christ. The context is the resurrection of believers, and the order and progression in which it takes place. A difference between the two passages is that in 1 Corinthians the emphasis is upon the question of Christ's resurrection and its implications. The Church at Corinth appears to have had some internal dispute over the nature of Christ's resurrection. This dispute probably reflects a difference of opinion between Gentiles and Jews over the nature of the resurrection, whether it was bodily or spiritual.[62] Paul affirms that 'Christ has indeed been raised from the dead, the firstfruits of those who have fallen asleep' (v. 20; NIV; note the use of the language of sleep for death, similar to that in 1 Thess. 4). He then gives a brief comparison and contrast of Adam and Christ in regard to the origin of death. He says that 'in Christ all will be made alive. But each in his own turn: Christ, the firstfruits; then, when he comes, those who belong to him' (vv. 22-23; NIV). Then, in one of the relatively few references in the Pauline writings to the kingdom and certainly one of the few references to the kingdom of Christ,[63] Paul says that the end will come 'when he hands over the kingdom to God the Father after he has destroyed all dominion, authority and power. For he must reign until he has put all his enemies under his feet' (vv. 24-25; NIV). The last enemy is said to be death. Then 'When he has done this, then the Son himself will be made subject to him who put everything under him, so that God may be all in all' (v. 28; NIV).[64]

61. For overviews of the issues involved, see L.J. Kreitzer, *Jesus and God in Paul's Eschatology* (JSNTSup, 19; Sheffield: JSOT Press, 1989), pp. 134-45; C.E. Hill, 'Paul's Understanding of Christ's Kingdom in 1 Corinthians 15.20-28', *NovT* 30 (1988), pp. 297-320, esp. pp. 297-98; and Holleman, *Resurrection and Parousia*, pp. 4-31.

62. Holleman, *Resurrection and Parousia*, pp. 35-40.

63. The term βασιλεία appears in Paul in the following places: Rom. 14.17 (of God); 1 Cor. 4.20 (of God); 6.9, 10 (both of God); 15.24 (of Christ), 50 (of God); Gal. 5.21 (of God); Eph. 5.5 (of Christ and of God); Col. 1.13 (of his son); 4.11 (of God); 1 Thess. 2.12 (of God); 2 Thess. 1.5 (of God); 2 Tim. 4.1 (of Christ), 18 (of the Lord).

64. Hill ('Paul's Understanding', pp. 298-300) relies upon a chiastic structure of the passage to reinforce his analysis; however, J. Lambrecht ('Structure and Line of Thought in 1 Cor. 15.23-28', *NovT* 32 [1990], pp. 143-51) shows that this is not necessary, to say anything of correct.

Several observations may be made about this passage as well. The most obvious one is that there is no clear specification of a thousand-year intermediate period. In fact, there is no clear specification of any period of any length. Nevertheless, that has not prevented a number of scholars from proposing such a millennial scheme. There are several issues that are often raised. The first is concern for those who are not 'of Christ'. Some have proposed that the two uses of 'all' (πάντες) in v. 22 draw a contrast between all dying in Adam and all being made alive in Christ, with the question of whether the second 'all' implies all people universally saved or all resurrected, some believers and others non-believers, though at separate times.[65] Then, in the sequence in vv. 20-24, Christ is raised first, the firstfruit (vv. 20, 23), 'then' (ἔπειτα) those in Christ at the time of his return (παρουσίᾳ),[66] and then (εἶτα) the end—but then what of those not in Christ, already possibly introduced in v. 22? There have been several solutions to these problems. Some take τὸ τέλος (the end) to refer to 'the rest', those who are not 'of Christ'.[67] Most commentators reject this understanding, since there is virtually no other Pauline usage to support it, and argue that here it is synonymous with the return of Christ.[68] Others take the word 'then' (εἶτα), following on from ἔπειτα, as implying a gap between the resurrection of those 'of Christ' and the resurrection for judgment of those who are not 'of Christ'. This intervening period would be the millennial kingdom. This sequence has been supported to the satisfaction of some by the interpretation of the two following 'when' (ὅταν) clauses (v. 24). Most interpreters take these as parallel in time, but the proposal has been made that they are in inverse order, with the handing over of the kingdom to God occurring after the destruction of every ruler, authority and power. This position has been supported by the use of the aorist

65. See W.B. Wallis, 'The Problem of an Intermediate Kingdom in 1 Corinthians 15:20-28', *JETS* 18 (1975), pp. 229-42, esp. p. 234.

66. It must be admitted that there has been a gap betwen Christ's resurrection and his return, but this is probably not one anticipated by Paul (it has also been 2000 years, and cannot be equated with the millennial period being discussed here).

67. H. Lietzmann, *An die Korinther* (HNT, 9; Tübingen: Mohr Siebeck, 3rd edn, 1931), p. 80.

68. Paul also uses the term in Rom. 6.21, 22; 10.4; 13.7; 1 Cor. 1.8; 10.11; 2 Cor. 1.13; 3.13; 11.15; Phil. 3.19; 1 Thess. 2.16; 1 Tim. 1.5, none of them with the sense of 'the rest'. Some have taken τὸ τέλος to mean 'finally', a usage attested in 1 Pet. 3.8, but not apparently in Paul.

tense form in the second clause as indicating antecedent action, and taken as further indication of an intermediate period between the two events.[69]

There are a number of comments that should be made here. With regard to the argument based upon the verb tenses, this argument simply cannot be sustained solely on the basis of the verb tense forms, since it has been recognized by numerous grammarians since at least the beginning of the century that verb tense forms in Greek, certainly in the non-indicative moods, do not have temporal reference.[70] Even if one interprets the two events as being in inverse order in the 'when' clauses,[71] this does not imply a gap between the events, and certainly not one of a thousand years. They seem, instead, to be two events that take place at 'the end'. The word 'then' has more merit for suggesting an intermediate period, since, in its only other use with ἔπειτα in Paul, it is used in somewhat similar syntax in 1 Cor. 15.5-7, where a sequencing is specified. However, one instance is not sufficient to form a rule. As Robertson and Plummer say, 'then' 'may introduce what is subsequent or what is immediately consequent'.[72] Also, there is no indication of the length of this fixed period of time, still leaving the definition of this period imprecise.[73] There is the further problem that if Paul were intent upon making clear this tripartite sequence, he could easily have

69. Wallis, 'Problem', pp. 230-31. Wallis ties this analysis to the theologically motivated linear view of time argued for by, for example, O. Cullmann, especially in his *Christ and Time: The Primitive Christian Conception of Time and History* (trans. F.V. Filson; London: SCM Press, 1962 [1946]), soundly criticized by J. Barr, *Biblical Words for Time* (SBT, 33; London: SCM Press, 2nd edn, 1969 [1962]), esp. pp. 50-85.

70. See S.E. Porter, *Idioms of the Greek New Testament* (Biblical Languages: Greek, 2; Sheffield: JSOT Press, 2nd edn, 1994), p. 52, citing Schwyzer, Robertson, Moulton, Dana and Mantey, Moule and Gonda. It is unfortunate that Kreitzer (*Jesus and God*, p. 145) commends Wallis on his interpretation of the two 'when' clauses, calling it 'the most significant contribution he has to make to the study of the passage'.

71. See G.D. Fee, *The First Epistle to the Corinthians* (NICNT; Grand Rapids: Eerdmans, 1987), p. 752.

72. A. Robertson and A. Plummer, *A Critical and Exegetical Commentary on the First Epistle of St Paul to the Corinthians* (ICC; Edinburgh: T. & T. Clark, 2nd edn, 1911), p. 354.

73. See Hill, 'Paul's Understanding', p. 308; Holleman, *Resurrection and Parousia*, pp. 53-54.

done so more explicitly. If, as has been argued, this explicit description is not Paul's concern in this passage, since he is dealing at this point only with those 'in Christ', then this also takes away the argument for seeing the intermediate period spoken of here. What of those who are not 'in Christ'? This does not appear to have been a concern for him in this passage, since he was concerned to outline the effects of the resurrection for those 'in Christ'.[74] At best, this passage offers a hint at an intermediate period of Christ's rule, but nothing more, even with a charitable interpretation. He does not appear to speak of two resurrections,[75] and it is probably best to say that Paul certainly does not argue for, and probably does not even refer to or even hint at, a millennial period in 1 Cor. 15.20-28.

2 Corinthians 5.1-10. This passage, 2 Cor. 5.1-10, can be divided into a number of subsections, but each approaches the human situation from a similar perspective. In the first, 2 Cor. 5.1-5, Paul draws a number of contrasts between the earthly life, which he depicts as a tent or earthly clothing, and an eternal house in heaven that is not made by hands. The major debate here is between whether this section argues for a disembodied intermediate state after death and before the resurrection,[76] one which Paul wishes to avoid, or whether the 'building from God' in v. 1 is a resurrection body that believers inhabit upon death until the parousia.[77] Both positions have had a number of influential and important exegetes who have defended them. The important interpretative issue is

74. See Fee, *First Corinthians*, pp. 753 n. 38, and 750 n. 19, where he attacks Wallis's logic; J. Héring, *The First Epistle of Saint Paul to the Corinthians* (trans. A.W. Heathcote and P.J. Allcock; London: Epworth, 1962), p. 166; cf. Hill, 'Paul's Understanding, pp. 304-307; S.E. Porter, 'The Pauline Concept of Original Sin, in Light of Rabbinic Background', *TynBul* 41.1 (1990), pp. 3-30, here pp. 15-16.

75. Even Schweitzer admits that this is the case in 1 Cor. 15.20-28 (*Mysticism of Paul*, pp. 67-68).

76. The classic statement of this position is O. Cullmann, *Immortality of the Soul or Resurrection of the Dead? The Witness of the New Testament* (London: Epworth, 1958), esp. pp. 52-55.

77. See M. Harris, *Raised Immortal: Resurrection and Immortality in the New Testament* (Grand Rapids: Eerdmans, 1983), pp. 220-26. For a thorough survey of the various opinions, which number far more than two, see M.E. Thrall, *A Critical and Exegetical Commentary on the Second Epistle to the Corinthians* (ICC; 2 vols.; Edinburgh: T. & T. Clark, 1994–2000), I, pp. 363-70, and her conclusions on p. 397, similar to those of Harris.

how the term 'naked' is understood in v. 3.[78] The latter position seems most likely. Harris gives five lines of support for the position: (1) when v. 1 refers to 'having' a building from God, it refers to believers possessing this body at the time of death, when the earthly tent is destroyed;[79] (2) Paul's use of 'put on over' in v. 2 (ἐπενδύσασθαι) refers to putting on the resurrection body without shedding the earthly body; (3) vv. 6 and 8, like vv. 1-4, speak of present and future conditions; (4) in v. 8, the contrast is between earthly existence and spiritual existence, with the latter required to be with the Lord (not a disembodied state); and (5) there is no interruption between the two states suggested.[80] The term 'naked' in this view means that at death the believer is clothed with the resurrection body, not left bodiless. If this position is correct, then it is difficult to find evidence for an intermediate, earthly millennial kingdom. Even if this position is not correct, and the disembodied state is posited for dead believers, it is difficult to see how this argues for an intermediate millennial kingdom for all of his followers, with Christ reigning. The contrast in these verses appears in any case to be between the earthly present kingdom and some form of either disembodied, intermediate state, hardly the millennial kingdom, or the resurrected, spiritual body, anticipating the parousia and judgment.[81]

Philippians 1.21-23. The last passage to consider is Phil. 1.21-23, which is very similar in some ways to 2 Cor. 5.6-8. Paul draws a contrast in his desires between living in the body, his current state, and his dying and being with Christ, a condition that he says that he prefers. Two major critical issues with bearing on our discussion here are, first, whether this passage expresses a genuine choice, and, secondly, what

78. On various options, see Thrall, *Second Corinthians*, I, pp. 374-80.

79. The issues of the conditional clause, and the uses of the aorist and present tense forms have led to unnecessary confusion on the part of some commentators. For example, see P. Barnett, *The Second Epistle to the Corinthians* (NICNT; Grand Rapids: Eerdmans, 1997), p. 257.

80. See Harris, *Raised Immortal*, pp. 98-101; cf. Holleman, *Resurrection and Parousia*, pp. 72-74; and A. Plummer, *A Critical and Exegetical Commentary on the Second Epistle of St Paul to the Corinthians* (ICC; Edinburgh: T. & T. Clark, 1915), p. 163, for a concise summary.

81. The question of whether this introduces contradictions with Paul's eschatological positions elsewhere, in particular 1 Cor. 15, is beyond the scope of this study. See R.P. Martin, *2 Corinthians* (WBC, 40; Waco, TX: Word Books, 1986), pp. 97-101.

bearing it has on Pauline eschatology, in particular on the issue of the millennium. As to the second question, Hawthorne takes the phrase 'to be with Christ' in v. 23 as descriptive of an intermediate period, after death and before the resurrection of believers, but he must admit that Paul 'does not speculate on the nature of this "intermediate condition"'.[82] The vast majority of scholars, however, do not take this as a passage bearing much weight on the issue of Pauline eschatology. As Collange states,

> the meaning of the text is being somewhat forced when it is over-exploited as source material for a reconstruction of Pauline eschatology. Not that the text is silent on this point or that the '*sun Christō einai*' ('to be with Christ') of v. 23 does not correspond to the apostle's actual thought...[83]

In other words, there may be some reference to Paul's eschatological position, but the idea is not developed in any significant way. Bringing in reference to the resurrection seems to be foreign to this passage, especially since the phrasing is that which is used elsewhere when Paul speaks of being with Christ after his return.[84] Besides, there is certainly no clear indication of a millennial kingdom. As to the first question raised above, many scholars take this as a genuine choice that the apostle is facing,[85] even that of voluntary death,[86] but a good case can be

82. G.F. Hawthorne, *Philippians* (WBC, 43; Waco, TX: Word Books, 1983), p. 50.

83. J.-F. Collange, *The Epistle of Saint Paul to the Philippians* (trans. A.W. Heathcote; London: Epworth, 1979), p. 62.

84. See P.T. O'Brien, *The Epistle to the Philippians* (NIGTC; Grand Rapids: Eerdmans, 1991), pp. 132-37, esp. p. 137. This passage also raises issues regarding consistency in Pauline eschatology. Many commentators focus upon this issue (e.g. U.B. Müller, *Der Brief des Paulus an die Philipper* [THNT, 11.1; Leipzig: Evangelische Verlagsanstalt, 1993], pp. 61-64), while others leave the tension (e.g. A. Plummer, *A Commentary on St Paul's Epistle to the Philippians* [London: Robert Scott, 1919], p. 30).

85. M. Silva, *Philippians* (Wycliffe Exegetical Commentary; Chicago: Moody, 1988), p. 81, who waxes lyrical on the emotional language in the passage. Cf. Holleman, *Resurrection and Parousia*, p. 199, who states, 'Paul's idea of his own afterlife here is that of a martyrological resurrection taking place immediately after his death.'

86. See C.S. Wansink, *Chained in Christ: The Experience and Rhetoric of Paul's Imprisonments* (JSNTSup, 130; Sheffield: Sheffield Academic Press, 1996), pp. 96-125.

made that this is either a hypothetical choice or one that he conceives himself making in the future, since he looks forward to his release in vv. 24-26.[87] In any event, although the reign of Christ is clearly expressed in this passage, again it does not fit the definition of millenarianism that has been put forward above. Paul's alternation is apparently a hypothetical choice between an earthly existence and an existence with Christ, with there being no other clearly postulated intermediate condition.[88]

Like the other New Testament writers, Paul too does not provide evidence for a clear, earthly intermediate millennial kingdom of a thousand years, in which Christ reigns before the final judgment. Instead, although he apparently speaks of Christ's reign in 1 Cor. 15.24, this reign is not clearly defined, and may well approximate to Jesus' ministry on earth, which culminated with Christ's resurrection and the defeat of death. In the other passages, there seems to be an alternation between an earthly and a non-earthly (heavenly) kingdom, with the two either overlapping now or the non-earthly following immediately from the current, which is the less desirable.

Conclusion

The result of this study of the earliest Christian documents indicates that one must define millenarianism before one can decide whether Christianity was a millenarian movement. If one defines the term very broadly, as is done in social-scientific criticism, then one might well argue that early Christianity was a millenarian movement—it was indeed a movement that expected some kind of imminent, this-worldly salvation. However, this definition must be used with caution. The authors of Revelation, Hebrews and 2 Peter clearly were anticipating such imminent salvation. Paul, on the other hand, in some places looks for such an imminent intervention but in other places is content to

87. See G.D. Fee, *Paul's Letter to the Philippians* (NICNT; Grand Rapids: Eerdmans, 1995), 140-50, esp. pp. 147-48 n. 38; Collange, *Philippians*, p. 62. Again, how this relates to Paul's eschatology elsewhere is beyond discussion here. See Fee, *Philippians*, pp. 149-50.

88. See J.B. Lightfoot, *St Paul's Epistle to the Philippians* (London: Macmillan, 1913), p. 93.

realize that his death may well precede such an occurrence. It is clear that the later, social-scientific definition of millenarianism is a development from the earlier, more traditional Christian theological concept. One is therefore begging the question of whether early Christianity was a millenarian religious movement according to social-scientific criteria until one actually analyses the movement in terms of the narrower, traditional definition.

If one defines the term millennium in a more traditional way, one must conclude that on these terms earliest Christianity was not, properly speaking, a millenarian movement. The little evidence that there is for such belief in a literal, future thousand-year reign of Christ as an intermediate period before the final judgment is only possibly found in one passage (Rev. 20). However, this passage itself is fraught with difficulties, including those of interpretation and reception. The marginal place that Revelation maintained for a number of years, besides its relatively late date of composition in comparison with other New Testament books, minimizes its place as an indicator of the belief of earliest Christianity. The same can be said for Hebrews and 2 Peter. It is only with Paul that one can entertain the possibility of Christianity as a millenarian movement. Here, too, the evidence is ambiguous. There is no doubt that Paul saw Christ as the Messiah, and entertained a kingdom or reign of God (or Christ) and the final judgment of God, but it is unclear whether this period of reign was terminated with the return of Christ or whether it continued for the indefinite future. There also is no indication of the timescale for the length of this period of God or Christ's reign, and certainly no consistent or specific indication of where or when it occurs. Sometimes Paul seems to think of it as imminent and within his lifetime, and sometimes he anticipates his death before it occurs, even though he maintains his belief in its occurrence.

Perhaps a better way of examining the evidence is to see a trajectory of belief. The earliest writers of the New Testament did not strictly conceive of Christianity as a millenarian movement, even though they clearly believed in the reign or kingdom of God (and, occasionally, of Christ), and depicted some of this belief in apocalyptic language on occasion. Instead, when/if at least some elements of Christianity did develop millenarian belief, this was apparently the result of further reflection and development by later Church thinkers, especially those of the second to third century, possibly involving reflection on Revelation 20 and other apocalyptic writings (see, for example, *Barn.* 15, with reference to a thousand years, but which merges into eternity; Justin, *Dial.* 80-81; Tertullian, *Adv. Marc.* 3.24).[89] So, in answer to the question of whether early Christianity was a millenarian movement, the answer is probably no, but that it may have become one soon after.

89. See Swete, *Apocalypse*, pp. 261-62; Court, *Myth and History*, pp. 2-3.

THE BIBLE, THE TRINITY AND HISTORY: APOCALYPTICISM AND MILLENNIALISM IN THE THEOLOGY OF JOACHIM OF FIORE*

Anthony R. Cross

While the Calabrian Abbot Joachim of Fiore is to many an unknown figure of the past, his obscurity belies his significance for the theory of history and for the development of Christian apocalypticism in general and millennialism in particular. He 'discerned in the events of the Bible the hidden outlines of a cosmic drama which was to haunt Western minds for centuries'.[1] In his own lifetime and the early thirteenth century he was primarily known for his concordances between the Old and New Testaments and his predictions of the coming of the Antichrist,[2] and it was only later that his views of the future progress of the earth gained widespread influence.[3] Not only did he develop one of the most

* I am grateful for the constructive comments and help of Marjorie Reeves, Sean McGlynn and Arthur Gibson.

1. C.H. Lawrence, *The Friars: The Impact of the Early Mendicant Movement on Western Society* (London: Longman, 1994), p. 54.

2. M. Reeves, *The Influence of Prophecy in the Later Middle Ages: A Study in Joachimism* (Oxford: Clarendon Press, 1969), p. 14; B. McGinn, 'Joachim and the Sibyl', *Cîteaux Commentarii Cistercienses* 34 (1973), pp. 97-138 (97); R.E. Lerner, 'Refreshment of the Saints: The Time after Antichrist as a Station for Earthly Progress in Medieval Thought', *Traditio* 32 (1976), pp. 97-144 (138-40), who argues that people in the later Middle Ages believed that the time of the Antichrist was imminent.

3. M. Bloomfield and M. Reeves, 'The Penetration of Joachism into Northern Europe', in D.C. West (ed.), *Joachim of Fiore in Christian Thought: Essays on the Influence of the Calabrian Abbot* (2 vols.; New York: Burt Franklin, 1975), I, pp. 107-28. E.g. p. 127: 'Universally he appealed to [his early thirteenth-century admirers] as one who, living in a day of impending crisis, had been endowed with the *spiritualis intellectus* to open the mystery of the Seven Seals, map out the course of history and foretell the advent of Antichrist... [T]he men who lived in [the next two generations after his writing] would very naturally tend to be obsessed by the "crisis aspect" of Joachism and to focus their attention wholly on the

influential theories of history, but his influence has continued to the present day, even though the way he has been used would often have horrified him. His theory of the three ages of history has not only influenced Christians for nearly eight hundred years, but also theologians and philosophers such as G.E. Lessing (1729–81), F.W.J. von Schelling (1775–1814) and J.G. Fichte (1762–1814), while it has been questionably claimed for G.W.F. Hegel (1770–1831), Auguste Comte (1798–1857) and Karl Marx (1818–83), movements including the New Age movement, and even, if indirectly, Hitler's Third Reich.[4] In popular genres, a good case can be made for his influence on J.R.R. Tolkein's *Lord of the Rings* and the modern cult television science fiction series *Babylon 5*. It is important, then, to examine his ideas, for the 'strong popular tendency to read current historical events into books such as Daniel and Revelation' is a legacy of Joachim's work.[5]

The Development of Apocalyptic from the First to the Twelfth Century

While Ernst Käsemann's statement that 'Apocalyptic was the mother of all Christian theology'[6] is clearly an overstatement, it can nevertheless

expected Antichrist. In the first phase of Joachism, then, little attention is paid to the Abbot's trinitarian doctrine of history, with its promise of fruition in the third *status*.' (This article was originally published in *Speculum* 29 (1954), pp. 772-93.) See also Lerner, 'Refreshment', pp. 119-20; and Reeves, *Influence*, pp. 37-58.

4. For these and others who have been influenced by Joachim, see Lerner, 'Refreshment', p. 98, and the literature cited in n. 7; N. Cohn, *The Pursuit of the Millennium: Revolutionary Millenarians and Mystical Anarchists of the Middle Ages* (London: Pimlico, 3rd edn, 1970), pp. 108-109; D.C. West, 'Introduction', in *idem* (ed.), *Joachim of Fiore*, I, pp. i-xiii (viii); M.W. Bloomfield, 'Joachim of Flora: A Critical Survey of his Canon, Teachings, Sources, Biography, and Influence', in West (ed.), *Joachim of Fiore*, I, pp. 29-91 (86-89) (originally published in *Traditio* 13 [1957], pp. 249-311). For his influence on the New Age movement, see R. Kyle, *Awaiting the Millennium: A History of End-time Thinking* (Leicester: Inter-Varsity Press, 1998), p. 48, citing his own *The New Age Movement in American Culture* (Lanham: University Press of America, 1995), p. 21.

5. G. Bray, *Biblical Interpretation Past and Present* (Leicester: Inter-Varsity Press, 1996), p. 152.

6. E. Käsemann, 'The Beginnings of Christian Theology', in *idem*, *New Testament Questions of Today* (Philadelphia: Fortress Press, 1969), p. 102. J. Pelikan, *The Christian Tradition: A History of the Development of Doctrine*. I. *The Emergence of the Catholic Tradition (100–600)* (Chicago: University of Chicago Press, 1971), p. 123, concurs with Käsemann.

be accepted that 'almost all [scholars] are agreed that the earliest members of the Jesus movement were apocalyptists who saw his resurrection as the beginning of the new aeon'.[7] The prevalence of eschatology[8] throughout the New Testament shows how important an understanding of the place of the end times, and the end itself, was to the earliest Christian writers and communities.[9] Apocalypticism continued throughout the early centuries of the Christian Church, as did a literal, historical

7. B. McGinn, 'Introduction: John's Apocalypse and the Apocalyptic Mentality', in R.K. Emmerson and B. McGinn (eds.), *The Apocalypse in the Middle Ages* (Ithaca, NY: Cornell University Press, 1992), pp. 4-19 (10).

8. Definitions of terms used here need to be made explicit. P. Fredriksen, 'Tyconius and Augustine on the Apocalypse', in Emmerson and McGinn (eds.), *Apocalypse*, p. 20 n. 1, offers the following: eschatology refers to 'those beliefs concerned with the end of time and the final destiny of humankind' without implying a timetable; apocalypticism means that 'the End, however conceived, is imminent'; millenarianism 'holds that the redemption brought by the End, whenever it comes, will be collective, historical, and earthy (as opposed to heavenly or exclusively spiritual)', adding, 'The idea of a thousand-year period implied by the term is less essential to its import than is its focus on the earth, and human history, as the ultimate arena of redemption'; apocalyptic millenarianism 'holds that such a redemption is imminent'. Robert E. Lerner, 'The Medieval Return to the Thousand-Year Sabbath', in Emmerson and McGinn (eds.), *Apocalypse*, p. 51 n. 2, takes millennialism, millenarism, millenarianism and chiliasm as synonymous, a position that is adopted here, though, in this essay, millennialism is the preferred term understood as belief that in, adopting the words of J. Pelikan, *The Christian Tradition: A History of the Development of Doctrine*. III. *The Growth of Medieval Theology (600–1300)* (Chicago: University of Chicago Press, 1978), p. 42, the period 'between the two comings of Christ, the first in the incarnation, the second in the judgment, there is a middle age'. On p. 2, Pelikan cites Julian of Toledo (seventh century), *Antitheses* 2.69, and Albertus Magnus (1192–1280), *Commentary on the Minor Prophets* Habakkuk 3.2, as mediaeval proponents of this view.

9. From among the vast literature see D. Hellholm (ed.), *Apocalypticism in the Mediterranean World and the Near East: Proceedings of the International Colloquium on Apocalypticism, August 12–17, 1979* (Tübingen: J.C.B. Mohr, 1983); A.Y. Collins (ed.), *Early Christian Apocalypticism: Genre and Social Setting* (Semeia, 36; Atlanta: Scholars Press, 1986); J. Marcus and M.L. Soards (eds.), *Apocalyptic and the New Testament: Essays in Honour of J. Louis Martyn* (JSNTSup, 24; Sheffield: JSOT Press, 1989); G.W.E. Nickelsburg, *The Apocalyptic Imagination* (New York: Crossroads, 1989); J.J. Collins and J.H. Charlesworth (eds.), *Mysteries and Revelations: Apocalyptic Studies since the Uppsala Colloquium* (JSPSup, 9; Sheffield: Sheffield Academic Press, 1991); N. Cohn, *Cosmos, Chaos and the World to Come: The Ancient Roots of Apocalyptic Faith* (New Haven: Yale University Press, 1994).

understanding of the millennium first prophesied in Rev. 20.1-2. Apocalypticism, often but by no means exclusively in the form of millennialism, was encouraged by the Christians' use of, not only the book of Revelation but also the Sibylline Oracles (a mixture of Jewish and Christian prophecies) and the development of their own Sibyllines[10] (a process that continued during the Middle Ages),[11] and by the outbreak of persecutions, such as those at the turn of the third century.[12] Its prevalence was witnessed to by many leading theologians, including Papias (c. 60–c. 130), Justin Martyr (c. 100–165), Irenaeus (d.c. 195), Tertullian (c. 160–c. 220), Hippolytus (d.c. 235/6), Commodian (variously dated between the mid-third to mid-fifth century) and Lactantius (c. 240–c. 320), and is clearly seen in the heterodox Montanists (late second to early-mid third century), whose most famous convert was Tertullian.[13]

10. B. McGinn, *Visions of the End: Apocalyptic Traditions in the Middle Ages* (Records of Civilization: Sources and Studies, 96; New York: Columbia University Press, 2nd edn, 1998), pp. 18-21; see also B. Thompson, 'Patristic Use of the Sibylline Oracles', *Review of Religion* 16 (1952), pp. 115-36.

11. Various Sibylline oracles and the book of Revelation were the most influential texts in mediaeval apocalyptic speculation. See Cohn, *Pursuit*, pp. 30-33, who writes, 'save for the Bible and the works of the Fathers [the Sibyllines] were probably the most influential writings known to medieval Europe' (p. 33). On their influence and use, see also Reeves, *Influence*, *passim*; Lerner, 'Refreshment', pp. 99-100; McGinn, 'Sibyl', pp. 116-22, and *Visions*, pp. 43-50 and *passim*.

12. R.M. Grant, *Augustus to Constantine: The Thrust of the Christian Movement into the Roman World* (London: Collins, 1970), p. 165. This was equally true during the Diocletian persecutions in the early fourth century when Victorinus of Pettau wrote his *Commentary* on Revelation. On Rev. 1.1's 'the things that must shortly come to pass', Victorinus understood 'soon' to mean 'now', and his interpretation of Revelation was chiliastic, looking forward to the literal thousand-year millennium before the end. Later, after the Constantinian settlement, Jerome thoroughly revised Victorinus's work to reflect the situation of the Church at peace in the empire. On this see E. Ann Matter, 'The Apocalypse in Early Medieval Exegesis', in Emmerson and McGinn (eds.), *Apocalypse*, p. 39, and McGinn, *Visions*, pp. 25-26.

13. E.g. Papias in Eusebius's *Ecclesiastical History* 3.39.11-12; Justin Martyr, *Dialogue with Trypho* 80–81; Irenaeus, *Against Heresies* 5.35.1; Tertullian, *Against Marcion* 3.24; Hippolytus, *Commentary on Daniel* 4.18-19 (see also his *Treatise on Christ and the Antichrist*, written c. 200); Commodian, *Instructions* 1.44; Lactantius, *Epitome of the Divine Institutes* bk 7, chs. 14-19 and 24, written between 304 and 313; and for the apocalypticism of the Montanists, see, e.g., Eusebius, *Ecclesiastical History* 5.14-18. For discussion of these and other texts, see Pelikan,

However, a number of factors have been suggested that contributed to a major reaction against apocalypticism in general and millennialism in particular.[14] For over two and a half centuries the Roman empire had been viewed in a very negative light, as is reflected in the book of Revelation itself,[15] but with the 'conversion' of the emperor Constantine in 312 this inevitably had to change. From this point onwards, the life of the Church and the Roman state seemed inextricably linked. Further, a literal-historical reading of apocalypticism seemed to many to be too 'Jewish'. Jerome believed that 'to take John's Apocalypse to the letter is to Judaize'.[16] No longer was Revelation to be read as a prophecy of the events of the end, nor as revealing its timetable, for such was excluded by Acts 1.7's 'It is not for you to know the times or dates the Father has set.' Rather, Revelation was to be read as an allegory of the Church, and particularly its struggle with good and evil. In the third century, Origen (c. 185–c. 254) had attacked the literal historicizing of apocalyptic in favour of an allegorical and spiritual interpretation,[17] and in this he was followed by the great historian of the early Church, Eusebius of Caesarea (c. 263–c. 339),[18] and Methodius of Olympus (d.c. 311).[19] But the problem with this was allegory's ahistorical nature. This fact was recognized by Tyconius (c. 330–c. 390) and Augustine of Hippo (354–430). Paula Fredriksen writes:

Emergence, pp. 124-30; J.N.D. Kelly, *Early Christian Doctrines* (London: A. & C. Black, 5th revised edn, 1977), pp. 465-69; M. Reeves, 'The Originality and Influence of Joachim of Fiore', *Traditio* 36 (1980), pp. 269-316 (272); Cohn, *Pursuit*, pp. 24-29; McGinn, *Visions*, pp. 21-25. On the Montanists see Grant, *Augustus to Constantine*, pp. 157-70; R.L. Fox, *Pagans and Christians in the Mediterranean World from the Second Century* AD *to the Conversion of Constantine* (London: Penguin Books, 1986), pp. 404-10.

14. McGinn, *Visions*, p. 25, but see the whole of his discussions on pp. 25-27; also see Cohn, *Pursuit*, pp. 29-30.

15. Rev. 14.8; 16.19; 17.5; 18.2, 10, 21.

16. This view was also held by Julian of Toledo. On both, see Lerner, 'Medieval Return', p. 53 and n. 8.

17. Origen, *On First Principles* 2.11.2-3. See Kelly, *Doctrine*, pp. 472-73, and Pelikan, *Emergence*, pp. 125. On pp. 128-29, Pelikan critically notes the opinion of many who trace the view that the parousia had already taken place in the coming of Christ as the Word made flesh from Clement of Alexandria (c. 155–220) through Origen to Gregory of Nyssa (c. 330–95).

18. McGinn, *Visions*, pp. 25-26.

19. Methodius, *Symposium* 9.1, see Pelikan, *Emergence*, p. 125.

> Many earlier theologians had either allegorized any historical and temporal reference out of John's prophecy or repudiated the text altogether. Other Christians, and most especially those in North Africa, had on the authority of the Apocalypse asserted an enthusiastic and socially disruptive millenarianism. Against these two extremes, Tyconius and, following him, Augustine introduced in the late fourth and early fifth centuries a reading of John that affirmed its historical realism while liberating it from the embarrassments of a literal interpretation.[20]

In order to avoid a literal millennium on the one hand and ahistorical allegory on the other, Tyconius[21] pioneered a typological reading of Revelation which did not deny its historical significance, yet permitted him to assert that the time of the end and the identity of the saved could not be known. This dual approach was important, as he was trying to correct his fellow Donatists, who had adopted a separatist ecclesiology coupled with a millennial expectation of the end within a hundred years.[22] To this end he developed seven rules that he believed were 'the compositional principles of Scripture, encoded in the text itself, which conceal or obscure its meaning'.[23] Tyconius was an anti-apocalypticist; and his seven rules, which complicated the biblical text, enabled him to preserve the historical significance of some of the most apocalyptic and millennialist passages of Scripture, while obscuring their eschatological import. For instance, his fifth rule enabled him to interpret the numbers and dates of Revelation, including the thousand-year millennium, as symbolic and indicative of spiritual truths, rather than literally.[24]

In his early years Augustine had held to a millennialist interpretation of Rev. 20.1-10,[25] but his becoming bishop of Hippo in North Africa coincided with the expected realization of numerous apocalyptic dates and events, some of which believed that the year 400 was the year 6000 from creation—and therefore the date of the end.[26] In his *City of God*,

20. Fredriksen, 'Tyconius and Augustine', p. 21.

21. Tyconius's *Commentary on Revelation*, written c. 385, has not survived, but has been reconstructed from later writers; see McGinn, *Visions*, p. 27, especially n. 118 (on p. 292) for these later writers.

22. For details see Fredriksen, 'Tyconius and Augustine', pp. 21-24.

23. Fredriksen, 'Tyconius and Augustine', p. 26.

24. Fredriksen, 'Tyconius and Augustine', pp. 27-28.

25. Augustine, *Sermons* 259.2. See Pelikan, *Emergence*, p. 129; Fredriksen, 'Tyconius and Augustine', p. 29 and n. 28; McGinn, *Visions*, p. 26 and n. 112.

26. Fredriksen, 'Tyconius and Augustine', pp. 29-30 and n. 29.

Augustine[27] rejected the idea of an earthly millennium, and argued that the thousand years referred to the present dispensation of the Church; therefore, 'It follows that the Church even now is the kingdom of Christ and the kingdom of heaven.'[28] In his systematic review of eschatological ideas, Robert Lerner notes that Augustine

> reprehended any hope for miraculous collective betterment on earth. Since faith and charity required Christians to despise delight in earthly existence and to live solely for the end of enjoying God in heaven, there could be nothing superior to the Church militant as an earthly institution designed to forward that end. Therefore it followed that when Saint John told of a thousand-year earthly reign of Christ and the saints (Apoc. 20.1-6), he could not have been referring to a coming dispensation but had to be telling of the present Church.[29]

Augustine[30] strongly rejected a literal reading of the one thousand years of Rev. 20.1-2[31] so that believers would not attempt to calculate the end by working out the date of the origin of the Church, because Christ had declared that no one would know the time of the end:[32]

> If the Apocalypse's thousand years could be interpreted literally, they had to stand figuratively for the world's last thousand years, of which the Church's reign would be a part, or else they had to be taken as a perfect number representing an indeterminate totality.[33]

27. For Augustine's anti-literal, anti-millennialist position see *City of God* 20.7, 9 and 13, which is discussed by Fredriksen, 'Tyconius and Augustine', pp. 29-35; and McGinn, *Visions*, pp. 26-27.

28. Augustine, *City of God* 20.9; see Augustine, *Concerning the City of God against the Pagans* (London: Penguin Books, 1972), p. 915.

29. Lerner, 'Medieval Return', p. 52.

30. Augustine's views are discussed by Reeves, 'Originality', pp. 272-75.

31. P. Brown, 'Saint Augustine', in B. Smalley (ed.), *Trends in Medieval Political Thought* (Oxford: Basil Blackwell, 1965), p. 11, writes that there are 'no verbs of historical movement in the *City of God*, no sense of progress towards ends that may be achieved in history. Augustine defused the dangerous idea of millennium by declaring that it had already begun with the Incarnation and quenched an optimistic view of secular history by declaring that the world was growing old. The *saeculum* was doomed to remain incomplete, for no human potentiality could ever reach its fulfillment within time' (cited by Reeves, 'Originality', p. 273).

32. Augustine, *City of God* 18.53, on the basis of Mt. 24.36 and Acts 1.7. See Lerner, 'Medieval Return', p. 52.

33. Lerner, 'Medieval Return', pp. 52-53.

However, Augustine did make a concession in that he conceded that belief in a spiritual millennium was less reprehensible than the materialistic alternative.[34]

Other leading scholars also adopted this spiritual reading, including Jerome (c. 347–c. 419) and, much later, Gregory the Great (540–604);[35] it was this position which became 'orthodox doctrine'.[36] Julian of Toledo said that the millennium denoted 'the church of God, which, by the diffusion of its faith and works, is spread out as a kingdom of faith from the time of the incarnation of Christ until the time of the coming judgment', and Ambrose Autpert (d. 784) could refer to '[Christ's] kingdom, which is the church'.[37] So far as the book of Revelation is concerned, it was transformed from a book of 'apocalyptic fervour into an extended allegory of the Church'.[38]

However, during the fourth and fifth centuries 'a theological basis for undermining the prohibition [of applying Rev. 20.1-10 to the future] was created unwittingly, on technical grounds, by a few exegetes who themselves were ardent antimillennialists'.[39] Jerome was the first to suggest a short interval (45 days) of earthly 'silence' or 'peace' between the death of the Antichrist and the final judgment. However, this 'peace' was understood negatively, and was seen not as a time of blessing, but one of trial. With Jerome's authority behind it, this brief period became common in the writings of later theologians, including Bede (c. 673–735), Alcuin (d. 804), Haimo of Auxerre (d.c. 860), the writer of the Old Saxon *Genesis* (ninth century) and Adso of Montier-en-Der (c. 910–92).[40] In the early twelfth century this final age took on a positive sense, designated by the *Glossa Ordinaria* (early twelfth century) on Dan. 12.12[41] as a time of 'refreshment of the saints',[42] and it

34. Augustine, *City of God* 20.7, on which see Lerner, 'Medieval Return', p. 53.

35. See Lerner, 'Medieval Return', pp. 51-54; Matter, 'Apocalypse', pp. 38-40. See also Kelly, *Doctrine*, pp. 479-80.

36. Cohn, *Pursuit*, p. 29.

37. Julian of Toledo, *Antitheses* 2.69, and Ambrose Autpert, *Commentary on the Apocalypse* 1, both cited by Pelikan, *Medieval Theology*, p. 43.

38. Matter, 'Apocalypse', p. 38.

39. Lerner, 'Medieval Return', p. 53.

40. For detailed discussion of Jerome to Adso, see Lerner, 'Refreshment', pp. 101-109, 129, and also his 'Medieval Return', pp. 53-57; Reeves, 'Originality', p. 276.

41. For details see Lerner, 'Refreshment', p. 109 n. 39.

42. For the development of this, see Lerner, 'Refreshment', pp. 109-15, who

received 'epoch making' treatment from Joachim of Fiore.[43] Joachim developed this period between the death of Antichrist and the end, though he agreed with Augustine in interpreting the thousand-year reign of Revelation 20 as a perfect number that expressed a time of fullness.[44]

Therefore, in spite of the various attacks on apocalyptic, the literal reading of Revelation never altogether disappeared and neither did its corollary—belief in the historical and material coming of the millennium,[45] whether the thousand years were understood literally or, as in Joachim, symbolically.

The Immediate Historical Context of Joachim of Fiore

There is no doubt that Joachim of Fiore was a Church reformer, but not in the conventional sense. He was not seeking a return of the contemporary Church to the idealized perfection of the primitive Church, but looking to the future Church in the third age of the Holy Spirit, which

notes that it came to be understood as the time in which the conversion of the heathen and Jews would take place, as well as a time in which the ministers of Antichrist could repent. This notion was taken up from the *Glossa* by Honorius Augustodunensis c. 1107, Otto of Freising in the 1140s and 50s, Hildegard of Bingen in the 1140s and Gerhoh of Reichersberg (1093–1169). On the conversion of the heathen, the bringing back of the Greeks into union with Latin Christendom and the final salvation of the Jews in Joachim's predictions, see E.R. Daniel, 'Apocalyptic Conversion: The Joachite Alternative to the Crusades', *Traditio* 25 (1969), pp. 127-54.

43. Lerner, 'Medieval Return', p. 57. For details of how Joachim developed this period see Lerner, 'Refreshment', pp. 115-20.

44. R.E. Lerner, 'Joachim of Fiore's Breakthrough to Chiliasm', *Cristianesimo nella Storia* 6 (1985), pp. 489-512 (507 n. 42), citing Joachim, *De vita Sancti Benedicti* (*The Life of St Benedict*, written in 1187); C. Baraut (ed.), 'Un Tratado Inédito de Joaquín de Fiore', *Analecta Sacra Tarraconensia* 24 (1951), pp. 33-122 (102) (c. 32). Lerner also refers to Joachim's *De Ultimis Tribulationibus* 11.5-11, the text of which is in E.R. Daniel, 'Abbot Joachim of Fiore: The *De Ultimis Tribulationibus*', in A. Williams (ed.), *Prophecy and Millenarianism: Essays in Honour of Marjorie Reeves* (Harlow: Longman, 1980), p. 187. On the general issue of *The Life of Saint Benedict*, see S. Wessley, '"Bonum mutare locum": The Role of the "Life of Saint Benedict" in Joachim of Fiore's Monastic Reform', *Revue Bénédictine* 90 (1980), pp. 314-28.

45. E.g. in Adso of Montier-en-Der in the tenth century, see Lerner, 'Medieval Return', pp. 51-52 n. 3, 'Refreshment', pp. 97-144 and 'Chiliasm', pp. 489-512. See also Cohn, *Pursuit*, pp. 30-36.

was soon to dawn.[46] Joachim believed that the contemporary Church had lost its spiritual vitality, applying to it the words of Isa. 1.21 about Jerusalem, 'How has the faithful city become a harlot!'[47] His view of the corrupt Church led to his belief that it needed to be 'resurrected, as it were, from the grave'.[48] In the third age, which he saw as about to dawn, a new Church was going to be born of the old one:

> It is our intention...to comprehend the end of the temporal realm, which is properly called Babylon, and to disclose in the clearest possible words that which is near, the birth of the Church, which will take place at the same time.[49]

The eleventh-century reforms championed by Gregory VII had raised the expectations of many Christians with regard to the nature and state of the Church, and, while there continued to be those who worked for reform from within the Church, there were increasing numbers of those who took it upon themselves to realize the revival in the contemporary Church of the pristine, apostolic Church.[50] Some of these developed naturally heterodox tendencies, such as the Cathars,[51] while others were

46. E.R. Daniel, 'Joachim of Fiore: Patterns of History in the Apocalypse', in Emmerson and McGinn (eds.), *Apocalypse*, p. 85, states 'The *status* of the Holy Spirit was Joachim's vision of the goal desired by the reformers of the eleventh and twelfth centuries.'

47. Joachim, *Tractatus super quatuor evangelia* (*Treatise on the Four Gospels*) 1, cited by Pelikan, *Medieval Theology*, p. 301. On Joachim's ecclesiology see Pelikan's discussion on pp. 301-303.

48. Joachim, *Tractatus* 3, cited by Pelikan, *Medieval Theology*, p. 301.

49. Joachim, *Liber concordie novi et veteris testamenti* (*The Book of Concordance of the Old and New Testaments*) 1.1, cited by Pelikan, *Medieval Theology*, p. 302.

50. Various reform and heretical movements arose between the eleventh and the end of the twelfth century when Joachim was writing. On these, see, especially noting his subtitle, M. Lambert, *Medieval Heresy: Popular Movements from the Gregorian Reform to the Reformation* (Oxford: Basil Blackwell, 2nd edn, 1992), 'Orthodox reform and heresy', pp. 35-43 and *passim*; G. Constable, *The Reformation of the Twelfth Century* (Cambridge: Cambridge University Press, 1996), e.g. pp. 166-67 and *passim*; and B. Bolton, *The Medieval Reformation* (Foundations of Medieval History; London: Edward Arnold, 1983). On the new religious orders see below, and on the 'heresies' see also W.L. Wakefield and A.P. Evans (eds.), *Heresies of the High Middle Ages* (Records of Western Civilization; New York: Columbia University Press, 1969); R.I. Moore, *The Origins of European Dissent* (Oxford: Basil Blackwell, 1985).

51. On the Cathars see B. Hamilton, *The Albigensian Crusade* (London: His-

forced by Catholic opponents into heresy, for example, the Waldensians.[52] That it is right to see Joachim within the context of the rise of heresy is supported by the observation that, when Joachim's trinitarian doctrine was condemned in 1215 by the Fourth Lateran Council (canon 2), it was sandwiched between the first new creed for, in Colin Morris's words, 'a very long time' that was 'directed against the wave of heresy' (canon 1) and a canon that set out a programme of action against heretics (canon 3).[53] Gordon Leff has argued that Joachim's prophecies of the opening of the seventh seal and the final age of history were the most pervasive influence on the 'growing sense of apocalypticism' in mediaeval heresy from the thirteenth to fifteenth centuries.[54]

Joachim was particularly concerned with the reform of monasticism.[55] His own Cistercian order[56] had been formed at the very end of

torical Association, 1974), and *The Medieval Inquisition* (Foundations of Medieval History; London: Edward Arnold, 1981); E. Le R. Ladurie, *Montaillou: Cathars and Catholics in a French Village 1294–1324* (London: Penguin, 1978); J. Sumption, *The Albigensian Crusade* (London: Faber & Faber, 1978); M. Lambert, *The Cathars* (Oxford: Basil Blackwell, 1998), and *Heresy*, pp. 44-61, 105-46. While there were certainly cross influences between them, the dualistic heresies, such as the Cathass, had different origins to those groups of reformers, such as the Waldensians, who started within the Church but were excluded on the issue of obedience, rather than doctrine. Innocent III, e.g., tried to keep the Waldensian inside the Church. I am grateful to Marjorie Reeves for this qualification.

52. See Lambert, *Heresy*, pp. 62-87, 147-71; G. Audisio, *The Waldensian Dissent: Persecution and Survival, c. 1170–c. 1570* (Cambridge Medieval Textbooks; Cambridge: Cambridge University Press, 1999).

53. C. Morris, *The Papal Monarchy: The Western Church from 1050 to 1250* (Oxford History of the Christian Church; Oxford: Clarendon Press, 1989), p. 448.

54. G. Leff, *Heresy in the Later Middle Ages: The Relation of Heterodoxy to Dissent c. 1250–c. 1450* (2 vols.; Manchester: Manchester University Press, 1967), I, p. 5.

55. So much was this so that B. McGinn, *Apocalyptic Spirituality: Treatises and Letters of Lactantius, Adso of Montier-en-Der, Joachim of Fiore, the Franciscan Spirituals, Savonarola* (London: SPCK, 1980), p. 108, writes that monasticism and his reforming zeal combined in that it was 'the future, not the past, of monasticism' that was his real concern.

56. G. Strauss, 'Ideas of *Reformation* and *Renovatio* from the Middle Ages to the Reformation', in T.A. Brady, Jr, H.A. Oberman and J.D. Tracy (eds.), *Handbook of European History 1400–1600: Late Middle Ages, Renaissance, and Reformation*. II. *Visions, Programs, and Outcomes* (Grand Rapids: Eerdmans, 1996), p. 6, remarks that in the twelfth century 'it was above all the Cistercians who stood for a thoroughgoing attempt to undertake a restoration of the authentic spirit of

the eleventh century (f. 1098 at Cîteaux),[57] and the twelfth century saw the founding of many new religious orders, including the Augustinian Canons, the Canons of St Victor and Order of Fontevrault (each c. 1100), the Templars (c. 1118), the Premonstratensians (1120) and the Carmelites (1154).[58] While some earlier monks viewed the new orders as the only positive prospect for the future, Anselm of Havelberg gave them a role 'at the culmination of what he considered to be a progressive unfolding of the faith "from good to better to best" '.[59] Lerner believes it most likely that, even before Joachim went to Casamari seeking the full admission of the monastery of Corazzo into the Cistercian order, he was already exploring the idea that the whole of salvation-history was

> a steady advance toward ever more dominant and 'spiritually' perfect monasticism in which the imminent future would see the culmination of trends initiated by the proto-monks Elijah and Elisha, then vastly extended by St Benedict, and then extended still further in his own day by Cistercians, Templars, and Hospitallers.[60]

Once he had become abbot of the small house of Corazzo, Joachim sought to bring it '"up to date" in the most ascetic usages then gaining ground in the world of Benedictine monasticism by introducing Cister-

pristine Christianity: renunciation, labor, imitation of Christ in all things. To "reform" individuals and institutions, i.e., "make them better [*reformare in melius*]", it was necessary to "restore [*restaurere*]" them to these original virtues'. The characteristics of the Cistercians were poverty, simplicity and eremitical solitude. On the Cistercians in general see, e.g., C.H. Lawrence, *Medieval Monasticism: Forms of Religious Life in Western Europe in the Middle Ages* (London: Longman, 2nd edn, 1989), pp. 174-205; S. Tobin, *The Cistercians: Monks and Monasteries of Europe* (London: Herbert Press, 1995).

57. Daniel, 'Joachim of Fiore', p. 73, writes, '[T]he twelfth century was optimistic about history and the future. The Gregorian reformers certainly believed that they could dramatically reform and purify the Church on earth. Joachim, who was clearly Gregorian in his sympathies, believed that history was evolving towards the *status* of the Holy Spirit...when the Church would enjoy a historical era of peace and spiritual attainment that would far surpass anything achieved in the past.'

58. Orders founded in the eleventh century included the Camaldolese (c. 1012), Vallambrosians (1036), Carthusians (1084) and Grandmontines late in the century.

59. See Lerner, 'Chiliasm', p. 491, on Otto of Freising in the 1140s see n. 5 for details, and n. 6 on Anselm of Havelberg in 1149.

60. Lerner, 'Chiliasm', pp. 491-92. Detailed discussion of Joachim's views of the steady progress of monasticism can be found in Reeves, *Influence*, pp. 135-44.

cian customs'. But frustrated by the slowness of gaining the house's acceptance into the Cistercian order and as he began to see that the Cistercians needed reforming, Joachim founded a new monastery, and the fact that he named this new eremitic house 'San Giovanni in Fiore' after the contemplative visionary St John is taken by Robert Lerner as evidence that he hoped it would '"flower" into a new order to set the fullest spiritual standard for the coming Sabbath age'.[61]

A second outcome of the eleventh-century Gregorian reforms was that the pope[62] received a place within apocalyptic speculation, something which had warrant in neither Scripture nor the patristic Church: in fact there was 'no hint of any special place for the papacy in the drama of the end for almost the first millennium of Christian history'.[63] As early as the 1160s the prominent Bavarian Augustinian canon and advocate of the Gregorian reforms, Gerhoh of Reichersberg, had attacked the place that financial dealings had come to hold in the affairs of the twelfth-century papacy,[64] but it was Joachim who first developed the role of the papacy in the imminent crisis of history. While dissatisfaction with the papacy as an instrument of reform blossomed after the Fourth Lateran Council, Joachim lived at the beginning of this process, and the position he adopted fuelled anti-papal feelings over the next century.[65] From the controversy surrounding the election of Honorius II in 1124 and the eight-year schism of Analectus II, which began in 1130, the papacy had been plagued with debates over the nature of reform.[66] This was followed by a debate during Joachim's lifetime on the relationship between the papacy and the Holy Roman Empire that lasted from the death of Alexander III in 1181 to the accession of Innocent III in 1198. One party opposed the empire's growing influence on

61. Lerner, 'Chiliasm', pp. 509-10.

62. For discussion of the papacy from Gregory VII to the end of the twelfth century, including many of the issues and people mentioned in this paragraph, see I.S. Robinson, *The Papacy 1073–1198: Continuity and Innovation* (Cambridge Medieval Textbooks; Cambridge: Cambridge University Press, 1990).

63. B. McGinn, 'Angel Pope and Papal Antichrist', *Church History* 47 (1978), pp. 155-73 (156-57, quotation from p. 157). On the origins and development of the idea of the Angel Pope, see Reeves, *Influence*, pp. 401-15, and McGinn, *Visions*, pp. 186-95.

64. See McGinn, *Visions*, pp. 94-107.

65. McGinn, 'Angel Pope', pp. 157-58.

66. On these events, see Morris, *Papal Monarchy*, pp. 182-84; and on their significance as background to Joachim, see McGinn, 'Angel Pope', p. 158.

the papacy, the other sought to accommodate the emperor and to focus on internal Church affairs. It was this latter view that Joachim held: in fact he became 'a kind of apocalyptic adviser to the peace party in the curia during these years'.[67] His views on the role of the papacy in the coming third age is ambiguous. He saw a pope as the one who would guide the new society through the crisis of the period of the Antichrist,[68] yet if we can accept Roger Howden's late twelfth-century account of Joachim's conversation with Richard I in 1190, he also believed that the Antichrist would be a pope.[69] Joachim did not believe that the papacy would disappear in the third age, but that it would be 'spiritualized and monasticized'. McGinn writes,

> Joachim's vision of history in which the crisis of the persecution of the Antichrist would be followed by a time of peace, contemplation and spiritual enlightenment within a monasticized society can be seen as an original variation upon the theme of reform that had been so essential to Christian society since the eleventh century. For the Abbot of Fiore, reform was not essentially man's work in the present but rather the irruption in a new way of the divine life of the Trinity into history.[70]

The Church of Joachim's day had 'increasingly accepted a pragmatic utilization of institutions of effective government (e.g., bureaucratic organization, the use of highly-trained personnel, especially Canonists, and better organized systems of taxation and judicial process) as the model of ecclesiastical order', a model that was threatened by Joachim's

67. McGinn, 'Angel Pope', p. 158, and *Visions*, p. 126. On the political context of Joachim's thought, see McGinn, 'Sibyl', pp. 102-16.

68. Joachim, *Liber* (Venice edn., 1519), f.[folio] 56rb.

69. On the authenticity of this account, see Reeves, *Influence*, pp. 6-10, who argues that the same position is hinted at by Joachim, *Expositio in Apocalypsim* (Venice, 1527), f. 168ra. For Roger of Howden's account, see *The Annals of Roger de Hoveden Comprising the History of England and of other countries of Europe, Volume II, part I, 1181–1192* (trans. H.T. Riley; Felinfach: Llanerch Publishers, 1997), pp. 177-80. Also see J. Gillingham's *Richard Coeur de Lion: Kingship, Chivalry and War in the Twelfth Century* (London: Hambledon Press, 1994), pp. 150-51 (pp. 141-53 for discussion of Roger of Howden's writing on the crusade), and his *Richard the Lionheart* (London: Weidenfeld & Nicolson, 2nd edn, 1989), pp. 156-57; R. Payne, *The Crusades: A History* (Wordsworth Military Library; Ware: Wordsworth Editions, 1998), pp. 219-26 (originally published under the title *The Dream and the Tomb* [1986]); McGinn, 'Angel Pope', pp. 158-59, especially n. 14.

70. McGinn, 'Angel Pope', p. 159.

'apocalyptic vision of the reformed Church'. Joachim's ideas and those of the Church were inevitably at odds with each other.

> The clash of his theory of reform and the institutional context in which it found itself is clear in Joachim's own works; it would become explicit in terms of social and political action as the Abbot's ideas were taken up by various groups who came to believe that the Third Age had already dawned and that the ecclesiastical organization of the time was a force blocking its realization.[71]

Joachim's theories were taken on board by many, particularly by the Spiritual Franciscans, as well as many other Joachites,[72] who developed his ideas, invariably in ways not to the liking of the Church.[73]

71. B. McGinn, 'Apocalypticism in the Middle Ages: An Historiographical Sketch', *Mediaeval Studies* 37 (1975), pp. 252-86 (281). The whole of this article is a most useful survey of mediaeval apocalyptic historiography. Also see the two surveys specifically on Joachim provided by Bloomfield, 'Joachim of Flora', pp. 29-91, and 'Recent Scholarship on Joachim of Fiore and his Influence', in Williams (ed.), *Prophecy*, pp. 21-52.

72. So B. McGinn, 'The Abbot and the Doctors: Scholastic Reactions to the Radical Eschatology of Joachim of Fiore', *Church History* 40 (1971), pp. 30-47 (35), draws a clear distinction between those ideas that are Joachimite, i.e. authentically Joachim's, and Joachite, i.e. developments of his views in directions he frequently would not have wished to take them. In this he is followed by West, 'Introduction', pp. v-xiii. However, many writers on Joachim and his 'successors' do not make this distinction despite its obvious advantages, e.g., Reeves, 'Originality', p. 297 n. 107.

73. For these developments and reactions against them, see the magisterial volume by Reeves, *Influence, in toto*; but also Bloomfield, 'Joachim of Flora', pp. 74-87, and 'Recent Scholarship', pp. 32-38; Leff, *Heresy, passim*; J. Moorman, *A History of the Franciscan Order from its Origins to the Year 1517* (Oxford: Clarendon Press, 1968), *passim*; Cohn, *Pursuit*, pp. 108-13 and *passim*; F. Oakley, *The Western Church in the Later Middle Ages* (Ithaca: Cornell University Press, 1979), pp. 185-89, 205-206, 305-306; S. Ozment, *The Age of Reform: An Intellectual and Religious History of Late Medieval and Reformation Europe* (New Haven: Yale University Press, 1980), pp. 103-15; Reeves, 'Originality', pp. 297-316; Lambert, *Heresy*, pp. 194-214; Strauss, 'Ideas', pp. 7-11. McGinn, 'Angel Pope', p. 159, states that Innocent III was perhaps the last successful reforming pope, his support of the mendicant orders and summoning of the Fourth Lateran Council being evidence of this. But it was a reform very different in kind from Joachim's. He and his thirteenth-century successors 'looked less and less like reformers or men of sanctity and more and more like the able lawyers, administrators and politicians they were'. Little wonder that Innocent III was identified by the Joachite *In Hieremian* (Venice edn, 1516), f. 23r, written in the 1240s, as a papal villain (see McGinn, 'Angel

> The prodigious spiritual ferment of the twelfth century that had led to the creation of so many experimental forms of the perfect life, both orthodox and heterodox, had whetted the hopes of men rather than exhausted them. Such hopes usually centred on the image of the 'apostolic life', the imitation of Christ and the apostles, and were, for the most part, backward-looking, given life by their attempt to revive a golden past. For Joachim, however, the renewal of monasticism was to be a new eruption of the Holy Spirit within history—a *renovatio* from the future rather than from the past.[74]

Two other important historical factors need to be noted. Joachim lived in the days when the Levant was under constant threat from the Saracens. The First Crusade had been called by Urban II in 1095, the second followed in 1147, and the third was consequent on the fall of Jerusalem to Saladin in 1187.[75] The success of Islam[76] under Saladin clearly suggested to Joachim that the third age was near.[77] From the time of the early Middle Ages and such notable writers as Gregory the Great (540–604), Isidore of Seville (c. 560–636) and Bede, expectation of the Antichrist figured prominently in Christian literature and, from c. 800, particularly in Spain, his coming was linked to the presence and threat of Islam. In the writing of Agobard (c. 779–840), bishop of Lyon, there arose the figure of the Last World Emperor who would reign immediately before the appearance of the Antichrist. In such speculations Jerusalem came to occupy a key place,[78] and all together, these factors led to a heightened sense of the imminence of the end. Joachim

Pope', p. 159 and n. 17). On Innocent III, see J. Sayers, *Innocent III: Leader of Europe 1198–1216* (Medieval World; London: Longman, 1994).

74. McGinn, *Spirituality*, p. 108. See also Reeves, *Influence*, pp. 505-508.

75. On the place that Jerusalem held in mediaeval Christendom, see A.H. Bredero, *Christendom and Christianity in the Middle Ages: The Relations between Religion, Church, and Society* (Grand Rapids: Eerdmans, 1994), pp. 79-104. On these first crusades, see J. Riley-Smith, *The Crusades: A Short History* (London: Athlone Press, 1987); H.E. Mayer, *The Crusades* (Oxford: Oxford University Press, 2nd edn, 1988).

76. For discussion of Joachim and Islam, see Daniel, 'Apocalyptic Conversion', pp. 131-39.

77. Lambert, *Heresy*, p. 199. Daniel, 'Apocalyptic Conversion', pp. 133-35, discusses in some detail the place of Saladin in Joachim's thought.

78. Bredero, *Christendom*, pp. 97-98. See the whole of his discussion of eschatology and Jerusalem on pp. 95-99. On Jerusalem, Antichrist and the Last World Emperor, see McGinn, *Visions*, *passim*.

identified Saladin as the sixth of the seven heads of the red dragon mentioned in Rev. 12.3.[79] Marjorie Reeves notes that Joachim

> lived at a point where western Europe thrusts out into a Mediterranean menaced by Saracens, where, in Messina, pilgrims, travellers and crusaders gathered and every rumour of the great conflict with the 'Beast from the Sea' was echoed. The drama of the times, the sense that events were moving to a great climax, must have impressed itself on his imagination.[80]

The twelfth century also witnessed 'a quickened interest in the meaning of history and prophetic destiny', with Rupert of Deutz (c. 1070–1129) and Anselm of Havelberg (c. 1100–58) developing understandings of history as a developmental, progressive revelation of the Trinity.[81] 'Each of them saw progressive stages of illumination, the work of the Holy Spirit in history, but neither clearly projected the final fruition of history in its last stage. Anxiety about the future was in the air.'[82] It is into this context that Joachim first appears.

79. Joachim identified the seven heads with the great persecutors of the Church: Herod, Nero, Constantius Arrianus, the Persian King Cosdroe (sometimes seen as Mahomet), Mesemothus (or Rex Babilon), Saladin and the Antichrist who was yet to come. The tail he labelled Gog, the final persecutor. See M. Reeves, *Joachim of Fiore and the Prophetic Future* (London: SPCK, 1976), p. 22 (this has recently been revised, *Joachim of Fiore and the Prophetic Future: A Medieval Study in Historical Thinking* [Stroud: Sutton Publishing, rev. edn, 1999]; the first edition is used throughout this paper).

80. Reeves, *Prophetic Future*, p. 3. R.W. Southern, 'Aspects of the European Tradition of Historical Writing: 3. History as Prophecy', *Transactions of the Royal Historical Society* 5th series 22 (1972), pp. 159-80 (176), notes that 'Innocent III, of all the popes of Joachim's lifetime the least inclined to encourage him, believed that the Number of the Beast denoted the 666 years that Islam was destined to last. Since nearly six hundred years of this allotted period had now passed, the end of the world was near', citing *Registrum* 16.28 in *PG*, CCXVI, cols. 817-22.

81. Reeves, *Prophetic Future*, p. 2. On Rupert of Deutz, see McGinn, *Visions*, pp. 95-96, 108-10; E. Breisach, *Historiography: Ancient, Medieval and Modern* (Chicago: University of Chicago Press, 2nd edn, 1994), p. 140. On Anselm of Havelberg, see McGinn, *Visions*, pp. 109-10, 114-16, 128; Lerner, 'Chiliasm', p. 491; Breisach, *Historiography*, p. 141. On Rupert, Anselm and other mediaeval historians who developed similar theories, see Reeves, 'Originality', pp. 281-87. On mediaeval historians and mediaeval historiography in general, see B. Smalley, *Historians in the Middle Ages* (London: Thames & Hudson, 1974); Breisach, *Historiography*, pp. 88-152.

82. Reeves, *Prophetic Future*, p. 2.

Joachim of Fiore (c. 1135–1202)[83]

Joachim of Fiore was born in Celico in Calabria, the son of a Sicilian official who hoped his son would follow in his footsteps. At an early age he went on pilgrimage to the Holy Land (c. 1167), and aged fifteen joined the Cistercian abbey of Sambucina and was ordained into the priesthood in 1168. By the time he entered the Benedictine monastery of Corazzo (not earlier than 1171), where he became abbot in 1177, he had lived as a hermit on Mount Etna and been an itinerant preacher in Calabria. For most of the 1180s he worked towards getting Corazzo accepted into the Cistercian order.[84] To this end he visited the Cistercian house at Casamari, remaining there for a year and a half in 1183–84,[85] where he received two visions, the first of which enabled him to understand a passage he had been studying in the book of Revelation: he called it 'a revelation of the fullness of the Apocalypse and of the complete agreement of the Old and New Testaments perceived with clear understanding by the mind's eye'. The second vision concerned the nature of the Trinity.[86] It was during this period that he came to the

83. McGinn, *Visions*, p. 314 n. 5, notes that the most important study of Joachim of Fiore's life is H. Grundmann, 'Zur Biographie Joachims von Fiore und Rainers von Ponza', *Deutsches Archiv für Erforschung des Mittelsalters* 16 (1960), pp. 437-546. But also see Bloomfield, 'Joachim of Flora', pp. 29-91, and his later 'Recent Scholarship', pp. 23-52; D.C. West and S. Zimdars-Swartz, *Joachim of Fiore: A Study in Spiritual Perception and History* (Bloomington: Indiana University Press, 1983); and B. McGinn, *The Calabrian Abbot: Joachim of Fiore in the History of Western Thought* (New York: Macmillan, 1985); and his *The Presence of God: A History of Western Christian Mysticism*. II. *The Growth of Mysticism: From Gregory the Great to the Twelfth Century* (London: SCM Press, 1995), pp. 337-41 and *passim*. The biographical sources for Joachim are discussed by West, 'Introduction', p. ii (a biographical account is included on pp. ii-iv).

84. On Joachim's relation to the Cistercians, see Reeves, *Influence*, *passim*, and 'The Abbot Joachim's Disciples and the Cistercian Order', *Sophia* 19 (1951), pp. 355-71.

85. On this period see Lerner, 'Chiliasm', pp. 490-91.

86. On the revelation concerning the Apocalypse, see Joachim of Fiore, *Expositio* f. 39v, and on the Trinity see *Psalterium decem chordarum* (Venice, 1527), f. 227r-v, both cited by McGinn, *Spirituality*, p. 99 nn. 7 and 10. For detailed discussion of the visions, see Reeves, *Influence*, pp. 21-25, and her *Prophetic Future*, pp. 4-5, where, p. 5, she discusses the possibility that Joachim had 'other moments of vision'; Lerner, 'Chiliasm', pp. 492-512, in which he discusses not just the content of the visions and their dating, but also their influence on his development of

attention of Pope Lucius III, who, in 1184, encouraged him to write down his apocalyptic revelations.[87] In time Joachim came to be held in such high regard that he advised the likes of Richard the Lionheart, the Emperor Henry VI and Pope Innocent III.[88]

By the time the Cistercians accepted Corazzo in 1188, Joachim and some of his followers had already begun to separate themselves from the monastery, having become disillusioned by what they considered the laxity and indiscipline of the order, and, sometime between 1190 and 1192, he founded a new house at San Giovanni da Fiore, for which he was condemned by the Cistercians in 1192.[89] While the Florensians initially enjoyed popularity, receiving the approval of Celestine III in 1196, they nevertheless went into sharp decline in the early thirteenth century, never having realized their founder's aspirations of reform.[90]

concordances, understanding of Revelation and the Trinity, and the composition and dating of his three major works.

87. On this occasion, Lucius tested Joachim's prophetic abilities by asking him to explain some Sibylline fragments. On this incident see McGinn, 'Sibyl', pp. 97-138; Reeves, *Influence*, pp. 3-4, 21; Southern, 'Aspects', pp. 167-68. Later Joachim also received encouragement to write from Urban III and Clement III (see Reeves, *Influence*, p. 28). McGinn, 'Sibyl', e.g. p. 119, believes that Joachim was asked to interpret the *Sibilla Samia*, and that his short commentary on the Sibyl, the *Expositio de prophetia ignota Romae reperta* is authentic (pp. 99-102) and was written in 1184 (p. 99). McGinn also provides a commentary and the text, pp. 122-38.

88. See Reeves, *Influence*, pp. 3-15, and, on his conversation with Richard I, also her 'History and Prophecy in Medieval Thought', *Mediaevalia et Humanistica* NS 5 (1974), pp. 51-74 (60-61); Morris, *Papal Monarchy*, pp. 518-19.

89. Geoffrey of Auxerre, one of the leading Cistercians at the time and a former close friend of Bernard of Clairvaux, launched a violent attack on Joachim for his chiliasm, excoriating him for his 'Judaism', claiming that he was a baptized Jew, employing the argument of Jerome that belief in an earthly millennium was 'Jewish' (see Lerner, 'Chiliasm', pp. 510-11, and his 'Refreshment', p. 101, and the reference in n. 16, where he discusses Jerome's views). On the accusation that Joachim was a Jew, see the study by B. Hirsch-Reich, 'Joachim von Fiore und das Judentum', in West (ed.), *Joachim of Fiore*, II, pp. 473-510 (originally published in *Judentum im Mittelalter* [Miscellanea Mediaevalia 4, 1966], pp. 228-63), who argues decisively against his Jewish parentage, and in this is followed by many, including Reeves, *Influence*, pp. 14-15. Joachim did, however, write *Adversus Iudaeos*, on which see Bloomfield, 'Joachim of Flora', pp. 32-33, and 'Recent Scholarship', pp. 24 and 31.

90. The Fourth Lateran Council (1215) included the Florensian order as one of the four pillars of the Church. On the order see F. Russo, *Gioacchino da Fiore e le Fondazioni Florensi in Calabria* (Naples: Fiorentino, 1959); Bloomfield, 'Joachim

Joachim of Fiore has been described as 'not only the most important author of the Middle Ages, but one of the most significant theorists of history in the Western tradition'.[91] He wrote three major works, which he began in the early 1180s: *The Book of Concordance of the Old and New Testaments*, *Exposition of the Apocalypse* and the *Ten-Stringed Psaltery*.[92] These major works have been described as 'lengthy, repetitious, and difficult for those not well acquainted with his intricate exegesis and symbolism'.[93] In these and his other works,[94] Joachim deals with three major issues, which will be the focus of our attention in the rest of this paper: the interpretation of Scripture, his doctrine of the Trinity, and the meaning of history; though it must be noted that these issues frequently overlap and at times Joachim's thought is not always wholly clear.

of Flora', pp. 73-74; and Morris, *Papal Monarchy*, pp. 522-23. In 1570 the order was reunited with the Cistercians.

91. McGinn, *Visions*, p. 126, citing in support of this claim the conclusions of K. Löwith, *Meaning in History: The Theological Implication of the Philosophy of History* (Chicago: University of Chicago Press, 1949); F.E. Manuel, *Shapes of Philosophical History* (Stanford: Stanford University Press, 1965); E. Bloch, *Man On his Own* (New York: Herder & Herder, 1970); and E. Voegelin, *The New Science of Politics* (Chicago: University of Chicago Press, 1952).

92. The *Liber concordie novi et veteris testamenti*, the *Expositio in Apocalypsim* and *Psalterium decem chordarum*. On these and other works, see Reeves, *Prophetic Future*, p. 17, where she describes them thus: '[T]he *Liber Concordie* makes the most intensive study of the Old Testament as prefiguring the second and third *status*, while the *Expositio* naturally centres on the Risen Christ of the Apocalypse and is deeply concerned with the second *status*, and the *Psalterium* is focused on the *Spiritualis Intellectus* [spiritual intellectual/man] of the third *status*. Around this Trinitarian sequence smaller works, sermons and poems can be grouped...' On his writings/canon, see Bloomfield, 'Joachim of Flora', pp. 30-40, and 'Recent Scholarship', pp. 24-26.

93. McGinn, *Spirituality*, p. 97.

94. Joachim was a 'picture thinker', 'whose mind moved according to the rich combinations of symbolic thought rather than the clarity of the logical or discursive mentality' (McGinn, *Spirituality*, p. 103, citing M. Reeves, 'The *Liber Figurarum* of Joachim of Fiore', *Mediaeval and Renaissance Studies* 2 [1950], pp. 59-81 [65]). These figures were collected after his death into the *Book of Figures*, on which see M. Reeves and B. Hirsch-Reich, *The Figurae of Joachim of Fiore* (Oxford: Clarendon Press, 1972). In all Joachim wrote some dozen works, later supplemented, in time-honoured apocalyptic fashion, by a considerable number of pseudonymous works credited to him after his death (see, e.g., McGinn, *Visions*, p. 126).

The Interpretation of Scripture

The main stimuli of Joachim's thought were the Scriptures, particularly the book of Revelation,[95] and the Latin Fathers; there is little evidence that he had much knowledge of contemporary writers.[96]

While the central feature of his thought was the imminent appearance of the Antichrist and the dawning of the third age of history, Joachim did not see himself as a prophet, even though kings, emperors and popes eagerly listened to his predictions.[97] For him, these predictions did not come through the gift of prophecy but through the gift of understanding (*intelligentia spiritualis*, 'special insight') that he had received from God in his two visions in 1184. He therefore saw himself 'as an interpreter of the Scriptures'.[98] He wrote,

> [The] God who once gave the spirit of prophecy to the prophets has given me the spirit of understanding to grasp with great clarity in His Spirit all the mysteries of sacred scripture, just as the prophets who once produced it in God's Spirit understood these mysteries.[99]

95. Lerner, 'Chiliasm', p. 500, writes, 'Revelation...was the text most likely to offer guidance about the future beyond what could be learned from concordances' (on which see below).

96. Reeves, *Prophetic Future*, p. 2 and n. 6 (on pp. 176-77), in which she lists the chief influences on him. On the question of sources, see also Bloomfield, 'Joachim of Flora', pp. 51-68; Lerner, 'Refreshment', pp. 116-17.

97. Lerner, 'Chiliasm', p. 499, notes, 'In the twelfth century expressing any prophecy whatsoever was controversial since prophetic gifts were assumed to be rare.' On mediaeval prophecy and history, including discussion of Joachim, see Southern, 'Aspects', pp. 159-80; Reeves, 'History and Prophecy', pp. 51-74.

98. Morris, *Papal Monarchy*, p. 519. Reeves, *Prophetic Future*, Preface [p. ii], refers to it as natural that 'in the great Cistercian tradition' he should become 'a biblical exegete'. As well as the influence of scripture, the Fathers and Sibylline oracles, some have suggested that Joachim's understanding of God at work in history may have been influenced by Jewish ideas. Joachim acknowledged his indebtedness to the Spanish Jewish convert Petrus Alphonsi, one of the few contemporaries he did acknowledge (see Reeves, *Prophetic Future*, p. 3; also P.J. Alexander's paper 'The Diffusion of Byzantine Apocalypses in the Medieval West and the Beginnings of Joachimism', in Williams [ed.], *Prophecy*, pp. 53-106).

99. Joachim, as recounted by the early thirteenth-century Cistercian Ralph of Coggeshall in his *English Chronicle*, cited by McGinn, *Spirituality*, p. 100. For discussion of Ralph of Coggeshall, see Bloomfield and Reeves, 'Penetration', pp. 110-15.

In this Joachim was being traditional in that he was concerned with Scripture, but at the same time he was distinctive in the way he developed it: what McGinn calls 'its hermeneutical nature'.[100] This God-given illumination, however, was not his peculiar gift, but 'a foretaste of the Spiritual Intelligence to be poured out on all men before the end of history'.[101] Joachim was, then, an exegete, and in this he was continuing the literary character of apocalyptic from some of its origins within Judaism. McGinn notes that

> in his claim to found his vision of history not on a new divine communication, but on understanding the scriptures, Joachim was a faithful witness to this tradition. But the abbot of Fiore's theology of history was a new creation in many respects, and therefore it should not surprise us that the hermeneutical theory underpinning it was also novel.[102]

As with his understanding of the Trinity, Joachim's view of Scripture was both conservative and radical.[103] It is clear that Scripture was central to his theology,[104] as is clear in his opposition to Scholastic theology,[105] and his exposition of Revelation. In the Middle Ages the most important hermeneutical tool was the *lectio divina*, the 'spiritual reading' of biblical passages.[106] In the main, mediaeval theologians recognized and employed four senses in the interpretation of Scripture: the literal, tropological or moral, allegorical or mystical, and anagogical or revelatory. But Joachim developed these into a complex scheme of 12, emphasizing in particular seven 'typical' senses by which events in the seven ages of history had literal 'concordances' in the other six.[107]

100. McGinn, *Spirituality*, p. 100.

101. Reeves, *Prophetic Future*, p. 5. For fuller discussion see her *Influence*, pp. 16-20, 395-96.

102. McGinn, *Spirituality*, p. 101.

103. McGinn, *Visions*, p. 127.

104. Reeves, *Prophetic Future*, p. 4, states, 'The groundwork of all Joachim's doctrine was the study of the Scriptures'.

105. See McGinn, 'Abbot and the Doctors', pp. 32-33, and see the discussion on the Trinity below.

106. On this see B. Smalley, *The Study of the Bible in the Middle Ages* (Oxford: Basil Blackwell, 1952), pp. 26-36 and *passim*; Bray, *Biblical Interpretation*, pp. 145-47, and the whole of his discussion of the mediaeval period, pp. 129-64.

107. McGinn, 'Abbot and the Doctors', p. 31. The seven 'typical' senses are discussed, e.g., in Joachim's *Liber* f. 61r-v, and *Psalterium* ff. 265r-266r. For discussion of Joachim's use of the four senses and examples of how he used them, see Reeves, 'History and Prophecy', pp. 56-59; Daniel, 'Joachim of Fiore', pp. 79-80.

Some earlier twelfth-century writers had already begun to move away from the spiritualized, non-historical interpretation of the book of Revelation that had come to dominate the Church's theology since the time of Tyconius and Augustine. They saw it instead as a prophecy of historical events, some already fulfilled, others yet to be so, but it was Joachim who 'formulated this tendency into a coherent new theory of hermeneutics'.[108]

There is no denying that the 'abbot's theory of interpretation is notoriously complex'.[109] Marjorie Reeves and Beatrice Hirsch-Reich contend that there is a consistency in Joachim's historical schemata;[110] I believe this to be rightly challenged by Bernard McGinn, who maintains that

> the mixture of patterns, especially the all-important two's and three's, is an indication both of the logical inconsistency of Joachim and of the unique place that he holds in the history of medieval apocalyptic. If the pattern of two's may be said to represent his debt to the past and the starting point of his speculations, the pattern of three's indicates the transformation that was his real contribution to apocalypticism—his own creation out of the vivid experience of history of the latter part of the twelfth century.[111]

Reeves has drawn attention to the fact that Joachim was a picture thinker,[112] even a 'poet rather than a theologian—a poet of the meaning of history'.[113] McGinn adds that 'Joachim's somewhat confused verbal

108. McGinn, *Spirituality*, p. 101.

109. McGinn, *Spirituality*, p. 101.

110. Reeves and Hirsch-Reich, *Figurae*, pp. 7-11.

111. McGinn, 'Apocalypticism', p. 284.

112. Reeves, 'The *Liber Figurarum*', pp. 67-74. Joachim's pictorial thought was expressed most vividly in the collection of diagrams *The Book of Figures*. Reeves, *Influence*, p. 505, suggests that 'perhaps the basic reason for the popularity of Joachim's doctrine was his skill with the symbolism of patterns and the visual imagination which could translate history into *figurae*'. While there are many 'figures' from Joachim and his successors, the present essay has focused on his written ideas, though many of the books and articles on Joachim either discuss or reproduce many of the *figurae* or set out his thought diagramatically. For discussion and examples of Joachim's use of *figurae*, e.g. the Tree, Eagles, the Circle, a spiral, four square oratories and the ten-stringed Psaltery, see Reeves, *Prophetic Future*, pp. 16-22.

113. Reeves, *Influence*, p. 132, and she is followed by Oakley, *Western Church*, p. 186.

attempts to portray his vision of history cry out for visual presentation'. Many of his images reflect traditional apocalyptic symbolism and imagery, in particular those to be found in the book of Revelation: trees, circles, eagles, the Alpha and Omega and the ten-stringed Psaltery; and McGinn could well be correct in his belief that these came 'prior to verbal presentations in the development of Joachim's thought'.[114]

Focusing, then, on the complexity and even at times inconsistent nature of Joachim's work,[115] we nevertheless need to attempt to understand the basics of his views.

In the Middle Ages it was widely held that the Old Testament provided both parallels and prophecies of the New, and this particularly complied with the dominant mediaeval interest in discovering the spiritual, inner meaning rather than the literal, historical interpretation of Scripture. This approach employed a presuppositional use of concordances, which are tantamount to symbolic meanings, correspondences or types, which exist between the various ages.[116] Joachim's originality lay in using them as a method of understanding the future,[117] for he believed that in the same way that the Holy Spirit proceeds from the Father *and* the Son, so the spiritual understanding of the Scriptures pro-

114. McGinn, 'Apocalypticism', p. 284. See also his paper 'Symbolism in the Thought of Joachim of Fiore', in Williams (ed.), *Prophecy*, pp. 143-64, which focuses in particular on the significance of the symbols. West, 'Introduction', p. v, writes, 'Joachim's writings are a nightmare of apocalyptic allegory and exegesis, for his philosophy of history rested not only on the Dispensations and three *status*, but also upon the imagery of the apocalyptic scriptures, the genealogy of Christ, and the symbolism of numbers and letters.'

115. Leff, *Heresy*, p. 77, remarks, 'It is not easy to unravel much of Joachim's meaning over the order of events or the possible identity of his scriptural symbols in the transition to the third age and beyond.' Marjorie Reeves's forthcoming paper, 'Joachimist Christology and Progressive Revelation', *Florensia*, touches on the question of the consistency and inconsistency of Joachim's thought. I am grateful to Dr Reeves for allowing me to see a copy of his paper prior to publication.

116. Daniel, 'Joachim of Fiore', p. 73, believes that Joachim's concords 'had no real antecedents', adding, p. 83, 'The concept of *concordia* was innovative, having no real parallel in the thinking of Christian exegetes.'

117. Morris, *Papal Monarchy*, p. 519. Daniel, 'Joachim of Fiore', p. 76, draws attention to the historical role of concordances when he writes, 'Joachim's interpretation rested on principles of biblical exegesis the truth of which could be demonstrated historically. The *concordia*...was just such a proof of Joachim's conclusions.' See also p. 83.

ceeds from both the Old and the New Testaments. Concordances[118] were like a highway: 'Every traveler who goes forward until the route ahead is unclear finds the correct way to proceed by looking backward.'[119] As there was a concordance between the Old and New Testaments, so there was a concordance between the New Testament and what followed it, and 'Joachim worked indefatigably on traditional exegetical principles to solve the riddle of the future',[120] for, as '[c]ontemporary events illumined the concords of Scripture; the study of the Testaments gave the clue to the vast events on the threshold of which Joachim believed he stood'.[121] These 'concords', then, were the gift that enabled him to know the future. 'For him prophecy was not needed; the secret was there in the *sacra pagina* for the man that God had enlightened.'[122] Marjorie Reeves writes,

> The medieval approach to history which sought in each episode an inner meaning which linked it by concord with events of another era is, of course, quite foreign to us. It is as if each happening had a vertical point of reference, a 'thread' in the hand of God who combined threads into patterns on the inner side of history, whereas we look only for the horizontal connections and the pattern of visible cause and effect spun out along the time span.[123]

It quickly becomes clear that numbers were of the utmost importance to Joachim. In true apocalyptic manner, patterns of numbers proliferate—twos, threes, fives, sevens and twelves,[124] and these complex patterns of numbers both overlap and complement each other. McGinn observes that, while the patterns of sevens retain importance throughout his

118. Joachim, *Liber* (Venice, 1519), 2.1.2, f. 7rb, defined a concordance as 'a similarity of equal proportion between the New and Old Testaments, equal, I say, as to number, not as to dignity' (cited by Daniel, 'Joachim of Fiore', p. 78).

119. Joachim, *Liber*, 2.1.4, reproduced by McGinn, *Spirituality*, p. 123.

120. Lambert, *Medieval Heresy*, p. 198.

121. Reeves, *Influence*, p. 10. The basis of Joachim's traditional exegesis is also discussed on pp. 16-17.

122. McGinn, 'Abbot and the Doctors', p. 31.

123. Reeves, *Prophetic Future*, pp. 10-11.

124. M. Reeves, 'The Abbot Joachim's Sense of History', in M.M. Mollat (ed.), *1274: Année Charnière: Mutations et Continuités, Lyons-Paris 30 septembre–5 octobre 1974* (Paris: Centre National de la Recherche Scientifique, 1977), pp. 781-96 (789), and her 'Originality', p. 311, also draws attention to the importance of fours for Joachim.

works, threes eventually dominate,[125] and this reflects the centrality of the Trinity in his thought.

While the main pattern of history is his three *status*, Marjorie Reeves notes that Joachim nevertheless maintained that there are two dispensations in history, as there are two biblical covenants and two testaments, the old extending from the creation to the first advent, and the new from the incarnation to the second advent. This distinction, Marjorie Reeves notes, is demonstrated in that Joachim never uses *etas* or *tempus* for the threefold pattern, but *always* uses *status* in the pattern of threes. 'Thus "third age" is really incorrect.' She writes, 'History is, in one sense, completed in its two parts, but hovering over each there is a third development, a new quality of life rather than a third set of institutions, a quasimystical state rather than a new age.'[126] We will look at the three *status* in more detail later.

Sevens are also important in Joachim's thought. From Augustine he could adopt seven ages, corresponding to the seven days of creation, five leading up to the incarnation, the sixth lasting up to his own day, and the seventh, the Sabbath rest, would begin soon. This would then be followed by the eighth day of eternal bliss. For Augustine and all those who followed him, the seventh lay beyond history, but for Joachim it was historical. The tribulation under the Great Antichrist would conclude the sixth age, while the seventh age would precede the Last Judgment.[127] Joachim's use of concords also helped him when he

125. McGinn, 'Abbot and the Doctors', p. 32. However, Reeves, in M. Reeves and B. Hirsch-Reich, 'The Seven Seals in the Writings of Joachim of Fiore', *Recherches de théologie ancienne et médiévale* 21 (1954), pp. 211-47 (214), notes that the patterns of twos, not threes, were initially most widely known. 'A study of Joachim's writings suggests that this was the right order, that the abbot himself was at first much occupied with the conception of the two great parallel streams of history symbolised by the two Testaments, while later the Trinitarian view of history,—always present in his thought,—came to the fore', and she goes on to suggest that the germ of this pattern of twos originated in Rev. 5.1's 'a Book written within and on the backside, sealed with Seven Seals', which is mentioned at the beginning of the *Book of Concordance* (see Reeves and Hirsch-Reich, 'Seven Seals', p. 214, and especially n. 10). Reeves, '*Liber Figurarum*', pp. 74-77, suggests that the twofold concordance was meant to be more historical and the threefold more mystical, but Daniel, 'Apocalyptic Conversion', p. 130 n. 17, is more cautious.

126. Reeves, *Prophetic Future*, pp. 6-7.

127. For this section I am summarizing Reeves, *Prophetic Future*, p. 8. Joachim

divided the Old and New Testaments into seven parallel periods, each pattern in the former corresponding to one in the latter. Abraham, Isaac and Joseph, for example, correspond to Zechariah, John the Baptist and Christ, and with the three persons of the Trinity.[128]

We have already mentioned how Joachim developed 12 senses of Scripture, but he also used the concordance between the 12 patriarchs or tribes of the Old Testament and the 12 apostles and Churches. From meditating on the 12 tribes he discovered that 5 received their inheritance first, 7 later. Developing his concords of twos he noted that the 5 Churches associated with Peter (Jerusalem, Antioch, Constantinople, Alexandria and Rome) were founded first, followed by the 7 Churches of Asia Minor in Revelation 2–3. 'This division of the mystic twelve into five "prior" and seven "posterior" came to him as a revelation about time and its promise for the future', and whenever it is used by him it is done so in a prophetic statement about the future.[129]

The Trinity

Much of Joachim's understanding of the Trinity lies beyond the scope of the present study and so it need only be briefly summarized here, but two aspects of it are of direct relevance to us. First, his theology of the Trinity by-passed the logical categories and fine distinctions characteristic of the Scholastics and can be seen as archaic: '[s]trongly scriptural and symbolic in outlook, displaying an adequate, though not profound, knowledge of the Fathers'.[130] Joachim focused his misinformed attack on Peter Lombard in his *The Necessity of a United Trinity*,[131] which was

focused on seven in his *The Seven Seals* (*De septem sigillis*), based on the book of seven seals in Rev. 5.1 (see Reeves and Hirsch-Reich, 'Seven Seals', pp. 211-47). Reeves and Hirsch-Reich, 'Seven Seals', p. 220, note that one of the links connecting the *Book of Figures* with the *Expositio* and *Concordie* 'is its frequent use of the double pattern of sevens' (i.e. the parallels between the seven periods of the Old Testament and seven ages of the Church in the New Testament).

128. For other examples and discussion of such concordances, see Reeves, *Prophetic Future*, pp. 10-13.

129. Reeves, *Prophetic Future*, p. 10. Reeves examines the number-symbolisms, especially the 5+12 in her 'Sense of History', pp. 787-95, giving examples of his method and exegesis in relation to Sarah and Hagar, the seven days of creation, and Abraham and his family.

130. McGinn, 'Abbot and the Doctors', p. 32.

131. *De essentia seu unitate Trinitatis*. On the question of the authenticity of *De*

condemned by the Fourth Lateran Council in 1215[132] and has not survived. But, secondly, Joachim tried to do what the Scholastics had failed to do; that was to explore the Trinity's involvement in history.[133]

Many scholars have sought to determine whether it was his theology of the Trinity that provided the basis for his understanding of history or vice versa.[134] Bernard McGinn believes that the two developed simultaneously, each feeding the other,[135] while Marjorie Reeves has championed the view that it was his Trinitarian speculations that were formative,[136] but this has been challenged by Robert Lerner, who believes that it was his attempt to understand the book of Revelation that led him to his theory of history.[137]

essentia, the gist of his criticisms reconstructed from his other works, and his confusion over the theology of Peter Lombard, see McGinn, 'Abbot and the Doctors', pp. 32-33. McGinn describes Joachim as 'a traditionalist speaking out against new theological trends from a not very well informed position' (p. 33). For further discussion of Joachim against Peter Lombard, see Reeves, *Prophetic Future*, pp. 24-26, and her 'Sense of History', pp. 782-87; H. Lee, 'The Anti-Lombard Figures of Joachim of Fiore: A Reinterpretation', in Williams (ed.), *Prophecy*, pp. 127-42; Ozment, *Age of Reform*, pp. 106-107.

132. On the condemnation, see Reeves, *Influence*, pp. 28-36. See also Morris, *Papal Monarchy*, p. 448, and on the council and its aftermath focusing on the role of Innocent III, see pp. 447-51. In 1263 Joachim himself was condemned by a provincial council in Arles, but this was a local action and he was never officially proscribed by the Church (see Ozment, *Age of Reform*, p. 110).

133. See Reeves, *Influence*, pp. 20-21, 31.

134. See the discussion in Bloomfield, 'Joachim of Flora', pp. 43-45.

135. McGinn, 'Abbot and the Doctors', p. 33: 'Joachim's theology of history depends on his theology of the Trinity throughout, but his theology of the Trinity would not have been what it was had he not seen the history expressed in the Scriptures as the revelation of the Trinitarian mystery and had he not found the key to the interpretation of this mystery in a more adequate theory of the senses of Scripture.'

136. Reeves, 'Originality', pp. 287-93.

137. Lerner, 'Refreshment', pp. 115-19, and more recently in the whole of his article 'Chiliasm', pp. 489-512, in which he supports his argument by discussing the chronology of Joachim's writings, and the meaning and implications of his 'full' reading of Revelation. He persuasively, to my mind, argues that Joachim began writing his commentary on Revelation around the spring of 1183, but, when he had come to a dead end, he turned his attention to the *Book of Concord* in April 1184, and it was after this that he received his Easter vision concerning the 'plenitude' of the book of Revelation, which was followed by the second vision on the Trinity.

The Meaning of History

Joachim presented a revolutionary theory that explicated God's role in human history. In his understanding of history

> [a]ll three Persons operate all the time, from history's inception to its consummation, the activity of the Trinity is progressively drawing mankind on to a higher spiritual level: history is neither static nor repetitive, but the ongoing work of the living God.[138]

It is in this theology of history that Joachim's originality is most evident. Reeves believes that

> The originality of his structure lay chiefly in the fact that whereas others had seen the three stages in time in simple progression, Joachim believed that the very inner relations of the Trinity were at work in the time-process. Thus the third age must not simply follow the second, but proceed equally from both the first and the second. This entailed giving the second a time span parallel to the first, so that the concords between them could be drawn out, not in two parallel lines running to a horizon of Last Judgment, but in two converging lines meeting in the third *status*.[139]

History was, therefore, divided into three states (Latin *status*), each corresponding to one person of the Trinity, though in the same way that the Son and the Spirit proceeded from the Father, so too the ages overlapped. There was no danger of Joachim falling into the heresy of modalistic monarchianism in which the Father, Son and Holy Spirit were seen as different successive modes in which the one God revealed himself, for, as the Three Persons of the Trinity are One, so all are active in each *status* while each has his own distinctive work.[140] The first *status* was that of the Father, stretching from creation to the second *status* of the Son, which commenced with the rise of the messianic hope in the Old Testament, through the incarnation and New Testament period, down to Joachim's day. The third age of the Holy Spirit would be the culmination of history, in which humanity would enjoy the peace of God. Joachim illustrated this threefold, Trinitarian pattern of history

138. Reeves, 'Originality', p. 289. She also deals with his theology of history in *Influence*, pp. 16-27.

139. Reeves, 'History and Prophecy', p. 56. On his originality, see the whole of her article 'Originality', pp. 269-316.

140. Reeves, *Prophetic Future*, pp. 5-6. On his Christology, see Reeves, 'Originality', pp. 289-90.

by various three-part analogies, including winter, spring and summer, and starlight, dawn and the perfect day.[141]

The key was the book of Revelation, 'the key of things past, the knowledge of things to come; the opening of what is sealed, the uncovering of what is hidden'.[142] He discovered parallels between the opening of the book/scroll with writing on both sides and seven seals in Rev. 5.1, and the tribulations associated with them, and the history of Israel. This same pattern was being repeated in the history of the Church, which was about to witness the opening of the sixth seal. When that time came to an end, the seventh seal would be opened and the Church would enter into the sabbath rest of God,[143] represented in Rev. 8.1 by the half-hour silence.

Each of the three ages would have distinguishing characteristics.[144] In the first age the leaders were married men, typified by the 12 patriarchs; the second was led by clerics, exemplified by the 12 apostles; but the third age, of which Benedict of Nursia (c. 480–c. 547) had been the herald, would be led by 12 religious leaders, perhaps 12 abbots.[145] In terms of institutions, the sequence of the ages was 12 tribes, 12 Churches and 12 monasteries.[146] The pattern of 5 plus 7 reappears at this point, for as 5 tribes and Churches were followed by 7 later ones, so Joachim listed 5 great Cistercian abbeys as the first stage of the third *status*, but wisely refrained from specifying the subsequent 'seven mystical and spiritual houses which will characterize the real age of the Spirit'.[147] A series of images convey the movement of history through these three *status*: the first is characterized by the law and flesh, knowledge, chastisings, fear and will be lived as slaves in the servitude of slavery; the second is under grace and flesh and spirit, characterized by wisdom, action and faith, and will be lived as sons in filial obedience; the third is under greater grace, an age of spirit, with greater spiritual understanding, contemplation and love, and will be lived as friends in

141. Reeves, *Prophetic Future*, pp. 14-15.

142. Joachim, *Expositio* (Venice, 1527), f. 3r, cited by McGinn, 'John's Apocalypse', p. 19.

143. On the place of the thousand-year sabbath, see the whole of Lerner's article, 'Medieval Return', pp. 51-71, and specifically on Joachim, pp. 57-60.

144. See Reeves, *Prophetic Future*, pp. 14-15.

145. Reeves, *Prophetic Future*, p. 13.

146. For references see Reeves, *Prophetic Future*, pp. 13, 177 n. 28.

147. Reeves, *Prophetic Future*, p. 13.

freedom. In the third *status* the 'eternal gospel' of Rev. 14.6, which was associated with the sixth seal, would finally be disclosed. Joachim believed that two new transitional and intermediary orders of spiritual men/monks, an eremitical order and a preaching order, would be raised up by God to lead the faithful into the third age and be the agents of a new spiritual understanding[148] between God and humanity.[149] The reason for there being two orders was because of the double procession of the Spirit from the Father and the Son.[150] The hermits would agonize for the Church during the tribulation suffered under Antichrist, the preachers would labour in the world.[151]

Further, each of the three *status* was divided into 7 ages corresponding to the 7 angels of the book of Revelation, or 42 generations from Adam to Christ on the basis of Matthew 1, and 42 from Christ to the new age, and, with a generation calculated as 30 years,[152] this suggested the date of 1260 for the beginning of the third age, though Joachim himself demurred from making this definite. Further, the third age would be preceded by a terrible tribulation when the Antichrist[153]

148. See Reeves, *Influence*, Part Two, 'New Spiritual Men', pp. 133-292. It was chiefly the Franciscan order, and particularly the Spiritual Franciscans, who took on Joachim's ideas, seeing themselves as the spiritual men of whom he had spoken, and who circulated and developed his writings, though clearly the Florensian order would also have studied, copied and imitated their founder's writings and figures (so Reeves, 'Joachim's Disciples', p. 362). Reeves, 'Joachim's Disciples', p. 368, notes that Joachim's later followers came to associate the two third-age orders as the Franciscans and Dominicans, though a role was also claimed for the Cistercians, p. 366, adding on p. 369, 'Joachim's promises of new orders were, indeed, so varied in phraseology and so rich in conception as to allow ample scope for a variety of claimants.' She then remarks that 'it is curious that his order made so little effort to embody [his dynamic conception of new spiritual men] or to express the contemplative life of the third *status* more fully than those around them', suggesting that perhaps they shared their master's attitude of standing on the threshold of the third age.

149. Reeves, *Prophetic Future*, p. 13.

150. For discussion of the concept of the spiritual men and full references in Joachim's works, see Reeves, *Influence*, pp. 140-44.

151. Reeves, *Prophetic Future*, p. 13 n. 30 (on p. 178), citing Joachim, *Expositio* ff. 175v-176r.

152. Oakley, *Western Church*, p. 186, comments that on a generation being 30 years Joachim was 'unclear'.

153. For detailed studies of the Antichrist, see Reeves, *Influence*, Part Three, 'Antichrist and the Last World Emperor', pp. 293-392; R.K. Emmerson, *Antichrist*

would be loosed on the world. In contrast to Augustine and the Scholastics, Joachim did not believe that once the Antichrist had been judged the end of the world would immediately follow, contending, 'The End of the world and the last hour are not always to be taken for the very last moment', using 1 Jn 2.18 in support. A little later he adds, 'After the destruction of this Antichrist there will be justice on earth and an abundance of peace',[154] during which time the 'Jews and many unbelievers will be converted to the Lord'. This would be of unknown duration, for 'The number of years, months and days of that time are known only to God.'[155]

While Joachim's understanding of history has been described as generally 'optimistic',[156] a position he shared with some other mediaeval writers,[157] there was also a pessimistic dimension to it, reflected in his introduction of Revelation 20 as a description of the end times with its final onslaught of evil prior to the end: 'the purified last age itself would end in times of trial'.[158] The *status* of the Spirit will be followed by the final persecution at the hands of Satan:

> When they [the years, months and days] will have been completed and led to their end, Satan again will be released from his prison to persecute

in the Middle Ages (Seattle: University of Washington Press, 1981), *passim*; B. McGinn, 'Portraying Antichrist in the Middle Ages', in W. Verbeke, D. Verhelst and A. Welkenhuysen (eds.), *The Use and Abuse of Eschatology in the Middle Ages* (Mediaevalia Lovaniensia, I.15; Leuven: Leuven University Press, 1988), pp. 22-24, and also his *Antichrist* (San Francisco: Harper, 1994), *passim*.

154. Cf. Joachim's remark that 'after this little while is finished [the Lord's people] will begin to see a time of peace like nothing that has been since men began to exist on earth', from his Letter to the Abbot of Valdona, reproduced by McGinn, *Spirituality*, p. 119. He used the image of Satan bound for a thousand years (not understood literally) in his *Expositio* ff. 210v-212r, cited by Reeves, 'Originality', p. 287 n. 68.

155. On the unknown duration of the last age, see *Expositio* f. 210d (Venice, 1527), cited and discussed by Lerner, 'Refreshment', p. 119, especially n. 71.

156. Reeves, 'Seven Seals', p. 225.

157. See Lerner, 'Refreshment', p. 98.

158. Lerner, 'Refreshment', p. 119. Lerner adds that 'Joachim may even have thought that the final persecution of Gog and Magog would be partially deserved, for occasionally he made suggestions that at the end of the last age...there would be a cooling of charity and defection from the faith'. Also see Reeves, *Influence*, pp. 132, 305, and 'Seven Seals', pp. 222-24.

> God's elect since there will still be that remaining Antichrist signified by the tail of the dragon [Rev. 12.4].[159]

But in the end, after Judgment Day, the eighth day of eternity, God will triumph.

The question arises from Joachim's scheme of history as to what place was there in this reborn Church for the old Church, particularly the papacy[160] and sacraments? The answer is somewhat confused, since scholars are not agreed on the evidence, which is open to various interpretations.

Jaroslav Pelikan believes that Joachim saw the Church as a kind of John the Baptist:

> For even if, with the substitution of the things that are new, the things that are old were to pass away, this was not as though these things had not in their own time been instituted by God for righteousness, but rather because lesser things are to be left behind so that more powerful mysteries might be given to the faithful for their salvation.[161]

The 'new religion, which will be altogether free and spiritual', would supersede the 'ecclesiastical order, which struggles over the letter of the Gospel'.[162] He believed that this transition would be accompanied by a changed attitude to the present institutions: '...men will cease being zealous for those institutions that have been established temporarily.'[163] In the new spiritual Church 'a new leader, a universal pontiff of the new Jerusalem'[164] would replace the present papacy. But this raises the question of the nature of the supercession.

159. Translated from L. Tondelli, M. Reeves and B. Hirsch-Reich, *Il Libro delle Figure dell'Abate Gioachino da Fiore* (Torino: SEI, 2nd edn, 1953), pl. xiv, abstracted from lines 9-55 *passim*, reproduced by McGinn, *Visions*, pp. 137-38. Lerner, 'Refreshment', p. 119, notes that Joachim's introduction of Rev. 20 in his description of the last times brought with it the idea of a terrible onslaught of evil before the end, and the 'logic' of this led him to a theory of two final Antichrists: one identified with the Satanic beast defeated before the time of peace, and the other with Gog defeated immediately before the end. Lerner writes, 'Thus the purified last age itself would end in times of trial.'

160. McGinn, 'Sibyl', p. 127, admits 'there are few more complex areas in Joachim's thought than that of his views on the papacy'.

161. Joachim, *Tractatus* 1, cited by Pelikan, *Medieval Theology*, p. 302.

162. Joachim, *Liber* 5.65, cited by Pelikan, *Medieval Theology*, p. 302.

163. Joachim, *Tractatus* 3, cited by Pelikan, *Medieval Theology*, p. 303.

164. Joachim, *Liber* 4.31, cited by Pelikan, *Medieval Theology*, p. 303.

Some scholars maintain that Joachim's vision of the new spiritual Church that will come with the third age did not invalidate the existing institutional Church. Reeves adds the cautionary note that '[a]lthough there is certainly ambiguity in Joachim's statements about the Church of the third *status*, it must be asserted firmly that institutionally this was never anything but the Roman Church in his mind'. Although Joachim did speak in terms of the Church of Peter and the Church of John, and this certainly did come dangerously close to implying that the latter would replace the former in the third age, yet Marjorie Reeves asserts that 'these contrasts are qualitative, not institutional'. Peter represents the Church as it preaches and labours, John symbolizes the contemplative Church.[165] Elsewhere, she argues that for Joachim it was the people not the offices (of the papacy and clergy) that would yield.[166] However, McGinn criticizes Reeves's position on the survival of the papacy despite the changes it would undergo in the third age,[167] commenting that 'the meaning of these texts must always be viewed in the light of other texts that seem to indicate such a reduced role for the papacy that one is justified in speaking of a fundamental change'.[168]

165. Reeves, *Influence*, p. 395. Elsewhere, *Prophetic Future*, p. 7, Reeves writes, 'Institutionally, the Latin Church will stand until the Second Advent just as the Synagogue did until the First, but its quality of life will be transformed from that of the *ecclesia activa* to that of the *ecclesia contemplativa.*' On p. 14 she comments that 'it is difficult to discover what kind of institutional change Joachim expected'. Later she adds: '[u]nder the figure of Joseph's domination over his brethren, Joachim speaks of a final succession of Roman pontiffs who will reign from sea to sea, and he uses the figures of Mordecai and Judas Maccabaeus in the same way [*Liber* ff. 89r, 132v]. The Roman pontiff will be the Mount of the Lord to which all the nations will flow, for Joachim's third *status* is not only one of spiritual understanding and holy liberty, but also of ecumenism. The combination of immutability and transformation is summed up thus: the Church of Peter which is the throne of Christ cannot fail...but changed into greater glory it will remain unshaken for eternity [*Liber* f. 95v].'

166. Reeves, 'Originality', p. 295. She goes on to note that when Joachim speaks of *dissolutio* and *successio* he is thinking of 'orders', and *ordo* 'always seems to mean a type of religious life lived by a body of people rather than a formally constituted institution' (pp. 295-96).

167. Reeves, *Influence*, pp. 132, 395-97.

168. McGinn, 'Apocalypticism', p. 282. A summary of the various positions can be found in Bloomfield, 'Joachim of Flora', p. 46; Reeves, *Influence*, pp. 126-32.

Similarly, the interpretation of the place of the sacraments in Joachim's thought is far from clear. Pelikan believes that they would be replaced, just as they had replaced the rites of the first *status*.[169] However, Leff notes that Joachim frequently referred to these earthly symbols being consumed in fire.[170] The sacraments represented Christ's condescension to humanity, providing means by which people might reach him. As such they 'belonged...to the state of carnal understanding. With the clarification of the Holy Spirit they would not disappear but, rather, the spirit would pass beyond the symbol.'[171]

Conclusion

Joachim of Fiore was clearly an apocalyptist. This is demonstrated by the centrality of the book of Revelation for his theology, his use of symbols so familiar in apocalyptic literature, and his eschatology, which saw the third age as about to dawn. But was he a millennialist? This question is less clear. Marjorie Reeves believes he was not. She argues that Joachim's third age was not a supernatural millennium coming from above, nor was it a 'pause' granted by God somewhat arbitrarily, but 'the logical climax of the whole historical process, but because it is still part of time it does not embody final perfection'.[172] However, Robert Lerner disagrees. He notes, surely rightly, that when read literally, Rev. 20.4-5

169. Pelikan, *Medieval Thought*, p. 303, referring to Joachim, *Liber* 5.74. Reeves, on the other hand, believes that the only reference in the *Tractatus* to the transitoriness of the sacraments is an obscure one ('Originality', p. 296).

170. Leff, *Heresy*, I, p. 78, referring to Joachim, *Liber* 5.74.136.

171. Leff, *Heresy*, I, p. 78, citing Joachim, *Liber* 5.74.102vb. On the 'spiritualization' of the sacraments in the third age, see Bloomfield, 'Joachim of Flora', pp. 46-47.

172. Reeves, 'Originality', p. 293. Daniel, 'Joachim of Fiore', p. 86, agrees that the third *status* is not chiliastic/millennial, on the grounds that a new beginning is not implied by it, adding later, p. 87, that 'Joachim's thinking is evolutionary, not revolutionary. He was a reformer, not a millennialist. The most original and important contribution of the abbot of Fiore, therefore, was to make the vision of a reformed and purified Christendom the goal of an evolutionary process and to show how its roots were already there in the days of Abraham.' However, in his 'Apocalyptic Conversion', p. 130, Daniel admits that Joachim's third *status* 'has millenial characteristics', and, on p. 139, he refers to 'the millenial *status*', which suggests that in the time between the writing of these two works he has changed his mind.

> must refer to an earthly kingdom transpiring at the end of human history before the Last Judgment because John goes on to conclude with the report that after the thousand-year reign of the saints all the last things will transpire: Satan will be consigned eternally to the lake of fire and brimstone, all who had ever lived will be judged 'according to their works', and the heavenly Jerusalem, 'prepared as a bride adorned for her husband', will descend.[173]

He believes that as soon as one reads Revelation developmentally, 'with the last chapters standing in sequential order for earthly history's final events', one will necessarily become a chiliast. The words themselves, chiliasm and millennialism, the Greek and Latin respectively for 'thousand-yearism' were 'coined to describe belief in the literal prophetic meaning of Revelation's chapter 20'.[174] This Joachim did, following Augustine, understanding the thousand years symbolically.[175] Earlier Lerner takes chiliasm to mean 'the expectation of any imminent, supernaturally inspired, radical betterment on earth before the Last Judgment, regardless of the length of time assigned for such a final dispensation', and as such is synonymous with millenarianism.[176]

Joachim's contributions to history and theology, directly and indirectly, have been many. David Bebbington declares that he was the 'most significant mediaeval Christian theorist of history, second only to Augustine in influence amongst post-biblical writers',[177] and he also revived the historical interpretation of the book of Revelation.[178] Bebbington also draws attention to the fact that millenarianism 'has in practice fostered confidence in the future', and that this is evident in groups in the early Church as well as among those influenced by Joachim.[179] He was also the first mediaeval thinker to have a clear idea of a great social transformation which will take place in history.[180] Delno West

173. Lerner, 'Chiliasm', p. 503.

174. Lerner, 'Chiliasm', pp. 502-503.

175. On the brevity of this period and Joachim's following Augustine, see Lerner, 'Medieval Return', pp. 58-61.

176. Lerner, 'Chiliasm', p. 489.

177. D.W. Bebbington, *Patterns in History* (Leicester: Inter-Varsity Press, 1979), p. 58. Cf. his earlier comment on p. 18, that Joachim 'was to have almost as much influence on men who wrote history within a Christian framework in subsequent generations' as Augustine had.

178. Lerner, 'Medieval Return', pp. 51-71; Daniel, 'Joachim of Fiore', p. 73.

179. Bebbington, *Patterns*, p. 65.

180. Morris, *Papal Monarchy*, p. 521.

writes that '[t]he sum of Joachim's thinking reveals a belief that human society was becoming increasingly better'.[181] He continues later:

> Joachim's importance to history writing is that he strongly influenced the idea that history is an ongoing process. The conclusion that a wonderful spiritual age will come, in time, denied the cyclic pattern of history which taught the recurrence of an ancient Golden Age. Thus, Joachim combined the biblical motif of irreversible history with man's desire to recover a lost age of peace, prosperity and tranquility.[182]

In this regard, Abbot Joachim also contributed to the language of revolution, though it has been used in ways that would have appalled him. Colin Morris notes that up to his time *revolutio* (and its cognate *revolvere*) had only been used to describe the revolution of the stars, but Joachim

> gave it a solidly historical meaning by using it to describe the turning of the pages of sacred history, and he is reasonably consistent in this usage: semantically, the language of revolution is more common in his pages than the language of reform. God's purpose in history is *revolvere* not *reformare*.[183]

Bernard McGinn agrees:

> Joachim was in many ways a part of the great movement for the reform of the Church which had been active in western society since the mid-eleventh century. His originality in terms of the reform tradition lay in its emphasis upon the direction from which reform was to come. For the Abbot of Fiore reform was not by means of a return to the past, a *renovatio* of the pristine state of the Church in morals, laws, and institutions. Though others had stressed the breaking-in of the future as an important element in reform ideology...it was Joachim who provided the most complete theory of a *renovatio*, forward-looking and perfective, that was to take place in a new and better age to come.[184]

181. West, 'Introduction', p. vi.

182. West, 'Introduction', pp. viii-ix. For discussion of the cyclical and lineal understandings of history, Joachim falling within the latter, see Bebbington, *Patterns*, pp. 17-18, and chapters 2–3, pp. 21-67, with specific discussion of Joachim's contribution to historical thinking on pp. 58-61.

183. Morris, *Papal Monarchy*, p. 522. The many revolutionary movements of the Middle Ages have been well rehearsed by Cohn, *Pursuit*, *passim*.

184. McGinn, 'Apocalypticism', p. 281.

The importance of studying Joachim of Fiore, then, has been well summed up by McGinn:

> [T]he Abbot's organic and melioristic vision of history was to have many heirs in the West, even if few of them were in any sense direct. Joachim marks the beginning of a new stage in the history of the apocalyptic tradition and in European philosophy and theology of history.[185]

185. McGinn, *Visions*, p. 130.

READING THE SIGNS OF THE TIMES: MILLENARIAN AND APOCALYPTIC MOVEMENTS THEN AND NOW

Andrew Bradstock

Not unsurprisingly, the 1990s saw a revival of millenarianism, belief in the imminent return of Jesus Christ to earth to reign for a thousand years. As the second millennium of Christian history drew to a close, and anxieties increased about the supposed significance of the moment through which we were passing, so new movements and 'prophetic' figures emerged, some eagerly tooling up for Armageddon and staking out their space at key religious sites in anticipation of the impending end. In January 1999 an American group called Concerned Christians attracted the attention of the Israeli police with their plans to provoke a shoot-out in Jerusalem 'to hasten the second coming of Christ', and in the same month the *Guardian* (5 January 1999) reported evangelist Jerry Falwell's attempts to rally support in the United States for his pro-Netanyahu stance, based on a premiss that 'the security of Israel is an essential ingredient in the Second Coming when Christ will establish a kingdom centred on Jerusalem'. In 1997 the entire membership of the 'Heaven's Gate' movement committed suicide during the appearance of the Hale–Bopp comet, describing their mission as having been to offer 'a doorway to the Kingdom of God at the end of this civilization, the end of this millennium'.[1] The Branch Davidians in Waco, Texas, and Solar Temple sect in Canada and Switzerland are just two other (tragic) examples of contemporary apocalyptic movements convinced that the 'end-time' foretold in Holy Scripture had arrived. In addition to these more conventionally structured movements, millennial cults formed in cyberspace and recruited through the Web.

Such phenomena are, of course, hardly new, and appear with regularity at times of crisis and/or supposed historical significance; and this

1. S. Jay Gould, *Questioning the Millennium: A Rationalist's Guide to a Precisely Arbitrary Countdown* (London: Jonathan Cape, 1997), p. 53.

essay will explore, albeit briefly, some of the earlier millenarian movements of which we have record. But it will also ask why millenarianism has survived, why it continues to surface at certain times, and whether it should always be dismissed as a diversion of the mad, bad or dangerous. First, however, a brief reminder of its nature, origin and not untroubled history.

The roots of millennial belief can be traced back to ch. 20 of the book of Revelation in the New Testament, the apostle John's account of a vision he received on the isle of Patmos around the end of the first century. According to this passage, a pivotal phase in the countdown to the end of the world and the final judgment will be a thousand-year period during which two important developments will occur: the 'dragon', the Devil, will be bound and sealed up in a bottomless pit, unable to continue his art of 'deceiving the nations'; and women and men martyred for their witness to the faith will be brought back to life to 'reign' with Christ. The remainder of the faithful will be resurrected after this period, though they must first endure further onslaught from the Devil, who, duly released from his term of imprisonment, joins forces with Gog and Magog to wage war on the nations. The Devil's parole will last only for 'a little season', however, and he will finally get his just desserts in the form of eternal torment in the lake of fire and brimstone, following which the books will be opened revealing the fate of all humanity.

In some strands of the Christian tradition the concept of the millennium has loomed large, providing a key to understanding not just the timetable of the end of all things, but the pattern of history itself. At various times believers have speculated whether the thousand-year period might precede or follow the final return of Christ—post-millennialists believing the former, pre-millennialists the latter—but either way it has provided an important framework against which to read 'the signs of the times' and discern at what stage of history one might be living (notwithstanding that, for all types of millenarian, this generally turns out to be one near to the end). Further help in the task of interpreting the times has also been obtained by drawing upon other periods given prominence in apocalyptic literature, not least the 42 months during which, according to Revelation 13, 'the beast' is given licence to blaspheme against God and wage successful war on the saints.

A little reflection will reveal that there is something potentially subversive, not to say revolutionary, about this whole concept of a coming millennium: first, it gives sure ground for hope that all earthly socio-political orders, over which the Devil may be thought presently to be holding sway, will be brought to nothing and replaced by a new and perfect one; secondly, it promises a privileged place in the new order to those who have hitherto been effectively powerless, and who may have suffered persecution and even martyrdom on account of their faith in Christ and resistance to evil; and, thirdly, given the implication in other Scriptures that it is to be expected more or less imminently, it presents a threat to *present* governments and powers, not those which may or may not appear at some future, far-off date. It seems clear that the earliest Christian communities expected the new age to be inaugurated with minimal delay, encouragement being found in, for example, hints in Paul's early writings that he himself expected to be alive to see the return of Christ and the final resurrection (1 Thess. 4.17), and words attributed to Jesus in the Gospels of Mark (9.1) and Matthew (16.28) that some who had actually heard him speak would also see these events in their own lifetime.

What further sharpens the political 'cutting edge' of belief in the millennium is the implication in the Revelation passages that the new order it anticipates will be set up on earth, or at least a newly constituted earth. It has generally been assumed that most Christians in the first century thought in such terms.[2] The idea was firmly rooted in the soil of Jewish messianism, and they may have been further encouraged by sayings of Jesus like 'the meek...shall inherit the earth' (Mt. 5.5) and references in Paul to the whole creation waiting with eager longing for the birth of a new age (Rom. 8). Belief in an earthly millennium also appears to have been widely held among their successors in the second century, with Montanus and his (mainly female) devotees expecting, on the basis of a divine revelation, the arrival of the new Jerusalem in mid-second-century Phrygia, and Justin Martyr anticipating a thousand-year period of peace and prosperity in a restored and expanded Jerusalem. Irenaeus, Hippolytus and Tertullian were among many others confidently awaiting the realization on earth of the divine promises about the end time. Yet within another hundred years or so belief in a literal millennium on earth had been pushed to the margins of the Church where, on the whole, it has remained to this day.

2. See Stanley Porter's contribution to this volume for a more detailed examination of this belief among first-century followers of Christ.

We need not go too deeply into the reasons for this: in part it was to do with the millennium's delayed appearance, and in part with the radical change in the Church's fortune in the fourth century, the raising of its status from minority persecuted sect on the margins of society to virtually that of custodian of the 'civil religion' of the empire. The change did not occur overnight with the 'conversion' of the emperor Constantine to the Christian faith, and may not have been completed until two centuries later, but, more quickly than it could ever have imagined (or dreaded?), the Church found itself a powerful actor on the world stage. No longer did it find solace in the promise of an imminent, better order: it became rather comfortable with the present one. Something had to be done about the millennium, though, and since it could not be written out of the script (notwithstanding that some in the Church have expressed unease about the inclusion of the book of Revelation in the canon of the New Testament) it became redefined in essentially spiritual and ahistorical terms. The writings of Augustine in the fifth century reveal this process at its most subtle, the bishop of Hippo arguing in his magisterial *De civitate Dei* that the reign of the saints with Christ was now in process through the Church. Thus was the authority of the Church and its leadership enhanced, and the idea that the millennium might herald the dawn of a new era of divine rule on earth undermined.

Once Augustine's 'amillennialist' position became orthodoxy—a development not unconnected with the emergence of Rome as the dominant see in Christendom—belief in a coming perfect age on earth was sidelined; and it was not long before references to a literal millennium in early Christian writings were suppressed and millenarianism declared a heresy (a duty undertaken by the Council of Ephesus in 431). Despite a few dissenting voices—most notably that of the twelfth-century abbot Joachim of Fiore—Augustine's remained the mainstream position in the Church for centuries to come; and perhaps the English divine Thomas Burnet, writing more than 1,200 years after the Ephesian Council, is not overstating much when he asserts that the more the Church grew in 'splendour and greatness' the more 'she eclipsed and obscured' the doctrine 'so that it would have been lost out of the World as an obsolete error, if it had not been revived by some of the Reformation'.[3]

3. Cited in Gould, *Questioning the Millennium*, p. 47.

In fact it surfaced a little before the Reformation, both in Joachim (about whom a little more later) and, in a particularly militant form, among a group known as Taborites in early fifteenth-century Bohemia. Claiming some affinity to the reformer and martyr Jan Hus, this movement believed not just that the millennium was imminent, but that in order for it to materialize the world had first to be purged of all evil and sin. Troubled particularly by the level of corruption they observed in the Church and secular authorities of their day, they set about ridding the world of all its sinners and purifying it in readiness for the return of Christ. Not dissimilar ideas were espoused during the early Reformation period by the mystic German pastor and peasant leader Thomas Müntzer: an apocalyptic figure in the tradition of Daniel, Müntzer discerned in the degenerate state of the Church around him, and the growing restlessness of the peasants, signs that the world was moving toward a final transformation, and assumed responsibility himself for ushering in the new age. The time of the eschatological harvest, the rooting out of the tares from the wheat, was now here, he argued, and he himself had been appointed a wielder of the heavenly sickle. Under conviction that the final overthrow of the old order could be achieved on the back of the peasant uprisings going on around him, he assumed leadership of one of their bands; but, despite the appearance in the sky, at a very timely moment, of what had to have been a sign of divine approval for his stand, he and his followers failed in their mission and with few exceptions lost their lives in the process. Ten years after Müntzer a group inspired by the millenarian prophecies of Melchior Hofmann stormed the city of Münster, attempting to transform it into the New Jerusalem. There they established a socio-political order on pseudo-Old Testament lines, with 12 elders or 'Judges of Israel' to oversee all aspects of daily life, and a long list of sins punishable by death (which interestingly did not include polygamy, towards which they had a very relaxed attitude). Perhaps unsurprisingly, though, this venture, like Müntzer's, ended in slaughter and retribution at the hands of the authorities.

Millenarianism also flourished in England a little over a hundred years later: John Milton spoke of Christ as 'shortly-expected King', and almost everyone in the 1640s and 1650s seems to have assumed that they would witness his return in their own lifetime—even if opinions varied as to whether he would come 'in person' to set up a new kingdom, reigning perhaps through his saints, or 'in spirit', rising up in some mystical sense in his sons and daughters.[4] Date-setting—an activity associated nowadays mainly with so-called Jehovah's Witnesses and marginal fundamentalist sects—was widely practised, and not just by the eccentric or seventeenth-century equivalent of the 'anorak', but by eminent mathematicians and scholars like Joseph Mede and Sir Isaac Newton. The year 1666 was, in view of its similarity to the number of the 'beast' in Rev. 13.18, a much-discussed year, but so too was 1656, which many believed corresponded to the number of years that had elapsed between the Creation and the Flood. The 'Two Last Witnesses', the figure of Antichrist and the apocalyptic periods of 42 months and 1,260 years mentioned in Daniel and Revelation also featured prominently in calculations. Most Puritans took the pope to be Antichrist and estimated that, if his rise to prominence were dated to around the end of the fourth century, and he were allowed by God to exercise power in the world for 1,260 years, his destruction could be expected towards the middle of the 1660s.[5] Since it was also widely believed, on the basis of a prophecy in Daniel 2, that the return of Christ would occur following the collapse of the last of the four great (and corrupt) historical earthly kingdoms, expectations reached fever pitch around the time of the execution of Charles Stuart in 1649.

Thus we find Fifth Monarchists and others viewing the king's execution as clearing the way for the reign of King Jesus, and the Two Last Witnesses appearing in 1652 in the form of John Reeve and his cousin Ludowick Muggleton. Reeve and Muggleton's particular gift was to enlighten people as to their eternal state, the saved being those who accepted their status as the Witnesses, the damned those who did not. Like some millenarians they adopted the dispensationalist view of history advocated by Joachim of Fiore, also known as the 'Everlasting Gospel', which divided time into three stages each associated with a person of the Trinity—the Age of the Father equating essentially with the Old Testament dispensation, the Age of the Son with the Gospel period, and the Age of the Spirit (the final dispensation, which would lead up to the return of Christ and inauguration of the last judgment) with the period from the first century down to the present, which was

4. For a more detailed discussion of Milton and others awaiting the millennium in mid seventeenth-century England, see Pat Pinsent's contribution to this volume.

5. For a typical contemporary discussion of this topic, see M. Poole, *Commentary on the Holy Bible*. III. *Matthew to Revelation* (McLean, VA: MacDonald, nd [1683–85]), pp. 976-82.

characterized by fuller spiritual illumination, liberty and love. This 'spiritual' age, which Joachim envisaged would be preceded by intense activity by Antichrist, was the one in which Reeve and Muggleton (like all millenarians) were living, and was indeed ushered in by them as the Two Witnesses. Though Reeve was to die shortly after his adoption as a Last Witness, his cousin went on to build and hold together a movement that took his name and that survived, incredibly, until the late 1970s.[6]

Anticipation of a coming reign of Christ on earth also underpinned the programme of the True Levellers or 'Diggers', a movement that, led by the visionary writer and activist Gerrard Winstanley, equated the millennium with the remaking of the earth as a 'common treasury'. Winstanley saw evidence that the new order was beginning in the degree of support the Diggers initially received for their programme of planting the common land and living in community. According to his schema, as Christ effected his work of 'rising up' in his sons and daughters—this being his 'second coming'—so they would be drawn together to live again in the spirit of true community not known since before the Fall, sharing the earth among themselves and holding nothing to be their peculiar possession.[7] It was nothing less than a hope of regaining Paradise (Milton's vision of this event being rather different, of course) but it proved too heady an ideal for those whose earthly privileges it threatened—those with property and power—who chose, instead, to trample it out of existence. Echoes of the vision of Winstanley and other civil war radicals may be found a century later in William Blake—who probably encountered Muggletonian and other writings of that earlier period—with his desire to build the new Jerusalem in England's green and pleasant land. Blake's poem 'Night' from his Songs of Innocence, with its depiction of the lion laying down with the lamb drawn from Isaiah and Revelation, also suggests a hope of a literal New Jerusalem.

6. The history and survival of the Muggletonians is discussed in C. Hill, B. Reay and W. Lamont, *The World of the Muggletonians* (London: Temple Smith, 1983), and E.P. Thompson, *Witness against the Beast* (Cambridge: Cambridge University Press, 1993).

7. For a fuller discussion of Winstanley's millenarianism, see my *Faith in the Revolution: The Political Theologies of Müntzer and Winstanley* (London: SPCK, 1997), pp. 109-25; as its title suggests, this study also contains a consideration of Müntzer's apocalypticism.

A study such as this, albeit selective and sketchy in form and content, raises a number of questions. Why, given that the focus of its concern is still to arrive, has millenarianism survived? What is its attraction, particularly at times of uncertainty? And does it always give rise to a distorted view of reality, to a mistaken sense of the significance of the 'now', or can it contribute anything 'positive' to an understanding of the 'signs of the times', of the actual possibilities of the given historical moment? One could begin to answer the question about its survival simply by pointing to its inclusion in Scripture, for it *is* in the source text of Christianity whether the 'mainstream' of the Church chooses to recognize it or not. If the Church now considers it to be of marginal importance, that is, as I suggested earlier, simply a commentary on the extent to which that institution has accommodated itself in, with and to the world. For Christians committed to the vision that was arguably at the core of the early Church's eschatology, the reign of God *on earth*, the millennium remains of crucial importance. Only those who see human history as being of little or no interest to the divine mind, preoccupied as it supposedly is with matters spiritual and eternal, find millennial hopes an embarrassment.

But millenarianism also provides a basis for understanding and interpreting the world, particularly in times of upheaval, distress and uncertainty. That it played this sort of role in the mid-seventeenth century—a period punctuated by poor harvests, near-starvation, dislocation of communities, three civil wars and the execution of the monarch—is easy enough to understand, given the Bible's central place in all discourse of the time; though perhaps even today it has, for those weighed down with the complexity and uncertainty of what might lie ahead, also a function. Fitting events into a divine framework, perceiving that history is working out in accordance with scriptural prophecies, can bring an extraordinary sense of certainty at times when such a commodity is at a premium. It is often remarked upon that, for all that humanity has supposedly 'come of age', attraction to the irrational—astrology, the occult, new religious movements, the prophecies of Nostradamus and so on—has never been stronger. And the millennium offers, in addition to the 'certainty' also provided by other ideas and movements, a heady mix of salvation and power that is particularly attractive to those without either in this world. Come the millennium, not only will there be an end of suffering, but a new order in which the faithful will play a key—and, according to some interpretations, authoritative—role.

Of course, millenarians have been consistently wrong in their assumption that the end is not too far off, yet still the belief at the core of their message lives on. In part, as we have noted, this is because it is an important promise of Scripture, but its survival is also a testament to the triumph of hope over experience, as the history of many latter-day millenarian groups bears out. Followers of the nineteenth-century figures Edward Irving (Irvingites), William Miller (Adventists) and Charles Taze Russell (Jehovah's Witnesses), to name but three, have all lived through the disappointment of seeing their leaders' promises about the return of Christ come to nothing, and all have rationalized this disappointment and kept their hopes alive.[8] The North American writer Hal Lindsey, though not the founder of any movement, is another whose prophecies concerning the end time have been seen with hindsight to have been a little rash, but who has also succeeded in dusting himself off and coming back with more. He offers a clear example of how the business of rewriting prophecy in the light of changing world events might be approached. In his extraordinarily popular *The Late Great Planet Earth*, published in 1970, he predicted, using as a base line the establishment of the State of Israel in 1948, that the countdown to the end had begun and that we, his readers, were effectively the 'generation' that Christ had said would not pass away until the end had come (Mt. 24.34).[9] Playing a key role in this build-up to the end would be the USSR, the powerful enemy from the north described in chs. 38 and 39 of the book of Ezekiel. By 1994, however, with the Soviet empire in tatters and no longer a superpower on the world stage, Lindsey had discerned the real enemy of Israel to be Islam, and, in particular, the state of Iran. Russia would still play a part in the upcoming denouement, not least since it was still in possession of a significant nuclear arsenal, but only as junior partner in an alliance with its Muslim neighbour.[10] Disappointment in the wake of failed expectations may

8. For brief summaries of the ideas of these movements and their leaders, see R.J. McKelvey, *The Millennium and the Book of Revelation* (Cambridge: Lutterworth, 1999), pp. 33-36. The classic study is L. Festinger, *When Prophecy Fails* (Minneapolis: University of Minnesota Press, 1956).

9. H. Lindsey with C.C. Carlson, *The Late Great Planet Earth* (London: Lakeland, 1970).

10. H. Lindsey, *Planet Earth—2000 AD: Will Mankind Survive?* (Palos Verdes, CA: Western Front, 1994). See the useful brief discussion of Lindsey's views in McKelvey, *Millennium*, pp. 36-37.

provoke a period of re-evaluation and reinterpretation, but seldom a loss of faith altogether in the eventual appearance of the millennium itself. The signs and portents of its imminence are just too all-pervasive to be ignored: it's just a case of working out exactly what these signs and portents mean.

The general point to which this rewriting and date-juggling bears witness, that millenarians have, to a person, been consistently mistaken in their belief that the end is nigh, has of course led to criticism that religion in general, and Christianity in particular, cannot but give a distorted picture of reality and must be therefore either dangerous or foolish or both. Millenarians might be in principle revolutionary in that they seek a new social order here on earth, but they are, in practice, not so since they do not—and cannot—show how this order relates to the course of history. One particularly vigorous rehearsal of this view is Friedrich Engels's treatise on the peasant struggles in Reformation Germany and Müntzer's role in them, to which we have already alluded.[11] Although Müntzer was undoubtedly revolutionary in his aims and vision, admits Engels, his new society was conceived as the materialization of the prophesied, and imminently close, millennium, and therefore his programme amounted to no more than a 'sally beyond both the present and even the future'. Müntzer's preoccupation with the fulfilment of prophecy obscured the necessity for him to relate his programme to the process of history, which for Engels is a necessary characteristic of *all* Christian-inspired ventures. Christianity might inspire hope of a better future, and even active commitment to bring it about, but when it does it inevitably gives rise to a distorted understanding of the situation to be transformed and an inability to read the real possibilities of the present historical moment. Yet an alternative interpretation might be that the root of the mistake in many millenarians is not to be found in their Christian perspective of the world, nor in Christian eschatology per se, but in the demands which they place upon that eschatology, specifically that the millennium be realized 'for them'. On this reading, the effectiveness of Christian attempts to change the world need not depend on the abandonment of a Christian world-view, nor even an eschatological perspective, but the construction of a more balanced or measured eschatology which sees the coming reign of God both as a process within history and a perpetually future phenomenon.

11. F. Engels, *The Peasant War in Germany* (Moscow: Progress Publishers, 1956 [1850]).

Thus the key to reading the Apocalypse might lie in seeing its symbolism as always relevant to every period of human history, as providing a language and interpretative framework for contemporary events of any and every period; which is to say that, if the tendency of some millenarians to narrow the interpretation of apocalyptic images to definitive figures in (their own) history is avoided, such images can be powerful tools with which to critique contemporary forces opposed to the reign of God. The African theologian Teresa Okure is one who has demonstrated how this might be done in our own day: if the image of the beast, for instance, drawn from Daniel, appears to have been used by the writer of Revelation to identify the exercise of Roman power in his own day, then in a similar way the economy, the 'god' of today, may be critiqued by drawing on the image of 'the dragon and its beasts' in Revelation 12 and 13. Okure writes,

> Like the dragon, [the economy] has its beasts and false prophets, to whom it has delegated its powers, this time of the market and free trade. Its promoting agents might be the G7, the International Monetary Fund, the World Bank, the Paris Club and multi-national corporations. They know how to prevent people from buying and selling unless they worship this modern dragon.[12]

Other Christians in the two-thirds world have drawn on apocalyptic imagery to identify causes of oppression, like believers in revolutionary Nicaragua who identified the beast of Revelation with 'US imperialism', and other theologians in the region who have described aggressive, neo-liberal capitalism in similar terms.

Taking the millennium seriously does not therefore imply a preoccupation with the future, even less with bringing the future into the present, as has largely been the tendency of the historical and contemporary examples we have cited here. Completely the reverse, in fact, for genuine millenarianism is a response to the biblical call to men and women to live in a 'tension' between the present and the future, the 'already' and the 'not yet'. Paul's writings are clearly informed by both an expectation of the coming new age *and* a commitment meanwhile to live out its values here and now, and the Epistle of Peter also exhorts Christians 'wait[ing] for new heavens and a new earth, where righteousness is at home', to 'strive to be found by [God] at peace, without

12. T. Okure, 'From Genesis to Revelation: Apocalyptic in Biblical Faith', *Concilium*, no. 4 (1998), p. 29.

spot or blemish' (2 Pet. 3.13-14; cf. 3.11). Millenarian hope infuses the present with greater significance, not when the present is understood as the full realization of the future, but when the 'now' is understood in the light of the future, from the perspective of the coming reign of Christ. It is only on that basis that one can say that no action to further that reign, however apparently ineffective, can ever be considered lost or meaningless.

NEW RELIGIONS IN THE NEW MILLENNIUM

Elizabeth Puttick

Introduction

Does Christianity have a monopoly on the millennium? Arguably on the date—as corroborated by the almost total absence of other religions in this volume!—but not on millennialism per se. Millennialism may be a feature of any religion; it is more typical of newer and marginal groups, but is increasingly affecting even mainstream religion. Consequently, it is a key concept in the sociology of religion.

There are two parts to this paper: first, an overview of millennialist beliefs and tendencies in new religions; secondly, predictions concerning the significance of new religions in the post-millennialist world.

Church-Sect Theory

The main framework for the study of New Religious Movements (NRMs) is Church-sect theory, as expounded by Ernst Troeltsch in 1931, and since developed by other sociologists.[1] 'Church' as a sociological term refers to any large religious organization. Its chief characteristics are that members are born into it, hence do not have to demonstrate their faith—which may legitimately be lukewarm. Churches are closely related to the state, and may be the established state religion. In any case they usually have claims to universality, even if in practice there may exist substantial minorities of non-members. They draw their membership from all social classes, but are often associated with the ruling class. Management is through a hierarchy of paid professional

1. The most significant advances in Church-sect theory are in the work of B. Wilson, *The Social Dimensions of Sectarianism* (Oxford: Clarendon Press, 1990) and R. Wallis, *The Elementary Forms of the Religious Life* (London: Routledge, 1984).

officials. The danger of establishment is routinization: Churches are prone to becoming overly institutionalized, bureaucratic and dogmatic—which, under certain conditions, may lead to sectarianism.

Sects are almost diametrically opposed to Churches, even though historically they are offshoots. They are small, closely knit and deeply committed about their faith. Their membership is typically drawn from the poor, dispossessed, and minority or oppositional groups. Sects are founded and led by charismatic leaders, and management is informal, usually unpaid. Over time, the more successful sects are likely to stabilize and grow into denominations or even Churches, and the cycle begins again.

The most prominent difference between Churches and sects is ideological. The social function of Churches is to provide stability and social control. Consequently, they are conservative and 'world-affirming'.[2] Sects, on the other hand, often rebel against the perceived overformality, rigidity and dearth or death of inspiration in the Churches. In its place they offer a millennial vision. Their 'world-rejecting' attitude leads to an oppositional stance, which creates instability and antinomianism. Hence they have often been persecuted, which serves to further strengthen bonding within the group.

New Religious Movements

NRMs are a contemporary variant of sects. Some of them are literally sects of world religions, while others have rather tenuous connections, and may even be rejected by the parent religion if they deviate too far from orthodoxy. For example, most Christians disassociate from the Unification Church ('Moonies'), though Unificationists themselves claim kinship. The Nine o'Clock Service in Sheffield was widely admired by the Anglican establishment until its leader, Chris Brain, was exposed by his female parishioners for sexual misdemeanours, when he was condemned as a 'cult leader'. Other NRMs arise out of the broader New Age movement or are simply based on the syncretic vision of their founder.

Until recently, deprivation was the favourite theory of why people join NRMs in the West. This theory derives from the study of millenar-

2. The categories 'world-affirming', 'world-accepting' and 'world-accommodating' are taken from Wallis's typology of sects and new religious movements in his *Elementary Forms of the Religious Life* (1984).

ian groups in societies undergoing colonization. In such societies, there is often an acute contrast between the wealth and power of the invaders, and the poverty and oppression of the natives. Hence, millennialism is interpreted sociologically as a response by native peoples to the impact of western culture. Awareness of 'relative deprivation' leads to an awakening of what Engels called 'proletarian self-consciousness'. The most famous examples of this are the cargo cults.[3]

However, the typical membership of Western NRMs is white, middle-class, well educated. In America, even apocalyptic faith, traditionally the preserve of lower-class Pentecostalists, has spread to more prosperous creeds, such as Mormons, Adventists and Southern Baptists.[4] Consequently, both deprivation and the related Weberian theory of social marginality have been discredited.[5]

It has been widely noted that sects and NRMs flourish during periods of rapid social change, arising as vehicles of protest, deviation and challenge. They are responses to but also agents of transformation, experimenting with new ideas and practices, often in sealed-off communities, isolated from the norms, conventions and restrictions of society. In this respect they function as laboratories, crucibles for new experiments of which the more successful are taken up—usually in a more diluted, digestible form—by mainstream society. They offer a critique of family and society as well as established religion, and substitute *gemeinschaft*: an alternative loving community. They may also provide women with an alternative destiny to motherhood or career in the form of a spiritual path.[6]

Characteristically NRMs are radical, but they are not all on the cutting edge. Just as they may be perceived as either a threat or a hope for the future, so they themselves tend to adopt one of two responses to social change. Some see it as an opportunity for growth, experimen-

3. It should be noted that millenarianism is not the only possible response to colonial oppression. Other responses include political agitation, armed aggression, a new way of life, a retreat into resignation or a passive, introversionist form of religion.

4. H. Bloom, *Omens of Millennium* (London: Fourth Estate, 1997).

5. P. Worsley, *The Trumpet Shall Sound* (London: Paladin, 1970). See R. Wuthnow, *The Consciousness Reformation* (Berkeley: University of California Press, 1976) and R. Stark and W. Bainbridge, *The Future of Religion* (Berkeley: University of California Press, 1985).

6. E. Puttick, *Women in New Religions* (London: Macmillan, 1997).

tation, and rebellion against old norms and paradigms. In contemporary religion, this trend is exemplified by the eastern-based counter-cultural NRMs of the 1970s and the current New Age and pagan movements. However, change is also sometimes feared as leading to instability and chaos, though the fear may be rationalized as moral opposition to a perceived over-liberalism in mainstream society. In such cases, social change is resisted by reverting to puritanical social, sexual and religious values.[7]

I have typologized the different types of sect and other religious groups in terms of Abraham Maslow's 'hierarchy of needs', a 'holistic-dynamic theory' that can accommodate both the social and experiential dimensions of religion. Maslow distinguishes five levels of need that must be satisfied to produce a healthy, fully functioning human being: physiological; safety; belongingness and love; esteem; self-actualization. The evidence demonstrates that westerners join movements that directly affirm their personal values. These interrelated needs and values may be combined into two main groupings, which I call 'traditionalism' and 'personal development'.[8]

As might be expected, millennialism in western NRMs tends to take different forms from religions in colonized societies, but they all contain a number of the following features.

(1) Dissatisfaction or rejection of society ('world-rejecting').
(2) Awareness of relative deprivation (socioeconomic) leading to distress, anxiety.
(3) Vision and hope of a new/better world, often expressed in prophecy.
(4) Promise of rewards/salvation to faithful/elect.
(5) Expectations of imminent overthrow of present system of government.
(6) Millennium may be preceded by apocalypse/total confrontation.
(7) Catalyzed by divine/extraordinary intervention (for example, God, prophet, UFOs).

7. For example, at the 1971 Jerusalem prophecy conference, the evangelical leader Harold Ockenga cited the rising tide of 'sodomy, homosexuality and lesbianism' in support of his declaration that 'between 1965 and 1970 the moral dam gave way and...the resulting flood has played havoc with civilization' (P. Boyer, *When Time Shall Be No More* [Cambridge, MA: Harvard University Press, 1992]).

8. E. Puttick, 'A New Typology of Religion Based on Needs and Values', *Journal of Beliefs and Values* 18.2 (1997), pp. 133-45.

(8) Living in end time.
(9) Prophet or charismatic leader (expresses and mediates vision).

Millennialism in New Religious Movements

Millennialism is more typical of sects and NRMs, but is currently spreading throughout the Churches and even secular society, for example, within the environmental movement. All world religions contain some millennialist characteristics. Most NRMs are offshoots of or display some kinship with world religions, and may take on or develop these tendencies, especially at the present time, and among NRMs based on monotheistic traditions.

Monotheistic NRMs tend to have a more apocalyptic eschatology, developed by the Jews in the second century CE, and catalyzed by their experience of relative deprivation over the next few centuries. There has been a resurgence of hope for the Messiah since the founding of the State of Israel in 1948, intensified by the success of the Six Day War in 1967, which has also been a significant factor in the rise of Christian evangelical millennialism. The primary candidate was Rebbe Menahem Schneersohn, the late Lubavich leader, but since his death the messianic fervour has subdued.

Muslims have a millennialist tradition of the Mahdi ('rightly guided one'), an ideal leader related to the Jewish concept of the Messiah, as well as to the Christian belief in the Second Coming of Christ and the battle with the Antichrist. The Mahdi will usher in 1,000 years of peace on earth before the end of time. This belief is prominent among the Twelver Shiites. The Nation of Islam (the most controversial NRM in the American Black Muslim movement) have a prophecy that in 2000 Allah will destroy the whites and their religion. However, the American Muslim Mission, the majority group of this movement, have tried to improve relationships with the American government.

Millennialism is predictably most widespread among Christian-based groups, including the so-called 'destructive cults' that have hit the headlines over the last 20 years, most notoriously the People's Temple and the Branch Davidians. It was the tragedy of the mass murder and suicide of the followers of the Revd Jim Jones in Guyana that precipitated anti-cult prejudice and intolerance, particularly among evangelical Christians. However, it should be noted that, like Chris Brain, Jim Jones was widely admired as a Christian leader and viewed as a model of messianic socialism. In 1977 he won San Francisco's Humanitarian of the Year award, but a year later was being vilified as the Antichrist for his role in the movement's tragedy.

The Branch Davidians are an offshoot of the Seventh Day Adventists, hence in the mainstream of American millennialism. It is a classic example of a millenarian sect, displaying most of the key characteristics. Its leader David Koresh,[9] the 'sinful messiah' who died with his followers in the Waco conflagration in 1993, was a charismatic prophet who predicted that 1993 would be the year of the Second Coming of Christ. He developed a highly convoluted form of apocalyptic theology based on Seventh Day Adventist teachings, which he would preach to his followers for hours on end. In common with the Solar Temple and Heaven's Gate (see below), as well as many other less controversial NRMs, his eschatology also featured UFO fantasies, including his own UFO abduction by angelic beings. A modern variant of biblical visions and visitations? The group were isolated in Mount Carmel, the Waco compound, bound together by their distrust of civil authority as they awaited the end time. The FBI bombardment of Mount Carmel, the Waco compound, was interpreted as Apocalypse—a purifying fire through which Koresh and his followers would pass to Heaven. Although this violent attack endorsed their end time scenario, it is clear that the Branch Davidians did not set fire to themselves. The evidence is now overwhelming that the fire was caused by the FBI's tank bombardment of the buildings.[10]

Hinduism has a more cyclical view of history, so the concept of end time is not terminally catastrophic. However, according to Hindu cosmology, we are currently living in Kali-yuga—the last and lowest of the four ages. One Hindu-based NRM, the Brahma Kumaris, has a theory that when Kali-yuga ends, the new golden age will begin in New Delhi, and the Brahma Kumaris will be its chosen leaders. Fortunately, Hindus think in vast aeons of time, and Kali-yuga—though a brief moment in the grand cycle of ages—still has around 350,000 years to run.

The New Age promotes a more optimistic, upbeat form of post-millennialism, which may encompass but never dwells on the more lurid

9. David Koresh was the self-given name of Vernon Howell, a variation of Cyrus, the sixth-century BCE conqueror of Babylon believed to be a Zoroastrian fire-worshipper.

10. See D. Thompson, *The End of Tiime* (London: Random House, 1997) for an extended account of this movement.

and distressing aspects of apocalypse. New Agers prefer to interpret the millennium as a peaceful transformation of human consciousness, which can be prepared for through meditation and other techniques of self-development. Like Hinduism, the New Age adheres to a cyclical model of history, which is astrological, but based on the astronomical theory of the precession of the equinoxes. Approximately every 2,000 years, the sun moves into a new constellation at the spring equinox. Currently this is Pisces, but the new Age of Aquarius is imminent. Unfortunately, there is no agreement on the precise date of this change, which was prematurely welcomed in the 1960s, but may miss the obvious date by around 200 years. The main significance attributed to the Age of Aquarius is that it will usher in a new paradigm, which will become the foundation of a new, universal religion. This may be one reason why Christians are not partial to the Aquarian model of religious history, although there is much overlap between New Age and Christian occult symbolism.[11]

Harold Bloom, in his book *Omens of Millennium*, argues that this shared symbolism is at the heart of millennialist eschatology, particularly in the form of angelology, prophetic dreams and the near-death experience. He concludes: 'The most authentic omen of the Millennium could be named as our emergent dream of a guardian angel of personal resurrection, since the three most pervasive of current omens—angels, dreams, not dying—meet in that composite image'.[12]

However, there are also more apocalyptic groups, such as Elizabeth Clare Prophet's Church Universal and Triumphant, which is stockpiling weapons and building bomb shelters in Montana. Prophet is a prophet, and after her 1990 warning of imminent nuclear war, her followers sold up and retreated to the underground shelters. When prophecy failed, they rejoiced that their prayers had averted disaster—a common response to the failure of prophecy.

Less fortunate were the followers of Heaven's Gate, who carried their fantasies through to the bitter end in a mass suicide, one of the more

11. For example, the Church of Scotland minister Gordon Strachan believes that the ruling sign of an astrological age becomes the 'ascendant' of the following age, whose ruler only becomes dominant in the final stage (Wrekin Trust conference, London, 27 October 1990). This theory is unique to Strachan, and may serve to synthesize his Christian and New Age beliefs by promoting the continuing ascendancy of Christ (closely associated with the sign of Pisces) into the Aquarian age.

12. Bloom, *Omens of Millennium*, p. 227.

shocking manifestations of millennial fervour. The leaders of the Solar Temple and Heaven's Gate were both strongly influenced by Christianity, though developed their groups in a more esoteric or New Age direction. Marshall Applewhite, their leader, prophesied that the Hale–Bopp comet in 1997 was the harbinger of total apocalypse, but that his followers would escape to the UFO following it, thus ascending to a higher level of consciousness. This has parallels with the Solar Temple, whose members saw death as regenerating them into solar beings in another dimension beyond Sirius.

UFO cults have been prevalent in less disastrous forms since the 1940s, but as a separate phenomenon from New Age spirituality until the 1980s upsurge of belief in the paranormal within secular society. At this time, psychics and mediums, who had previously been concerned mainly with relaying messages from dead relatives to the bereaved, began to 'channel' warnings from higher entities existing on other planets and levels of consciousness. These new messages are apocalyptic in tone, prophesying that disaster will ensue unless we begin to raise our consciousness, work for peace and care for the environment. There is still a big divide between New Agers, who value the spiritual content of the 'messages', and more traditional UFO enthusiasts, who are obsessed with alien abductions.

Charismatic Leadership and Millennialism

It is the leader of a millennialist sect who interprets the teachings, gives its followers their thrust towards fear or hope, and initiates action (if any). One of the key characteristics of charismatic leadership is that the leader 'is set apart from ordinary men and treated as endowed with supernatural, superhuman, or at least specifically exceptional powers or qualities... [which] are regarded as of divine origin or exemplary'.[13] Once his followers accept his special status, a charismatic leader is able to set himself above and beyond the law, and becomes prone to acting unpredictably according to the inspiration of the moment. The consequences of charismatic leadership may be fatal, as in the 'cult tragedies' of recent years, or may lead to the creation of a new world religion.

13. M. Weber, *The Theory of Social and Economic Organization* (New York: Free Press, 1964).

Many members of NRMs believe that their leader is the designated leader of whatever New Age is to come, a belief that may have been initiated and/or encouraged by the leader himself—or herself, for a minority of these leaders are women. Sometimes the status of the leader rises with the expansion of the movement.

The early years of a charismatic religious leader are important in the mythologizing process, and are often linked to prophesies of the coming of a messiah or avatar. Miraculous stories have proliferated around such Indian gurus as Osho Rajneesh, Sathya Sai Baba, Muktananda, Mother Meera, often referring back to previous incarnations. It is relatively common for Indian gurus to change their names and titles, usually to mark a rise in status. Guru Maharaj Ji, leader of Elan Vital (formerly Divine Light Mission), gave himself a minor name-change but an enormous leap in status to Maharaji, which allowed his disciples to identify him as Kalki the tenth incarnation of Vishnu, Buddha Maitreya, and the Second Coming of Christ. Sathya Sai Baba has not changed his name, but his status rose from simple guru first to the incarnation of the nineteenth-century saint Shirdi Sai Baba, then to an *avatar* (incarnation) of Shiva, the highest god in the Hindu *Trimurti* (trinity); finally to universal God and ultimate receiver of all forms of devotion to other godheads.

New Religious Movements in the New Millennium

The last 30 years have seen many changes in religion and society. The secularization thesis has been widely discredited in the light of the enormous growth in both alternative/New Age and evangelical religion. This is sometimes perceived in terms of a sharply demarcated opposition between the postmillennialist optimism of the New Age and the apocalyptic gloom of the fundamentalists: the angels of light against the forces of darkness, except that nobody agrees on who is which.[14] However, the two types of religion correspond to my typology of traditionalist versus personal development religion.[15] Correspondingly, the growth of both types is happening in different ways. The evangelical movements are becoming more restrictive, more patriarchal, and certainly

14. New Agers certainly see themselves as light-bearers, harbingers of the millennium, but are sometimes seen by fundamentalists as 'part of a cosmic conspiracy to install the Antichrist' (Boyer, *When Time Shall Be No More*, p. 233).

15. Puttick, 'A New Typology of Religion'.

more actively proselytizing. The influence of the more liberal NRMs—the Human Potential Movement, New Age, eastern and pagan movements—is more subtle but pervasive. Long-term changes in ideas, attitudes and practices can sometimes be traced at least partly to the influence of NRMs, such as the widespread belief in reincarnation, the fast-increasing use of complementary medicine and health approaches, vegetarianism, meditation, body-positive spirituality and sacred sex. 'Personal development' originated in a psychospiritual context but has now become a fundamental concept in mainstream society, including the new business philosophy, with its growing emphasis on empowerment, human values and ethics. Other ideas have a reciprocal influence, emerging in secular form but developing a sacred dimension in alternative religion. For example, ecology has transmuted from a scientific discipline into sociopolitical activism and then into ecospirituality. In this form it influenced the new religions, particularly paganism, but has now also become a major force in mainstream religions.

It is sometimes observed that the current religious situation in the West has many parallels with religion in the Roman empire at the time of early Christianity. Whereas at that time paganism was in decline, its gods losing credibility, its rituals perfunctory, its hegemony challenged by other religions, including Christianity, the situation is now in reverse. Now as then there is a proliferation of 'cults' and competing belief systems, with a resurgence of inspiration from the East, creating a fertile 'cultic milieu'.

There are currently three major contenders for spiritual hegemony in the West: Christianity, Buddhism and the nature religions, particularly paganism and shamanism.[16] There are also three major social and religious trends, which I propose will strongly influence, if not determine, the relative success and outcome of religions in the postmillennial

16. There is some disagreement about the precise application of the terms 'paganism' and 'shamanism', and the relationship between these traditions. 'Paganism' refers to NRMs claiming to derive from pre-Christian European religions, of which the main ones are Druidry, Wicca and the Nordic tradition. 'Shamanism' strictly refers to the indigenous tribal spirituality of Siberia (now almost eradicated). It is often also generally applied to other living tribal traditions, including Native American spirituality, though Native Americans tend to reject the term. Shamanism is also sometimes erroneously classified under paganism as an umbrella term, and pagans themselves sometimes apply the term very widely, including even Hinduism (P. Jones and N. Pennick, *Pagan Europe* [London: Routledge, 1995]).

world. These trends are (1) spirituality, (2) feminism, (3) environmentalism. I shall discuss these in terms of the three front-runner religions.

Spirituality

Alternative spirituality in the 1990s has learned and absorbed much from the 1970s counter-culture. In many ways it is a revival of the experimental idealism of that period, but is creating a more integrated, feminized, politicized, and westernized spirituality. Whereas the 1970s saw a move away from ritual, tradition and social action to an individualistic, inner-directed search, the pendulum has swung back again but with a difference. The emphasis is now more on functionalist syncretism (sometimes disparagingly termed the 'spiritual supermarket', which is legitimated by whether it works). The New Age is still influenced by eastern mysticism but also more now by Celtic spirituality, which is even more influential on nature religions and Christianity.

In the 1970s Christianity was almost universally rejected by members of non-Christian NRMs, often with some vehemence, as outdated, sterile, hierarchical, misogynistic, fear-based and sin-obsessed. Some of these criticisms are still voiced, and mainstream Christianity is still in decline, particularly among the intelligentsia, who are mainly either entrenched in scientific rationalism or moving into religions based on personal development and eastern philosophy. But Christianity has also been influenced by the search for mystical spirituality, and is increasingly syncretizing meditation practices from Asian religions as well as revitalizing itself through the Celtic tradition.

Buddhism is the fastest growing of the world religions in the West and, in so far as it may be classified as an NRM (i.e. as practised by Westerners), the most respected and admired. Over the course of its long history it has developed probably the most sophisticated philosophy, mysticism and praxis of any religion. Buddhism also has many admired and influential teachers, pre-eminently the Dalai Lama, who received massive, enthusiastic media coverage when he visited the UK in 1999.

The nature religions have benefited from a widespread grass roots movement of 'return to our roots'—a pendulum swing from the 'turning East' of the 1970s.[17] Paganism is particularly rich in rediscovered

17. H. Cox, *Turning East: The Promise and Peril of the New Orientalism* (London: Allen Lane, 1979).

and reinvented rituals to mark and celebrate seasonal festivals and rites of passage. However, the main pagan praxis is magic, which has a low status in western society compared to Buddhist meditation, being widely viewed as crude and primitive superstition. It has an exotic appeal in some spiritual circles, but is unlikely to gain greater acceptance without modernizing, for example, through psychology or positive thinking. Shamanism, on the other hand, has a range of techniques for healing, self-healing and attaining altered states of consciousness, which are more adaptable to the conditions of contemporary western society. This greater relevance, combined with a freedom from occult trappings and more democratic social structures, may account for the faster growth rate of shamanism than paganism. Pagan doctrine is also somewhat underdeveloped and incoherent compared to Buddhist philosophy and meditation, which provide an ancient yet advanced and relevant spiritual methodology in tune with philosophy, psychology and new science.

Feminism and Women's Spirituality

Women's spirituality is one of the most significant religious trends. All liberal and progressive old and new religions in the West have modernized their attitudes towards women and offer a greater parity in gender roles, including at least some degree of participation in priestly functions. On the whole, women are drawn in greater numbers to these groups, though a minority are attracted by a perceived greater security and clarity in gender roles offered by more conservative groups. Christianity and Buddhism contain a fairly similar spectrum of attitudes ranging from misogyny to equality, though on the whole Western Buddhism at least offers greater opportunity to women for teaching and leadership. There are also some eastern-based NRMs, pre-eminently the Osho movement and the Brahma Kumaris, who actively discriminate in favour of women.[18]

Paganism scores highest of all on gender policy, being the only western religion with a developed thealogy. One of the three principles of the Pagan Federation is: 'Honouring the totality of Divine Reality, which transcends gender, acknowledging both the female and male

18. For detailed accounts of the women's spirituality movement see U. King, *Women and Spirituality: Voices of Protest and Promise* (London: Macmillan, 1989) and Puttick, *Women in New Religions*.

aspects of deity.' In practice this also means that women are given equal or superior spiritual status as priestesses. Wiccan covens are typically headed by a high priest and priestess, but the priestess tends to take precedence. It is also the only religion that contains a specifically, consciously feminist branch: feminist witchcraft, which believes in the supreme power of the Goddess and promotes women in all the key leadership and sacerdotal roles. The appeal of nature religions to women also lies in their praxis. Whatever its practical efficacy, magic can be an important means of personal development and empowerment for women, which is often its main attraction to the disempowered. Shamanism in particular contains ancient yet sophisticated and efficacious techniques for healing and therapy. Some of these, such as soul retrieval and 'journeying', are beginning to be used within mainstream psychotherapy.

Environmentalism and Ecospirituality

The one point all religions are agreed on is the need for an environmental awareness or dimension within spirituality. All world religions, including Christianity, have records of domination and exploitation of the environment legitimated by their theologies but are now busy 'greening' their theologies. Buddhism has a generally less violent history than Christianity, and superior credentials within the peace and environmental movements, advocated in the West particularly by 'engaged' Buddhists. Nature religions have embraced ecospirituality as a central doctrine, reclaiming a mythology evolved from ancient fertility cults and tribal religions, and rituals based on seasonal rites and worship of nature deities. Some pagans and shamans are active in the environmental protest movement. The grounding of nature religions and other NRMs in environmentalism, integrated with other social and gender issues as well as spirituality, could well become an important factor in their survival and growth into the next millennium.

The Future of Religion

One non-politically correct but fundamental question is, Who will win? Whether the New Age and evangelical movements will clash in a final Armageddon that leads to apocalypse, the return of the Dark Ages, or a New Age of sweetness and light, is hard to predict. The shadow of nuclear conflagration has retreated, but been replaced by fear of environmental catastrophe, fuelled not only by manmade destruction and pollution but also by increases in earthquakes, tornadoes and other natural disasters in a world where comets may be once again interpreted as omens.

For the foreseeable future the likeliest outcome is the continued growth of both alternative and fundamentalist religion, accompanied by the continued decline of mainstream Christianity. It may be that there will be no outright winners, but increasing pluralism and globalization, especially among the most popular religions, caught between deconstructive postmodernism and holistic syncretism. Syncretism has traditionally been condemned by theologians, although Christianity has survived partly through its skills in absorbing, borrowing and adapting from other religions and social trends. The New Age and nature religions make a virtue of syncretism, which is the leading mode for the appropriation and development of ideas in our postmodern age.

There are many signs of formal and informal interfaith dialogue between all three traditions, as well as some syncretism, even between pagans and Christians. As one neo-shaman has expressed it, 'Christ was a great shaman, healer and teacher, connected with spirits, possessing extraordinary powers. So I see no contradiction between Christ as avatar and the shamanic tradition.'[19] If a new world religion were to emerge from this new religious consciousness, it would be likely to contain elements of all these strands. It would certainly need to feature mysticism, personal development, social activism, Goddess spirituality and ecospirituality. Yet just as nations refuse to surrender their identity in a greater confederation, so more likely than a grand syncretism of religions is a continuing, increasing diversity. In religion as in nature, diversity is strength.

19. Interview with the author, 16 May 1996.

'AT THE CUTTING EDGE OF WHAT GOD IS DOING': MILLENARIAN ASPECTS OF BRITISH NEO-PENTECOSTALISM

Stephen Hunt

Since 1989, the annual 'Marches for Jesus' have become a familiar sight in Britain's towns and cities. Those involved are largely evangelical Churches, particularly of a charismatic (neo-Pentecostal) persuasion. The motivation for charismatics with such an evangelizing strategy is not merely to bear witness to Christ and the hope of renewal and revival, but reflects a distinct set of eschatological teachings. This is evident in that some of the organizers of the marches have argued that taking to the streets was a way of 'shifting demonic atmospheres': a belief that neighbourhoods, cities and regions of the world are controlled by 'territorial spirits'. These doctrines, often perceived by their critics as curious, unorthodox and even heretical, have increasingly become significant in obvious and sometimes less obvious ways—sometimes spreading beyond the borders of the Charismatic movement to influence non-charismatic mainline Churches.

Not all that take part on such marches are aware of the initial doctrinal impetus behind them. Nonetheless, the 'Marches for Jesus' are indicative of the growing influence that post-millenarianism has had on evangelical quarters in Britain over the last 30 years. Another has been the so-called 'Toronto Blessing'—the esoteric phenomenon that rapidly spread globally through charismatic Churches and impacted on some four thousand Churches in the UK.[1] Even the *Alpha* initiative, the large-scale evangelizing strategy endorsed by thousands of British Churches at the end of the 1990s, belied the tendency of charismatic evangelicals to endorse post-millenarian aspects, since it carried the core themes of revival and renewal and the emphasis upon the charismata, healing and spiritual warfare.

1. This is according to the charismatic-orientated magazine *Alpha*, May 1965, pp. 6, 9.

Like other forms of millenarianism, particularly within the Protestant evangelical community on both sides of the Atlantic, the emergence of post-millenarianism is best explained by two key overlapping considerations. First, the relationship of the Protestant evangelical constituency to its broader social environment. Here, a distinct, largely fundamentalist-orientated movement responds to the immediate and even global context in which it finds itself—making sense and negotiating with the world outside its boundaries.[2] Secondly, post-millenarianism marks the adaptation of evangelicalism to wider social and cultural trends, which help forge particular eschatological scenarios within the broad theme of the coming millennium of Christ. These two factors may seem mutually exclusive but they are not. Rather, they interplay in complex and subtle ways so that biblical references related to the millennium are shaped and moulded by a range of broader social and historical factors.

The Rise, Fall and Return of Post-Millenarianism

Post-millenarianism is merely one expression of Christian millenarianism. Among Protestant evangelicals it has long vied for legitimacy alongside a-millenarianism, and pre-millenarianism, although each has displayed overlapping themes and frequently culled theological constructs from a rival strand. Along with pre-millenarianism, post-millenarianism accepts the literal thousand-year reign of Christ in the coming kingdom of God. Hence, it rejects the a-millenarian position, which insists that the millennium is a symbolic and spiritual concept where the events spoken of in the Scriptures take place in heaven rather than on earth, and which marks the period between Christ's first and second coming.[3] On the other hand, the major departure with pre-millenarianism is that post-millenarianism sees Christ's return before the millennium rather than after it. In contrast to pre-millenarianism then, post-millenarianism presents a far more sanguine, but no less vigorous, eschatological scenario. In particular, it carries the core dogma that the Church will be perfected as the 'bride without blemish' and that evil

2. R. Bellah, F. Masden, W. Sullivan, A. Swidler and S. Tipton, *Habits of the Heart: Individualism and Commitment in American Life* (New York: Harper & Row, 1985).

3. W. Hood, *The Plan of the Apocalypse* (York, PA: Anstadt, 1900), pp. 164-77.

will be overcome at the same time that the ranks of the elect are swelled by a vast worldwide revival.

Although appearing periodically throughout Church history from the third century, post-millenarianism remained largely peripheral to established Christian theology. Where it was to find a home, however, was within factions of Protestant evangelicalism. From the nineteenth century, much like its rivals, it came and went out of fashion according to wider social and cultural circumstances.[4] From the mid-nineteenth to the early twentieth century, for particular historical reasons, post-millenarianism almost supplanted pre-millenarianism as the commonly received doctrine in the USA and considerably influenced Protestant evangelical thinking in Europe. The subsequent decline of post-millenarianism by the early twentieth century was no less due to a further set of historical transformations.[5]

The short-lived popularity of post-millenarianism was a result of a number of factors. First, post-millenarianism was squeezed out in the fundamentalist versus liberal debate.[6] By the late nineteenth century many of the core doctrines of post-millenarianism became increasingly difficult to sustain in the light of biblical studies (particularly those conducted in the German universities). The main critique was that the Bible yielded no single eschatology and that the highly dualistic theology espoused by post-millenarianism was an aberration from the main direction of biblical thought.[7] Moreover, in the eyes of conservative theologians its inherent optimism concerning a worldwide revival appeared to concede too much to modernity and all its ills. Simultaneously, the erosion of post-millenarianism was part of the waning perceptions of the supernatural in the same modernity. The rejection of apocalypticism within liberal theological thinking meant that rationality superseded the supernatural. From the liberal viewpoint then, post-millenarianism retained too much precritical biblicism and antiquated supernaturalism.

4. C. Patrides, 'Renaissance and Modern Thought on the Last Things: A Study in Changing Conceptions', *HTR* 93 (1958), pp. 169-86.

5. L. Chafer, 'Foreword', in C.L. Feinberg (ed.), *Millennialism* (Chicago: Malstrom, 1936).

6. J. Moorhead, 'The Erosion of Postmillenialism in American Religious Thought, 1865–1892', *Church History* 53 (1984), p. 76.

7. J. Carpenter, *The Bible in the Nineteenth Century* (London: Molbray, 1963).

Post-millenarianism also looked increasingly implausible because events had stubbornly refused to follow its scenario. The modern world was becoming profoundly secular and secularized, and disbelief and scepticism became the hallmarks of the emergent culture. Above all, revival was not forthcoming. It simply was not the case that evangelism was winning. Rather, the evangelical cause became increasingly socially and politically peripheral and found itself reduced to almost a relic in a lost world. This marginalization and resultant pessimism increasingly fed off a wider cultural despair that was wrought by global conflicts, revolutionary upheavals and the economic disasters of the early twentieth century.[8] Much of this fulfilled the teachings of one of the principal early exponents of dispensational pre-millenarianism, John Nelson Darby (founder of the Brethren movement), who espoused its innate pessimism by claiming that the second coming of Christ would be preceded by 'wars and rumours of wars', of global plagues and famines, moral depravity and religious decline. As a result of these developments post-millenarianism was overtaken, once again, by pre-millenarianism as the most legitimate eschatological framework among Protestant evangelicals. This was especially the case in North America, where pre-millenarianism's principal precepts become eulogized in the Schofield version of the Bible and were enshrined in the constitution of numerous fundamentalist Churches.

Throughout the second half of the twentieth century there was much to sustain the theological hegemony of pre-millenarianism. After all, for the first time the world threatened to be ended, not from natural forces, but from nuclear weapons and manmade environmental catastrophe.[9] However, during these decades post-millenarianism appeared to have gained a new lease of life among Protestant evangelicals, especially within the Charismatic movement that had grown rapidly on a global scale since the 1960s. This is not to say that all Pentecostals are post-millenarian, nevertheless the movement has been the major carrier of the core doctrines. Indeed, the impressive dissemination of post-millenarianism, albeit in different forms and through various theological trajectories within the broad contemporary Pentecostal movement means that, in terms of Christian eschatology, it is increasingly the success story of the modern or even post-modern world.

8. P. Creelan, 'Watson as Mythmaker: The Millenarian Sources of Watsonian Behaviour', *JSSR* 24.2 (1985), pp. 194-216.

9. M. Barkun, 'Divided Apocalypse', *Soundings* 65 (1983), pp. 257-80.

In the UK, it might be argued, there was much in the emergent Charismatic Renewal movement of the 1960s that implicitly and sometimes inadvertently carried some of the key tenets of post-millenarianism; those of revival, renewal and the return of the charismata to the Church. In addition, many Renewalists, in a self-reflective way, saw the Charismatic movement as a sign of the Last Days. Like the Latter Day movement that seceded from the established Pentecostal Churches in the 1940s and 1950s, revival and renewal were believed to be an indication of God pouring out the Holy Spirit before Christ's second coming. However, while the Renewal movement evolved some post-millenarian themes, a more explicit articulation came through UK Restorationism, which may even have predated the rise of its cousin in the mainstream Churches. In terms of its impetus, the Restorationist movement peaked in the mid-1980s, somewhat later than its denominational counterparts. However, its impact upon the wider charismatic scene was significant, not least of all in the influence of its pronounced post-millenarian doctrines.

This was not, however, the end of the story. Throughout the 1980s and 1990s, both Churches within the mainline denominations, and those of the various streams of the 'New' Churches that evolved out of Restorationism, were significantly influenced by teachings from the USA. Above all, there were the innovating doctrines of contrasting strands of dominion theology and especially the Third Wave movement. The latter, epitomized by the late John Wimber's Association of Vineyard Churches, impacted upon the neo-Pentecostal scene in Britain in the 1990s in no uncertain terms, not least of all through the 'Toronto Blessing'. Yet even the 'Blessing', as it was more colloquially known, has proved to be part of the on-going impression of post-millenarianism upon the Charismatic movement. This development, however, was by no means limited to Britain. Indeed, on a global scale Vineyard and similar ministries and confederations of Churches born within Third Wave theology have proved to be among the most significant movements in the contemporary Christian Church. This was so even in the USA where they have come to increasingly rival the hegemony of pre-millenarian fundamentalism.

Neo-Pentecostalism and Post-Millenarianism

This rise of post-millenarianism in the second half of the twentieth century, as in the mid-nineteenth century, could be attributed to specific developments that largely related to the wider cultural milieu and the response of evangelicalism to profound social and political changes. There was something unique about post-millenarianism in reacting to these changes. While millenarianism in terms of apocalyptic or 'end time' thinking is central, indeed imperative to the more fundamentalist and sectarian expressions of Protestantism, post-millenarianism has continued to prove that it can steer a course between espousing a reactionary fundamentalism and worldly accommodation by endorsing wider social trends and cultural developments.

Nineteenth-century post-millenarianism contained both reactionary and modernizing components and may be interpreted as taking a middle way between conservative and liberal theology. Essentially, it was a form of millenarianism that sustained a view of history that was characterized by both a belief in supernatural events and one that embraced natural laws of organic development and mirrored ideas of secular progress, optimism and rationalism. If pre-millenarianism reflected the trauma and upheavals of the modern world, to some extent at least, post-millenarianism reflected the hope of progress and the spirit of Enlightenment.[10] Symbolic of this was that early advocates, such as Jonathan Edwards and other revivalists, could provide frightening sermons of God's wrath and eternal perdition, but were not opposed to science, critical rationality and the faith in progress.[11]

10. Neither was the triumph of secular progress lost on the advocates of a-millenarianism, at least in the nineteenth century. A-millenarianism took a position between post and pre-millenarianism and looked towards the world with neither extreme optimism nor extreme pessimism. Here, progress is neither inevitable nor impossible. A-millenarianism frequently perceived a series of cycles through Church history that, more often than not, involved increased satanic activity. It has frequently fitted well into the Protestant Reformed tradition in that the Reformation itself signified a cycle of restoration and revealed truths. As Fulop shows for the black evangelical movement of the nineteenth century, a-millenarianism did not translate into a quietism or withdraw from social criticism. History is divinely ordained, moving towards its fulfilment, but allowed blacks to make sense of their history and allowed criticism of white Christian America (T. Fulop, ' "The Future Golden Day of the Race": Millennialism and Black Americans in the Nadir, 1877–1901', *HTR* 84.1 [1991], pp. 75-99).

11. A. Walker, 'Thoroughly Modern: Sociological Reflections on the Charismatic Movement from the End of the Twentieth Century', in S. Hunt, M. Hamilton and T. Walter (eds.), *Charismatic Christianity: Sociological Perspectives* (Basingstoke: Macmillan, 1997), pp. 17-42.

While post-millenarianism carried the liberal's preoccupation with optimism, it did not conspire to demythologize the Scriptures in an attempt to retain any plausibility for the disenchanted modern world. A hard residue of apocalyptic thought was sustained. Indeed, translated into Christian eschatology, progress was expressed through revival and the conversion of souls in order to bring the millennium about. In short, the saints were to be coworkers in the creation of the New Jerusalem.[12] The major thrust of post-millenarianism was to postpone history's cataclysmic end until after the millennium and therefore allowed the Church an interval necessary for the gradual evangelical conquest of the world. In turn, this reflected economic and political changes, in particular, economic expansion and a widespread ideology of social and political egalitarianism that was expressed through its Armenianism and its ecclesiastic disestablishmentarianism. Post-millenarianism therefore engendered the proliferation of voluntary societies to support domestic and foreign missions, establish evangelical colleges, promote temperance and launch public campaigns to enforce the Sabbath.

Like their nineteenth-century predecessors, the post-millenarians of the latter half of the twentieth century have been Janus-faced in being both fundamentalist and world-affirming. While displaying the clear fundamentalist credentials of a literal interpretation of Scripture, a profound dualism, and frequently a tendency towards exclusivism, post-millenarianism also takes on some modernizing tendencies. This explains, to a great degree, why it has been carried by the neo-Pentecostal movement and, arguably, why neo-Pentecostalism has become the rump faction of UK evangelicalism, while conservative evangelicals have spiralled into decline. Hence, unlike the 'classical' Pentecostals of earlier years,[13] the coteries of neo-Pentecostals have not been afraid of the new and innovating in terms of new technologies and cultural adaptation, at least as long as they could be moulded into a distinct world-view.

As in the nineteenth century, then, the new variety of neo-Pentecostalism rides the contours of the early twenty-first century. At one level this world-accommodating stance indicated a further development within the broader process of secularization, in that fundamentalist factions are faced with making some concessions to the contemporary

12. Moorhead, 'The Erosion of Postmillenialism', pp. 61, 73.
13. B. Wilson, *Patterns of Sectarianism* (London: Heineman, 1967).

world if they are not to be forced into decline and even oblivion.[14] Accommodation to the contemporary world has eased the tensions that exist because of the growing incongruities Protestant evangelicalism has faced in modernity and has allowed participation in society through cognitive bargaining. Yet this is by no means a straightforward process and there are stark contradictions and incongruities. There is, simultaneously, both a sectarian/fundamentalist backlash and compromising inclinations.

Although compromise might be a general tendency within the fundamentalist evangelical constituency, there is a distinctiveness about Pentecostalism in forging a post-millenarian scenario culled from both reactionary and worldly themes. This predilection is not merely limited to the context of advanced industrial societies. Hence, there is something innate relating to latter-day Pentecostalism that allows it to be perceptible to post-millenarian themes, in short, its cultural adaptability. As David Martin suggests, the strength of the Pentecostal movement on a global basis lies in the way that it has responded to the cultural environment in which it is embedded. More implicitly, Pentecostalism is best understood as *both* a reaction against society, and at the same time a product of it, and continually adaptive to its trends.[15] The reason for this, as Harvey Cox points out, is its fluid theology. To put it succinctly, Pentecostalism provides pliability derived from the emphasis upon the charismata and spiritual experience, which has rendered the theology frequently open to reinterpretation.[16] In many areas of the world, then, the march of Pentecostalism could partly be attributed to its syncretic tendencies, which allowed some principal tenets of fundamentalist dogma to be merged with cultural themes, which, in turn, appealed to the needs of particular social collectives.

14. D. Bebbington, *Evangelicalism in Modern Britain* (London: Cambridge University Press, 1989); J. Hunter, *American Evangelicalism: Conservative Religion and the Quandary of Modernity* (New Brunswick, NJ: Rutgers University Press, 1983).

15. D. Martin, *Tongues of Fire: The Explosion of Pentecostalism in Latin America* (Oxford: Basil Blackwell, 1990).

16. H. Cox, *Fire from Heaven: The Rise of Pentecostal Spirituality and the Reshaping of Religion in the Twenty-First Century* (Reading, MA: Addison-Wesley, 1994), p. 216.

UK Restorationism

So how have neo-Pentecostals merged fundamentalism with worldly accommodation in such a way as to forge distinctly post-millenarian themes? The answer is by no means straightforward. Certainly, it is not merely observable in terms of the apparently inevitable transformation of sectarianism into more complaisant forms of Christianity. Indeed, there has always existed among Pentecostals in western societies a confluence of reactionary predispositions and cultural adaptation. At first this might not seem obvious. In many respects the early expressions of neo-Pentecostalism in the UK appeared to be overtly reactionary and sectarian. This was perhaps not so evident with the Renewal movement in the established denominations, but the more virulent strain of post-millenarianism in the form of British Restorationism. Developing from the independent fellowships, such as those of Sidney Purse and G.W. North, Restorationist factions developed sectarian characteristics and embraced a theology that was aggressive and challenging to those outside its boundaries. Unlike the 'little remnant' mentality of pre-millenarianism, the Restorationists believed that God would not let his Church be swamped by sin or the devil. On the contrary, God would restore the Church to her original splendour not only by imparting upon her the full power of the charismatic gifts, but also equipping her with the government and ordinances of God's kingdom.[17]

Restorationism was influenced by different theological traditions, including classical Pentecostalism, Edward Irving's Catholic Apostolic Church, the Brethren movement and the overarching theological inspiration of Arthur Wallis.[18] At the same time its was inspired by theological strands from the USA, especially those espoused by Derek Prince and other members of the group known as the 'Fort Lauderdale Five'.[19] These theological threads fused to provide early Restorationism

17. A. Walker, *Restoring the Kingdom: The Radical Christianity of the House Church Movement* (Guildford: Eagle, 1998), p. 138. In the USA, Restorational teachings are emphasized in several Charismatic groupings, including a nation-wide network of Churches known as the People of Destiny International, and the North Carolina-based National Leadership Conference (E. Pousson, 'A "Great Century" of Pentecostal/ Charismatic Renewal and Mission', *Pneuma* 16.1 [1994], p. 96).

18. Walker, *Restoring the Kingdom*, pp. 228-67.

19. Walker, *Restoring the Kingdom*, pp. 92-101.

with overtly sectarian credentials. Not least of all was the Restorationists' claim that they were restoring the pattern of New Testament Christianity. This included a form of religiosity that rigorously circumscribed every aspect of the believer's existence and drew strict boundaries between life in what was perceived as the restored Church and the emerging kingdom, on the one hand, and the outside world, 'Babylon', on the other.

Perhaps above all it was the eschatology developed by Restorationism that belied its inherent sectarianism. In fact, Andrew Walker has argued that *the* key to understanding the emergence and significance of the Restorationist movement was its eschatology—a Last Days scenario in which the early Restorationists saw themselves at the forefront of God's plans. The Restorationists interpreted the Renewal movement as just a few showers of 'blessing' before the real deluge of the Holy Spirit in the end times, but believed that their movement would mark the final move of God and would take on a concrete expression through unique ecclesiastical structures. The kingdom would not be of this world but would exist as an alternative society, run according to God's rules by his people. Despite the apostasy of the historical Church, the kingdom of God was destined to be restored. Denominations would be abolished and the new Church would establish a substantial and glorious witness to the power and holiness of God. His people in the Last Days would prosper and become victorious over their enemies. The rest of the world would begin to disintegrate and look on in wonder.[20] The role of the Church led by the Restorationists, therefore, was to usher in the kingdom of God prior to the historical return of Christ to earth.

As Walker points out, Restorationism moved from sectarianism to 'New Church' in a rapid period of time. This suggested that the sociological principle that over a period of time sects tend to undergo transformation to denominations, was a process that was speeding up in the late twentieth century.[21] This is not to say, however, that more sectarian forms of New Church, such as Bryn Jones's Community Church and the intentional community of the Jesus Fellowship, do not remain. Nonetheless, such Churches have opened themselves up to a wider popular

20. Walker, *Restoring the Kingdom*, p. 139.

21. Walker, *Restoring the Kingdom*, pp. 262-66. This theory of sect development is probably most associated with the work of Neibuhr (H. Neibuhr, *The Social Sources of Denominationalism* [New York: World Publishing, 1929]).

appeal. As the Restorationist Churches developed organizational structures, they become less theologically exclusive, ecumenical, and sensitive to utilizing business-growth strategies and wider cultural developments in order to retain appeal and evangelizing outreaches. They also came to befriend their neo-Pentecostal counterparts in the denominations. In turn, the denominational charismatics adopted at least some of the practices and theology of the New Churches to the extent that the differences between them could scarcely be discerned.

Yet to argue that somehow early Restorationism was 'outside of culture' would be misleading. In the 1970s, Restorationism was undoubtedly one of the most successful contemporary forms of religiosity in Britain. There were good reasons for this. From one perspective the post-millenarianism it advanced reflected developments in the so-called New Religious Movements (NRMs). At a time of a decline of established religions the new, often syncretic, forms of religiosity filled the vacuum. Eileen Barker argues along these lines when she speaks of the attractions of the new religions to those who sought a dynamic expression of faith. The successful new religions were often those who were attractive in terms of what they offered the individual believer, especially by way of human fulfilment. What such new forms of religiosity had in common was the promise of community and a sense of belonging, of creativity, self-development, religious experience and the endeavour to build one variety or another of the kingdom of heaven on earth.[22] Moreover, the theme of overcoming the forces of darkness and the expected mass revival central to Restorationism was indicative of the triumphalism and success-orientated philosophies of so many of the forms of NRMs.

Many of these tendencies became even more apparent in the way that the New Churches were transformed in the 1980s. There was much that mirrored the development of so many new forms of religiosity which have emerged against the backdrop of the entrepreneurial culture.[23] Hence, as Harvey Cox has observed, the preoccupation with Church growth, rather like the compulsion for business expansion, appears to be a necessary condition for many neo-Pentecostal congregations and is itself a legacy of the enterprise culture. The 'designer Church', bearing

22. E. Barker, *New Religious Movements: A Practical Introduction* (London: HMSO, 1992), pp. 25-31.

23. R. Roberts, 'Religion and the "Enterprise Culture": The British Experience and the Thatcher Era (1979–1990)', *Social Compass* 39.1 (1992), pp. 15-33.

all the distinguishing features of success, is an essential imperative; a modern building, of large and ever-growing congregations, plenty of funds and the like are very often the hallmarks by which contemporary Churches are judged and the image frequently flaunted by neo-Pentecostalism.[24]

The Third Wave

As Restorationism in its pure form declined, other expressions of post-millenarianism, mostly from the USA, influenced the UK neo-Pentecostal scene. The most significant was the Third Wave movement. Here, the most important figure, at least in the UK charismatic milieu, was undoubtedly the late John Wimber, who headed the Association of Vineyard Churches. His link with leading members of the Charismatic movement in Britain and the distinct doctrines that he espoused meant that his impact could never be underestimated. Mainline charismatics, particularly Anglicans, and those New Churches, such as New Frontiers and the Pioneers, took on board Wimber's kingdom theology in no uncertain way. His impact was particularly significant not only because his doctrines frequently overlapped with theirs, but because he advanced the extra dimension of 'signs and wonders' through healing, exorcisms and various esoteric phenomena. Moreover, these ideas impacted at a time when the Charismatic movement, both denominational and New Church, was beginning to stagnate.

It is usual to place Wimber's own kingdom theology within the context of what came to be known as the Third Wave movement. Much like Restorationism, Third Wave dogma encompasses a distinct elucidation of Church history and is typical of the growing tendency of neo-Pentecostal groups to see themselves as reflecting the will of God in a more advanced and dynamic form. This was tantamount to constructing a theological framework that advanced a fresh rendering of Church history. Again this reflected a wider tendency among new forms of religion. Such sociologists as Jim Beckford and Richard Fenn[25] have argued that a major characteristic of modern forms of religiosity in late industrial society or, for Fenn, the postmodern world, is that religious

24. Cox, *Fire from Heaven*, p. 272.

25. J. Beckford, *Religion and Advanced Industrial Society* (London: Unwin Hyman, 1989); R. Fenn, 'Pre-modern Religion in the Postmodern World: A Response to Professor Zylerberg', *Social Compass* 37.1 (1990), pp. 96-105.

chronicles may be reinvented. The speed of social change and decline of cultural continuity breeds an ignorance of history, including religious history. In turn, new narratives are constructed by which religious collectives frequently perceive themselves as restoring, reforming or reviving the true faith.

The Third Wave movement epitomized such developments. As articulated by one of its leading exponents, Peter Wagner,[26] the Third Wave was meant to describe the beginning of the third great out-pouring of the Holy Spirit for revival in the twentieth century. The First Wave was identified as the rise of classical Pentecostalism. After centuries of complacency and spiritual powerlessness the Church was understood to be emerging with the power of the Holy Spirit and an enlightened comprehension of its historical role. Wagner interpreted the Second Wave as a major working of God among evangelicals, from the early 1960s, in the form of the Charismatic Renewal movement. This evidently brought many mainline Churches into line with the will and purpose of God. The Third Wave was identified as originating around 1980. The evidence of this was believed to be observable in the uniting of charismatics and traditional evangelicals as the essential core of the 'true' Church that would precipitate a global revival before the second coming of Christ. Wagner made it clear that such international Church organizations as Vineyard were more in tune with God's plan and at the 'cutting edge' of what God was supposed to be doing at the end of the second millennium.

The post-millenarian theme of Vineyard has been played out on more than one occasion. At the beginning of the 1990s, the British Charismatic movement had become preoccupied with the spiritual gift of prophecy, which was largely perceived as a specialized ministry returning to the Church. This concern with prophecy was largely initiated by Vineyard, which, in turn, was influenced by the self-designated circle of prophets that came to be known as the Kansas City Prophets (KCP). The KCP claimed a unique prophetic insight into the purposes of God in the next generation that included the outpouring of the Holy Spirit in an unprecedented manner as a prelude to the coming of Christ. The KCP predicted that there were 40 years left before the second coming of Christ. During this time, they argued, the elite believers of the 'Latter Rain' would perform signs and wonders, stretching out their hands to

26. P. Wagner, *The Third Wave of the Holy Spirit* (Ann Arbor, MI: Servant Press, 1988).

immobilize the enemies of Christ and would gain power in the nations to prepare for the second coming of the messiah.

In the early 1990s, Wimber, in association with Paul Cain and other members of the KCPs, espoused erroneous prophecies of a worldwide revival commencing in London. In 1990, the KCP ministered to a representative gathering of leaders of both mainline and New Churches at Holy Trinity, Brompton. In the Dockland arena in London a meeting was meant to signify the revival which was predicted to spread across the world as possibly the last great move of God. True to the psychology of cognitive dissonance, there followed elaborate attempts to explain why the revival had not occurred. John Wimber's reputation was seriously damaged by his association with the KCP, nonetheless since the early 1980s his specialist interests—whether healing or prophecy—had caught the attention of UK charismatics. The Toronto Blessing proved to be the final episode in Wimber's colourful and controversial ministry.[27]

Theological Dualism

Like Restorationism, the Third Wave movement is both fundamentalist and world accommodating. The fundamentalist element is discernible in its profound dualism. Dualist theological constructs are an integral element of millenarian dogma, whatever the precise rendition, in that the activities of Satan and his minions are given significant recognition. However, post-millenarianism, through its neo-Pentecostal prism, has tended towards a distinctive dualism and the creation of a world-view that insists that there exists two mutually exclusive realms of good and evil.[28] In Restorationism there was the overarching belief that as the

27. D. McBain and S. Hunt, 'Mainline Charismatics: Some Observations of Baptist Renewal', in Hunt, Hamilton and Walter (eds.), *Charismatic Christianity*, pp. 43-59.

28. S. Hunt, 'The Devil's Advocates: Demonology, Deviance and Religious Pluralism', in M. Percy (ed.), *Fundamentalism, Church and Society* (London: Cassells, forthcoming). The historical relationship between the perception of the demonic as largely responsible for the evil that confronted the Church was dominant, although not exclusively so, for some five centuries. Womack argues that it may chiefly be attributable to the experience of persecution and the relationship with the outside, often pagan, world (D. Womack, 'Divine Healing in the Post-Apostolic Age', *Paracete* 2.2 [1968], pp. 28-35 (34). A similar conclusion can be made concerning the nascent Charismatic movement in the mid-1960s. Facing

kingdom of God began to rapidly grow before the second coming of Christ, so it would meet with great opposition from the powers of darkness. Indeed, the very establishment of God's alternative society, it was argued, would inevitably polarize the world into the forces of good and evil.[29] The theology of the Third Wave went further. It articulated a more detailed demonology and infused an obsession with some UK neo-Pentecostals that bordered upon the paranoid.

Frequently, the near-total preoccupation with all things demonic was to discover the reality of the supernatural and marked a reaction against a secular and rational world that stubbornly resisted the prediction of an impending revival. This was certainly evident in John Wimber's teachings. Wimber insisted that it was necessary for the Church to harness God's power in order to be rescued from its impotence and numerical decline. As part of the dualist construct the 'Holy War' had a central place and constituted the relentless struggle between the forces of good and the powers of darkness. Taking the tone from the earlier theology of C.H. Kraft,[30] Wimber insisted that it was imperative for the Church to rediscover the supernatural and the reality of the demonic. The failings of the evangelizing endeavour into the Third World was, according to Wimber, because of satanic opposition and he claimed that this was also the case in western societies where the demonic influence appeared as rational scepticism.[31] The acceptance of Wimber's teachings by many UK charismatics meant that post-millenarianism, in the late twentieth century, developed into a war with the demonic that has been transformed into an action-orientated belief system which often looked

opposition from established Church hierarchies, it forged the imagery where a benevolent God had always been accompanied by the perception of an on-going warfare between the supernatural forces of good and the forces of evil (M. Neitz, *Charisma and Community: A Study of Religious Commitment within Charismatic Renewal* [Oxford: Transaction Books, 1987]).

29. Most Restorationists believed that the secret rapture of the Church that allows the saints to miss the tribulation, so popular with the pre-millenarians, was an unfounded biblical inference. Rather, the so-called 'great tribulation' was to be endured by the saints before the second coming of Christ. Restorationists, however, believed that the kingdom of God, which will be attacked by the Antichrist and his forces, would withstand all opposition as it was ushered in by the restored Church.

30. C. Kraft, *Christianity with Power: Your Worldview and your Experience of the Supernatural* (Ann Arbor, MI: Servant Press, 1989).

31. J. Wimber, 'John Wimber Calls It Power Evangelism', *Charisma* (September 1985), pp. 26-34.

rather like the fantasy game of *Dungeons and Dragons* played out through a kind virtual reality Bible writ large. The imperative was to hasten the kingdom of God, to bring mass revival by actively forcing back and overcoming the powers of darkness through aggressive spiritual warfare.

This theological cauldron was also influenced by the cultural dynamics of globalization. As Albrow points out, in the contemporary global context religion becomes a 'cultural site', since, in any social order, it can be influenced by the ebbs and flows of various expressions of religiosity across the world, which subsequently generate infinite variations and localized expressions of faith.[32] In turn, the interchange of cultural genres may generate complex currents of mix 'n' match religiosity.[33] This has had significance for the theology developed by post-millenarianism, since it has come to embrace religious dogma outside its immediate western cultural milieu and perhaps alien to orthodox Christianity.

Hinting at the consequences of globalization, Hiebert[34] argues that the western world has witnessed the return of forms of animism which have also come to influence the contemporary Church to the extent of subverting traditional Christianity. Cox similarly maintains that, in common with other NRMs, neo-Pentecostalism embraces a world-view where events are guided by spirits, ancestors, ghosts, magic and witchcraft.[35] This may be most clearly displayed not only in forms of animism, but the attempt at the metaphysical manipulation of concealed natural or spiritual forces. Put succinctly, Pentecostalism has succumbed to new theologies that have the effect of enhancing numerical growth of the movement, but at the expense of conventional theology. As Cox succinctly puts it, in the West the movement has a preoccupation with dominion theology, an excessive demonology and a constant reference to the spiritual world impinging upon this one in a way that borrows heavily from non-Christian religions and New Age teachings accompanied by various expressions of shamanism.[36]

32. M. Albrow, 'Globalization', in R. Brym (ed.), *New Society: Sociology for the 21st Century* (Toronto: Harcourt Brace, 1995), pp. 1-25 (20).

33. M. Featherstone, 'Introduction', in *The Global Culture: Nationalism, Globalization and Modernity* (London: Sage, 1990), p. 10.

34. P. Hiebert, 'The Flaw of the Excluded Middle', *Missiology: An International View* 10.1 (1982), pp. 35-47.

35. Cox, *Fire from Heaven*, p. 281.

36. Cox, *Fire from Heaven*, p. 213. The 'prayer warrior' has developed into a

Worldly Accommodation

There is still more to the post-millenarian equation à la Third Wave. Wimber's kingdom theology advanced the view that, as part of eschatological developments, God was providing the saints with new insights into not only the demonic, but prophecy and healing. Some of these themes followed the trajectories of contemporary western culture. Perhaps above all, much is indicative of David Martin's claim that the proliferation of Pentecostalism in the West is due to a culture of mass consumption and the participation in a 'free spiritual market'.[37] The preoccupation with Church growth, which so excited both mainstream and New Church charismatics, epitomized much. In the late 1970s, many took notice of the teachings of Donald McGavran at California's Fuller Theological Seminary. The strategy for Church growth he endorsed was not so much an art as a science. McGavran called for concessions to cultural traditions and endorsed the virtues of the academic disciplines of psychology and sociology.[38] Wimber adopted such teachings of Church growth but they became enmeshed with issues of divine power through his emphasis upon 'signs and wonders', including healing and exorcisms, and the enduring theme of revival. In turn, this emphasis on divine power reflected the tendency of modern evangelism, particularly in the USA, to become preoccupied with notions of power.

specialized ministry as a result of the influence of dominion theology, particularly those inspired by the teachings of Peter Wagner. As part of spiritual warfare, 'prayer warriors' can fight against satanic forces, pray for the sins of nations, or for the repercussions of ancestral sins (see, e.g., C. Jacobs, *Possessing the Gates of the Enemy* [London: Marshall Pickering, 1992]). There are those intercessors who pray from the top rooms of skyscrapers in order to be closer to the spiritual realm, while in Paul Yonggi Cho's Church in Korea (allegedly the world's largest Church) hundreds of intercessors pray 24 hours a day, 365 days a year, to break 'spiritual bondages' across the globe. Those Christians especially trained in discerning the 'spiritual atmosphere' claim to ascertain whether demonic forces are present. This can either be through divine revelation or by reading historical books and discovering the sins committed over previous generations that lead to an area succumbing to prostitution, drugs, crime, homosexuality and so forth. Whole neighbourhoods of cities can be explored with a procedure that is sometimes referred to as 'spiritual mapping'.

37. Martin, *Tongues of Fire*, p. 52.

38. D. McGavran, *Understanding Church Growth* (Grand Rapids: Eerdmans, 1970).

Forbes interprets this development as reflecting contemporary cultural values, which place considerable emphasis upon social, economic and political aspects of power.[39] In charismatic Churches, power may be seen in terms of the realization of success; of winning converts and success in the religious marketplace. Signs and wonders were an integral part of this.

At the same time, there are other clear concessions that neo-Pentecostalism has made to modern culture in the spiritual marketplace that have clear parallels with other NRMs. Perhaps the most obvious has been the development of a narcissistic and individualistic form of Christianity that tended to merge religious beliefs with contemporary concepts of health and healing. As Jim Beckford has impressively argued, modern forms of religiosity frequently attempt to conflate spiritual growth and the western cultural value of personal growth and healing at the level of the individual development, culture and the cosmos.[40] In many such new expressions of religiosity, human beings are perceived as moving towards a cosmic perfection within the context of an unfolding drama, and are frequently the recipients of the attention of supernatural forces or beings. These themes lent themselves well to the proactive dimension of human potential, which is among the key attractions that the new religions offer the adherent. In particular, there is the promise of being successful by unlocking alleged spiritual powers dormant in the individual (albeit couched in spiritual terms with the accent upon charisma) with conversion as the essential starting point for personal growth and fulfilling potential.[41]

In neo-Pentecostal circles, teachings of human potential are translated into a form of spiritual perfectionism and cleansing that dovetail with the post-millenarian precept that Christ would return to a Church unblemished, his purified bride. Hence, for charismatics the inner cleansing of the emotions and the eradication of 'demons' from God's saints reflects the preference for therapeutic techniques. These healing strategies clearly appealed to the core middle-class values of charismatic congregations, which essentially combined utilitarian and expressive styles and addressed emotional and psychological maladies. The

39. M. Forbes, *The Religion of Power* (Grand Rapids: Zondervan, 1983), pp. 17, 76.

40. J. Beckford, 'Holistic Imagery and Ethics in New Religious Healing Movements', *Social Compass* 31.2-3 (1984), pp. 259-73.

41. Beckford, 'Holistic Imagery', p. 267.

merging with post-millenarian themes again comes into clear relief, in that spiritual warfare is transformed into a power encounter between the forces of light and 'demons' that afflict the saints; demons of spoilt relationships, past traumas, and preconversion sexual misdemeanors.[42]

If such themes meant that post-millenarianism lent itself well to the cultural idioms of modernity, there have also been developments that hint at accommodation to the emergence of a postmodernity. In terms of religiosity, one of the themes that appears to be peculiarly conducive to the growth of innovating new religions is the emphasis upon individualistic religious experience.[43] In its contemporary guise, such experience has increasingly been transformed into a kind of religious commodity.[44] By the late twentieth century neo-Pentecostalism appeared to exploit and repackage some key characteristics of classical Pentecostalism, to which had been added the experience of the novel and the experiential. The Toronto Blessing exemplified much since it seemed to be encoded with the re-enchantment of the world that typifies postmodernity.[45]

In the mid-1990s, the Toronto Blessing spread rapidly throughout numerous charismatic Churches and others previously untouched by the charismatic movement. One in ten Churches in the UK was involved to one degree or another. The 'Blessing' became associated primarily with outbursts of uncontrolled, if not hysterical laughter during Church services. While some members of a congregation sank to the floor 'slain in the Spirit', allegedly under the power of God, others claimed to experience 'a spiritual drunkenness'—hysterical laughter or slurred speech and uncontrollable spasms of the limbs, gentle weeping, running on the spot and the 'Toronto Twitch'. This was accompanied by claims of experiencing prophecies and visions. At a leading charismatic Anglican

42. S. Hunt, 'Letting the Devil Get More than his Due. Some Problems with the Deliverance Ministry', in A. Walker (ed.), *Harmful Religion* (London: SPCK, 1997), pp. 43-65; *idem*, 'Managing the Demonic: Neo-Pentecostal Deliverance Ministries', *Journal of Contemporary Religion* 13.2 (1998), pp. 215-30.

43. W. Roof and W. McKinney, *American Mainline Religion: Its Changing Shape and Future* (New Brunswick, NJ: Rutgers University Press, 1987).

44. R. Warner, 'Work in Progress towards a New Paradigm for the Sociological Study of Religion in the United States', *American Journal of Sociology* 98 (1993), pp. 1044-93.

45. P. Freston, 'Charismatic Evangelicals in Latin America: Mission and Politics on the Frontiers of Protestant Growth', in Hunt, Hamilton and Walter (eds.), *Charismatic Christianity*, pp. 184-204.

Church, several individuals claimed visions of large angelic figures bathed in orange light.[46] Much was symbolic of how heaven had the appearance of continuity with the present life, in what was developing into an over-realized post-millenarian eschatology.

To be sure, the Toronto Blessing was many things and several explanations have been forwarded to explain its appearance. One was that charismatics were investing in a new enterprise of esoteric phenomena for their share of a relatively static religious market, or at least safeguarding the gains that had been made in terms of numerical growth.[47] Another was that in return for sometimes travelling long distances to experience the Toronto Blessing and surrendering to God, the psychological 'reward' was a range of subjective esoteric experiences.[48] These explanations, however, do not explain the significance of the theological framework in which the Blessing was cast. The expectation of revival placed it firmly within the post-millenarian framework. Admittedly, as the Toronto Blessing developed it was not clear whether those involved believed that a revival was occurring or whether the 'true elect' was merely being repaired for an imminent revival. Nevertheless, revival and the arrival of the kingdom of God were the key theological constructs. In the words of a leading figure of the Vineyard organization at the time; the Church was experiencing renewal for 'probably the greatest harvest in the world...we could be moving towards the last move of God...the real power is coming. God is just saying get used to it...'[49]

Conclusion

I have argued that, as in the nineteenth century, the late twentieth century and early twenty-first century variant of post-millenarianism has been contingent upon the social and cultural forces that have shaped it.

46. S. Hunt, 'The "Toronto Blessing". A Rumour of Angels', *Journal of Contemporary Religion* 10.3 (1995), pp. 271-80.

47. P. Richter, 'God Is Not a Gentleman', in S.E. Porter and P. Richter (eds.), *The Toronto Blessing: Or Is It?* (London: Darton, Longman & Todd, 1995), pp. 5-37.

48. M. Percy, 'The Toronto Blessing', *Latimer Studies* 53/54 (Oxford: Latimer House, 1996).

49. J. Arnott, 'Receiving the Spirit's Power' (audio tape, Toronto Airport Vineyard, June 1994).

To be sure, post-millenarianism twentieth century-style does display some overlaps with the variant a century earlier. This is both in terms of theological structures and the cultural dynamics that have helped forge its central doctrines—not least of all its abounding optimism. At the same time, however, there is something unique about post-millenarianism in the UK that reflects the marginalized position of the evangelical constituency from the second half of the twentieth century. This marginalization could have been reflected in various ways. UK neo-Pentecostals have inclined towards a preference for esoteric expressions of millenarianism above aggressively confronting the contemporary world. Hence, it has tended to be apolitical. In contrast, in the USA, post-millenarianism could become as politically active as pre-millenarianism. Since the 1970s in the USA, fundamentalism has gone through a significant rebirth after decades of marginalization that so many evangelical groups suffered between the ending of prohibition and the mid-1970s.[50] From that time, fundamentalism came out from the periphery and challenged social ills. Many clung doggedly to pre-millenarian precepts.[51] However, this political dimension was also

50. G. Kedal, *The Revenge of God: The Resurgence of Islam, Christianity and Judaism in the Modern World* (Cambridge: Polity Press, 1994), pp. 21-22.

51. That pre-millenarianism reflected the world-view and the experience of marginalization and persecution of evangelicalism had strong precedence among numerous Protestant sects. Such a millenarian view reflected a pessimistic theology where salvation not only meant spiritual salvation but salvation from the evil apparent in the world of what is often designated as the 'world system' (B. Wilson, *Sects and Society: A Sociological Study of Three Religious Groups in Britain* [London: Heineman, 1970]). Although theologically diverse, in the USA, under the influence of the Millerites, the early Mormons and the Jehovah's Witnesses, Christadelphians, Seventh Day Adventists and most strands of 'classical' Pentecostalism offered their own variety of pre-millenarianism. The predominance of pre-millenarianism from the mid-twentieth century in the USA was a result of Protestant fundamentalism yielding to an ethnocentric view of the world where the forces of darkness in the eschatological drama become personified in godless communism. Thus, USA culture and the fundamentalist cause converged in an eschatological framework where 'America' became ritually recreated as the Christian Leviathan where external forces threatened to attack the 'righteous' (L. Lindermayer, 'The Beast of the Revelation. American Fundamentalist Christianity and the European Union', *Etnofoor* 8.1 [1995], pp. 27-46). Other 'signs of the End' for pre-millenarianism in the USA include economic crisis, the spread of AIDs and the collapse of family life, the European Community, the United Nations and the New Age Movement. While British post-millenarianism have incorporated such sign-

expressed by post-millenarianism through dominion theology, especially through Christian Reconstructionalism.

As a wing of the Christian right, Reconstructionism maintained that conservative (Protestant) Christians could transform North American society (and ultimately the world). This would create the basis for Christ's millennial kingdom on earth through a God-mandated set of social, economic, educational, political and legal principles of the books of the Pentateuch.[52] British post-millenarianism, by contrast, has proved to be practically void of such political concerns. There were factions that were involved in the Festival of Light in the 1970s, and those that have joined moral campaigns against abortion, liberal laws on homosexuality and so forth. However, neo-Pentecostals in the UK are largely distinguished by their lack of political activism. The reality is that the broad evangelical constituency was too small and politically ineffectual in a nation that in many respects was far more secularized than the USA. The alternative was a tendency to embrace esoteric aspects that reflected the marginalized position of evangelicalism in civic life and to which post-millenarian themes conveniently yielded. Hence, in the UK, charismatics were more likely to attempt to 'pray out' evil in a geographical area than engage in outright political struggles.

The reality is that the self-reflective world-view that is post-millenarianism allows contemporary Pentecostals to come to terms with their peripheral position through an esoteric form of triumphalism; to believe that they are at the 'cutting edge' of what God is doing in the

watching into their world-view, they tend to endorse a much more optimistic scenario whereby these 'evils' are overcome by the 'true' Church as God poured out his spirit in the Last Days and the Kingdom of God began to spread across the world.

52. B. Barron, *Heaven on Earth? The Social and Political Agendas of Dominion Theology* (Grand Rapids: Zondervan, 1992). Such a society would constitute a theocracy where there would be no room for the evils of modern society, such as abortion or homosexuality, and no quarter given to pluralism—secular or religious (A. Shupe, 'Christian Reconstructionism and the Angry Rhetoric of Neo-Postmillennialism', in T. Robbins and S. Palmer [eds.], *Millenium, Messiahs, and Mayhem: Contemporary Apocalyptic Movements* [New York: Routledge, 1997], pp. 195-206). As Paul Freston shows in his study of Latin American Pentecostals, the political activities of Reconstructionists to control the state and government offices could be part of a wider strategy of spiritual warfare in that they are frequently accompanied by 'prayer marches' and intercessory prayer (P. Freston, 'Charismatic Evangelicals', p. 192).

world. The Toronto Blessing was symbolic of this development. It reflected the marginalization of a cognitive minority. At the same time, however, it supported Peter Berger's view as to the limits of secularization: in order that, in his words, 'the supernatural, banished from cognitive respectability by the intellectual authorities, may survive in hidden nooks and crannies'.[53] This of course begs the question of the likelihood of the endurance of post-millenarianism. In the nineteenth century the resurgence of post-millenarianism was short-lived. It may well be that post-millenarianism, like the neo-Pentecostal movement in Britain will be much the same and on a global scale may prove to be a very small paragraph in the story of Christianity. In some ways it has already been discredited. Revival tallies and the Third Wave have been dashed upon the rocks of secularist disbelief. The hope for revival, however, continues as an enduring theme for many charismatic Churches, albeit in a more measured and cautious way. Anyone for *Alpha?*

53. P. Berger, *A Rumour of Angels* (Harmondsworth: Penguin Books, 1969), pp. 18-19.

Part III
ARTS AND LITERARY PERSPECTIVES

'SUCH BEAUTIFUL DIGNITY IN SELF-ABUSE': MILLENNIAL REFUSALS AND THE APPETITES OF SOMATOCRACY

Michael Kirwan

'An Exchange of Reflections between Free Men'

A Manic Street Preachers' ballad about teenage eating disorders, '4st. 7lb' traces the complicity of the supermodel cult in reinforcing impossible ideals of female beauty and body shape (hence this article's title). The turbulent recent history of the Preachers, with the disappearance of the band's guitarist and lyricist, Ritchey Edwards, in 1995 stands as a powerful illustration of this essay's theme: the search for authenticity through corporeality. Perhaps this is the single most pervasive preoccupation of our current intellectual and cultural climate, and deserves a label that to my knowledge has not yet been coined: 'somatocracy'. A graphic intimation of what 'somatocracy' might mean is offered by a study from Elaine Showalter,[1] who surveys a number of contemporary functional psychopathologies as pandemic hysterias or 'psychological plagues'. Her analysis daringly links together such recent psychogenic phenomena as chronic fatigue syndrome, Gulf War syndrome, recovered memory, multiple personality syndrome, satanic ritual abuse and alien abduction; these hysterical expressions, according to Showalter, demonstrate the human capacity for converting emotional pain and conflict into the camouflaged, but culturally acceptable, language of body illness. Only when people deny the emotional and psychological sources of their symptoms and accede to a biological cause can they be regarded as 'legitimately' ill. Indeed, in a secular culture, spiritual causes, even more so than emotional or psychological, need to be translated into somatological language. To give this a formulaic expression, 'the body never lies'.[2]

1. E. Showalter, *Hystories: Hysterical Epidemics and Modern Culture* (London: Picador, 1997).

2. B.D. Shaw, citing Martha Graham, in 'Body/Power/Identity: Passions of the Martyrs', *JECS* 4.3 (1996), pp. 269-312 (269).

One reason, of course, for the intensity of the phenomena that Showalter discusses is the onset of the new millenium, a theme made explicit in a series of exchanges between Cardinal Carlo Maria Martini and Umberto Eco.[3] In this 'exchange of reflections between free men', Eco opens the dialogue by choosing a subject 'which, while truly current, extends its roots quite a distance and has inspired fascination, fear and hope in all members of the human family over the last two millennia': he selects the biblical image of the Apocalypse. What concerns Eco is a secular apocalypticism that pretends to ignore the end time while being thoroughly obsessed by it:

> We are living out—even if we do it in that unmindful way to which the mass media have accustomed us—our terrors of the end. We can even claim to live them out in a spirit of *bibamus, edamus, cras moriemur,* 'eat, drink, for tomorrow we die', toasting the end of ideologies and of solidarity in a vortex of irresponsible consumerism. So, everyone plays with the phantasm of the Apocalypse and all the while exorcises it, and exorcises it all the more, the more unconsciously it is feared, and projects it onto screens in the form of cruel spectacle, with the hope of thus having rendered it unreal. But the power of the phantasms lies precisely in their unreality (p. 25).

This 'desperate millenarianism' either announces (and celebrates) itself as the 'end of history', or else appeals to an archaic and timeless tradition beyond enrichment by any reasonable reflection. Eco contrasts this fever with the traditional Christian conception of history:

> Only those with a sense of the direction of history (even for someone who does not believe in the Parousia) can love earthly realities and believe—with charity—that there is still room for Hope. Is there a notion of hope (and of our responsibility regarding tomorrow) which can be shared by believers and non-believers? What can it still be based on? What critical function can be assumed by a way of thinking about the end which does not imply disinterest in the future but constantly puts the errors of the past on trial? (p. 28).

Martini's response to this secular reading of the book of the Apocalypse is to appeal to the text's 'interpretive key', the New Testament as a whole. The secularist use of apocalyptic is a 'flight from the present in order to take refuge in a future'; in other words, a reservoir of hope in

3. U. Eco and C.M. Martini, *Woran glaubt, wer nicht glaubt?* (Vienna: Paul Zsolnay Verlag, 1998); Original: *In cosa crede chi non crede?* (Rome: Atlantide Editoriale, 1996).

the future, but combined with desolation and resignation concerning the present. But in the light of the gospel, this projection of present frustrations is transformed into the prolongation of the experience of fullness, of 'salvation'. I merely draw attention to this common interest—shared by believer and non-believer—in searching for 'a way of thinking about the end which does not imply disinterest in the future but constantly puts the errors of the past on trial'. It is very interesting that Eco, from a secularist perspective, should be the one to choose the biblical theme, just as Eco is the first in the discussion to capitalize the word 'Hope'; it is just as interesting that the response from Martini is a 'playing down' of the apocalyptic theme, or what we refer to more precisely as a shift from apocalypse to eschatology. Note, in both cases, the surprising trajectory of thought: a secularist introduces a religious conceptual framework and terminology, the believer tries to play down the significance of that framework. In any case, both thinkers are united in a refusal of the nihilistic, celebratory strains of postmodernism.

Postmodern Bodies

It is impossible to deny the importance of corporeality as a theme in postmodern discourses; here, if anywhere, it seems to be the case that 'the body never lies'. Such an interest is justified above all in terms of *jouissance*, an alleged strategy of political or sexual emancipation. As the discussion of Eco and Martini makes clear, however, both believer and secularist may find grounds for concern in our ambiguous situation: the culture of excess on the one hand, and of denial or abnegation on the other, seem to be two sides of the apocalyptic coin, an ambiguity that is a genuine resource for theological reflection. I am tempted to read Eco's comments in the light of Gillian Rose's description of postmodernism as 'a process of endless mourning, lamenting the loss of securities which, on its own argument, were none such';[4] it is a refusal to let go, a static condition between the desire for presence and the acceptance of absence. Such attenuated grieving, of course, happens in any number of ways, even finding apparently contradictory expressions, and here I think Rose has presented us with a powerful metaphor for the apparently contradictory cultural impulses we are examining: a Dionysian celebration of excess and search for transcendence, and yet a

4. G. Rose, *Mourning Becomes the Law* (Cambridge: Cambridge University Press, 1996), p. 11.

refusal of the spiritual and its consolations, in what Cesario Bandera has elsewhere called 'sacred allergy'. Our condition, it seems, calls for a phenomenology of distorted or dysfunctional modes of 'consumption'; we speak in general of 'consumerism', 'materialism', 'addiction', etc. with reference both to the excessive dependence of individuals (upon substances, drugs, sexuality, etc.), and the mechanisms of excess that govern our culture and economy. Is it plausible that western culture's asceticism and refusals, as well as its enthusiasms, might be incorporated into a single paradigm? Is there a unitary explanation, an interconnnectedness between our culture of excess and our refusal of transcendence?

René Girard has spoken of the asceticism of what he calls the 'new puritanism', our culture's implacable hostility towards, and refusal of, meaning—a 'castration of the signified'. This asceticism he relates to the theme of consumption in an essay on eating disorders,[5] in which he argues that the apparently opposite conditions of anorexia and bulimia—self-emaciation and binge eating—are two sides of the same coin. Girard cites Kafka's short story, *Der Hungerkünstler*, 'The Hunger Artist', as a crucial parable for our time: a man whose feats of self-starvation draw crowds of admirers to the fairground, where he is exhibited as a 'living skeleton'. As time goes by, the crowds lose interest and start to dwindle. The hunger artist pushes himself to greater and more extended fasting, but to no avail. Finally, he lies forgotten under the straw in his cage, and is discovered just on the point of death. With his last breath, he whispers that the reason for his extraordinary asceticism was that he had never discovered a food that he enjoyed. If he had, he would have filled his stomach just like everyone else.

What, then, is this nourishment that is so elusive? Here, it seems to me, is a choice between those discourses of postmodernism that merely celebrate or extol the potentiality of the body for emancipation or gratification, and those which attempt to elucidate the full implications of the ambiguity outlined above; to recognize our situation as one of mourning, of absence of bodies.[6] Most recently, the authors of the

5. R. Girard, *Things Hidden since the Foundation of the World* (London: Athlone Press, 1987), p. 442; 'Eating Disorders and Mimetic Desire', *Contagion* 3 (Spring 1996), pp. 1-20.

6. W. Cavanaugh, *Torture and Eucharist* (Oxford: Basil Blackwell, 1998), and G. Ward, 'Bodies: The Displaced Body of Christ', in J. Milbank *et al.* (eds.), *Radical Orthodoxy* (London: Routledge, 1999).

'Radical Orthodoxy' movement attempt a theological recovery of precisely those areas that secular postmodernism has claimed as its own: corporeality, sexuality, 'the city'. Thus, in the volume of the same name, Gerald Loughlin essays a consideration of the erotic nature of God, while Graham Ward uses the displacements of the Paschal body of Christ as the source of a reflection upon corporeality. Here is the nub of the Radical Orthodoxy project, as we find many themes of traditional theology coming once more to the fore: liturgical and eucharistic explications of participation and 'real presence', but in such a way that the supremacy of the Christian metanarrative is vigorously affirmed and upheld.

There is no doubt that this project is immensely provocative and challenging, although there are those among us who perhaps think that supping with the postmoderns requires a longer spoon.[7] At the very least, the refusal by 'Radical Orthodoxy' to succumb to modern theology's pathos—its 'false humility'[8]—strikes a confident, very different tone from the theological reticence of Cardinal Martini in the dialogue we noted above. It is hard to argue with the assertion that a responsible Christian discourse on the body must include, and conclude with, the Eucharist and ecclesiology; but where is the starting point, or even the 'broken middle', of such a discourse? Do we not have to stay a while longer with our mourning and our hunger?

A Return to Martyrdom

A more fruitful discourse, I would suggest, is the recent flourishing of the theme of Christian corporeality *par excellence*: martyrdom. Karl Rahner called in 1983 for a renewed appreciation of the doctrine of martyrdom,[9] a call that has been met by enriched historical and contemporary perspectives, especially in the light of the massive political violence of this century. Ever since W.H.C. Frend's classic study of

7. For accounts of 'postmodernism' that stress its negative, anti-emancipative reality rather than its liberative potential, see F. Jameson, 'Postmodernism, or the Cultural Logic of Late Capitalism', *NLR* 146 (1984), pp. 55-93, and T. Eagleton, *The Illusions of Postmodernism* (Oxford: Basil Blackwell, 1996).

8. J. Milbank, *Theology and Social Theory: Beyond Secular Reason* (Oxford: Basil Blackwell, 1990), p. 1.

9. K. Rahner, 'Dimensions of Martyrdom: A Plea for the Broadening of a Classical Concept', in 'Martyrdom Today', *Concilium* 163 (1983), pp. 9-12.

martyrdom and persecution in the early Church set out to tell 'the story of the successful Christian revolution against the Roman Empire'[10] we have had a renewed appreciation of martyrdom as a praxis with political as well as theological implications. Here, of course, Latin American liberation theology is witness to a massive contribution, both in terms of the many thousands who have died in the struggle for social and human justice, alongside a number of more prominent figures, and in terms of those theologians who have thematized the immense suffering but also the hopeful witness of a whole continent.[11] An important recent text here is Cavanaugh's *Torture and Eucharist,* which combines a theological analysis of the conditions of political modernity that make state terror possible (an analysis which is broadly in alignment, therefore, with the 'Radical Orthodoxy' critique of modernity), and a case study of torture and resistance in Pinochet's Chile in the seventies. Cavanaugh notes the importance of the theme of martyrdom in Latin American ecclesial consciousness, citing but also critiquing Jon Sobrino and Leonardo Boff.[12] Under the chapter heading 'Habeas Corpus' he makes clear how the theme of martyrdom relates to his overall project:

> Martyrdom makes the body of Christ visible. To the world, the death-acts of the martyrs make visible a disciplined community that will not be conformed to the world... As such, martyrdom recalls into being a people, the people of God, and makes their life visible to themselves and to the world... The body of the martyr is thus the battleground for a larger contest of rival imaginations, that of the state and that of the church. A crucial difference in these imaginations is that the imagination of the church is essentially eschatological; the church is not a rival *polis* but points to an alternative time and space, a mingling of heaven and earth.[13]

The wealth of other recent material on martyrdom deserves closer inspection. In contrast to Radical Orthodox confidence that Christian

10. W.H.C. Frend, *Martyrdom and Persecution in the Early Church* (Oxford: Oxford University Press, 1965).

11. Most prominent here are the writings of Jon Sobrino upon Archbishop Romero, upon his assassinated Jesuit colleagues, and upon the 'crucified peoples' of Latin America; for a detailed study of how the symbolism of martyrdom operated at a popular level in El Salvador, see A. Peterson, *Martyrdom and the Politics of Religion: Progressive Catholicism in El Salvador's Civil War* (New York: State University of New York Press, 1997).

12. Cavanaugh, *Torture and Eucharist*, pp. 58-62.

13. Cavanaugh, *Torture and Eucharist*, p. 65.

symbols speak unambiguously and clearly,[14] we find the discourse of martyrdom, even from its inception, to be riven with contradictions. Recent historical studies have shown the origins of the phenomenon to be shrouded in uncertainty, for example, regarding the Jewish or specifically Christian provenance of the notion of martyrdom.[15] Even within the early Church there is a wide divergence between, for example, Tertullian's extreme sectarian views and more conciliatory 'eastern' ones, as Frend's dialectical scheme makes clear. James F. Keenan refers to martyrdom in the context of Christian attitudes to bodiliness,[16] and confirms the thrust of recent historical studies that 'religion and the state wrestled through a kind of dialectic for the socal construction of the body', a struggle that focused especially upon the bodies of women.

To select just one of these recent studies, Brent D. Shaw's 'Body/Power/Identity: Passions of the Martyrs' indicates the Jewish and Christian contribution in late antiquity to a transvaluation of the body in terms of an appreciation of bodily passivity as a form of resistance. Shaw indicates just as strongly how this is one factor in a wider cultural shift, and perhaps it is his description of this wider perspective that is most illuminating for our purposes, by which 'the problematic issues of the time seek definition through the public rituals of trial and torture, come to be expressed in an explicit terminology of their own, and are consciously reflected upon in written texts', though not so much in the public writings on the city-state as in more marginal texts, such as epic and lyric poetry, or medical treatises.

14. A confidence shared, it might be said, by Karl Rahner, who, in an earlier work, speaks of martyrdom as a 'supra-sacrament': 'If it is asked where is the point in human life where the sign will be absolutely true and the truth absolutely signified, where is the point at which both become one, action and suffering, the commonplace and the incomprehensible, death and life, freedom and violence, the most human and the most divine, the dark sinfulness of this world and the grace of God embracing it in mercy, cult and reality—then there is but one answer: in martyrdom' (*On the Theology of Death* [Freiburg: Herder, 1961], p. 111).

15. See, especially, G.W. Bowersock, *Martyrdom and Rome* (Cambridge: Cambridge University Press, 1995), and M. Lamberigts and P. van Denn (eds.), *Martyrium in Multidisciplinary Perspective: Memorial Louis Reekmans* (Leuven: Leuven University Press, 1995).

16. J.F. Keenan, 'Current Theology Note: Christian Perspectives on the Human Body', *TS* 55 (1994), pp. 330-46.

> These stories have embedded in them paradigms of how to confront power in situations where silent scripts, both individual and collective, become public. Such a point is reached when individuals or communities are driven beyond the point of any endurance, where their fundamental elements of identity are publicly questioned precisely in order to be effaced, and there are, so to speak, no options left except to die in silence or, in death itself to express some type of opposition to the imposition of overwhelming force.[17]

Shaw (here following Frend) cites the accounts of the Maccabean revolt as 'a classic instance of a public "no"—the open rejection of a ritualistic litmus test of types of sacrifice and publicly performed ceremonials that constituted an essential surrender of community and the self'. Most moving, perhaps, is Shaw's explication of the notion of *hypomēnē,* or endurance (*patientia*), a central feature in the developing doctrine of martyrdom in the first century CE. Shaw traces a shift from a 'feminised' understanding of *hypomēnē* (literally meaning 'to lie beneath something'), which contrasts the proneness of suffering female bodies (for example, in childbirth) with the erect male body, which inflicted pain and died on the field of battle. This 'subservience' is reflected in both sacred and profane motifs of torture and physical abasement, and reflects also the hierarchical stratification of male participation, and female non-participation, in the public life of the *polis*. However, the transvaluation of endurance that comes about in Jewish and Christian martyrologies, in which a purely passive endurance of suffering comes to be appreciated as a virtue, and not as weakness, brings about a loosening of rigid gender categories and the private/public dichotomy to which they had been anchored. Endurance *per se* is worked out as a consciously elaborated ideology charged with political and religious significance:

> Patience or the simple ability to outlast the persecutor was also inextricably linked to the other 'feminine' virtue of hope—hope for a better life, a divine promise of what was there for the patient, if only one could wait. This quasi-millenial expectation gave a larger, more-than-personal element to Christian endurance. It was the new body that would benefit from a reversal of present conditions. No pain, no suffering: the body would become impatient. The Apocalypse of John envisages this transcendent state when 'he will wipe away every tear from their eyes, there

17. Shaw, 'Body/Power/Identity', p. 275.

shall be no more death, no more grief, crying or pain—for those earlier things will have passed away'.[18]

The political resonances of this new valuation of the suffering body are most acutely felt because they coincide with a crisis of the Roman state. With its ideological foundations under threat, the state is forced to break, physically and visibly, any challenge to its authority; in a way that is similar to Cavanaugh's description of the exercise of torture in Pinochet's Chile, 'the body became central to demonstrations of power'; though indeed actual bodies found themselves caught in the crossfire of contradictory discourses of power. 'Every trial was therefore a matter of fixing identities',[19] both in terms of the reversal of power relations implied by the Christian revaluation of humiliation and abasement, and the claim to be a Christian that constituted the martyr's confession. Nevertheless, Shaw warns us against a too easy forgetting that this transvaluative power of individual bodies has its limits. He insists instead on a nuanced account of the dialectical relation between bodies—finite, mortal, isolated and weak—and institutions that contained a more enduring power:

> It was these institutional forces—an organisational apparatus, a program of education, policing functionaries, a body of servitors, pervasive writings and records, an hierarchical membership and officialdom—that remembered, conferred and supported public identities, classified, and, not inconsequentially, made enduring life and death decisions that were successfully enforced. The evidence of this investigation, therefore, points forcefully in the direction of the strong dialectic between individual and structure, in both space and time. The residual problem was that, although the body might well 'never lie', the variant truths embedded in it were often as contradictory and conflict ridden as those in the world outside it.[20]

18. Shaw, 'Body/Power/Identity', pp. 297-98.
19. Shaw, 'Body/Power/Identity', p. 301.
20. Shaw, 'Body/Power/Identity', p. 402. Shaw has elsewhere drawn attention to the specific paradox of martyrdom that is implicit here, that the witness of the martyr is totally dependent on the martyrologist. This paradox is especially poignant in the case of the third-century martyr St Perpetua, whose account of her visions and suffering in prison is 'framed' by an avalanche of not always sympathetic male commentators. See B.D. Shaw, 'The Passion of Perpetua', *Past and Present* 139 (1993), pp. 3-45.

Conclusion

Once again, a comparison with Cavanaugh's conclusions is instructive, since *Torture and Eucharist* is an attempt to diagnose the Chilean Church's initial failure to resist state terrorism as a misrecognition of the nature and significance of social bodies. Only by a twofold eucharistic praxis is the existence of the Church as 'body' made visible and effective: both in terms of the gathering of bodies, which is the essence of eucharist, and by way of excommunication as a sanction against practitioners of the 'anti-liturgy', which is torture. I would wish to indicate that this eucharistic retrieval of 'bodiliness' is enriched and supplemented by a new awareness of martyrdom as a discourse of theological and political transformation.

The 'ecumenical' possibilities for this kind of theological perspective—a theologically responsible somatology—are considerable. Need it be pointed out that a common reflection upon state torture versus ecclesial resistance, along the lines of Cavanaugh's case study, would bring liberation theologians into conversation with the former Silent Church of post-communism—a dialogue that, ten years after the fall of the Berlin Wall, still seems to be nonexistent? What has been more evident in this essay, however, is the possibility of a bridge or common ground between the traditional concerns of liberation theology and more abstruse 'northern' themes. The crisis of representation and of meaning which is at the heart of alleged 'postmodernism' has its corporeal turn, which needs to be addressed as such. What opens up, perhaps, at least for the present, is a responsible theological style, in an age when talk of the 'soul' or 'spirit' seems to carry increasingly little weight. Which brings us back to the Manic Street Preachers, the nihilist rock band from a former mining town in Wales. Their lead guitarist, Ritchey Edwards, had been treated for manic depression, a condition that left its mark on many of the songs he wrote for the band before his disappearance. After one press conference, Edwards responded to one journalist who questioned the integrity of the band's aggressive nihilist posture by taking a razor blade and carving the figures '4 real' on his forearm. In 1995 Edwards went missing and has not been seen since, though media scepticism has frequently regarded this as a pop star's publicity stunt.

How are we to read this 'text'? What 'truth' is attempting to come to light here? We have a disappeared body, and a real absence: not, to be sure, a human tragedy on the scale of the thousands of victims of torture, disappearance and execution on the South American continent and elsewhere; but a significant cultural icon, nevertheless, for many rock fans. Once again, a story of

> how to confront power in situations where silent scripts, both individual and collective, become public...when individuals or communities are driven beyond the point of any endurance, where their fundamental elements of identity are publicly questioned precisely in order to be effaced.[21]

What has captured people's imagination is the remarkable recovery of the band's remaining members. Their production of two prize-winning albums and retreat to some extent from the nihilist darkness of their previous material is something of a secular 'salvation narrative'. For an age and a culture seeking 'ontological density'[22] and yet not ready or able to receive the full nourishment of the gospel, this may be the nearest many will get to the 'real thing'. To acknowledge this much is at least to discover once again the value of *hypomēnē,* recast here as 'a way of thinking about the end which does not imply disinterest in the future but constantly puts the errors of the past on trial'; it is to keep on searching for that elusive theological register, which needs to include both the reticence of a humble waiting and the confident proclamation of a 'radical orthodox' hope, to take with all theological seriousness the predicament of the Hunger Artist, who is both refuser and assertive witness.[23]

21. Shaw, 'Body/Power/Identity', p. 275.

22. J.L. Marion's phrase—is this Milan Kundera's 'unbearable lightness of being'?

23. My thanks to James Hanvey SJ, for his comments on a previous version of this paper.

'FABULOUSLY TEXTUAL': RELIGION AND THE FUTURE IN SPECULATIVE FICTION

Kevin McCarron

> The Church could no more prevent outbreaks of Pelagianism than it could contain an even more dangerous heresy, and one which, of all the heterodox currents in Christianity, was the most replete with utopianism: the idea of the millennium.
>
> Krishan Kumar, *Utopia and Anti-Utopia in Modern Times*

> Francis Ford Coppola once jokingly encouraged George Lucas to make a religion of *Star Wars*; by the millennium's end, the process has taken care of itself.
>
> Brian Logan, *Guardian*

> 'So what's missing?' she asked.
> 'God,' he said, simply.
>
> Colleen McCullough, *A Creed for the Third Millennium*

Tom Woodman begins his illuminating essay 'Science Fiction, Religion and Transcendence' with these words:

> In an article in *Books and Bookmen* for February 1971, J.G. Ballard stated that science fiction was 'totally atheistic'. Darko Suvin's important article 'Science Fiction and the Genological Jungle' (*Genre*, Fall, 1973) has argued the theoretical case for this viewpoint: the conceptual frameworks of science, the real basis of the genre, forbid any dabbling with religion beyond its purely historical or anthropological interest.[1]

Although Colleen McCullough's protagonist in the quotation used as an epigraph above laments the absence of God in the year 2034, God is actually represented in three specific ways in the futuristic texts I want to discuss. These manifestations I want to describe as 'Circular Christianity', 'Old Testament Christianity' and 'New Age Christianity'. The

1. P. Parrinder (ed.), *Science Fiction: A Critical Guide* (London: Longman, 1979), p. 110.

cult television science-fiction series *Babylon 5* falls into the last of these categories and a substantial portion of the paper will be devoted to the role of religion in this programme. The two primary reasons, which are linked, for this emphasis are, first, the extraordinary success of this show; it is somewhat melancholy for a lecturer in literature to acknowledge that more people would have seen the last episode of the third series of *Babylon 5* than have probably read all the novels I'll be discussing put together. The second reason for devoting a disproportionate section of this essay to *Babylon 5* is that the series seems to me to reflect very accurately the growing tendency in the West to appropriate a religious discourse for ends that are essentially secular. With the most extraordinary confidence, *Babylon 5* extrapolates from this tendency and projects it into the twenty-second century—and across the entire universe.

In the first of the categories of texts I want to discuss, 'Circular Christianity', the world, at some undefined futuristic period, has been devastated by nuclear war, so much so that the extreme future actually resembles the extreme past. The novels are animated by dramatic irony; as they progress, the reader watches humanity reproduce the slow, painful evolutionary steps that will enable them to arrive at the stage where they are once again capable of destroying themselves. Steven Connor summarizes the plot of Russell Hoban's *Riddley Walker* (1980) with admirable economy:

> This novel is set some 2,500 years in the future in the aftermath of nuclear war. Human life has been reduced to an Iron Age condition, although the inhabitants of this civilization have preserved the memory of the more developed civilization whose destruction has led to their own condition, in the myth of Eusa, a strange amalgam of the story of St Eustace and a fabular account of the events leading to the splitting of the atom and use of the nuclear bomb by the USA.[2]

In the course of his persuasive analysis of *Riddley Walker*, Connor refers to David Cowart's 1989 book *History and the Contemporary Novel*: 'David Cowart, in the course of an interesting and elaborate reading of the circular and progressive models of history in *Riddley Walker* concludes that both are debased, since both "lack an adequately developed spiritual or sacral dimension" '. Connor goes to suggest,

2. S. Connor, *The English Novel in History: 1950–1995* (London: Routledge, 1996), p. 218.

however, 'But the point is not so much the relative value of "archaic" and "civilized" modes of temporal consciousness, as the fact that they necessitate and lead to each other...'[3] Equally, one can agree with Cowart that the 'point' of *Riddley Walker* does indeed include a distinction between circular and progressive models of history, and the absence of the sacral dimension in either of them. The book's attitude, overall, to Christianity is hostile and God and nuclear power are rhetorically and conceptually conflated throughout the novel, implying that Christianity has been complicit in the world's destruction, and may well be again. Traditional Christian eschatology and annihilation narratives are, of course, similar in that both are 'fabulously textual' in the famous phrase of Derrida's that I have used as the title of this paper.

While less rhetorically ambitious than *Riddley Walker*, Walter M. Miller's *A Canticle for Leibowitz* (1960) is considerably more sophisticated, theologically. This novel describes the time after a nuclear holocaust when a monastic order is the sole preserver of scientific knowledge. After the nuclear disaster a movement called 'The Simplification' had blamed science, and tried to stamp it out. This response, however, is depicted as misguided, and Tom Woodman writes, 'Miller's point is that the Church cannot set herself against any real truth, for all truth bears some relationship to the Logos. It is not science that is wrong but men's hearts.'[4] Science is only a tool, given by God as a compensation for the Fall. The mistake humanity has made, the novel suggests, is believing that science could, and should, replace religion, rather than insisting that science remain the handmaiden of religion:

> Too much hope for Earth had led men to try to make it Eden, and of that they might well despair until the time toward the consumption of the world... The closer men came to perfecting for themselves a Paradise the more impatient they seemed to become with it and with themselves as well.[5]

At the novel's conclusion, the earth is to be totally destroyed in a final holocaust but the representatives of the Church leave earth on a spaceship, in a final dramatic twist taking with them, as they must, the scientific learning they possess. Within such narratives Christianity is, strikingly, depicted as somehow fated, inextricably bound up with the

3. Connor, *The English Novel in History*, p. 222.
4. Parrinder, *Science Fiction*, p. 120.
5. W.M. Miller, *A Canticle for Leibowitz* (London: Corgi, 1975), p. 287.

fate of the world. *Riddley Walker* is unequivocally uneasy at this inevitability, while *A Canticle for Leibowitz* is quietly optimistic, but, irrespective of their particular attitudes to Christianity, all such narratives place Christianity, even in the extreme future, at the very centre of western experience.

In the second of my categories, and the least complicated, 'Old Testament Christianity', God is seen only in his (always 'his') most wrathful and violent manifestations. In Bernard Malamud's *God's Grace* (1982), God speaks to the only human survivor of a thermonuclear war, Calvin Cohn:

> 'The present Devastation, ending in smoke and dust, comes as a consequence of man's self-betrayal. From the beginning, when I gave them the gift of life, they were perversely greedy for death. At last, I thought, it will give them death because they are engrossed in evil.'[6]

Although I will argue later that, in essence, *Babylon 5* is an example of 'New Age Christianity', its references to Christianity invariably focus on the anger of God. Generally, in *Babylon 5* the name of God is associated with the most fearsome violence, suffering and death. The space station's commander, Susan Ivanova is described, for example, in the novel *Voices*, as thinking, 'Vengeance was better left to the Lord, or so she'd been taught as a child',[7] while later she pursues an escaping pirate 'like divine vengeance'.[8] In the television episode 'Between the Darkness and the Light' (419), she says of herself as she gives the order to destroy all the surviving fighters, 'I am the right hand of vengeance. I am Death incarnate. God sent me.' In the *Times Literary Supplement*, Heather O'Donoghue wrote of a recently published novel (1998) by Reg Gadney,

> *Mother, Son and Holy Ghost* is a millennial novel in two senses: its subject is the Trinity—a batty and sinister religious cult of the kind supposed to flourish in the run up to millennia—and its narrative culminates on December 31, 1999, when the Inner chapter of Trinity plan a bloody sacrifice and resurrection in Trafalgar Square on the last stroke of midnight.[9]

6. B. Malamud, *God's Grace* (New York: Avon, 1983), p. 4.
7. J. Vornholt, *Voices* (London: Boxtree, 1995), p. 14.
8. Vornholt, *Voices,* p. 198.
9. H. O'Donoghue, *Times Literary Supplement*, 23 October 1998, p. 25.

Christianity is represented throughout the novel as a source of deception and illusion, and its inherent and extreme violence is inevitably linked to the terrorist violence committed in its name.

In Margaret Atwood's critically acclaimed *The Handmaid's Tale* (1985), we are offered a vision of the near future in which the only remnants of Christianity are its most baleful and intolerant manifestations. Peter G. Stillman and S. Anne Johnson write:

> Facing plagues and ecological crises that caused widespread sterility, the founders of Gilead generated a right-wing fundamentalist reading of the Bible, grafted it onto patriarchal attitudes and imposed it throughout society. Gilead is devoted to reproduction—white, Christian, misogynist, stratified reproduction. Fertile women are rare (men, by patriarchal definition are not infertile), and Commanders, the rulers of the society, want children. If a commander's wife is unable to bear children, a fertile woman must be brought in to be impregnated by him. These women are the handmaids, prepared only for pregnancy, their status and purpose made evident by their uniforms and their names.[10]

Clearly emerging from a background of 1980s North American revivalist fundamentalism, Atwood's one-sided critique of Christianity envisions the religion of the future as a mixture of the politically expedient and a convenient outlet for the essential misogyny of virtually all men. This lurid, and ludicrous, paranoid fantasy owes much of its enormous success to its uncontested equation of the masculine drive for power with God's own universal authority and omnipotence. The future, in such texts, is always seen as a space within which a capricious, punitive and wrathful God plays far too large a part in human affairs. No God at all would be preferable, and this is indeed the ideal for the great majority of texts that constitute my third and final category, 'New Age Christianity'.

So, finally, I want to refer to several texts in which Christianity is represented as an anachronism; often one which has been, or is being, superseded by a humanism that has retained the vocabulary of religion, if nothing else. In Brian Appleyard's *The First Church of the New Millennium* (1994), set in the near-future, the architect Steven Rix's vision of a soaring Gothic cathedral to inaugurate the millennium is wrested from him by developers, who intend to recast it as part of a giant theme

10. P.S. Stillman and S.A. Johnson, 'Identity, Complicity, and Resistance in *The Handmaid's Tale*', *Journal of the Society for Utopian Studies* (1994), pp. 70-86 (75).

park, the only possible way in which a cathedral can be seen as legitimizing its existence in the twenty-first century:

> 'You mean you could build my church as a cover for a leisure centre because they like the look of Gothic cathedrals. Of course! How could I be so blind? That is the only way you could build it today, as a leisure centre. And, of course, the only way you could get permission for a leisure centre is by building a Gothic cathedral. Brilliant.'
>
> I moaned and dropped my forehead into the palm of my hand.[11]

In Colleen McCullough's *A Creed for the Third Millennium* (1985), the splendidly named Joshua Christian is cynically used by a presidential committee to pacify the masses by charismatically offering them a secularized Christianity; all redemption and forgiveness, Christianity without tears. In an address televised to the nation Christian announces: 'I am not a religious man, if by that you envision a man who observes an established religious regimen. Yet I believe in God. *My* God. Not anybody else's God. And God is the crux of my life.'[12] Religion here is subjective, undemanding, and actually very contemporary. In P.D. James's *The Children of Men* (1992), set in a near-future in which no children at all have been born for decades, the narrator muses on the new nature of religion:

> During the mid-1990s the recognized churches, particularly the Church of England, moved from the theology of sin and redemption to a less uncompromising doctrine: corporate social responsibility coupled with a sentimental humanism... The change was immediately popular. Even to unbelievers like myself, the cross, stigma of the barbarism of officialdom and of man's in-eluctable cruelty, has never been a comfortable symbol.[13]

Here, too, Christianity has become acceptable within a futuristic society only when vitiated and, in essence, secularized.

In some texts, while religion has almost completely vanished from the culture in terms of practice, the rhetoric of religion is still pervasive. In William Gibson's *Neuromancer* (1984), for many critics the exemplary 'cyberpunk' novel, Gibson describes what happens when his protagonist, Case, has his ability to work in cyberspace destroyed by toxic drugs administered to him for stealing. The language is theological:

11. B. Appleyard, *The First Church of the New Millennium* (London: Bantam, 1994), p. 130.

12. C. McCullough, *A Creed for the Third Millennium* (London: Futura, 1991), p. 248.

13. P.D. James, *The Children of Men* (London: Faber, 1993), p. 15.

> For Case, who'd lived for the bodiless exultation of cyberspace, it was the Fall. In the bars he'd frequented as a cowboy hotshot, the elite stance involved a certain relaxed contempt for the flesh. The body was meat. Case fell into the prison of his own flesh.[14]

Throughout Gibson's subsequent novels, the language becomes even more overtly theological. In *Count Zero* (1987), Gibson writes, '[T]he Wig had become convinced that God lived in cyberspace, or perhaps that cyberspace was God…'[15] In *Mona Lisa Overdrive* (1988), during a discussion about the precise nature of cyberspace, one of the characters asks, '[T]he matrix is God?'[16] But God is merely a word in cyberpunk; a word, moreover, emptied of all sense of sacrality.

A similarly casual attitude to the language of religion can be seen in comments made by fans of George Lucas's *Star Wars*, and its 'prequel' *The Phantom Menace*. Brian Logan, in the *Guardian,* quotes a fan who downloaded the trailer for the new *Star Wars* film from the internet: 'It was as if someone deeply religious who has only ever known of the New Testament finally gets to read the Old Testament.'[17] Elsewhere in the article, Logan notes that 'Luke Skywalker was voted a more popular role model than Christ in a recent American poll', and quotes an English fan who intends to go to America to see *The Phantom Menace*: 'Hollywood is the Rome of cinema, and we international fans are pilgrims.' The secularization of religion is seen not just in the speech of the fans, of course, but is a significant aspect of the *Star Wars* films themselves, which infantilize religion, clearly perceiving it only as a powerful social process that can usefully promote sound moral behaviour.

Christianity is also seen in a number of futuristic texts as a constituent part, and by no means the strongest part, of a pot-pourri of 'mystical' beliefs. In Louise Lawrence's *Children of the Dust* (1985), for example, another post-holocaust narrative, vaguely positive aspects of Christianity are merged with pantheism to offer the reader a comforting vision of the future that is, characteristically, enthusiastic about the 'spiritual' life, while disinclined to suggest any process of religious reciprocity. It is in *Babylon 5*, however, that the contemporary practice of secularizing religion can be seen in its most persuasive form.

14. W. Gibson, *Neuromancer* (London: Grafton, 1984), p. 12.
15. W. Gibson, *Count Zero* (London: Grafton, 1987), p. 173.
16. W. Gibson, *Mona Lisa Overdrive* (London: Grafton, 1988), p. 138.
17. B. Logan, *Guardian*, 6 April 1999, pp. 8-9.

In his book *Understanding the New Age*, Russell Chandler writes:

> Many are embracing a more open, yet elusive movement that lies abroad in the land. Collectively, this ideology is known as the New Age. This introspective movement, which embraces 'Higher Consciousness' as the supreme quest of humankind, is shaking loose an avalanche of ideas that question our traditional Western philosophies and our long-held Judeo-Christian ethos.[18]

Babylon 5, although set in the middle years of the twenty-third century is very much a product of the time in which it was being produced: the 1990s. J. Michael Straczynski, the writer and producer of the series, stressed the plurality of his own creation when he wrote, 'The thematic structure of *Babylon 5* is a hodge-podge of philosophical positions, Biblical allusions, Jungian archetypes, hero-myth, Greek tragedy, socio-political extrapolation, comparative religions, literary metaphor...'[19] Chandler writes, 'New Age is a hybrid mix of spiritual, social, and political forces, and it encompasses sociology, theology, the physical sciences, medicine, anthropology, history, the human potentials movement...'[20] In New Age thought, in fact, conventional, restricting boundaries collapse in what amounts to a linguistic free-for-all.

In his book on translation, *After Babel*, George Steiner writes:

> The perennial question whether translation is, in fact, possible is rooted in ancient religion and psychological doubts on whether there ought to be any passage from one tongue to another. So far as speech is divine and numinous, so far as it encloses revelation, active transmission either into the vulgate or across the barrier of languages is dubious or frankly evil.[21]

However, by the sixteenth century the postulate of untranslatability has a purely secular basis. In *Babylon 5* a simple computer software program renders all alien speech perfectly comprehensible and, in effect, the series rejects both the sacred and the secular objections to translation.

Steiner suggests that 'the utopian and the messianic are figures of syntax',[22] and later he quotes from the Old Testament scholar Franz

18. R. Chandler, *Understanding the New Age* (Reading: Word, 1988), p. 9.
19. A. Lane, *The Babylon File* (London: Virgin, 1997), pp. 22-23.
20. Chandler, *Understanding the New Age*, p. 17.
21. G. Steiner, *After Babel* (Oxford: Oxford University Press, 1992), p. 251.
22. Steiner, *After Babel*, p. xiv.

Rosenzweig: 'Every translation is a messianic act, which brings redemption nearer.'[23] Jeffrey Sinclair, the series' protagonist, is himself a messianic figure, as is Joshua Christian in *A Creed for the Third Millennium,* and during the ceremony in which Sinclair is confirmed as 'Entil'Zha—the One', Catherine Sakai looks on:

> Rathenn began to read in a loud, rhythmic voice page after page from the ancient texts, all in a language so old, only a few Minbari still understood it... Jeff had already taught himself to read it, but he had a natural gift for languages she lacked.[24]

Sinclair, characteristically, reads religious texts so as to understand the language; he does not learn the language so as to understand the religious texts. Similarly, the head of security, Michael Garibaldi, studies the Book of G'Quon, a word very similar to the Hebrew word for sacred 'qu'dosh', and is 'justified' when he discovers from it that the Shadows can be defeated through telepathy. Religion is depicted as having value only when it leads to directly practical results. Here is a description of Sinclair's room on Minbari: 'It always reminded Sinclair of a hotel room in New Vegas, but somehow more spiritual.'[25] The room manages to be a combination of one of Earth's fleshiest cities and yet 'somehow' more spiritual. The vagueness of this 'somehow' is characteristic of considerations of religion in *Babylon 5.* Usually, alien religion is represented as idiosyncratic and harmless. The Minbari religious caste, for example, is vegetarian. It would be, of course. This is New Age shorthand for indicating spiritual enlightenment. As is well known, vegetarians are so much more ethereal than carnivores. Minbari religious belief seems to be a fusion of western perceptions of Hindu philosophy and vitiated Kantian ethics. It is exotic and undemanding—much like the perfect alien, in fact.

Christianity is only one of numerous religions in *Babylon 5.* It is rarely practised, and is consistently criticized. In the episode entitled 'Passing through Gethsemene' (304), the Minbari ambassador Delenn offers a clear critique of Christianity:

> We do not believe in any individual god or gods... We believe that the universe itself is conscious in a way we can never truly understand. It is

23. Steiner, *After Babel*, p. 257.

24. K.M. Drennan, *To Dream in the City of Sorrows* (London: Macmillan, 1997), p. 273.

25. Drennan, *City of Sorrows*, p. 10.

> engaged in a search for meaning, so it breaks itself apart, investing its own consciousness in every form of life. We are the universe, trying to understand itself.[26]

The Minbari are emphatically represented as the most spiritually 'advanced' of the four main alien cultures: Narn, Centauri, Vorlon and Minbari. The views expressed here by Delenn, which firmly reject Christianity's monotheism, are characteristic of New Age thought. Chandler writes: 'The New Age bottom line can be stated in three words: "All is One." The cosmos is pure, undifferentiated, universal energy—a consciousness or "life force". Everything is one vast, interconnected process.'[27]

Although tolerant of Christianity, *Babylon 5*, quite consistent with its New Age leanings, is actually opposed to it and the association of an Old Testament Christianity with wrath and violence is implicitly criticized by Sinclair's more 'evolved' religious views. Sinclair was educated by Jesuits and he is fond of discussing religion, but his interest in the subject is overwhelmingly practical and ethical. Theology is nearly always depicted as pointless and arid in futuristic societies and probably the principal reason for this is the contemporary passion for practicality and efficiency—indeed, I would argue that a Pelagian subtext underlies all negative portrayals of theological discussion in futuristic fiction. There are exceptions, of course, and these include, obviously, *A Canticle for Leibowitz*, as well as Brian Moore's *Catholics* (1972) and Walker Percy's *Love among the Ruins* (1971). In the case of the two latter novels it is worth noting that theological discussion is taken seriously throughout both of them. Kieran Quinlan, for example, writes of *Love among the Ruins*: 'One of the questions in the novel...is whether More will open himself to the grace of religious belief in its *fullest* sense and return to the fold.'[28] Percy's novel opens with these words, making explicit its religious concerns: '[I]n these dread days of the old violent beloved U.S.A. and of the Christ-forgetting Christ haunted death-dealing Western world.'[29] However, the settings of both *Love among the Ruins* and *Catholics* are extremely un-futuristic, in effect supporting my argument rather than refuting it.

26. Cited in Lane, *The Babylon File*, p. 270.

27. Chandler, *Understanding the New Age*.

28. K. Quinlan, *Walker Percy: The Last Catholic Novelist* (Baton Rouge: Louisiana State University Press, 1996), p. 128.

29. W. Percy, *Love among the Ruins* (London: Paladin, 1976), p. 3.

In the *Babylon 5* episode 'By Any Means Necessary' (112), the Narn ambassador, G'Kar, says to Sinclair, 'You are a far more spiritual man than I gave you credit for.' Sinclair replies, with a rueful smile, 'I know a couple of Jesuit teachers who might disagree with you.' Although the episode implies otherwise, the Jesuits would be right to disagree with G'Kar. Sinclair's understanding of the importance of a religious ritual to G'Kar is certainly sympathetic, but Sinclair is 'spiritual' only in the vaguest, most New Age, and thoroughly indeterminate manner.

In *To Dream in the City of Sorrows*, a character enters a temple and sees Sinclair:

> 'Sorry Ambassador. I didn't mean to disturb your prayers.'
> Sinclair smiled. 'I wasn't praying. I come here to read or just sit sometimes. Just to be alone.'[30]

Sinclair's smile indicates his amusement at the idea of prayer. The temple, traditionally a formalized space for communal worship, has been transformed utterly here; it is now a private, solipsistic space, where 'aloneness' is not a state to be overcome through an act of communal worship, but one to be celebrated. *Babylon 5* wears the robes of the sacred while articulating the beliefs of the secular. The series enjoys the exoticism of alien temples, chanting, robes, ancient texts; all the accoutrements of religious practice, but 'God', in the series' evolutionary model of religion, is a cold abstraction, an ethical framework upon which can be draped various, and tautologous, injunctions to be tolerant of other religions, while the individual strives for individual perfection. This may be commendable, but it is humanism, not religion. The 'Ideal' religion in *Babylon 5* is actually remarkably similar to the idea of an 'atheistic religion', offering a complete system of belief and ritual, with liturgy and sacraments, priesthood and pontiff, but founded on humanist principles, advanced by Auguste Comte in his *System of Affirmative Politics*, published in 1854.

The title of the episode 'The Quality of Mercy' (121) is taken from Shakespeare's *The Merchant of Venice* and there are numerous literary allusions throughout the series. There are also a large number of biblical references. Overall, however, within *Babylon 5* the literary and the biblical references are not separated into a profane/sacred dichotomy; conflation is the primary allusive dynamic. The biblical references point only to an absence. The numerous references to Ezekiel and to

30. Drennan, *City of Sorrows*, p. 252.

Jeremiah, for example, have the same intertextual significance as references to Tennyson and Homer; religion is seen solely as a cultural practice, it forms part of a rational discourse, not a supernatural or sacred one. In *Violence and the Sacred*, Rene Girard writes, '[T]he Latin *Sacer*, which is sometimes translated "sacred", or sometimes "accursed"...encompasses the maleficent as well as the beneficent.'[31] *Babylon 5*, like *Star Wars,* has no sense of the sacred. It is, instead, comfortable with New Age beliefs in the importance of raising the individual consciousness so as to become one with the universal All.

The title of the episode from the first series entitled 'A Voice in the Wilderness' (118/119) is an unaccredited reference to Isa. 40.3: 'The voice of him that crieth in the wilderness, Prepare ye the way of the Lord.' But, significantly, the Lord does not appear. What does occur is that a Minbari named Draal sacrifices himself for the good of others while invoking the sententiously named 'Third Principle of Sentient Life', which simply suggests that sacrificing oneself for the good of others is a very good thing to do. Why this should be so is not taken up by Sinclair, Delenn, or by Draal himself. 'The Third Principle of Sentient Life' is actually very similar to Kant's 'Categorical Imperative', admittedly no mean comparison, but Kant's injunction was philosophical, not spiritual or religious. This distinction is one of many that *Babylon 5* refuses to make. The book of Isaiah actually describes the Babylonian captivity, an episode that Martin Luther refers to in his *The Babylonian Captivity of the Church* (1521). Here, Luther is primarily critical of Catholicism's use of the priesthood to establish an illusory equivalence between ideas and matter through the medium of representation, and the inevitable fetishizing of human activity that accompanies the belief. He links this fallacy to the equally erroneous belief that grace can be earned by human actions. *Babylon 5* fetishizes human activity and has no concept of grace without human actions.

The title of the series necessarily invokes the Tower of Babel, described in Gen. 11.1-9, but while the biblical narrative is preoccupied with hubris, guilt, punishment and confusion, *Babylon 5* offers its viewers a reassuring dichotomy between darkness and light, a phrase that actually provides the title for a recent episode. *Babylon 5* is fundamentally optimistic, locating all evil in the unenlightened views of others. *Babylon 5* rejects a transcendent God, one who exists outside

31. R. Girard, *Violence and the Sacred* (trans. P. Gregory; Baltimore: The Johns Hopkins University Press, 1977), p. 257.

humanity, and instead locates God within the individual and evolved consciousness. Chandler notes, 'New Age transcendence revels in innate human potential.'[32] So too does *Babylon 5* and perhaps it is, above all, hubris that characterizes most writing on religion and futurity. Religion in the new millennium, at least according to writers of speculative fiction, will be either violently anachronistic, or so vitiated as to cease to be religion in any meaningful sense of the word. One wonders whether the future will have any conception of the phrase 'Hobson's choice'.

32. Chandler, *Understanding the New Age*, p. 305.

Grim Present, Glorious Future: Millennial Implications in the Novels of Ngugi wa Thiong'o

John A. Anonby

As the new millennium began, the anticipated disasters failed to materialize, and the sun rose as usual on 1 January 2000. Nevertheless, too casual an approach to this significant time line could blind us to the opportunity for some panoramic retrospection, particularly of the past century, and for a glimpse of some exalting hopes for the future. The year 1900 can, for instance, be conveniently marked as the culmination of the period of European colonial domination of the globe. Literally, at that time, 'the sun never set on the British Empire', as I was reminded when standing in front of a statue of Queen Victoria erected in Auckland, New Zealand, on the occasion of her diamond jubilee as monarch, in 1897. Now, one century later, it is evident that the age of colonialism has been replaced by the voices of indigenous and marginalized peoples everywhere demanding a hearing. What are some of the opportunities unfolding before our eyes? And what mistakes from this past century should we seek to avoid in our common future? Challenges facing the Christian Church at this time are formidable and daunting; nevertheless, the opportunity for Christians to implement the principles of the kingdom of God have perhaps never been greater. Christians, however, are not in agreement as to the appropriate response to this challenge.

At the risk of oversimplification, I would like to suggest that the crux of the matter lies in the tendency of Christians to define salvation in polarized terms: individual regeneration or social redemption. Is the biblical 'kingdom of God' primarily apprehended in terms of individual experience, or is it realized as communal transformation?

This tension, perhaps reflecting in some measure the traditional emphasis on the role of good works as an expression of faith in the Roman Catholic apprehension of salvation in varying degrees of contrast to the Protestant predilection towards the role of faith as an expression of good works, is also detectable among African theologians.

Jean-Marc Éla of Cameroon, for example, in commenting on the Pan-African Conference of Third World Theologians in Accra, Ghana, in 1977, argues in 'Christianity and Liberation in Africa' that 'African theology must...be *liberation* theology' (Éla's emphasis), that 'salvation in Jesus Christ is liberation from every form of slavery', and that 'the church ought to signify this salvation concretely, by creating conditions that liberate human beings and enable them to grow'.[1] This, he contends, will require 'increased militancy' in the 'political, economic, cultural' spheres of local activity.[2] Closer to the other end of the spectrum is the more cautious approach of François Lumbala of Zaire, who, while conceding that the Churches of Africa 'must assume the task of guiding the peoples to socio-political liberation', feels that it is not their 'main job'; pushing his point even further, he contends that 'if the management of the temporal becomes a church's main enterprise, we may doubt the Christian authenticity of that Church'.[3] For Lumbala, liberation in the arena of health, nutrition and politics, while a 'manifestation of the coming Reign of God', is secondary to our relationship with God; the paramount activity of the Church is the 'praise of our divine Parent'.[4]

Some biblical parameters might be useful here. In perusing the Old Testament, I was struck in a fresh way, while preparing this essay, at the resonant arrangement of that ancient code, the ten commandments of Exodus 20. The first four commands involve the relationship between the individual and God, whereas the last six challenge the individual in his or her relationship to other human beings. To put it another way, the first four imply the centrality of a God-focused piety, but the horizontal outworking of such religious devotion embraces the last six. There is no room for eclecticism here—all of the commands are given to all of the people.

Another biblical corollary is the historical context of the exodus, whose main event can easily be identified as the deliverance of the Israelites from their political oppressors in Egypt. Ngugi wa Thiong'o, whose works will be discussed in more detail below, continually

1. J.-M. Éla, 'Christianity and Liberation in Africa' (trans. R.R. Barr), in R. Gibellini (ed.), *Paths of African Theology* (Maryknoll, NY: Orbis Books, 1994), pp. 136-53 (140, 142).

2. Éla, 'Christianity and Liberation', p. 150.

3. F.K. Lumbala, 'Africans Celebrate Jesus Christ' (trans. R.R. Barr), in Gibellini (ed.), *Paths of African Theology*, p. 81.

4. Lumbala, 'Africans Celebrate', p. 82.

describes his political heroes in his early novels as Moses figures who are attempting to cast off the yoke of British colonial subjugation of Kenyan national peoples.

An equally fascinating Pentateuchal detail is the divinely instituted year of Jubilee, described in considerable detail in Leviticus 25. This 'golden' anniversary—an appealing archetypal model for the new millennium?—involved a proclamation of 'liberty throughout all the land unto all the inhabitants thereof' (v. 10).[5] It provided opportunities for universal repatriation, for the freeing of slaves, and for the setting of limits on the economic shackles anyone could place on another individual. Even more profound is the rationale given for this radical kind of social redress: the Israelites were not to perpetuate the kind of bondage they had been forced to endure in Egypt (vv. 42, 55). A further resonance, with anticipatory links to the New Testament, is that the trumpet sounding of the announcement of the year of jubilee was to take place on the day of atonement (v. 9), thereby implicitly linking social and political freedom with the spiritual freedom of forgiveness provided by the atonement.

Is it any wonder, then, that the Prophetic tradition picked up the connection? In Isaiah 61 we read the emancipating message that Jesus recited as he announced the purpose of his mission on earth (Lk. 4.18-19):

> The Spirit of the Lord God is upon me; because the Lord hath anointed me to preach good tidings unto the meek; he hath sent me to bind up the broken-hearted, to proclaim liberty to the captives, and the opening of the prison to them that are bound; to proclaim the acceptable year of the Lord (Isa. 61.1-2).

It should not come as a surprise that Jesus' proclamation of his message of salvation validated and preserved the lofty perspective of the inextricable link between individual salvation and social emancipation. His imprimatur on the connection is also implicit in his reduction of the entire Old Testament law into two timeless mandates:

> Thou shalt love the Lord thy God with all thy heart, and with all thy soul, and with all thy strength, and with all thy mind; and thy neighbour as thyself (Lk. 10.27).

Jesus then coalesces his point with its immediate application in the account of the good Samaritan, whose presumed faith manifested itself

5. I am using the KJV throughout, as it dominates Ngugi's biblical citations throughout his works.

in good works—a major issue in the epistle of James. Justification by works (Jas 1.21) clearly counterbalances the theme of justification by faith in Romans 4 and, interestingly, both the Jacobean and the Pauline perspectives appeal to the archetypal example of Abraham.

There are, however, indications in the Gospels that Christ's methods for addressing social and political oppression transcend coercion, retaliation and violence. As we all know, the Sermon on the Mount (Mt. 5–7) admonishes us to love our enemies and to pray for those who despitefully use us (5.44). Jesus also radically alters the nature of rulership and authority by redefining it in terms of service to others instead of demanding servitude from others:

> Ye know that they which are accounted to rule over the Gentiles exercise lordship over them...but so it shall not be among you... And whosoever of you will be the chiefest, shall be servant of all (Mk 10.42-44).

Though consummately desirable, not merely as an ideal but as an earthly reality, the kingdom of God is not attainable by violent means—if we are hearing Christ's words accurately:

> My kingdom is not of this world: if my kingdom were of this world, then would my servants fight... (Jn 19.36).

Nevertheless, is it not our supreme longing to see God's will 'done in earth, as it is in heaven' (Mt. 6.10)?

Having been educated in schools founded by missionaries in Kenya, Ngugi was highly cognisant of the teachings of Scripture, as is readily apparent in the profuse number of biblical allusions in all of his novels. Two of his titles—one directly and the other obliquely—encapsulate overt scriptural motifs (*A Grain of Wheat* and *Devil on the Cross*). Ngugi's personal life, however, true of so many other members of the Kikuyu tribe, was greatly disrupted by the conflicts that emerged between the colonial government of Kenya and the Kikuyu-dominated Mau Mau guerrilla activities, which ultimately resulted in the dismantling of the shackles of colonial domination celebrated in Kenya's achievement of political independence in 1963. Ngugi's early novels, such as *The River Between*,[6] *Weep Not, Child*[7] and *A Grain of Wheat*,[8]

6. N. wa Thiong'o, *The River Between* (Nairobi: Heinemann, 1965). Though his first novel, this work was published after the appearance of *Weep Not, Child.*

7. N. wa Thiong'o, *Weep Not, Child* (Nairobi: Heinemann, 1964).

8. N. wa Thiong'o, *A Grain of Wheat* (Nairobi: Heinemann, 1967).

trace the history of some of the major issues at stake, up to Kenya's emergence into nationhood. His last three novels, *Petals of Blood*,[9] *Devil on the Cross*,[10] and *Matigari*,[11] reveal Ngugi's disappointment with the limited achievements of independence; the political blossoms have borne bitter fruit; the foreign political domination has been replaced with the external economic control defined as neo-colonialism, eloquently imaged in the title of *Petals of Blood.*

In looking back over this past century through Ngugi's eyes, we can detect three transgressions for which Ngugi would arraign the western world in its dealings with East Africa: cultural intrusion, political domination and economic exploitation. The first of these is the dominating theme of Ngugi's *The River Between.* An exquisite and lyrical work, this novel traces the powerful but invasive impact of the early missionaries on the indigenous culture of the Kikuyu tribe by means of the tool of education, the 'white man's magic' (p. 21). Part and parcel of this kind of education were the cultural, religious and even political values of the missionaries, who transmitted into the African setting the foreign perspectives of Europe, particularly of the UK. The central image of the novel, featured in the title, is the river of life, the Honia, the shared boundary of the two clans that comprise the tribe. Their common heritage begins to divide them, however, as the people on the Kemeno Ridge resist the proselytizing work of the missionaries, whereas the Makuyu inhabitants embrace these Christian endeavours. The complexity of the plot intensifies when one of the chief dignitaries from Kameno, Chege, sends his son, Waiyaki, to the missionary school to learn the 'white man's magic' in order to counteract this foreign intrusion. The characterization techniques also add richness to the novel, as the Christian tribal leader of Makuyu, Joshua, like his namesake from the Old Testament, is determined to 'serve the Lord' (Josh. 24.15) but, unlike his prototype, is a bigoted, unsympathetic and repellent individual. Waiyaki, while dedicated to the traditional values of his tribe, is depicted as a black messianic figure whose fame as a teacher and whose

9. N. wa Thiong'o, *Petals of Blood* (Nairobi: Heinemann, 1977).

10. N. wa Thiong'o, *Devil on the Cross* (Nairobi: Heinemann, 1982). Ngugi initially wrote this novel in his native Gikuyu, and subsequently translated it into English.

11. N. wa Thiong'o, *Matigari* (Oxford: Heinemann, 1989). Written in Gikuyu by Ngugi, this novel was translated into English by Wangui wa Goro.

magnanimity as a person earn him the love of Nyambura, Joshua's daughter. In keeping with his messianic role, Waiyaki's attempts to reunite these tribal factions lead to his rejection by both groups and to his presumed execution. Killam, in his *Introduction to the Writings of Ngugi*, has noted that Ngugi has 'exploit[ed] similarities' between Waiyaki and Christ, 'against a legendary history which reveals a strong association between the Gikuyu and the Christian myths'.[12]

Although panoramic, the novel also focuses on some very specific issues that separate traditional tribal cultural values from the entrenched customs of the western world, such as polygamy, male circumcision, and female circumcision. Joshua acknowledges that polygamy must be sinful, as it is denounced by the missionaries, though he wonders why it was acceptable to some of the Old Testament patriarchs. Male circumcision, though universally practised by the Jews, becomes suspect to Mr Livingstone, the missionary, when he responds in horror to the dances held on 'the eve of circumcision' (p. 56). The most controversial issue, female circumcision, a ceremony launching young females into womanhood in the Kikuyu tradition, is tied to the traumatic experience of Joshua's younger daughter, Muthoni, who escapes from her home to visit her aunt in Kameno in order to undergo this procedure. Unfortunately, she develops an infection, is taken to the missionary hospital, and dies, though maintaining to the end her conviction that she had not violated her personal belief in Christ. In all of these issues, Ngugi implies that the timeless tribal customs of the Kikuyu community have experienced unnecessary interference and disruption by external intrusions. He is more unequivocal in a speech on 'Church, Culture and Politics', presented at the Fifth Assembly of the Presbyterian Church of East Africa in Nairobi in 1970:

> The coming of Christianity...set in motion a process of social change, involving rapid disintegration of the tribal set-up and the frame-work of social norms and values by which people had formerly ordered their lives and their relationship to others.[13]

12. G.D. Killam, *An Introduction to the Writings of Ngugi* (London: Heinemann, 1980), p. 33.

13. N. wa Thiong'o, *Homecoming: Essays on African and Caribbean Literature, Culture and Politics* (Nairobi: Heinemann, 1972), p. 31.

Ngugi employs even harsher words as he synthesizes his views on the European political domination of Kenya, a process complicated by 'the contradiction inherent in colonialism and its religious ally, the Christian Church'.[14] He sees an irony in the fact that

> Christianity, whose basic doctrine was love and equality between men, was an integral part of that social force—colonialism—which in Kenya was built on the inequality and hatred between men and the consequent subjugation of the black race by the white race.[15]

The essence of this passage is distilled throughout his next novel, *Weep Not, Child.* The similarity of the name of the protagonist, Njoroge, to Ngugi conveys the author's personal feelings on the heart-wrenching events depicted in the novel. Njoroge is thrilled to be selected by his parents as the only child in his family to attend school. He 'came to place faith in the Bible and with his vision of an educated life in the future was blended a belief in the righteousness of God' (p. 49). A precocious pupil, Njorogi progresses rapidly in his studies, but ominous events begin to develop. His father, Ngotho, a humble labourer on a large farm owned by a colonialist, Mr Howlands, becomes involved in a strike in which Howlands' land manager, Jacobo, a black man, is wounded by the mob. Njoroge's brother, Boro, joins the Mau Mau resistance movement, and a state of emergency is declared when the popular Kikuyu patriot, Jomo, is arrested. For Njoroge, this news is devastating, for he had come to identify the Gikuyu people, 'whose land had been taken by white men', as none 'other than the children of Israel about whom he read in the Bible' (p. 49). The involvement of Njoroge's family in the resistance movement brings him to the attention of the police, who take him out of school, torture him and eventually release him—but all of his hopes have been crushed. These events cause him to lose his Christian faith, and the novel closes with his failed attempt at suicide.

The incongruity between the biblical perspective of social justice and the violent political conflict in Kenya that ended with Kenya's achievement of *Uhuru* (freedom) is a central issue in what many scholars have assessed as Ngugi's finest novel, *A Grain of Wheat.* Early in the work, Ngugi incorporates a resonant messianic/millennial passage from Psalm 72:

14. Ngugi, *Homecoming*, p. 31.
15. Ngugi, *Homecoming*, p. 31.

> He shall judge the poor of the people, he shall save the children of the needy, and shall break in pieces the oppressor. For he shall deliver the needy when he cometh; the poor also and he that hath no helper (Ps. 72.4, 12).[16]

This passage encapsulates both Ngugi's preoccupation with oppressive political regimes as well as his irrepressible vision of a society characterized by egalitarianism and justice. These biblical flashes of hope, however, do not inform the tactics of the ostensibly 'Christian' colonial powers in the novel; they are—rather significantly—found in the Bible that had belonged to Kihika, the Mau Mau freedom fighter, who had underlined these passages in red ink. By means of this literary stratagem, Ngugi has metaphorically disarmed the British-empowered colonial régime by turning their major spiritual weapon—the Scriptures—against them. It is, of course, not surprising that Ngugi's appeal to the Scriptures has aroused some heated criticisms. Peter Nazareth, for instance, points out the 'central irony'[17] involved in the biblical inspiration attached to Kihika; similarly, Gakwandi regards Ngugi's perception of the conflict as a 'bizarre interpretation of Scripture...reinterpreted to suit the people's own aspirations'.[18] Killam, somewhat more sympathetically, concedes that Ngugi 'has written this novel to explain, in artistic terms, and through a sustained comparison with Christian teaching, action and theology, the origins of the struggle and especially its legitimacy'.[19] In any case, Ngugi clearly condones force, if necessary, as a means of translating the biblical vision of social justice into a political reality:

> Violence in order to change an intolerable, unjust social order is not savagery: it purifies man. Violence to protect and preserve an unjust, oppressive social order is criminal, and diminishes man... The British perpetrated violence on the African people for fifty years.[20]

The central image of the novel, encapsulated in the title, is also featured in Kihika's Bible, where he had underlined Jn 12.24:

16. Ngugi, *A Grain of Wheat*, p. 22.

17. P. Nazareth, *Literature and Society in Modern Africa* (Nairobi: East Africa Literature Bureau, 1972), p. 144.

18. S. Gakwandi, *The Novel and Contemporary Experience in Africa* (New York: Africana, 1977), p. 113.

19. Killam, *An Introduction*, p. 55.

20. Ngugi, *Homecoming*, pp. 28-29.

> Verily, verily, I say unto you, Except a corn of wheat fall into the ground and die, it abideth alone: but if it die, it bringeth forth much fruit.[21]

Kihika had, in fact, fastened on the sacrifice of Jesus on the cross as the paradigm to be followed by the Kenyan freedom fighters: 'We have to be ready to carry the cross. I die for you, you die for me... Everybody who takes the Oath of Unity to change things in Kenya is a Christ' (p. 83). The Uhuru celebrations depicted at the conclusion of the novel focus primarily on honouring the memory of patriots like Kihika who had made the supreme sacrifice; their willingness to lay down their lives did not, however, signal defeat, but had rather opened the way for an abundant harvest of national freedom—a metaphorical resurrection patterned on the example of Christ.

Also juxtaposed to Kihika's 'corn of wheat' passage in the novel is the apocalyptic prophecy from Rev. 21.1, 'And I saw a new heaven and a new earth: for the first heaven and the first earth were passed away.'[22] As glorious as this distant prospect seems, it is not Ngugi's intention to replace earthly potentialities with heavenly escapism. Ngugi has here, as elsewhere, transmuted the Christian eschatological vision into earthly political concerns. A just society, for Ngugi, will usher in a 'new heaven and a new earth' or, more precisely, bring heaven to earth. In his famous speech to the Presbyterian General Assembly, this same kind of language appears:

> ...working in alliance with the socialist aspirations of the African masses, we might build a new society to create a new man freed from greed and competitive hatred...in a just socialist society. Remember that Book of Revelation: 'I saw a new heaven and a new earth...'[23]

A supporting corollary to the this-worldly focus of Ngugi's concerns is his distrust of what he would regard as a self-focused concept of salvation. This is clearly implied in one of the most grim incidents interwoven into *A Grain of Wheat.* A black revivalist by the name of Jackson publicly denounces politics, declaring, 'My home is in heaven: here on earth I am a pilgrim' (p. 74). This kind of detachment during the state of emergency aroused the wrath of the freedom fighters, who hacked him and other groups of Christians to pieces (p. 74). It is apparent that,

21. Ngugi, *A Grain of Wheat*, p. 175.
22. Ngugi, *A Grain of Wheat*, p. 175.
23. Ngugi, *Homecoming*, p. 36.

for Ngugi, political involvement is a necessary tool for implementing social justice.

The third major concern of Ngugi, as reflected in his last three novels, is what he regards as the economic exploitation of Africa, and this theme dominates these final works. Neo-colonialism, the overarching and widely employed term for this phenomenon, basically signifies that the political subservience previously endured by African nations has been replaced by such pervasive economic dependency that the disparities between the wealthy and the impoverished are as wide now as they were in the colonial era. The dedicatory page in *Devil on the Cross*, for instance, contains the blazoned words, 'To all Kenyans struggling against the neo-colonial stage of imperialism' (p. 5).

Worth noting is the fact that, while the central issues in the last three novels are virtually identical, these thematically related works demonstrate remarkable divergences in their plot and structure, thus attesting to Ngugi's ingenuity as a literary artist. *Petals of Blood*[24] has an enigmatic and richly ambiguous title combining plant and fire imagery, which Ngugi develops in his analysis of the blossoming of the plant of Uhuru and the burgeoning of the conflagrating forces that simultaneously threaten this freedom. The journey motif unites the plot, while also symbolically tracing Kenya's faltering progress in the brave new world of economic controls.

There are three major characters, all of whom represent segments of the society of post-independence Kenya. Wanja vacillates between the revolutionary spirit of her grandparents, who had fought for freedom, and the opportunistic expediency of her money-loving father; in effect, hers is a choice between an allegiance to socialistic ideals or to the capitalistic forces enveloping the new Kenya. The most enigmatic major character is Munira, a schoolteacher with emotional and psychological struggles who, prior to burning down Wanja's whorehouse, becomes a convert during a revival. Ngugi's portrayal of Munira has elicited the criticism that Munira is a 'fragment' rather than a fully rounded character',[25] while Palmer similarly argues that Ngugi's depiction of Munira is

24. The phrase, 'Petals of Blood', is Ngugi's conscious borrowing from a poem by the Caribbean poet, Derek Walcott, entitled 'The Swamp' (Introductory page of Ngugi's novel).

25. C.B. Robson, *Ngugi wa Thiong'o* (London: Macmillan, 1979), p. 99.

'one of the novel's major weaknesses'.[26] It can be argued, however, that Ngugi's resistance to any kind of faith is not rooted in earthly affairs and induces him to regard Munira's 'talk about new worlds with Christ' (p. 314) as an aberration and an unconscionable repudiation of personal responsibility. This is consistent with Ngugi's contemptuous depiction of a minor character in the novel, a black Anglican priest, Rev. Jerrod Brown, who offers the spiritual 'bread and fish of Jesus' (p. 149) to a destitute delegation of starving people instead of attending to their deplorable condition. Ngugi's protagonist is clearly the worker, Karega, who clings to his 'vision' of a 'kingdom of man and woman... of all the Kenyan working and peasant masses' who will create 'a new earth' in which 'all flowers' will 'ripen and bear fruits and seeds' (pp. 344, 294, 303), no longer drooping with petals of blood.

Ngugi returns to the issue of neo-colonialism in *Devil on the Cross*, but he moves from the intense seriousness of his previous novels to satire, parody and inversions, though without jeopardizing his underlying concerns. The links between the ruling forces in society and institutionalized Christianity are imaged in the title of this bizarre novel, and symbolic elements intrude throughout. The protagonist of the novel is a young woman named Wariinga, whose desperate attempt to commit suicide is thwarted by an alert stranger; in her subsequent dazed state, she has a nightmare of the Devil on the cross. In her reverie, she sees a 'crowd of people dressed in rags' who nail the Devil to the cross 'singing songs of victory' (p. 13). A parallel to Christ's resurrection follows, however, when, three days later, some wealthy, well-dressed men lift 'the Devil down from the Cross' (p. 13), and then continue their economic machinations at the expense of the poorest people around the world. The thematic implications of this nightmare are far-reaching; for most of the poverty-stricken peoples of the globe, destitution is a perpetual reality, not merely a bad dream. For Ngugi, the unholy alliances of the capitalistic countries of the world hold the Third World communities in lingering financial thralldom. The object of western devotion is not Christ, whose life and death exemplified a sacrificial love for others, but rather monetary power, imaged in Ngugi's devil.

Ngugi's penchant for employing Scripture as a tool is worked out in the ostensible biblical justification for capitalistic enterprises in Christ's parable of the talents in Matthew 25. His focus, however, is not on the

26. E. Palmer, 'Ngugi's *Petals of Blood*', *African Literature Today* 10 (1979), pp. 153-66.

servants who have successfully managed their master's affairs, but on the 'unprofitable servant' who accused his master of reaping where he had not sown. The master of the international 'Competition in Modern Theft and Robbery' (p. 76) boasts that the secret of his success is precisely his ability to reap what others have sown (p. 85), thus profiteering from the sweat and toil of others.

Ngugi's recurring depiction of social or political liberators as either Moses or Christ figures[27] recurs in *Matigari*, but in this novel the experiences of the protagonist, Matigari, are tied to the events in the life of Christ throughout the entire work. As in the Gospels, there are reports of miracles, proclamations of freedom and phenomenal appearances. In its unrelenting attack on the blatant economic inequities perpetuated by neo-colonialism, this novel is, in effect, the Gospel according to Ngugi.

And what are some of the essential features of Ngugi's 'Gospel'? In Christ's parables, there is a sharp contrast drawn between the jurisdictions of this world and the kingdom of Heaven. Matigari also speaks in parables, as in this example of neo-colonial disparities:

> The worker produces goods.
> Foreigners and parasites dispose of them.
> The worker is left empty handed.
>
> Where are truth and justice on this earth?

Both the New Testament Gospels and Ngugi's 'Gospel' also contain an eschatological message. Jesus prophesies that the 'distress of nations' will terminate when 'they shall see the Son of man coming in a cloud with power and great glory' (Lk. 21.25, 27). Matigari shares with some inquiring youths his conviction that there is a 'God' within humans who some day 'will come alive and liberate us who believe in Him', and thereby bring an end to the 'imperialism' that has 'tried to kill that God within us' (p. 156).

Ngugi's vision of an egalitarian society in which there is no discrimination on the basis of 'tribe, race or colour' and where the earth will 'return to the tiller' and 'the worker...to whom it belongs' (p. 156), is not predicated on any kind of faith in either credal or institutionalized Christianity, however. Matigari clearly declares, 'I don't belong to your

27. This motif has been explored in my previous article, 'Images of Christ in East African Literature', in S.E. Porter, M.A. Hayes and D. Tombs (eds.), *Images of Christ: Ancient and Modern* (RILP, 2; Sheffield: Sheffield Academic Press, 1997), pp. 239-58.

religions or to your churches' (p. 94). His message is not doctrinal, but political and social; the 'God' within human beings represents all of the possibilities and potentialities of the peoples of the earth to bring about their own emancipation. As symbolized in the name of the protagonist of this novel, Matigari ma Njiruungi, 'the patriots who survived the bullets' (p. 20), this kind of liberation, for Ngugi, manifests the highest form of patriotism.

As we absorb some of the implications of Ngugi's criticisms and concerns relating to institutionalized Christianity, while maintaining our faith in the integrity of the Scriptures, how can we most salutarily 'prepare the way of the Lord' (Isa. 40.3) for this new millennium? And how can we, following the footsteps of Christ, proclaim 'the acceptable year of the Lord' (Lk. 4.19)? What are the essential features of a truly integrated and wholistic gospel that addresses the 'whole spirit and soul and body' (1 Thess. 5.23) of people whom we are attempting to reach?

Perhaps the best place to begin is to revisit Ngugi's three major historical concerns: cultural intrusion, political domination and economic exploitation. Regarding the first, Ngugi's arraignment must be acknowledged. In the words of François Lumbala, we hear the lament, 'our cultural elements have been rejected and disparaged by colonialism',[28] and from Patrick Kalilombe we begin to see that 'the real tragedy is that traditional culture has been practically discredited'.[29] In response to such concerns, we must enlarge our appreciation for cultural diversity and approach such differences with greater sensitivity. Some missionary organizations have been more successful than others in accommodating tribal customs that, while divergent from western patterns, cannot be regarded as a violation of Scripture. And there is also room for re-evaluating one's own culture in the light of Scripture. Byang Kato's categorical dictum applies to us all: '[Biblical] Christianity is absolute'.[30] Nevertheless, this limitation is not antithetical to the worthy goal, for instance, of what Rosino Gibellini terms as an 'authentically African...Christianity'.[31]

28. Lumbala, 'Africans Celebrate', p. 80.

29. P. Kalilombe, 'Spirituality in the African Perspective', in Gibellini (ed.), *Paths of African Theology*, pp. 115-35 (131).

30. B.H. Kato, *Theological Pitfalls in Africa* (Kisumu: Evangel Publishing House, 1975), p. 168.

31. R. Gibellini, 'African Theologians Wonder...and Make Some Proposals', in *idem* (ed.), *Paths of African Theology*, pp. 1-8 (7).

The sordid history of the external political domination of Africa is an even sadder issue, in spite of the dismantling of colonial regimes in the last half of this past century. While it would be hard to deny that missionary activity was generally supported by foreign political governments, it is refreshing to encounter Kalilombe's opinion that 'Christian evangelization' has largely been 'in opposition to...the "spirituality" of colonialism'.[32] This tallies with a comment shared with me by a fellow doctoral student from Sierra Leone studying at the University of Alberta to the effect that 'missionaries were the only bright spot in the sordid history of colonialism'. It is also encouraging to see how much national Christian communities have grown and developed subsequent to independence, largely through the efforts of their own leaders. Another delightful development is the increasing numbers of Africans doing missionary work in, for example, Canada—a tacit recognition that our common citizenship as members of the universal Church of Christ transcends earthly political boundaries and jurisdictions.

Ngugi's distress over neo-colonialism is as pressing an issue as ever, with widening internal economic gaps within countries and increasing disparities between the 'have' and 'have not' nations of the globe; Africa is an acute example of this phenomenon. Kalilombe's analysis of the spirit of neo-colonialism is particularly insightful. He sees it, in effect, as the spirit of materialism, which 'promises attractive, immediate, and palpable results', but which is 'in opposition' to the love of God and neighbour.[33] Kalilombe points out that 'traditional African spirituality (ideally, though perhaps not always in fact)'[34] has valued human relationships above material goods, and that this provides a pattern for the Christians of the world to emulate in their priorities, as they keep the needs of the disadvantaged in mind. Reminding us that God chooses what is weak to shame the strong, Kalilombe concludes with a challenge and a hope that we might well consider as we enter the next millennium:

> In our present world, cultures of greed and violence are creating death while people long for peace, security, and joy. It may be that simple spiritualities, based on more human and humane values, like those

32. Kalilombe, 'Spirituality', p. 133.
33. Kalilombe, 'Spirituality', p. 133.
34. Kalilombe, 'Spirituality', p. 133.

> coming from the weak and poor nations of the world, are the hopeful reserves for humanity's future survival.[35]

Ngugi's appeal to the apocalyptic vision of 'a new heaven and a new earth' (*Homecoming*, p. 36) resonates around the globe, as in the challenge of Bonino of Argentina, who contends that the Christian gospel must be formulated

> in terms of the kingdom and the history of salvation, of the proclamation of the jubilee of the grace of Jesus, of the hope for new heavens and a new earth... Jesus Christ is the archetype and mediator of a true human life—personal and collective—not a means to achieve some subjective superhuman exaltation.[36]

The kingdom of God must be realized both individually and socially, as those who become new creations in Christ (2 Cor. 5.17) translate their love for God into redemptive social action: 'Inasmuch as ye have done it unto one of the least of these my brethren, ye have done it unto me' (Mt. 25.40).

35. Kalilombe, 'Spirituality', pp. 134-35.

36. J.M. Bonino, 'Conversion: A Latin American Rereading', in D. Kirpatrick (ed.), *Faith Born in the Struggle for Life* (trans. L. McCoy; Grand Rapids: Eerdmans, 1988), pp. 3-14 (9, 12).

A Theology of the Other: Some Postcolonial Themes in Brian Moore's Late Twentieth-Century Fiction

Liam Gearon

Introduction

Much of Brian Moore's fiction, from 1955 until the author's death in 1999, was concerned with a portrayal of Catholicism.[1] This preoccupation is in some ways surprising for a writer whose personal relationship with Catholicism demonstrated a lifetime of ambivalence if not open antagonism to the religion of his birth.[2] Setting aside the relationship between the author's life and his literary work, this essay examines some of Brian Moore's final writings, which throw light on his preoccupations not only with Catholic theology but Catholic encounter

1. The novels of Brian Moore in chronological, first publication order are: *Judith Hearne* (London: Andre Deutsch, 1955); *The Feast of Lupercal* (Boston: Little, Brown, 1957); *The Luck of Ginger Coffey* (London: Andre Deutsch, 1960); *An Answer from Limbo* (Boston: Little, Brown, 1962); *The Emperor of Ice-Cream* (Boston: Little Brown, 1965); *I Am Mary Dunne* (London: Jonathan Cape, 1968); *Catholics* (London: Jonathan Cape, 1972); *The Mangan Inheritance* (London: Jonathan Cape, 1979); *Cold Heaven* (London: Jonathan Cape, 1983); *Black Robe* (London: Jonathan Cape, 1985); *The Colour of Blood* (London: Jonathan Cape); *Lies of Silence* (London: Vintage, 1990); *No Other Life* (London: Bloomsbury, 1993); *The Statement* (London: Bloomsbury, 1995); *The Magician's Wife* (London: Bloomsbury, 1997). Original dates of publication have been retained to avoid confusion when referencing but page references (where relevant) are to these most recent and easily available editions.

2. See D. Sampson, *Brian Moore: The Chameleon Novelist* (Dublin: Marino, 1998). Also H. Dahlie, *Brian Moore* (Toronto: Copp Clark, 1969); H. Dahlie, *Brian Moore* (Boston: Twayne Publishers, 1981). In addition to the biocritical studies of Dahlie and Sampson, J. O'Donoghue, *Brian Moore: A Critical Study* (Dublin: Gill & Macmillan, 1990), and R. Sullivan, *A Matter of Faith: The Fiction of Brian Moore* (Westport, CT: Greenwood Press, 1996), are major studies of Moore's fiction and include bibliographical sources.

with the cultural and specifically *religious* other; and I want to show ways in which the notions of identity set against alterity, otherness and difference are key themes too in both post-Vatican II theology and postcolonialism. The essay will thus demonstrate how the latter two perspectives—of some import for defining the theological and ideological landscape of the early third millennium—are provided with a reflective, literary space in the novels of Brian Moore.

From Colonialism to Liberation: Post-Vatican II and Postcolonial Perspectives[3]

It might be useful from the outset to clarify further some basic terms and intentions, for this essay. First, I want to address the parameters for the postcolonial theory/criticism as well as the variant uses of terms, such as postcolonial/postcoloniality/postcolonialism. Secondly, I want to establish some parameters for an outline discussion of post-Vatican II theology. I want then to focus on the fiction of Brian Moore, and in the main consider his late twentieth-century fiction, to provide a literary demonstration of some potentially common ground between postcolonial criticism and post-Vatican II theology.

First, then, we need to distinguish between postcoloniality, as historical and political state of the post/colonial, and postcolonialism, the theory of postcoloniality within the academy.[4] Within this context, it is an emerging assumption within the field that a distinction also needs to be made between postcolonial *theory*, as cultural *commentary* on power imbalances between the the colonized and colonizer, and postcolonial *criticism*, as more (actively) political and *engaged involvement in overcoming such power imbalances*. This is perhaps best illustrated by distinguishing between seminal texts, say between the postcolonial *criticism* of Fanon's *The Wretched of the Earth*,[5] and the postcolonial *theory* of Said's *Orientalism*.[6] Both centre concerns around power imbalances

3. E. Dussel, *The Church in Latin America, 1492–1992* (London: Burns & Oates, 1992).

4. B. Moore-Gilbert, G. Stanton and W. Maley, *Postcolonial Criticism* (London: Longman, 1997), pp. 57-62; L. Gandhi, *Postcolonial Theory* (New York: Columbia University Press, 1998), pp. 1-24.

5. F. Fanon, *The Wretched of the Earth* (trans. C. Farrington; Harmondsworth: Penguin Books, 3rd edn, 1990).

6. E. Said, *Orientalism: Western Conceptions of the Orient* (Harmondsworth:

and the oppressive use of such power for domination—territorial gain, cultural and political imperialism, but the two have differences of emphasis and approach, illustrated well by their respective influences: Fanon's by Marx and Said's by Foucault.[7]

More broadly, we can recognize here the central but often uneasy alliance within postcolonialism of Marxism and poststructuralism.[8] The 'alliance' between Marxism and poststructuralism arises in postcolonialism because of the latter's concerns for (a) social/economic/political reform in the context of exploitative inequality (central to Marxism)[9] and (b) affirmation of cultural difference in the face of universalism that defines the marginal as 'other' (a feature of post-

Penguin Books, 1995 [1978]); also *idem*, 'Orientalism Reconsidered', in F. Barker, P. Hulme and M. Iversen (eds.), *Colonial Discourse/Postcolonial Theory* (Manchester: Manchester University Press, 1994), pp. 210-29.

7. We might as easily contrast A. Cesaire's *Discourse on Colonialism* (Paris: Editions Presence Africaine, 1955) and the representative selection of essays in H.K. Bhabha's *The Location of Culture* (London: Routledge, 1994), extracts reprinted in Moore-Gilbert, Stanton and Maley, *Postcolonial Criticism*, pp. 73-90, 166-90, respectively. On pp. 248-72, with useful commentary, is an extract from A. Ahmad's *In Theory: Classes, Nations and Literatures* (London: Verso, 1992), a critical stance against Said and Bhabha particularly and postcolonialism as a whole for its failure to recognize ongoing inequality in West/non-West international relations. Ahmad's position neatly illustrates the Marxist influence of the more radical postcolonial critics, to the extent that Ahmad largely dissociates himself from postcolonialism altogether. See also Gandhi's summary of Said's critics in *Postcolonial Theory*, pp. 65-80.

8. Marxism has thus often charged poststructuralism, with its emphasis on the ending of grand narratives so well exemplified by Lyotard, as a neglect of the progress of history through socio-economic change. In other words Marxists charge poststructuralists with undermining Marxist grand narrative. Indeed, the charge is often made specific to show the political damage of poststructuralism in the 1980s' ascendancy of the right, especially the transatlantic alliance of Thatcher and Reagan. Poststructuralists argue in turn that Marxism imposes an enlightenment-derived universalism in its global socio-economic analysis and ignores the importance of cultural difference, and arguably religious difference in particular. Marx is thus often cited pejoratively as having seen the value of British empire-building as a necessary stage in the socio-economic reform, highlighting in particular Marx's negative view or attitude to Indian culture. See Gandhi's critical overview of postcolonialism intellectual history and current relation within the academy in *Postcolonial Theory*, pp. 1-64; also Moore-Gilbert, Stanton and Maley, *Postcolonial Criticism*, pp. 1-72.

9. See A. Brewer, *Marxist Theories of Imperialism: A Critical Survey* (London: Routledge and Kegan Paul, 1980).

structuralism).[10] We can postulate a scale dependent upon the emphasis placed upon either an 'engaged' (Marxist) stance or more 'detached' cultural criticism (poststructuralist) position. Such a scale might also, if simplistically, be described as ranging from a politically engaged anti-colonial/imperial nationalism (postcolonial criticism) to transnational cultural commentary (postcolonial theory). If we again compare Fanon and Said, it is the difference between the postcolonial *criticism* of Fanon's anti-imperialist revolutionary stance against French colonialism in Algeria in *The Wretched of the Earth* and the postcolonial *theory* of Said's (post-/transnational) cultural analysis of *Orientalism*, further exemplified, even typified by *Culture and Imperialism*.[11]

It is appropriate now to move postcolonialism to a post-Vatican II perspective, and I am here following McBrien's definition of Catholicism as a Church and a faith, an ecclesiology and a theology that epitomizes a universalist soteriology by the very nature of its own self-definition *as* catholic.[12] I want, however, to distinguish between a pre- and post-Vatican II understanding of this soteriological universalism in both ecclesiological and theological terms.

Vatican II is defined—as we may define postcolonialism—through seminal texts, those primarily of the Council itself, as well as postconciliar documents that arose from the Council's new theological direction.[13] This new theological direction was as much pastoral as it was doctrinal, unlike the preceding others into which context it must be put.[14] The Council was thus concerned with a re-orientation to a world

10. For instance, H. Bhabha, 'The Other Question: Difference, Discrimination and the Discourse of Colonialism', in F. Barker, P. Hulme and M. Iversen (eds.), *Literature, Politics and Theory* (London: Methuen, 1986), pp. 148-73.

11. E. Said, *Culture and Imperialism* (London: Vintage, 1994 [1993]).

12. R.P. McBrien, *Catholicism* (New York: HarperCollins, 1994).

13. See Appendix at the end of this chapter for a list of the documents of the Second Vatican Council and their respective dates of publication. See A. Flannery (ed.), *Vatican Council II: The Conciliar and Post Conciliar Documents* (Dublin: Dominican Publications, 1992). For an overview of trends in post-Vatican II theology, see M.A. Hayes and L. Gearon (eds.), *Contemporary Catholic Theology: A Reader* (Leominster: Gracewing, 1998; New York: Continuum, 1999); also see A. Hastings, 'Catholic History from Vatican I to John Paul II', in *idem* (ed.), *Modern Catholicism: Vatican II and After* (London: SPCK, 1991), pp. 1-13. For an approach to 'Evaluation and Interpretation of the Documents of Vatican II', see F. Sullivan in Hayes and Gearon, *Contemporary Catholic Theology*, pp. 335-48.

14. See M. Walsh, 'Councils in Church History', in Hastings (ed.), *Modern*

from which, since Vatican I, the Church had separated itself, essentially in epistemological distance from 'Modernism', post-Enlightenment developments per se.[15] Like all universalist doctrines, however, the pre-Vatican II Catholic Church, confident of its own identity, secured such assured self-understanding in part at least through the often pejorative definition of the non-Catholic 'other'. In the case of Catholicism, such an ecclesiology was marked by an equally stringent theology, classically stated by the formulation that 'there is no salvation outside the Church'.

This changed with the Second Vatican Council (1962–65). Three key areas are of most relevance for our present discussion. First, the Church redefined itself as an institution from a hierarchical to a more egalitarian (if as yet far from democratic) ecclesiology, from a 'Church militant' to the 'People of God'. The key document here is *Lumen Gentium*.[16] It is *Lumen Gentium* that illustrates too the second development, a theology also arising from more moderate ecclesiology, that is, a radical redefinition of soteriology. Essentially the shift from 'no salvation outside the Church' to a universal model of salvation could not be more marked. Here (even though some may find this patronizing), the Church recognized the possibility of salvation for those *outside* the Church, a doctrine incorporating ecumenism in *Unitatis Redintegratio*, and, in *Nostra Aetate*, the possibility of salvation *through* the religious other of Buddhism, Hinduism, Judaism and Islam, and even atheism in *Lumen Gentium*. Thirdly, even with a strong history of social teaching, the Church demonstrated a growing awareness through the Second Vatican Council that a post-Vatican I 'separation' of the Church from 'the world' prevented a full involvement with issues of social, economic and political import. *Gaudium et Spes* is generally recognized as the document that most fully exemplifies this new spirit of active socio-economic engagement and Christian responsibility.[17] The latter, for instance, is accredited, particularly post-Medellín,[18] with the develop-

Catholicism, pp. 14-19; also T.P. Rausch, 'The Church and the Council', in Hayes and Gearon (eds.), *Contemporary Catholic Theology*, pp. 258-78.

15. See Hastings, 'Catholic History', pp. 1-13.

16. For a critical overview of this document, see R.P. McBrien, 'The Church', in Hayes and Gearon (eds.), *Contemporary Catholic Theology*, pp. 279-93.

17. For commentary, see E. McDonagh, 'The Church in the Modern World', in Hayes and Gearon (eds.), *Contemporary Catholic Theology*, pp. 294-315.

18. See A.T. Hennelly (ed.), *Liberation Theology: A Documentary History*

ment of liberation theology's conjoining of a 'people of God' ecclesiology with a pastoral theology of social justice.[19]

It is this identity with the poor against injustice and oppression in which inheres a potential degree of commonality in approach and ideological orientation between post-Vatican II theology and postcolonialism. That liberation theology and postcolonialism share varying degrees of emphasis on Marxist analysis is an obvious point of such theological/ideological reference. Such an identity is, however, more significantly reinforced when the analysis of oppression is rooted in the history of the colonial and *especially where liberation is defined through its postcoloniality.*[20] With a key emphasis upon the historical context of soteriology, such theological/ideological analyses naturally lead to an examination of the structural roots of injustice in historical as well as contemporary context. In many theological communities, often but not exclusively in former colonies, the re-examination of biblical scholarship in the context of histories of oppression thus leads, perhaps inevitably, to analysis not simply of present-day injustice but the historical roots of inequality. The historical irony here, of course, is that in so many colonial histories, the imperialism of economic and political might was vouchsafed by theologies of superiority, with colonization often accompanying and consolidating supposed soteriological conquests.[21]

Tentatively, then, I am suggesting then that post-Vatican II theology and postcolonialism (theory and criticism) share a common stance on a

(New York: Orbis Books, 1990), especially 'From Vatican II to Medellín', pp. 39-119, and particularly the text from the Second General Conference of Latin American Bishops, 'The Church in the Present-Day Transformation of Latin America in the Light of the Council' (26 August–6 September 1968), pp. 89-119.

19. See R. Charles SJ, *Christian Social Witness and Teaching: The Catholic Tradition from Genesis to Centesimus Annus*, in two volumes, but especially vol. II, *The Modern Social Teaching—Context: Summary: Analysis* (Leominster: Gracewing, 1998). For a useful juxtaposition of Catholic sexual morality and social teaching, see T.P. Rausch, 'Sexual Morality and Social Justice', in Hayes and Gearon (eds.), *Contemporary Catholic Theology*, pp. 403-33. For a wider overview of moral theology, see T.E. O'Connell, 'The History of Moral Theology', in Hayes and Gearon (eds.), *Contemporary Catholic Theology*, pp. 389-402.

20. A notable demonstration of this point is the manner in which Enrique Dussel's influential history of liberation theology in South America deals precisely with the movement from 'colonialism to liberation'.

21. For a global, historical overview, accompanied by extensive bibliographies, see A. Hastings (ed.), *A World History of Christianity* (London: Cassell, 1999).

number of grounds, and here I identify three: an emphasis on historical perspective in the analysis of social-structural inequality; an identity with the marginalized and oppressed 'other'; and a radical, *social* interpretation of texts. Thus, in identifying the historicity of oppression, Vatican II theology and postcolonialism both provide ideological and theological focus on (and give voice to) the marginalized other; providing for religious and ideological readings of texts as economically and politically transformative *or* inherently conservative,[22] either upholding the colonial or subverting the imperial.[23]

A Theology of the Other: Religion, Ideology and Alterity

Broadly following Said's line of analysis in *The World, the Text and the Critic*—that in fact all writings as cultural artefacts are inevitably rooted in the historical moment of particular communities—I want to develop this congruence of ideas, ideological and theological, and attempt to characterize Brian Moore's late twentieth-century fiction as a

22. See, for instance, B. Ashcroft, G. Griffiths and H. Tiffin (eds.), *The Empire Writes Back: Theory and Practice in Postcolonial Literature* (London: Routledge, 1989); H.K. Bhabha (ed.), *Nation and Narration* (London: Routledge, 1990); H. Tiffin (ed.), *De-scribing Empire: Postcolonialism and Textuality* (London: Routledge,1994). The expression of empire through aesthetic is of course definitively presented in Said's *Culture and Imperialism.* I have already hinted at degrees of radical interpretation within postcolonialism and the divisions incurred, and the move from commentary to political engagement is potentially a long one, or a journey not undertaken, which is the critique of Ahmad's *In Theory: Classes, Nations, Literatures.*

23. See, for instance, the section headed 'Biblical Books Favoured by Liberation Theology', in L. Boff and C. Boff, *Introducing Liberation Theology* (trans. P. Burns; Tunbridge Wells: Burns & Oates, 1987), pp. 34-35. There are always historical caveats, of course. 'Postcolonialism' could argue that Catholicism maintains a patriarchal hold on many oppressed societies. Liberation theology might argue by way of return that its intention to make the Church a Church of the poor, its option for the poor, should be interpreted in the widest possible sense, that a theology of poverty needs to be widened to include minorities and the marginalized, including women, and that liberation theology is the process of overcoming oppression of any kind. It is a tension which has led to conflict, of course, within the Church itself. Again, see Hennelly, *Liberation Theology*. Also of interest, M. Prior, *The Bible and Colonialism: A Moral Critique* (Sheffield: Sheffield Academic Press, 1995). For a critical assessment of the influence of theology on postcolonial writing, see S. Gupta's 'Post-Colonial Literature and Metaphysics', in L. Gearon (ed.), *English Literature, Theology and the Curriculum* (London: Cassell, 1999), pp. 348-71.

similar, literary unification of post-Vatican II and postcolonial perspectives. A long-time lapsed Catholic, Moore's interest in Catholicism demonstrates a peculiar literary dependence on a grand narrative long since abandoned.[24] Moore had also early resisted a political stance in relation to the staunch Irish nationalism he had inherited from his Catholic Belfast family and rejected too a youthful flirtation with Marxism.[25] Moore's lifelong, if paradoxical, preoccupation with Catholicism can and should, though, be seen in wider ideological context.

Since *Judith Hearne* and his early Irish novels, Moore demonstrated a literary interest in the relationship between the religious and the political, a theology of the pulpit that is rarely emphasized in studies of Moore's early Belfast novels, while more obvious in later Irish works.[26] Further, though, not only is this joint theological/ ideological perspective apparent (if largely unexamined) in such obvious Irish settings but it persists on the margins of much less likely contexts in Moore's early North American novels. Take, for instance, the historical background to Mary Dunne's family as Irish immigrants from the Irish Famine of the 1840s:

> Father Malone, according to Grandma Dunne, was the name of an Irish cardinal. It seems the cardinal led thousands of Irish emigrants to Australia to save them from the famine. My great-grandfather was to have gone to Australia with the cardinal's group and had christened his new baby in honour of the cardinal. But, at the last minute, Great-grandfather Dunne changed his mind, raised his own passage money, and sailed to Quebec instead. If he had sailed to Australia I would not have been. Sometimes, I think of that.[27]

However, most significantly, where post-Vatican II and post-Medellín Catholicism developed its global ideological involvement, Moore *also* found renewed theological meaning in issues of social justice. Moore's post-Vatican II novels demonstrate, then, not only continued preoccupation with Catholicism but increased awareness of theology's political dimension and active ideological commitment, the link between political and salvation history; and, in his concern for justice (more humanistic than religiously committed), Moore nevertheless demonstrates an interest in post-Vatican II theology and post-coloniality.

24. See Sampson, *Brian Moore*, pp. 34-35.
25. Again, see Sampson, *Brian Moore*, pp. 34-35.
26. Such as Moore, *Lies of Silence*.
27. Moore, *I Am Mary Dunne*, p. 15.

Moore's novel *Catholics* can be seen as a turning point in Moore's consideration of Vatican II theology in a political context. In this novella the post-Vatican IV emissary Kinsella is sent to reform the traditionalist community of monks on the Island of Muck off the West Coast of Ireland, itself a richly symbolic place for Irish nationalist struggle, which becomes the confluence of religious struggle too between the political and liturgical conservatism of the old tradition and the new revolutionary Church. Significant here are seminal references to liberation theology. The publication of *Catholics* so close to seminal work of liberation theology, close to works by (for instance) Gutierrez[28] and Boff,[29] is likely to be coincidental but Moore has picked up on a new revolutionary spirit of the Church at the time.[30]

The history of Catholic oppression also persists as an often neglected backdrop to *Catholics*. Thus the 'out of print' *Weir's Guide to Religious Monuments* presents the monastic community of Muck in wider historical context, one which has persistently demonstrated the clash between political and theology:

> MUCK ABBEY, Kerry, Ireland. On a small island off the rocky panoramic coastline of the Atlantic Ocean known as 'The ring of Kerry'. The Monastery (Albanesian Order), founded 1216, rebuilt 1400–70, has a dependency, or cell, on the mainland, the priory of Holy Cross, at Mount Coom near the village of Cahirciveen. This priory, sacked by Cromwellian troops, was, in Penal times, a site for clandestine mass, conducted in the open air on a 'mass rock' altar. The Abbey itself (on Muck Island) escaped Cromwellian despoliation...[31]

It is against this historical metatext that *Catholics*' liberation theology references might also be read, as we might surmise a postcolonial reading (a state of postcoloniality) for 'post-Vatican IV' Ireland.

A further development in Moore's fiction towards a congruence of theology and postcoloniality is shown in *Cold Heaven* (1983). In ways which prefigure *Black Robe*, *Cold Heaven* presents the roots of North American Catholicism within the historical context of Church mission and early colonial enterprise, here late seventeenth-century Spanish

28. G. Gutierrez, *Teología de la liberación* (Lima: CEP, 1971), ET *A Theology of Liberation* (New York: Orbis Books, 1973).

29. L. Boff, *Jesus Cristo Libertador* (Petropolis: Vozes, 1979), ET *Jesus Christ Liberator* (New York: Orbis Books, 1978).

30. See Boff and Boff, *Introducing Liberation Theology*, pp. 66-77.

31. Moore, *Catholics*, p. 7.

imperialism.[32] Despite its contemporary setting, then, Marie Davenport's experience of the numinous, a vision of the Virgin Mary around which the novel's plot turns, takes place on the Monterey Coast. The following serves not simply as a metatext for the reading of Marie Davenport's experiences but a wider history of ideological and theological grand narrative of which they form a part:

> Our Lady of Monterey
> On an expedition to the Monterey Peninsula in 1780, the Archbishop of Merida sent this statue in care of the Franciscan monks to be conquistador of this new land. On arrival the monks placed it in a temporary altar and later installed it in the mission in this place.
>
> In 1799 Captain Portillo gave the statue a silver crown in thanks for the miraculous relief of his vessels when they were almost shipwrecked on the cliffs near this chapel. An invocation to our Lady of Monterey produced a sudden, total calming of the elements for several minutes during which the vessels were enabled to come about and the crews and vessels were saved.
>
> When the mission was abandoned after secularization, the statue was cared for by local Indians in their homes. After the Sisters of Mary Immaculate established their convent here in 1921, the statue was found in the home of one of the surviving Indian families. It was restored to its original chapel in 1937.[33]

Locale is important here for the novel, as it is in post-Vatican II thinking, because of a decentralized emphasis on the specificity of pastoral need;[34] and in postcolonialism because territory is at the heart of colonization.[35] When Marie Davenport's vision is transferred to the nun

32. For an introductory overview of the history of Christianity in North America, see R.B. Mullin, 'North America', in Hastings (ed.), *A World History of Christianity*, pp. 416-57; also the classic work by R.T. Handy, *A History of the Churches in the United States and Canada* (Oxford: Clarendon Press, 1976).

33. Moore, *Cold Heaven*, p. 64.

34. See E. McDonagh, 'The Church in the Modern World', in Hayes and Gearon (eds.), *Contemporary Catholic Theology*, pp. 294-315.

35. Said comments: 'It is difficult to connect these different realms, to show the involvements of culture with expanding empires, to make observations about art that preserve its unique endowments and at the same time map its affiliations, but, I submit, we must attempt this, and set art in the earthly, global context. Territory and possessions are at stake, geography and power. Everything about human history is rooted in the earth, which means we must think about habitation, but it has also meant that people have planned to *have* more territory and therefore must do something about its indigenous residents. At some very basic level, imperialism means

Sister Anna towards the novel's close, the latter's comment that this 'would be a place of reverence' adds to Marie Davenport's testimony about the purpose of the vision. More important, though, is the stated, physical appearance of the Virgin in the latter's vision: 'Her skin is dark, like a Mexican's.'[36] This provides a narrative circularity to the visionary. It was, after all, in the process of Spanish mission to the indigenous peoples that the Virgin first appeared and 'when the mission was abandoned after secularization', the commemorative statue 'cared for by local Indians in their homes'.

Significantly, then, this prefaces Moore's post-Vatican II shift in locale and focus of his portrayal of Catholicism. From *Cold Heaven* Moore no longer examines the place of Catholicism, as institution and world-view, through western culture and society. Such treatment was previously focused, often in cross-cultural ways, on Ireland and North America. If Moore uses these settings again, though, it is to look at their social and cultural margins: to indigenous peoples in the history of the colonial Canada of New France (*Black Robe*), to the struggle against Communist imperialism (*The Colour of Blood*), to the oppressed in the Caribbean (*No Other Life*), to Jewish persecution (*The Statement*) and, in his final novel, to French colonial incursion into Islamic Algeria (*The Magician's Wife*). With a post-Vatican II portrayal of Catholicism increasingly losing its Eurocentric focus, especially post-Medellín, it is entirely natural that Moore's novels should themselves reflect, in the novelist's continuing preoccupation with religion as favourite metaphor,[37] an increasing geographical and theological diversity.

Theologically and ideologically, then, Moore's most notable interests in his late fictions reflect a convergence of post-Vatican II Catholic and

thinking about, settling on, controlling land that you do not possess, that is distant, that is lived on and owned by others. For all kinds of reasons it attracts some people and involves others in untold misery. Yet it is generally true that literary historians who study the great sixteenth-century poet Edmund Spenser, for example, do not connect his bloodthirsty plans for Ireland, where he imagined a British army virtually exterminating the native inhabitants, with his poetic achievement or with the history of British rule over Ireland, which continues today' (Said, *Culture and Imperialism*, p. 5).

36. Moore, *Cold Heaven*, p. 233.

37. See T. Brown, 'Show Me a Sign: The Religious Imagination of Brian Moore', *Irish University Review* 18 (1988), pp. 37-49, and P. Gallagher, 'Religion as Favourite Metaphor: Moore's Recent Fiction', *Irish University Review* 18 (1998), pp. 50-58.

postcolonial thinking, perspectives especially apparent in *Black Robe* (1985) and in Moore's final novel, *The Magician's Wife* (1997), two novels whose historical settings predate both postcolonial criticism and the Second Vatican Council but, significantly, whose ideological and theological positions do not. Both *Black Robe* and *The Magician's Wife* provide a treatment of cultural, religious and ideological otherness in historical context while demonstrating a wider authorial presentation of a more contemporary shift from pre- to post-Vatican II theology and from a colonial to postcolonial perspective.

Black Robe

Moore's story of seventeenth-century French colonial and missionary enterprise in Quebec tells of the journey of a Jesuit priest, Father Laforgue, to the northern outpost of Ihonatiria.[38] Laforgue's is a journey of personal transformation through encounter with the (indigenous) 'other'. I argue that this transformation in Laforgue marks (however anachronistically) the later historical shift in post-Vatican II theology as well as a postcolonial perspective: from a distinct otherness ('there is no salvation outside the church') to identity, an empathetic respect for difference, a stance in favour of those marginalized in the history of imperialism.[39]

The preparatory 'Author's Note' makes plain the sources of historical research for *Black Robe*: Graham Greene's *Collected Essays*, the latter's discussion of *The Jesuits of North America*, deriving in turn largely from the work of Francis Parkman (1823–93) who in his turn had consulted the Jesuits' letters to their supporters in France, the *Relations*.[40] From the outset of his novel Moore contextualizes the cultural

38. Again, for an overview of the period, see Mullin, 'North America', pp. 416-57, as well as Handy. For a recent treatment of writing and identity in Canada, including postcolonial perspectives, see C. Verduyn (ed.), *Literary Pluralities* (Ontario: Broadview Press; Journal of Canadian Studies, 1998).

39. For an early 'pre-postcolonial' reading of theology and imperialism, see H. Camara, *Church and Colonialism* (London: Sheed & Ward, 1969).

40. See, for instance, R.G. Thwaites (ed.), *The Jesuit Relations and Allied Documents: Travels and Explorations of the Jesuit Missionaries in New France, 1610–1791*, XXII (New York: Pageant Book Company, 1959). See also F. Parkman, *The Jesuits in North America in the Seventeenth Century* (Toronto: George N. Morang, 1907). For an early treatment of the archaeological evidence of the Huron, see W. Jury and E. McLeod Jury, *Sainte-Marie among the Hurons* (London: Oxford

encounter between the French Jesuits and 'Les Savages'—as the confederacies of indigenous tribes were collectively known to the French—in colonial Canada:

> The Huron, Iroquois, and the Algonkin were a handsome, brave, incredibly cruel people who, at that early stage [that is, the seventeenth century], were in no way dependent on the white man and, in fact, judged him to be their physical and mental inferior. They were warlike; they practised ritual cannibalism and, for reasons of religion, subjected their enemies to prolonged and unbearable tortures. Yet, as parents, they could not bear to strike or reprove their unruly children. They were pleasure-loving and polygamous, sharing sexual favours with strangers as freely as they shared their food and hearth. They despised the 'Blackrobes' for their habit of hoarding possessions. They also held the white man in contempt for his stupidity in not realizing that the land, the rivers, the animals, were all possessed of a living spirit and subject to laws that must be respected.[41]

This pervasive sense of complete otherness is reinforced as Father Laforgue progresses towards the Ihonatiria Mission before the full onset of the harsh Canadian winter. This 'otherness' was largely down to the Jesuits' description of difference between Christian Europe and

> this Country,—and with Nations who do not differ from us more in Climate and in Language than they do in their nature, their way of acting, and their opinions, and in everything that can exist in Man, except body and Soul...[42]

Accompanied by Algonkin guides, they encounter the feared Iroquois. Escaping the horrors of cannibalism, torture and the certainty of death at the hands of Iroquois tormentors, the much reduced party of travellers encounter the fur traders Casson and Vallier returning from the Huron country down river with six Algonkin paddlers. Illustrating the post-

University Press, 1953). From amongst the extensive literature on Canadian First Nations, see the anthropological treatments of A.D. McMillan's *Native Peoples and Cultures of Canada* (Vancouver: Douglas & McIntyre, 2nd rev. and enlarged edn, 1995), and J.W. Friesen, *Rediscovering the First Nations of Canada* (Calgary: Detselig Enterprises, 1997).

41. Moore, *Black Robe*, p. 8, essentially a summary of mutually uncomprehending attitudes expressed in the *Relations* but with Moore's authorial overview from a 'postcolonial' perspective.

42. The opening of a letter from Revd Father Barthelemy Vimont to Revd Father Jean Filleau, 'Provincial of the Society of Jesus, in the Province of France', 1642, in Thwaites (ed.), *Jesuit Relations*, p. 205.

Reformation as well as early colonial context, Casson, the Huguenot, and Vallier, the Catholic, have set aside religious difference in their trade expedition but it is the Huguenot Casson who admits of the strength of the theological underpinning of imperialism:

> The Jesuits were the real rulers of this country. Champlain was completely under their thumb. He was like a priest himself, now, in his old age, lecturing everybody on the importance of saving the Savages' immortal souls.[43]

As it was to the Jesuit correspondents to France in the seventeenth-century *Relations*, Laforgue's mission is one in which 'the dangers of this journey were transformed miraculously into a great adventure, a chance to advance God's glory here in a distant land'.[44]

The notion of otherness is reciprocal. In the perception of the indigenous peoples, the culture of the priests is different from the traders':

> What sort of men are you? You don't come here, as other Normans do, to trade furs. You ask to live with us in our villages, and yet you stay apart in this house. No one may sleep here and you hide your nakedness from us. Why?

Still, eventually, the motives of religion and trade (theology and economic imperialism) become confused. Thus the shaman Mestigoit remarks to Laforgue, 'I see it now. You are just another Norman pig, a greedy fucker in love with furs',[45] and, as Chomina also later admits to Laforgue, 'Norman' greed becomes the source of personal and collective corruption: 'I have become as you, greedy for things.'[46]

Still, Laforgue eventually reaches the Ihonatiria Mission to find Father Duval dead and Father Jerome stroke-damaged, and he decides to stay 'in this land God gave to Cain, the devil's land, living among barbarians' for the sake of their salvation; but this traditional soteriology (evident in the seventeenth-century *Relations*), the quest for souls and mass baptisms, is increasingly making less sense. In the encounter between First Nations and Jesuit at the Ihonatiria Mission, Aenons, a friend of (now also murdered) Father Jerome speaks with prophetic intensity of mutual cultural difference and of the manner in which religious conversions make vulnerable people of the indigenous tribes:

43. Moore, *Black Robe*, p. 178.
44. Moore, *Black Robe*, p. 47.
45. Moore, *Black Robe*, p. 69.
46. Moore, *Black Robe*, p. 152.

> You and your god do not suit our people. Your ways are not our ways. If we adopt them we will be neither Norman nor Huron. And soon our enemies will know our weakness and wipe us from the earth.[47]

Struck by metaphysical doubt Laforgue's faith is restored by a compassionate transformation, as soteriological as it is personal:

> He looked up at the sky. Soon, winter snows would cover this vast, empty land. Here among these Savages, he would spend his life. He poured water on a sick brow, saying again the words of salvation. And a prayer came to him, a true prayer at last. *Spare them. Spare them, O Lord.*

There is a decided shift away from a traditional understanding of mission as soteriological conquest to empathy, compassion, and, finally, at the conclusion of the novel, identity. Father Laforgue's concluding stream of consciousness leap to identification with the indigenous people previously seen as other is summed up by the litanic conclusion of the novel and takes Moore's novel beyond the comparisons with Conrad's *Heart of Darkness*:[48]

> *Do you love us?*
> *Yes.*[49]

In the journey of Laforgue from the early settlement of Quebec to Ihonatiria, Moore's wider authorial stance marks a transition (anachronistic as it might be) from pre- to post-Vatican II and from colonial to post-colonial perspective. Indigenous people are no longer 'Savages', neither civilized nor transformed by Christianity. Mission is thus differentiated in the end from colonization,[50] though perhaps ambivalently.[51] Still, in

47. Moore, *Black Robe*, p. 220.

48. See H. Dahlie, '*Black Robe*: Moore, "Conradian" Tale and the Quest for Self', *Irish University Review* 18 (1988), pp. 88-95.

49. Moore, *Black Robe*, p. 224. The odd literary anachronism, the repeat of Joyce's conclusion to *Ulysses*, is unlikely to be accidental.

50. Indeed, if we take Verduyn's collection, readings of contemporary Canadian identity are discussed in terms where ethnicity, race and culture predominate and religion is very much in the secular sidelines.

51. Being wary of universalizing the diverse patterns of colonization and liberation, histories of the Canadian First Nations nevertheless rarely reflect such a positive view of early seventeenth-century Catholic encounter and, indeed, enigmatically, the post-Vatican II Church maintains too its commitment to 'mission' while retaining a universal soteriology. See *Ad gentes divinitus*, in Flannery (ed.), *Vatican Council II*, pp. 813-56.

terms of a move from pre- to post-Vatican II theology, this is an emphatic shift from the salvific subjugation of the other through the universal imposition of Christian uniformity to the celebration of difference through identification. Again, in terms of the move from colonial to postcolonial, theology is finally (if ambiguously) differentiated from imperialism.[52]

The Magician's Wife

Moore's final novel confirms the importance of colonial geography in the representation of religious and ideological space. It looks at the historical roots of Catholic cooperation with the processes of imperialism but again finally contextualizes the process within both a postcolonial and post-Vatican II perspective. A French magician, Henri Lambert, is enticed into the court of Napoleon III and his skills as a conjuror are to be employed in the process of colonial subjugation in nineteenth-century Algeria.[53]

Here, in classical colonial fashion, Europe meets Africa, the contrasting territories highlighting cultural otherness as much as physical difference. Thus, a waning, post-Enlightenment French Catholicism oddly combined with pseudo-scientific 'magic' meets a seemingly credulous, essentially pre-scientific and African Muslim 'other'. The historical context, despite a vastly different physical and ideological landscape, is reminiscent of *Black Robe*: it seems that Moore has again looked to the past for a physical place to experiment with the ambiguities of contrasting and conflicting belief systems—in *Black Robe* between the French Jesuits and the First Nations, and in *The Magician's Wife* between the modern scientific rationality (and residual Catholicism) of the French and the pre-modern faith of Islamic Algeria.[54] Moore risks

52. For further discussion, see P. Mota Santos, 'Good Indians and Bad Indians: The European Perspective of Native Americans as Depicted in "The Mission" and "Black Robe"', in S. Castillo and V.M.P. Da Rosa (eds.), *Native American Women in Literature and Culture* (Porto: Universidade Fernando Pessoa, 1997); also J. O'Donoghue, 'Historical Themes, Missionary Endeavour and Spiritual Colonialism in Brian Moore's *Black Robe*', *Irish Quarterly Review* 23 (1993), pp. 131-39.

53. For an accessible overview of the period dealt with in Moore's novel, see R. Price, *A Concise History of France* (Cambridge: Cambridge University Press, updated edn, 1997), pp. 142-208.

54. Said's discussion in *Orientalism*, p. 209, of the often hostile 'Christian' representation of Islam.

here a dangerous homogenization, something of which Said warned in *Orientalism*.[55]

Moore finally avoids such by the ambiguities of his characterization. There is no little irony here, for instance, in that Lambert represents from the outset of the novel a man who has aspiration to all the scientific rationality that the Enlightenment can afford. The preoccupation with clocks (there are 40 of them in Lambert's Tours residence) is largely symptomatic of this, as is the predominance of mechanical gadgetry in the household. These devices which tell the head of the household if intruders or visitors are present, suggests a struggle to omniscience, a clear analogy to powers of a scientific modernity to replace a pre-modern religiosity. Still, it is Colonel Deniau, the key instigator in using Lambert for political ends, who plays upon the potential perceptions of Lambert's 'magical' skills as *spiritual* authority among the Arab population, a rhetoric that Lambert himself takes to heart:

> Fear mixed with awe and reverence for the unknown, for something we do not understand. That's at the heart of all magic... But in Africa...the Arabs will never have seen illusion such as I can devise. Believe me, to them I will be the most holy of marabouts.[56]

That electricity is used as part of the demonstrations to impress and frighten the 'unscientific' Arabs indicates then a colonial use of *modernity* under the guise of a superstitious, pre-modern religiosity, Lambert being described as 'a great Christian sorcerer';[57] as Deniau claims:

> What we need to convince the Arab is something even more spectacular, something which will both frighten and amaze them...supernatural powers.[58]

55. Said comments in *Orientalism*: 'I have been arguing that "the Orient" is itself a constituted entity, and that the notion that there are geographical spaces with indigenous, radically "different" inhabitants who can be defined on the basis of some religion, culture, or racial essence proper to that geographical space is equally a highly debatable idea' (p. 322).

56. Moore, *The Magician's Wife*, p. 76.

57. Moore, *The Magician's Wife*, p. 112.

58. Moore, *The Magician's Wife*, p. 58.

In contrast to an expanding but secularizing French empire,[59] Algeria represents a reverse demarcation between religious (marabout) and secular (sheik) authority. It is the marabouts' capacity to declare jihad on the French that is central to Deniau's colonial manipulations, as he explains to Lambert:

> Muslim countries are very different from ours. Their marabouts or saints have a political and spiritual influence which is greater than the power of any ruler... An unfortunate situation for the sheiks.[60]

From French recognition of marabouts' political influence through religious authority, Deniau sees nationalism epitomizing the true faith of imperialism: 'Todays's true devotion was reserved for the flag':[61] 'I have great plans for Algeria. I see it as the meeting ground between East and West and the key to our empire's economic expansion.'[62] Already declining in post-Enlightenment France, Catholicism retains then a merely nominal role in Napoleon III's colonial advancement; but attempts to convince the Arabs of the spiritual superiority of 'Christianity' over Islam with no more than Lambert's electrical trickery does indicate the role religion played in the imperial process. It is of course a perverse 'theology of imperialism' that thus provokes Lambert to admit:

> I am a sorcerer. I am Christian. I am French. God, whom you call Allah, protects me. As he will protect my country from any enemy who dares to strike a blow against France.[63]

It is, though, the magician's wife (her designation a sign of derivative status and social marginality[64]) who reveals the trickery behind the sur-

59. See Gandhi's discussion (her only major comment on religion) of how 'the birth of nationalism in Western Europe is coeval with the dwindling—if not the death—of religious modes of thought'. Of course, such a perspective naturally neglects religion in global context, as Hastings' historical overview mitigates against such Eurocentrism, at least in the history of Christianity. More broadly, see J. Casanova, *Public Religions in the Modern World* (Chicago: University of Chicago Press, 1994), and J. Haynes, *Religion in Global Politics* (Harlow: Longman, 1998).

60. Moore, *The Magician's Wife*, p. 58.

61. Moore, *The Magician's Wife*, p.109.

62. Moore, *The Magician's Wife*, p. 58.

63. Moore, *The Magician's Wife*, p. 119.

64. Cf. G. Spivak, 'Three Women's Texts and a Critique of Imperialism', *Critical Inquiry* 12 (1985), pp. 242-61; also J. Sharpe (ed.), *Allegories of Empire: The Figure of Woman in the Colonial Text* (Minneapolis: University of Minnesota

face 'spiritual' power of her husband's magic to the leading marabout, Bou-Aziz, thereby exposing the bankruptcy of this complicity between 'theology' and imperialism.

In the encounter between the magician's wife and Bou-Aziz, two figures on the imperial margins, Moore focuses on 'otherness', giving voice and finally power to disempowered: the female other within the physical bounds of imperial France but beyond influence there now given the narrative opportunity to subvert Empire; the Islamic other, geographically 'external' to North Africa, but open to imminent subjugation and territorial incorporation. Here, though, is presented Islam's weakness and strength: in accepting the will of Allah and not exposing Lambert, Algeria *receives* but finally *resists* French colonialism. This strength is recognized by the magician's wife, woman and herself other:

> Their faith was not more spiritual than Christianity, but it was stronger, frightening in its intensity, with a certitude Christianity no longer possessed (p. 198).

With an authorial foresight on history, both flag and faith and nationalism and religion are thus seen as twin forces that eventually win Algeria's independence. Moore's sentences of italicized conclusion to *The Magician's Wife* thereby contextualize the novel in events that give credence to an historical, metafictional and postcolonial reading of his fiction:

> *The following year, in the summer of 1857, French armies under the command of Marechal Randon and General MacMahon subdued the tribes of Kabylia, thus completing the conquest of Algeria by France.*
>
> *In the summer of 1962, Algeria officially declared its independence, ending the French presence in that country.*

It is coincidental perhaps but 1962, the year of Algerian independence, is that of the opening of the Second Vatican Council. It might be argued that Moore's novel attempts to link explicitly a new post-Vatican II theological thinking with a postcolonial perspective. Interpreting the relationship with Islam as 'people of the Book', the Second

Press, 1993); and A. Blunt and G. Rose (eds.), *Writing Women and Space: Colonial and Postcolonial Geographies* (New York: Guildford Press, 1994). Gandhi's chapter headed 'Postcolonialism and Feminism' (pp. 81-101) has obvious relevance too. Also of broader interest to the terrain of women, travel, writing and the colonial, see S. Mills, *Discourses of Difference: An Analysis of Women's Travel Writing and Colonialism* (London: Routledge, 1991).

Vatican Council provided a radical reidentification with Islam in a relationship as historical as textual—a universal soteriology accepting difference and celebrating the other.[65] Moore presents the history of Catholicism as complicit in French colonialism but, taking the wider post-Vatican II and postcolonial perspectives, it is a Catholicism implicitly rehabilitated by a new allegiance with the oppressed and the marginalized, even in the context of a fundamental sense of religious alterity.

Conclusion

Eagleton's ideological (broadly Marxist) literary theory maintains that no text can be hermetically sealed from history.[66] This provides for interesting parallels with Said's critique of Derrida (in *The World, The Text and the Critic*) that poststructuralism lacks engagement with political actuality, thereby justifying Said's 'postcolonial' readings in *Orientalism* and *Culture and Imperialism*. In turn, however, this reminds me of the earlier contrast between the postcolonial *theory* of Said as cultural commentary and the Fanon's revolutionary postcolonial *criticism* as politically engaged. We see similar degrees of theological engagement with the political post-Vatican II, and especially post-Medellín, but, to take one notable example of liberation theology, the latter is concerned not simply with a radical reading of biblical texts but an ecclesiological *praxis* in constructing a Church of and for the poor, the marginalized, the oppressed.

At the opening of a millennium the novelist never lived to witness, Moore's juxtaposition of the social and the (post-)metaphysical[67] enables his literary treatments of colonial history to be interpreted through these wider post-Vatican II and postcolonial perspectives for a twenty-first century readership. In this regard, I stated earlier that post-Vatican II theology and postcolonialism (theory and criticism) might be said to share a common stance on the three possible grounds: an emphasis on

65. For an overview of official teaching on such theological transformation, see F. Gioia (ed.), *Interreligious Dialogue: The Official Teaching of the Catholic Church* (Boston: Pauline Books & Media, 1997).

66. T. Eagleton, *Literary Theory* (Oxford: Basil Blackwell, 2nd edn, 1996).

67. See my 'Catholics: Sexuality and Death and Catholicism in the Novels of Brian Moore', in M.A. Hayes, W.J. Porter and D. Tombs (eds.), *Religion and Sexuality* (Sheffield: Sheffield Academic Press, 1998), pp. 272-84.

historical perspective in the analysis of social-structural inequality; an identity with the marginalized and oppressed 'other'; and a radical, *social* interpretation of texts. Moore's late twentieth-century fiction, especially in its self-conscious theological/ideological intertextuality, presents a similar literary and postcolonial 'theology of the other'. Yet, as fictions, Moore's novels finally remain ambivalently poised, between 'engagement' and 'commentary'. Moore's appropriation of history thus remains both *conservative*—in using the colonized 'other' for aesthetic ends—and *radical*—in the appropriation of a postcolonial (and post-Vatican II) perspective on alterity. Perhaps it is this ambivalent relationship to the world that unites and disunites *any* literary text to political and theological history; an ambivalence that makes the text itself *other* than that which it attempts to represent.

APPENDIX
Documents of the Second Vatican Council

December 1963

Constitution on the Sacred Liturgy
Sacrosanctum Concilium
Decree on the Mass Media
Inter mirifica

21 November 1964

Dogmatic Constitution on the Church
Lumen Gentium
Decree on Eastern Catholic Churches
Orientalium ecclesiarum
Decree on Ecumenism
Unitatis redintegratio

28 October 1965

Decree on the Pastoral Office of Bishops in the Church
Christus dominus
Decree on the Sensitive Renewal of Religious Life
Perfectae caritatis
Decree on Priestly Formation
Optatam totius
Declaration on Christian Education
Gravissiumum educationis
Declaration on the Relation of the Church to Non-Christian Religions
Nostra Aetate

18 November 1965

Dogmatic Constitution on Divine Revelation
Dei Verbum
Decree on the Apostolate of the Laity
Apostolicam actuositatem

7 December 1965

Declaration on Religious Freedom
Dignitatis humanae
Declaration on the Missionary Activity of the Church
Ad gentes
Decree on the Ministry and Life of Priests
Presbyterorum ordinis
Pastoral Constitution on the Church in the World of Today
Gaudium et spes

Some Reflections of Millenarianism in Seventeenth-Century Literature

Pat Pinsent

The usage of the word 'millennium' simply to mean the year 2000 would have seemed strange and inadequate to seventeenth-century thought, which interpreted the term in the light of the book of Revelation:

> And I saw an angel come down from heaven, having the key of the bottomless pit and a great chain in his hand. And he laid hold on the dragon, that old serpent, which is the Devil, and Satan, and bound him a thousand years, And cast him into the bottomless pit, and shut him up, and set a seal upon him, that he should deceive the nations no more, till the thousand years should be fulfilled... I saw the souls of them that were beheaded for the witness of Jesus and for the word...and they lived and reigned with Christ a thousand years (Rev. 20.1-4).

While many orthodox believers of the seventeenth century expected the thousand years or millennium of Christ's reign and Satan's captivity to begin about the year 2000, many pundits identified it as happening in their own lifetimes, to be presaged by a number of signs, such as cosmic disturbances (which can always be observed by those who are looking for them), the apostasy of the Church (easily located by Puritans as characterizing the Roman or even the English Church) and the advent of 'the man of sin', who could be seen as the monarch or the Pope.

Such readings of the book of Revelation certainly lent strength to the anti-monarchist movement of the mid-seventeenth-century, but they can also be detected at a significantly earlier date. One of the most evident results of the Protestant Reformation was the opening up of the Bible to reading and private interpretation by those who had not necessarily been schooled in traditional doctrines, for, as Christopher Hill remarks, 'Any careful reading of the Bible gives rise to thoughts about the end of the world.' He also observes, 'The accredited preachers of God's word not only proclaimed that the millennium was approaching but told "you that are of the meaner rank, common people" that they were to take the lead in forwarding Christ's cause'.[1] Well before the Civil War, millenarianism was abundant among the members of minority sects, and was deplored by writers whose political and religious persuasions differed from theirs; their hostile reactions are even to be found as early as the end of the previous century.

The controversialist and proto-journalist Thomas Nashe (1567–?1601) seems to have written his prose work *The Unfortunate Traveller* (1594) partly for entertainment and partly to further his own strongly anti-Puritan views. His 'hero', Jack Wilton, is portrayed as wandering sixteenth-century Europe and encountering savagery that Nashe seems to delight in recounting. In his travels, Wilton witnesses an outbreak of millenarianism, the Radical Anabaptist establishment of a 'New Jerusalem' at Münster in 1534 and its subsequent downfall. He berates its exponents, 'all the crew of Cnipperdollings and Muncers' (the names of two of the Anabaptist leaders) for not forsaking all and following Christ:

> They did not serve God simply, but that He should serve their turns... They took not up their crosses of humility and followed him, but would cross him, upbraid him and set him at nought if he assured not by some sign their prayers and supplications.[2]

Because of their self-delusions, leading to the expectation that God is at their beck and call, they interpret the sudden appearance of a rainbow as a sign from heaven, and run headlong towards destruction, a sight to which Wilton responds with paradox: 'Pitiful and lamentable was their unpitied and well-performed slaughter.' He goes on to compare his reactions to the ensuing massacre to the compassion that spectators feel in spite of themselves at the painful death of 'the most cruellest of all beasts', a baited bear:

> Those that, beholding him at the stake...wished him a suitable death to his ugly shape, now...re-call their hard-hearted wishes and moan him suffering as a mild beast, in comparison of the foul-mouthed mastiffs, his butchers. Even such comparison did those overmatched ungracious Munsterians obtain of many indifferent eyes, who now thought them, suffering, to be sheep brought innocent to the shambles, whenas before they deemed them as a number of wolves up in arms again the shepherds.

1. C. Hill, *The World Turned Upside Down* (Harmondsworth: Penguin Books, 1975), pp. 34, 95.
2. T. Nashe, *The Unfortunate Traveller* (ed. J.B. Steane; Harmondsworth: Penguin Books, 1977), pp. 284-86.

Wilton concludes: 'Hear what is it to be Anabaptists, to be Puritans, to be villains. You may be counted illuminate botchers for a while, but your end will be "Good people, pray for us".' While this moralizing comes oddly from a character who throughout the text reveals himself as an unfeeling prankster and a fornicator, it would appear that Nashe's reader is being encouraged to take care lest the sympathy which might be engendered by the harsh punishments meted out, not only in Münster but also in contemporary England, on those who rejected the traditional structures of Church and state, might all too easily lead to acceptance of their false opinions.

The hostility of Ben Jonson (1572–1637) to any hint of anti-nomianism is particularly apparent in *The Alchemist* (1612). Like Nashe, and perhaps even on his model, he tends to associate Puritanism with millenarianism; one of the rogues, the pseudo-alchemist Subtle, describes the two Amsterdam Puritans, Tribulation Wholesome and Ananias, who become his clients, as 'knipperdolings'.[3] The audience of this play, as often happens in Jonson's work, is prevented from undue adverse criticism of the villains by the contemptible and hypocritical behaviour of those they dupe, who deserve all they get. The Puritans' hopes that base metal will be transmuted to gold to further the finances of 'the saints', like the aspirations of the nobleman Sir Epicure Mammon, are doomed from the beginning, so that the audience's interest lies mainly in how and when their downfall will be achieved. After all the dupes have been adequately fleeced, Subtle and his henchman Face engineer a great explosion of the alchemical furnace, which is prefigured by a lengthy passage in which Jonson lampoons the notions of the Fifth Monarchy Men. These millenarianists, depending on the work of Hugh Broughton (1549–1612), believed that after the fall of the four monarchies (often interpreted as those of the Assyrians, the Persians, the Greeks and the Romans), as foretold in the book of Daniel (2.36-43), there would arise the kingdom of Jesus. In Jonson's play, the prostitute Doll Common, disguised as a noblewoman, drowning Mammon's feeble expostulations, rants in what can only be described as an explosion of absurd language, derived from Broughton:

3. B. Jonson, *The Alchemist* (ed. F.H. Mares; London: Methuen, 1971), act II, scene 5, line 13.

Doll	For after Alexander's death...
Mammon	Good lady—
Doll	That Perdicas and Antigonus, were slain, The two that stood, Seleuc' and Ptolemy—...
Mammon	Madam.
Doll	Make up the two legs, and the fourth Beast. That was Gog-north, and Egypt-south: which after Was call'd Gog Iron-leg, and South Iron-leg—
Mammon	Lady—
Doll	And then Gog-horned. So was Egypt; too. Then Egypt clay-leg, and Gog clay-leg—...[4]

Jonson's hostility to millenarian ideas is very evident, but he was too early to witness the short-lived jubilation of the Fifth Monarchy Men, who, in their expectation of 'the direct intervention of King Jesus in English politics', were later joined by 'many men [to whom] the execution of Charles I seemed to make sense only as clearing the way for King Jesus'.[5] The hopes engendered by the Civil War among such egalitarian groups as the Levellers and Diggers, and indeed some Puritan women who optimistically thought equality could be extended to their sex, were to some extent shared even by more scholarly writers, such as Milton, who, even before the execution of Charles I, in his treatise 'Of Reformation' (1641), after he has vituperated against contemporary English bishops for their pomp and luxury, looks forward to the time when this 'great and warlike Nation...casting farre from her the *rags* of her old *vices'* [emphases here and below Milton's] may press on to the day '[w]hen thou the Eternall and shortly-expected King shalt open the Clouds...shalt put an end to all Earthly *Tyrannies*, proclaiming thy universal and milde *Monarchy* through Heaven and Earth'.[6]

Like many of his less articulate contemporaries, Milton seems to imply that part of the joy that the righteous will take in the establishment of Christ's kingdom will be seeing the casting down to hell of those who have acted counter to God's kingdom 'by the impairing and diminution of the true *Faith*': 'After a shamefull end in this *Life,* (which God grant them) [they] shall be thrown downe eternally into the *darkest* and *deepest Gulfe* of Hell.'

4. Jonson, *The Alchemist*, act IV, scene 5.

5. Hill, *Upside Down*, pp. 72, 96.

6. J. Milton, *Complete Prose Works*, I (ed. D.M. Wolfe; New Haven: Yale University Press, 1970), p. 616.

I am not, however, concerned here so much with the political ferment of the period as with the way in which aspects of millenarianism are to be found in some of the poetry of the period. I have found it useful to employ a sociological definition of 'millenarianism', derived from Norman Cohn's *The Pursuit of the Millennium*, which

> begins by defining the term 'millenarian' as including any religious movement that pictures salvation as: (a) collective, in the sense that it will be enjoyed by all the faithful as a group; (b) terrestrial, in the sense that it will be realized on this earth rather than in some other worldly heaven; (c) imminent, since it will come soon and suddenly; (d) total, because it will completely transform life on earth and bring complete perfection rather than some lesser improvement; (e) miraculous, in the sense that it will be accomplished by, or with the help of, supernatural agencies.[7]

I am not suggesting that the poets I shall be discussing below exhibit all these characteristics, but rather that the concept of millenarianism was so pervasive in the seventeenth-century political and religious climate that its validity tends to be assumed, particularly among those of a Puritan persuasion.

George Wither (1588–1667) was earlier in his life a fairly orthodox Anglican but his developing Puritan sympathies led him to be one of the few poets celebrating in verse the execution of Charles I. In 'Vox Pacifica' (1645), a poem admired by the Levellers and Diggers, notably John Lilburne,[8] he voices in an apocalyptic tone his desire for democratic reform; he enjoins 'King, priest and people' to listen:

> For, if your pride, and follie, shall despise
> The gentle VOICE, that now salutes your eare,
> Ere long, there shall another VOICE arise,
> Which will not such a peacefull note preferre.
> It shall not move with so becalm'd a Breath,
> Nor be dilated through so milde an ayre,
> But, from the wombe of *Hell*, and Jawes of *Death*,
> Be thund'red forth, with horrours and despair.[9]

7. Summarized in M. Hill, *A Sociology of Religion* (London: Heinemann, 1973), p. 207.

8. See Hill, *Upside Down*, p. 96, and D. Norbruck and H. Woudhuysen, *The Penguin Book of Renaissance Verse* (Harmondsworth: Penguin Books, 1992), p. 848.

9. In Norbruck and Woudhuysen, *Renaissance Verse*, p. 748.

Like many others, Wither seems more interested in the preceding cataclysm than the ensuing millennium, but the collective, terrestrial, imminent, total and miraculous qualities of the divine intervention which he anticipates are evident.

While the nature of the situation in England lent itself to the denunciatory tone of Wither's outburst, concentrating more on the threat of the signs that would precede the period of millennium than on the settled period to follow, it was nevertheless possible for optimists to look elsewhere for the location of a true terrestrial paradise. The New World could easily be seen to have many of the characteristics of the earthly paradise, especially if seen from afar. Andrew Marvell (1621–78), despite at one point in his youth wavering in his allegiance and temporarily acceding to Roman Catholicism, was for most of his life committed to a Puritan political and religious stance. At different periods of his life he was tutor to General Fairfax's daughter Mary and Latin secretary to the Council of State, as well as being MP for Hull. His poem 'Bermudas'[10] was probably composed sometime after July 1653, while he was tutoring Oliver Cromwell's ward William Dutton, and living in the house at Eton of the Puritan divine John Oxenbridge. Twenty years previously, Oxenbridge had been a member of a group seeking refuge in the Bermudas from the Laudian persecution. Marvell, whose long poem about General Fairfax's estate, 'Upon Appleton House', can be seen as furnishing proof of his desire to image in poetry that perfection that real life denied him, creates in 'Bermudas' an earthly paradise that images the millennial ideal of salvation. The exiles, rowing a small boat, are heard by the 'listning Winds' while singing:

> What should we do but sing his Praise
> That led us through the watry Maze
> Unto an Isle so long unknown,
> And yet far kinder than our own?

The miraculous nature of the divine providence which has led them to this haven is made evident:

> Where he the huge Sea-Monsters wracks
> That lift the Deep upon their Backs.

The recollection here of Ps. 74.13, 'Thou brakest the heads of the dragons in the waters', suggests an affinity between the song of the

10. Quoted from H. Kelliher, *Andrew Marvell: Poet and Politician* (London: British Library, 1978), p. 58.

exiles and the way in which God's power is celebrated in the Hebrew Bible; Puritans, especially in exile, often seem to have seen themselves as kindred to the wandering Israelites. The flora with which Marvell endows the island, while presumably dependent on Oxenbridge's description, is both exotic and almost pre-lapsarian; it suggests something almost beyond Nature but within the power of the God of nature:

> He [God] hangs in shades the Orange bright,
> Like golden Lamps in a green Night,
> And does in the Pomegranates close,
> Jewels more rich than Ormus show's [sic].
> He makes the Figs our mouths to meet;
> And throws the Melons at our feet.
> But Apples plants of such a price
> No Tree could ever bear them twice.
> With Cedars, chosen by his hand,
> From Lebanon, he stores the Land.

Again here with the reference to Lebanon, Marvell ensures that the links between the experience of the exiles and that of the children of Israel is not overlooked. The God-given fruit here is less assertive than that which almost aggressively forces itself upon the stroller in Marvell's rather better-known poem, 'The Garden':

> Ripe apples drop about my head;
> The luscious clusters of the vine
> Upon my mouth do crush their wine;
> The nectarine and curious peach,
> Into my hands themselves do reach;
> Stumbling on melons, as I pass,
> Ensnared with flowers, I fall on grass.[11]

The element of threat in the more secular poem would be out of place in 'Bermudas', but the sense of abundance is equally overt. The wanderers in 'Bermudas' find that God

> ...in these Rocks for us did frame
> A Temple where to sound his name.

Thus it is clear that this new Eden will not be a site for a new Fall.

Marvell, more than most poets, maintains a detachment from the action of his poems, often to the extent of irony, so that it is impossible

11. Quoted from A. Marvell, *Poems* (ed. F. Kermode and K. Walker; Oxford: Oxford University Press, 1990), p. 48.

to be certain about the tone in which this earthly paradise is described. It is however interesting to note that as far as can be determined it was written at a time both when he himself was enjoying the favour of Cromwell and when the ideas which he had espoused were in the ascendant, yet the picture it conveys is nevertheless escapist; perhaps he had realized that heart's desire, once attained, is never so satisfying as it appeared when it was elusive.

The attraction of a terrestrial paradise may also be seen in the context of the stridency of contemporary Puritan preaching about hell, which generated such fear that people were prepared 'to accept either the idea of a material heaven on earth in an imminent millennium, or the idea that heaven and hell were internal states of mind'; Lodowick Muggleton's response to such threats was 'I cared not for heaven so I might not got to hell'.[12] Certainly the picture Marvell creates could well be more attractive to many people than the traditional and more static view of heaven.

Those who lived in the realities of the new colonies, of course, already knew this. Not experiencing so idyllic a climate as the Bermudas, the New England colonists seem to have a more realistic attitude to the hardships of nature and are less likely to envisage their surroundings as representing the earthly paradise. Rather, they continued in expectation of its imminent arrival. As Peter Conn suggests:

> Feeling that they knew history's inevitable destination, Puritan believers searched for millennial signs and often found them... They expressed their apocalyptic expectations in a language that superimposed the imagery of the Bible's prophetic books upon the phenomena of New England experience... Millennial preoccupations fixed themselves firmly in the American imagination.[13]

Probably the most notorious of the New England poets who expressed this apocalyptic was Michael Wigglesworth (1631–1705), whose lugubrious long poem *The Day of Doom* (1662) was compulsorily committed to the memory of subsequent generations of New England school children. Conn states, 'The argument of this poem was that God had turned New England into "a waste and howling wilderness" to punish the spiritually bankrupt behavior of his chosen people'.[14] As another

12. Quoted in Hill, *Upside Down*, p. 174.

13. P. Conn, *The Cambridge Illustrated History of American Literature* (Cambridge: University Press, 1989), p. 48.

14. Conn, *Cambridge Illustrated History of American Literature*, p. 48.

critic says, 'It was intended to renew in them a sense of their obligations as Puritans and of the justness of God's way with both the elect and the damned.'[15] It might be claimed, however, that there is more emphasis on the damned than the elect, together with more stress on the apocalyptic signs than on the millennial bliss to follow. It begins:

> Still was the night, Serene and Bright,
> when all Men sleeping lay;
> Calm was the season, and carnal reason
> thought so 'twould last for ay...
> Wallowing in all kind of sin,
> vile wretches lay secure...[16]

As a light breaks forth at midnight, they hear 'an hideous cry' and rush from their beds:

> Viewing this light, which shines more bright
> Then doth the Noon-day Sun.
> Straightway appears (they see't with tears)
> The Son of God most dread;
> Who with his Train comes on amain
> To judge both Quick and Dead.

Wigglesworth's repetitive beat enforces his message strongly, intensified by the plethora of biblical echoes from both the Gospels and the book of Revelation.

Not everything from the New World was gloom and doom and the more justly distinguished work of Anne Bradstreet (1612–72) conveys relatively little warning of apocalyptic signs or promise of millennial bliss. Her work includes long poems entitled 'The four elements', 'The four humours', 'The four ages', 'The four seasons', and, with the promise of more relevance to the fifth monarchy, 'The four monarchies'. Bradstreet however provides no hint of interest in a fifth monarchy; while it might be conjectured that she simply avoided it because it would have spoiled the symmetry of her work, this may not in fact be the case. She concludes this piece, by far the longest of her 'Fours', with 'An Apology':

15. R.H. Pearce, *The Continuity of American Poetry* (Princeton, NJ: Princeton University Press, 1987), p. 20.

16. Quoted from G. Moore, *The Penguin Book of American Poetry* (Harmondsworth: Penguin Books, 1977), pp. 51-53.

To finish what's begun, was my intent
My thoughts and my endeavours thereto bent;
Essays I made but still gave out,
The more I mused, the more I was in doubt;
...At length resolved, when many years had past,
To prosecute my story to the last;
...But 'fore I could accomplish my desire,
My papers fell a prey to th' raging fire.[17]

It appears that the preoccupation with the here and now that characterizes many of her best poems, those about her family, may have led to a reluctance to undertake a fifth monarchy theme, well before the conflagration that destroyed her papers.

More germane to the present subject is Bradstreet's 'A dialogue between Old England and New; concerning their present troubles, anno, 1642'. Old England laments the 'contention grown, 'twixt subjects and their master', which has led to '[m]y weeping virgins and my young men slain', but New England, after reproaching her mother's 'fearful sins', especially the lack of adequate prosecution of those too much under the sway of popery, has a more encouraging message, which begins in apocalyptic terms:

When thus in peace, thine armies brave send out
To sack proud Rome and all her vassals rout;
...And on her pour the vengeance threat'ned
Bring forth the beast that ruled the world with's beck,
And tear his flesh and set your feet on's neck;
...And do to Gog as thou hast done to Rome...

It does however seem a little facile to enjoin Old England to a far-reaching holy war (the imagined bounds of which stretch as far as Turkey) from the relative safety of New England. Interestingly, Bradstreet also includes in her millennial vision the conversion of the Jews,[18] possibly accompanied by a return to their 'homeland':

17. A. Bradstreet, *Works* (ed. J. Hensley; Cambridge, MA: Belknap Press, 1967), 'An Apology', p. 177, and 'A Dialogue between Old England and New', pp. 179-88.

18. It is interesting to recall the well-known lines in Marvell's 'To his coy Mistress': 'And you should, if you please, refuse/ Till the conversion of the Jews', quoted from Marvell, *Poems*, p. 24. The implication here is that such an event is very far from immediate!

Oh Abraham's seed, lift up your heads on high,
For sure the day of your redemption's nigh;
The scales shall fall from your long blinded eyes,
And Him you shall adore who now despise.
Then fullness of the nations in shall flow,
And Jew and Gentile to one worship go;
Then follows days of happiness and rest;
Whose lot doth fall to live therein is blest:
No Canaanite shall then be found i' th' land...

Bradstreet's vision of millenial bliss is certainly terrestrial, collective and total, relatively imminent and partially miraculous, though it seems also to demand action from 'Old England', who can anticipate with confidence the support of God in this action.

With the Restoration of the monarchy in 1660, the hopes of minority groups for the imminent establishment of Christ's kingdom on earth inevitably receded. After a relatively brief period during which millenarianist thinking had been represented in sectors associated with power, it tended to become submerged beneath both the secularism and the development of scientific investigation that characterized the new reign, though it would be naïve to deny its existence totally. Additionally, it is claimed by Worsley that 'it is amongst people who feel themselves to be oppressed and who are longing for deliverance that they [millenial movements] have been particularly welcomed'.[19] In the immediately preceding period there had been some opportunity for people of lower class to have a voice, in some of the minority religio-politico movements, but it may be conjectured that after 1660 they again needed to look for fulfilment within a world other than this. John Bunyan (1628–88), who in 1658 had announced that 'the judgment day is at hand',[20] seems by the time he wrote *Pilgrim's Progress* (1678) to have by and large transferred this concept to another world. A significant scene is the point at which Christian is admitted to the heavenly Jerusalem and the narrator sees through the gates that '[t]he City shone like the sun; the streets also were paved with gold'. There is evident intertextual reference here to the biblical words 'the city was of pure gold' (Rev. 21.18) and 'the city had no need of the sun...for the glory of God did lighten it' (Rev. 21.23), but a key difference occurs when

19. P. Worsley, *The Trumpet Shall Sound* (London: MacGibbon and Kee, 1968), quoted in M. Hill, *A Sociology of Religion* (London: Heinemann, 1973), p. 212.

20. Hill, *Upside Down*, p. 97.

the narrator finds himself excluded: 'They shut up the gates; which, when I had seen, I wished myself among them.'[21] This contrasts with the biblical 'And the gates of it shall not be shut at all' (Rev. 21.25) and clearly marks the fact that Bunyan presumably no longer views the coming of Christ's kingdom as either immediate or terrestrial.

The writings of Thomas Traherne (1637–74) take a different stance towards the concept of an earthly paradise, that of demonstrating its reality in the here and now. Traherne, an Anglican clergyman whose education and subsequent appointment as Rector of Credenhill during the Commonwealth and Protectorate period may evidence some early Puritan leanings, of which, however, there is little evidence in his writing, produced a large number of poems and prose meditations, most of which were not discovered until the twentieth century. One of the most recently discovered of these, in 1967, is *Commentaries of Heaven*, not identified as Traherne's until 1982. The poems in this manuscript are arranged in alphabetical order, from the first, 'Upon Abhorrence', to the ninety-seventh and last, 'Baseness', which suggests that had he lived to complete the series it might have constituted nearly 2,000 poems by the time he reached, perhaps, 'Zeal'. The sentiments expressed in number 46, 'Ambassadors', typify Traherne's recognition of God's immanence in this world; the unorthodox spellings are Traherne's own:

> God out of Zion shineth in Compleat
> And perfect Beauty: He did never cheat
> The soul of any: His diviner Light
> His Truth as well as Lov is infinit.
> Such Worlds of Glory doth his Skill display
> In the Divine Proportions of the Way
> And the Sweet Methods which salute mine Eys
> With Endless infinit Varieties…
> And so doth Beautifie the Times and Lands
> Wher in my GOD in all his Glory Stands
> That all the World is a New Paradice
> Of Joy and Bliss to me beyond all Price
> And Time it self a most Celestial Sphere
> As if the Way to Heaven, were Heaven here.[22]

21. J. Bunyan, *The Pilgrim's Progress* (London: George Routledge, 1864), p. 240.

22. T. Traherne, *Commentaries of Heaven: The Poems* (ed. D.D.C. Chambers; Salzburg: University of Salzburg, 1989), p. 57.

The unusual emphasis placed by Traherne on this world as God's abode is more striking if comparison is made between his work and that of Henry Vaughan, a poet who also rejoices in the natural world but who stresses the ultimately other worldliness of God's dwelling to which his dead brother and friends have departed:

> They are all gone into the world of light!
> And I alone sit lingring here;[23]

By contrast, Traherne sees nature as charged with God and all humankind as heirs of 'Felicity' in a universe alive with divinity. The main area in which Traherne's vision seems to me deficient in its millenarianism is in its strongly individualistic aspect. His use of the pronoun 'we' is sparse by comparison with 'I', and while in no sense does he exclude the rest of humanity from his conviction about his divine inheritance, the collective aspect sometimes defies logic. In one of his prose meditations he claims:

> You never enjoy the world aright, till the sea itself floweth in your veins, till you are clothed with the heavens, and crowned with the stars; and perceive yourself to be the sole heir of the whole world: and more than so, because men are in it who are every one sole heirs, as well as you.[24]

The notion of each person individually as a 'sole heir' is surely the obverse of a communal millennial vision. In other respects, however, 'Ambassadors', like much of Traherne's writing, seems to encapsulate aspects of such a vision, for his message is that God's power has provided paradise here and now, but that it needs to be recognized before it can be realized in the individual.

By the end of the seventeenth century, religious poetry seems to show relatively little trace of millenarianism. Where the major poet of the period, Alexander Pope, touches on religious matters, his tone is one of a safely detached deistic generalism, far from the intense involvement of the earlier period. His 'The Universal Prayer' begins:

23. H. Vaughan, *The Complete Poetry* (ed. F. Fogle; New York: Doubleday, 1964), p. 270.

24. T. Traherne, *Selected Poems and Prose* (ed. A. Bradford; Harmondsworth: Penguin Books, 1991), p. 197.

> Father of all! In every age,
> In every clime adored,
> By saint, by savage, and by sage,
> Jehovah, Jove, or Lord![25]

Such a deity is certainly not expected to intervene to establish an earthly kingdom. The fervour of the seventeenth century, with its intense belief in the reality of God's soon to be established kingdom, was seen as dangerous and inappropriate to a period to which the epithet Augustan or the term 'Enlightenment' might aptly be applied.

The obverse of this is the intense concern with personal salvation to be found in some of the eighteenth-century hymns, especially those emanating from the Methodism of the Wesleys or from Evangelicals like Newton and Cowper. Here again are to be found an emphasis on individual rather than collective salvation, the use of the singular rather than the plural pronoun.

The equation by millenarianist movements of the year 2000 with the millennium of the book of Revelation would have been unintelligible to those seventeenth-century thinkers whose vision of the coming of Christ's kingdom on earth was far too immediate for them to contemplate its advent being delayed by as much as 350 years.

25. A. Pope, *Collected Poems* (ed. B. Dobree; London: Dent, 1956), p. 216.

Sacred Music at the Turn of the Millennia

Wendy J. Porter

Introduction

It is common to approach music historically by seeing a work in the context of its immediate surroundings, including the music that just precedes and follows it, in order to discern the advances or innovations that a particular composer or period brought to the development of music. But is there something to be gained by comparing three widely disparate points in the history of sacred music? Can these points in history provide windows of access into or illumination of the Christian faith that is represented through its music? I think that indeed they can provide these very things—an opportunity to see the changing elements of faith over the span of two millennia. Obviously, these brief glimpses in no way give a full or complete picture of the given time period, but they do provide some details that ultimately contribute to a more comprehensive view of the history of sacred music within the tradition of the Christian Church.

The three historical points that I have selected occur roughly at the beginning, middle and end of two millennia. The span of time is from the first century after Christ to the end of the twentieth century. I focus first on what is considered by many to be the earliest Christian hymn in the New Testament, and which was undoubtedly written in the first century. Secondly, I look at a tenth-century manuscript that is representative of New Testament passages, preserved by scribes and marked with ekphonetic notation for some sort of liturgical chant or cantillation of the text. Thirdly, I discuss a choral work that is based on New Testament texts, and which was published in 1990. These three works represent different strands of the history of sacred music, and yet also have some common foundations. They also show a certain shifting in the history of interpretation as it is seen through the hand of the composer. All three works are intricately connected with the New Testament and each represents at least some aspect of the faith of the time in which it was written.

A New Hymn in Philippians (First Century)

Philippians 2.6-11 is often referred to as an early Christian hymn. What is usually meant by 'early' is that it is a quotation from something written earlier than the writing of the epistle;[1] I will discuss this briefly below. The decision about whether it is technically a hymn has not reached a consensus,[2] but most would certainly agree that the writing style of these six verses is very different from the style that precedes and follows them.

ὃς ἐν μορφῇ θεοῦ ὑπάρχων οὐχ ἁρπαγμὸν
ἡγήσατο τὸ εἶναι ἴσα θεῷ,
ἀλλὰ ἑαυτὸν ἐκένωσεν μορφὴν δούλου λαβών,
ἐν ὁμοιώματι ἀνθρώπων γενόμενος·
καὶ σχήματι εὑρεθεὶς ὡς ἄνθρωπος
ἐταπείνωσεν ἑαυτὸν γενόμενος
ὑπήκοος μέχρι θανάτου, θανάτου δὲ σταυροῦ.
διὸ καὶ ὁ θεὸς αὐτὸν ὑπερύψωσεν
καὶ ἐχαρίσατο αὐτῷ τὸ ὄνομα τὸ ὑπὲρ πᾶν ὄνομα,
ἵνα ἐν τῷ ὀνόματι Ἰησοῦ πᾶν γόνυ
κάμψῃ ἐπουρανίων καὶ ἐπιγείων καὶ καταχθονίων,
καὶ πᾶσα γλῶσσα ἐξομολογήσηται
ὅτι κύριος Ἰησοῦς Χριστὸς εἰς δόξαν θεοῦ πατρός.

Who, being in very nature God,
did not consider equality with God something to be grasped,
but made himself nothing,
taking the very nature of a servant,
being made in human likeness.

1. For example, see R.P. Martin, *Carmen Christi: Philippians 2.5-11 in Recent Interpretation and in the Setting of Early Christian Worship* (SNTSMS, 4; Cambridge: Cambridge University Press, 1967; Grand Rapids: Eerdmans, rev. edn, 1983), p. xxxiv: 'We are on firm ground in stating that Philippians ii.6-11 represents a hymnic specimen, taken over by Paul as a *paradosis* from some early Christian source with a Jewish background.'

2. See, e.g., G.D. Fee, 'Philippians 2.5-11: Hymn or Exalted Pauline Prose?', *BBR* 2 (1992), pp. 29-46 (30), where he states, 'primarily I want to call into question the whole matter of the passage as a hymn, which, despite most scholarship to the contrary, it almost certainly is not'.

> And being found in appearance as a man,
> he humbled himself
> and became obedient to death—
> even death on a cross!
> Therefore God exalted him to the highest place
> and gave him the name that is above every name,
> that at the name of Jesus every knee should bow,
> in heaven and on earth and under the earth,
> and every tongue confess that Jesus Christ is Lord,
> to the glory of God the Father (NIV).

The understanding of the word 'hymn' or ὕμνος from the perspective of Greek classical culture is a song of praise addressed to a god or gods. However, as with the passage in 1 Tim. 3.16,[3] the Philippians hymn is not addressed *to God*, but is specifically *about Christ*.[4] An alternate sense for the term 'hymn' from the context of a Greek-speaking Jew would distinguish a second kind of hymn—and that would be of the kind referred to in the headings of some of the Psalms, which are not songs of praise, but are nonetheless addressed to God.[5] Here again, the distinction is that the Philippians passage is not addressed *to God*, but is *about Christ*.[6] In neither sense can this Philippians passage be considered a hymn.[7] However, Stephen Fowl's comment on this problem of terminology is that it

3. For similar discussion on 1 Tim. 3.16, see W.J. Porter, 'The Composer of Sacred Music as an Interpreter of the Bible', in M. O'Kane *et al.* (eds.), *Interpreting the Bible: Breaching Borders, Crossing Boundaries* (JSOTSup, 313; Sheffield: Sheffield Academic Press, forthcoming).

4. See discussion in R.P. Martin, 'Aspects of Worship in the New Testament Church', *Vox Evangelica* 2 (1963), pp. 6-32 (8-9), although Martin writes that both Greek and Christian hymnody as 'songs of praise were addressed to the Deity', which does not seem to be the case here (p. 8).

5. See S.E. Fowl, *The Story of Christ in the Ethics of Paul: An Analysis of the Function of the Hymnic Material in the Pauline Corpus* (JSNTSup, 36; Sheffield: JSOT Press, 1990), pp. 31-33; see also W.S. Smith, *Musical Aspects of the New Testament* (Amsterdam: W. Ten Have, 1962), p. 20, who says, 'The word "hymn" was in common use in the pre-Christian Orient, being used to indicate a general song of praise to the divine being(s), a usage well known to the Jews.'

6. See discussion in M. Hengel, *Between Jesus and Paul: Studies in the Earliest History of Christianity* (trans. J. Bowden; London: SCM Press; Philadelphia: Fortress Press, 1983), pp. 78-96, *passim*.

7. See R.C. Trench, *Synonyms of the New Testament* (London: Macmillan, 9th edn, 1880), p. 299, who observes that, apart from Paul's use, the noun ὕμνος is not

> in no way invalidates the use of the term hymn… Rather, it means that in calling these passages hymns we are using a term that is the construction of a later, critical community, and not a straightforward translation of ὕμνος in either its specific or generic sense.[8]

I would suggest that this passage was later recognized as a new kind of hymn.

After seeing that Phil. 2.6-11 does not fit within these early definitions of 'hymn', a second grey area of categorization is the understanding of the traditions of music that may have been used in the early Church. Scholars frequently write that the music of the early Christian Church came directly from the ancient synagogue. Paul Bradshaw points to the widespread influence of Gregory Dix,[9] and says the following: 'Dix shared the standard scholarly consensus that the first half of the rite was "in its Shape simply a continuation of the jewish [sic] synagogue service of our Lord's time" '.[10] Dix's statement has specific implications for music, as he includes psalmody in his reconstruction of the synaxis,[11] and there has been widespread acceptance of his view. His own further statement is that this early part of the rite 'was carried straight over into the christian Church by its jewish nucleus in the

used in the Apostolic Fathers, not in the writings of Justin Martyr, nor in the Apostolic Constitutions. He provides the possible explanation that the word 'was for the early Christians so steeped in heathenism, so lined with profane associations, and desecrated by them, there were so many hymns to Zeus, to Hermes, to Aphrodite, and to the other deities of the heathen pantheon, that the early Christians shrunk [sic] instinctively from the word'. If Trench is correct in his assessment, it also provides an interesting insight into the mind of Paul, who is obviously undeterred by these associations, and seeks to redefine the word by employing it on two occasions as a noun. Its use as a verb, as in P.Oxy. 1786, is found not only in the parallels of Mt. 26.30 and Mk 14.26, but also in Acts 16.25 and Heb. 2.12.

8. Fowl, *Story of Christ*, p. 33.

9. Dom Gregory Dix, *The Shape of the Liturgy* (Westminster: Dacre Press, 1954 [1945]).

10. P.F. Bradshaw, *The Search for the Origins of Christian Worship: Sources and Methods for the Study of Early Liturgy* (Oxford: Oxford University Press, 1992), pp. 137-38.

11. W. Jardine Grisbrooke, 'Synaxis', in J.G. Davies (ed.), *A Dictionary of Liturgy and Worship* (London: SCM Press, 1972), pp. 353-54 (353): 'The name *synaxis*…is today normally used only of that service which is the most ancient and archetypal of them all, the office of readings and prayers which precedes the celebration of the eucharist.'

decade after the passion',[12] later referring to its 'original unchanging outline' as it was found 'everywhere'.[13] However, recent study from musicological, liturgical and Jewish historical perspectives has not only called into question the thought that the early Church simply took over the music of the synagogue,[14] but also raises questions about whether there was an established synagogue liturgy existing in such a precise form before the destruction of the Temple in AD 70.[15] This research has cast some doubt, for instance, on whether there was established and formal psalmody in the synagogue at this point. There seems to be no documentary evidence for believing that psalmody existed in any kind of structured form in the synagogue that Jesus would have known. This does not mean that the early Christian Church in no way carried on Jewish patterns of singing psalmody as it was practised in the Temple, but it does leave the much larger question of what is meant by the statement that the music of the early Church was taken over from the synagogue. Some have thought that psalmody would have been less like song and much more in the nature of chant or cantillation.[16] What is

12. Dix, *Shape of the Liturgy*, p. 36.

13. Dix, *Shape of the Liturgy*, p. 38.

14. It should be noted here that earlier biblical scholarship did refer to this possibility, i.e. R.P. Martin, *Worship in the Early Church* (London: Marshall, Morgan & Scott, 1964; Grand Rapids: Eerdmans, 2nd edn, 1978), who, although he writes on p. 40 that the 'Church was cradled in Judaism, and borrowed many of its forms of worship from the Temple and synagogue', also mentions on p. 41 that 'we admit that there is some doubt as to the extent to which the singing of divine praises had developed in the Palestinian synagogues of the first century'. See also Hengel, *Between Jesus and Paul*, p. 90, where he says that 'so-called "official" Pharisaic Judaism did not have any singing of hymns in its synagogue services, leaving aside say the recitation of the hallel psalms on certain feast days'.

15. For discussion of this point, see J. McKinnon, 'Christian Antiquity', in *idem* (ed.), *Antiquity and the Middle Ages: From Ancient Greece to the 15th Century* (Man and Music; London: Macmillan, 1990), pp. 68-87 (69): '[I]t is unlikely that there was already in place a formal service of the word that could be adopted *en bloc* by the first Christians. Such a synagogue service began to take shape only after the destruction of the Temple by the Romans in AD 70'; see also Bradshaw, *Search for the Origins*, pp. 18-19, who questions a formal synagogue liturgy in the entire first century.

16. However, see Augustine, *Confessions* 10.33.49-50, where he refers to the practice of Athanasius, 'who required the reader of the psalm to perform it with so little inflexion (*flexu*) of voice that it was closer to speaking (*pronuntianti*) than to singing (*canenti*)', cited in J. McKinnon (ed.), *Music in Early Christian Literature*

largely accepted, at least about the psalmody of the early Christians, is that it would have incorporated a type of responsorial singing,[17] and it would likely have been monophony, that is, sung in unison (or in octaves, given the different voice ranges).[18]

The subject of music in the early Christian Church has provoked a century of lively, even heated, debate.[19] Many pieces of the puzzle have

(Cambridge Readings in the Literature of Music; Cambridge: Cambridge University Press, 1987), p. 155. Based on Athanasius's requirement, the 'readings' were too musical, otherwise there would have been no need for this guideline. A question this raises is, was this a characteristic even in the earliest days of the Christian Church or a development much closer to the time of Athanasius? In either case, whether the earliest forms were more along the lines of chant or of song, this does not exclude either classification from discussions of 'music'—on the contrary, they are critical to discussion of music in the early Church. It is likely that most readings were done in some manner of chant or cantillation, e.g., see J. McKinnon, 'Early Western Civilization', in *idem* (ed.), *Antiquity and the Middle Ages*, pp. 1-44 (10), and Hengel, *Between Jesus and Paul*, p. 189 n. 23.

17. See Smith, *Musical Aspects*, pp. 16-17, who gives some of the historical background to this thought: 'It seems that in general among the ancient Jews, the extent of the congregation's participation in the musical part of the worship service was relatively slight. The burden for the musical part of the service, apart from any help from a choir, seems to have rested upon an individual cantor or precentor. The share of the congregation was apparently in large part merely the answering of the solo voice of the precentor at appropriate places with short responses as "Amen", "Hallelujah", or "Hosanna", or at greater length, participating responsively in the *Shema*, the *Shemoneh 'Esreh*, the *Hallel*, and other Psalms and parts of the liturgy chanted responsively. The simple musical *response* (of a group to an individual) is of very ancient origin and was in general use among the nations of antiquity.'

18. P. Westermeyer, *Te Deum: The Church and Music* (Minneapolis: Fortress Press, 1998), p. 62, writes that '[h]owever diffuse the practice of the early church, it included the ideal of singing "with one voice"', which is thought to mean unison singing. Westermeyer points to two first-century sources that may indicate this, first, that of Clement, who flourished c. 96: 'Let us, therefore...cry out earnestly to him as if *with one voice*' (*1 Clem.* 34.5-7; *PG*, I, cols. 276-77; trans. in McKinnon [ed.], *Music in Early Christian Literature*, p. 18); and Ignatius, c. 35–c. 107: '...you might sing *in one voice* through Jesus Christ to the Father' (Ignatius, *Eph.* 4.1-2; *PG*, V, cols. 733-36; trans. in McKinnon [ed.], *Music in Early Christian Literature*, p. 19).

19. For some discussion of the debate, see W.J. Porter, 'Misguided Missals: Is Early Christian Music Jewish or Is It Graeco-Roman?', in S.E. Porter and B.W.R. Pearson (eds.), *Christian–Jewish Relations through the Centuries* (RP, 6; JSNTSup, 192; Sheffield: Sheffield Academic Press, 2000), pp. 202-27.

been found for later periods of liturgical music[20] and many clues are still being pieced together to answer numerous questions regarding the particularly cloudy part of the earliest musical history of the Christian Church.[21] Documents have been found this century that have added greatly to the corpus of musical knowledge about the first few centuries after Christ, such as Oxyrhynchus Papyrus 1786, the earliest known fragment of a Christian hymn with musical notation, dating to the late third century.[22] Based on it, questions have been raised as to whether the roots of Christian music are to be found in the ancient Greek modes and notation,[23] or, as some have thought, whether this papyrus is simply the attempt of someone who knew Greek notation to try to record a hymn that would otherwise not be found with this notation.[24] Meanwhile, there has been ongoing questioning about the music of the earliest Christian Church, going back to basic questions, such as the one mentioned above: did the music of the early Church actually come directly from the synagogue, and would it have included formal psalmody if it did not come from the synagogue? What kind of music was

20. For instance, a document that explained much of Byzantine musical notation was discovered in the 1880s, virtually unlocking a thousand or more years' worth of musical secrets. See the brief synopsis of the discovery of the most important clues to the deciphering of Byzantine music in C. Høeg, *La notation ekphonétique* (Monumentae Musicae Byzantinae, Subsidia, 1.2; Copenhagen: Levin & Munksgaard, 1935), pp. 18-19.

21. See, e.g., Smith, *Musical Aspects*; E. Werner, *The Sacred Bridge: The Interdependence of Liturgy and Music in Synagogue and Church during the First Millennium* (vol. 1: London: Dennis Dobson; New York: Columbia University Press, 1959; vol. 2: New York: Ktav, 1984); J. McKinnon, 'On the Question of Psalmody in the Ancient Synagogue', in I. Fenlon (ed.), *Early Music History: Studies in Medieval and Early Modern Music*, VI (Cambridge: Cambridge University Press, 1986), pp. 159-91; M.L. West, *Ancient Greek Music* (Oxford: Clarendon Press, 1992); J.E. Scott, 'Roman Music', in E. Wellesz (ed.), *Ancient and Oriental Music* (New Oxford History of Music, 1; London: Oxford University Press, 1966 [1957]), pp. 404-20.

22. B.P. Grenfell and A.S. Hunt, 'Christian Hymn with Musical Notation', in *The Oxyrhynchus Papyri*, XV (Egypt Exploration Society Graeco-Roman Memoirs; London: Egypt Exploration Society, 1922), no. 1786, pp. 21-25 (21).

23. E.g. P.H. Lang, *Music in Western Civilization* (London: Dent, 1963 [1941]), who says that P.Oxy. 1786 'testifies to the fact that the educated Christian Greeks accepted and transplanted the musical system of their ancestors' (p. 23).

24. See discussion of this in M.L. West, 'Analecta Musica', *ZPE* 92 (1992), pp. 1-54 (36-46).

there? Was it all vocal (the most common consensus) or were there instruments to accompany the singing? The Church Fathers, for instance, have much to say about the evils of musical instruments, but do their statements also represent the opinions or practices of the Christian Church in the first century? Eric Werner argues that the apostle Paul detested musical instruments, although his case is not entirely convincing on this point.[25] These and numerous other questions have created a lively discussion, to say the least. Obviously, simple answers to these questions will not be found in this essay.

Leaving aside the question of what the music may have sounded like, I return to the possibility that Phil. 2.6-11 can qualify as a hymn, not because it was already being sung in the early Church, but because it had just been written and was therefore incorporated into the developing Christian liturgy as a new hymn.

Many scholars think that this passage is a quotation of some sort, and many would say that it is a quotation by Paul of someone else.[26] I find it less and less convincing that Paul quoted a hymn that was previously known to the early Christians or even that he quoted some poetic passage from a contemporary,[27] partly because of the difficulty of reconstructing who this writer may have been. It seems increasingly more likely that Paul wrote the passage himself. For one thing, casual reference is sometimes made to the 'hymns' of the early Christian Church,

25. E. Werner, '"If I Speak in the Tongues of Men...": St Paul's Attitude to Music', *Journal of the American Musicological Society* 13 (1960), pp. 18-23.

26. Although there are several who argue that Paul may have written it. See recent discussion along this line in N.T. Wright, 'ἁρπαγμός and the Meaning of Philippians 2.5-11', *JTS* NS 37 (1986), pp. 321-52 (352) (reprinted in revised form as 'Jesus Christ Is Lord: Philippians 2.5-11', in *idem*, *The Climax of the Covenant: Christ and the Law in Pauline Theology* [Edinburgh: T. & T. Clark, 1991], pp. 56-98 [98]): '[I]f someone were to take it upon themselves to argue, on the basis of my conclusions, that the "hymn" was originally written by Paul himself... I for one should find it hard to produce convincing counter-arguments.' See also M. Silva, *Philippians* (Wycliffe Exegetical Commentary; Chicago: Moody Press, 1988), p. 105; and Martin, *Carmen Christi*, pp. 42-62.

27. See R.H. Gundry, 'Style and Substance in "The Myth of God Incarnate" according to Philippians 2.6-11', in S.E. Porter, P. Joyce and D.E. Orton (eds.), *Crossing the Boundaries: Essays in Biblical Interpretation in Honour of Michael D. Goulder* (Leiden: E.J. Brill, 1994), pp. 271-93, who writes: '[T]he concentricity, chiasms, and related other parallels in Phil. 2.6-11 rather favor the view that this passage represents Paul's own exalted prose (a view gradually regaining favor) rather than an early Christian hymn' (p. 288).

but the Church had only existed for about 30 years by the time of Paul's writing; this is very early for the Church to have had an established set of hymns of this nature. Furthermore, who besides Paul is known to have written at this developed theological level by this time? Surely if there was someone who was writing new hymns, this person would be known by name, at least, if not by the writings.

Stephen Fowl argues that the primary focus of the discussion of the hymn should be its function within the argumentation of Paul in Philippians, rather than where the hymnic material originated. Fowl discusses the use of hymns as concrete entities or exemplars, which could be 'extended by analogy to offer solutions to particular problems' being experienced by the Christian community—in this case, persecution of the Church.[28] Fowl clarifies that it can only be called an exemplar in retrospect, after it has been used to solve a problem. The possibility this raises, however, is that in this case Paul has composed and introduced in his letter a hymn—not one that has been known previously and used in the Christian community, but one that will become known and used as a result of his having introduced it. Just as Fowl's exemplar can be used by analogy to solve current problems, so the use of this hymnic passage as an actual hymn, not simply something to be read aloud in a letter format, but sung by the community in whatever form it may have taken musically, results in a hymn that can be of use to all those who perform or hear its vocalization. This hymn then may have become the heart of the message to the Church at Philippi, that is, the model of Christ's obedience even to death, rather than simply being a reminder of something that they already knew.

In sum, it may be that the Philippians hymn is not the earliest Christian hymn in the sense of it representing a previously known hymn in the Church at Philippi, nor in the Christian Church at large, but it may be at the very beginning of the formal christological hymns of the Christian Church. It does not neatly fit the Greek definition of the word, nor does it fit the theological concepts of either the Greek hymn or the Jewish psalm of praise to God. What it does do is represent a template for Christian theology and hymn-writing, one that reflects a ternary pattern of Christology, that is, Christ's pre-existence, his incarnation and death on a cross, and his resurrection and ultimate exaltation. In this hymn, we see the newness of the Christian faith, and the establish-

28. Fowl, *Story of Christ*, p. 93.

ment of a corresponding new hymn. The newness of both the faith and the hymn is evidenced in the new way that the ideals of a hymn are presented and in its new interpretation of the characteristics of God as manifested in Christ Jesus.

A New Testament Lectionary with Ekphonetic Notation (Tenth Century)

This tenth-century document is comprised of four folios, or eight pages, from a parchment codex.[29] The biblical text of this parchment is Jn 6.71–7.46. The pages are part of a gathering, the first page beginning in the middle of a pericope or scenario. The pages are of roughly equal size, about 24 × 31.5 cm (10 × 13 in.). The manuscript has been damaged by having been folded in half, which makes reading certain letters and marks of notation difficult on the middle line, particularly on the fourth or outer sheet. There are many indications that this text was originally used in a liturgical context, including the headings that divide the units according to a liturgical calendar. Nomina sacra include ιc, χc, πνα, πνc, πρων, ανον, shortened forms for 'Jesus', 'Christ', 'Spirit' (two forms), 'the Fathers' and 'man'.

C.R. Gregory speculated that the manuscript originated in eastern Asia Minor or perhaps Armenia,[30] while Herbert Hunger thought on the basis of the decoration that it originated in Egypt.[31] The provenance remains unknown. The hand is in a pronounced Coptic style or Alexandrian majuscule, which is identifiable by thick horizontal and thin vertical strokes. The letters are formed in a very regular, upright fashion. Each line averages 10 characters and the columns are approximately 24 lines long, with an average of 3 verses per column, 6 verses per page.[32]

29. Austrian National Library Suppl. Gr. 121. Gregory-Aland 0105. Edition: C.R. Gregory, *Textkritik des Neuen Testaments* (3 vols.; Leipzig: Teubner, 1909), III, pp. 1066-74. Cf. H. Hunger with C. Hannick, *Katalog der Griechischen Handschriften der Österreichischen Nationalbibliothek* (Vienna: Österreichischen Nationalbibliothek, 1994), Part 4, p. 208. See also a new edition of this parchment, in S.E. Porter and W.J. Porter, *New Testament Greek Papyri and Parchments: New Editions* (Mitteilungen aus der Papyrussammlung der Österreichischen Nationalbibliothek [Papyrus Erzherzog Rainer] New Series, 28; Vienna: Österreichische Nationalbibliothek with Verlag Brüder Hollinek, forthcoming 2001), no. 39.

30. Gregory, *Textkritik des Neuen Testaments*, III, p. 1066.

31. Hunger with Hannick, *Katalog der Griechischen Handschriften*, p. 208.

32. The text is divided into two columns on each page as follows: 1: Jn 6.71–

This parchment, with its 8 pages, is comprised of just over 46 verses. Decoration of the manuscript, which is typical of the period, includes large decorated letters, which are the first letter of a section and are much larger in size than the regular lettering of the text. These letters are written ekthesis, that is, extending well into the margin to the left of the column.

Two of the common marks written on this manuscript are marks of punctuation: the most common is a small cross, the teleia; a second is a combination of two dots that looks much like the present-day colon. These signs usually occur at the ends of short or long units. Marks of punctuation also include a raised dot and low dot. It is these, in conjunction with the diacritical marks known as ekphonetic notation, that are of interest to me here. The markings are musical-rhetorical, as first speculated by Gregory.[33] Some of the ekphonetic notation includes signs called *oxeia*, *apostrophos*, *apeso exo*, *kentemata*, *bareia*, *hypokrisis* and *kremaste*, which will be explained briefly below.[34]

It is likely that the ekphonetic markings, except the small crosses or teleia, have been added by one or more later hands, through the course of the manuscript being used in a liturgical context over a number of years, although the markings are very consistent throughout. Abbreviations for αρχη and τελοc are written beside the columns to mark the beginning and ending of reading units, which consist of about 13-16 verses.

Wellesz writes that

> hardly any two codices containing the same pericopes have exactly the same ecphonetic notation throughout the text: there are many divergencies to be found, but only in small details. In the main there must have been, from the beginning, a single tradition for chanting the pericopes.[35]

7.3, 7.3-6; 2: Jn 7.7-10, 7.10-13; 3: Jn 7.13-16, 7.16-18; 4: Jn 7.18-22, 7.22-24; 5: Jn 7.24-27, 7.27-30; 6: Jn 7.30-32, 7.32-35; 7: Jn 7.35-37, 7.37-39; 8: Jn 7.40-42, 7.43-46.

33. Gregory, *Textkritik des Neuen Testaments*, III, p. 1066; see E. Wellesz, *A History of Byzantine Music and Hymnography* (Oxford: Oxford University Press, 2nd edn, 1961 [1948]), pp. 284-300.

34. See G. Engberg, 'Greek Ekphonetic Neumes and Masoretic Accents', in M. Velimirovic (ed.), *Studies in Eastern Chant*, I (London: Oxford University Press, 1966), pp. 37-49 (38-39), where he describes the 'classical' period of the use of ekphonetic notation, in which they are customarily used in pairs.

35. Wellesz, *History of Byzantine Music*, p. 256; cf. H.J.W. Tillyard, *Handbook of the Middle Byzantine Musical Notation* (Monumentae Musicae Byzantinae,

This is one of the reasons that scholars think that the signs represent known melodies or melodic formulas prescribed for certain kinds of phrases and to be used at certain points in the musical-reading.[36] In the four folios or eight pages that are preserved in this particular gathering, the text is divided into four pericopes or scenarios, only three of which are notated ekphonetically. The first pericope is that of Jesus going to the Feast of Tabernacles; the second is Jesus teaching at the Feast (up to the point where someone tried to seize him); the third is further discussion about whether Jesus was the Christ, but this pericope is not notated ekphonetically. The fourth is Jesus' declaration that if anyone is thirsty he should come to him for living water, ending with the guards saying that they have never heard anyone speak like this, although the page following this last one of the parchments would have had further verses to complete the pericope. Wellesz writes that normally there is a formulaic introduction to a reading from the Gospel, delivered in a narrative style without accentuation (*kathiste*) and consisting of the words τῷ καιρῷ ἐκείνῳ, meaning 'at that time',[37] although this does not appear to be the case in this manuscript. Similarly, at the end of a reading, there would often be increased variety in the notation, which is in evidence in this manuscript, although not following exactly the formula described by C. Høeg.[38] This coincides with at least two kinds of liturgical factors, one being the possible climax of the reading itself and the other being the musical or non-musical elements of the liturgy that are to follow, where the implementation and realization of the ekphonetic notation would provide clues to those who would follow the reading, perhaps providing pitch and opening formulas for music that is to follow.

Subsidiae, 1.1; Copenhagen: Levin & Mundsgaard, 1935), p. 13, who writes that 'Byzantine Hymnody is more like recitative than melody'.

36. See the useful discussion of melodic formulas in a related context in M. Velimirovic, *Byzantine Elements in Early Slavonic Chant* (Momumentae Musicae Byzantinae, Subsidiae, 4, main volume; Copenhagen: Ejnar Munksgaard, 1960), ch. 5, 'Melodic Formulae', pp. 61-67.

37. Wellesz, *History of Byzantine Music*, p. 253.

38. For description of a normal formula at the end of a pericope, see Høeg, *La notation ekphonétique*, pp. 22-23: '[D]ans les leçons, l'ordre des groupes est libre et dépend des constructions syntaxique, sauf à la fin, où l'on trouve généralement la suite que voici //…// \\…\\ ¨¨…¨¨ ,,…,,//.' Here Høeg has written the progression of signs found in pairs.

For the sake of brevity, my remarks are confined to one pericope, which falls almost entirely on page five of the eight. It contains a representative sampling of the markings of ekphonetic notation. The text begins midway through Jn 7.24 and ends at v. 30:

> ...make a right judgment. 25 At that point some of the people of Jerusalem began to ask, 'Isn't this the man they are trying to kill? 26 Here he is, speaking publicly, and they are not saying a word to him. Have the authorities really concluded that he is the Christ? 27 But we know where this man is from: when the Christ comes, no one will know where he is from.' 28 Then Jesus, still teaching in the temple courts, cried out: 'Yes, you know me, and you know where I am from. I am not here on my own, but he who sent me is true. You do not know him, 29 but I know him because I am from him and he sent me.' 30 At this point they tried to seize him, but no one laid a hand on him, because his time had not yet come (NIV).

The full realization or understanding of these markings is not entirely certain yet, although much progress was made last century in determining various features of them, as mentioned above.[39] Following the identifications as Wellesz has outlined them, the reading has the following characteristics.[40]

(oxeia) ...MAKE A RIGHT JUDGMENT. (teleia and colon) (= the voice rises to a higher note and remains there until the end of the phrase)

25. (apostrophos) AT THAT POINT WERE ASKING (apostrophos) (= a lower pitch of voice but spoken without emphasis; it can also indicate taking a breath, which delineates shorter phrases in a way that it does not with longer ones)

(oxeia) SOME OF THOSE FROM JERUSALEM, (teleia)

(double apostrophos) 'ISN'T THIS THE MAN (oxeia) (= apeso exo, as with the single apostrophos, indicating a rise from the beginning of the phrase to the end of the phrase)

(hypokrisis) THEY ARE TRYING TO KILL? (hypokrisis) (= a full stop according to Wellesz)

26 (bareia) AND HERE HE IS, (bareia) (= indicates lowering the voice on the words between the encompassing marks, but lowering in such a way as to give emphasis)

39. For a more complete treatment of the signs and how they are used, see Høeg, *La notation ekphonétique*, ch. 4, 'L'emploi des signes', pp. 43-70.

40. For greater ease of reading I have aligned the text to correspond with the notation, as opposed to keeping it in its original columns; for plates and diplomatic and reconstructed texts, see Porter and Porter, *New Testament Greek Papyri and Parchments*, no. 40. I have also used a fairly literal word-for-word translation in order to keep the comparison of the notation straightforward.

(apostrophos) SPEAKING PUBLICLY, (apostrophos)
(oxeia) AND THEY ARE NOT SAYING A WORD TO HIM. (teleia)
(kremaste) THEY DON'T REALLY KNOW, DO THEY (kremaste) (= the voice rises and gives slight accentuation to the words)
(apostrophos) THE AUTHORITIES (apostrophos)
(kathiste) THAT HE IS THE CHRIST? (kathiste) (= a narrative style without emphasis, although this does not seem appropriate at this point in the text)
27 (bareia) BUT THIS MAN (bareia)
(apostrophos) WE KNOW (apostrophos)
(oxeia) WHERE HE IS FROM: (teleia)
(kathiste) BUT WHENEVER THE CHRIST MAY COME, (kathiste) (= a narrative style without emphasis, but again, it does not seem to match the sense of the text at this point)
(oxeia) NO ONE WILL KNOW (oxeia) (= the voice rises to a higher note and remains there until the end of the phrase)
(oxeia) WHERE HE IS FROM'. (oxeia)
28 (apostrophos) THEREFORE CRIED OUT IN THE TEMPLE COURTS, (oxeia) (= apeso exo, indicating a rise from the beginning of the phrase to the end of the phrase)
(apostrophos) JESUS WHO WAS TEACHING (apostrophos)
(oxeia) AND SAYING: (teleia)
(bareia) 'YOU KNOW ME (bareia)
(kremaste) AND YOU KNOW WHERE I AM FROM. (kremaste)
(apostrophos) I HAVE NOT COME OF MYSELF, (apostrophos)
(kentemata) BUT HE WHO SENT ME IS TRUE. (kentemata) (= a form of an ascending third)
(oxeia) WHOM YOU DO NOT KNOW. (teleia)
29 (kremaste) I KNOW HIM (kremaste)
(apostrophos) BECAUSE I AM FROM HIM (apostrophos)
(oxeia) AND HE SENT ME'. (teleia)
30 (bareia) AT THIS POINT THEY TRIED TO SEIZE HIM (bareia)
(bareia) AND NO ONE LAID A HAND ON HIM (bareia)
(apostrophos) FOR IT HAD NOT YET ARRIVED (apostrophos)
(kentemata) THE HOUR (kentemata)
(apostrophos) OF HIM. (apostrophos)

Some of these phrases clearly are paralleled with that of a present-day reading. For instance, the use of the *apeso exo*, rising from the beginning of the sentence to the ending, occurs on the following statement: 'Isn't this the man?' (οὐχ οὗτός ἐστιν). The rising motion throughout the phrase is indicated visually by a mark below the first letter (*apostrophos*) upwards to the mark above the final letter (*oxeia*); this matches the natural rising intonation of a question. A second statement that uses this combination of *apostrophos* below the first letter and *oxeia* above the final letter (*apeso exo*) is 'Therefore [Jesus] cried out in the temple courts' (ἔκραξεν οὖν ἐν τῷ ἱερῷ). Here the rising intonation also matches the sense of this phrase, with a rise in intensity as Jesus prepares to make his announcement.

The *oxeia* is one of the most common forms of ekphonetic notation and can encompass many kinds of statements. The fact that the voice is elevated does not necessarily imply heightened accentuation, but rather may be seen as the equivalent of a voice required for a public audience, one that naturally is more elevated than the voice one uses in one-to-one dialogue. *Hypokrisis* seems to mean a lengthy separation of words, a pause that delineates the section. The phrase found within two hypokrisis signs is 'the one they are trying to kill' (ὃν ζητοῦσιν ἀποκτεῖναι). The combination of its preceding phrase (see above, with the use of *apeso exo*) and this one is that of rising intonation on 'isn't this the man…', followed by a significant pause separating it from the completing phrase '…they are trying to kill?'

Use of the *bareia* in this passage is also interesting and seems appropriate to the sense of the words. The phrases that are found within sets of *bareiai* are: 'And here he is' (καὶ ἴδε), 'But this man' (ἀλλὰ τοῦτον), '(and) you know me' (κἀμὲ οἴδατε), and 'at this point they tried to seize him' (ἐζήτουν οὖν αὐτὸν πιάσαι). In each of these cases, the phrase gains a degree of intensification by dropping the pitch, giving added emphasis to the words in the process. All four instances of the use of *bareia* in this particular pericope are appropriately placed on phrases that are significant factors in the story.

The final mark that I will call attention to is the *kremaste*, which indicates that the voice rises and gives slight accentuation to the words. The two phrases that use this form of notation are 'and you know where I am from' (καὶ οἴδατε πόθεν εἰμί) and 'I know him' (ἐγὼ οἶδα αὐτόν). Again, these are short phrases, but pivotal in the context of this particular pericope.

Even without knowing the exact sound of these musical-ekphonetic units, it can be recognized that the markings are not random, that there is a very specific plan.[41] Some of it is formulaic, and formulas that can often be found at the endings of pericopes or lectionary readings are in evidence in this manuscript. There are varying degress of accuracy in manuscripts of this nature, but in this particular parchment, the mark-

41. See, again, Wellesz, *History of Byzantine Music*, p. 256.

ings are consistent and occur in logical divisions, if not always identical to the ones a modern-day interpreter would use. The shape of the text is clear and it becomes increasingly obvious that both the text itself and the meaning of the text are held in high regard, with the text elucidated by its notation. The particular focus on single words or groups of two words often gives an indication of emphases that were considered important, perhaps giving more clarity to the text than the longer phrases one might commonly use today.[42] In either case, there is evidence of very close readings of the text[43] and an expectation that the person who was to deliver these musical readings would accurately interpret and deliver the text as the ekphonetic notation prescribed.[44]

At this point in the history of sacred music, we see tremendous adherence to the biblical text, with it providing the foundation on which musical delivery was based. Musically, there may have been much more freedom than the notation and the idea of musical formulas suggests, and some freedom of interpretation may well have been common within the confines of the formulas and textual fidelity. The ekphonetic notation, as it is written in this manuscript, indicates that while there are some obvious correlations with modern speech, it does not correspond exactly with modern-day emphases, particularly in that very small phrases are treated independently and with great attention to detail, not making use of the longer phrases that we would delineate today.

John Tavener: 'We Shall See Him as He Is' *(Twentieth Century)*

The leap to this late twentieth-century choral work is large, to say the least, and yet some of the features of this composition fit closely with that of the preceding discussion. The particular composition, John Tavener's hour-long choral work entitled 'We Shall See Him as He Is',

42. In contrast to later Byzantine notation, where the meaning of the text and the words themselves sometimes become more obscure as melodic embellishment or ornamentation reaches its highest proportions; this is a feature similar to what occurred at the height of the development of Latin Renaissance polyphony.

43. See Wellesz's statement, *History of Byzantine Music*, p. 251: 'The cantillation followed the syntactical structure of the phrase in every detail.'

44. Or 'reminded', for there is still speculation as to how much was specifically indicated in this notation and how much was simply a reminder or clue to the formulas that were already familiar to those who would deliver these lectionary readings.

was published in 1990. Tavener's sacred choral works have incorporated representations of Byzantine musical idioms and theological ideas of the eastern Christian Church, and presented them to an unusually receptive western Christian Church.[45] He depicts—in discussing his own music, he intentionally uses language that has a visual characteristic—some of the features of an ancient practice of worship, but in a form of music that sounds new to the contemporary listener. In a review of a live performance of this work, Richard Langham Smith writes that it 'evoked an hour's devotion in the various chapels of a basilica'.[46] Tavener definitely attempts to present an element of the visual symbols and visual forms of ritual in his music. The review further describes Tavener's manner of alternating 'between the powdery thirds of Anglican church music and the inflections of Byzantium',[47] with recognition of an intermingling of East and West. David Wright, in his review, writes that the problems of reception that this work presents 'tends to be glossed over because of the approachability of its surface'.[48] The lack of musical development and the imagery can seem simplistic and perhaps too easily accessible. Wright goes on to say, however, that explicit in this work 'is a musical and conceptual disdain for the easy-listening apparatus of post-modernity' and that it 'demands an act of concentrated listening by its audience', in part because there are such small changes over such a long period of time.[49] So, what seems simple in one respect, is perhaps more difficult in another.

The work is scored for a main tenor soloist, as well as additional tenor and soprano soloists, a chorus and an orchestra consisting of strings, organ, two trumpets and two sets of timpani. Andrew Burn writes, 'With these forces Tavener creates a score of idiosyncratic timbres for each principal idea, a process which may be likened to the

45. See discussion of the dichotomy of eastern and western perspectives on Christianity and Tavener's own contribution to this discussion in A. Wilson-Dickson, *The Story of Christian Music: From Gregorian Chant to Black Gospel: An Authoritative Illustrated Guide to All the Major Traditions of Music for Worship* (Oxford: Lion, 1992), pp. 166-67.

46. R.L. Smith, review, 'A Winning Path', *Musical Times* 133 (1992), pp. 475-76.

47. Smith, review, p. 475.

48. D. Wright, review, '1992 Prom premières (2)', *Tempo* 183 (Dec. 1992), pp. 33-34 (34).

49. Wright, review, p. 34.

different mosaics or paints that make up the colours of an ikon.'[50] It should be mentioned here that the idea of a mosaic is not only found in the musical timbres, but also in the compilation of the text, as will be discussed below. Tavener has made much use of the term 'ikons' in his music, reflecting his interest in the painted ikons of the Orthodox Church. The settings in this work are often deceptively simple, as noted above, although often extreme in vocal and instrumental range, using single changes in orchestration, ornamentation, or dynamics. Burn describes it thus: 'There is little development in terms of the "Classical" western music tradition; the ideas are static and ritualistic, varied primarily through subtle changes of instrumental or choral scoring.'[51]

It is interesting to see that what Tavener calls ikons would in most liturgical settings be called pericopes or readings. Having said that, the text is both straightforward and not-so-straightforward as it seems, based largely on the way in which Mother Thekla, the compiler of the text, has arranged it. Features of her contribution to this choral work are noteworthy, for the text itself and the combination of the words and music are important features of the present discussion. For instance, there is no question that the text comes from the New Testament. However, while she has not exactly rewritten it, she has seriously reduced it, to the point of being extremely sparse, even minimalistic. While it appears at first that the text is simply from the Gospel of John, she has actually conflated several books of the New Testament—three books that are traditionally thought to be written by the same author, but which have very different styles of writing and very different roles in the New Testament. These three books include not only the Gospel of John, but the First Epistle of John and the book of Revelation or the Apocalypse of John. Obviously, John is the perceived author and, in fact, he is the main character of this musical work. The interesting merging of these three books, however, can be observed first in the two phrases that comprise the refrain. The first phrase, which forms the title of this work, is 'we shall see him as he is'. It comes from 1 Jn 3.2: 'Dear friends, now we are children of God, and what we will be has not yet been made known. But we know that when he appears, we shall be like him, *for we shall see him as he is.*' This, however, is the only part of the text that comes specifically from 1 John (although the first lines

50. A. Burn, notes to CD recording of 'John Tavener: "We Shall See Him as He Is" ' (Chandos [Chan 9128], 1992), p. 3.

51. Burn, notes, p. 3.

of Ikon 1 have some resemblances). The second phrase of the refrain, 'Amen, come Lord Jesus', comes from the penultimate verse in the book of Revelation, or the Apocalypse of St John, 22.20, 'He who testifies to these things says, "Yes, I am coming soon". Amen, come Lord Jesus.' Interestingly, however, the refrain is sung only in Greek throughout the piece until the very last line of the work, where it is sung in English. The rest of the text is all in English and comes almost entirely from the Gospel of John, in reduced form, and, apart from the final section, is chronological as it appears in the Gospel. Again, it is evident that the text is not completely straightforward, for although it at first glance appears simple to the point of being extreme, it in essence gives the full outline of a portrait without filling in the details.

The work, set out in 11 'ikons' or pericopes from the Gospel of John, follows this pattern: Refrain, Ikons 1–3, Refrain, Ikons 4–5, Refrain, Ikons 6–7, Refrain, Ikons 8–9, then a Refrain integrated within Ikon 10, and finally Ikon 11 (a modified version of the refrain, but in English instead of Greek). In Ikon 1, for example, the text is: 'I heard: Before time was. Time within. Time beyond. Created. Uncreated. Bodiless Body.'[52] The words for Ikon 9 are: 'I saw: The cross. His body crucified. The Blood. The Water. Linen clothes. Napkin.'[53]

As I mentioned, the text of the ikons or pericopes is almost entirely from the Gospel of John. However, the introductory phrases with which each pericope or ikon is opened—either 'I saw' or 'I heard'—are not a noticeable feature of the Gospel of John. They are, instead, very visible phrases in the book of Revelation; in fact, these two phrases in one form or another appear about 75 times throughout the book, as opening formulas for various visions or audible events that John introduces. It is intriguing that this form of presentation has been used to introduce each ikon in the musical work, for the style of presentation in the Gospel is quite different from that of Revelation. One thing this style provides, however, which is essential to the idea of an ikon depicted in music, is that of an easily recognizable formula. The opening phrase, 'I saw' or 'I heard', has that quality of familiarity both in its brief wording and in the repetition of the musical formula with slight variations or decorations. These give a stylized form of development, but do not detract from a recognizable similarity.

52. The biblical text for this ikon is taken from Jn 1.1-4 and 1 Jn 1.1-2.

53. This is from Jn 19.16, 17–20.9. The other ikons are largely from chs. 2–6 and 19 of John.

It is also noteworthy that the text only gives the outline of each pericope or so-called ikon. The descriptive words, though sparse, are not obscure (see examples given above of Ikons 1 and 9). They serve as succinct, even poignant, reminders for the reader who is familiar with these stories; by their brief symbolic words they allow one fully to recall the events that are depicted. These features are in keeping with the idea of a musical depiction of the visual form of the ikon: representation of the form with familiar style and familiar techniques, never full detail, never life-like recreation of the image, never innovation to draw attention to the innovation itself.

There are many levels at which this work is symbolic and picks up the mannerisms of certain formulas of Byzantine music and eastern Christianity. The declamation of the phrase 'I saw' or 'I heard' is formulaic. It provides what one might expect if the same ekphonetic sign were written above the phrase every time it occurred in a sacred text, such as was explored above in the portions of John with ekphonetic notation. However, the form of the delivery also has some similarities to the setting of Bach's St John Passion. Both use the pattern of a tenor narrator, extra soloists who act as specific individuals, and a chameleon-like choir that can be the crowd at a marriage feast and can also provide the ambience of a musical halo, an effect that occurs at the entrance of certain ikons in this work.

Does Tavener's work, 'We Shall See Him as He Is', give us some insight into faith at the beginning of this millennium? Although it can at first hearing strike the listener as contrived, its features provide us with valuable insights into the Christian faith at the beginning of the twentieth-first century and, perhaps, views into similar practices of faith nearly a millennium ago. For instance, Tavener has chosen simple lines, lines that are frequently set to be sung in unison, which is reminiscent of an ancient practice of singing. Although Mother Thekla has provided a text that has been highly edited, streamlined and compiled in a mosaic-like way, it does not deviate from the actual depiction of the pericope or ikon, in its own way reflecting the ancient practice of holding the text in high regard. This cleanness of line, both in the music and in the text, projects an image of timelessness, which is undoubtedly what Tavener was hoping to achieve. Similarly, the use of the Greek language as the refrain and title is another feature that draws this modern-day work back to the inception of Christianity, and certainly to the height of Byzantine chant. In a stylized way, through means that some might call simplistic or mannered, Tavener has nonetheless drawn a full circle that brings the end of a millennium back to its beginning. By bringing it back to the biblical text and unison singing, which has characterized the music of the Christian Church for most of the millennium that preceded it, he has also provided a larger full circle that brings us back to the very inception of Christianity. Certainly he has given us insight into the present-day penchant to reread and reinterpret old texts, rearranging then in new kaleidoscopic ways. By taking on ancient forms, or at least modern representations of ancient forms, he has reworked the old in such a way as to present a work that seems quite new.

Conclusion

The three points in the history of sacred music that have briefly been discussed here are in no way representative of the greatest works in sacred music, for the parameters of this discussion have completely bypassed all of those compositions that would traditionally be considered the greatest choral works, including those of Palestrina, Tallis, Byrd, Mozart, Bach, Beethoven, Schubert, and so on. Nonetheless, these three works represent significant characteristics of sacred music at the beginning, middle and end of two millennia. The first, as one of the most highly discussed passages in the New Testament and one that many have thought may be an older hymn, has created great interest for those scholars who have tried to determine of what the music of the New Testament may have consisted. Most of all, it represents aspects of the newness that was inherent at the inception of the Christian faith and Church, both newness in defining what a hymn is and newness in presenting Christ. The second, the Gospel of John passage, by means of its ekphonetic notation, gives us some clues to its musical presentation in a liturgical setting. It is a stage in Byzantine chant that is foundational for later developments in sacred chant, providing insights into the musical practices of the Byzantine Church and other Christian Churches in the ninth to thirteenth centuries. It also gives us a view of the Church at a point when faithfulness to the text was perhaps more straightforward than in later periods, where individuality has been developed to a great extent. Having said this, there is no definite indication that there was not some degree of spontaneity involved or some level of personal interpretation by the performer within the confines of the formulas of the notation. Nonetheless, the formulas also show us that the text was revered and preserved, perhaps giving us some idea of the ideals of faith in the Christian Church at the time. The third work, Tavener's choral composition, written at the end of the second millennium after Christ, represents the continuing musical and liturgical need to reinterpret a fundamental text of the Christian Church, the story as presented in the Gospel of John. By taking on some characteristics of ancient musical formulas, trying to imbue them with visual characteristics, and redefining and reshaping the basic text, this work provides some direct ties to the Byzantine Church and to the early Christian Church, providing a window into these earlier cultures. At the same time, the work stands on its own as a window into faith at the end of a millennium, a work in which some features of the faith of East and West are merged through a collage or mosaic of text fragments and musical-formulaic fragments. Perhaps in this work, in which something new is created out of those things that are most ancient, we see a recent example of a genuine attempt to describe the faith of today that is trying fully to exist in the present but to not lose hold of the most valuable things of its history. In this way, Tavener's work successfully completes a millennium by bringing modern-day faith back to the practices of one thousand years ago and back to the precepts of the beginning of Christianity.

SACRED ART IN A NEW AGE: A VIRTUAL REALITY ROSE WINDOW CELEBRATING THE FEMININE

Delia Whitbread

Introduction

> Is it mere nostalgia to look to the cathedrals, and ponder a new but equivalent unity of art and architecture, of private reverie and public rite, based on a new and secular commonwealth of symbolic imagery?[1]

Malcolm Miles, in his book *Art for Public Places*, asks this question in his analysis of the relative success and failure of contemporary public art in creating the unifying power of the great mediaeval cathedrals. His answer to this question by the end of the book is to speculate that there might be a language for such artwork in myth where symbols and dreams often have common roots. He hopes that we might return to the 'great subjects' of traditional sacred art without succumbing to romanticism and nostalgia—as the Victorians so often did. As he says, 'Revivals are an expression of poverty of thought, a compensation for a notion of something lost.'[2]

The question is, How can such a revival be accomplished in the public spaces that might become the 'cathedrals' of the new millennium? And what of the past in craft and symbol can be built on and renewed without recourse to mere imitation and cliche? We are in need of new directions in our public art that do not discard the power of our traditional past in either craft skills or imagery. We now have a medium accessible through computing technology that can rival the art forms of the past in international scope if not physical size. It is the marriage of the primary visionary medium of the mediaeval world, stained glass, with the visionary power of the Internet that is the subject of this essay.

The project I am researching is an attempt to use the Internet and advanced computer graphic technology to design a modern equivalent

1. M. Miles, *Art for Public Places* (Winchester: Winchester School of Art Press, 1989), p. 5.
2. Miles, *Art for Public Places*, p. 216.

to the great mediaeval rose windows of the past. Taking a new theme with an ancient but lost history—that of female imagery—and using women artists from all over the world in collaboration, I intend to construct a design on the scale of the great rose windows of Chartres in virtual reality. These windows are 15 metres in diameter and a computer graphic collage on a scale of 1:12 using a geometric template was designed as part of my MA project at the Royal College of Art. This was accompanied by a thesis on gender and iconography that examined the history and variety of female imagery in a number of archaic and current religious traditions. It is part of the brief of the design that it should be rooted in an understanding and appreciation of the past. The intention is to create icons of the feminine from the refiguring of the old in a new context that offers a more multicultural framework than that of the Christian Middle Ages.

The success of such an undertaking will be judged in its final outcome but the justification of the enterprise is outlined here. I would like to discuss both what we can learn from the principles of sacred art that governed the making of the significant 'public' art of our heritage and the modern use of the female body in relation to female imagery of other cultures and times.

A Virtual Reality Rose Window: Geometry as Transcendental Perfection

In the Middle Ages rose windows first appeared after the conquering of Moorish Spain and the translation of Arab books on sacred geometry—knowledge of which had been lost to the West since the Dark Ages. The term 'rose'—first used in connection with Aphrodite and later with the Virgin Mary—became the prime expression of divine love in Christian iconography.

As an image of wholeness the circle has always been the perfect symbol of sacred unity in every religious tradition and is the form of every mandala for meditation in the East. The rose windows of Northern Europe were mandalas on a grand scale using the craft of glass with its orchestration of light (also an important Christian metaphor for God) to an effect unparalleled in any other tradition. As such it seemed the 'perfect' form and medium to express and celebrate the diverse nature of the feminine principle. The various figures are contained within a harmonious whole by both the geometry of the pattern and the coloured glass by which they are rendered.

The design is structured around a geometry of sevens. Seven is the number that has always been associated with the feminine in sacred geometry. It was used in connection with Pallas Athena in Ancient Greece and the Virgin Mary in the later Christian tradition. 'Seven' also relates to the seven visible planets, which are seen as aspects of the human psyche that, in the Virgin Mary, symbolized the perfection of the human soul. Seven is known as the 'Virgin' number within the primal decad, because it can be neither divided equally nor multiplied equally to make any other number. As a geometric equation it is an 'irrational', or perhaps more mysteriously and positively, a 'supra-rational' form because it is impossible to construct a heptagon accurately by the use of a compass. The final adjustments have to be made by hand, as the measurements are never absolutely accurate.

Plate 1. *In the Womb of the Rose.* Collage of computer graphic images. IBM paintbox outputting to a thermal wax printer. 150 × 150 cm. MA(RCA)

Plate 1 shows a computer graphic collage of the design that is approximately 1:12 in scale. The full-scale version would be equal to that of the great windows of Chartres—approximately 15 metres in diameter. In the design there are 28 major panels revolving around a central seven-petal heart. This numerology relates to the 28 days of the lunar month—the moon and the menstrual cycle have links in all traditions. Plate 2 shows the whole of one section of the design in line before scanning into the computer. The base unit for the design of all the figurative panels is a geometry of a large circle with a smaller satellite circle to reflect a sun–moon relationship common to ideas of the feminine in all cultures. As a symbol it is less pejoratively weighted than the traditional biological and cosmic sign of the circle of Venus above the cross of matter. The cosmic egg from the Hindu tantric tradition occupies the heart of the window. The egg is a symbol common to all traditions and represents hope and the creative potential for change and growth. In this image, free of any gender distinctions, are the seeds of all beginnings—it represents the raw elements of matter floating in primaeval chaos that have yet to be given form. It also echoes the biological egg in the physical womb. The window is a metaphor for the womb of the feminine.

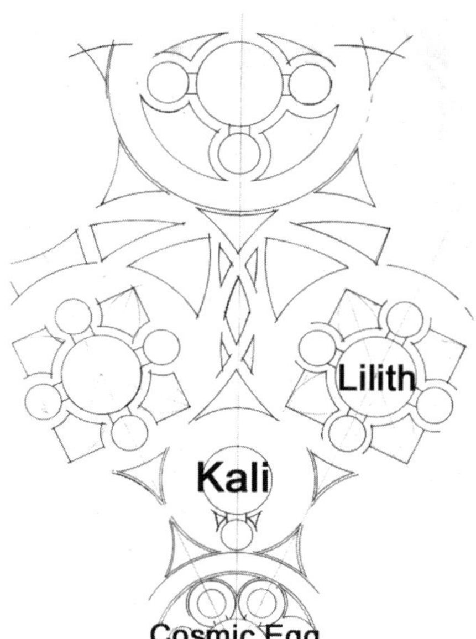

Plate 2. Section of geometry of circle showing placement of *Kali* and *Lilith* panels. MA(RCA)

The panels for Kali and Lilith are marked on the drawing in Pl. 2. From the cosmic egg panel seven archetypal 'goddess' images radiate. The figures are torsos and grow both out of the earth and from the geometric principle that is the abstract initiator of their birth in the centre of each of their 'moons'. They emerge into a landscape that is presided over by a progressively waxing and waning moon. The landscape correspondingly echoes this in a seasonal change in which the trees grow, bloom; fruit fade, die and decay as one moves clockwise around the circle. Each goddess is chosen to represent an equivalent aspect of woman's experience of life from her girlhood to her death.

I have chosen these archetypes in the full knowledge that for the ancient goddesses such a separation in nature would not have been possible, as they expressed a reality that encompassed all aspects of being. Kali, as beginning and end of time, heads the circle. She is followed by Artemis, the independent 'virgin',[3] symbol of freedom and individuality. Inanna/Aphrodite represents relationship with the other, love and sexuality. Other figures suggested are Isis (the nurturing mother with her child); Kuan Yin (the compassionate image of mature maternal love); Cybele (the wisdom of the old earth mother); Hecate (the crone who sees three ways and guides the knowledge of past, present and future).

In the next circle of seven panels are allegorical figures from myth and tradition that have shaped our metaphors of femininity both positively and negatively. They are contained within a square that represents their effect on material reality despite their fantastic origins.[4] These would include Eve and Lilith (respectively the 'good' and 'bad' wives of Adam). Also represented would be the opposing images of the Divine Sophia and the Dreadful Medusa as inspiring and petrifying of human endeavours respectively. The outer 14 panels are contained within a triangle of 3 moons. In sacred/Platonic geometry the triangle traditionally represents human consciousness.[5] Here the work of real

3. The ancient goddesses were not virgin in the sense we understand today—meaning chastity or lack of sexual experience. They often had many lovers, some sacrificed in spring rituals of fertilization of the soil. However, they were never 'married' and had no regular consort. Virgin here means more like 'one-in-herself' (see E.M. Harding, *Women's Mysteries: The Inner Life of Women in Religious Myths and Ritual* [London: Rider, 1986]).

4. In Platonic geometry four represents the world of being with its four dimensions and four directions, north, south, east and west.

5. In the ancient world the triangle was a symbol of female genitalia and is

women in the physical world is celebrated, whether it is on the assembly lines of the industrialized nations or carrying water for hours each day in parts of Africa or India. These panels would also include women's participation in the traditional fields of nursing, education and agriculture as well as their creativity in the 'fine' and craft arts of the world. The various moons of the outer panels could contain vegetable and animal forms appropriate to each image.

The tracery patterns of the design are made up of various experiments in collage translated into computer graphics and pasted into the geometric patterns that make up such elements as the spokes in the 'wheel'. As the levels of manifestation move outward the individual elements increase in size very slightly. The outer panels appear largest as the action moves out of the controlling frame of the geometry. This is intended to give an explosive effect but also creates the impression of a sphere seen from the inside. Thus the paradox of the womb as both a container and also the dynamic agent of birth is given expression in form.

In using the ancient craft of stained glass I am anchoring this new perspective in a traditional base and putting a great Gothic visionary art (still loved and revered despite loss of meaning in its inspiring faith) into the context of a modern, multicultural society. In the interests of redressing the present grave imbalance between male and female values, I am emphasizing the feminine—hopefully for the illumination of men's inner worlds as well as women's outer realities. By redeeming the 'ideals' of the feminine from the limitations imposed on them by patriarchal ideology, and combining their figurative images with uniting abstract principles of geometry, it is possible to celebrate a wholeness in the experience of being female that has been lost to the individual religious traditions since the era of the Great Goddess. However, this is not the whole of the story—next we have to give these old images new life within the medium of glass. Just how are we to reconstruct those icons from the misrepresentation of the past and the misunderstanding in the present?

Icons Versus Images in the Twentieth Century

First, we need to define what we mean by sacred art and the term 'icon'. The mediaeval Christian would have had no confusion concerning such

represented as such in Kali's *Yantra*. *Yantra*s are geometric symbols used in meditation and particular to each deity in the Hindu pantheon.

terms. The pilgrims of mediaeval Europe would, whatever the language differences encountered in their travels, have instantly recognized the characters and stories of biblical narratives in the glass and architecture of the Churches they visited. All over Christendom—from Iona to Rome and beyond—the conventions of clothing, posture, halo and attributes would have been recognizable to a population that was more visually literate than our own.

All religious art was controlled by the Church and was part of a recognized ritual that gave it meaning and function. Whether monastic or lay the craftsmen followed the pattern of forms dictated and designed by the Church in the previous centuries, and even after the split with the Eastern Orthodox Church a continuity of image continued until the Renaissance. The idea of a personal religious art would have been unthinkable, which is why the artists and craftsmen who created the illustrated manuscripts and great cathedrals have not signed their work.

Nowadays the word 'icon' does not have the particular significance of a prescribed image of a holy figure like the Virgin Mary and Child Jesus, which are still reproduced according to the dictates of the Eastern Orthodox tradition. These early Christian icons are intended to be supra human rather than non-human—they symbolize the transcendence of the human spirit rather than a personalized image of a human mother. Titus Burckhardt, in his seminal work *Sacred Art of East and West*, describes the phenomena thus:

> In the icon the only perspective is the logical; sometimes the optical perspective is deliberately reversed; modeling by superimposed 'highlights' inherited from Hellenism, is reduced until it no longer disturbs the flat surface of the picture; often it is translucid as if the persons represented were penetrated by a mysterious light.[6]

The stylized and two-dimensional features of icons are meant to represent a meaning greater than their substance—and the gold leaf and rigid but rhythmical arranged drapery emphasize their other worldliness in order to encourage contemplation. In comparison post-Renaissance work with its celebration of the individual and physical perfection of the real human body creates a new aesthetic not covered by the same definitions.

6. T. Burckhardt, *Sacred Art in East and West: Its Principles and Methods* (London: Perennial Books, 1986), p. 68.

The Craft Process as Discipline in Sacred Art

The recreation of an icon is not a matter of pure personal expression. Burckhardt introduces his book as follows:

> When a historian of Art applies the term 'sacred art' to any and every work that has a religious subject, they are forgetting that art is essentially form. An art cannot properly be called 'sacred' solely on the grounds that its subjects originate in a spiritual truth; its formal language also must bear witness to a similar origin...a spiritual vision necessarily finds its expression in a particular formal language; if that language is lacking, with the result that a so-called sacred art borrows its forms from some kind of profane art, then it can only be because a spiritual vision of things is also lacking.[7]

Essentially conservative and dogmatic by nature, Burckhardt values the crafts of the older sacred traditions because they involved a discipline that demanded the surrender of ego for mastery of practice. Burckhardt consequently values sacred art as a craft-based discipline that used formal means to bring geometry, symbolism, medium and ornament into a whole expression of a non-personal deity. For this reason artists were to copy and reinterpret older icons—not to create new images of their own. Such discipline was normally controlled by a rigorous monastic life and still is in the Hindu/Buddhist and Orthodox Christian monasteries of the East. Similarly, successful icons in any religion are usually governed by a controlling geometry that harmonizes the proportions of the figures and their gestures. Thus there is created in the figure and the face a still point around which all activity flows, reminding the viewer of their own centre, around which they can compose their own emotions.

'Religious' art, on the other hand, however noble the sentiment that inspires the work, has developed more personal modes of expression since the secularization of art in the Renaissance. The appeal of such art is often dependent on fashion and the culture of the time and has no traditional formal language. Despite its apparent conformity good sacred art is as dependent on the skill and sensitivity of an individual as any secular art. In a room full of icons of the same theme, it is usually not hard to pick out the most powerful, which draw us by a combination of artistic skill and spiritual presence. However, the discipline involved in the application of the craft and the continuity in the formal language of

7. Burckhardt, *Sacred Art*, p. 7.

the images renders disparate works harmonious and creates the necessary link with the history of the religion or culture to which it belongs.

Some of the skills employed in the craft of traditional sacred art are not available to the artist in an ordinary art school setting. Not many secular artists are trained, for instance, in the egg tempera painting with gold leaf that is necessary for the creation of orthodox icons. By comparison stained glass has always had a tradition of non-monastic practice and is still a living craft. By the power of its association with the religious, and the fact that, as a craft, it has changed little as a technique since the Middle Ages, it is a perfect medium for the creation of a new form of sacramental work, as discipline is essential for its creation. However inspired one is by the vision of the whole, the making of the piece is laborious and full of pitfalls—blood, sweat and tears are spilt, and cuts, burns and breakages an inevitable part of the process. The necessary fragmentation and reassembly of an image makes non-attachment and faith almost a prerequisite for the task.

Kali and Lilith: The Process of Making 'Icons' in Stained Glass

As Pere Couterier said in his book *Sacred Art* about images made for contemporary Christian settings: 'Mark well where purity has its true domain. It is far less in the subject than the style. A clothed statue can be impure, a nude miraculously pure. There is a kind of religious sentimentality that is impurity itself.'[8]

Sentimentality is a problem that bedevils most modern western attempts to recreate the power so evident in the images of the old mother goddesses. The languorous, sexless prettiness of some New Age 'goddesses' reveals how hard it is to shake off our old concepts of the ideal feminine—still rooted in Christian dualism and a romantic Victorian tradition of female perfection. Modern western feminists grapple with the problem of how to express a female sexuality not open to exploitation but rarely in a traditional religious context. Couterier highlights the fact that 'purity' in a sacred image is not contingent on it being clothed or not, however the ideas of purity meaning 'chastity' inform the image of the sacred feminine. Compassion and virtue are still the favoured depictions of female in most of the world's cultures, not sexuality and power. Women who do not conform to the model risk censure and, in

8. M.-A. Couterier, *Sacred Art: Texts Selected by Dominique de Menil and Pie Duploye* (trans. G. Ryan; Austin: University of Texas Press, 1989), p. 22.

some extreme situations, even imprisonment and death. These limited images of female, in which sexuality and aggression are only seen in the context of the demonic world of temptation and sin, deny the reality of all human nature. If purity is equated, as it is in the Christian tradition, with 'truth', then only the whole, with all its contradictions, is an honest representation of both the human condition and divine love. Rather than 'reinventing the wheel' in these matters it seems more expedient to use the precepts of traditional sacred art to reinterpret images that, although shocking, are already partly 'sanctified' by their antiquity and/or current usage. I turned to images from archaic or eastern traditions for my inspiration. As Zimmer says of Hindu art,

> Hindu...in its great period, rested on those intimate experiences of the living organism and mysteries gained through yogic experiences—and simultaneously had a definitely heterosexual flavour, distilled and refined to a subtle enchanting fragrance. Greek Art was derived from experiences of the eye; Hindu art from those of the circulation of the blood.[9]

By using such images with an informed understanding of their success, the female icons of the future can be resurrected with their proper power. As sample pieces for my project I have made two images using historical sources: *Kali—Mistress of Life and Death* (Plate 3) and *Lilith—Spirit of Instinctual Wisdom* (Plate 6). The research, and the reinterpretation into another medium, glass, have been useful exercises in my knowledge of both processes.

The principles of sacred art dictate that the artist must efface ego in the creation of an iconic image whose form has been handed down by tradition. The discipline of the craft involved is also important in the evolution of the 'perfect' icon in that, however fearful the image, the artist tries to render it as beautifully as possible within the limitations of the medium—thereby to make an object worthy of representing a divinity. But it is the personal surrender and involvement of the artist alone that is able to give the image numinous life rather than just imitative excellence. In transferring the image of Kali into the Northern European craft of stained glass I have adhered as closely as I can to these principles. I hope in the process that I have both respected her nature within the context of her origins and given her real life in the context of my own tradition.

9. H. Zimmer, *Myths and Symbols in Indian Art and Civilisation* (ed. J. Campbell; Bollingen Series, 6; London: Pantheon Books, 1948), p. 190.

Kali—Mistress of Life and Death

> Hindu art far surpasses Greek Art in its exultation of feminine beauty. The spiritual ideal of Greek art, progressively lowered towards a purely human ideal, is the *cosmos* as opposed to the indefinity of *chaos*... It catches no glimpse of the 'prakritic' plane, that is to say the inexhaustible ocean of forms... In Hindu art, on the contrary, the feminine body appears as a spontaneous and innocent manifestation of the universal rhythm, like a wave of the primordial ocean or a flower on the tree of the world.[10]

Notwithstanding the hyperbole of Burckhardt's expression, there are few images more indicative of chaos than that of the Hindu goddess Kali, whose origins probably predate the other Vedic gods. In the design Kali occupies the 'no-moon' phase of the lunar cycle that is traditionally associated in all traditions with change and dissolution—a mysterious and powerful time of creative power that could bring on either madness (lunacy) or initiation and enlightenment. In the Hindu tradition it is the female principle called *Shakti* that manifests the whole of the universe by the activity of her dance, while the masculine principle is the passive principle that merely initiates the process. Neither aspect is ever conceived of as having a totally separate existence and Hindu myths do not place a high value on celibacy or abstinence, which, on the contrary, is seen as dangerous to the balance of the cosmic order.

Kali symbolizes the cosmic power of creation. As nature both gives life and takes it away, Kali marks both the beginning and end of time. She represents all three aspects of life—creation, preservation and destruction. As such she has the same ambivalent aspect as the ancient goddesses of the European tradition and is a living representative of their power who is still revered in India today. In her upper left hand Kali carries a bloody axe with which she has severed the head of a giant. The giant's head is held in her lower left hand and shows her as the destroyer of life. However in her upper right hand she holds a lotus and is making the *mudra* (gesture) of blessing, while her lower right hand makes the *mudra* of granting boons and illustrates her life-giving aspect. Her hair is wild to show her state of abandon[11] and her tongue is

10. Burckhardt, *Sacred Art*, p. 37.

11. K. Lang, 'Shaven Heads and Loose Hair', in H. Eilberg-Schwartz and W. Doniger (eds.), *'Off with her Head': The Denial of Women's Identity in Myth, Religion and Culture* (Berkeley: University of California Press, 1995), pp. 41-42.

extended as if to lick up the world but her mouth is slightly smiling. She is often shown as both seductive and destructive at the same time.[12] But whatever the strength of the figurative image it is represented equally powerfully in the geometric descending triangles of the Kali *yantra* that lies in the heart of her 'moon'.

Plate 3 is based on a nineteenth-century gouache image from the Kalighat temple complex in Calcutta (Plate 4). The flat colour and strong decorative detail of the original made this a comparatively easy image to transform into glass. I worked from collage to create the necessary fragmentation. I used the decorative features of the original to good effect in the translation of the jewellery into rich details with the employment of flash glass that has been etched, stained and painted. The controlling geometry governing the proportions of the figure and its features is centred just below the open mouth—the orifice most often equated with the vagina in a female face. The completed piece in two panels is a full-scale version measuring approximately 75 × 120 cm.

The one aspect of the original not translated in this process was the black face. Although many mediaeval stained glass images appear to have black faces, this is an accumulation of centuries of smoke from candles rather than the deliberate intent of the artist. A dark face in glass would run counter to the need for illumination, especially if it was the focal point of the image. Fortunately, in the tantric tradition Kali has many faces, each associated with a particular aspect and governed by a different colour. Her black face is associated with death and is usually seen in her mad dance among the corpses in the cremation ground. Her white face is the more stable aspect and is associated with liberation.[13]

The story most famously associated with her is that she was created by the collective meditative power of the gods in order to subdue demons that were threatening the existence of the world. She was so beautiful and so powerful that all the gods wanted her as a wife but Shiva (the Destroyer) was chosen as her consort. She set about her bloody task with great glee, however, she became blinded by the joy of killing and began to destroy the good as well as the bad. Shiva could

12. D.R. Kinsley, *The Sword and the Flute: Kali and Krisna—Dark Visions of the Terrible and the Sublime in Hindu Mythology* (Berkeley: University of California Press, 1975), p. 142.

13. S. Chattopadhyaya, *Reflections on the Tantras* (Delhi: Motilal Banarsidaas, 1978).

Plate 3. *Kali.* Stained glass panel. 120 × 75 cm. 1989. MA(RCA)

only stop her by lying down as if dead in her path where she danced among the corpses on the battlefield. When she stepped on him and recognized her husband, and thus her relationship to existence, she came to her senses and order was restored to the cosmos.[14]

As the manifestation of the all-powerful mother, Kali is both a positive and negative symbol. However, her ambivalence is balanced by the transcendent symbol of the lotus that she carries—upon which she also usually stands. In my glass panel I have added a snake around her right arm and hand to represent her consort Shiva as the 'hidden' masculine principle. The snake as a traditional symbol of sexual energy and instinctual knowledge has been lost in our Christian tradition. *Kundalini* energy in the tantric tradition is symbolized by the snake and is the primal sexual force that is roused from its sleep in the *chakra* at the base of the spine to ascend to the top of the skull and engender enlightenment.[15] It is often described as female and in the panel the motif of serpentine energy also appears in the border.

In the tantric tradition love of the 'Terrible Mother' in her most fearsome aspect means the conquering of the fear of death. 'She may be hideous but she may be no less loved!'[16] This is the liberation that contemplation of her image offers. In view of our capacity to create an impersonal extinction for the whole of the planet, she seems a timely reminder of our human limitations.

> 'I am not one of those,' he chanted,
> 'Who put the garland of skulls round thy neck and look back in terror
> And call thee "the Merciful".
> The Heart must become a burial ground
> Pride, selfishness and desire all broken into dust.
> Then, and only then, will the Mother dance there!'
>
> Vivikenanda[17]

14. Kinsley, *The Sword and the Flute*, p. 92.

15. *Kundalini* is the name given to sexual energy in its cosmic nature. According to tantric belief, sexual energy in its base primal form resides at the base of the spine but can be raised, via meditative and/or sexual practices, through the seven gates to consciousness known as *chakras* that mark its stages up the spine. At the higher levels this energy is transmuted into cosmic power until enlightenment is reached at the top of the head. See P. Rawson, *Tantra: The Indian Cult of Ecstasy* (London: Thames & Hudson, 1973), p. 27.

16. W. Doniger O'Flaherty, *Women, Androgynes and Other Mythical Beasts* (Chicago: University of Chicago Press, 1975), p. 142.

17. Quoted in Kinsley, *The Sword and the Flute*, p. 144.

Plate 4. The goddess Kali. Gouache on paper.
Kalighat, Calcutta, India. c. 1845. V. & A. Museum

Lilith—Spirit of Instinctual Wisdom

Lilith (Plate 6) was a more difficult piece to interpret as the source was a three-dimensional relief. 'Lilith' was the Judaic name given to the Sumerian goddess Ishtar/Inanna, whose powers were associated with animals and the knowledge and creative force of instinctual sexuality. In the Burney Plaque (Plate 5)—a clay relief dating from 2,000 BCE—she wears the horned head-dress that denoted divinity and is supported by two lions as was common to all images of ancient goddesses. She is shown holding symbols of power—the rod and circle—in a form similar

Plate 5. Inanna/Ishtar. The Burney Plaque. Clay relief. 2000–1800 BCE Sumerian. Formerly British Museum

to the Egyptian *ankh* which meant 'life'. She is attended by two owls that symbolize her association with the powers of darkness and the unknown.[18] Ishtar was both the sweet maid and the warrior goddess that the Babylonians appealed to for both justice and compassion. She was not only associated with sexuality and fertility but vengeance and war. In the earliest poetry addressed to a deity she is appealed to thus:

> She made the night come forth like the moonlight,
> She made the morning come forth like bright daylight...
> Against the evildoer she renders a cruel judgement, destroys the wicked,
> She looks with kindly eyes on the straightforward, gives him her blessing.
>
> My Lady looks on in sweet wonder from heaven's midst,
> They parade before the holy Inanna,
> The Lady who reaches Heaven, Inanna, is lofty,
> The Maid, Inanna, I would praise as is fitting.[19]

The most famous of the earliest texts found from that period deals with Inanna's descent to the underworld to visit her sister Erishkigal. It is told in a number of forms and is the first example of a moon myth using the motif of judgment, death and resurrection. In the process of her journey, Inanna, the Queen of Heaven, has to relinquish her royal regalia and attendant powers at each of the seven gates to the underworld until she is 'naked and brought low'. She is finally judged, condemned and executed by Erishkigal and her corpse is hung to rot from a peg. After three days she is rescued with the aid of Enki, her father and god of the Underworld Sea, who creates two beings from the dirt under his fingernails to plead for her. Their sympathy for Erishkigal's pains (labour or otherwise) allows them to claim Inanna's corpse as a gift and she is redeemed from death. On her way back from the underworld Inanna retrieves all her powers at the seven gates. However, she also comes back with 'the eyes of death' and all the knowledge that entails. Once returned she finds her lover Dumuzi reigning on her throne in her stead and he is the only one who fails to kneel to her on her return. In her anger she wishes to sentence him to death but he is saved by the

18. A. Baring and J. Cashford, *The Myth of the Goddess: Evolution of an Image* (London: Penguin Books, 1993), pp. 216-18.

19. Quoted in Baring and Cashford, *The Myth of the Goddess*, p. 200. Originally cited in S.N. Kramer, *From the Poetry of Sumer: Creation, Glorification, Adoration* (Berkeley: University of California Press, 1979), p. 86.

Plate 6. *Lilith.* Stained glass panel. Computer image composite of stained-glass panel 135 × 85 cm. 1999

intervention of his sister, who pleads for him and shares his fate each of them having to spend six months in the underworld.[20]

So powerful was the cult of Ishtar/Inanna—with its emphasis on sexuality and the independent power of the feminine—that while the Jews dwelt in Babylon the Judaic tradition had to demonize the image to prevent its adherents from being seduced away from the true faith. Lilith's name comes from the ancient non-Semitic Mesopotamian word *lil* meaning breath or spirit of life in the sacred sense. *Lilit* were spirits of the night. In Jewish myths written long after Genesis Lilith becomes the 'bad' first wife of Adam, who was created from the same dust at the same time but refused to be subject to him sexually or spiritually and demanded equality. She escaped into the desert by uttering the secret name of God and is reputed to haunt the night, tempting men in their dreams and fathering demons from their spilt seed.[21] Lilith's positive connection with life and conception was sacrificed to the new patriarchal order and her name became synonymous with all demons and the dark. However, when we look at her attendant owls we might surmise that her memory is preserved in our folklore image of the owl as wise bird of the night that has a fearsome reputation as a hunter.

The Burney Plaque is not coloured and so I invented a symbolic use of colour in *Lilith* that seemed appropriate. The red background is to be common for all 'heroine' figures, so I used blue and gold on the body and wings, as a suitably powerful contrast. The blue also offsets the nakedness of the figure and allows for a more symbolic representation of the details of nipples and pubic hair, which then take on the same weight as the clawed talons, jewellery and crown. As this is a full figure, the head, so that it can be seen clearly at a distance of 30 feet from the ground, is proportionally bigger than the figure. The controlling geometry governing the proportions of the figure and its features is centred just below the navel, on the womb.

The symbol of the eight-petal star/flower in the four 'moons' is commonly found in Sumerian decorative art as a symbol of Ishtar. It represents both the planet Venus (her ruling planet, also represented by the seven-pointed star in the figurative panel) and the balance of heaven and earth as material forces. The geometry of the eight-pointed star is a combination of two squares, one at a 45 degree angle to the other. Here

20. D. Wolkstein and S.N. Kramer, *Inanna: Queen of Heaven and Earth* (London: Rider, 1984), pp. 22-30.

21. Baring and Cashford, *The Myth of the Goddess*, pp. 510-13.

the blue cruciform petals act as the static, stable element and the red diagonal petals as the dynamic, energizing element. The eye in the centre is also a common feature of the goddess imagery of the region where simple 'eye-goddess' figures abound.[22] In the square tracery pattern is the image of the snake—commonly associated with the early goddess cults where it symbolized hidden knowledge and immortality—as it lived underground and also shed its skin regularly to be 'reborn'. Before the writing of Genesis snakes were not associated with evil but wisdom and were the guardians, not the despoilers of Paradise.[23]

In Plate 7 *Lilith,* with her beautiful body and bird's wings, soaring from clawed feet that are anchored in two lions, is a powerful symbol of an ancient wisdom we no longer understand. Lions have always been solar symbols and thus part of a masculine mythology. Here they are her vehicle and means of support, but as much as she is carried by them she also keeps them 'down to earth'. Thus masculine principles can inform and direct the physical world rather than soaring unchecked, bringing about all sorts of dangerous consequences. With her clawed feet in the ground of being and her head in the heavenly principles of *logos* (the world of abstract thought and ideals), Lilith is a perfect symbol of the feminine in the role of mediating between the material and the spiritual realms. She represents a wisdom that comes from an understanding of instinctual forces that we no longer know how to respect or govern.

The Internet and Beyond: Expanding the Parameters for a Participatory Project

Much of the initial design work for this project was done on computer and the finished the plans already exist on disk. This information will be revised for inclusion on the World Wide Web. As in the mediaeval tradition, the window is designed to be a source of information as well as inspiration, and it is important that the main panels are figurative and legible. There will be guidelines on proportions, colours and symbolic details to be used to create harmony within the individual panels. The project is intended to attract as wide a cultural mix as possible—as the

22. This is a symbol also found in the cult of the Indian goddess *Kali*, where it is said that should the 'Great Mother' close her third eye for one second the universe would cease to exist.

23. Baring and Cashford, *The Myth of the Goddess*, p. 497.

Plate 7. *Lilith.* Detail of figure. Stained glass panel 135 × 85 cm. 1999

window is intended to reflect global experience, it should not be defined by any one culture. Designs for the 28 major figurative panels that conform to the specifications will then be submitted to a panel of independent judges and displayed on the website. Those selected for the rose window will be chosen for artistic merit and to reflect the need for cultural diversity. I hope to have at least 14 artists involved in the final production of designs.

Once selected the designs will be assembled as a whole, using computer technology. This will enable the piece to be colour balanced and rendered artistically compatible. The editing of the process will need to be done on a single computer, as software colours vary according to the technology used. The tracery panels will then be completed with sponsors' logos and imagery as appropriate. This will enable a high degree of participation from all levels of the community, for example, women's groups and organizations, industry, educational institutions. The website will contain details of all participating artists and institutions as well as information about the images and their source.

After the staging of a virtual reality exhibition of the completed design, there could also be an exhibition of a full-scale hardcopy. This could be assembled in various parts of the world at the same time. There would be scope for different versions of the design in different situations, for instance, non-figurative in the case of Islamic countries. Although the finished design will never equal the quality of a stained glass window, it would be able to convey some of the grandeur of the vision. On-line the light of the screen gives a very similar radiance to glass and the imagery used can be seen in detail as well as from a virtual distance. The creation of a virtual reality environment for the piece would be the next logical step towards the creation, perhaps in later years, of a real architectural environment for the real rose window.

Conclusion

We are told repeatedly in the media that 'the future is female', yet no one seems to be able to define what this means in practice or whether it is to be desired or feared. It may mean the end of the patriarchal culture of competitive power and domination in the economic and material realms. The beginning of a more 'feminine' relationship to the world based on cooperation among people might be essential in order to nurture this sadly ravaged environment in which we are all struggling to live.

The old ways of seeing will not promote survival of our species or the planet, but perhaps the Internet offers us a new view. It is feared for its capacity for spreading evil, as in the easy access to pornographic, fascist and racist material of all kinds, but it is also a tool that has the potential to be educative and productive of unity. As Edward Whitmont says in his book, *The Return of the Goddess*, 'The patriarchal Gods said "Thou shalt and thou shalt not" but the Goddess says "You may, but be careful" '.[24] We are all, male and female, called to greater awareness of the possible consequences of our actions.

Whatever the outcome of the New Age, its artwork will become its legacy. If we want that legacy to be as lasting and powerful as that of the past millenniums we will need to be as exacting and united in our vision of the new as were our ancestors. *In the Womb of the Rose* is a project with its roots in an older tradition but with a more complex symbolism than our immediate monotheistic past provides. The rose window is an attempt to give expression to the multi-cultural consciousness of our current understanding of our modern world. It uses a geometric form that in all traditions symbolizes unity and allows contradictory images of the feminine expression in a context that gives each equal weight and meaning. Lack of balance is a symptom of the conflicts endemic in modern society and this threatens the world of female and male alike, affecting both the way we see ourselves and each other. There is a place for an understanding of diverse iconic imagery in a new context and this project is intended to be both a celebration of the past and a contribution to its recreation.

24. E. Whitmont, *The Return of the Goddess: Femininity, Aggression and the Modern Grail Quest* (London: Arkana, 1982), p. 189.

TIWI CATHOLICISM: DANCE AND RELIGIOUS SYNCRETISM AMONG A NORTHERN ABORIGINAL PEOPLE*

Andrée Grau

The Tiwi World

The Tiwi, a Northern Aboriginal people, live on Bathurst and Melville Islands, off the Northern Territory of Australia. Although relatively isolated from the rest of the world because of the dangerous currents surrounding much of the islands, contacts always existed with other Aborigines from the mainland and over the centuries visitors came from Asia (trepang fishermen from Macassar and pearl divers from Japan) as well as Europe (the Dutch made contact first in 1635 then in 1705, the British in 1818).[1]

Occasionally conflicts arose from these encounters: for example, when Tiwi men went to steal women on the mainland or when in 1823 the British tried in vain to establish a settlement on Melville Island. On the whole, however, contacts were generally friendly: intellectual and artistic exchanges as well as social obligations were established with mainland Aborigines and the Asian visitors went back home happy with their cargo and left behind them new techniques (dugout canoes against the indigenous bark canoes, for example) and new ideas. They also occasionally left children, and hence Asian features are characteristic of some Tiwi people today.[2]

* Almost two years were spent among the Tiwi of Melville Island over three visits between 1980 and 1984. I returned in 1998 for a five-week period. The research and fieldworks were funded by the Australian Institute of Aboriginal and Islanders Studies. I am grateful for the help, support and advice that has been given to me by the Institute and its staff throughout the years.

1. The name Melville and Bathurst were given then to the islands to honour Viscount Henry Dundas Melville, first Lord of the Admiralty and the Right Honourable Earl Bathurst, Principal Secretary for the Colonies.

2. The oral tradition does not speak of rapes but of mutual agreements. Women

Despite their regularity the contacts were nevertheless fairly sporadic and their impact was easily absorbed into the social fabric. With the arrival of Father Gsell, an Alsatian priest from the Mission of the Sacred Heart, and the subsequent establishment of a Catholic mission on Bathurst Island in 1911, however, the Tiwi way of life was transformed in a way that had never happened before.

Until 1911 the Tiwi were self-sufficient, with a hunting and gathering economy in a rich and fairly reliable environment. Theirs was typical of 'the original affluent society' that the American anthropologist Marshall Sahlins talked about.[3] In Sahlins's argument, if a society has more than enough of whatever is required to satisfy its consumption needs, then it can be described as affluent.

Different paths can be taken in order to create affluence: western capitalist society, for example, needs to produce much because constant scarcity is the tenet of its ideology: it is assumed that people will always want to consume more of everything than there is to go round.

Another path, which Sahlins called the Buddhist path, could be to desire little. This is the road that had traditionally been taken by hunters and gatherers: their needs were few and nature supplied them abundantly. It is not, to use Emily Schultz's words, that

> foragers have suppressed their natural greed; rather their society has simply not institutionalized greed or rewarded the greedy. As a result, foragers cannot be considered 'poor', even though their material standard of living is low by Western standards. Poverty is not an absolute condition, nor is it a relationship between means and ends; it is a relationship between people.[4]

Abundance depends not only on material wealth but also on subjective satisfaction. This is important because these opposite perspectives have been at the basis of much misunderstanding between the Tiwi on the one side and missionaries and administrators on the other. The latter ethnocentrically believed, without a doubt, that they were better off. They saw themselves as belonging to the 'haves' while the Tiwi were seen as belonging to the 'have-nots'. This attitude is still pervasive today. To quote economic anthropologist Allen Johnson,

today talk, for example, about Japanese as being considerate and generous. Some also mention that missionaries disrupted a system that was working well.

3. M. Sahlins, *Stone Age Economics* (Chicago: Aldine, 1972).

4. E. Schultz and R. Lavenda, *Cultural Anthropology: A Perspective on the Human Condition* (New York: West, 1990), p. 415.

> 'Primitive' society is seen in polar contrast to our own. If we are high-tech, they are technologically simple. If we live long, they die young. If we are free, they are slaves to tradition. If we are a society blessed by an abundance of leisure, then they must be constantly pressed by the never-ending struggle for survival. These contrasts are so obvious that they are seldom questioned. Our beliefs legitimate our quest for progress and our desire to transfer our technological skills...[5]

Yet an archaeologist, for example, applied his knowledge of Maya stone tool-making to manufacture surgical scalpels and his obsidian blades were found to be more than 200 times sharper than the surgical steel scalpels used in the late 1980s[6] showing that ancient technologies can be more efficient than contemporary ones.

When the French anthropologist Barbara Glowczewsky started work in Australia in the late 1970s she felt that 'the self-referential allusion to memory, language and image in Australian spirituality, and its bodily and territorial expression, seemed to me very modern, which is what made me speak of "tribes of the cybernetic Dream" '.[7] We needed to reach the age of virtual reality in order to find images able to translate into our world the complexity of Aboriginal cosmology.

Anthropologists the world over have shown that hunting and gathering economies rarely required more than three to four hours work per adult per day, while modern technological advances have rarely resulted in more free time. Indeed much of our contemporary lives seems to be spent trying to fit everything in and most of us battle with an increasing scarcity of time. Even in our holidays we are pressured to consume, to see more sights, to gets our money's worth of entertainment. In contrast, among the Tiwi the notion of 'wasting time', for example, is new and entirely alien to their traditional conceptual framework, because time is not a commodity to be wasted or not, time simply is and just sitting is doing something.

5. A. Johnson, 'In Search of the Affluent Society', in A. Podolefsky and P.J. Brown (eds.), *Applying Anthropology* (Mountain View, CA: Mayfield, 1989 [1978]), pp. 157-64 (157).

6. P.D. Sheets, 'Dawn on a New Stone Age in Eye Surgery', in Podolefsky and Brown (eds.), *Applying Anthropology*, pp. 111-13.

7. B. Glowzcewsky, 'Dynamic Cosmologies and Aboriginal Heritage', *Anthropology Today* 15.1 (1999), pp. 3-9 (6).

Early Contact with Missionaries

It is said by the order that when the first Convent of the Sacred Heart was founded in Sydney in 1888, the continent was recognized 'as limitless hunting grounds teeming with souls to be won to the love of their crucified Redeemer'.[8] Therefore, when Father Gsell arrived on Bathurst Island he met what were, for the majority of people of the time, 'pristine natives' whose souls could be saved once they were incorporated into a more 'civilized' lifestyle and once the 'unsavoury' bits of their culture were eliminated.

Hunting and gathering had to be replaced by a more controllable settled economy based on agriculture. Among most missionaries of the period, there was an unshakeable belief that if one generation could be taught to cultivate the soil, their descendants would follow and they all would enjoy the benefits of civilization. Never, it seems, did it occur to them that foraging was maybe the best ecological and cultural strategy for a people.

In terms of cultural habits that were deemed offensive and had to be eliminated, the twin institutions of gerontocracy and polygyny were undoubtedly the first to draw Father Gsell's attention.

Tiwi marriage practices are extremely complex and would require a great deal of time to describe, but for this discussion it suffices to say:

(1) The Tiwi generally practised, and still practise today, country endogamy, that is, they marry people linked spiritually to the same territory of the islands as themselves.

(2) They also practise matrilineal clan exogamy, that is, they marry someone who belongs to another clan, usually the clan of their father.

(3) As marriages should be reciprocated, this often leads to brother and sister exchanges within countries.

(4) Marriages were organized through a form of prenatal betrothal, where a young girl, often no more than an infant, was bestowed as a mother-in-law upon a young man. All the progeny of the bestowed woman then became potential wives of the young man.

8. Anonymous, *Other Worlds: The Extended Apostolate of the Society of the Sacred Heart* (New York: Manhattanville College of the Sacred Heart, 1951), p. 1.

As a result of such practices, the age difference between spouses could be up to 30–40 years, and some men acquired many wives, indeed the more wives, the more prestige. Furthermore, the Tiwi also practised a form of levirate, whereby a man married his deceased brothers' widows. Theoretically at least, then, a Tiwi woman could only be a wife, being married before her birth to the day of her death.[9]

Father Gsell interpreted the situation as one of women living a life of drudgery, being pawns in men's power struggle for prestige. He saw it as his duty to emancipate Tiwi women into a modern way of life.

If one takes into account his religious order, his attitude towards women is not surprising. According to Reverend Mother Stuart, who was writing at the time Father Gsell established the Bathurst Island mission, the Society of the Sacred Heart had always sought 'in its whole tone and spirit and training and manner of life a woman's excellence, the perfection of womanhood'.[10] For her, at the time of the foundation of the order at the turn of the eighteenth and nineteenth centuries,

> [It] was realized...how much of the future, for good or evil, hung on the influence of women, and that a systematic education preparing them for their responsible charges in life, was one of the most powerful means of directing the course of the coming time.[11]

Father Gsell, with the nuns who joined him later, set out, genuinely I am sure, to ameliorate the position of women. For them only monogamy and marriage between partners of the same generations could achieve this. Gsell's strategy, then, was somehow to 'buy' girls and the rights over their female progeny and to raise these girls in the mission's convent. At the height of his 'purchasing' career in the late 1920s and 1930s he had acquired 150 'wives'.[12] As the girls became adults they married, in Church, men of their generation. Thus the power of old men was undermined, and as under a catholic marriage a husband could not acquire other wives, monogamy was established.

9. It was this situation that led the anthropologist Jane Goodale, for example, to entitle her book on Tiwi culture from the perspective of its women folk, *Tiwi Wives: A Study of the Women of Melville Island, North Australia* (Seattle: University of Washington Press, 1971).

10. J.E. Stuart, *The Society of the Sacred Heart* (London: Convent of the Sacred Heart, Roehampton, 1914), p. 96.

11. Stuart, *Society of the Sacred Heart*, p. 4.

12. Hence the title of his autobiography published in 1956, *The Bishop with the 150 Wives.*

Father Gsell certainly changed the face of Tiwi society in his 50 years as a missionary. In his eyes he had been instrumental in a move from feudal lordship to a Christian brotherhood where men and women enjoyed equal rights and obligations.[13] Having established this, the Tiwi then could be led into a manufacturing capitalist society with the establishment of a number of craft-based enterprises, which succeeding generations of missionaries helped create.

Father Gsell and later missionaries, however, did not realize the resilience of indigenous culture. While doing extensive genealogical work for my PhD in the early 1980s, it became quite clear that the women allowed 'free choice' of marriage partner did it within very confined limits. Indeed I only recall very few marriages that were not within the rules. Women always 'selected' youths belonging to the right categories in terms of land and clans, and more often than not married men they had been tentatively promised to by a relative. Once married, young men established households that were often joined by their female relatives, the younger of whom they could later 'give away' to men of their 'choice', preserving then the pre-mission day situation in an altered form.[14]

Because today the age differential between spouses is lower than at the turn of the century, a new system seems to have replaced the old. This is, however, not the case. When discussing marriages during fieldwork in 1998, women were adamant that if the Tiwi rules were not followed only calamities could happen to the couple. They gave a young couple who has had more than its fair share of grief and difficulties as an illustration to prove their points. This was also how some people explained the tragic wave of suicides among young men on Bathurst Island in the 1990s.

13. F.X. Gsell, *The Bishop with the 150 Wives: Fifty Years as a Missionary* (Sydney: Angus & Robertson, 1956), p. 11.

14. See also the excellent discussion in D. Bell, 'Choose Your Mission Wisely: Christian Colonials and Aboriginal Marital Arrangements on the Northern Frontier', in T. Swain and D. Bird Rose (eds.), *Aboriginal Australians and Christian Missions* (Adelaide: Australian Association for the Study of Religion, 1988), pp. 339-54.

Tiwi and the Mission

Although the Tiwi never experienced the massacres of the mainland, they did see their culture being constantly devalued and their language undermined. (Because of its complexity very few non-Tiwi ever manage to become fluent in it.) Those Tiwi brought up at the mission also experienced strict discipline. According to Reverend Mother Stuart discipline was something all the Sacred Heart Schools were occasionally criticized for by some people, but according to her 'self control is so vital to the conduct of life that no price is too great to pay for the acquiring of the habit'.[15]

Sometimes discipline led to harsh punishments. I was told, for example, of girls made to stand all day in full sun because they had escaped to visit their family. Furthermore, although the missionaries may not have been directly responsible for the policy devised by the Australian government of kidnapping children of mixed parentage in order to raise them within a so-called European context, they nevertheless colluded with it by raising up this 'stolen generation'—as these children are now being referred to—in their institutions. Pularumpi, my place of fieldwork, for example, had been a mission dedicated to them. Yet despite all this I never heard a word of reproach against the mission during both my periods of fieldwork of the 1980s and 1998. This often puzzled me.

In Tiwi ideology there is no notion of good and evil corresponding to the Christian ideology. Neither is there a notion of guilt, or of original sin. Happy things and bad things are seen to coexist. They are part of life, and human beings have to deal with both. Laughter, love for one's children, pleasure with one's lover, satisfaction with hunting may be more enjoyable than jealousy or murder, but the latter belong to life as well and there is no point in ignoring them. Missionaries brought both positive and negative things and both have to be accepted.

Furthermore, along with other Aborigines probably, the Tiwi can be said to be extremely pragmatic. If something is seen to work, they seem quite happy to adopt it creatively, developing new possibilities in their lives, providing it is not entirely contradictory to their ideology.[16] Very

15. Stuart, *Society of the Sacred Heart*, p. 87.

16. Furthermore innovation has always been intrinsic to Tiwi culture. Every year, for example, men have had to create new song cycles as part of the *Kulama* yam increase ritual. Similarly new songs and dances have to be composed and

quickly they became aware that, unlike the British soldiers who had established a settlement on Melville Island in the late nineteenth century and had left because of disease and constant attacks from the Tiwi, the missionaries with their life-long commitment were more resilient and were here to stay. They also realized that, although patronizing, the attitude of the missionaries was less exploitative than that of the soldiers.

One could also say that they showed more creativity than the missionaries in the sense that they saw possible links between Catholicism and the Dreaming, which, to my knowledge, was not really reciprocated. Throughout the century missionaries and administrators have been convinced of their own superiority and of the need to admit the Tiwi into this superior world. In a 1950s book looking at the schools of the Society of the Sacred Heart around the world, one can read in the Australian section:

> All the schools have vigorous Mission Societies. The aim of the small people at *Kerever Park* is to buy at least eighty black babies each term; and they do it... Zeal is maintained by visits from missionaries, for example... Bishop Gsell...from [his] aboriginal mission in the North-west of Australia.[17]

Dreaming and Catholicism

A number of analogies can be made between aspects of Catholic life and Catholic Faith and Tiwi life and Dreaming. The Dreaming is undoubtedly the key concept underlying Aboriginal spirituality. I can not do justice here to its complexity. For the sake of my discussion I will say that the Dreaming is both the time when the world was created as well as a parallel contemporary world, a sort of cosmic memory where everything that has been, is or will be exists and that can be reached through the art in general and dance in particular.

choreographed for specific moments of mortuary rituals. Tiwi people often comment that people on the mainland 'use the same songs all the time' while they 'make new ones all the time'. This importance of creativity undoubtedly led to the easy incorporation of many new ideas and artefacts. During fieldwork, for example, I recorded songs and dances about electricity and beer, as well as about the 'big house of the Queen of England'.

17. Anonymous, *Other Worlds*, p. 29.

In both Tiwi and Catholic worlds two orders of knowledge are recognized: one that is intellectual, the *ratio* of Christianity, and one that is supernatural, the *fides* of Christianity.[18] In both cases the supernatural is the 'truer' knowledge and in both instances it needs experiencing. In Christianity faith entails trust, whereby individuals commit themselves and assent to truths that are not seen or cannot be proved. Among Aborigines trust is not really relevant because the separation between what we call *fides* and *ratio* is only used for argument's sake, in philosophical discussion with outsiders, such as myself. They are perceived as two aspects of the same phenomenon.[19]

In the Tiwi world-view masculine and feminine principles are not only complementary but both exist within each human being. For example, I, as a woman, am a mother for my own children and my sisters' children, but I am also a father for my brothers' children, the opposite being true for men. I have discussed elsewhere, for example, how men dance that they are pregnant with, giving birth to, or breastfeeding their sisters' children.[20] There is no doubt that within such a system, a new religion showing strong women as well as men would have had a better chance than one representing mainly one sex. Although nuns and priests professed celibacy, quite an alien concept for the Tiwi, there were analogies in other places. The nuns offered a unique vision of womanhood, for example, in the sense that, like Tiwi women, they undertook any task necessary for survival. They also maintained an independence of spirit, just like Tiwi women.

In addition, the Tiwi world was created by Pukwi or Imunga, the Sun-woman. Metamorphosed into a turtle, she descended to the then amorphous earth and created the islands through her journey. On her way she left her daughters at different places around the islands, all 'watery' in nature.

18. This distinction came about, for example, when discussing the dance repertoire. Individuals would explain to me the differences between dances that had been choreographed ('I think it myself') and dances that were seen to be part of their biological make up ('It's my Dreaming').

19. It is also worth noting here, I think, that Aboriginal people throughout Australia generally seem to hold the view that westerners are incredibly simplistic and unsophisticated regarding issues of spirituality, to the extent that, to them, it is sometimes hardly worth the effort of engaging in such a discussion.

20. A. Grau, 'Gender Interchangeability among the Tiwi', in H. Thomas (ed.), *Dance, Gender and Culture* (London: Macmillan, 1993), pp. 94-111.

The image of Mary, mother of God, although very different in concept and nature, can nevertheless finds resonance within Tiwi cosmology. Similarly, the image of Christ, the God-Man, could provide a cultural analogue with the Dreaming overlapping everyday life and the world of the spirits.

Reading about the devotion to the Sacred Heart, I was struck too by the many biblical images of the Holy Spirit as the living waters flowing from the pierced heart of Jesus. The waters found near the homes of the daughters of Pukwi mentioned earlier is where Tiwi men find the unborn spirit of their children, so that for the Tiwi too some waters have a life-giving quality. Looking at the iconography of the Sacred Heart, it was interesting too to note that in some paintings, such as in Odilon Redon's *The Sacred Heart*,[21] for example, the 'heart' is placed lower and more centrally than the anatomical heart, much closer in fact to where the Tiwi place Imunga, the source of life, and where Tiwi dancers say they draw their energy from when they perform.

These latter remarks are informed speculations on my part. I am no theologian and I have only rarely discussed Christian theology as such with the Tiwi. Furthermore, living on Melville Island, which at the time of my more intensive periods of fieldwork had no permanent Catholic presence, I never really had a proper conversation with any of the priests or nuns. Our exchanges were rarely more than greetings and a few words after or before funeral, wedding or christening services.

Comparison between Catholic services and Tiwi rituals were often made to me, however, by some of my Tiwi friends. For example, they often commented on the use of incense by the Catholic Church to 'smoke the devil away', as they said, and compared it with their own use of fire and smoke for purification. They also commented on the theatricality of the Catholic service, with its use of ritual gestures, with the priest facing different directions at different times, just like they themselves face specific directions in rituals and use gestures and dances to mean very specific things.

I would argue that the success of Catholicism among the Tiwi—today most Tiwi would label themselves Catholic even if they are not regular Church attenders—in contrast to other Aboriginal places, has been because of the possibility of establishing some analogies between the systems.

21. The French painter Odilon Redon (1840–1916) is better known for his visionary and symbolist paintings.

Dreaming-Catholicism Syncretism

What is interesting to note is how over the past 80 years the Tiwi negotiated with the intruders and managed to establish 'deals' with them in order to keep a sense of integrity. Unable to establish exchanges on an equal basis with the missionaries, because these were steeped in prejudices and their own sense of superiority, the Tiwi tried to establish bridges of understanding. Until the 1960s and 1970s they could only operate within a fairly restricted framework. With self-determination established in 1967 and the passing of the Aboriginal Land Rights Act of 1976, however, a new era began.[22]

Changes of policies and ideology within the political sphere were paralleled with changes within the missionary movement. Indigenization of Churches was encouraged and the arts were seen as an appropriate channel to do so. Little by little the Tiwi were encouraged to create art—in the form mainly of paintings, but also sculpture and some pottery—to be placed in the Church. In the 1990s, the congregation in Bathurst, for example, was literally surrounded by Tiwi art. Old hymns were translated into simple Tiwi[23] and new ones were written.

As the Church became more open to Tiwiization, the Tiwi became more and more proactive. Rather than use only the schema offered by missionaries (decorations on the wall and the altar, simple songs using

22. Australia was annexed to the British crown in 1770, without any recognition that Aboriginal people had ever had any sovereignty over the land. Indeed it was considered *Terra nullius*—the land of no one. Although legally considered British subjects, Aborigines only gained citizenship in 1949, and this only in theory, as the constitution of 1901 denied them all rights and specifically excluded them, for example, from the national census. They had to wait until 1967 to be integrated within Australian society as full citizens.

23. Tiwi is a polysynthetic agglutinative language, that is, it is a language in which all the elements of a sentence may be combined in a single highly complex morphological structure. In effect the Tiwi verb is a sentence in miniature. The verb may contain within itself not only pronominal reference to subject and object, or markers of tense or mood, which are fairly common in the world's languages, but it may contain many other types of information, such as proximity or time of day. In addition nouns can be incorporated as well, and when they are incorporated they are transformed. Because of this, individuals take time to master the language and different levels of Tiwi can be identified: from what can be labelled 'children Tiwi' to what one can call 'classical Tiwi'. Very few non-Tiwi go much further than the children version of the language.

western melodies), a few individuals well-versed in traditional performance style and fluent in classical Tiwi started to compose Tiwi songs according to Tiwi rules and aesthetic criteria as well as to introduce dancing for specific occasions. During my fieldwork of the 1980s, for example, the Christmas and Easter festivals incorporated Tiwi performances.

I have described elsewhere that the dancers' bodies literally embody the Dreaming as well as their daily reality.[24] For the Tiwi there is neither separation between the body and the self, nor separation between the body and the world at large. Bodily, social, ecological, and spiritual worlds are all interconnected and part of a single cosmological universe given signification through the dancers' bodies, which embody land, social relationships and spiritual beliefs.[25]

24. A. Grau, 'Dancers' Bodies as the Repository of Conceptualisations of the Body, with Special Reference to the Tiwi of Northern Australia', in *Proceedings of International Association for Semiotic Studies, 5th Congress, 1994, University of California, Berkeley* (The Hague: Mouton, 1997), pp. 929-32; *idem*, 'Danse et "pensée" symbolique: Danser la parenté chez les Tiwi de l'Australie du Nord', in A. Montandon (ed.), *Sociopoétique de la danse* (Paris: Anthropos, 1998), pp. 15-26; *idem*, 'On the Acquisition of Knowledge: Teaching Kinship through the Body among the Tiwi of Northern Australia', in V. Keck (ed.), *Common Worlds and Single Lives: Constituting Knowledge in Pacific Societies* (Oxford: Berg, 1998), pp. 71-94; *idem*, 'Paysage, corps et poésie: Une esthétique intégrée de la danse chez les aborigènes Tiwi', in *La Danse: Une Culture en Mouvement* (Strasbourg: Université Marc Bloch, Centre de Recherches Européennes en Education Corporelle, 1999), pp. 377-86; *idem*, 'Land, Body and Poetry: An Integrated Aesthetic Among the Tiwi', in S. Kleinert and M. Neale (eds.), *The Oxford Companion to Aboriginal Art and Culture* (Oxford: Oxford University Press, 2000), pp. 356-62.

25. For other aspects of Tiwi dance, see also A. Grau, 'Sing a Dance—Dance a Song: The Relationship between Two Types of Formalised Movements and Music among the Tiwi of Melville and Bathurst Islands, North Australia', *Dance Research* 1.2 (1983), pp. 32-44; *idem*, 'Les danses rituelles Tiwi', *Cahiers de Musiques Traditionelles* 5 (1992), pp. 205-16; *idem*, 'Gender Interchangeability among the Tiwi', in H. Thomas (ed.), *Dance, Gender, and Culture* (London: MacMillan, 1993), pp. 94-111; *idem*, 'Dance as Politics: The Use of Dance for the Manipulation of the Social Order among the Tiwi of Northern Australia', in *Proceedings of the 17th Symposium of the International Council for Traditional Music, Study Group on Ethnochoreology* (Nafplion: Folklore Museum, 1994), pp. 39-44; *idem*, 'Dance as Part of the Infrastructure of Social Life', in J. Baily (ed.), 'John Blacking: The Belfast Years', *World of Music: Journal of the International Institute for Traditional Music* 37.2 (1995), pp. 43-59; *idem*, 'Ritual Dance and Modernisation: The Tiwi Example', in *Proceedings of the 18th Symposium of the ICTM Study Group on*

Dancing in Church, therefore, is more than, say, incorporating a Tiwi design on the cloth covering the altar or hanging a Tiwi painting on the Church's wall. Similarly, composing Tiwi songs for use within a Christian framework is more than singing translations with a guitar accompaniment. Tiwi people always talk about the importance of 'big words', and about how happy they feel when ritual calls are heard, reverberating through the landscape, filling the space between performers and the sacred places they are directed to. They feel very deeply for language, all languages. They delighted in hearing my husband and me converse in French, for example.[26] Similarly, they told me in 1998 how much they had enjoyed listening to Eric Venbrux, an anthropologist working among them in the 1990s, speaking Dutch with his wife.

Language and dance for them are best seen as summarizing symbols, in the sense that, as a flag among some people may summarize all the emotions they may have towards a nation, Tiwi language and dance are emblems of Tiwi identity. When I first worked among them, my hosts always introduced me to newcomers, saying, 'She comes to study language', even though we spent hours talking about dance! Similarly, Tiwi people often said to outsiders, 'We will never give up our dancing', when discussing the fact that they would never give up their culture.

Composing songs and dancing in Church could be seen as an attempt by the Tiwi to integrate Catholicism into the Dreaming. Are the present-day missionaries aware of the possible implications of what is taking place? I do not know. Because their own society sees the arts as luxuries human beings can indulge in once the necessity of making a living has been dealt with, will they miss the Tiwi perception that sees them as a path essential for the continuation of human life, just as they seem to have missed the way Tiwi people renegotiated their marriage arrangement in light of the changes enforced on to them? Only time will tell.

Ethnochoreology (Warsaw: Polish Academy of Science, 1995), pp. 89-96.

26. Whenever they heard us speak French, they always commented to each other 'they speak language'. Somehow English did not seem to fall into the category of language.

Indexes

Index of References

Old Testament

New Testament

OTHER ANCIENT REFERENCES

INDEX OF AUTHORS